THE BATTLE OF BERLIN

For Paula

THE BATTLE OF BERLIN

Bomber Command Over The Third Reich 1943–1945

Martin W. Bowman

AIR WORLD

First published in Great Britain in 2020
and reissued in this format in 2026 by
Pen & Sword Air World
An imprint of
Pen & Sword Books Ltd
Yorkshire – Philadelphia

ISBN 978 1 52679 793 3

A CIP catalogue record for this book is available from the British Library.

Typeset by Mac Style
Printed and bound in the UK by
CPI Group (UK) Ltd, Croydon, CR0 4YY.

MIX
Paper | Supporting responsible forestry
FSC® C013604

The Publisher's authorised representative in the EU for product safety is Authorised Rep Compliance Ltd., Ground Floor, 71 Lower Baggot Street, Dublin D02 P593, Ireland. | www.arccompliance.com

For a complete list of Pen & Sword titles please contact

PEN & SWORD BOOKS LIMITED
47 Church Street, Barnsley, South Yorkshire, S70 2AS, England
E-mail: enquiries@pen-and-sword.co.uk
Website: www.pen-and-sword.co.uk

or

PEN AND SWORD BOOKS
1950 Lawrence Road, Havertown, PA 19083, USA
E-mail: uspen-and-sword@casematepublishers.com
Website: www.penandswordbooks.com

Contents

'...the book I'd write would not be a novel, but simply a true tale cut from the cloth of reality, concocted out of true events and characters.

***Soldiers of Salamis*, a novel about the Spanish Civil War published in 2001 by Spanish author Javier Cercas**

Chapter One

Berlin Season

'It has been decided that the primary objective of your operations should now be focused on the morale of the enemy civil population and in particular, of industrial workers. The aim is the destruction of German cities, the killing of German workers and the disruption of civilised community life throughout Germany. It should be emphasised that the destruction of houses, public utilities, transport and lives; the creation of a refugee problem on an unprecedented scale; and the breakdown of morale both at home and at the battle fronts by fear of extended and intensified bombing are accepted and intended aims of our bombing policy, they are not by-products of attempts to hit factories.'

Air Marshal Sir Arthur Travers Harris CB OBE, who once declared that the Germans living under a savage tyranny were 'not allowed the luxury of morale'.

'Achtung, Achtung!' Major Eckart-Wilhelm 'Hugo' von Bonin listened impatiently but attentively to the long litany of instructions from his bordfunker (radio-operator) crouched in the cockpit of their Bf 110G-4 night-fighter as they continued their Helle Nachtjagd ('night chase') across the Belgian countryside. Thirty minutes earlier the 24-year-old Staffelkapitän (Squadron Commander) had lifted the Messerschmitt with its deadly electronic wizardry and heavy firepower off from St. Trond/Sint-Truiden and he had then climbed at maximum rate to an operational height of 5,300 metres. Their route was to take them to one of the Himmelbett Räume ('four-poster bed boxes'), each one of them a theoretical spot in the sky, in which one to three fighters orbited a radio beacon waiting for bombers to appear.

Each box, about 20 miles square, which had names like 'Hamster', 'Eisbär' ('Polar Bear') and 'Tiger' (around Terschelling Island), was a killing zone in the path of hundreds of incoming prey. All approaches to occupied Europe and Germany were divided into circular and partly overlapping areas, which took full advantage of Bomber Command's tactic in sending bombers singly and on a broad front and not in concentrated streams. The 'Himmelbett Räume' and the Nachtjäger were orchestrated by Jägerleitoffiziers (JLOs or GCI-controllers) in 'Battle Opera Houses'. Though the JLOs were far removed from the actual battles, high tiered rows of Leuchtspukers or 'Light Spitter girls' projected information onto a huge screen for them and operators moved the plots on the Seeburg plotting tables.

The Jägerleitoffizier announced monotonously at regular intervals, 'No Kuriere in sight' and von Bonin had to continue orbiting. 'Hugo's brother, Oberstleutnant Hubertus von Bonin (Knight's Cross of the Iron Cross recipient) was killed in action on 15 December 1943. 'Hugo', who lost two other brothers on the Eastern Front, had twenty-three confirmed night abschüsse (victories). He was impatient to add to his score and probably did not concern himself with the bombers' destinations on Thursday 18/Friday 19 November 1943. He was not to know that it marked the start of the 'Main Battle of Berlin'. Some 440 Lancasters had been dispatched to the 'Big City'. Although the Nachtjagdgeschwader did not know the actual numbers involved, the night predators were unconcerned, satisfied in the knowledge that there would be scores of ubiqutous black 'Fat Cats' for them to aim for.

Von Bonin was one of many who eagerly awaited the code-word from the Jägerleitoffizier that would send him scurrying into action in his alloted box. Suddenly, as if by magic, 'Have Kurier for you, Kirchturm 10 (1000 metres), course 300°.' Using the figures on a clock face, i.e. east to west in the northern part of the night-fighting area, he added helpfully: 'Kurier flying from two to eleven.'

Startled but composed, the three-man crew reacted with excitement and enthusiasm. According to the information from the Jägerleitoffizier they were only a few kilometres behind a British bomber! The enemy aircraft had been picked up on Würzburg ground radar, fixed on the plotting table and transmitted to Major von Bonin and his crew stalking the bomber. As soon as Oberfeldwebel Friedrich Johrden, his bordfunker, picked up contact on his Lichtenstein radar set, he transmitted 'Emil-Emil' to alert his JLO, but there was no indication yet on the Lichtenstein. It was 0220 hours. They hoped to reach the 'Fat Cat' before it left the range of the Würzburg ground radar.

'1,000 metres, 800 metres, 500, 400, 300 metres!' Power off and minimum speed in order not to overtake him, von Bonin had to attack from behind and that at the dangerous rear turret of the 4-mot [four-motor]. 'There he is!' Their eyes looked out and focused on a black shape of the Britisher. Small, blueish exhaust flames made it easier to keep the target in sight. Four engines, twin-tail, were recorded almost subconsciously. No sudden movement that might attract their attention. Calm now! Guns armed? Night sight switched on? Everything OK! Now von Bonin could see that it was a 'Lanki'. He applied a little more power and approached the Lancaster cautiously. Now he was exactly behind him at about 100 metres' range. The rear turret was clearly recognizable. His bordfunker remained silent.

'Pauke! Pauke!' ('Kettledrums! Kettledrums!'). Von Bonin had obtained visual contact of his target, crossing gently from starboard to port. It was 'L-London' of 115 Squadron which was skippered by 20-year-old Australian Pilot Officer Raymond Ernest Lee Peate. Born in North Sydney, he was employed as a motor body painter at Highgate Hill in Brisbane before his posting to England. Peate had taken off from Little Snoring airfield north of the Norfolk village at 1803 hours.

Friedrich Johrden immediately transmitted 'Ich beruhe' and von Bonin closed in rapidly for the kill. The equipment was checked and the four machine guns and two MG-FF 2cm cannon were loaded and cocked. At the bordfunker's feet were ammunition drums with seventy-five rounds each for the pair of deadly cannon. Now the Lichtenstein screen was aglow with the green time base and the ground blips, which also showed their altitude.

'250, 200, 150 metres.' A slipstream shook the Messerschmitt. They were close! At 100 metres von Bonin pressed the gun-button on the stick and was startled at the rattle of the cannon. He stayed behind the great night bird, firing and observing the projectiles striking the rear turret and the fuselage. Strikes peppered the fuselage and danced along the wing root. An equally short burst of brightly-coloured tracer disappeared into the Lancaster's wing and fuselage. He must have been hit! The Lanc burst into flames. Doomed, it fell away to port in a flaming death dive, impacting in a field at Hermée in Belgium 4 kilometres north-west of Herstal. 'Horrido!' ('Tallyho'), exclaimed von Bonin over R/T to ground control to announce his success.

None of the Lancaster crew survived the encounter. Sergeant Neil Mackay, the 25-year-old second pilot, was from Paisley in Renfrewshire. Sergeant Hugh George Bannister, the flight engineer, only 19 years old, a former Halton apprentice, was on his eighteenth op. Pilot Officer Noel Reginald Shaw, the 27-year-old navigator, was from Oldham in Lancashire. Canadian Pilot Officer Murray Lincoln Richardson was the bomb-aimer. Flight Sergeant François Benigne Collenet, the 22-year-old Belgian wireless-operator, never had the chance to radio base before he died at his post. Warrant Officer 2 Sidney Andrew Anderson, the 23-year-old mid-upper gunner who was born in Cromer, Manitoba, and Sergeant George Vivian Sharratt, the 21-year-old rear gunner, had no time to open fire on their attacker before they too were killed. They were all laid to rest at Heverlee War Cemetery.

At Little Snoring Peake's flight commander, Squadron Leader Jim Starkie had seven letters of commiseration to write to the next of kin. Telegrams had already been sent to Ernest Rory and Mary Peate in Australia, to Alexander and Adamina Stewart Mackay in Paisley and to George and Constance Bannister in Romford. Hugh Bannister's mother had died when he was only 3 and his father then married his late wife's sister. In Oldham Walter and Susan Shaw were no doubt heartbroken to receive the news they had been dreading; likewise the Collenets domiciled at Shoreham-by-Sea in Sussex. In Canada, Murray Richardson's kith and kin received word of his untimely death. At Radville, Saskatchewan Sarah Anderson, a widow who had remarried, now had the sad task of passing on the bad news to Sidney's sister and his four brothers that he had been killed on operations. In Tamworth, Staffordshire, George Sharratt's young wife Margaret Edwina Olga no doubt tried to come to terms with the heartache of knowing that she was now a widow.

Von Bonin's Viermot [four-engined bomber] took his score to twenty-four and counted towards the major's coveted Ritterkreuz. The highly-prized Knight's Cross was awarded to von Bonin on 5 February 1944 when he had gained thirty-one victories.

'Naxos' and 'Flensburg' equipment homing onto the H2S airborne, ground-scanning radar system and the 'Monica' tail-warning device might have identified von Bonin's victim. They had become a poisoned chalice and bomber crews were instructed not to leave sets on too long.

None of this technical wizardry had been available in the early part of the war when raids on Berlin were few and infrequent and when they did materialize, numbers were small and navigation and bombing aids were almost unknown. Not that Germany was prepared for bombing raids at night. When the subject of night-fighting was raised at a conference of German service chiefs just before the war, it was dismissed out of hand with the words: 'Night fighting! It will never come to that!' Up until May 1940 the night air defence of the Reich was almost entirely the province of the flak arm of the Luftwaffe.

After Neville Chamberlain had resigned the premiership on 10 May 1940 and Winston Churchill had become prime minister of Great Britain, Nazi dictator Adolf Hitler realized there would be no peace deal and the Battle of Britain began in mid-July. Often outnumbered and nearing exhaustion, RAF fighter pilots did not win the conflict but they prevented the Luftwaffe from winning it. Without air superiority, Hitler tried a different tack; one which he no doubt came to rue. In July Winston Churchill had addressed the Chief of Air Staff in these words:

'In case there is an attack on the centre of Government in London, it seems very important to return the compliment the next day upon Berlin. I understand you will have by the end of this month a respectable party of Stirlings ready. Perhaps the nights are not yet long enough. Pray let me know.'

On the night of Friday 23/Saturday 24 August 1940 the Luftwaffe rained bombs on London; the first to fall on the capital since 1918. Little damage was done, but Londoners were as one with Churchill. American foreign correspondent John Negley Farson summed up the prevailing mood:

'I have never thought of the English as a revengeful nation – a conquering race seldom is – yet one of the most menacing things for Hitler was the way that everyone dispassionately discussed the urgent need for the immediate bombing of Berlin. There was no false sentiment; it was just that no one there believed there was any other answer to the indiscriminate German night-bombing than to bomb Berlin off the map.'[1]

Bomber air crews too were particularly keen to 'dish out' some form of retribution for the blitz on British cities. On 14/15 November 1940 Robert Kee never forgot seeing the bombing of Coventry from Upper Heyford airfield where he was learning to fly twin-engined bombers. Born on 5 October 1919 in Calcutta where his father ran a jute business, Kee read Modern History at Magdalen College, Oxford before leaving in 1940 to join the RAF. He trained as a pilot and in July 1941 was commissioned and joined 44 'Rhodesia' Squadron at Waddington, 4 miles south of Lincoln, flying Hampdens. 'The feeling was "I wish I could bomb Berlin and get our own back a bit",' Kee wrote. He did bomb Berlin twice. 'I think there was pleasure in the thought that we were reciprocating after the bombing of places like Coventry and London.'[2] Some 449 bombers dropped 30,000 incendiary bombs which killed 568 people and damaged 71 factories and 41,500 homes, of which 2,306 were destroyed. The devastation was so great that the Nazi Minister of Propaganda Doktor Joseph Goebbels coined the phrase 'Koventrieren' or 'Coventrate' to describe the utter destruction of a city by bombing attack with an excessive amount of bombs.

The RAF bomber crews, who had generally been instructed to aim for targets of industrial or military importance, noted that the attack on Coventry and those on a host of other British cities that followed seemed to bring about a change of policy. The effects of the bombing and the possible breakdown in civilian morale was not lost in the minds of the senior members of the government and Bomber Command, but Britain had neither the aircraft nor the capacity to retaliate other than the ability to make 'pin-prick' raids on towns and cities in the Reich. By the end of 1940 the 'Big City', as it was known, was bombed on only ten occasions and from January to early March 1941 there were no further trips to the city, but Berlin was never left untouched for long.

On 12/13 March Bomber Command flew 257 sorties against targets in Hamburg, Bremen and Berlin. These raids came after the second blitz on Portsmouth on 10/11 March when more than 1,000 people were rendered homeless by thousands of incendiaries and hundreds of HE bombs dropped on the city. The raid, like the one on Coventry, which had remained uppermost in Robert Kee's mind, had a profound effect on George Carter, a navigator on a Whitley bomber, who wrote:

'It is the first time I have been to the 'Big City' and…. I hope we knock the blazes out of the target (which incidentally is the post office in the centre of the city). Before, I have always felt sorry for the people down below, but the other night I came over Portsmouth on the way home and saw it afire. I saw an explosion about 2,000 feet high. So now I feel different about it and I shall not be too careful to hit the post office. I have got one bottle, one brick and one piece of concrete to throw out with some personal messages to the Hun.'

It was not until 14 February 1942 when the famous 'area bombing' directive, which had gained support from the Air Ministry and the prime minister, was sent to Bomber Command. Air Marshal Sir Arthur Travers Harris CB OBE, who arrived at High Wycombe on 22 February to take up his duties as commander-in-chief, was directed by Marshal of the RAF Sir Charles Portal, Chief of the Air Staff, to break the German spirit by the use of night area rather than precision bombing and the targets would be civilian, not just military. Harris, a compact, silent, bull-terrier of a man with one outstanding characteristic, a bitter hatred of the 'Hun' and all that he stood for, was 48 years old, born in Cheltenham, Gloucestershire on 13 April 1892, the son of a member of the Public Works Department of the Indian Civil Service. In 1910, aged 17, Harris had emigrated to Southern Rhodesia. He joined the 1st Rhodesia Regiment but returned to England in 1915 to join the Royal Flying Corps, with which he remained until the formation of the Royal Air Force in 1918. No.44 Squadron had been formed at Hainault in Essex on 24 July 1917 and by the end of the war it was commanded by Harris. He remained in the Air Force throughout the 1920s and 1930s and when he assumed command of RAF Bomber Command, among the squadrons he inherited was 44 Squadron, which became the first to convert completely to Lancasters, flying their first operational sorties in this aircraft with a mine-laying sortie in Heligoland Bight on 3 March 1942 and 97 (Straits Settlements) Squadron, which became the second Lancaster squadron after beginning conversion in January 1942. The first night-bombing operation was on 10/11 March when two of 44 Squadron's aircraft took part in the raid by 126 aircraft on Essen.

Known variously as 'Butch', 'Bomber' or 'Bert' (as Churchill, using naval slang, would often address him in private conversation), he has been described as 'a rough, tough, vulgar egomaniac'. To his crews, who he fondly referred to as his 'old lags', he was simply 'the 'guv'ner'. 'If he had put out the word, his squadrons would have flown up to and through the gates of Hell,' wrote one of his pilots. 'What stopped us in our tracks was the speed at which he was asking our crews to ride up to one of those gates.'

Whether you liked him, whatever the appellation, or despised him, Harris was just what Bomber Command needed. He feared no foe, senior officers or politicians. He brooked no arguments from juniors and pooh-poohed any from those of equal or senior status who held a contra opinion. Harris knew what he was going to do and proceeded to move Heaven and Earth to do it. Woe betide anyone who stood in his way. He was a firm believer in the Trenchard doctrine and with it he was going to win the war. According to Professor Solly Zuckerman, technical advisor to those responsible for the bombing policy, Harris 'liked destruction for its own sake'.

Sir Arthur warmed to the task, announcing: 'The Germans entered this war under the rather childish delusion that they were going to bomb everybody else and nobody was going to bomb them. At Rotterdam, London, Warsaw and half a hundred other places, they put that rather naive theory into operation. They sowed the wind and now they are going to reap the whirlwind.... We are going to scourge the Third Reich from end to end. We are bombing Germany city by city and ever more terribly in order to make it impossible for her to go on with the war. That is our object; we shall pursue it relentlessly.'

Furthermore he said later: 'There are a lot of people who say that bombing cannot win the war. My reply to that is that it has never been tried ... and we shall see.'

In the summer of 1941 RAF Bomber Command had, on paper, a nominal strength of 49 bomber squadrons or almost 1,000 aircraft but 8 of these squadrons were equipped with Blenheim light bombers and Harris's predecessor had been forced to rely mainly on the Wellington squadrons, for so long the backbone of Bomber Command operations. However, new, four-engined bombers like the Manchester, Stirling and the mighty four-engined Lancaster, which would enter service in early 1942, were coming off the drawing board. In May and June that same year Harris unleashed the first 'Thousand' raids on Cologne, Essen and Bremen. During March to July 1943 the Battle of the Ruhr followed and in July-August Hamburg was obliterated by fire of biblical proportions.

The fate of Hamburg aroused great anxiety in Berlin, especially when RAF aircraft dropped leaflets that called upon all women and children in the capital to leave at once, as they had done before the raids on Hamburg had begun. On 6 August Goebbels, deeply worried that the RAF would repeat the threat that they would 'Hamburgise' Berlin, caused panic by ordering an immediate partial evacuation of the city. By September 1943, 800,000 people had left Berlin. Over the coming months, until March 1944, a further 400,000 people were evacuated as the population of the capital dropped from 4 to 2.8 million. By the end of the year there were more than 6 million German evacuees from the bombing nationwide.[3]

Harris considered that the recent successes in both series of attacks confirmed his views that the time was ripe for the 'Final Battle': the destruction of the capital of the Third Reich. With the aid of H2S Berlin was easily identifiable from the air at night and the long winter nights made the deep penetration flights to the 'Big City' possible. When the weather forecast predicted not only favourable conditions over the target but acceptable landing conditions for the returning bomber fleet, which usually numbered between 400 and 700 aircraft, Bomber Command would go to war from scores of aerodrome villages carved out of farmland that had been lifted from pre-war obscurity and gave the impression that after the RAF had passed by they would lapse into obscurity again.

In a message to his crews that was read out at briefings before one particular raid on Berlin 'Bomber' Harris announced in a quiet but forceful tone: 'Tonight you are going to the "Big City". You will have the opportunity to light a fire in the belly of the enemy that will burn his black heart out.'

To reinforce his obsession to destroy the capital of the Third Reich, in a minute to Churchill on 3 November 1943 Harris said:

'We must get the USAAF to wade-in in greater force. If they will only get going according to plane and avoid such disastrous diversions as Ploesti, and getting 'nearer' to Germany from the Plains of Lombardy (which are further from 9/10th of war productive Germany than is Norfolk) we can get through it very quickly. We can wreck Berlin from end to end if the USAAF will come in on it. It will cost, between 400-500 aircraft. It will cost Germany the war.'

However, the USAAF could not attack a long-range target like Berlin for another ten months, by which time their fighters were able to escort the bombers on this long trip. So Bomber Command would have to undertake the Battle of Berlin on its own. All that was needed were a fair wind and good weather but October followed the same pattern as September, with more raids on German cities and some French targets and the first two weeks of November 1943 were a cold, dank and misty time. The Lincolnshire Fens lay swathed in fog for days on end and frost gleamed on the fields and hedges, warmed now and again by fitful bursts of sunshine, which made it possible to fly. Then the vibration from 2,000 Merlin engines running at climbing power (2,850 revs and +9 lb boost) would make the glasses dance on the bars of Lincolnshire's pubs, much to the wonder of those whose wartime role was possibly more permanent than that of the air crews who rode the sky above them.

A few nights before the Battle of Berlin began, American war correspondent Martha Gellhorn visited a Lancaster station in Lincolnshire to witness the squadrons' departure and return from a raid on Modane in France. Martha was not permitted to fly on raids like her male colleagues. She was a woman who maintained a certain emotional detachment in her personal life but who also wanted to engage in the world of action, to be a part of great events, to write about them, to do the work she had committed herself to, even when, or especially when, those events were tragic and heartbreaking. She loved being with exciting men who were also at the centre of things.[4]

The scene Martha described might just as easily have been a round trip to Berlin: 'The Lancasters looked like enormous deadly black birds going off into the night,' she wrote; 'somehow they looked different when they came back. The planes carried from this field 117,000 lbs of high explosive and the crews flew all night to drop the load as ordered…. Here are the men who did it, with mussed hair and weary faces, dirty sweaters under their flying suits, sleep-bright eyes, making humble comradely little jokes and eating their saved-up chocolate bars.'

Berlin was all this and more.

Finally, after a spell of bad weather had grounded the Main Force, at 'morning prayers' on Thursday, 18 November 'Bomber' Harris announced that 835 bombers would be over Germany that night; 440 of them Lancasters and four Mosquitoes heading for Berlin almost exactly due west of Lincoln, while another 395 aircraft, mostly Halifaxes and Stirlings, would fly a diversionary raid on Mannheim and Ludwigshafen 300 miles away. The total effort for the night would be a new record for a non-1,000 raid night but only by one, with 884 aircraft (including 45 aircraft engaged on minor operations) being dispatched.

Though 106 Squadron was in the process of moving from Syerston to Metheringham, they were still on the battle order. On 11 November the squadron's Lancasters were loaded with air and ground crew (plus a few hitch-hikers), suitcases, kitbags, bicycles and various impedimenta stashed in the fuselages for the squadron move. W.R.P. Perry, one of the pilots on the squadron, wrote:

'Chocks away – and so are we. My faithful ZN-Z was fully laden.

'Two friends of mine, Johnny Forsyth and Colin Storer were to formate on me and we proposed to announce our arrival with a gentle 'beat-up'. Metheringham R/T call sign was 'Coffee-stall', so we intended also to broadcast a rendering (literally!) of the Java Jive. The new Station Commander was not amused – and said so! We had joined the Squadron in June. Our 'own' first aircraft had been *'Admiral' Dumbo* (the flying elephant and it was!) and then a new ZN-Z *Admiral Shyte-Awk2*. Why the 'Admiral' prefix? At the time 106 was still the 5 Group designated ship attack squadron, and we had two Fleet Air Arm observer lieutenants attached to us. Every time we bombed a port they came along to identify what German naval ships were there. By November we were two-thirds through our first tour.

'On the 12th of November the Squadron and Station started 'working up'. We did an hour's local flying, checking new landmarks, noting our proximity to Coningsby, Woodhall Spa, Bardney and Waddington. Flying continued: ammunition, bombs and fuel stocked up and then we were ready to go on November 18th. I was told that I was not flying that night, but a brand new Lancaster was at Waddington awaiting collection. I could 'take a day off' and collect same. Taking Les Blood my wireless-operator and Doug Cunnison, bomb-aimer, we duly arrived at 'Waddo' and it then being lunchtime arranged to pick up the aircraft in the afternoon. I had barely started my meal when I was called to the phone and my flight commander informed me that the aircraft was now required for ops that night and that I was to fly it. I protested that if I was on ops I wanted my own 'Z'. It was to no avail. I could do the NFT (night flying test) on the way back 'and be quick about it!'

'At briefing at East Kirkby halfway between Spilsby and Coningsby in Lincolnshire there was a feeling of deep apprehension when the CO of 57 Squadron, Group Captain Taft announced, 'Well, gentlemen, your target tonight is "Whitebait".' (On behalf of Harris Air Marshal Sir Robert Henry Magnus Spencer Saundby KCB KBE MC DFC AFC who became Deputy AOC in Chief in 1943, had selected 94 German towns which were ripe for carpet bombing. A keen fly fisherman, he gave codenames to each of them known as 'Fish code'. For example Nuremberg was 'Grayling' and Berlin was 'Whitebait'.)

'For a few moments, 'Geoff' King the observer/bomb-aimer on George Lang's crew wrote, 'you could have heard a pin drop. Then, as our individual briefings commenced, the volume of noise increased – and so did our nervousness.'

'King had enrolled in the RAF in April 1940 at Cambridge, firstly serving on ground staff as a flight mechanic until re-mustering and being posted onto his initial air-crew training in January 1942. The training of pilots and navigators usually took about two to two and a quarter years. An 'Air Bomber' (the correct term for bomb-aimer) was about eighteen months. Wireless-operators and air gunners took about nine months to one year and an engineer usually took from six to nine months. George Lang was a young Canadian, who had told his new crew at OTU (Operational Training Unit), 'Well, you sons of bitches, you'll be flying with me.' And that's how they met their skipper. 'Lang loved the ladies; a devil in that respect and was as cool as a cucumber and remained in efficient overall control in all circumstances throughout the time we would fly together,' says King. 'Jock' (Robert) Burns, the flight engineer, quiet as a mouse, a real staid Scotsman, was a man whose ability more than lived up to his reputation. Australian 'Flash' ('Frank') Green, mid-upper and part-time rear gunner, was quietest of all, always on top of his job and he helped to save our bacon early on in our operational experiences. They were all quiet, unless we were having a booze-up. But they were few and far between. Wireless-operator Vince Day, a little cockney, full of life, kept us in close contact with base at all times and fed us any relevant information. Tommy Thomas, a typical Welshman but very quiet, and Dickie Poulson, rear gunners, were always efficient and always warned of any likely danger.'[5]

The crew skippered by Flying Officer Anthony Francis Gobbie was even more cosmopolitan. Gobbie was born in London on 24 November 1919. His father is thought to have been of Italian extraction. For a time the family lived in New England and Tony Gobbie attended Harvard University for a year before returning to England in about July 1939 and he joined the RAF where he became operational during the 'Battle of the Ruhr'. On 18 November he went to the briefing for the raid on Berlin, knowing that next morning the *London Gazette* would publish the citation for the award of his DFC. His navigator, Flying Officer Alfred Edward Walter Gardner, who hailed from Norbury, Surrey was also a recipient of the award of the DFC. Richard William Newcomb, the bomb-aimer who was from Olmué in the Marga Marga Province, Valparaíso Region in Chile, had unfortunately caught tonsillitis and missed some operations and had been assigned to the crew as the bomb-aimer. He had just been promoted to pilot officer and probably did not have time to buy his uniform.

Having by now survived two months of operations, George Lang's crew had moved up from the fourth bombing wave to the second. The crew would be flying 'lucky Charlie' that had arrived on the squadron two weeks before.

'"C-Charlie" became a true and trusted friend,' wrote 'Geoff' King. 'She was fitted with H2S and so my operational in-flight position now moved from the nose to the small (and very uncomfortable) bench seat beside "Curly" (Roy) Davis, who was quiet and a damn good navigator; 100 per cent competent and he would always keep them on course. My equipment was fixed to the right-hand side of his navigator's table. The H2S proved invaluable on long trips: not only did it provide constant fixes that I could pass to "Curly", it also let us map-read our way (literally) along the route thus enabling us to remain on track within the bomber stream and avoid the more heavily defended areas. Although we didn't know it at the time, the 18th November was to be the first of ten trips we were to make to Berlin.'[6]

At Wickenby, about 10 miles north-east of Lincoln, close to a brace of villages with names such as Rand, Fulnetby and Holton-cum-Beckering, whose publicans, when the RAF arrived, must have thought their dreams had come true,[7] 19-year-old flight engineer Brian Edward George Soper on 12 Squadron was a little shocked. Not having done any ops, he was called into the Chief Flight Engineer's office and told that he would be flying that night; not with his crew skippered by Warrant Officer Arthur Rew but with 30-year-old Flight Lieutenant Benjamin Edward McLaughlin DFC whose flight engineer had been recently commissioned and was away getting 'kitted up'. McLaughlin had served in the Portsmouth and Palestine Police forces before the war. Later at the briefing, Soper received another jolt when he saw that the target was the 'Big City'; 'the first time for me of many,' he wrote.

'Old Man Luck' was still pointing Warrant Officer Eric Jones's crew on 49 Squadron in the correct direction. The thin, 6 feet 5 inches tall former builder's clerk from Newent in Gloucestershire had not been to the 'Big City' since his 'second dickey' trip on 23/24 August 1943 and his crew had not been there at all.[8] In the early days heavy bombers carried second pilots or 'second dickies' as they were known. The idea was not so much as a reserve but rather to give the newcomer to the squadron a chance to learn his job thoroughly before taking on a crew of his own. As time went on the number of 'second dickey' trips was reduced to a couple, just to give the 'sprog driver', the inexperienced pilot, an idea of the 'score'.[9]

Jones's crew had survived their first sortie over Germany with a trip to Nuremberg on 27 August and confidence had probably increased by .01 per cent, and the pattern of visits into Lincoln, operating whenever the moon and weather and sleeping permitted, had begun to take shape.

"The very mention of the name Berlin,' Eric said, 'created a certain tension and apprehension amongst all those present at briefing. There were to be a further three raids on Berlin in that week and we participated in all of them. This raid on Berlin was my 14th and the crew's twelfth, so we were almost halfway through our tour. "Steve" Stevenson, my bomb-aimer, when approaching the city on his bombing run said, "Sorry Skipper, dummy run, go round again" and I put the Lanc into a 360° turn to come round onto the same heading. Well, we nearly finished our tour there and then and, I might add, some other poor devil's as well. When I had gone through 180° and facing the oncoming stream I was left in no doubt where the rest of the stream was. Lancs were visible all round and on a reciprocal heading. How we escaped a collision I will never know. Flying to the target one rarely saw another bomber unless they were being attacked by a fighter or coned by searchlights. To find the stream, fly on a reciprocal course. I said to "Steve"; "Don't you ever ask me to go round again. You make sure you line up correctly and we drop 'em first time." We did and that was the first and last time we went round again.

'After "Steve's" call for a "dummy run" over the target and turning to set course for home we hoped that no further problems lay ahead. Our wish was not granted. As the homeward trip progressed Ken Blackham my 26-year-old navigator, who was an ex-London policeman, started to calculate very high winds. At first he thought he had got it all wrong but eventually established that we were running into a 100 mph headwind and it was cutting our ground speed back to a comparative snail pace; I doubt if we were moving over the ground any quicker than 120 mph. This situation had Ron Harris, the 19-year-old engineer, doing rapid petrol calculations and as the homeward journey progressed it was obvious we were not going to make base and we might not even make England. Our luck lasted out and we crossed the coastline but it meant getting down onto the "deck" as quickly as possible and this turned out to be an American base.

'That night the main Bomber Force was scattered all over Eastern England, obviously seriously disrupting any operational plans for the following night. Our American hosts, delighted at having a Lancaster in their midst, feted us with a cracking meal and excellent overnight accommodation (for what was left of the night). When we flew out the following morning we noticed that our night flying rations had been stolen from our Lanc, we suspected by American ground crew as some kind of souvenir. So who cared? They had looked after us so well.

'There were to be a further three raids on Berlin in that week and we participated in all of them; then Berlin again the following week.'

All told, Eric Jones and his crew would take part in twelve raids on the German capital.

At Warboys in Huntingdonshire Bill Porter, a flight engineer on 156 Squadron in the Pathfinder Force, was down to fly 'P-Peter', the crew's 'old pal' and favourite Lancaster.

"We always had confidence in her and everything seemed right,' wrote Porter. 'Briefing informed us that the target for that night was the "Big City" – well named as it was thirty-three miles across: a long way, after dropping your bombs, to the relative safety of darker skies.

'We drew our parachutes from the store. Printed on mine was "Squadron Leader Brian Duigan DFC". I knew he had finished his second tour of ops shortly after we started on ours. He was a tough Australian and a lucky one. I hoped his luck would be carried in his parachute. Was it some kind of omen? A lucky charm? It was a cheering thought.'

Pilot Officer John C. Adams, an Australian pilot serving on 50 Squadron at Skellingthorpe just outside Lincoln, was down to fly 'S-Sugar', a brand-new Lancaster, one of twenty-one aircraft his squadron were contributing to the Berlin raid:

'Our Lancasters had been loaded to an all up weight of 65,000lb. This consisted of enough fuel for us to stay airborne for nearly nine hours and our bomb load was the usual 4,000lb 'cookie' surrounded by nearly 6,000lb of incendiaries. We had been briefed to take the most direct route to the target – 'straight in' – which took us over Holland and north of most of the defended areas such as the Ruhr and the cities east of it. Our return track was to take us north after leaving the target. When we reached the Baltic we were to fly due west over Denmark.

'We left the English coast near Mablethorpe and headed across the North Sea until we came to the coast of Holland. By this time we had climbed to 18,000 feet. After a short time over land we were again over water, the Zuider Zee. It was a very dark night and we were only just able to make out shorelines. There were no features on the ground which we could distinguish. By this time we had left the effective area of our 'Gee' navigation system so that the coast of the Zuider Zee was the last chance we had of fixing our position. From there to the target it would be a matter of flying by dead reckoning using the wind strength and direction obtained from the last position fix.

'The weather had been fairly clear over England but as the flight progressed we found patches of cloud at around the height we were flying. I was flying the Lancaster for most of the time on instruments. There was very little to be seen by looking out. On clear nights I looked on the Pole Star as a good friend. It was very often nicely positioned just over my left wingtip on our way to the target. However, on this occasion there was too much cloud around for it to be visible.

'We were well into Germany, somewhere to the north-west of Hanover, when I was startled by another aircraft which flashed in front of my windscreen. It was close enough for me to see that it was twin-engined and it seemed to be travelling very fast, about 100 mph faster than we were. It came into my field of vision from our left and disappeared off to the right a few metres in front of my right wingtip. I think that its course would have been at an angle of about sixty degrees to our own. It was close enough for me to see the flames from its engines and, whether I imagined it or not, I believed that I heard their roar as it was crossing in front of us. This close encounter happened so fast that 'Tom' Midgely, our flight engineer was the only other member of the crew who saw it. When the other members of the crew heard what had very nearly happened, there was some excited chatter over the intercom but it soon died down. I told the boys to forget about it. That one had missed us!

'I wondered if the enemy pilot had another Lancaster on his radar and was hurrying to catch up with him or whether he had just been vectored into the bomber stream. To this day I wonder if that enemy pilot was aware that he had come within a split second of being part of a fireball in the sky.

'When we arrived we found the city covered in cloud and because of the difficulty of accurately identifying the target area, the markers were quite scattered. We bombed on what appeared to be the main concentration of reds and greens. With the cloud cover, searchlights were not a problem but the defences put up a very heavy barrage of predicted flak. We had no chance of obtaining a picture of the aiming point; we just came back with a nice picture of cloud which was lit up by the fires under it and some lines of light which represented the target indicator flares. We saw no fighters and we managed to come through the flak barrage without damage although some bursts were fairly close.

'Despite our confidence things quickly began to go wrong,' wrote Bill Porter on 'P-Peter' on 156 Squadron. 'The weather forecast was for clear skies over Germany but it proved to be 10/10ths cloud up to 12,000 feet and the forecast wind strength was way out. Either King, our navigator, didn't spot it or Doug our wireless-operator didn't pick up a broadcast of altered wind speed from Bomber Command HQ. Consequently, King said, "Navigator to pilot: time to target is now..." He was rudely interrupted by a burst of anti-aircraft fire around us. Buffeted around in the hail of ack-ack fire and hearing the clangs of shrapnel hitting old "P-Peter", I thought, "We're for it now. They've got us on the hook with their radar-predicted flak." But, thanks to George, our skipper, jinking the Lanc around we eventually got away. Once clear George said, "Pilot to navigator: where was that?"'

'"Brandenburg, skip," replied King.

'From Brandenburg we were supposed to make a timed run to Berlin but, because of the wind strength, we were at the target already – ahead of everybody else! At the briefing we had been told the time over the target would be sixteen minutes with twenty-seven aircraft bombing every minute. If we went round again we would be late and the anti-aircraft guns would have us on our own again.

'"That option's out," decided George, much to our relief although to my surprise he then said, "Navigator: give me a reciprocal course back over Berlin." King did so and we swung round 180 degrees and back we went.[10]

'By this time the target was well alight. Our planes, silhouetted against this and the searchlights on the thick cloud beneath us, looked like strange insects crawling over a vast table top. Those that spotted us going the wrong way must have thought us very foolish, or that we had a duff navigator aboard. But we dropped our bombs and left, inwardly congratulating ourselves that we had got away with it and that the worst was over. We had to fly south-west to pick up the main bomber stream heading home. Everything was remarkably quiet.

'"Christ!" yelled George suddenly over the intercom as he sent "P-Peter" into a nose dive.

'"What the hell?"

'There was a deafening bang and we plummeted like a broken lift. My feet left the floor. I hung on to the canvas back of my seat and saw my parachute pack apparently floating in mid air. After what seemed like an age, when I felt sure we would hit the ground and that would be it, George pulled "P-Peter" out of the dive.

'"Everyone OK?" he asked over the intercom. Doug, regaining his composure at his wireless-operator's panel, ignored the question and said, "All the internal fuselage lights have come on. We'll look like a Christmas tree from outside. I want something to smash the bulbs."

'"Use the hammer in my tool kit," I indicated to Doug as I was busy checking the engine gauges.

'"All engines seem all right. Exhaust stub flames OK for colour, skip," I said.

'"That's a relief," replied George.

'Doug's voice came again over the intercom. "Just been down the back. Al's heading this way," he said referring to our rear gunner, "he's hurt his hands."

'It turned out that in the nose dive "Al" had thought we were going down for good and had taken off his gloves to open his turret doors to get his parachute in readiness for baling out. As he had held on to the metal to pull himself out, his hands had been severely frost-bitten and he had pulled all the skin off his palms and fingers. Doug installed him on the rest bed and he remained there holding his painful hands in the air for the rest of the trip home. Doug borrowed my hammer and hit the light bulbs. (He took a kind of fiendish pleasure in smashing up Air Ministry property, he said later.) He had tried to man the rear turret but it was useless and would not rotate at all. Fortunately, it was not needed for the trip back home was uneventful.'

As Flying Officer William H. Baker of Hull, the pilot of 'V-Victor' on 207 Squadron began his bombing run, his aircraft collided with the rear of 'Z-Zebra', the Lancaster skippered by Pilot Officer Frank Lees on 9 Squadron at Bardney.

According to Baker's 23-year-old navigator, Flight Sergeant Thomas Gedling of South Shields, they were 'zigging' and Lees' plane was 'zagging'!

Gedling's fingers and feet became frostbitten before the Lancaster reached the target, but he wrapped a sweater round his hands and continued his work. Baker's Lancaster suffered severe damage to the nose and port propellers and Flight Sergeant Jim Shimield his bomb-aimer fell to his death when the forward escape hatch was lost. On 'Z-Zebra' Sergeant Leonard Stanley Harris, the 20-year-old rear gunner, was killed. Lees, a policeman from Manchester, could not maintain height so he ordered his crew to abandon 'Z-Zebra'. Flight Sergeant H. Fisher from Huddersfield and D.T. Cordon the navigator walked for five days before being arrested by a German policeman.

Bill Baker flew his crippled Lancaster over the target, but only then did the crew discover that the bomb-release gear was out of action. Baker turned for home on three engines. The wind that blew through the open nose of the bomber was bitterly cold at 20,000 feet and the crew were soon numbed by the elements. While his crew huddled for warmth in the fuselage, Baker was exposed to the full blast of the biting wind. By the time he landed back at Spilsby where his wife was an MT driver on the squadron, Baker had badly frostbitten fingers on both hands and he would never fly on operations again. 'Tom' Gedling also had badly frostbitten fingers, but continued his allotted task until the English coast was safely reached. For his courage and fortitude, which 'contributed to the safe return of his aircraft' he was awarded the DFM. Bill Baker was awarded an immediate DFC. 'V-Victor' was repaired and a few days later, on 22 December, Baker took the aircraft on a cross-country test flight. There was an engine fire which could not be extinguished and the crew was ordered to bail out. Three of Baker's crew were killed.[11] The story of the collision broke when the flight engineer on Baker's aircraft later ended up in Stalag Luft IVB, the same prison camp as five members of Lees' crew.

Tony Gobbie's crew on 'I-Ink' on 57 Squadron were shot down at Barnsdorf about 11 kilometres from Dresden. Alfred Gardner and Richard Newcomb were killed; the rest of the crew were taken prisoner. Two years after repatriation to England, in 1947 Tony Gobbie yet again crossed the Atlantic to America and migrated to Florida where he married Lorraine Albin in Broward County in 1953.[12]

None of the crews saw the 'Big City' through the thick cloud that carpeted Berlin and the winds proved to be far stronger than predicted. The bomber stream became scattered and bombing was carried out blindly. Tens of thousands of incendiaries and 2- and 4-ton HE (high-explosive) bombs were dropped within a period of barely thirty minutes. One of the Pathfinder aircraft dropped a yellow TI [Target Indicator] in error, confusing the Main Force bomb-aimers who had been instructed to bomb on the green TIs only.[13] According to the post-raid report:

'the TIs could be seen cascading to the ground and much of the effort undoubtedly fell on Berlin but the comparative failure of this operation resulted from unserviceable H2S sets – of which nineteen out of twenty-seven failed; an unexpectedly light wind en route delaying the backers-up so that for five or six minutes only one Green TI could be seen burning; and a smokescreen hampering visibility.'

Only one aircraft on the raid – a Mosquito – had been equipped with the new Mk III H2S on which so many hopes were pinned, but that set became unserviceable en route to the target. The pilot obeyed orders and returned to base. No serious damage was inflicted to major industrial premises, although considerable damage was caused by fire in residential suburbs.

'We had our usual uneventful trip until the approach to the target,' wrote 'Geoff' King on 'C-Charlie' on 57 Squadron. 'This was from the north-west. It took an eternity, for we hardly seemed to be moving. Ahead of us lay what appeared to be an impenetrable screen of anti-aircraft fire from ground level to well over 20,000 feet, bursting in sequence every so many seconds at all levels. I thought, "My God! How in hell's name are we going to get through this lot?" On our starboard side were two aircraft burning from stem to stern. As we neared our aiming point I concentrated on our bombing run and not on the hell that was going on outside the aircraft.

'"Bomb doors open. Left, left – steady, steady." As the illuminated cross on my Mk XIV bomb sight criss-crossed the green target markers, I pressed my bomb release. At that moment, you could feel the bomb load leave the bomb bay and immediately the aircraft wanted to rise. "Bomb doors closed."

'Below, one could see some of our own Lancasters and Halifaxes silhouetted against the inferno. I often wondered how many of these aircraft were hit by bombs from above. (In theory, most of them should not have been there, because each bomber wave had its own height and time of attack – essential with the number of aircraft taking part.) There were also enemy fighters flying with us. If the anti-aircraft fire eased, you knew that fighters were there in numbers but usually they ignored their own defences and pressed home their attacks on some unfortunate aircraft. It was just like a boiling cauldron below and fires were visible a hundred miles away from the target. I usually remained in the nose until we were clear of the target, keeping an extra eye open for fighters and other aircraft. This trip, with a loss of nine was to be one of the lowest losses on this target.

'At about this time the German night fighters were becoming more visible and more efficient. (What we didn't then realise was that some of them could home in on our H2S and precautionary warning systems.) Some were equipped with fixed upward-firing cannons ('Schräge Musik'; 'Jazz' or 'slanting' or 'Oblique Music'): devastating weapons that could cut a Lancaster apart (they could also be a bit hazardous for the fighter pilot, if he got too close to an exploding aircraft). Fortunately, we didn't at that time realise the full potential of this type of fighter but it may explain a few of the little mysteries, such as damage and losses that we attributed to other causes or to bad luck.'

'P-Peter' on 156 Squadron joined the circuit over Warboys: 'We were told to take our place in the queue and circle while waiting to land,' wrote Bill Porter. 'My heart sank. The petrol gauges were showing almost empty now. Ten minutes later we were still circling and I had to tell George of my worries.

'Be safest to use the transfer cock and feed all engines from the starboard main tank – that's got most in,' I said.

'"OK, Bill," said George; "go ahead."

'I held my breath and crossed my fingers (not literally) as I turned over the feed controls to that tank. The engines continued to purr without faltering but even so, I was desperately worried about the petrol. Five more minutes went by and we were still circling.

'I hope these gauges are accurate or else we're in real trouble,' I told 'George'. That spurred him into action and he called control to tell them. They insisted we wait and continue circling.

'We can't,' I said, 'we've no juice!'

'"George" called control again. "We are short of petrol and we're coming in."

'He headed for the downwind leg of the runway watching for other planes landing as we were jumping the queue. I put the undercarriage down and checked the tyres with an Aldis lamp. We couldn't check whether the tail wheel was there or not.

'"Bill, cut the throttles," said "George". I did so and hung on for a rough landing but all was well and we taxied back to our pan, shut down the engines and all was quiet.

'When I emerged from "P-Peter" the sergeant in charge of the ground crew was standing at the bottom of the ladder. "All engines OK, 'Chiefy'," I told him confidently.

'"Wanna bet? Come and have a look."

'The side cowlings on both port engines had been ripped off and the outer one had about eight feet of the flexible alloy air intake branch hanging down. The propeller blade tips on both airscrews were bent.

'"Ignore my remark about the engines 'Chiefy'," I said.'

Brian Soper would have worse trips later, but this first one was memorable: 'For the first time I experienced the flak, the searchlights, the fires, the bombs bursting on the ground and the Lanc shaking when the flak was close. I saw the brilliant colours of the target markers on the ground and experienced the long, long wait over the target while the bomb-aimer identified the target and gave his instructions to the pilot. I felt the great lift of the Lanc when the bombs were released and then the two minutes flying on straight and level for the camera to check where our bombs had gone. And finally to dive and turn away on a course for home. I had to wonder what this experienced crew thought of this new 'sprog' engineer on his first trip, the crew that I hadn't even really met. It seemed like hours before we got away from the target.'

Unfortunately, Flight Lieutenant McLaughlin, his pilot on this trip, was killed on 5 July 1944 during dual-instruction training on a Halifax on 1667 HCU at Sandtoft in Lincolnshire.

Pilot Officer John Adams on 50 Squadron had left the target area and the trip home to Skellingthorpe from then on was without incident:

'When we reached our dispersal, we were greeted by the ground staff, who anxiously asked if all was well with their lovely new 'S-Sugar'. We told them that she had performed perfectly except that 'Monica' was u/s. They said that it was not their worry – the radar people would have to fix that. We were discussing this when the crew bus arrived to pick us up. As we piled in, the ground crew were already starting to work on servicing 'S".

At the debriefing at Wickenby Brian Soper enjoyed a cigarette and a tot of rum. 'It was like living again – but for how long?' He would follow this trip with three more to Berlin, flying with his own pilot and crew.

At Warboys 'P-Peter's crew on 156 Squadron surveyed the damage to their Lancaster in the cold light of day:

'The ground crew told us,' wrote Bill Porter, 'that on dipping the tanks there had been only thirty-five gallons of petrol left. I went round to the rear turret. "Al" had been lucky that it (and he) hadn't been cut off entirely – even the ammunition belts were severed. He and our mid-upper gunner had been fortunate in that the nine flak holes in the fuselage were between their positions. The astrodome had been sliced off – another foot or two further forward and I'd have had it – so too would George. So, what exactly had happened? It seemed that we had collided with two aircraft: the one George saw to port when he had instinctively taken evasive action by shoving the control column forward and sending us into a dive but close enough for the other aircraft to wipe off the astrodome. In diving we had hit another aircraft but how the side cowlings came off remained a mystery. It was extraordinary that a plane had been directly underneath us. It dawned on us that it could well have been an enemy fighter with upward slanting guns just ready to have a go at us when we fell out of the sky on top of him! We could well have written him off. It was a cheering thought out of such a close run thing. It was then I thought about my parachute: had the tough Australian, Squadron Leader Duigan, been watching over me last night?'[14]

A mid-upper gunner on 44 ('Rhodesia') Squadron at Dunholme Lodge who was on his first trip to Berlin wrote later:

'The night was a cold night with big patches of cloud. About five minutes after take-off, I saw ice was forming on the guns. As we left the cloud the ice disappeared, but I had to keep a watch-out for it the rest of the trip. As we reached the enemy coast, flak opened up and a stray piece hit the exhaust on the starboard inner engine, which burst into flames. From the mid-upper turret, I could see the flames shooting out for nearly two feet and lighting up the clouds around us. I reported to the skipper, who could also see the damage from his cabin.

'The great danger was that the flame might reach the petrol tanks, but as it was not blowing that way and the engine was still working, we decided to carry on, the flight engineer keeping a careful watch on the temperature of the engine. No one made any suggestion of turning back.

'We went on and made our bombing run. Cloud was thicker over the city, but this was to our advantage, because their searchlights couldn't get through to us. Flames were still streaming from the exhaust, lighting up the clouds around us, and my turret in particular; I felt conspicuous but luckily, cloud kept the fighters down. We didn't see one – only a couple of fighter flares on the way back. By the time we got to base, the exhaust was burning merrily, but we landed safely and were pretty glad to see the ground again. But taking it all round it was one of the quietest trips I ever made.'[15]

The headlines in the *Daily Mail* on Saturday, 20 November announced: 'It has entered the realm of possibility that Berlin may be approaching the end of its days as a capital city, due to the fearful rain of bombs that fell on it Monday night. The RAF has devised means to level targets the size of Berlin. The raid was by far the heaviest that that city has ever experienced'.

RAF Headquarters reported: Last night Bomber Command sent to Germany the largest contingent of heavy bombers ever deployed in a single night. It divided up into two formations which operated independently. One formation attacked Ludwigshafen, the other Berlin, which lay under a pall of cloud so that the damage could not be accurately observed. A stream of several hundred four-engined bombers reached the German capital along the Havel river (in eastern Germany) and then split into groups that bombed Siemensstadt, Neukölln, Mariendorf, Steglitz, Marienfelde and other districts of Berlin. Tens of thousands of incendiaries and two- and four-ton high-explosive bombs dropped on Berlin within a period of barely thirty minutes. The reflection of huge fires lit up the clouds, revealing that severe damage must have occurred in the industrial districts.

The Air Ministry said: 'More than 2,500 tons of bombs were dropped in the raids on Berlin and Ludwigshafen. Two important targets were raided simultaneously; simultaneous raiding is a new tactic of Bomber Command. Recently the Luftwaffe has concentrated extremely strong formations of night fighters around probable target zones. Aerial reconnaissance informs Bomber Command of the positions of the German night fighters and Bomber Command then tries to strike at places where there is inadequate fighter protection. For example, last night the RAF deployed its formations simultaneously over two cities approximately three hundred miles apart, so that the German night fighter defences found it impossible adequately to protect both targets. Naturally these new tactics require the deployment of formations that are as large as possible, because despite everything the German Luftwaffe remains a formidable enemy that is quite capable of warding off twin attacks of limited force'.[16]

German fighter controllers were unable to bring any significant number of 'Wild Boar' ('Wilde Sau') and 'Tame Boar' ('Zahme Sau') night-fighters employing freelance or Pursuit Night Fighting tactics into action against the bomber stream bound for Berlin. Only nine Lancasters were lost from this force, all to flak; just 2 per cent. (On Ludwigshafen losses were 5.8 per cent.)

One of the missing on Berlin was a 'special' Lancaster on 101 Squadron at Ludford Magna. Ludford was better known as 'Mudford Magma' and 'Mudford Stagna' because it was still marshy, although built on one of the highest stretches of the Lincolnshire Wolds. The Special Squadron's Lancasters were armed and loaded with bombs just like the other heavy bombers but carried an extra crew member who operated 'ABC' or 'Airborne Cigar' equipment to jam enemy radio transmissions.

Lancaster III LM370 SR-K2 piloted by Flying Officer Charles Patrick McManus who was from Eire was shot down and crashed SSE of Emmen in Holland and the radar-jamming equipment was examined by the Germans. All the crew were killed and are buried at Schoonebeek, Holland.

As 101 Squadron losses mounted it was later suspected that German fighters were homing in on the emissions from the 'ABC' equipment in the aircraft. From October 1943 until the end of the war all Main Force attacks on German targets were accompanied by the 'ABC'-equipped Lancasters, sometimes up to twenty-seven on one raid. Between 18 November 1943 and 24 March 1944 101 Squadron lost seventeen aircraft. The 'ABC' aircraft were stationed in pairs at regular intervals in the bomber stream so that if one was shot down, other parts of the stream would still be covered.

An effective 'Tame Boar' operation mounted against the second force destroyed ten bombers, while flak destroyed another thirteen bombers.

'The RAF's twin assault was so carefully timed and so well concentrated,' went another official report, 'that only thirty-two bombers were lost – a very small percentage of the total used. The effects of this twin raid, greatest military operation of its kind in history, will go far beyond the enormous havoc wrought to German war production. It has shown the Nazis that during recent bad weather lulls the RAF's bombing strength has been built up into a mighty weapon capable, in time, of paralysing their entire war machine. It has, too, completely falsified the recent assurances of Nazi leaders that new defensive tactics and secret weapons would give immediate immunity from large-scale raids. The operations were another triumph for the RAF's weather men, who accurately predicted conditions which would give our Berlin raiders cloud cover and ensure clear visibility for our bombers on their return to base.'

One report said: 'The main weight of the attack is reported to have fallen on the south-west of the capital. The Hochbahn (subway) had direct hits in several places. Railway sidings and goods yards were smashed. Bombs fell on the centre of the city. The Army, SS and police are busy sheltering thousands rendered homeless. More than 350 4,000lb 'blockbusters' rained down on Berlin. The number of four-engined bombers used to set this new Bomber Command record was probably not far short of 1,000. It is possible that well over 2,500 tons of high explosives and fire bombs were showered on the two German targets. The attack proved as never before the value of Pathfinder squadrons. Berlin was attacked by an all-Lancaster force that had to battle through ice and cloud to the hidden target. They dropped their bombs within the gaudy patterns of target indicators dropped by the Pathfinders, which cascaded through the clouds. As the 'blockbusters' fell, fires glowed over a wide area. Series of violent explosions burst through the clouds, even when the bomb flashes were hidden. The Germans call our 4,000lb explosives 'Bezirkbomben' – district bombs. One of them can make a whole block of buildings disappear. Every plane in one squadron carried a 'blockbuster'.

'The Lancasters were over Berlin for half an hour, beginning just before 9 pm. But many crews reported there was no sign of fighters. Cloud protected our planes and prevented the thousands of British and Empire airmen engaged from seeing the effects of their onslaught.[17]

'Another report – headlined BIGGEST BLITZ: RAF OUT AGAIN ALL EUROPE OFF THE AIR LAST NIGHT: BERLIN HIT BY 350 'COOKIES' – appeared in the press after Leverkusen was bombed on the night of 19/20 November when bad weather on the continent prevented many night-fighters from operating and only five bombers were lost. It was reported that

'Waves of Britain's biggest bombers streamed out towards Europe last night less than twenty-four hours after the RAF had sent its greatest-ever force of heavy bombers to launch its first twin 'thunderbolt' assault with Berlin and Ludwigshafen the targets. Over the south-east coast the procession, starting early, took close on three-quarters of an hour to cross. The size and direction of the force indicated another big raid on Germany. All over Europe there was a radio black-out and Berlin, Deutschlandsender, Bremen, Leipzig, Hamburg, Cologne were off the air. All day yesterday fires started by our bombers on Thursday night burned unchecked in Berlin. That was made clear by a German High Command announcement last night. The fires, they stated, 'have now been brought under control.' First reports from the German frontier state that traffic has been paralysed by 'the hardest attack the German capital has suffered.'

'After 'P-Peter' on 156 Squadron landed at Warboys an ambulance had whisked away the crew's injured rear gunner for an MO's inspection and he was later admitted to the RAF hospital in Ely. Middleton St George reported three Canadian crew members suffering frostbite as a result of temperatures as low as -40°C. One was a rear gunner who had cut a clear-vision panel in his turret, while the other two were navigators whose photo-flash camera hatches were 'exceedingly draughty'.

'On 106 Squadron W.R.P. Perry's new aircraft had proved a success: 'We bombed Berlin from 25,000 feet (the higher the fewer) and came back at 27,500 feet. Pilot Officer 'Miff' Mifflin (whose flight engineer, Norman Jackson later won the VC) who had taken 'Z' that night had the pilot's side window blown out. He said that it was a bit chilly! The next two months passed quickly and we finished our tour'.

Airmen who were badly injured and badly burned were treated as in-patients at Ely for two months before becoming some of Sir Archibald McIndoe's 'guinea pigs' at East Grinstead Hospital. McIndoe was a New Zealander and the father of skin grafts. Fellow Kiwi Flight Sergeant Ivan Williamson, a wireless-operator on 115 Squadron at Little Snoring, was the victim of a horrific crash in a Lancaster on 14 September 1943 after two engines were feathered at 1,200 feet during an air test in which he sustained grave facial burns as well as a broken shoulder blade, six broken ribs and a sizeable lump of flesh gouged out of his groin. If that were not enough, he had a perfect print of a Lancaster spar, including two bolt-heads, imprinted in his back. He was photographed every morning and received a copy of his early grafts. He healed 'like a healthy animal' and it wasn't long before he was disgracing himself, 'getting a hard on in my saline bath'.

'Life was cheap in those pretty hard days. I went back to the squadron as a lost soul and crewed up twice with new crews but was taken off the Battle Order both times. Neither crew survived their first op. I later crewed up with a crew who had seven trips on Stirlings but the pilot and bomb-aimer went LMF ('lack of moral fibre'; in other words 'a coward').[18] They were stripped of all rank and the crew was finally broken up after six trips, four of which were to Berlin. I went on with 75 (New Zealand) Squadron later and in all did 44 operations. I had incredible luck all the way through. It would be no exaggeration to say that I missed death at least ten times during the war and since.'

Chapter Two

Ordeal by Fire

'Everything suddenly went all white. The brilliance stayed in the sky for a long time and then coloured to a reddish glow, which went on as long as we were over the target. It was like a terrific sunset.'

Sergeant G.K. Chapman of Tynemouth, Northumberland, a Lancaster navigator.

The 23-year-old Ursula Gebel, a Berlin secretary, was very fond of animals. Fortunately, her family were shareholders in the Zoologische Garten (Bahn Zoo) off the Kurfürstendamm in the Tiergarten district, which meant that they all had free entrance at any time. During the afternoon of Monday, 22 November 1943 Ursula stayed for a long time at the elephant cage, wistfully watching performing tricks and stunts with the keeper. There were six females and one baby elephant. Just before closing time, the baby elephant turned the handle of a barrel organ and played a goodbye melody.[1] Momentarily the war seemed far away; however, Berliners lived in constant fear of air-raids on their city. They were terrified of the blast effects of a 4,000lb 'cookie' bomb and the air pressure of the explosions that burst lungs and internal organs. They were frightened too of the incendiaries filled with 11lb of phosphorous, which penetrated to lower floors so that a dwelling could burn from the bottom upwards and from the top downwards at the same time until the roof beams fell and crumbling walls crushed them. The death that came from the sky killed defenceless people, especially women, small children and old people. Unlike the soldiers in the field, they did not have the opportunity to surrender and places to safely take shelter were few.

Work had begun on an extensive system of public air-raid shelters before the war, but by 1939 only 15 per cent of the planned 2,000 shelters for Berlin had been built. Other shelters were built under government buildings, the best-known being the so-called 'Führer bunker' under the Reich Chancellery building. In addition, many U-Bahn stations were converted into shelters.[2] In an air-raid shelter Berliners could suffocate, burn or drown in fire-fighting water. Much of the population had to make do with their own cellars. However, even before the procession of RAF British bombers bent on raining destruction on the Reich capital headed their way, thousands of Berliners knew they had a better chance of survival if they could take cover on the lower floors inside the three enormous 'Gustav' twin flak fortifications in the city. With concrete walls up to 3.5 metres (11 feet) thick, they were considered to be invulnerable to attack from the air and much like the keeps of medieval castles, they were some of the safest places in a fought-over city.

Known officially as 'G' (Gefechtsturm or 'combat') towers or Flaktürme, their construction had been ordered by Hitler after the RAF raid on Berlin in 1940. In

May 1941 the Führer gave his approval to the final design submitted by Professor Friedrich Tamms, the chief architect. From the outset the plan was to utilize the above-ground Hochbunker (blockhouse) bunkers as a civilian air-raid shelter with room for 10,000 civilians inside. There was also space to house the most priceless and irreplaceable holdings of fourteen museums from Berlin, while on the third floor was an eighty-five-bed hospital. The rooms were climate-controlled. Joseph Goebbels said that they were 'true wonders of defence'. The Führer wanted six towers in Berlin[3] but only three were built. The first of these, Flakturm I at the Bahn Zoo was in Hitler's favoured Neo-Romantic style with some elements of medieval fortresses. The flakturm site was flood-lit nightly despite the blackout, except during actual raids. By pouring cement around the clock, construction was completed in six months. Its location in the Tiergarten in a busy part of the city gave the tower its name and its presence would raise morale.[4]

Once the hunting-ground of Prussian kings, the Tiergarten had been chosen by Hitler as the new Nazi government diplomatic district and work started in 1938 on an ensemble of new embassies. All of these were in the impersonal monumental style chosen by the Führer and Albert Speer, his 38-year-old chief architect and the Nazi Armaments Minister who had overseen the construction of the New Reich's Chancellery in the remarkable time of just under a year for the Führer's diplomatic New Year reception on 10 January 1939. Speer enjoyed the trappings of a private office in his War Industry Ministry next to the Hotel Adlon on the Unter den Linden, the main boulevard in the central Mitte district at the corner with Pariser Platz directly opposite the Brandenburg Gate. Early in the war Hitler would make his way discreetly via a series of gardens to the government ministerial buildings fronting Wilhelmstrasse to Speer's private office.

For Jews the life-saving concrete 'castles' like the 'Gustav' were verboten (forbidden). There were no shelters for these wretched people. In 1943 they lived only as forced labourers, in Mishhen with Aryan spouses or as illegals in Berlin. Joel King was one of them. His biggest problem was not the bombs; he hoped they would bring liberation. Until then, he had to hide from the Nazis. At night he slept in a kind of bunk room; during the day he had to make himself invisible. In March 1943 he discovered the Bahn Zoo as a refuge. In the aquarium house it was quiet and warm; here he could rest a little.

The four twin 128mm (5 inch) guns on the roof had effective range to defend against the RAF and USAAF heavy bombers. Crewed by 350 anti-aircraft personnel and assisted by the Hitler Youth, the flak towers were able to sustain a rate of fire of 8,000 rounds per minute from their multi-level guns with a range of up to 14 kilometres (8.7 miles) in a 360-degree field of fire. From 1943 the lower platforms of the zoo facility had four twin mounts of 12.8cm Flak 40. As soon as Flakturm I was completed, contractors started on Flakturm II at Friedrichshain and Flakturm III in the Volkspark at Humboldthain on the outskirts of Berlin to create a triangle of anti-aircraft fire that covered the centre of the city. Building the towers was a serious diversion from Hitler's primary war effort. Each day trains and barges needed to deliver 2,000 tonnes of concrete, steel and timber. Germany's national rail timetable was adjusted to give the flak materials priority. By 1942 the five huge public shelters (Bahn Zoo; Anhalt Bahnhof close to the Potsdamer Platz;

Volkspark Humboldthain; the Turmpaar II in the Volkspark Friedrichshain; and the Heinrich von Kleist Park) were complete, offering shelter to 65,000 people.

The lowest two floors of each tower pair were designed for up to 15,000 people, but had to cope with as many as 40,000. Crowds queued on suitcases outside during the day to get inside during night raids but the conditions became appalling with foul air, hospital corpses, vermin and concrete dust. Armin Lehmann, a junior courier moving in and out of Hitler's bunker, later related:

'Men, women and children would exist for days on end, squashed side by side like sardines along every corridor and in every room. The lavatories would very quickly cease to function, clogged up by overuse and impossible to flush because of lack of running water. The passageways of the hospital units became make-do mortuaries for the dead – the nurses and doctors fearing death themselves if they dared venture out to bury the corpses. Buckets of severed limbs and other putrid body parts lined all the corridors.'

Harry Schweizer, a 17-year-old flak auxiliary with the Hitler Youth, wrote of his experiences at the Zoo Bunker which he considered the most comfortable of the three big flak towers in Berlin:

'It was well equipped with the best available materials, whereas the interior fittings of the Friedrichshain and Humboldthain Bunkers had been skimped, only the military equipment being first rate. The Zoo Bunker's fighting equipment consisted of four twin 128mm guns on the upper platform and a gallery about five metres lower down with a 37mm gun at each corner and a twin-barrelled 20mm gun in the centre of each side flanked by solo 20mm guns left and right. The twin 128s were fired optically (by line of sight) whenever the weather was clear enough, otherwise electronically by remote control. The settings came from the smaller flak bunker nearby, which only had light flak on its gallery for its defence, but was especially equipped with electronic devices. Long-range Blaupunkt radar was installed there and our firing settings came from 'Giant Würzburg' radar as far away as Hanover. That bunker also contained the control room for air situation reports and was responsible for issuing air raid warnings.

'Our training went along simultaneously with action with the heavy and light artillery pieces. We also received some basic training on radar and explosives. We suffered no casualties from air attacks, but comrades were killed by gun barrels exploding and recoils. The shells for the 128s relied on the radar readings for their fuse settings and were moved centrally on rubber rollers up to the breech. If there was only the slightest film of oil on the rollers, the already primed shell would not move fast enough into the breech and would explode.... The 128s were used mainly for firing at the leading aircraft of a group, as these were believed to be the controllers of the raid and this would cause the others to lose direction. Salvos were also fired, that is several twins firing together, when, according to the radar's calculations, the circle of each explosion covered about fifty metres, giving the aircraft in a wide area little chance of survival.

'When we were below on the gallery with the 37s or 20s driving off low-flying aircraft, we would hear the din and have to grimace to compensate for the pressure changes that came with the firing of the 128s. We were not allowed to fasten the chinstraps of our steel helmets so as to prevent injury from the blast. Later when we fired the 128s at clusters of tanks as far out as Tegel, the barrels were down to zero degrees and the shock waves were enough to break the cement of the 70cm high and 50cm wide parapet of the gallery five metres below, exposing the steel rods beneath.

'The 37s and 20s were seldom used against British and American aircraft as they flew above the range of those guns and low-flying aircraft seldom came within range. The fighting bunker had been built with an elastic foundation to take the shock of the discharge of the 128s. Two twin 128s firing alone would have been sufficient to break a rigid foundation. The bunker had its own water and power supplies along with an up-to-date and well-equipped hospital in which, among others, prominent people like Hans-Ulrich Rudel, the famous Stuka pilot, could be cared for. Rudel had a 37mm cannon mounted in his aircraft, but we had later versions of the gun on the tower and he often came up to the platform to see the weapons in action during our time there. Normally only the gun crews were allowed on to the platform, but our superiors made an exception in his case.'[5]

The smoke and shock waves produced by the large-calibre multi-level guns on the 'G-towers' meant the 'Gustav's' aiming data had to be generated off-site using radar and detection equipment so each 'G-tower' had a more compact structure called the 'L' (Leitturm or 'leadership') or 'Lower' tower within half a kilometre, connected by underground cables. This tower rose to roughly the height of a thirteen-storey building (40 metres), but with sides only 50 by 23 metres compared with 70 by 70 metres for the mighty gun towers. There was one cellar floor and six upper floors above that. On the roof was an observation cabin and small 'Freya' radars. Teenage boys of the Luftwaffenhelfer's Oberschüler from Zwickau in Saxony manned a 'Würzburg-Riese' ('Giant') which could be retracted behind a thick concrete and steel dome for protection.[6] All the radars were controlled from the zoo's lower floors where a radio transmitter and headquarters control rooms carried out the central direction of the whole of Berlin's flak and searchlight units. On occasion Berliners could receive ample warning of a raid on their city by listening in to the broadcast on the special short wave-length used by the staff of the 1st Flak Division under Generalmajor Otto Sydow and the Flakscheinwerfergruppe Berlin under Colonel Paul Hasenfusse. Another indication was the arrival of the Hilsszug Bayern (Bavarian Relief Column), bringing food to the Hochbunker when a big raid was expected.

'You may be interested to know that the flak guns in Berlin are being fired by 15-year-old boys as fast as Russian PoWs can load them,' said a briefing officer at Wickenby, as if to lessen the tension. Reaction around lunchtime on Monday, 22 November when the bomber crews began to arrive at their briefing rooms to learn the details for that night's raid was little different at all the bases.

At Kirmington at 1315 hours on 22 November twenty-two Lancaster crews on 166 Squadron, having been checked through the door by the SP (RAF Service Policeman), started to give vent to their feelings as they saw the target on the map. Most of the 154 air crew had been on the Berlin raid four nights before. Although the squadron had 'got away with it' on that occasion, it was anyone's guess what would happen this night.

The 30-year old Wing Commander Reginald John Twamley told his crews to be seated and then started off with general matters: petrol, bomb-load, take-off, etc.[7] Then he motioned to Flying Officer William E. 'Jonah' Jones of the Intelligence/Operations staff: his turn. Born in Salford, Lancashire on 14 October 1916, Jones had volunteered for the RAF as air crew on the outbreak of war but was re-mustered on medical grounds and subsequently re-commissioned in the Intelligence branch. He had tried hard to get permission to go on this operation but Group would not sanction it. Having arrived in the operations room by 0830, at 0940 he had taken down the details from the Group broadcast. Group had required a 'Goodwood' or 'maximum effort' on 'Whitebait' (Berlin). This was the first occasion that Jones had been called on to brief on the 'Big City' and it had to be good.

Although he had his briefing notes in his hand, 'Jonah' always made sure that he could do the briefing without having to read from them. If he had to read his notes, he could not look at the crews, and in any case, it gave the impression that he was simply reading a prepared 'speech'.

As 'Jonah' took the platform with his 3 feet-long black pointer in his hand, he gave a quick look around. 'How many of them would return to be interrogated in the early hours of the morning?' he wondered.[8]

H-Hour was set for 2000 hours which meant take-off at 1645 for the first aircraft, followed at one-minute intervals by the other aircraft. The bombers, 469 of them Lancasters, 234 Halifaxes (in the middle wave sandwiched between the Lancasters), 11 Mosquitoes and 50 Stirlings of 3 Group flying their last Main Force operation to the 'Big City' would again use the same direct route in and out.

Final briefing had been fixed for 1500 hours so the Intelligence officers collected their notes and envelopes to take valuables from the crews or to collect letters for posting in the event of non-return and they made their way to the crew room. Last minute 'gen' was put on the blackboard and final questions answered. They wished everyone 'Good Luck' or 'Happy Landings' and watched the crew buses take the crews out to their aircraft where last-minute inspections and final preparations were carried out. 'God help Berlin tonight,' someone said.

In Berlin the Jägerleitoffizier made an early identification of Berlin as the probable target.

During the early evening of Monday, 22 November, sitting in his favourite restaurant on the Kurfürstendamm, Konrad Warner, a journalist, had just begun to eat when the waiter said confidently, 'If they do not come at half-past eight, they will not come today.' It was at 7.30 pm when the air-raid alarm sounded. This November night would see the greatest force sent by Bomber Command to the capital so far in the war, numbering as it did 764 aircraft. Warner left the very broad, long boulevard and went to the large bunker at the Bahn Zoo. 'People were talking a lot; some women were busy working; most expected the alarm to be over soon. Suddenly, the building vibrated down to the foundation walls, cracks appeared and the lights went out. Every conversation was silenced. Women were crying; men were looking rigidly at each other.' Warner also was worried. He feared for his wife who was with her mother in Charlottenburg.

Ursula von Kardorff, a 33-year-old journalist working for the Deutsche Allgemeine Zeitung in Berlin, wrote the following:

'... a herd of people in the darkness, running like animals towards the entrances – too small and much too narrow. Rude police and officers herd the unwilling crowd up the stairs for distribution on the various floors. For every new floor the crowd grinds to a halt. A woman broke down, screaming. She was convinced she would be in greater danger on the upper floors. 'I have a husband at the front,' she shrieked. 'I am not going up there.' At long last she was taken away. The towers have spiral staircases. Loving couples seek them out – a travesty on a carnival. When the anti-aircraft guns on the roof are firing, the building trembles and all heads duck as if a reaper was swung over them. People are standing pell-mell; scared bourgeois, weary wives, shabby foreigners dragging all their belongings with them in huge sacks and soldiers emitting an air of embarrassment. I thought: God have mercy upon us if panic strikes.'[9]

Gertrud Kahlke, after twice being 'bombed out' and narrowly escaping death, lived in the apartment of another woman named Gitta, where she experienced the first heavy attack at the zoo. Gertrud heard the panic; 'a hellish concert of tortured poor animals' where 'screaming monkeys snapped around in the burning cages.'

The raids were nervy for Berliners and German air crews alike. One of the pilots reported: 'The anti-aircraft started firing about 180 miles outside Berlin, so that we had to fly for a total of 360 miles through a more or less dense barrage, which was hard on the nerves.'

Albert Speer was informed immediately when the first Luftgefahr (air-raid threat) signal warned of a large fleet of bombers heading towards Berlin and the western part of the capital with its three large rail installations – Westend, Bahn Zoo and Bahnhof Charlottenburg – in particular. When the bombers reached Potsdam and the anxious Berliners heard the clear, sonorous sound of the Fliegeralarm (air-raid alarm), Speer decided he wanted to see the 'Terrorangriff' from the safety of the observation cabin on the roof of the 'L' tower at the Bahn Zoo with Ritterkreuzträger Oberst Hans-Joachim 'Hajo' Herrmann, a 29-year-old single-minded, high-ranking and influential member of the Luftwaffe with stern Aryan good looks and piercing blue eyes.

Herrmann left his Battle Headquarters at a villa near the Olympic Stadium west of Berlin which he shared with the Luftflotte and drove to the zoo to meet Speer. What he said to Herrmann shortly before they watched the attack about further increases in production, coupled with his friendly exhortation to hold out, made Speer feel bitter. 'It seemed to me that before any action could be taken aerial mines had to strike home on the very walls of the bunkers, by which time it would be too late.' The spectacle that unfolded made a lasting impression on both of them.

Speer scarcely reached the top of the tower when he had to take shelter inside it. In spite of the stout concrete walls, heavy hits nearby were shaking it. Injured anti-aircraft gunners, having difficulty breathing and covered in gunpowder smoke and steam, crowded down the stairs behind him; the air pressure from the exploding bombs had hurled them into the walls. For twenty minutes explosion followed explosion. From above Speer looked down into the well of the tower, where a closely-packed crowd stood in the thickening haze formed by cement dust falling from the walls.

The first Pathfinders arrived over the 'Big City' just before 2000 hours to find the city covered by ten-tenths cloud. The forecast had been for clear conditions over the home airfields, broken to medium-level cloud over Berlin and low cloud or fog over much of the rest of Germany. Three Pathfinder Squadrons – 7, 83 and 156 – had an unhappy night. Three of the five Lancasters equipped with the new 3cm H2S Mk III sets had to turn back after their equipment failed. They bombed Texel on the way home but under the rules at the time, this did not count towards the crews' tour of operations. The two other sets showed a clear outline and the raid opened with the blind markers accurately dropping four red TIs at the AP slightly to the east of the centre of the capital and this was maintained without a break until the close of the planned period. Six blind markers had marked the target area and release point by zero hour.

The 15-year-old Gerda Kernchen who lived with her parents in a cottage in the Kleingarten (small garden) area called Wittenau on the north-west edge of the capital recalled:

'When the final alarm sounded, you could already see the 'Christbaum' ('Christmas trees'; a popular German name for a Target Indicator) being dropped by the Pathfinders to mark the target for the bombers. You could see the searchlights streaming up from the ground, searching for the aircraft. The city was surrounded by a ring of white light.'

One of the Mosquito sky-markers on 139 Squadron was flown by Group Captain Leonard Cain Slee DSO DFC with Major John Mullock of the Royal Artillery and latterly the 5 Group Flak Liaison Officer occupying the navigator's seat. Slee had gained fame for his role in Operation 'Robinson', a low-level daylight attack by Lancasters on the large Schneider armament factory Le Creusot, France in 1942. On 17 May 1943, he was posted to become the station commander at RAF Dunholme Lodge as an acting group captain, but he had little time to undertake the 'normal' command duties of a station commander as he was called upon to pioneer the new role of 'Master Bomber' being developed by Bomber Command.

Mullock had flown with Guy Gibson to Italy in 1942 and had participated in raids on Lübeck, Rostock, the Renault works and Genoa but this was his first trip to Berlin and his second with Slee, who he last flew with on his Lancaster on the 20/21 June 1943 operation on the Zeppelin works at Friedrichshafen.

Slee took off from RAF Wyton at 1812 hours carrying twelve white drip flares known as 'spoofs'. They were to release them at twenty-second intervals while over the centre of Berlin. The markers and flares were concentrated, although the absence of any photographic evidence made it impossible to assess their accuracy. One of the pilots gave this account: 'The coloured flares from the Pathfinders showed us our way as clearly as we could wish.' Bomber crews noticed that flak over the target, which was again cloud-covered, was 'unusually restrained' and the Pathfinders carried out sky-marking but many of the Main Force crews aimed their bombs through the cloud at the glow of the fires burning from the previous night. Despite the risk of collisions, the rate of aircraft over the target was increased to thirty-four a minute.

Mullock was kept busy dropping "Window"; one bundle of which represented one aircraft echo on enemy radar screens (thin strips of aluminium which on Nachtjagd and Flakwaffe radar screens either appeared as a cluster of primary targets or swamped the screen with multiple returns). The major was also trying to rub ice off the inside of the Perspex in the nose of the aircraft, which he found exhausting; it was -47° outside and very warm inside, resulting in heavy condensation. Slee dropped their white flares at 2012 hours from a height of 32,000 feet. Mullock saw them ignite and thought how they compared with the ones the Germans used.

Mullock would report that 'after the attack had been going for four to five minutes the flak was entirely barrage, spread over a vast area and wildly dispersed in height. No bursts were seen above an approx height of 23,000 feet. There seemed to be no attempt to fire a barrage over any one part of the city as might have been expected. The rate of fire of most of the guns would appear to have been something in the region of five to six rounds per minute. Several of the blind markers were undoubtedly shot down in the early stages by predictor control (unseen fire). This was due to the fact that the backers-up were late and thus did not provide any cover. When the attack on Berlin had developed, concentration and 'Window' cover obviously precluded the use of radar. The impression gained was that the defences were in a state of utter confusion and were firing blindly and wildly.'[10]

Flight Sergeant Les Bartlett, the bomb-aimer on Flying Officer Mike Beetham's crew on 50 Squadron was making final adjustments on his bombing panel. Beetham, a 'compact, precise man who would later earn a fierce reputation as a young squadron commander', was born in London on 17 May 1923 and educated at St Marylebone's Grammar School. His father had been awarded the Military Cross in the Great War as an army major in the trenches. In 1940 Major Beetham was stationed at Hillsea Barracks on the hills overlooking Portsmouth and father and son spent the summer holidays watching RAF fighters in the Battle of Britain tackling German bombers trying to destroy the local docks. Major Beetham wanted his son to go into the army but after watching the dogfights overhead Michael was determined to be a fighter pilot. In 1941 he joined the RAF straight from school, but by then the service needed bomber pilots and he trained as a pilot in America and entered Bomber Command to fly Lancasters in the autumn of 1943. He loved the Lancaster; 'it felt right, it handled beautifully and was a delight to fly. If it was heavier on the controls than we now consider proper, back then this weight gave a young pilot confidence and you got used to it.'

It was fifteen minutes to zero hour. Then the first TIs went down, yellow ones, followed by reds, cascading into greens, which gradually descended into the clouds, which were the ones they were to bomb on.

The first wave started their bombing at the same time as a line of fighter flares went down in brilliant white parallels to their track. It was about 2 miles away, but it had been laid by the Mosquito boys as a decoy.

In the final turn, Les Bartlett was straining to try to see everything at once, trying to decide which of the TIs were most accurate. He then gave the necessary corrections to Beetham so as to get to the chosen TIs. He ordered bomb doors open, but then way down below he saw a Halifax bomber. Beetham made a quick weave, ending up on a parallel course and with a final, 'Left, left, steady ...' Bartlett pressed the 'tit' and the Lancaster lurched as 4,000lb of bombs left the bomber. He quickly threw the jettison bars across to ensure that there were no hang-ups in the bomb bay. Beetham kept the Lancaster straight and level for about thirty seconds, which seemed like thirty minutes, while the camera photographed the aiming point of their bombs. He then yelled, 'OK, camera operated, bomb doors closed.'

The clouds themselves were insufficient to hide the destruction going on. Everywhere for miles around seemed to be burning, throwing up a pink and scarlet haze through the cloud. It was so light that one could read in the bombing compartment. The flak was moderate but falling short, bursting some 3,000 feet below them.

On their port bow Beetham's crew saw an aircraft out of control falling earthwards with smoke pouring from it but no fire as far as could be seen. In this case the crew had a fair chance of bailing out. Beetham set course out of the target area. Everything ahead looked black and very uninviting from a crew's point of view. This was the danger area where fighters would be waiting. They could see red Very lights used by the fighters to attract each other's attention in the air all around them. To avoid being jumped, Beetham did a steady weave for about five minutes. With over 600 miles to go there was no need to get too anxious.

Things began to quieten down, but to be on the safe side they would make a banking search occasionally, mainly to avoid being attacked from below. At 8,000 feet they were able to release their oxygen masks and breathe freely again, which was always a great relief after having had them clamped on their faces for several hours. Flasks of hot coffee were passed around and Beetham allowed a little conversation. They began to see other aircraft around them as the English coast was reached. All around was a great armada, as hundreds of red, green and white navigation lights could be seen. A message was sent to base: 'Hello "Black Swan", this is "Pilgrim D for Dog". May I pancake, please, over?' This was acknowledged and a glow of relief felt throughout the crew.[11]

Irmgard Heidelberg living in Wormserstrasse 4 was in the Volksoper on Kantstrasse in Charlottenburg when the raid began:

'The opera was over and I wanted to go down to the subway. Suddenly the siren sounded. Now I was looking for shelter, but where? I wanted to go to the Kaiser Wilhelm Gedächtniskirche [Kaiser Wilhelm Memorial Church] at the end of Kurfürstendamm, but the air-raid shelter was already crowded, so I had to go on. I finally found a public shelter in Budapeststrasse. When I had sat down for quite a long time I realized that there was already a lot of smoke in the cellar. Luckily there was a water pipe in it. I wetted my handkerchief because I had no gas mask. After a short time all the people still in the cellar were told that they should leave. As I stepped out into the street, I saw a picture to shudder. Everywhere I looked there was nothing but fire, fire and fire. I wanted to go home and went to the Kurfürstendamm where there was also fire, smoke and dust.

'The Joachimsthalerstrasse was on fire, but I wanted to go to the subway. When I was finally at the entrance I could not get into it. I looked around; saw that the Wilhelmshallen, Ufa Palast am Zoo [an important film theatre] and the whole row of houses were a sea of flame. I returned to the Kurfürstendamm and then I saw that the church was burning. Now I ran on to Tauentzienstrasse. There too I tried to escape through small side streets, but the English had also dropped their firebombs there and it burned wherever one went. Finally I had arrived at Wittenberg Platz.

Suddenly a wind fanned the fire but I wanted to go home and I ran along the Kleiststrasse. There was fire all the way up Nollendorf Square. In the Bülowstrasse I ran because many houses were burning. At last I reached Potsdamer Strasse and I thought it would get better and quieter, but it was exactly the same; only rubble and fire. When I was across the Potsdamer Bridge, the siren sounded the second time. I could not get into a house so I ran on to Potsdamer Platz and I waited in the subway until the all-clear. Then I went on and saw that the Potsdam station was in flames. I walked along Leipziger Strasse to Charlottenstrasse. I could not go any further because everything was burning. Now I had to go to Hausvogteiplatz, from there a crossroad to the Lustgarten; from there along the castle and the Neue Königstrasse. When I arrived at the town hall it had already fallen prey to the flames.'

From 1958 to 2020 hours 753 bombers dropped 2,500 tons of blast bombs and approximately 150,000 incendiaries on Berlin in barely thirty-five minutes. One pilot said:

'We had no problems as we released more than fifty two-ton bombs on the city centre, which the flares had divided into sectors. Only one of our bombs hit outside the area marked by the flares. Suddenly, about twenty minutes after the first bomb was released, there was a gigantic explosion whose effects were clearly visible from an altitude of over 21,000 feet and a blazing light shot up turning the horizon fiery red.'

Hundreds of air crews confirmed that they had never felt such a shock wave on any previous operation. The explosion was the huge Neukö blln gasworks blowing up; 105 people were crushed in a panicked rush at a shelter next to the gasworks. At a public shelter in the basement of the Joachimstal School it was said that 500 people were killed, probably by blast from a 4,000lb 'cookie' bomb which dropped just outside the building. Air crews reported that large fires spread through the city.

Following his talk with Speer and while the attack was still under way, 'Hajo' Herrmann went up to the roof of the tower and looked around:

'Incendiary bombs were lodged high in the trees and burning on the pavements. There was a shrill organ concert of thousands of flak splinters whistling down and striking sparks from the concrete as they landed, punctuated by the cracking of bombs and the pressure waves of aerial mines. All around them was a light grey to white, luminous sea of fog. In the centre of this chaos the young men [Luftwaffenhelfer] on their exposed tower carried out their duty.'

Herrmann was appalled. 'This was what terror looked like in the eyes of the defenceless victim,' he wrote later. 'I was not wearing a steel helmet and I withdrew to the protection of the thick concrete walls.'[12]

The previous year in Berlin Herrmann had begun to consider the problem of defence, working from theories and figures on paper:

'There too I had experienced heavy raids, the most recent of them in March 1943 when I had been able to see Rigoletto as far as the second act. From the steps I had watched the rest of the drama unfold in the sky. It had seemed to me to be a bad thing that night fighters had their command post in Holland. Now and then, at the very least, a leader should be in the middle of the action. Rear echelons, frequently but not always justly reviled, were of course usually behind the lines. Here, they were right up front. The flak was always in the thick of things while the kellergemeinschaft [cellar community] took cover in bunkers and cellars, in the middle of the rain of flak and bomb splinters. I had visited their senior commanders and had been able to form an idea of the sufferings of the armed forces and of the civilian population. I had also discussed ways in which there could be cooperation, especially with the Luftwaffe, a subject that until then had not been addressed. Following that March 1943 attack I cursed everything and everyone above me in rank and position that went under the name of leadership.'

Herrmann got into his BMW and drove westward through the city's burning streets. He felt completely overwhelmed and asked himself whether he should admit defeat. 'Who would want to go on? Who could go on? To my la in the Division, I said that, if the bombers came back the next day we must get into the air.'[13]

When the rain of bombs ceased, Speer ventured out on the platform again. His private office and his War Industry Ministry were one gigantic conflagration. Speer was driven there at once in his Mercedes. A few secretaries, 'looking like Amazons in their steel helmets', were trying to save files even while isolated time bombs went off in the vicinity. In place of his private office Speer found nothing but a huge bomb crater.

'From the flak tower the air raids on Berlin were an unforgettable sight,' wrote Speer later, 'and I had constantly to remind myself of the cruel reality in order not to be completely entranced by the scene: the illumination of smoke, the innumerable probings followed by flashes of explosions which were caught by the clouds of searchlights, the excitement when a plane was caught and tried to escape the cone of light, the brief flaming torch when it was hit. No doubt about it, this apocalypse provided a magnificent spectacle.'

As soon as the bombers turned back, Speer was driven to those districts of the city where important factories were situated. His extravagant W31 type G4 Mercedes, deemed too expensive for general army use, must have caused consternation in the streets strewn with rubble and lined by burning houses. The BMW 327/28 convertible which his wife Margaret used mostly to drive their four eldest children – Arnold, Fritz, Albert and Hilde – to school might have been openly more considerate. Speer wrote later:

'We drove over streets strewn with rubble, lined by burning houses. Bombed-out families sat or stood in front of the ruins. A few pieces of rescued furniture and other possessions lay about on the side of the road. There was a sinister atmosphere full of biting smoke, soot and flames. Sometimes the people displayed that curious hysterical merriment that is often observed in the midst of disasters. Above the city hung a cloud of smoke that probably reached 20,000 feet in height. Even by day it made the macabre scene as dark as night.'[14]

Flying Officer William Benjamin Stewart of New Richmond Station, Quebec piloting a 408 'Goose' Squadron RCAF Lancaster recalled:

'On the homeward journey, both gunners – Sergeants R.H. Rolph and Norman Varley – reported enemy aircraft and ordered evasive action. When avoiding a third enemy attack by a corkscrew the aircraft went into what could have been a high speed stall since ASI [Air Speed Indicator] indicated 210. The aircraft then spun to the starboard side with all four engines cut and dived from 18,000 to 13,000 feet when it recovered from the spin to the starboard and immediately went into another to port. Pull out from this spin was made at 8,000 feet in 10/10ths clouds. On recovery the aircraft continued to lose height down to 5,000 feet. At that altitude, control was maintained providing no violent corrections were made.'

Flight Sergeant Robert Duncan Ochsner, the 25-year-old wireless-operator of Olds, Alberta, was unable to obtain a fix when 20 miles from the enemy coast so this was crossed on dead reckoning at 4,000 to 5,000 feet. Stewart also noted that the navigator, Flying Officer W.C. Burns 'did a fine job'. Height was again gradually lost and the English coast was crossed at 2,500 feet. The crew was then ordered to be prepared to bail out as Stewart did not think he would be able to land safely. After a further examination of position, he decided that with extra careful handling the aircraft could be landed and this was done.[15]

Gerda Kernchen remembered the raid so well because it was the first time she saw a dead body:

'We were in our cellar and we heard a tremendous crash and the whole house shook. The biggest bomb called an air mine, or blockbuster, had landed in our neighbourhood. The earth was soft peat, so most of the houses just moved on their foundations, but the houses closer to the blast were destroyed. When we left our cellar, we went to see where the bomb had landed. Then we saw one of the neighbours. He was dead. It was a really frightening sight, because the percussion had mutilated him and his eyes were hanging out of his head. It was one of those images I will never forget. Everyone was so shocked and horrified by the first big raid, because we had been assured that Berlin was safe. My mother said: 'We must keep our faith in Herr Hitler. He will protect us!' My father, who was a first war veteran and had refused to join the Nazi Party, never said a word. I suspect that he knew that things were not going well. From then on, everyone was too frightened to stay at home and we headed to the neighbourhood bunker when the alarm sounded. The bunker had been built earlier in 1943 and it was just two blocks away. Our bunker could accommodate two hundred people. It contained a honeycomb of small rooms, each with a pair of bunk beds and two benches for sitting. There were also full kitchens and bathrooms. As the raids continued, some people lived there full-time because they had no homes. The maximum length of a raid was two hours. After it was over, people would go back to sleep. In the morning, I would go off to work although I never knew whether my factory where I sewed uniforms for the Luftwaffe would still be standing.'[16]

Finally in the fire-glow over Berlin the bomber crews were able to observe many details of the destroyed city districts. A Mosquito over the target at zero+7 reported that two main fire concentrations 7 to 10 miles apart were reflected on the clouds. This reflection could be seen for 80 miles on the way home. Returning crews could only estimate that the marking and bombing were believed to be accurate. 'It appeared to have been a concentrated attack,' stated 6 Group's ORB [Operational Records Book]. '"Sky markers" well placed. A number of large explosions.'[17] The reports generally suggested a highly successful attack; an opinion that was confirmed by the enemy's complaint of a 'heavy terror raid'.

In London RAF Headquarters announced: 'More than 2,000 tons of blast bombs and approximately 150,000 incendiaries were dropped on Berlin in barely 45 minutes. The air crews report that large fires spread through the city and that their glow lit the sky a fiery red. Repeated violent explosions took place that could not be attributed solely to the explosive effect of the bombs.'

Another announcement said: 'The air raid on Berlin on the night of Monday to Tuesday was comparable to the heavy grand assaults on Hamburg in summer of this year. Around 2,400 tons of blast and incendiary bombs were dropped on the German capital. The extremely misty weather hindered operations by the German searchlight batteries, so the German flak could only shoot aimlessly. We employed new tactics in this raid. A large number of Pathfinder aircraft flew with the bombers to light up particular districts of Berlin and then to mark the targets with coloured flares for each bomber wing. A new type of flare has been developed for this purpose which lit Berlin adequately despite the heavy clouds overhead. For example, the whole of the government office district was clearly discernible in the light of the flares.

The German flak divisions claimed twenty-three bombers shot down on the raid. Eleven of these were Lancasters and ten Halifaxes, including one on 51 Squadron skippered by Wing Commander Christopher Louis Yser Wright, which was shot down into the Grunewald on its run up to the target with just two of the crew parachuting to safety. The German night-fighters claimed just four of the bombers lost. Two Lancasters on 7 Squadron PFF at Oakington were shot down and a third, which was hit by flak over the target that shot away the elevators, limped home to base where five of the crew bailed out, while the pilot and navigator remained on the aircraft until they too had to abandon the bomber 20 miles north of the base.

Lancaster 'B-Bertie' on 83 Squadron PFF was probably downed by radar-predicted flak through the 10/10ths cloud and crashed in the Schiller Park in Berlin. The skipper, 33-year-old Pilot Officer Ralph Henderson DFM, a former flight engineer, had only just returned to his squadron via Spain on 6 June after evading capture after being shot down on the raid on Stuttgart on 11/12 March. All seven air crew were killed. Henderson left a widow, Muriel C.L. Henderson of Headington, Oxford.

On 156 PFF Squadron Flight Sergeant Trevor George Stephens and crew failed to return. On 23 August the 21-year-old skipper from Sutton Coldfield, Warwickshire had nursed a crippled Lancaster back to Warboys from Berlin and he was awarded an immediate DFM. Stephens was posthumously commissioned. The other Lancaster lost on the squadron was skippered by 23-year-old Squadron Leader Douglas Campbell 'Tiny' Anset DFC. His virtuoso performances on the piano, his clear tenor voice singing arias from La bohème, as well as cleverly-executed comic songs, would be sadly missed. 'Tiny' had been awarded the DFC only ten days earlier.[18]

At Middleton St George Air Vice Marshal George Eric Brookes, Air Officer Commanding of 6 Group RCAF had watched a record thirty-four Halifaxes – seventeen each from 419 'Moose' and 428 'Ghost' Squadrons – take off, two of the aircraft failing to return. There were no survivors on 'D-Dog' on 428 Squadron piloted by 22-year-old Sergeant Jack Morton Jacob. Also, all seven members of the novice crew on 419 Squadron skippered by 21-year-old Pilot Officer William Langenberg Hunter from Vancouver – whose average age was just 20 – died too. Warrant Officer2 Joseph Alexander Lesage, the Canadian rear gunner who had completed twenty-five trips in his nine months, had been drafted in as a last-minute replacement for an ailing crew member. The flight engineer, Sergeant Wilbert Blare Jones from Crayford, Kent, who was on only his second operation and had just turned 18, was one of the youngest members of RAF Bomber Command to die on operations in 1943. The mid-upper gunner, Sergeant George Alexander May from Hyde Park near London, Ontario was 19 years old. All the crew are buried at Diever General Cemetery in Holland. 'Jac' Jacob and crew including 19-year-old Air Canadian bomber Sergeant 'Rad' Radbourne are buried in Hanover War Cemetery.

Two Lancasters crashed on take-off for Berlin but there were no casualties. On return two Halifax crews perished when their aircraft collided over Yorkshire. The crew of 'K-King' on 102 Squadron at Pocklington skippered by 24-year-old Pilot Officer Walter Hughes of Walton, Liverpool returned to the Pocklington area and joined the landing circuit with landing lights on. They were flying in a clear sky with good visibility. While awaiting their turn to land and soon after crossing the airfield boundary, the Halifax was struck on the starboard side by a Halifax on 77 Squadron piloted by 23-year-old Flight Sergeant Cornelius Charles Linehan while in the landing circuit of Elvington airfield. Both aircraft fell to the ground from around 2,500 feet and crashed 500 feet apart on land around Newlands Farm, roughly between Barmby Moor and Wilberfoss. All fourteen airmen died as a result of the collision.[19] Three more aircraft were written off after crashes and other accidents.

The *Daily Telegraph* was one of the newspapers that carried stories of the raid under the banner headlines 'RAF's BIGGEST BERLIN RAID; REICH OFFICE HIT IN 2,3OO-TON ONSLAUGHT: PATHFINDERS LIGHT WAY FOR BOMBERS: OTHER GREAT FORCE OUT LAST NIGHT.' Air Commodore Ernest Leslie Howard-Williams,[20] the *Daily Telegraph* Air Correspondent, reported:

'Unbroken heavy cloud lay along the whole route, making it difficult for the enemy's night fighters to intercept, but despite the weather conditions navigation and aiming were completely successful, indicating the tremendous development that has taken place in area bombing by night.

'The Pathfinder force under Air Commodore Bennett is now able to use its special technique to such purpose that we have bombed Berlin 'blind'. The bombers followed the brightly-lit 'target indicators' these Pathfinders dropped, although the target area itself was not seen.

'It is early to talk of Berlin being 'Hamburged'. It has already taken approaching 4,000 tons in two raids within five nights of one another, but Greater Berlin covers about 340 square miles, compared to Hamburg's fifty and Greater London's 694.

'All crews when they went into their interrogation rooms shortly before dawn were confident of the results. None had any doubt that they had won a great victory. They had beaten the night-fighter of squadrons and also the massed gun batteries of AA guns which served as Berlin's second line of defence. Casualties were well below the average, even for attacks on much 'easier' targets.

'At one bomber group headquarters they were well satisfied when it was reported that only two aircraft were outstanding. Five minutes later they heard that one more had landed and a few minutes later that all were back from a whole bomber group; not a single aircraft was missing.

'It was another cloud-cover attack, like that of four nights ago. Both on the outward and homeward journeys the bombers flew for hundreds of miles over an unbroken sea of cloud.

'Over Berlin there was just an occasional gap through which crews caught a glimpse of what was happening on the ground – the vivid coloured lights of a marker bomb, a rising pillar of black smoke, a red patch of fire. But the bomb-aimers were not looking for such gaps.

'The Pathfinders, out in force, dropped in a dense concentration an unbroken succession of target indicators and pyrotechnic flares, from start to finish. Enemy guns were shooting at the flares as they fell but nothing stopped the Pathfinders from building up an unmistakable target of coloured lights and keeping it thick throughout the period of the attack for just over half an hour from eight o'clock.

'The clouds began to reflect the intense glow of the fires below, and even through cloud several thousand feet thick the light was so bright that crews saw each other's bombs as they fell. Twenty minutes after the first bombs had dropped, hundreds of crews saw one of the most violent explosions that had ever been reported from a German target.

'Sergeant G.K. Chapman of Tynemouth, Northumberland, a Lancaster navigator said: 'The attack was so well concentrated that while we were over Berlin we saw only one flash of a 4,000-pounder outside the main area of fires. We saw about fifty block-busters go off in that time.'[21]

'There was just one break in the cloud bank,' said a Halifax pilot. 'It took no more than a second or two to fly over it but that was long enough for us to see the punishment Berlin was getting. We saw great fires dancing on the ground and then the cloud shut off the picture again. But we could still see how much was burning. The clouds hung in the sky like a glowing target.'

'Very few night-fighters were over Berlin and the Germans were forced to let loose the great barrage which had once been the main defence of the capital before modern tactics forced the enemy to use so great a part of his air force to protect his cities. Searchlights were blocked by the clouds and without any hope of the bombers being coned, the gunners could only blaze away at all the sky above Berlin. There was enough heavy flak however to bring shells near many of the bombers.

'I knew we had been hit,' said Warrant Officer Raymond Bradley of Portsmouth, 'but I didn't know where, until I heard the rear-gunner.'

'"Brad," he called out indignantly, "look what's happened to my gun." Then he told me how the barrels had been twisted and bent. When we got back I looked at them and they were just like a melted candle. Bits of the shell dashed all over the aircraft, rattling against us like peas in a tin can but we got home without any difficulty.

'Just after that the gunner saw a twin-engined night-fighter, one of the few that were in the air. The rear gunner pressed the button – I didn't know what he expected to happen. Of course, nothing did. We swung into evasive action at once and threw the enemy off. He never knew what a chance he had missed.

'Single night-fighters which were over Berlin while the attack was on had to face their own barrage. Just as a Lancaster was on its bombing run with the bomb doors open, an Fw 190 was spotted by the mid-upper gunner. I warned the captain and opened fire. The rear-gunner also got in a burst. Our starboard fins and rudder were damaged, but I think the enemy was hit too. At any rate he drove off and dived away.'

'As during last week's attack on Berlin, most of the AA batteries on the route were in action. 'There was a long avenue of flak about 200 miles from Berlin,' said Sergeant R.V. Stevenson of Loughborough, a Lancaster rear-gunner. 'We turned away, but it followed us so we barged through it at high speed. Nothing hit us. It was not so cold as last week and I was sweating most of the way there in my electrically heated suit.'

The official communiqués (in which no mention is made of aircraft lost in crashes in England) and homilies to air crew to 'press on regardless' were all part of the military bureaucracy prevalent on operations. Although the losses were light in comparison to other raids at this time, it was scant comfort if you were one of those who were missing, believed killed, or one of the anxious relatives, waiting and fearfully praying for news of loved ones. In RAF parlance, 'Missing' at least gave loved ones a glimmer of hope. 'Missing, believed killed' did not. In air crew circles 'Missing' were those who had 'Gone for a Burton' (a beer) or more commonly 'gone for a shit'; 'bought it' or had got the chop; never 'killed'. Difficult targets were 'the arsehole of death'. Very seldom did crews say among themselves that they were on 'operations'. It was either 'dicing with death', 'juggling with Jesus' or 'gambling with God'. Meanwhile life had to go on and it was just as well to embrace that old secret air crew belief: 'Whoever it happens to, it won't be me.' The human cost permeated all corners of the British Empire.

At Bourn, Group Captain Neville Holroyde Fresson DFC had ten letters of commiseration to write to the next of kin that day as all seven men on the crew of Canadian Flight Lieutenant James Francis Munro DFC on 97 Squadron were KIA. They included Bill Waller and Frank Burbridge DFC who had been assigned to the crew after 'Johnny' Sauvage's crew had completed their tour in October. Both men were married.

When it was known that 'A-Apple', skippered by Pilot Officer Eugene Francis 'Frank' McEgan had failed to return from the raid on Monday night, Fresson signed a letter that was quickly dispatched to McEgan's mother Irene at 'Sorrento', 20 Margaret Street, Strathfield in Sydney on Wednesday, 24 November. In part the letter said:

'Pilot Officer McEgan took part in a raid on Berlin as Captain of his aircraft, no news having since been received. We can but hope that the aircraft was forced to land and that the crew are safe, even as prisoners of war. Your son had carried out twelve operational sorties since joining this Squadron.... He was very well liked by all of us and he and his fellow aircrew will be greatly missed.'

A cable was also sent to Mr McEgan serving in the Middle East. In time both parents would be informed by the Air Ministry when it was known that their son, known by his family as 'Possum' or 'Poss' for short, had been killed in action.

'A-Apple' had been hit by flak over Berlin and the return was made on two engines. They were hit again over Osnabrück and McEgan gave the order to bail out when they were at 18,000 feet. Pilot Officer Adrian Spencer the navigator made his way towards the front of the aircraft and found the pilot's seat empty. He and Flying Officer John Vincent Tyler the bomb-aimer tried to keep the aircraft on a reasonable straight and level flight path and found that Sergeant J.J. Johnson the wireless-operator and Sergeant W.S. Gibb, mid-upper gunner, had bailed out. McEgan had actually collapsed over the front hatch and Tyler tried to help him but by this time the aircraft was down to 200 feet. Seconds later it struck the ground at a farmyard at Achmer, 6 miles from Osnabrück airfield. Spencer, Johnson, Gibb and Warrant Officer J.R.A. Burke DFM, the Canadian rear gunner, survived and were taken prisoner.[22]

Frank McEgan had been obsessed with flying from a very early age: he was always making model aeroplanes and his room was festooned with the planes hanging from the ceiling. As soon as he could, at age 18 Frank had joined the RAAF. There, he and some friends built a full-sized glider with a 66 foot wingspan, which they called the 'Falcon'. It was only on his final leave, however, that he was able to fly the glider for the first and last time.[23]

Five Stirling IIIs that were lost took the total losses to twenty-six. Just before Stirling 'J-Johnny' on 214 Squadron skippered by 20-year-old Flight Sergeant George Addison Atkinson from County Durham reached the target area the oil pressure on the port outer engine began to drop and Atkinson noticed that the propeller was revolving at excessive speed. He completed the bombing run and Sergeant Johnny Friend the bomb-aimer sighted and released the bombs correctly one minute after ETA at 1906 hours from 12,000 feet, but the propeller was feathered to prevent a seizure with the result that the aircraft was dangerously low. At 9,000 feet it was dropping into icing cloud and Atkinson restarted the engine to gain more height for crossing a bad front. The engine had to be stopped almost immediately to prevent it catching fire and the propeller then failed to re-feather but continued to windmill. The aircraft lost height steadily until it was only 1,500 feet above ground 20 miles east of Hanover where the aircraft was engaged by flak. Sergeant Wilfred Sweeney, the 20-year-old Canadian rear gunner from Weyburn, Saskatchewan was wounded in the right leg, but he refused to leave the turret.

Sergeant 'Jock' Wilson the wireless-operator sent out an SOS at about 2145 hours and repeated it until it was acknowledged. It was picked up at 2230 as a very faint signal and he was given a fix. From then onwards, although reception was very bad, he maintained communication with the ground sending the height, speed, course and DR position obtained from the navigator, Sergeant Bruce Edwards at intervals. Near the Zuider Zee the aircraft was picked up by the searchlights which were attacked by the gunners. Crossing the island at about 50 feet the aircraft was again engaged by flak and searchlights; fifteen to twenty-five of the latter were shot at by the gunners and doused. An Fw 190 intercepted the Stirling but was claimed shot down in flames by 'Wilf' Sweeney in the rear turret. When Sergeant Des Hughes the flight engineer reported there was only ten minutes of fuel remaining, Atkinson ordered the crew to take up their ditching stations. Because of icing, a head wind and the windmilling airscrew, the speed had been very low.

Information of their plight was signalled to the ground station and the aircraft was fixed accurately 30 miles north-east of Cromer as Wilson pressed his key down when the aircraft ditched at 0034 hours in a choppy sea, on a dark night with no moon. The sea at the time had a 60 feet crest with waves across the swell at angles of 90 degrees. Prior to ditching, Atkinson called out the height of the aircraft as it approached the sea tail first. The aircraft bounced off a swell and then made a very heavy impact with the water, causing the nose to sink in and the fuselage to break in half about 1 foot 6 inches behind the mid-upper turret. Sergeant 'Ronnie' Boutell the mid-upper gunner had over-inflated his 'Mae West' inside the aircraft and had to be helped through the escape hatch. Atkinson was trapped in the nose and went under as the aircraft broke in two. Edwards jumped into the dinghy and dragged Boutell in out of the sea. Wilson was heard calling and the other survivors paddled up to him and helped him on board. Sweeney, who had been observed jumping into the sea, was also heard to call but they failed to find him. After drifting for about an hour 'Des' Hughes was picked up from his 'K'-type dinghy.

Johnny Friend got out of the astro hatch, but was swept into the sea by the waves. Hughes passed him a 'K' dinghy which was swept away. Friend re-entered the almost submerged fuselage, found another dinghy, held his breath and swam out again as the aircraft sank, three minutes after ditching. He inflated the dinghy and climbed in, but although he heard other members of the crew shouting and answered, he was too weak to paddle towards the sound and lost touch with them. After sunrise he hoisted a red sail and fired a star cartridge when an Air-Sea Rescue Hudson approached. The Hudson crew dropped smoke floats alongside and he was shortly after taken on board a high-speed launch from Great Yarmouth which continued the search and picked up the other four surviving members of the crew from the big dinghy about forty minutes later. Atkinson and Sweeney could not be found.

Only fifty Stirlings had taken off and once again their tonnage of bombs dropped had been negligible. The three raids they had made on Berlin were significant in the number of early returns (forty-six) and losses (thirty-seven). The Stirling losses since August now reached 109 aircraft in raids on German targets. A letter from Sir Arthur Harris to the Secretary of State for Air, Sir Archibald Sinclair sums up the despair felt at HQ Bomber Command and by Harris in particular at the thought of the continuing use of the Stirling:

'The Stirling and the Halifax are now our major worries. They presage disaster unless solutions are found. I understand that the Stirling is to go in favour of the Lancaster as fast as the changeover can be achieved. The Stirling Group has now virtually collapsed. They make no worthwhile contribution to our war effort in return for their overheads. They are at half strength and serviceability is such that in spite of the much-reduced operational rate and long periods of complete idleness due to weather I am lucky if I can raise thirty Stirlings from No.3 Group for one night's work after doing a week of nothing, or twenty the night after. There should be a wholesale sacking of the incompetents who have turned out approximately 50% rogue aircraft from Short and Harland's, Belfast and Austin's, not forgetting the Supervisors responsible at the parent firm. Much the same applies to the Halifax issue, nothing ponderable is being done to make this deplorable product worthy for war or fit to meet those jeopardies which confront our gallant crews.'

The raid on the night of 22/23 November marked the demise of the Stirling, the least effective of the British four-engined heavies. Never able to achieve the altitude performance that the Halifax and Lancaster could attain, the Stirling had a dismal ceiling of between 12,000 and 15,000 feet. Taking its poor performance and negligible tonnage of bombs dropped into consideration, Harris felt that he could no longer send his ten Stirling squadrons in 3 Group on raids on Germany and some units were posted to Transport Command. A few Stirlings were retained for use against fringe targets such as on Wednesday 1 and Thursday, 2 December when just nineteen Stirlings and a dozen Halifaxes were dispatched to the Frisians and to the east coast of Denmark while the Main Force rested. The last raid by Stirlings in Bomber Command was flown by four aircraft on 8 September 1944 on a raid on Le Havre. The Stirling's passing would only be mourned by the Lancaster and Halifax crews whose casualties would soon soar as a result.[24] The Merlin-powered Halifax Mk IIs and Vs, which equipped many of 6 Group RCAF's squadrons as well as those of 4 Group, could fly a little higher than the Stirling but not much.

It was not until 20 December 1943 that a photograph of the 'Big City' was obtained revealing damage caused by six major raids of which the operation of 22 November was the second and the most effective raid on Berlin throughout the whole war. A vast area of destruction stretched across the capital caused mainly by firestorms as a result of the dry weather conditions. From a distance of 30 miles the air crews could see a smoke cloud rising to 19,000 feet from the eleven major fires that had continued to smoulder since Monday night.

Approximately 2,000 people were killed (including 500 people in a shelter that received a direct hit) and 175,000 bombed out. More than 50,000 troops (equivalent to almost three army divisions taken from their normal duties) had to be brought in to help from garrisons up to 100 kilometres away in the following days. Erich Hampe in the standard work *Civil Air Defence in the Second World War* remarked in astonishment: 'Although the means of transport had failed, the Berlin workers both indigenous and foreign were pouring into the dawn, past burning rows of houses and over ruined streets in the outskirts.' Reich Minister of Propaganda Joseph Goebbels was always prepared to spend huge sums on live performance and he ordered the Komödie theatre to be put back into operation. The repair was only abandoned after it was hit for the fourth time in January 1944. 'A review was a better pastime than to stand for something edible. Every day could be the last and the people desperately wanted a last pleasure.'

A German report of the raid stated that 130 mines, 900 high-explosive, 200,000 incendiaries and 20,000 phosphorus bombs had been dropped as well as 60 flares. The casualty roll was 1,757 dead and 6,923 injured with 180,000 people made homeless, for in the attack 2,791 homes were destroyed with another 2,300 damaged. Industries and waterways had been destroyed or damaged, including the electrical firms of Osram and Telefunken severely damaged in addition.

Most of the damage was to the residential areas of Tiergarten and Charlottenburg, Schöneberg and the separate suburb city of Spandau. At least 3,000 houses and 23 industrial premises were completely destroyed or severely damaged and it was estimated that 175,000 people were left homeless. The Kaiser Wilhelm Gedächtniskirche was left in ruins. Much of the Unter den Linden was devastated and several other buildings of note were either damaged or destroyed, including the British, French, Italian and Japanese embassies on and around the thoroughfare. Charlottenburg Castle and Bahn Zoo, as well as the Ministry of Weapons and Munitions, the Waffen SS Administrative College, the barracks of the Imperial Guard at Spandau and several factories employed in the manufacture of material for the armed forces including five factories of the Siemens electrical group and the Alkett tank works which had recently moved from the Ruhr were hit. The whole complex around the Wilhelmstrasse, the Brandenburg Gate area and the Tauentzienstrasse, Potsdamer Platz, the Anhalter Strasse and many other building-lined streets were completely destroyed. Berliners once again began clearing away the debris and devastation as fire crews tried to extinguish the blazing fires.[25]

Goebbels was given a general picture of the situation in Berlin by his chief assistant Gerhard Schach, which Goebbels described as 'a sad one indeed'. Doktor Robert Ley, the besotted head of the German Labour Front and Reichsleiter of the political division of the Nazi party from 1933 to 1945, feebly paraphrasing Winston Churchill and Clemenceau, said defiantly: 'We will fight in front of Berlin, in Berlin, behind Berlin!' Ley, who was one of Hitler's inner circle, was reported to be furious because the German fighters did not take to the air during the 'unfortunate' night.[26] Goebbels added:

'What if the weather was bad! After all the English fly in bad weather from their southern English airports [*sic*] all the way to Berlin; but the German fighters can't rise from the ground in Berlin because the weather is unfavourable! You can't simply surrender the capital of the Reich to the terror of the enemy. If we conduct war on such squeamish principles we won't get very far.'

The Swiss *Gazette de Lausanne* commented that Berliners were 'completely stunned by the catastrophe' and 'everywhere were saying that their city "will become a second Hamburg".'

After being bombed out of a succession of flats, Marie (Illarionovna) Vassiltchikov, a 27-year-old high-spirited cosmopolitan member of European high society and an anti-Nazi émigré from Russia, was living as a paying guest in the villa of friends, Baron and Baroness von Gersdorff in the Woyrschstrasse just south of the Tiergarten together with her papa. Lieutenant Colonel von Gersdorff was an early military member of the conspiracy to overthrow Nazism and one of the few major conspirators in the plot to assassinate Hitler. 'Missie', as she was more familiarly known, grew up in Germany, France and Lithuania, where her father's family had owned property since before the Revolution of 1919, when they moved to Berlin. The city was one of the most cosmopolitan in the world at that time and attracted all nationalities and creeds, especially those who had money. There was a very active Russian 'colony' who revelled in the high culture the city had to offer. 'Missie' worked for the Information Department of the Foreign Ministry headed by her detestable superior, SS Brigadeführer Professor Doktor Franz Six. Through her contacts she had some advance warning of impending raids, but having friends in high places did little to help her.

In October, having written in her diary that 'there are air-raids now every night but they seem pretty harmless – they usually catch me in the bath tub'; 'Missie' wrote: 'Last night the greater part of central Berlin was destroyed.'[27]

Joseph Goebbels too was appalled at what he saw: 'Blazing fires everywhere.... Transportation conditions are ... quite hopeless.... Devastation is ... appalling in the government sector as well as in the western and northern suburbs.... Hell itself seems to have broken loose over us.'

'That second night we hit Berlin the temperatures were round about minus forty,' wrote 31-year-old Squadron Leader Joe Northrop on 83 Squadron. 'There was a bit of heating in the cockpit but the poor old gunners at the rear end had nothing. No heated clothing, no anything.

'On our squadron, ninety per cent of the rear gunners were out of action after the second night – they'd all got frostbite where the oxygen mask fitted; and the fingers and toes.

'To replace them we had to go to the OTUs and grab all people there – some had just started training – some had never been airborne. We made up the battle order with them. Some had never fired a gun. It didn't make much difference. They were only a pair of eyes. They couldn't do very much with .303s. But it was the principle of the thing that was so bad.

'It was Berlin every night from then on – even though we didn't go every night we were briefed and stood by and it was only the weather that stopped us. Harris was determined that we were going to hit Berlin. He'd got a phobia against the place. He'd a biggish force and he wanted to really hit them.'

Chapter Three

While Berlin Burned

'Greatest Raid in History Sets Berlin Aflame; 1000 Planes Hit Heart of Capital.'

Tuesday, 23 November morning edition of the New York *Sun*.

When Konrad Warner left the bunker at the Bahn Zoo, he was presented with an incomprehensible sight. Houses, public buildings and the Berlin Zoo like the Hagenbeck in Hamburg before it had suffered under the weight of the bombs. The Kaiser Wilhelm Memorial Church and the Ufa Palast am Zoo were on fire; everything burned brightly. At speeds of up to 15 metres per second, the firestorm swept through the streets, taking cars and passers-by with them and spreading black foul-smelling smoke. Raging fires could hardly be extinguished because the water mains had also been damaged in many places by the bombs. Warner had the impression that all of Berlin was destroyed. In less than fifteen minutes more than 1,000 incendiary bombs and canisters of phosphorus had set fire to fifteen of the zoo buildings where a third of the animals died. There were still 2,000 animals left, although many had been evacuated to zoos in other parts of Germany but the bombing killed most of the remainder and several large and dangerous animals – leopards, panthers, jaguars, apes – escaped and had to be hunted and shot in the streets.

The antelope house and the enclosure for the beasts of prey, the administration building and the director's villa were entirely destroyed, while the monkey house, the quarantine building, the main restaurant and the elephants' Indian temple were left in ruins or badly damaged. Deer and monkeys escaped, birds flew away through the broken glass roofs. The ornamental three-storey aquarium building and the 30-metre crocodile hall were also destroyed, along with the artificial jungle. The great reptiles, writhing in pain, now lay beneath chunks of concrete, earth, broken glass, fallen palms and tree trunks in water 12 inches deep, or crawled down the visitors' staircase while the firelight of the dying city of Berlin shone red through a gate knocked off its hinges in the background. Passers-by on the Budapesterstrasse were confronted with the gruesome sight of the lifeless bodies of four crocodiles. The reptiles had probably been flung out onto the street by the explosion. If they would have survived the blast, they must have died from the cold outside.

Over the next few days the elephants that had perished in the ruins of their sleeping quarters had to be cut up where they lay, with men crawling around inside the rib-cages of the huge pachyderms and burrowing through mountains of entrails.[1]

Fantastic rumours began circulating. An escaped tiger made its way into the ruins of the Café Josty[2] on the Potsdamer Platz and gobbled up a piece of Bienenstich pastry it found there, and promptly died. Someone who doubted the quality of the

Josty brothers' cake-making was sued for libel by the Konditorei's owner. The court ordered a post-mortem of the dead animal which found, much to the satisfaction of the confectioner, that the tiger's death had been caused by glass splinters found in its stomach![3]

Supposedly, lions on the loose were prowling around the nearby Kaiser Wilhelm Memorial Church, but they lay charred and suffocated in their cages. Crocodiles and giant snakes were said to be lurking in the hedgerows of the Landwehrkanal. 'Missie' Vassiltchikov heard that the crocodiles tried to jump into the River Spree and were hauled out and shot. Later, Berliners regarded bear hams and bear sausage as delicacies. The crocodile tails, cooked in large pans, tasted like fat chicken.

Ursula Gebel went back to the zoo because she had heard that it had been heavily bombed. It was closed, but she managed to get inside through a damaged entrance:

'I was amazed. There were water-filled bomb craters everywhere and all the buildings were destroyed and burnt out. All the big animal houses were gone. The six female elephants and the baby were nothing but blackened carcasses, roasted to death by phosphorus bombs. A terrible smell lingered above the total destruction of my beloved Zoo. There were blasted and dead animals everywhere. The only living thing, in his big pond, was a big bull hippopotamus called 'Knautschke', still swimming while above him his shelter burned down.

'I knew a lot of the keepers. With tears in their eyes, they told me about the horrible night. All the brown bears, the polar bears, the camels, the zebras, the antelopes, the ostriches and all the beasts of prey – lions, tigers, panthers, leopards and hyenas – were dead; the keepers had been forced to shoot many of the burning and crazed animals. All the wild birds were gone. Of the apes, only one orang-utan – a female called 'Cleo' – managed to escape into the nearby park. She had been found sitting in a big tree with her baby but she died from a heart attack and her body was hanging in the tree. Flak soldiers brought 'Muschi' the baby down the next day and sent it to the Zoo at Copenhagen. In the big aquarium, all the glass cases were broken and the water had poured out, sweeping alligators and crocodiles, as well as all the fish and snakes, out into the open where they perished in the November cold of this night.'[4]

After having weathered ashes and the red-hot glare of smouldering heaps of debris on her way to the zoo, Charlottenburg resident Josepha von Koskull, who was employed as a Luftschützwärtin (member of the air-raid protection), noticed an exhausted and distraught feral-looking Alsatian near a completely burned-out guard house lolloping towards her. She took pity on the exhausted and dazed animal and just as she was about to feed it with a bread roll, two uniformed zookeepers warned her that it was actually an escaped wolf.

Else Kurz reported that 'The heat of the fires had left a chestnut tree in leaf again in November. Someone using the pseudonym 'Embo Schiller' likened the conflagration to Nero's time. In Berlin-Spandau, on Seeburger Strasse 14, a woman whose property bordered on the barracks of a prison camp said that a neighbour was alarmed that the prisoners might escape. Like a gigantic fist, the bombs smashed everyone and everything.'

A 13-year-old boy wrote that his grandmother was wearing shoes on the wrong feet and we had to laugh about it very much. It was not the first time that the siren got us out of our beds; maybe it will be the last time for many. Bombs were whistling down, dust swirled and there was smoke everywhere. Everyone had put on gas masks or wet handkerchiefs around their nose and throat. A cry frightened us all: 'House is burning!' We all had to leave the cellar but when we got out there was fire everywhere; everything was on fire and the fire was crackling. Sometimes it was green, for there were phosphorus bombs. The splitter ditch was full of people, but more and more we heard that they had lost everything in Berlin. But we did not lose the courage to believe in the leader, the people and the victory.'

Returning to Berlin by train in the early dawn from Puddiger in Pomerania, 36-year-old Hans Georg von Studnitz endured an experience which to him seemed like 'the end of the world'. Born in Potsdam in 1907 of old Silesian stock and a journalist in Berlin since 1930, he now held a senior post in the German Foreign Office Press and Information Section. He and his companions had to leave the train and continue their journey by the S-Bahn suburban train service because the Stettiner station in Berlin had been put out of action. After an hour they gave up the attempt to reach the Alexanderplatz. The air was so polluted with the smell of burning and with the fumes of escaping gas, the darkness was so impenetrable and the torrents of rain so fierce, that their strength began to fail them. At about 5.00 am a newspaper woman showed them the way to the underground station in the Rosenthalerplatz to take the train to the terminus in the Alexanderplatz. The road leading to the Rosenthalerplatz consisted of nothing but a row of smouldering shops and offices. Through the flickering flames, the smoke and the showers of sparks Von Studnitz and his companions made their hazardous way to the underground station. Hundreds of people had taken refuge on the subterranean platforms, with such of their possessions as they had been able to salvage. Wounded, bandaged and their faces smothered in dust, they hunched apathetically on their bedding or whatever else they had been able to bring with them. At the Alexanderplatz they emerged into the 'burning hell that was Berlin'.

'Thus broke the grim morning of November 23rd,' wrote von Studnitz. 'All around the destroyed station in the Alexanderplatz the great warehouses were burning fiercely. Further towards the city stood the Schlüters Royal Palace, the former residence of the Hohenzollerns, in the middle of a tornado of fire and smoke. From one wing gigantic tongues of flame shot skywards. We crossed the Spree into the burning banking quarter. The Zeughaus, the university, the Hedwigskirche and the National Library had long since been reduced to ashes. From the Unter den Linden dense clouds of smoke obliterated the view into the Friedrichsstrasse and the Wilhelmstrasse. In the Pariser Platz the headquarters of IG Farben was burning. The Hotel Adlon opposite seemed to have escaped damage. The French Embassy, the Friedländers mansion, the Schautenkasino and the corner houses built by Schinkel which flank the Brandenburg Gate displayed the beautiful profile of their architecture for the last time against a background of flickering flame.

'On the other side of the Brandenburg Gate the Tiergarten looked like some forest battle-scene from the First World War. Between whole battalions of fallen trees stood the jagged stumps of oak and beech trees, bereft of the crowning glory of their foliage. The Charlottenburger Chaussee was strewn with torn camouflage-nets and the twisted wreckage of burnt-out cars and lorries, between which a mass of dazed and wandering people were stumbling along. The Siegessaule [the Victory Column designed by Heinrich Strack after 1864 to commemorate the Prussian victory in the Danish-Prussian War], still towered over the Grosser Stern [central square] like the Sword of the Day of Judgement. Around the mighty memorial the bronze busts of Moltke and the paladins of the 1870 war gazed down on the troubled mirror of an artificial lake, created during the night by the bursting of the water mains.

'Then we reached the Handelallee and our own home. Here, too, the park had been ploughed up by the bombs, the Kaiser Friedrich church had been reduced to ruins by a direct hit and the four- storeyed buildings to burnt-out shells. Our own house had escaped damage in the attack itself, but had succumbed to the flames consuming its neighbours. Of the thirty-three houses in the street only three had survived the night. And our own house was the last to catch fire. We gazed up at the windows of the second floor, behind which there was a ghastly, flickering glare. Like a six-armed torch, our Empire chandelier, the only thing inside the room which was still recognisable, swayed to and fro and then plunged like a shooting-star through the burnt ceiling of the first floor into the cellars below.'

The burning city made a clearly visible target for bombers returning that evening. When Von Studnitz and his companions left Berlin with the Italian ambassador two hours before this second attack, the streets were still 'lit up as bright as day by the glare of the still raging conflagrations'.

At around 7.00 pm 'Missie' Vassiltchikov rushed down the stairs of her office to go home when the hall porter intercepted her with the ominous words 'Luftgefahr 15 – höchste Alarmstufe' ['air-raid danger 15']. RAF bombers were on their way. The streets were full of people, many of them just standing around for the visibility was so poor that nobody expected the raid to last long or cause much damage. 'Missie' packed a few things into a small suitcase in case she and her father had to leave their house. She had just finished packing when the flak opened up. It was immediately very violent and they hurried down to the half-basement behind the kitchen where they usually sat out air-raids. They had hardly got there when they heard the first bombers approaching. They flew very low and the barking of the flak was suddenly drowned by a very different sound: that of exploding bombs, first far away and then closer and closer, until it seemed as if they were falling literally on top of them. At every crash the house shook. The air pressure was dreadful and the noise deafening.

For the first time 'Missie' understood what the expression 'Bombenteppich' ['bomb carpet'] meant; the Allies called it 'saturation bombing'. At one point there was a shower of broken glass and all three doors of the basement flew into the room, torn off their hinges. 'Missie' pressed them back into place and leaned against them to try to keep them shut. She had left her coat outside but didn't dare go out to get it. An incendiary flare fell hissing into the entrance and men crept out to extinguish it. After an hour or so it became quieter, but then it started all over again.... 'Only around 9.30 pm did the droning of planes overhead cease. The planes did not come in waves as they did usually but kept on droning ceaselessly overhead for more than an hour – there must have been several hundreds of them,' she wrote.[5]

Berlin was in fact the target for 383 bombers: 365 Lancasters, 10 Halifaxes and 8 Mosquitoes. The bombing force took the same direct route used twelve hours earlier and once again the Jägerleitoffizier made an early identification of Berlin as the probable target. From a distance of 30 miles the air crews could see the fires that had continued to smoulder since Monday. They noticed that flak over the target, which was again cloud-covered, was 'unusually restrained' and the Pathfinders carried out sky-marking but many of the Main Force crews aimed their bombs through the cloud at the glow of the fires burning from the previous night. This time the attack concentrated mainly on the western part of the capital with its three large rail installations: Westend, Bahn Zoo and Bahnhof Charlottenburg, which suffered more than in all the previous raids.

The Pathfinders carried out sky-marking but many of the bomb-aimers aimed their bombs through a smoke cloud almost 19,000 feet high from eleven major fires still burning from the previous night. Bomber crews noticed that flak over the target was 'unusually restrained', but the night was clear and there were only a few clouds to hinder visibility so that operational conditions were far more favourable to the German air defence than on the previous night.

'This raid was very similar to the previous one,' recalled Flight Sergeant Brian Soper on 12 Squadron at Wickenby, 'although both ground and "sky-markers" were used as there was a lot of cloud at lower levels. These took the form of flares, red, green, or yellow, the colours specified at the briefing, dropped by Pathfinder Lancs or Mosquitoes. "Sky-markers" called "Wanganui" flares were dropped by parachutes, with one colour dripping from the other. To bomb on these, the bomb-aimer would need to be sure of approaching from the right direction; height and wind speed calculations were important. These markers were only used when the ground markers could not easily be seen and were probably not too accurate.'

Only a handful of experienced Nachtjäger ('Tame Boar') crews – twelve who had braved the elements – shot down an estimated four to thirteen of the twenty bombers (all Lancasters) that were lost over Berlin. (A Mosquito marker aircraft was also lost to flak.) Gunners on some of the bombers fended off fighter attacks and saved their aircraft from becoming another sad statistic. Others were lucky. Two Lancasters on 50 Squadron were attacked around 2008 hours when the main body of fighters arrived over Berlin. The Lancaster flown by 22-year-old Pilot Officer Joseph Lloyd Dobbyn DFC of Melita, Manitoba was attacked by a Ju 88 which closed in from the port quarter and fired two bursts and then broke away underneath. Dobbyn's luck finally ran out on the night of 22/23 March 1944 when he was one of the fatalities of the raid on Frankfurt.

Flight Sergeant R.A. Leader was attacked by a Bf 110 and his mid-upper gunner, Sergeant D.R. Tupman, opened up with a very long burst. The fighter replied with a short burst of cannon fire and broke away to port. Flying Officer A.R. Candy the navigator then saw a Ju 88 overhead. Once again Tupman opened fire with a long burst. The enemy fighter moved to the starboard side and Tupman fired again. Sergeant T.F. Coulson the rear gunner was unable to fire as his guns had frozen up. Tupman claimed the Messerschmitt as 'damaged'.[6]

Untold losses were avoided by 'spoof' fighter flares dropped by Mosquitoes north of the bomber stream, which caused some diversion of the night-fighter effort and fake 'Corona' instructions ordering the German pilots to land because of fog at their bases. When the Nachtjagd introduced female commentators to give the 'running commentary' to the fighters to beat the 'Corona' interference, this was swiftly countered by a female voice from England. Later the transmission of three or four superimposed German voices would be used. Eventually, instead of attempting to imitate the German commentators, British operators would set out to simply irritate them by blocking the air waves by reading lengthy passages from the writings of Johann Wolfgang von Goethe or the speeches of Hitler. Gradually the Germans would overcome the worst effects of 'Corona' by increasing the frequency spread used and making rapid changes of frequency during operations, but in the meantime 'Corona' caused great confusion and on occasion exchanges between night-fighter pilots and the real controllers reached explosive levels.

Finally in the fire-glow over Berlin the Lancaster crews were able to observe many details of the destroyed city districts. The whole complex around the Wilhelmstrasse, the Brandenburg Gate area and the Tauentzienstrasse, Potsdam Square, the Anhalter Strasse and many other building-lined streets had been completely destroyed.

'The all-clear,' wrote 'Missie' Vassiltchikov, 'came only half an hour after the last planes had departed.' Berliners once again began clearing away the debris and devastation as fire crews tried to extinguish the blazing fires but the wind, thus far non-existent, suddenly rose and the fires spread. She continued:

'We went out into our little square and sure enough the sky on three sides was blood-red. This, the officer explained, was only the beginning; the greatest danger would come in a few hours' time, when the fire-storm really got going. Our square was already filled with smoke and one could hardly breathe…. Also the electricity, gas and water no longer worked and we had to grope our way around with electric torches and candles. Luckily we had had time to fill every available bath tub, wash basin, kitchen sink and pail. By now the wind had increased alarmingly, roaring like a gale at sea. When we looked out of the window we could see a steady shower of sparks raining down on our and the neighbouring houses and all the time the air was getting thicker and hotter, while the smoke billowed in through the gaping window frames. We went through the house and found to our relief that apart from the broken windows and the unhinged doors, it had not suffered any real damage.

'Just as we were swallowing some sandwiches, the sirens came on once more. We stood at the windows for about half an hour, in total silence. We were convinced it would start all over again. Then the all-clear sounded again. Apparently enemy reconnaissance planes had been surveying the damage.

'Towards 2 am I decided to sleep for a while. Every now and then a crashing building or a delayed time bomb would tear one awake and I would sit up with a pounding heart. By now the fire storm had reached its peak and the roar outside was like a train going through a tunnel.[7]

People deeply anchored in Nazi ideology took the opportunity to tell their stories simply. Marta Kissuth walked along the Rykestrasse and entered the street at the water tower. On the fence was furniture of the hard-hit population. The sight hurt so badly that she stopped and saw an old woman lifting her belongings on a hand-truck. Then she said to her, almost joyfully: 'A new life is blossoming from rubble. Our leader wins and wins.' Then she said to Marta again: 'Do you know what I wrote to my son? "Bomb-damaged, but I am healthy."'

Otto Krause from the Pilsator at Alexanderplatz, Gontardstrasse 3-5, stated: 'My work as an air defence officer was now in operation. Then I went to the beer cellar of Borchardt. It was getting worse and worse and only by the circumstance were we able to close the stable cellar door at the last moment that we all owed our lives. A thunder – crash – an earthquake; we heard the impact of the bombs or mines. The station was hit! We heard the low-flying bombers. Alexanderplatz – what devastation. There were only ruined and burning houses and shops.'

On 83 Squadron PFF at Wyton the loss of Lancaster III 'C-Charlie' was keenly felt. Wing Commander Ray Hilton DSO DFC*, who had returned to command 83 Squadron for his third tour in November and his crew, were killed after being hit by flak and crashing in the target area. Hilton, who was 27 years old and left a widow, 'Betty' Evelyn Hilton, had flown at least sixty-four operations.

On this night Flight Lieutenant Wilfred Cyril Riches and his crew on 97 PFF Squadron were detailed for a leading role within the Pathfinder Force, but the raid became a nightmare. It was Riches' twenty-third operation and four of these had been on Berlin. On a previous raid on Berlin on 3/4 September, his aircraft was attacked by an enemy fighter, the damage inflicted was severe and Sergeant Christopher Frank Nordhoff, his 20-year-old rear gunner was killed by cannon fire from an enemy fighter when over the target, but Riches avoided further attacks and made it home to Bourn.

Now, on the approach to the target Riches' Lancaster was repeatedly hit by flak with the result that the port inner engine caught fire and had to be feathered. Despite this, he persisted in pressing on with his attack and dropped his bombs and markers accurately. On the return flight, after flying on three engines for about two hours and when about to cross the Dutch coast, the starboard outer engine failed. At this time Riches was at 14,000 feet, but despite this he managed to get back across the North Sea to his base and make a safe landing, the third engine cutting out while still on the runway. He was awarded an immediate DFC. On the night of 2/3 December Riches' Lancaster was hit by heavy flak at Berlin and he was knocked unconscious but managed to come to and pull the aircraft out of a vertical dive. Unfortunately, Squadron Leader Riches DFC was killed in action on 635 Squadron on 6 July 1944.

Apart from the 20 Lancasters that were missing, 5 more had crashed in England with 11 men killed and another 14 injured. At around midnight 'S for Sugar', the Lancaster piloted by Flying Officer 'Don' Turner on 49 Squadron, was returning over the North Sea at 1,000 feet on track for Fiskerton 5 miles east of Lincoln, but the conditions were misty so Turner decided to let down a little in order to determine landfall. Just as he did, 'Sugar' suddenly struck the sea and then moments later it was careering up the beach at Chapel St Leonards on the Lincolnshire coast, 5 miles north of Skegness towards sand dunes. A startled but intact crew clambered out into waist-high freezing sea water. The crash was observed by Frank Raynor on duty at the ROC observation post. He was first to reach the aircraft on a bicycle, followed by Joe Kirk, on coastguard duty at the watch box, who he had alerted on the way. The crew members were all in shock and one asked Raynor to retrieve a white glove, a present from a girlfriend. All survived and they spent the next few days recovering in Scampton sick bay. They resumed flying within six months. Sadly, on 22/23 March 1944 'Don' Turner and five of the crew were killed on the raid on Frankfurt. While in England Flight Sergeant Jack Norman E. Bennett, the 30-year-old Canadian rear gunner who was born in Calgary, had met his grandparents Mr and Mrs Nash Downes, aged 85 and 83, residents of London, who had come through all the London blitzes.

In Norfolk Miss Marjorie Morton and her mother had a narrow escape when a 156 Squadron Lancaster crashed into High Acre House, Rudham Road, Harpley near Bircham Newton. The 23-year-old pilot, Flight Sergeant Gordon William Fordyce who was from Sarnia, Ontario and Sergeants George Johnson, the 34-year-old flight engineer, and Ronald Horace Hodges, the mid-upper gunner, died in the crash. Reginald Tipple, a 55-year-old lorry driver, Home Guard sergeant and special constable living in his cottage only 200 yards away, heard the crash and rushed out to find the Lancaster had smashed into High Acre House. 'Reggie' Tipple entered the burning aircraft and broke the cabin with bricks so that he could rescue Sergeant Lawrence J. Collins, the navigator who was trapped in the nose of the aircraft. He then rescued another member of the crew who was stuck under the wing with his clothes on fire. After putting out the flames, 'Reggie' helped a third member of the crew who had been flung out of the Lancaster and finally, Flight Sergeant James Steel Minogue, the Canadian rear gunner who was trapped in the broken tail. 'Reggie' was awarded the British Empire Medal for his bravery.[8]

'V for Victor', a 9 Squadron Lancaster skippered by Pilot Officer Norman John Robinson, a 26-year-old Irishman from County Kildare, was one of two Lancasters from Bardney that almost made it home, but at 11.45 villagers at Belchford near Ludford Magna heard the bomber circling low in the fog. They briefly caught sight of the Lancaster as it clipped the top of a row of trees close to the village church before 'V for Victor' roared up, stalled and then crashed nose-down into a field nearby. Robinson and five of the crew were killed instantly.

At South Norwood in London Vera May Pitman would wait for news of her husband Flight Sergeant Bertram John Pitman, the 21-year-old bomb-aimer. He and Flying Officer Charles Godfrey Hinton, the 25-year-old second pilot from Cheltenham, Sergeant Robert George Taylor, the flight engineer, Flight Sergeant Thomas Rhodes Davis, the 20-year-old navigator from Streatham and Sergeant Walter Espley Jones, the 23-year-old wireless-operator of Saughall Massie on the Wirral died with their pilot. Flight Sergeant L.E. Mitchell and Sergeant J. Casey, the two gunners, were thrown clear. Despite having facial burns, Casey went to the assistance of Mitchell who had a broken leg and burns to his face and hands. He had dragged himself clear before the Lancaster went up in flames. Villagers gave both men first-aid before they were taken to RAF Hospital Rauceby for treatment.[9]

The other Lancaster on 9 Squadron that failed to make it home was 'N-Nuts' flown by Pilot Officer Geoffrey Ward aged 23 from Dewsbury who crashed on making a turn to port on his second approach to land. 'N-Nuts' went into a shallow dive to starboard and, failing to respond to the controls it crashed, thankfully without injury to the crew. Three Lancasters on 44 ('Rhodesia') Squadron failed to return to Dunholme Lodge.[10]

At Kirmington 'Jonah' Jones and two other Intelligence officers were waiting impatiently to interrogate the returning crews. Jones had been 'duty dog', remaining in the Ops Room while the other two went off for a meal and had to be content with a mug of tea. It wasn't his night. Two Lancasters on 166 Squadron had failed to take off and two more aborted early on. These crews had to be interrogated; the two abort crews mostly for the benefit of the appropriate specialist officer who had been called when the reason for the return was known. One of the early returns was due to a fuel leakage and the aircraft was losing fuel at an alarming rate, so the skipper had decided to abandon the mission and jettison his bombs 'safe' in the North Sea before landing.

At 23.30 the noise of aircraft engines was at last heard approaching from the east. Control rang to tell Jones that 'Q-Queenie' was overhead. It was the signal to call the other Intelligence staff and get the tea urn delivered. The Lancasters started landing and the first crew to enter the briefing room came in, tired but looking quite pleased with themselves. They took a mug of tea and a cigarette and after a few preliminary 'unofficial' questions and comments, the interrogation began. According to this first crew, the trip was 'a piece of cake'.[11]

'C-Charlie' had crash-landed at a fighter station in the south and all the crew were safe. Combat reports included the loss of 'A-Apple' captained by Warrant Officer Eric F. Grove, which had taken off at 1702 hours. It is thought probable that this Lancaster was shot down 40 kilometres west of Berlin at 6,000 metres by Leutnant Peter Spoden. The German pilot had recently joined 5./NJG5 after a long period of convalescence, despite the surgeons' opinion that he would never walk again. Feldwebel Schmiedler had replaced Ballweg as his bordfunker. Spoden was still very angry at being shot down and wounded over Berlin on 23 August and was ashamed to say that he aimed not for the normal point of the wings but into the fuselage. Spoden fired a long burst with his forward-firing weapons, the salvo resulting in an explosion sending countless chunks of burning debris and wreckage down to earth. Both gunners – Sergeants John Francis Mathew Davies and James Edward William Iverson – were never seen again. Grove, Sergeant Alan Smith, navigator; Sergeants A. Rossi the flight engineer and S.G. Patterson the wireless-operator; and Flight Sergeant Ted Hunt the New Zealander air-bomber survived and they were held in captivity until the end of the war.

On the bomber bases in Eastern England, suddenly, interrogations were over. The last crew was interrogated at about 02.30 and the Intelligence officers settled down to compile the Group Raid report. Their task was to sort and collate all the information and assemble it in a special sequence as soon as possible before sending it over the teleprinter link to Group Headquarters at Bawtry. When completed, the Form-Y 'toilet roll' (frequently 3 or 4 feet long) was handed in to the Signals Section.

Finally, at 04.30 three weary Intelligence officers put on their caps and greatcoats. After making arrangements for the 'duty dog' to be called for morning duty, they bid the watch-keeper 'good night' – even though dawn was not far off – and walked into the bitterly cold morning air. Jones reached his billet just near the station entrance and crawled into his cold bed, thinking of his wife and baby fast asleep 200 miles away. Then he thought of Berlin 'hopefully blazing merrily and the bomb disposal squads dealing with unexploded or long-delay bombs' before falling asleep for a brief three or four hours before a new day of operations and the Group broadcast came over the 'blower': 'Hello Kirmington, Maximum Effort again on….'

At Spilsby Flight Lieutenant Ralph Allen's crew on 207 Squadron returned safely from Berlin and headed for their sleeping quarters in the Nissen huts on the station. Allen, who lived at Weston-super-Mare in Somerset, shared his hut with his navigator, Pilot Officer Eric Stephenson and another pilot, Flight Lieutenant Derek Edward Reay and his navigator, Flying Officer Robert Edward Mair. They each had a bed and mattress, a locker and a little hanging wardrobe and there was the usual large potbelly stove in the middle of the room for heating with a few chairs around it. They were not exactly impressed by this accommodation, but it was pretty standard fare for the RAF during the war.

'Ralph and I were not too worried when we got back to our hut and found that Bob and Derrick were not there,' says Stephenson, 'because they could have been further back in the bombing raid or they could just be late or were forced to land somewhere else. In the morning, however, we learnt that their aircraft was missing. Later it was confirmed that they were killed in action and that was a bit shattering. It probably influenced my action a day or so later.'[12]

Stephenson, a Geordie from Tyneside, was born in his maternal grandmother's house in the riverside town of Jarrow on 22 July 1922. His family moved to north-west London soon after and he completed his education at Kilburn Boys' Grammar School. He was offered a place in Medicine at University College London. At the end of the first year he was sent to Kingsbury County School to complete a short stint in Pure Science and it was here he was captivated by a long-legged girl in a brown pleated gymslip who was full of energy and fun. This girl was Freda and they quickly became friends, despite the disapproval of Eric's father who forbade his 19-year-old son from seeing her. Eric disobeyed his father, left home, put his medical training on hold and joined the RAF in late 1941. He would volunteer for air crew and get a pair of wings on his RAF tunic, grow a moustache, Brylcreem his hair, wear a casual silk scarf and be altogether irresistible to Freda. Stephenson had washed out of pilot training during which he had escaped death on the flip of a penny coin.[13]

RAF Headquarters announced: 'Last night Berlin was again the target of a grand assault by the RAF. On Tuesday night leading into Wednesday, the western part of Berlin suffered more than in all the previous raids. On Wednesday afternoon, Mosquitoes flew over the capital and reported having observed well over 200 giant conflagrations.'

'What the first attack spared was destroyed by the second,' wrote Hans Georg von Studnitz.[14] 'Those who lived through both say that the latter was the worse, since an even higher proportion of explosive bombs were dropped. Between the Charlottenburg and the Alexanderplatz stations practically everything has been destroyed. Only in the Kantstrasse, the Rankestrasse and along the Kurfürstendamm can one find a few blocks of houses still standing, like islands in a sea of ruins. The Gedachtniskirche is surrounded by ruins, the Zoo has been burnt out, the Aquarium and the Eden Hotel have been demolished, the old western sector, from the Budapester Strasse as far as the Potsdam bridge, has been wiped out, the Tiergartenstrasse and the northern edge of the Tiergarten had ceased to exist….

Of the hotels, only the Esplanade, the Adlon and part of the Kaisderhof remain standing. Nearly all the Ministries and banks, the old Reich's Chancellery, the Wilhelm I mansion, the Charlottenburg palace and the whole of the Lützowplatz quarter lie in ruins. With few exceptions, the embassies and legations have been reduced to smouldering ashes.... All plans for assembly areas and evacuation procedures have been completely nullified by the magnitude of the catastrophe. The streets are crammed with thousands of lorries and an army of soldiers, prisoners of war and convicts is at work, fire-fighting, salvaging furniture and conveying people to a place of safety. The behaviour of the population has been beyond all praise.'

At the home of the Reich Minister of Propaganda, Doktor Joseph Goebbels in Hermann Göring Strasse, the top floor was burned out completely and the whole house was filled with water. Goebbels considered it 'practically impossible' to live there. 'There is no heat, no water and all rooms filled with pungent smoke.' He noted in his diary on Wednesday, 24 November:

'Early in the morning I am already at work. Straightaway Schaub[15] gives me a report on the situation in Berlin, which is very sad. It is inexplicable how the British were able to destroy so much of the capital in one air raid. The Wilhelmsplatz is truly the picture of desolation. It is still blazing from end to end. The Propaganda Ministry has mainly been spared.... Now and then I am able to snatch half an hour's sleep; but then I am called back to work. Large formations of British aircraft are again set on an obstinate course for Berlin.... The raid begins shortly after the alarm siren. This time there are more blast bombs than incendiaries. Once again it is a first-class grand assault.... Mines and explosive bombs hail down incessantly on the government district. One after another the most important buildings start to burn. After the raid when I take a look at the Wilhelmsplatz, I find that the ghastly impression of the previous evening has grown even worse. I pass on into the Propaganda Ministry. The offices are burning in two places on the side of the Wilhelmsplatz.... The poor people, who are the victims of these low-down methods of English warfare, are really to be pitied.'

Towards 11.00 am that Wednesday 'Missie' Vassiltchikov decided to go out to try to reach her office. She had heard that the Unter den Linden area had suffered just as badly as her neighbourhood; the French and British Embassies, the Hotel Bristol, the Zeughaus (Arsenal) and the Wilhelmstrasse and Friedrichstrasse were all very badly damaged. The instant she left her house 'Missie' was enveloped in smoke, and ashes rained down on her head. She could breathe only by holding a handkerchief to her mouth and blessed her friend Heinz for lending her his fur-lined military goggles. 'At first the Woyrschstrasse did not look too bad,' she wrote, 'but one block away, at the corner of Lützowstrasse, all the houses were burnt out.'

As she continued down Lützowstrasse the devastation grew worse; many buildings were still burning and she had to keep to the middle of the street, which was difficult on account of the numerous wrecked trams. There were many people in the streets, most of them muffled in scarves and coughing as they threaded their way gingerly through the piles of fallen masonry. At the end of Lützowstrasse the houses on both sides of the street had collapsed and 'Missie' had to climb over mounds of smoking rubble, leaking water pipes and other wreckage to get across to the other side. Until then she had seen very few firemen around, but here some were busily trying to extricate people trapped in the cellars. On Lützowplatz all the houses were burned out. The bridge over the River Spree was undamaged but on the other side all the buildings had been destroyed; only their outside walls were still standing. 'Many cars were weaving their way cautiously through the ruins, blowing their horns wildly.' The whole district 'had been wiped out in just one night!'[16]

At noon, a spokesman for the German Armed Forces High Command (the Wehrmacht) stated to representatives of the foreign press concerning the raid on Berlin: 'These terrorist raids on German cities have expanded to such an extent that regrettably we are forced to deploy our retaliatory weapon.' However, when questioned by journalists, the spokesman expressed no details about the method or date of German retaliatory measures.

On Thursday, 25 November Goebbels wrote in his diary: 'Now we are gradually learning again to get used to a primitive pattern of life. Mornings in the Göringstrasse there is no heat, no light, no water. One can neither shave nor wash. One has to leave the bunker with a burning candle. At the crack of dawn I get up with the worst headache of my life. I am plagued with headaches non-stop. But what does that matter; it's time to get to work. I drive straight to the office where I can shave and wash.... Most of the Kaiserdamm is still burning; but the fire department hopes to get the fires under control in the course of the night. Isolated clumps of people flit over the streets making a genuinely ghostly impression. Your heart is wrenched when you drive through areas like this. How beautiful Berlin was once and how wretched and dilapidated it looks now.'

Following the raid 'Bomber' Harris received a message from Sir Archibald Sinclair, the Secretary of State for Air, which he instructed to be conveyed together with his reply to all ranks:

'My warmest congratulations to you and to all ranks serving under your command on two crushing attacks on the Nazi citadel. Berlin is not only the home of Prussian militarism and the capital of the Nazi government, but it is also the greatest single centre of war industry in Germany. Often before, your squadrons have hit it hard. The most convincing measure of this success has been the huge deployment of the enemy's resources for its defence. Nevertheless your attacks these last two nights have reached a new level of power and concentration and have proved that however much he may marshal his guns, searchlights and fighters, the enemy cannot match your skill and determination of your crews.'

Harris replied: 'On behalf of all ranks of Bomber Command I thank you for your encouraging message. The Battle of Berlin progresses. It will continue as opportunity serves and circumstances dictate until the heart of Nazi Germany ceases to beat.'

A foreign correspondent was reported to have said that the raid was 'the Twilight of the Gods'. In Stockholm vivid accounts of the scenes in the German capital after the raid were given in Wednesday's Swedish Press. The Berlin correspondent of the *Stockholm Aftonbladet* said that 'the raid was incomparably the largest ever made on the city and starting early, caught many people inside the city who would later have been in the suburbs. Throughout the whole night raging fires were visible in different parts of the city, which was covered by a mighty cloud of smoke.'

Svenska Dagbladet confirmed that the government districts had been hit hard: 'Hitler's residence near the Reich Chancellery received a direct hit and burnt fiercely and so did the Foreign Office. The French Embassy received a direct hit and was set on fire. It was useless to try to extinguish it. The [former] British Embassy was hot and a fire broke out.... The Armament Ministry ... was burned down to the first storey. The whole of the Tiergartenstrasse looked like a curtain of fire even several hours after the raid.'

Private reports to the Swedish *Afton Tidningen* stated that the first attack was made by a formation of Mosquitoes:

'When the all clear sounded and Berliners were leaving the shelters, a large number of heavy bombers swept over and dropped a devastating load of HE and incendiaries. The victims are thought to number thousands.

Unconfirmed reports quoted by the newspaper say the Mixnanan Genest Ludwig Loewe and Askania factories were razed. Other factories including the A.E.G. turbine works in Moabit; the Oberschöneweide and the Siemens plants are still burning. Street traffic is practically stopped. When the sirens wailed again people who had gone into the streets to see if their homes were still standing were forced to rush back to shelters. When the 'all clear' sounded a second time there were the strangest scenes in the streets, said the correspondent. Some people were trying to help the firemen; others were hurrying along with all their possessions in suitcases and duffel bags.

Later in the night one could see thousands of people who had obviously lost their homes or who were waiting for fires near their homes to be put out. They had gathered in the railway stations, the underground stations and other public places, with nowhere to go. A large number of residential areas, including the most densely-populated workers' quarters, were turned into an area of fire. A large number of official buildings were burned down and irreplaceable art treasures lost. Among the official buildings burned down are several of the foreign legations and embassies, including the Swedish one. Berlin's firemen and emergency rescue squads were sent immediately to the hardest-hit areas but the work was immeasurably difficult.'

Other Swedish newspaper reports from Berlin indicated that the city's fire-fighting apparatus and preparations were totally inadequate. 'German night-fighters and flak had great difficulty in attempting to stop the attack, especially because of the excellent cloud cover which the RAF had,' one report said. Another said

'Count Bernadotte, head of the Swedish Red Cross and Arvid Gustav Richert the Swedish Minister in Berlin, were both in the Swedish Legation when the alarm sounded. After the raid both assisted others from the Legation trying to rescue what they could from the fire. The Finnish Legation was also destroyed, it was said and the Hungarian and Danish Legations suffered more or less severe damage. Other bombs are reported to have fallen in the Albertstrasse, containing Himmler's Gestapo headquarters.

'Among the churches badly hit were the famous Gedaechtniskirche, the Kaiser Wilhelm Memorial Church, which dominates the eastern entrance to the Kurfürstendamm. The offices of the Stockholm Tidningen on the Pariser Platz were destroyed. Other buildings in the same area whose fate is not yet known include the Hotel 'Adlon', the offices of Speer, the Armaments Minister and the famous Brandenburger Tor [Brandenburg Gate]. When Berlin tried to go to work this morning great fires were burning across the city and clouds of smoke vomited into the already blackened skies. The transport system has broken down. Berlin walked to work. Tens of thousands who had been travelling out into the suburbs in the hope of escaping raids were caught there. In some areas gas and electricity supplies were smashed.'

Reports from German sources indicated this attack on Berlin was perhaps the heaviest of this war and it represented the most effective blow yet struck at the Reich capital. Other reports filtering through from neutral sources told of whole blocks of buildings on fire, of gas and electrical services cut off and transport paralysed.

The Berne correspondent of *Allehanda* said that 'the centre of Berlin, the areas round Alexanderplatz, Friedrichstrasse and Unter den Linden were hit and the western, northern and southern suburbs, including Siemensstadt, Spandau, Neukölln. Lichtenberg and Pankow severely damaged. The fire services, ARP rescue squads and pioneer troops were hard-worked and many were unable to assist at every place where help was needed. Many theatres were hit and the University Town library was still burning yesterday morning.

'The official German communiqués admitted that the attack was heavy and stated that 'tremendous damage was done, while there were big losses among the population.' The allegation was made that British bombers flew in to attack 'with the sky entirely over clouded and without being able to see the ground.'

'This statement, probably, is designed to explain to Berliners why the Luftwaffe fighters and flak failed to avert such vast devastation. I think it is accurate to state that never before have German official communiqués emphasised to such an extent the severity of the damage which it is admitted has been inflicted on a great number of districts of the capital. It is generally maintained that the Allied bombers were turned away by the German defences before passing over the Berlin suburbs. Even in the case of heavy attacks this claim has been made. There are no such pretensions today. Referring to the big Allied night air raid on Berlin on Monday, a German communiqué yesterday stated: 'Last night British bomber formations made a heavy terror attack on the capital of the Reich. Devastation was caused in several districts of the town by HE and incendiary bombs. A number of irreplaceable buildings of artistic value were destroyed. The population suffered casualties. Other enemy air forces attacked a locality in the Rhineland. According to reports to hand, the air defences brought down twenty-nine enemy bombers, although conditions were particularly difficult for the defence.'

Most Stockholm newspapers quoted the German Foreign Office spokesman as saying that 'The Wilhelmstrasse was living and working yesterday as usual. Round this famous street, site of the German Foreign Office and of several embassies, firemen were still working to put out the flames of the many fires,' it was stated.

In an effort to soften the blow at the German morale, Dr. Paul Schmidt, chief of the German Foreign Office Press Department said, 'Berlin is proud to stand now in the common front with many (other German towns). One sentiment shared by all of us in this hard and fateful struggle – indomitable hatred of the enemy, who strives to exterminate the German nation in his brutal will to annihilate.'

In Berlin the German News Bureau announced: '[The] British bombers … had no ground visibility because the sky was completely overcast, but the raid was a severe one that caused heavy damage and casualties in many districts of the capital, mainly in workers' districts. It is also reported that irreplaceable art-historical treasures were destroyed and damage was inflicted on offices belonging to the diplomatic representatives of several neutral nations. At today's foreign press conference, the head of the German Foreign Ministry press division stated his views of the air raid on Berlin last night. He emphasized that the most important thing about the raid had been the reaction of the Berlin population. He was proud to say that Berlin had honoured its role as the capital of the Reich. The people had defended their city in an exemplary way, often at risk of their lives. The spokesman mentioned several examples of the self-sacrificial conduct of the populace. There had been much suffering that night, he said; yet there had also been countless proofs of comradeship and unconditional will to serve. The British might believe that they can undermine German morale by destroying German homes and places of culture, but the events of this night bear out that the Berliner will emerge unbowed from these trials and that faith in our Final Victory cannot be shaken.'

In London the *Daily Mail* editorial took a more realistic view: 'It has entered the realm of possibility that Berlin may be approaching the end of its days as a capital city, due to the fearful rain of bombs that fell on it Monday night. The RAF has devised means to level targets the size of Berlin. The raid was by far the heaviest that that city has ever experienced.'

By now Doktor Goebbels in Berlin was inconsolable: 'Your heart is wrenched when you see all that has fallen victim to the air raids…. At last I have got the Führer to allow us two types of air raid siren, at least for Berlin: that is one genuine alarm siren to signal that bomber formations are approaching the city and a mere warning siren to warn of isolated offensive aircraft. This is essential because I cannot throw a city of four and a half million people into a violent turmoil every evening for the sake of two Mosquitoes. So far the Führer has given permission for these two distinct types of air siren only in Berlin; but I hope that they can soon be transferred to other districts as well. Also, in future the radio transmitters will no longer be turned off when individual offensive aircraft fly in. This was one of the worst nights of my entire life.'

Although the flames were still soaring skywards Goebbels hoped that Berliners would overcome the worst difficulties by noon and get ready for the next night. Fire engines were requisitioned from nearby towns and from as far away as Hamburg, while the Wehrmacht had to supply two and a half divisions – some 50,000 men – whose sole task was to clear the main streets to enable transport and food supplies to resume. 'It would be wonderful,' he added, 'if we had one night's rest.' Seemingly the Gauleiter's wish was heard on the night of Wednesday 24/Thursday, 25 November while the heavy bombers rested and a token six Mosquitoes bombed Berlin through cloud, perhaps just enough to keep the sirens wailing over the city to deprive Berliners of their much-needed sleep.

On the 24th the bomber crews were in their crew rooms at about 10.30 awaiting operation instructions when they were told that the operation to Berlin was cancelled and so Eric Stephenson decided to do a quick trip to London to see his fiancée Freda:

'I wanted to see her again as I was going to ask her to marry me. I had a nasty feeling I might not see her again if I did not get there quickly. With hindsight it was probably not a very sensible thing to do, as Spilsby was so isolated. I dashed back to our hut, changed my battle dress into walking out uniform and got to Boston somehow, before going onto Peterborough for a train to London.

Freda was now a 'Wren' in the Women's Royal Naval Service and stationed at Crosby Hall in Chelsea, a magnificent old building on the embankment, so I hot-footed it down there as soon as I got to London. I was overjoyed to be with her again. I calculated that I had not seen her since 17th August when we left OTU, which was the last period of leave that we had. I was sure we were due for some more leave now that we were on operations, so I asked her to marry me. She accepted my proposal and we decided to wed on 1st January 1944 at the Holy Trinity Church on Brompton Road, Chelsea, followed by a reception at the 'Blue Cockatoo', a restaurant we both liked quite near the 'Wrenery' not too far from the church.'

Eric Stephenson spoke to Squadron Leader Dudley Pike, who commanded 'B' Flight (to which his crew had been transferred a day or so before), to tell him of his marriage plans and desire for leave on 1 January:

'He assured me it would be okay. All aircrew were due to fly another operation against Berlin that night – Friday 26th November – after which the squadron could expect to get some more leave. The operation went without incident and on the Monday we proceeded on leave after completing the seven-hour trip to Berlin.'[17]

'Missie' Vassiltchikov, her father and her friend Loremarie Schönburg, each wearing tags inscribed 'bombengeschädigte' ('bomb victim') returned to Berlin on 26 November, dragging their luggage through the mud and ashes. They noticed that the houses on all sides of the Tiergarten were black and still smoking. The park looked like a battlefield in France in the 1914–18 war; the trees stark and gaunt and broken-off branches everywhere, over which they had to clamber. 'Missie' wondered what had happened to the famous rhododendrons and what it would be like in the spring. As transport was non-existent they had to walk all the way, but Berlin's traffic was assuming an almost pre-war appearance.

Cars that passed them were crammed. In the Bendlerstrasse the offices of the OKH (Army Command HQ) had been destroyed and dozens of officers and soldiers in the grey-green uniforms of the army were crawling about the debris, trying to salvage their archives. It was the same scene at the Ministry of the Navy further down the Bendlerstrasse, except that here naval officers and ratings in blue were performing the same aerobatics among the ruins. In the Landgrafenstrasse not a single house had survived and only the outer walls remained. In a large six-storey building the cellar had received a direct hit, killing 300 Berliners trying to shelter from the bombs.

In the Kurfürstenstrasse most of the houses there had been hit too. The corner of the Nettelbeckstrasse had been literally 'pulverized', with only small piles of rubble remaining. In front of another wrecked building a crowd was watching a young girl aged about 16 standing atop a pile of rubble, picking up bricks one by one, dusting them carefully and throwing them away again. Apparently her entire family was dead, buried beneath, and she had gone mad. This part of the town looked truly ghastly. In some places one could not even tell where the streets had been. 'Missie' and her companions 'no longer knew where they were'.[18]

Chapter Four

'No Enemy Plane Will Fly Over the Reich Territory!'

'His forehead was icy cold. The middle of his flying suit was badly torn and bloodstained. After examining him, one of the ambulance helpers suddenly became ill and had to walk away. The cannon shells had cut "Jerry" in half.'

Lieutenant 'Nick' Knilans USAAF, a pilot on 619 Squadron.

'There was no moon and there were three air-raids in the three nights that I was in Berlin,' wrote Christabel Bielenberg. This British writer – beautiful, headstrong and born to privilege in London – lived in Berlin and was married to a dashing German lawyer, both of whom were opposed to Nazism. 'The bombs fell indiscriminately on Nazis and anti-Nazis, on women and children and works of art, on dogs and pet canaries. New and more ravaging bombs – blockbusters and incendiaries and phosphorous bombs which burst and glowed green and emptied themselves down the walls and along the streets in flaming rivers of unquenchable flame, seeping down cellar stairs and sealing the exits to the air-raid shelters.'

Carl, a neighbour, had an air-raid trench dug between their two gardens, but he had not had time to cover the tin roof with earth, so every night his mother, who wore a huge steel helmet during the raids and looked like a 'ghost robin', sat together with Christabel in that trench, 'listening to the shrapnel splinters bouncing off the roof like "vicious hailstones".'

Christabel learned when she was in Berlin 'that those wanton, quite impersonal killings, that barrage from the air which mutilated, suffocated, burned and destroyed, did not so much breed fear and a desire to bow before the storm, but rather a certain fatalistic cussedness, a dogged determination to survive and, if possible, help others to survive, whatever their politics, whatever their creed.'[1]

On the night of Thursday 25/Friday, 26 November the Lancaster crews had been warned for Berlin and 236 Halifaxes and 26 Lancasters for Frankfurt but the Met forecast for the Berlin area was poor and finally, at 2200 hours, the Lancaster raid on the 'Big City' was cancelled. The Frankfurt force lost just twelve bombers: eleven Halifaxes and one Lancaster. In Berlin Goebbels tried to put a brave face on the recent bombing, writing on the morning of Friday, 26 November that there were signs that Berlin was beginning to recover:

'The Wilhelmplatz has already undergone quite a change. The fires are out, the atmosphere is clear, smoke has disappeared. There is no blaze left to extinguish. In short, although one sees the bare ruins of buildings … the most serious catastrophe has already been overcome. It is remarkable how fast everything goes. I thought it would take weeks; in reality, only two days were needed to get back to some semblance of order.'

RAF Headquarters was more clinical. It announced: '...although Berlin has already been bombed more heavily than Hamburg, the damage is comparatively less because the built-up area of Berlin is substantially larger. It would take approximately 50,000 to 60,000 tons of bombs to destroy the German capital to the same extent as Hamburg.'

That Friday morning at Woodhall Spa airfield, 1.5 miles from the peaceful Victorian spa town and a world away from the horrors of Berlin, 26-year-old Lieutenant 'Nick' Knilans USAAF was on the 619 Squadron battle order for that night as more favourable weather had been forecast. Hubert Clarence Knilans had left Delavan High School in Madison, Wisconsin in 1935 and in the summer months he milked cows and worked the horses on the family farm in Walworth County. Delavan was a thriving manufacturing town about halfway between Milwaukee and Chicago where Knilans looked for jobs when winter came, but his ambitions lay elsewhere. In October 1941 when his call-up papers had run out, the 24-year-old had driven up to Canada to join the RCAF with the intention of becoming a 'Yank' in Canadian clothing in Bomber Command.

At the time most Americans wished to remain neutral, millions choosing to follow the progress of the blitz and the war in Europe by tuning in to Edward R. Murrow, head of CBS European Bureau in London for his penetrating radio broadcasts. Millions more digested the column inches graphically written by reporters who were syndicated in many hundreds of newspapers throughout the USA, but not all columnists were as enthusiastic as Murrow when it came to championing the British cause. Boake Carter, who was syndicated in eighty-three newspapers with a combined circulation of more than 7 million readers asked: 'Where does the Roosevelt Administration drive the idea that Americans want to go gallivanting forth to play Sir Galahad again?' Walter Winchell, syndicated in 150 newspapers with 8½ million circulation, struck home, saying:

'The future of American youth is on top of American soil, not underneath European dirt. Attitudes had changed little after America entered the war. In April 1942 the American air attaché in London reported to Washington that 'The British public have an erroneous belief, which has been fostered by effective RAF publicity, that the German war machine can be destroyed and the nation defeated by intensive bombing.'

At Woodhall 'Nick' Knilans discovered that his USAAF first lieutenant's pay was roughly the same as the RAF group captain who commanded the station. A superb pilot, later in his career he would 'buzz' the officers' mess at the Petwood Hotel with only 2 or 3 feet to spare and so frightened a WAAF that she dropped the entire contents of a tea tray over the station CO, but he was deadly serious about operations: '...flying into combat night after night, to me, was not very funny. It was a cold-blooded battle to kill or be killed.' It was for just such reasons that he refused to have 'a scantily-clad girl' painted on the nose of his aircraft.

The strain of continuous operations had never been worse than on the night of 3/4 October when he had lost his 22-year-old rear gunner, Sergeant Gordon Hunter 'Jerry' Jackson, a Scot from Dumfries on the raid on Kassel. 'Jerry' had received a telegram from his wife Phoebe that he had a newborn son and had rushed over to see Acting Wing Commander William 'Jock' Abercromby to ask to be taken off flying duties. The 'Wingco' told Jackson that he was due for leave in a week's time and that he could see the baby then. Turning for the target, they were attacked by a night-fighter that poured tracer into the rear of the Lancaster from 300 yards causing an explosion. Knilans sent the flight engineer aft to check on Jackson. He found him slumped over his guns.

'When we landed,' recalls Knilans, 'I told the crew they need not stay on to see "Jerry" taken from his turret. The ground crew were unable to open the turret doors, as the force of the cannon shells had driven "Jerry" against them and I had to use a screwdriver to prise them apart. Then I got hold of "Jerry"'s collar and pulled him backwards, free of the turret. His body was stiff as I lowered it to the ground and took off his goggles, oxygen mask and helmet. His still features were unmarked. I brushed back a fallen lock of hair. His forehead was icy cold. The middle of his flying suit was badly torn and bloodstained. After examining him, one of the ambulance helpers suddenly became ill and had to walk away. The cannon shells had cut "Jerry" in half.'

Knilans stayed behind in the darkness, depressed at losing his friend: 'When I got to the briefing room the Squadron doctor told me that 'Jerry' must have died instantaneously. He gave me two sleeping pills but I gave them to a WAAF who was overcome with grief. She was a good friend of 'Jerry's and he had given her his personal effects to send to his parents if he failed to return. Before drifting off to sleep, I prayed that God would see 'Jerry' into heaven.'[2]

At briefings for the fourth and last of the great November attacks on the 'Big City', 443 Lancaster crews were given Spandau, Siemensstadt and Tegel as the primary targets. Both the Main Force and a smaller formation of 157 Halifaxes and 21 Pathfinder Lancasters were detailed to fly a common route across the Channel and then easterly over Northern France and Belgium to 30 miles north of Frankfurt to make the German defences believe that this was the intended target. The bomber stream would then fly off to the north-east on a heading for Berlin, the smaller force breaking off due south for Stuttgart. Three Mosquitoes on 139 Squadron were to attack the target before the Main Force at zero minus six minutes and dropping bundles of 'Window'. Four other Mosquitoes on 139 Squadron would fly to the target and then turn and fly for three and a half minutes before releasing 'spoof' fighter flares at twenty-second intervals. Three more Mosquitoes would attack after the Main Force at zero plus 120 minutes.

At Oakington halfway between Cambridge and Huntingdon Pilot Officer A.E. 'Ted' Ansfield lay in a hospital bed recovering from burns he had received on an operation earlier in the week. Ted was an observer (a navigator trained as a bomb-aimer and as operator of the air-to-ground radar used for blind marking when the target was under cloud) on 7 Squadron PFF. Casualties among Pathfinders at this time were heavy and on 7 Squadron the 'chop rate' was less than six trips per crew. Ansfield listened to the roar from the dispersals where the station's Lancasters were being run up and tested for the night's operation and it was enough to make him decide that he wanted to fly on that night's operation. Ansfield persuaded the MO to discharge him from hospital and let him take it easy in the mess. As he left, a quiet voice behind him said: 'Ansfield, briefing's at 1500 hours – good luck.' Ansfield said: 'Thank you, sir, thank you very much', and ran all the way to the briefing room. The crews were already assembling but he was just in time to get his name down on the list on Flying Officer Gerard 'Gerry' Beaumont's crew for the night's operation to Berlin in 'F-for-Freddie'.

As they prepared to go aboard their aircraft at dispersals in the winter darkness the 7 Squadron crews sang *Silent Night*, not because Christmas was only four weeks away but because the carol had become the squadron's departure theme song. Then as each crew climbed aboard, the singing died away and soon the last voices were drowned in the vibrant crescendo of the engines as one by one the Lancasters started up and taxied out for take-off. It was six o'clock when 'F-for-Freddie' climbed away from Oakington. Two hours later the crew were turning over Frankfurt and heading north-east for Berlin.

Inevitably, some aircraft did not make the take-off. At Wyton preparations were severely hampered when 'K-King' on 83 Squadron, which was being bombed up, exploded at dispersal just before 5.00 pm while an armourer crew was working on it. An electrician entered the aircraft to make final adjustments to the flare 'chute mechanism which contained a live and highly sensitive magnesium flare, commonly referred to as the photo-flash, which was released with the bomb load to record the point of impact of the bombs. An electrical failure caused the photoflash to explode and the fuel tanks and bombs exploded. It was said afterwards that the photoflash slipped from the launching tube and exploded immediately, setting off the 4,000lb bomb which atomized everything within range. Six personnel including the 22-year-old pilot, Flying Officer Jonah Alderson-Hiller and two of his crew were killed. Alderson-Hiller left a widow, Dorothy Mabel of Treforest, Glamorgan.

Among those missing was 24-year-old Marion White McDowell a popular WAAF corporal who drove the tractor which pulled the bomb trolleys. Her husband, Guardsman James Alexander McDowell of Irvine, Ayrshire was killed on active service with the 1st Battalion, Scots Guards on 6 July 1944 aged 30. Group Captain John Searby recalled that he saw Marion McDowell quite often as he made his rounds, hauling the string of five or six big bombs – each on its separate trolley – turning into the hardstandings one by one where the armourers unhitched the trolley and wheeled it under the waiting bomb bay. Then off she would go to the next hardstanding to repeat the process:

'A pleasant girl with a cheery word for everyone and we were all very sad at her death. Her contribution and that of the ground airmen killed with her should not be forgotten. It provided an example of men and a woman killed on active service doing a vital job which everyone took for granted.'

Crews on 61 Squadron at Syerston near Newark in Nottinghamshire had only arrived at Skellingthorpe ten days earlier to take their place alongside the Lancasters on 50 Squadron. When Jeff Gray's crew had packed their few possessions, waved goodbye to Nottingham and climbed aboard Lancaster 'G-George' for the short hop across to their new home, they said:

'Never mind, in Lincoln there are lots of pubs with lots of beer and the girls are just as pretty as the lace-making girls of Nottingham. All of which was probably true, but they forgot to mention that Lincoln was surrounded by at least ten other bomber stations and swamped by young men in blue. Soon the long dark winter nights came upon us, the moon faded and the 'Big City' awaited our coming.'

Friday evening was an opportunity for Pilot Officer Tony Bird to observe the expressions of his colleagues on 61 Squadron as they lounged in the crew room. Bird's DFC had been gazetted on 22 October 1943. He wrote:

'Pilot Officer Andrew Strange with whom I had flown on my first operation on the squadron was sitting alone with a look of great sadness which contrasted with his usual cheerful and outgoing nature. I was sure that he had experienced a strong premonition that he would not return and I was to treat such premonitions with great respect during the coming weeks.'

On his crew's sixteenth trip Australian Pilot Officer John Adams on 50 Squadron was taking Flight Sergeant G. Thomas, a Gunnery School instructor who needed to experience an operation. The episode of the near-miss on 18/19 November had made Adams even more nervous about the possibility of colliding in the dark with another aircraft and further dismay was caused when they were told that their regular Lancaster III 'S-Sugar' was unserviceable and they had to take 'N-Nuts', the squadron 'jinx', to Berlin instead.

'The night of 26th November was a particularly cold one,' wrote Adams. 'A cold front had come down from the North Atlantic. It was just after the shortest day of the year and Skellingthorpe was fairly dark by about 4.30 in the evening. However, at briefing we were told that we could expect reasonably clear conditions over the target but to conserve our fuel as we might find ourselves being diverted to another airfield on our return. Our route was to take us into Germany, south of the heavily defended Ruhr Valley. This route was chosen in the hope that the defences would expect an attack on one of the cities near to our track and that they would assemble their night fighters south of the route followed by our main force. The route home was to be directly west, taking us out over northern Germany and across Holland.

'All the 50 Squadron Lancasters were loaded to an all-up weight of 66,000lb. This consisted of around 2,100 gallons of fuel and 10,000lb of bombs – a 4,000lb "cookie" and the balance incendiaries. We were off the ground after using the full length of the runway at 1715. By this time it was quite dark and overcast. We were not too familiar with the aircraft and so I had "Tom" Midgely our flight engineer pay particular attention to the engine temperatures. Sure enough, by the time we were well clear of the ground, they were on their limits. I eased off the throttles while "Tom" reduced the engine revolutions to normal climb/cruise settings and settled down to see if the temperatures would come down. They remained fairly high but just within their operating limits and we resigned ourselves to a long period of slow climbing.'

The procession heading for the 'Big City' took forty-five minutes to cross the coast. The first wave of 'bombers' was picked up by German radar over the mouth of the River Somme flying a south-westerly course before branching off into the southern Ruhr and was identified as Mosquitoes by their air speed and flying without H2S. The diversion on Stuttgart, however, drew many night-fighters away from the bombers heading for Berlin. A small formation of nineteen Stirlings and fourteen Wellingtons penetrating as far as the Heligoland Bight to sow mines in the sea was picked up in time by radar at the time of the first crossings of the mouth of the Somme by the second wave of 'several hundred four-engined bombers'.

The JLO sent up a total of 545 twin-engined night-fighters which included 73 aircraft to patrol over Belgium, Holland and north-west Germany, but this resulted in complete failure due to bad weather and 'Windowing' by the RAF aircraft; however, faulty organization was just as much to blame. Simultaneously, twenty-nine night-fighters – twenty Bf 110s, eight Ju 88s and an He 219, all equipped with SN-2 radar – were scrambled as 'Tame Boars' and were directed into the bomber stream over southern Belgium. The bad weather over southern Germany restricted numbers of night-fighters scrambled there to just thirteen patrols and five aircraft on 'Wilde Sau' duties and only eighty-four night-fighters engaged the Main Force, which was 'Windowing' strongly and was plotted by H2S bearings.

Ted Ansfield on 7 Squadron heard 'Gerry' Beaumont warning the two gunners to keep a sharp lookout for fighters and Sergeant Phillip John Palmer, the mid-upper gunner, replied that all he could see was another Lancaster about 600 yards away to port. Flight Sergeant Dave Wilson operating the 'Fishpond' airborne interception radar confirmed that the Lancaster and another – which the gunners could not see – were showing as a blip running in line with them on his screen. A moment later something else came onto his screen. He just had time to shout over the intercom: 'There's a smaller signal moving fast towards us' when there was a great crashing, hammering noise which swamped the roar of the engines and the Lancaster lurched as a stream of cannon and machine-gun fire poured out of the darkness into them. Flight Sergeant 'Archie' Turner, the rear gunner, a New Zealander, saw the fighter and called to the pilot to dive to port, but it was too late. The damage was done. The Lancaster was mortally wounded. The four engines, the petrol tanks and the rear half of the fuselage was ablaze.

'Get the bombs off,' Beaumont shouted, but Ansfield had already thrown the jettison switch; nothing had happened. The electrical release gear had been damaged. He looked into his air-to-ground radar and from it fixed their position. They were 20 miles north-east of Frankfurt-on-Main at 23,500 feet. As he straightened up to reach his instruments he noticed that the sleeve on his flying suit was shot through. He tried to pass on the information but nobody heard him; the intercom wires to his helmet had been shot away. So he leaned out and shouted the position report to Bill Meek the navigator – who was from Newtongrange – who drew the centre-section curtains aside to relay it to Dave Wilson for transmission to base, but the wireless-operator was lying dead over his key. Ansfield went forward, the Lancaster was starting to go down and the pilot gave him a thumbs-down sign to bail out. 'Good luck Ted,' he said, 'see you in hell!'

Down in the nose Ansfield found Sergeant Denys Ashworth, the flight engineer, crouching over the escape hatch. He looked despairingly at Ansfield. 'The ruddy thing's jammed,' he shouted. 'Put your foot through it,' Ansfield yelled at him and then, impatient to get the job done, he pushed Ashworth aside and kicked it open himself. 'Out you go and good luck – see you below,' he said.

Ashworth, who was very young and very frightened, looked down at the black roaring void and backed away. 'I can't, sir,' he said. 'Don't argue, it's your only chance,' Ansfield snapped back. Reluctantly Ashworth sat on the edge of the hatch and hung his feet out. Ansfield gave him a push and he disappeared into the night. Ansfield checked his parachute and was about to follow him when above the noise of tortured engines and the roar of the flames further aft, he heard someone screaming, beseechingly, 'Oxygen! Oxygen!'

He crawled out of the nose back into the cockpit. Bill Meek told him it was Palmer calling from the mid-upper turret in the burning fuselage. 'The poor devil's in the middle of it. We can't get to him.' Ansfield knew that oxygen wouldn't help Palmer. He could only assume that the gunner believed it might give him added strength to struggle out, so he leaned across the pilot and turned the oxygen lever to 'emergency'. They were diving now. Standing by the pilot, Ansfield saw the airspeed indicator going up towards the danger line and the altimeter unwinding fast from 20,000 to 19,000 feet. He said: 'Can we pull her out together Skip?' Beaumont shook his head. 'Not a chance in hell – the controls are dead. Out you go. Meet you downstairs.'

'Archie' Turner maintained that while hanging from his parachute he observed a renewed night-fighter attack that led to the resulting explosion. Later it was discovered that they had been attacked by Oberleutnant Albert Walter. Making a textbook attack, he had come in from nowhere and blazed his cannons into the engines and fuel tanks. He would not survive the war, being killed on 24 February 1944.

Ansfield moved forward into the nose. There was a brilliant flash. The Lancaster's 5 tons of bombs and flares had exploded and the aircraft disintegrated. The next thing he knew he was lying on the ground in a forest in the darkness, numb with cold and his face badly frostbitten. The only sound was the distant barking of a dog.

For several minutes, as consciousness ebbed back, Ansfield lay there while his mind struggled to bring his situation into perspective. At first his last memory was of a hospital bed. Then he remembered the trip he needn't have flown on: the fighter, the fire and the flash. He knew he hadn't jumped out and because of that he couldn't at first comprehend why he was alive. Ted Ansfield remained at large for six days before hunger and bad weather forced him to surrender and he was later sent to Stalag Luft I. Beaumont, Palmer and Wilson were found in the district of Winkels. They found Bill Meek between Winkels and Probbach. Their parachutes had not opened. Ashworth was discovered in the district of Selbenhausen with an open parachute. They are all buried together in the British War Graves Cemetery in Hanover.

The outward trip, as far as Warrant Officer John Edwin Thomas DFC on 166 Squadron was concerned, was uneventful since he had taken his heavily-loaded Lancaster off the runway at Kirmington on what was his crew's twentieth trip, but over the 'Big City' they were caught in searchlights. Thomas was able to climb to about 28,000 feet and he got away from the beams but on the return and approaching the German-Dutch border, the Lancaster was attacked by a Bf 110, which riddled the bomber with cannon fire. Sergeant 'Jimmy' Edwards the bomb-aimer had part of his left hand shot away and he also suffered a gaping wound in his left thigh. Sergeant Wilfred O'Malley's voice announced over the intercom that he was trapped in his rear turret, whereupon Sergeant Arthur Victor Collins DFM immediately replied that he was going to help him. Thomas shouted that he was unable to hold the aircraft much longer and he gave the order to bail out. Five men bailed out successfully but the two gunners were killed in the aircraft when it crashed. Sergeant Bill Bell the navigator made three attempts to escape from captivity during 1944, but he was caught each time after being on the loose for a few days.

'This was my first exploit over Nazi Germany,' wrote Pilot Officer Gordon John 'Scuffy' Scuffins DFM of Ipswich, Suffolk, a bomb-aimer on 207 Squadron. Born at Brundish in 1923, he had been a lathe-turner at Ransomes, Sims and Jefferies in Ipswich before enlisting in the RAF in 1941.

'From 10.30 am on the morning before the trip was to take place, I felt very nervous about it all and had a feeling that I didn't want to fight anybody. However, after preparations were made and getting airborne I felt the worst was over. In what seemed like days to me we just stooged on with searchlights and flak popping up here and there, finding other less fortunate crewmembers of the force.

'Eventually we came to the target. As we approached it I was reminded of Butlins and Canvey Island all in one. The sight fascinated me but I as well as my crew realised that we had a job to do. We went in over the centre of the concentration with our fellow members of the force all around us. Then came the big moment of my career. I was to drop my first bomb load on the Reich capital. I dropped them in the orthodox manner and for all I cared in those three minutes, I could have been dropping practice bombs on a practice target in England.

'On the way back we had nothing to do except watch for fighters of which we were lucky not to encounter one. Not until we were safely in bed did I consider my job was done to the best of my ability.[3]

Once again Group Captain Slee flew in a Mosquito with Major Mullock as his observer. They had taken off at 1855 from Wyton. Over Cologne they saw several aircraft coned and surrounded by intense flak. As they neared Koblenz, searchlights could be observed as far as the eye could see. Just south of Koblenz, twenty searchlights made a determined effort to illuminate them and many fighters were seen around Frankfurt. They approached Berlin from the west and could see the defences of Brunswick and Magdeburg in action with their vast number of searchlights. One in particular – the master beam with its bright blue extra-wide light – could be seen in a dense and wide belt all around Berlin. Thirty-one beams were counted ahead of them; it seemed as light as day in the aircraft. They had arranged to communicate with a Mosquito flight commander over Berlin, but when they were coned, they called: 'Hello Junior, do you see that poor fellow cornered up there, well that's us!' After they had dropped their 'spoof' fighter flares they then dropped twelve bundles of 'Window'.

On his return Mullock reported that: 'Considering the heavy bombers were beneath the Mosquito, it was most remarkable that the searchlights were able to select targets above. It would appear radar could only operate successfully against aircraft considerably above the Main Force and out of the 'Window' cover. The initial pick-up must have been accomplished by means of radar after which it would appear that the control was visual. Condensation trails were a great help to searchlights. One pilot was coned at 28,000 feet over Berlin, escaping from the beams almost immediately after losing sufficient height to ensure that condensation trails did not occur. It was an old trick of the Germans to leave a gun blacked out until an unsuspecting aircraft was well within range of the majority of defences; many pilots were caught by this ruse.'[4]

The attack was delivered by 376 Lancasters and 7 Mosquitoes from a cloudless sky. The weather was clear over Berlin but, after their long approach flight from the south, the Pathfinders marked an area 6 to 7 miles north-west of the city centre and most aircraft bombed there. However, primary blind-markers were scattered short of the target and all but one of the secondary markers had become u/s. One of the Pathfinder aircraft was Lancaster 'Q-Queenie' on 405 'Vancouver' Squadron, better known as '*The Ruhr Express*', the first Canadian-built Lancaster X by Victory Aircraft. The aircraft's first operation on 22/23 November was with a crew captained by 21-year-old Flight Sergeant Harold Arthur Floren of Westbury, Saskatchewan along with a reporter and photographer to document '*Ruhr Express*'s' raid on Berlin. However, when the bad weather had conspired against 'Queenie', causing over half of the Pathfinder force to abort, Floren had tried to continue onto the target but engine problems that had begun as the aircraft crossed into enemy territory continued to worsen and finally forced him to return to base. Even though '*Ruhr Express*' had failed to reach Berlin, a fake briefing of the mission was held for the press for publicity's sake. Now, on 26 November Floren, who had just been promoted to the rank of pilot officer, captained '*Ruhr Express*' on its second trip to Berlin.

The raid itself went well because the German controllers thought that the bombers were heading for Frankfurt and only realized late on that the target was, in fact, Berlin. Damage was considerable and civilian casualties were high. Thirty-eight war-industry factories were destroyed and many more damaged. Goebbels wrote:

'…the English [*sic*] aimed so accurately that one might think spies had pointed the way…. Another grand assault comes due on the city. This time it is not the turn of the city centre so much as of the Wedding and Reinickendorf districts; the main target in Reinickendorf is the big industrial munitions plant.'

The Alekett factory, the most important German maker of field artillery, producing half of the entire output, was set on fire and despite attempts to put it out it was destroyed. Smaller amounts of bombing fell in the centre and in the Siemensstadt (with many electrical factories) and Tegel districts. The great Berlin Assembly Hall was burned to the ground.

'That is a heavy blow,' wrote Goebbels. 'Back to the bunker in the Wilhelmsplatz. The situation has taken a more threatening turn as one industrial plant after another has gone up in flames. The sky arches over Berlin with a blood-red eerie beauty. I can no longer stand to look at it. The Führer too is very much depressed. The situation has become even more alarming since one industrial plant after another has been set on fire.'

Flak was intense and nine of the losses occurred over Berlin, two of these to fighters. Nine aircraft were shot down on the outbound route, forty were damaged by flak and eleven damaged by fighters. The scattered condition of the bomber stream over the 'Big City' meant that the Lancasters became easy pickings for the night-fighters off track on the return flight. 1JD destroyed most of the twenty-seven Lancasters lost and seventy-nine damaged. Only two German night-fighter aircraft failed to return.

There were three collisions. One of them involved Pilot Officer John Adams on 50 Squadron flying the 'jinxed' 'N-Nuts' to Berlin. They had unloaded their bombs and continued north for a few minutes to clear the defences of the city and then turned for home when there was a crash and the Perspex above Adams head and the windscreen disappeared. Left sitting into a 200 mph -40°C wind, Adams flew in a north-westerly direction hoping to make the coast to the North Sea. Once over the sea, the plan was to head due west and then they were near to England. They never made it. Old 'N' crashed into Wilhelmshaven Bay where a German launch picked up the six survivors. Cyril Billet was swept away in the strong current and Bill Ward, who had received a blow to the head, also drowned. Adams reflected ruefully: 'We were sad at losing two good friends and bitterly disappointed to finish as prisoners of war because of a collision with one of our own aircraft.'

Also involved in a collision this night was a Lancaster on 61 Squadron and 'S-for-Sugar' on 467 Squadron RAAF piloted by Flying Officer John Alexander Jack Colpus. 'Sugar' had joined the Australian squadron in late September after flying sixty-eight ops on 83 Squadron as 'Q-Queenie'. The Goering quotation 'NO ENEMY PLANE WILL FLY OVER THE REICH TERRITORY!' had been added below the bomb log under the cockpit canopy by LAC Willoughby, one of the engine-fitters in mid-March 1944 around the time that 'Sugar' completed eighty-eight operations. Jack Colpus had been born on 11 November 1920 in Subiaco, Perth and he gained his pilot's licence before his driver's licence when he trained in Western Australia. He was one of the lucky ones and would survive thirty-one operations, always leaving his shoes outside his room after a raid; not to have them cleaned but to let the ground staff know he was safe.

'We arrived at the target on time at about 20,000 feet with no cloud cover – contrary to the met forecast,' he wrote. 'The whole Berlin area was a mass of waving searchlights about forty miles in diameter. We completed our bombing run and had just selected bomb doors closed when we were coned by searchlights. They seemed to come from all directions at once. Evasive action corkscrew turns, which were made in an attempt to escape, failed. Heavy flak thumped in all around us, with puffs of black smoke and cordite smell, indicating how close they were. After a while, which seemed like eternity, the flak stopped as if by magic, which meant only one thing. Fighters were coming in. I decided on desperate action and dived steeply down to the left and picked up speed to reach 300 mph at 10,000 feet before pulling out to the right and up. At that moment the searchlights lost us, although I was still dazzled.

'We were climbing as quickly as possible to gain height to get away from the light flak and back into the main bomber stream when suddenly the plane lurched and dived to port. I thought we had lost power on one engine but the rear gunner said we had hit another Lancaster. Full right rudder, full rudder bias and full aileron trim was applied but "Sugar" still kept turning to the left. Further action was necessary, so power on the engines on the port side was increased and on the starboard side decreased until we were able to fly on course. All four motors were then switched to run off the port wing fuel tanks in an effort to eventually raise the port wing to a near level position. We jettisoned the bomb containers to lighten the load. The plane was now under control flying at the slow speed of 140 mph and gradually losing height. We decided to fly straight home as we would soon be out of the bomber stream, which was taking a dog-leg route back. After about two hours, due to a lighter fuel load, we were able to maintain height at about 5,000 feet. The crew made ready to bail out if necessary, as the amount of damage sustained could not be ascertained and now that evasive action would not be possible, we would be 'sitting ducks' for flak or fighters. Full right rudder was required for the four-hour trip back. The engineer went into the bomb-aimer's compartment and assisted me by holding the rudder pedal with a strap around it, to give my leg a rest.'

'Nick' Knilans had an eventful trip, which started badly because 'Robbie' Robinson, his rear gunner who was on his second tour, had not shown up for the NFT (night flying test) earlier in the day and then got worse when they reached 20,000 feet:

'Robinson piped up: 'My turret's u/s.'

'"Monica" calling,' said Les [Knell, wireless-operator], 'about six hundred yards.'

'I just had time to ask Roy [Learmouth] the mid-upper if he could see anything when a bright stream of tracer shells zipped across the port wing and Roy shouted 'Corkscrew port'. I could hear his guns chattering as I tried some gymnastics with a kite full of bombs and petrol.

'It's a Junkers 88,' said Robinson.

'Feathering the port inner,' said Ken Ryall, my 18-year-old flight engineer.

'Marvellous, I thought, levelling out after losing a lot of height and in the corner of my eye I spotted the Junkers. 'Nine o'clock high,' I called. No reply from anyone. 'Can't you…' I didn't finish the sentence because his wing dipped as he turned to come in. I side-slipped hard to port as he flew right over us, all guns blazing. 'I hope you bleeders saw him that time,' said I.

'Standard tactics would be for the Junkers to make a wide circle and expect to find us again, still on our course. 'Roy, watch for him behind you. I'm going to turn all the way around.' 'Right ho, Skip,' said the Aussie. I did the tightest turn I could and must have got inside the bandit's circle. I heard Roy's guns. 'You got him,' yelled Robbie and I looked down and saw him falling straight down in flames.

'Another standard tactic was for the fighters to work in pairs. One would attack and draw fire. The other would hang back and see from our gun flashes exactly where we were. 'Watch out on the dark side,' I said, meaning the other side from the shining moon, but the second fighter wasn't orthodox. A dark shape hurtled towards us from directly in front. I put the kite in a dive and shouted: 'Fire straight up.'

'Bf 110,' said the excited voice of 'Robbie'. 'He flew right through the bullets.'

'Course for Berlin, Harry please,' I asked our jolly navigator [Harry Geller, a 'jolly, fat Jew' from Toronto], knowing his pencils and stuff would be all over the floor.'

The Junkers had shot away large pieces of elevator as well as disabling the port inner. Knilans was wrestling with a joystick that wanted to leap forward to smash into the instrument panel alternately with cracking back into his seat. All they could do was hold steady for a gentle descent over the 250 miles to Berlin.

The Lancaster was attacked three times by enemy fighters. One of Knilans' engines was damaged and the American pilot feathered the propeller, lost height but continued to the target. He approached Berlin out of the darkness, and the streets and the buildings began to take shape. Crossing the city amid heavy flak bursts, Robinson twice yelled: 'We're not going to make it.' Knilans 'shut him up'. Later he would have the gunnery leader replace him. For the moment Knilans had other things to think about:

'From our height, with the flares above and hundreds of searchlights below, the scene became increasingly clear. It was a vivid and dramatic moment. 'Blockbusters', looking like fifty-gallon oil drums, were tumbling down past us from the bombers above. Amid all the buffeting and noise of the light and heavy ack-ack, Ken Ryall spoke up. 'Should we pray, Skipper?'

'No,' I replied, 'not while we are about to kill more old men, women and children down there.'

Joe Tate got the bombs away at 13,000 feet in a brightly-lit hell of searchlights, flak, aircraft falling all around and a tumbling cascade of 4,000lb 'cookies' from the higher Lancs threatening to knock their wings off. Straining to keep up with the stream in their continuous slow descent, 'Nick' Knilans crossed the Dutch coast at 2,000 feet.

On arrival over Woodall Spa Knilans found the airfield shrouded in fog and was told by ground control to fly to Scotland. This was impossible and so they made for Spilsby, a new aerodrome at the southern end of the Lincolnshire Wolds near Skegness where Knilans approached on three engines.[5]

'It was just as foggy. I couldn't see the runway lights above 100 feet so I did my circuit hoping there were no church steeples. I slept on a snooker table in the mess while a van came for us from Woodhall and we went home at walking pace with a WAAF in front holding a torch.'[6]

The American was awarded the DSO and Roy Learmouth received an immediate DFM. Knilans had decided amid the flak and the searchlights to make a resolution. 'If I survive this trip tonight and then the rest of the war I'll try to do some public work – good deeds versus destruction…. Berlin told me where my destiny lay.' Post-war he became a teacher until his retirement.

En route to the target the Lancaster on 166 Squadron at Kirmington flown by 22-year-old Flight Sergeant Roy Barton Fennell from Bromham, Wiltshire was intercepted by a fighter over Belgium. New to the squadron, Fennell had flown his 'second dickey' trip to Berlin on 22/23 November with 22-year-old Sergeant Joe Horsley, who was from York and worked for Lloyds of London before joining the RAF and they made their debut together on Berlin the following night.

Now, on the crew's second Berlin trip, between Charleroi and Caen from 1935 to 2030 hours a Ju 88 first sighted at 400 yards on the starboard quarter slightly up attacked before breaking away to starboard beam level. Sergeant Charles Cushing, the mid-upper turret gunner, gave the evasive order: 'Corkscrew starboard – go!' On first sighing of the night-fighter, which fired one continuous burst until breaking away, Cushing fired 100 rounds at it until his ammunition in the right-hand gun was expended. His left-hand gun was put out of action when it was hit and also the servo ducts on the aircraft were damaged in the attack. Sergeant George William

Meadows, the 30-year-old Canadian rear gunner who came from the village of Bowsman, Manitoba was severely wounded when a bullet struck him in the back, was deflected by the wiring in his electrically-heated clothing and came out in the groin. Despite his wounds, Meadows remained in his turret and his excellent cooperation with the pilot, together with his good shooting, beat off a further eight attacks by fighters.

Cushing was hit above the eye by flying metal when a cannon shell exploded against his turret. The Lancaster's starboard propellers were holed and the navigational instruments, including the compass, were damaged. Fennell decided to drop his bombs on a target of opportunity, a German airfield, and return home steering westward by the North Star, but no sooner had he dropped his bombs than an Fw 190 'Wilde Sau' attacked and fired from behind. A cannon shell exploded between the flight engineer Sergeant William Pettis and the Irish navigator Sergeant James Smyth, the eldest son of the family who farmed at Moorfields, County Antrim about 6 miles east of Ballymena. As the cockpit filled with smoke, the nose suddenly dropped and the Lancaster dived. Wrestling with the controls as the airspeed indicator showed 350 mph, Fennell believed that the aircraft was doomed and he ordered the crew to bail out.

Later, however, he regained control and cancelled the order but discovered that the bomb-aimer Sergeant Ronald Alec Moodey had already left. Unfortunately, he did not survive the bail-out. Fennell found that now both Flight Sergeant Douglas B. Harvey, his Australian wireless-operator, and Jim Smyth had head wounds. Meadows, in spite of his painful wound, kept up instructions to Fennell to 'corkscrew' as the Fw 190 continued making persistent attacks on the battered Lancaster. Locating their position without instruments proved difficult and Fennell came down warily to 3,000 feet, where the crew sighted the lights of an airfield. Descending further to 2,000 feet to try to effect recognition, they were met with intensive fire from light flak. They struck out towards the west and came down thankfully at Ford airfield in the south of England.

George Meadows subsequently received the Conspicuous Gallantry Medal. Because of his wounds he did not return to operational flying until April 1944. A few pints were no doubt consumed later in the bar of the Georgian coaching inn in George Street, Barton-upon-Humber, which apart from going to the cinema several times is where Fennell spent his off-duty leisure time. A week after his last supper there on 30/31 March 1944, he and James Smyth, Bill Pettis and Doug Harvey were killed in the disastrous raid on Nuremberg.[7]

As the bombers returned home, fog covered much of eastern England with many squadrons being diverted. As midnight approached, conditions at Fiskerton were quite severe. Radiation fog was 1,200 feet deep and visibility down to 450 yards. At 0015 hours it was decided to light FIDO (Fog Intensive Dispersal Operation) for 49 Squadron's returning crews. This was the first instance during the war that FIDO was used operationally to bring down one complete squadron of bombers (Graveley had used its system the previous week to land four Halifaxes). FIDO was designed to disperse the lethal cloud and fog, but the mechanism by which it accomplished this was plain terrifying to the uninitiated. Vast pipes carrying thousands of gallons of petrol were installed down all sides of the runway. The pipes were pierced with holes, from which a fine jet of petrol spurted forth when the pumps were in operation. To fire up each section of the system, a man manually set light to the first burner and then ran like hell when it ignited with a whoosh. The heat dispersed the fog and cloud and the glow of the flames provided a flare-path.

'H-Harry' and two more Lancasters touched down safely and were followed by 'K-King' skippered by Warrant Officer Eric Jones.

'FIDO was a highly expensive way of dispersing fog. It was very simply a perforated pipe, one on each side of the main runway, for its full length. Raw fuel passing through the pipes was ignited and the resultant intense heat just burnt away the fog. Not many airfields were graced with this device so we were fortunate. When in use FIDO could be seen for miles. Not only by us, I always thought, but also by those damned intruders. Landing a Lancaster into the FIDO system seemed like a descent might be into Hades. It was only when the plane got reasonably close to the runway that a pilot realised there was indeed a space between the two strips of flame affording sufficient space to land. The process certainly kept pilots on their toes. No swinging off the runway in a crosswind unless they wanted to straddle those flames. Nevertheless it certainly got rid of the landing in fog problem. One operational night when the fog was very dense, we were the bolt hole for dozens of Lancs. Unable to get in at their bases they were diverted to Fiskerton. Lancasters were lined up on the runways not in use and on every available perimeter track. If Jerry had got wind of this he could have enjoyed a 'Hey-day' or 'Hey-night'.[8]

Four more Lancasters landed and at 0102 hours 25-year-old Australian Sergeant Roy Joseph Richardson flying 'C-Charlie' returning from the crew's first operation entered the 'funnel'. Next in the stack behind them was 'A-Able' flown by fellow Australian Flight Sergeant Clive Roantree, who recalled:

'We positioned ourselves to land immediately after 'C-Charlie' who would turn into the funnel whilst we were on the down-wind leg and should be clear of the runway as we touched down. The two parallel bars of fire, one on either side of the runway, could be clearly seen with bars of flame at each end to stop the fog rolling into the cleared area. On our practice on 3rd November we had found that after we turned into the funnel at six hundred feet and lined up with the runway, as we approached, the fire on the cross-bar reflected on the Perspex windshield so that it was impossible for the pilot to see out. To offset the problem my flight engineer called height and airspeed as soon as we lined up on the runway. For the inexperienced pilot it could be a frightening experience as it is not until the aircraft crossed the bar of flame at less than 100 feet that it was possible to see clearly and then make a visual landing. Subsequently a shield was placed in front of the bar of flame to prevent windscreen reflection.

'On this night, with wheels down, pitch in fully fine with twenty degrees of flap, we were at the end of the down-wind leg ready to make our turn across wind before entering the funnel, when there was a dull flash on the ground right at the beginning of the funnel. I knew that an aircraft had crashed and to my horror realised that it must be Richardson in 'C-Charlie'. I continued the landing procedure turning across wind and there, right below us was an aircraft on fire! Giving the crew the order that we were going to overshoot, I called flying control, 'Hello "Passout", "Bandlaw Able" overshooting – an aircraft has crashed and is on fire in the funnel

– I say again an aircraft has crashed and is on fire in the funnel.' At the time I was completely unaware of Sergeant Richardson's Lancaster crashing behind me in the approach funnel.'[9]

Richardson and four of his crew including Pilot Officer Harry Lowe RCAF, the 22-year-old American bomb-aimer of Harrison, New York, were killed. Sergeant M.O. 'Spud' Mahony RCAF, the American mid-upper gunner, and Sergeant Colin Winterborn, the rear gunner were the only survivors. Mahony recalled:

'The cockpit was a sheet of flame, but I could just make out the skipper still in his seat.... I went forward and could see his clothing was on fire ... grabbing him by his parachute harness I pulled like hell, but the harness had been burnt part through and it gave way, sending me tumbling back into the radio compartment. Regaining my feet, I went back into the heat again to try to get Roy out, but a stronger force seemed to be pulling me back; I then became aware of two figures holding me and one was shouting: 'It's too late mate, it's too late ... nothing can be done now.' The next thing I remember was being taken to the sick bay.'

Pilot Officer Johnny Stow, who had joined 100 Squadron in April 1943, crash-landed at Waltham 5 miles south of Grimsby on return. The wreckage caught fire, but the crew managed to scramble clear relatively unscathed. Two Lancasters on 626 Squadron failed to return to Wickenby and a third crashed while attempting to land. The 21-year-old Canadian Flight Sergeant Cecil John Edgar Kindt and crew were shot down about 20 miles north-east of Berlin with no survivors. The Lancaster piloted by 24-year-old Australian Flight Sergeant Keith Neville Windus of Boxleigh, Gumble in New South Wales crash-landed at Barton Bendish near RAF Marham. All the crew died.

Flight Lieutenant V. Wood on the same squadron was returning from his final operation, but despite the weather he was determined to land at his home airfield and was using the radio aid Beam Approach Landing System. Unfortunately, unknown to him, it was off calibration. The first thing he knew about it was when the aircraft touched down in the middle of the WAAF site, just north of the village of Holton-cum-Beckering and about half a mile short of the airfield boundary. One wing came within a foot of one of the huts, the other narrowly missing a haystack. Slithering at about 100 mph across the fields, ditches and fences quickly took the undercarriage legs clean off and the nose parted from the fuselage. The Lancaster was a complete write-off, but miraculously none of the crew was seriously injured.[10]

Returning in fog, Flight Lieutenant Anthony Herbert Tomlin DFC on 619 Squadron was diverted to Hutton Cranswick, Yorkshire; however, the weather was just as bad and he made at least one attempt at landing but with fuel running out there was not enough left to try again and he crashed around 1 mile east of the airfield, just missing Cranswick Common Farm. The Lancaster struck a haystack which removed the tail of the aircraft and came to rest when it crashed through into willow trees on the edge of a small pond. While two of the crew sustained injuries, all were able to climb clear.

Three Lancasters on 50 Squadron suffered fatal accidents on their return. 'X-X-ray' on 50 Squadron captained by Pilot Officer Edward Charles Weatherstone had endured an attack by a Ju 88 but Sergeant Collingwood the rear gunner had got in a shot and claimed the enemy aircraft as 'destroyed' despite only one of his four guns working. On return Weatherstone was diverted to Melbourne airfield in Yorkshire. On landing they struck an RAF Standard 8 van, killing the 29-year-old driver, AC2 William Irving Gregory before running into 'A-Apple' skippered by Pilot Officer Douglas Reginald Toovey of Noiwood, South Australia, which had become bogged down in the wet ground. A fire broke out and both aircraft were burned out. Amazingly, no-one on either crew suffered injury.

Low on fuel, 30-year-old Flight Sergeant Joseph Watson Thompson DFM of Sudbury Hill, London made several attempts to land 'K-King' at Pocklington before he crashed at Canal Head, destroying the village pub and also a number of cottages on Ramsdale Terrace. Joe Thompson and four of his crew died in the crash. The two other crew members were injured. A lodger, 41-year-old Percy Palucey Hopkinson of Sheffield, and 69-year-old Mrs Gertrude Bird, a widow, both died. Two other civilians, including a woman who was trapped in her bedroom, were badly injured and three other ladies suffered shock.

On 61 Squadron two Lancasters also failed to return to Skellingthorpe and 'H-Harry' captained by Pilot Officer Arthur James Douglas Eaves crashed into the Börgermoor south of Surwold with the loss of all seven crew. 'W-William' piloted by 22-year-old Pilot Officer John Gilbert McAlpine, a grazier from Nyah, Victoria, and 'O-Oboe' skippered by Pilot Officer Andrew Paul Edmund Strange were lost without trace. It is thought that 'Oboe' was hit by radar-controlled flak guns as no night-fighter claims were made for this Lancaster.[11]

'It was with great regret that on our return we discovered that Pilot Officer Strange and crew were listed amongst those missing,' wrote Tony Bird, with whom he had flown on his first operation on 23/24 August. Bird was destined to complete six bombing trips to the 'Big City'. It was after the crew had completed these six Berlin operations that a British Movietone News film crew took a short newsreel featuring crews on 61 Squadron on their return from the 'Big City'. Apparently, when his mother saw the newsreel at her local cinema she cried out in her excitement 'That's my Tony!', no doubt to the surprise of the surrounding audience![12]

Flight Lieutenant Charles Owen on 97 Squadron recalled in his log: 'Usual flares and aircraft shot down on way in. Target was clear and we could see fires burning from an attack on the previous night. Hundreds of searchlights and very heavy flak, firing mainly into the cones.' Born on 5 January 1923 in Barcelona, the second of five children to parents who ran a hotel in Algeciras, just across the bay from Gibraltar, after leaving public school he had worked at the Supermarine aircraft factory as a boy of 17 in 1940 and had been badly injured in an air-raid. He spent the winter in hospital and, when fully recovered, had been accepted by the RAF as a trainee bomber. On the operation to Berlin on 18/19 November he had overshot the target on the initial run and had turned back and bombed against the stream. He did not like it at all and made up his mind never to do it again if he could help it. On 22 November, Owen had written in his log book: 'First trip with my own crew and the "Big City" at that.'

Now, Owen flew over Hanover by mistake on the return journey and was coned for seven minutes. He lost height from 20,000 to 13,000 feet during evasive action from intense heavy flak. There were several holes in the starboard wing and roof of his cockpit and the bomb-aimer was wounded slightly in the leg. They were also attacked by a fighter when coned, but the only damage was 6 inches off one of the blades of the starboard outer prop and he landed safely back at Bourn.[13]

At Holme-on-Spalding-Moor 5 miles south of Market Weighton, a Lancaster on 630 Squadron undershot but the crew was uninjured. At Elsham Wolds, a comparatively rough-and-ready base 7 miles north-east of Brigg, 103 Squadron lost three out of the record thirty Lancasters dispatched and one Lancaster landed damaged at Croft, just over 4 miles south of Darlington, County Durham. ED417 piloted by 27-year-old Flying Officer Robert William Brevitt was involved in a collision with Halifax II 'V-Victor' on 428 'Ghost' Squadron RCAF piloted by 30-year-old Flight Sergeant Robert Moscrop Buck who was returning to Middleton St George from the diversionary raid on Stuttgart. Buck had permission to land and was at about 200 feet when the Lancaster, which did not have permission, also tried to land, colliding with the Halifax. All on Flight Sergeant Buck's crew were killed. The Lancaster went down north-east of the airfield with the loss of six of the crew. Brevitt left a grieving widow, Margaret Hill Brevitt from Newcastle-upon-Tyne. Sergeant Samuel Thomas Kyle Bowyer, the mid-upper gunner, managed to escape the crash but suffered serious burns.

On 12 Squadron Lancaster 'E-Edward' flown by 24-year-old Australian Pilot Officer Robert Spencer Yell of Murga, New South Wales swung off the runway at Wickenby on return and 23-year-old Sergeant Arthur George Twitchett landed wheels up at Binbrook. Both crews were uninjured.[14] Brian Soper on Warrant Officer Arthur Rew's crew was on his third Berlin raid:

'There were many searchlights around, both at the target and at Frankfurt, with many night fighters in the Frankfurt area. On return to Wickenby there was a problem getting the wheels to lock down. Having tried all the recommended procedures to no avail, they diverted us to another base, in case we messed up the runway for the others. After going through the final checks, Arthur landed 'tail heavy' and the locks came on. We stayed overnight and returned to the base the following day with the undercarriage checked out.'

One of Michael Bentine's friends on 12 Squadron was navigator Flight Lieutenant Arthur Walker, affectionately known as 'Pop' because he was 31 and considered to be senior air crew. Having just finished his tour of thirty operations, he was to become an instructor. That Thursday, Bentine, who was an Intelligence officer and blessed with a clairvoyant ability, was granted a forty-eight-hour pass. He spoke to 'Pop' before leaving and wished him well. On his return late at night, Michael cried out 'Hi 'Pop' as he made his way to his Nissen hut. 'Pop' gave a sign of acknowledgement from about 35 feet away as he made his way to his own hut. It was not until the next morning that Bentine learned that 'Pop' had been killed on returning from Berlin in which he volunteered to help a new bomber crew skippered by Australian Flight Sergeant Hugh Robert Hector Ross. At 2345 hours Lancaster 'U-Uncle' flew into trees in low cloud and crashed into army lorries parked in the grounds of Hainton Hall, 6 miles south of its base at Wickenby. All on board perished. 'Pop' Walker left a widow, Jean Walker, of Darlington, County Durham. He is buried in Whitehaven Cemetery.[15]

A 106 Squadron Lancaster flown by Pilot Officer Ronald Frederick Neil returned early with one starboard engine surging and he was unable to maintain height.

He jettisoned his bomb load and approached Metheringham, a 'drome with many Nissen huts, on the edge of the Fens 12 miles south-east of Lincoln, but overshot and crashed in a field nearby. Sergeant A.L. Parker, the rear gunner, was the only casualty, suffering a broken arm. He was absent on 2/3 December when Neil and his crew were killed over Berlin.

The Lancaster piloted by 28-year-old Wing Commander Alexander Campbell Mair DFC, commanding 408 'Goose' Squadron RCAF at Linton-on-Ouse was lost without trace and he and his seven crew are commemorated on the Runnymede Memorial. Mair, who was born in Scotland and educated in Windsor, Ontario, had been with the unit less than four weeks. He left a grieving widow, Janet Helen Mair of Oakville, Ontario.

Just before reaching Berlin the starboard outer engine had failed on 'G-George' flown by Canadian Flight Sergeant Robert T. Lloyd, followed by a malfunction in the rudder trim mechanism. This caused the aircraft to lose height, but from 18,000 feet they still managed to bomb at sixteen minutes after midnight, though the bombs fell some distance short of the aiming-point. The engine magically restarted but then the intercom to Sergeant M.A. Robert, the Canadian mid-upper gunner, failed. Near Magdeburg 'G-George' was hit by flak and Robert was badly wounded in the foot. They were then attacked by a Ju 88 night-fighter and the Lancaster was hit in the mid-upper turret. The engine pressure to the starboard inner engine fell and was feathered. Lloyd set course for Stradishall but on reaching it safely, he decided to go on to Fiskerton. On arrival the starboard outer engine cut and the rudder trim packed up, sending the Lancaster into a shallow spiral dive from 5,000 feet. Lloyd ordered his crew out, but this was countermanded as the escape hatch proved difficult to open and he decided to crash-land. A call of 'Darkie' [the RAF emergency service] and 'May Day' by the wireless-operator received no acknowledgment, but Sergeant L. Lane managed to pick up another aircraft and received some directions from them. Lloyd finally made a belly-landing in a sewage disposal ground 1.5 miles south-east of Lincoln with no further injuries to the crew.

On 405 'Vancouver' Squadron '*Ruhr Express*' and the crew returned unscathed but the cameraman found that his camera had frozen up during the flight so no photos were taken. This first successful operation would end up being the last for '*Ruhr Express*' on 405 Squadron. The unit was equipped with Lancaster Mk Is and the differences in the engines, electrical system and instruments between them and the Mk Xs would make maintenance and logistics problematic. KB700 was therefore transferred to a squadron that would be equipped with Canadian-built Lancasters. No. 419 Squadron would soon be one of those units as they were about to begin the transition from Halifax bombers to the new Mk X Lancasters that were now regularly emerging from the Victory Aircraft factory. Harold Floren would remain with 405 Squadron, but while flying Lancaster 'A for Apple' to Brunswick on 14 January 1944, his aircraft received a direct hit and the aircraft exploded. Floren and his crew were posted missing and later listed as presumed dead on 6 October 1944.

A Lancaster on 432 Squadron piloted by Canadian Sergeant Peter Woodrow Dennis of Fort William, Ontario was attacked three times over the target area by a trio of Me 210s which caused serious damage and put Sergeant Joseph Herve Leon Quesnel's rear turret out of action. Nevertheless, in the words of the official history: 'Quesnel coolly directed his pilot's combat manoeuvres and the attackers were evaded.' Dennis and Quesnel were awarded DFMs for their actions which resulted in the aircraft returning safely to East Moor. Later, on a sortie in December 1943 Joe Quesnel's aircraft was attacked by enemy fighters and he destroyed one of the attackers. Born at Parry Sound, Ontario in 1922, Quesnel later left to work in Reading, Berkshire as a lathe operator, returning home and enlisting in Toronto on 27 October 1941. He survived the war and received his DFM by post in 1950.

By 0100 hours the weather over eastern England had worsened, and nearing the coast Australian Flying Officer Jack Colpus was directed to land 'S-Sugar' at Linton-on-Ouse as Waddington was covered in fog:

'We were given priority landing behind a plane which was overshooting. We were about five hundred feet too high on the approach but I decided to land as fuel was getting short. As we touched down on the runway at 120 mph (about 20 mph too fast due to the steeper angle of descent) the port wing stalled. If I had made a normal approach at the correct speed, the plane would have stalled before landing and crashed. The aircraft ground-looped at the far end of the runway due to the high landing speed and excessive braking. Inspection of the damage revealed that about 5 feet of the wing-tip was missing and a portion of the remaining damaged area which was turned down at right angles caused the turning problem. 'S-Sugar' was sent back to the manufacturers and did not return to squadron operations until 15 February 1944. When the Skipper of the Lancaster on 61 Squadron we collided with [Canadian Pilot Officer Johann Walter 'Wally' Einarson DFM] landed at Waddington a few days later especially to see me to discuss circumstances he confirmed that they were coned in searchlights and he was taking avoiding action. We were all very lucky.'[16]

The foggy conditions were to prove fatal for thirteen Lancasters, low on fuel or badly shot up, that crash-landed at bases in Yorkshire. (A Stirling, which had been engaged on a mining operation towards the Frisians returned to Wratting Common (West Wickham) and made two attempts to land before crashing near Bury St Edmunds without injury to the crew.) The airfields were congested and Flight Lieutenant W.E.D. Bell on 619 Squadron could not obtain permission to land 'S-Sugar' at Woodhall Spa although his fuel was dangerously low. When down to the last few gallons he ordered his crew to bail out, pointed the Lancaster out to sea and abandoned the bomber over the Humber Estuary. All the crew survived and the Lancaster was found next morning on the Four Holme Sands.

The main body of 115 Squadron had begun the day by leaving Little Snoring for a new posting to Witchford, 2 miles south-west of Ely where 195 Squadron had re-formed using elements of 115 Squadron on 1 October. Twelve Hercules radial-engined Lancasters that took off from Little Snoring were to join 195 at the Cambridgeshire base after bombing Berlin, so the air crews took their bicycles and gear with them to prevent anything being 'pinched' by the ground crews during their absence. Eleven Lancasters duly touched down at Witchford but nothing was heard from 'L-London' which had taken off for Berlin at 1746 hours.

The crew, skippered by 21-year-old Flying Officer Edward Barrie Woolhouse from Bearwood, Smethwick in Staffordshire, included the usual mix of personalities and various ages and experience; Sergeant Joseph Pallanca the flight engineer being the oldest at 34 and Sergeant Tommy Monk of South Yardley in Birmingham the youngest at 19. Pallanca's father was Italian and his mother was German. In 1935 Joe had married Miriam Lorraine O'Gorman of Biggin Hill, Kent. William Alexander Mitchell, the 20-year-old Canadian bomb-aimer, was from Winnipeg, Manitoba.

'L-London' was one of five aircraft shot down north-east of Frankfurt when some H2S bearings continued as far as the Nürnburg area, Kitzingen and Stuttgart and German fighters may have homed on to the emissions. Two of these missing aircraft were claimed by Major Wilhelm Herget, who was known as 'Der Kleine' or 'the small one' because of his stature. He had destroyed twelve aircraft in May to September 1940 before becoming a night-fighter pilot in 1941. It is doubtful whether Tommy Monk and his fellow gunner, Sergeant Henri Hugh Falls even saw their attacker, who appeared out of the night and quickly shot the Lancaster down to crash at Stockheim, 35 kilometres north-east of Frankfurt. It is rumoured that three of the crew were shot in cold blood after bailing out. Tommy Monk, Sergeant Bill Bell the navigator and Sergeant Arthur Vernon Baker the wireless-operator are buried in a collective grave at Dürnbach War Cemetery where Mitchell, Pallanca, Falls and their skipper lie. What the Germans made of the bicycles in the wreckage of the aircraft is not known.

In Berlin that Saturday the German News Bureau reported: 'Yesterday evening the British made another terrorist raid on the German capital. Partly for reasons of weather, partly to mislead the German air defence, they chose to make a detour across south-western Germany. German night fighter aircraft fought the enemy along his lengthy run-in route and involved him in heavy aerial combats especially in the Berlin area, with support from German flak guns. Reports received so far indicate that fifteen bombers were observed to go down before this new raid began. We are still receiving reports of further shoot-downs.'

Hans Georg von Studnitz described the devastation caused on the night of the 26th/27th:

'The British press has been exultant. Air Marshal Harris has stated that twelve thousand tons of bombs have already been dropped on Berlin, or two thousand tons more than on Hamburg. To 'Hamburgise' Berlin, he says, a total of sixty thousand tons will be required. So I suppose we have another forty-eight thousand tons coming to us!.... The behaviour of the population has been exemplary. Although a few gruesome scenes have occurred, there has been no panic anywhere. The evacuation and care of those Ausgebombt [bombed out] is now proceeding in a better-organised manner and the train services have been restored with surprising swiftness. Soldiers and prisoners of war are engaged on clearing-up operations. By the third day after the catastrophe the main streets have already been cleared of rubble and we no longer go in fear of those irritating punctures. Notices on the walls give the addresses of assembly areas and food offices. Red placards in German, French, Russian and Polish issue warnings to would-be plunderers.... Many streets still remain closed. From the upper storeys of the Ministries and public buildings rubbish and rubble is being thrown down into the road below.... Estimates of the numbers killed vary greatly and the number of those rendered homeless is said to be between 400,000 and half a million.'

On 28 November Goebbels wrote that: 'The British are greatly overestimating the damage done to Berlin. Naturally it is terrible, but there is no question of twenty-five per cent of the capital no longer existing. The English naturally want to furnish their public with a propaganda morsel. I have every reason to want them to believe this and therefore forbid any denial. The sooner London is convinced that there is nothing left of Berlin, the sooner they will stop their air offensive against the Reich capital.'

Goebbels travelled through the damaged areas of Berlin in his plush Mercedes staff car with Julius Schaub, chief aide and adjutant to Hitler and Werner Naumann, State Secretary in the Ministry of Public Enlightenment and Propaganda, stopping at several ration distribution stations:

'The misery one sees is indescribable,' Goebbels wrote later. 'It breaks one's heart to see it; but all the same we must clench our teeth [and bear it]. Sometimes one has the impression that the mood of people in Berlin is almost religious. Women walk over to me and make signs of blessing and pray God to keep me safe. All this is very moving.... The food [being distributed to the people] is praised everywhere as excellent.... You can wrap these people around your little finger with small tokens of kindness. I can hardly believe that this city led a revolt in 1918. Under my leadership that would never have happened.'

'Missie' Vassiltchikov's journey was much more difficult. As she passed Wittenbergplatz, the whole vast square was strewn with the carcasses of burned-out trams and buses. Bombs had fallen everywhere, even on the S-Bahn station and the huge K.D.W. (Kaufhaus des Westens, 'Department Store of the West') on Tauentzienstrasse, a major shopping street, between Wittenbergplatz and Breitscheidplatz now merely a skeleton.[17] 'Missie' and her companions caught a train and fled the city wearing their 'Bombengeschädigte' tags. Reich Minister of Propaganda Goebbels had recently issued a proclamation ordering all young people to remain in Berlin and feared that they might be turned back at the station, but they got away safely.[18]

'Missie' spent all day Monday describing her adventures and tried to convey what Berlin now looked like to those who had not lived through it. After finally going to bed she found the total silence difficult to get accustomed to.

Goebbels wrote in his diary on Monday, 29 November: 'I went to Reinickendorf and especially to Wedding [in Berlin]. I took part in a public meal at the Gartenplatz. Male and female workers here received me with an enthusiasm that was as incredible as it was indescribable. Once that was the Reddest [most Communist] part of Wedding, around the Ackerstrasse. I would never have believed it possible for such a change in attitude to take place. The people made me eat with them. I was lifted onto a box to speak to them. I gave a very passionate and unrestrained talk that spoke to the hearts of the workers. Everyone addressed me in the familiar and called me by my first name. The people wanted to carry me across the square and I managed only with difficulty to prevent them. Women embraced me. I was forced to give out autographs. Cigarettes were handed out; we smoked one together. In short, everything was as jolly as an amusement park. Naturally the destruction is enormous. But as far as the public themselves are concerned, they are taking it in good humour…. In an extended discussion with Doktor Ley, I considered how we can get the workers to go back to the factories; because for the most part they have not returned there…. Tobacco is now the most approved luxury; a Berliner will stand on his head for a cigarette.'

Lord Sherwood, Under-Secretary of State in the Air Ministry, stated concerning the air war against Germany:

'In the past Berlin expressly ordered Warsaw, Rotterdam and Belgrade to be levelled. In their enthusiasm the Germans even made documentary films of these great deeds of the Luftwaffe so that they could be suitably admired. Now they are paid out in the same coin. The crocodile tears in the eyes of so many Germans can awaken no pity. The blows now being dealt to Germany are merely just punishment for the crimes that the Third Reich has committed against small nations, their unprotected cities and minority groups in many states. We can make Germany only one promise: Our blows will increase in power until the military capacity of the Nazi Reich has been broken.'

During November 1943 RAF Bomber Command carried out four big raids on Berlin, the last on 26/27 November at a cost of eighty-one aircraft. Combined casualties for the three raids on Berlin on 22/23, 23/24 and 26/27 November had resulted in the deaths of almost 4,500 people killed and more than 417,000 people rendered homeless for more than a month and more than 36,300 for up to a month.[19] The bomber losses on the two Berlin raids on 23/24 and 26/27 November cost Bomber Command forty-six aircraft. Overall, losses in November had been light and Lord Portal, the Chief of Air Staff, told Churchill that this was 'particularly encouraging'. Churchill's reply was: 'All very good. I congratulate you.'

In late 1943 the great loss of life in the Siemensstadt and Mariendorf districts and also to Lichterfelde had forced Goebbels, who had persuaded 1 million of its 4.5 million inhabitants to leave Berlin before RAF Bomber Command's main attacks began, to order the evacuation of all children and all adults not engaged in war work to country areas or to towns in Eastern Germany where air-raids were not anticipated. In Berlin on 2 December Goebbels received and addressed members of the Nazi Party Organisation, police and municipal authorities and thanked them for the excellent services rendered. He also expressed Hitler's appreciation. He also warned that further raids on the capital would follow.

Chapter Five

'An Orchestrated Hell'

'*...a terrible symphony of light and flame. It isn't a pleasant kind of warfare. The men doing it speak of it as a job.*'

The banner headline in the Friday morning edition of the *Daily Express* heralding Edward R. Murrow's account of the previous night's raid on Berlin.

Canadian Sergeant (later Flying Officer) Clayton Moore, a farm boy aged 19 years and 6 months from Saskatchewan, flew his first tour on 9 Squadron at Bardney 10 miles east of Lincoln in 5 Group as a rear gunner on the crew of Sergeant William E. Siddle. They would soon discover that Lincolnshire was mostly flat, with the triple towers of Lincoln cathedral dominating the skyline for miles around. The Canadian's first impression of Bardney village after alighting at the railway station, the predominant feature of which was the sugar beet processing plant at one end, was 'one of rural peace and tranquillity; the stillness of their placid surroundings interrupted only briefly by the raucous roar of a Lancaster from the airfield nearby as it clawed its way skywards over the rooftops.'[1]

Clayton Moore's first meeting with his pilot, who was from Penrith in Cumberland where his parents owned the Crown Hotel, had been during 'crewing up' at 16 OTU and it had been memorable:

'I was approached by a tall, slim and distinctly untidy individual, with a face that looked as if it had been slept in. I estimated his age to be somewhere in the mid to late twenties, a calculation which categorised him as something of a father figure, if not an antique.'

'I'm Bill Siddle,' the sergeant announced softly with a broad toothy grin. 'I'm looking for a gunner. Would you be interested in joining us?' he asked, indicating three other men who had followed him across the room.

'I had seen Sergeant Siddle at various times during the course but had only flown with him once. We had been detailed to do some bombing practice off the west coast on that occasion, after which I had let go a few hundred rounds of .303 at a smoke float. He had hedge-hopped the elderly Wellington most of the way back from the exercise and I had been impressed, not only by his sense of fun, but by his ability to handle the aircraft and it was the latter quality which prompted me to accept the invitation.'[2]

Siddle's crew flew their first op, to Hamburg, on 27 July. By the first week of September they had flown five trips and returned safely each time and their pilot had been granted his commission, but returning from their sixth trip, to Munich, on 6/7 September their Lancaster was hit when a flak shell burst a few yards from their right wing. At first the damage seemed superficial, but the Lancaster began losing fuel and the starboard outer engine began overheating as they cleared the French coast and had to be shut down. Within sight of Bardney the starboard inner engine was showing signs of losing power and Siddle requested landing priority which was granted. Suddenly the aircraft swung sharply to starboard, seemingly out of control, and crashed in a field at Minting in Lincolnshire. All seven crew were badly injured and all were taken the 20 miles to the RAF hospital at Rauceby near Sleaford. Clayton Moore was discharged after ten days and he returned to Bardney, but three of the crew including Sergeant Richard Emrys Jones, the crew's 22-year-old Welsh mid-upper gunner, required a longer spell in hospital because of their spinal injuries.

On 22 October most of the crew were once more on the squadron battle order: 'November 2nd proved to be something of a red letter day for us,' wrote Clayton Moore, 'because we were "issued" with our own aircraft and its ground crew. The aircraft bore the registration EE136 and the squadron letters "WS-R". It had emblazoned beneath the "driver's window" in "olde" English script the most unlikely name of "*Spirit of Russia*". Beneath the name were painted several rows of bombs, a record of the impressive number of trips she had so far completed. Although we had no way of knowing it then (otherwise we might have refused to fly in any other aircraft), "*Spirit of Russia*" was to complete 109 operational sorties before being withdrawn from active service and would ignominiously end her days as a practice hulk for fire-fighting crews before being sold for scrap.'

December beckoned after five nights of stand-down for Bomber Command and the C-in-C, Air Marshal Harris, was keen to get two more raids in on the 'Big City' before the moon rose. Some of his crews felt much the same way, although on Thursday, 2 December when the fifth heavy attack on Berlin within a fortnight was on the battle order they would have preferred it to be somewhere else.

Somewhere else is where Flying Officer Raymond Howitt Marshall DFC, a bomb-aimer on 44 Squadron at Dunholme Lodge, headed on 28 November when he was sent on a one-month Bomber Leader Course at No.1 Air Armament School (AAS) at Manby, Lincolnshire. Ray was born on 25 March 1918 in Upper Caldecote, Bedfordshire. He had an elder brother, Philip, a younger sister, June and a younger brother, David. Their father, Harry, died of pneumonia in January 1928. After being educated at Repton School, Ray continued the family tradition and took up farming. He built a 4,000 square feet glasshouse on the 6-acre property in Upper Caldecote. War clouds gathered just as this enterprise was becoming viable. Although in a 'protected' industry Ray could not resist the call to arms, especially as his elder brother Philip was evacuated from Dunkirk with the remnants of the BEF in June 1940. Leaving the business in the capable hands of his employees, Ray enlisted in the RAF in May 1941 but he 'washed out' of pilot training at Oklahoma and then in late 1942 he passed out as an air bomber in Canada.

Marshall's award of the DFC had been gazetted on 2 November for his actions on his seventh op on the Berlin raid of 31 August/1 September 1943 when soon after 'bombs away', the Lancaster was hit by machine-gun fire from a fighter. Some damage was sustained, while the mid-upper and rear gunners were wounded. Marshall promptly manned the mid-upper turret and used its guns most effectively to drive off an enemy aircraft which was rapidly closing in. In the words of Flying

Officer Parsons, his pilot that night, he 'put on an excellent show by removing the injured mid-upper gunner and manned the turret, while keeping excellent watch despite failure of guns.' As a result of their wounds the mid-upper gunner lost an eye and the rear gunner lost a foot.

A run of good fortune had seen Marshall survive eight ops including four raids on Berlin in November on the crew skippered by Flying Officer Gerald Arthur West DFM. In October his new pilot had spent twenty days at the Air Crew Rehabilitation School (the 'Glass House') at Sheffield as punishment for his poor landing on their return from Bochum on 29 September, or for another reason. With West absent Marshall did not fly on operations for more than five weeks, but rather than hanging around as a 'spare bod' to make up a crew in the event of sickness, he insisted on either being put with a permanent crew or being posted to another squadron. His persistence resulted in him being posted to the recently-formed 630 Squadron at East Kirkby. He credited his survival to this move.

Back on ops with West as his pilot again on 10 November, he flew three trips to Berlin, on 18 November – Marshall's thirteenth – and again on the 23rd and the 26th/27th in the reliable 'X-X-ray'. They took off at 1724 hours. It was just 12.05 am when Flying Officer West and his crew landed back in England after a flight of six hours and thirty-nine minutes. All the squadron crews returned safely.

Before he left for his course at Manby Ray Marshall's crew asked if they could take his good luck charm, his wife's signet ring, with them on operations during his absence. Ray had married his fiancée Joan Ann Kendall at the Holy Trinity Church in Bedford on 2 January 1943 after returning from North America. It would have been a great shock to Ray to learn later that his crew, with whom he had flown the last eight raids were all killed on 2/3 December.[3]

Dick Jones, the mid-upper gunner on Bill Siddle's crew, was now back at Bardney from leave after his marriage to Edith Malcolm, a breathtakingly attractive nurse from Easington Colliery, County Durham, who Clayton Moore had met during her hospital visits:

'I met Dick in the mess shortly after my return,' wrote Clayton Moore, 'and was privately treated to a detailed account of the marriage ceremony and the short but ecstatic honeymoon, which had been celebrated in York and Bridlington. His lucid and detailed account of the proceedings left me with little to imagine and I found myself possessed of mixed feelings of desire, envy – even jealousy – for my old friend. Nevertheless, I was pleased to see the effect that the event had produced. I had never known him to be so happy and contented.

'Because he was anxious to get his tour completed – and because we were still not fully operational – he had volunteered to fly as a spare gunner and had already notched up a couple of extra trips towards the required number of thirty. On the following day, I also put my name forward as a volunteer.

'It was to be December the second before weather conditions allowed the squadron to operate again. Once more, we were compelled to stand down because of crew shortages, but Dick Jones was on the battle order as spare mid-upper gunner with Pilot Officer Warwick's crew from "A" Flight. I was relieved on learning this because I knew the crew to be more experienced than ours, they being into the second half of their tour. In fact their operational standing was indicated by the fact that a "second dickey" would be flying with them that night.

'After the evening meal, I found Dick seated at a table in the bar lounge and he was busily writing a letter. After drawing a pint of beer from the bar, I walked over to join him.

'"Writing that last letter home, Dick," I smirked, but not without a feeling of remorse for having said it.

'Before making a reply, he smiled and aimed a playful swing in my direction. I side-stepped and sat down in the chair opposite.

'"Just writing to Edith," he said. "Third one this week. I'm not up to writing letters, but she's worth the effort." At this, he folded the unfinished letter and laid it on the table beside a photograph of her.

'I took a swig from my pint, then pulled a pack of cigarettes from my pocket and offered him one. After we had both lit up, I asked him what the target was.

'"It's the 'Big City' again," he replied with a grimace.

'"Never mind. You should be alright with Warwick. It's a good crew, anyway, Dick Lodge should be back soon, and we want you in the crew where you belong. Gerry's a good man, but I think we should stick together."

'After exhausting the subject of evasion techniques for the time being, Dick again steered our conversation back in the direction of his favourite topic – Edith. Then, in the midst of propounding her qualities, he grew suddenly serious and said: "Clayton, I want you to do something for me." At this he hesitated and added, "I want you to understand that I wouldn't ask this of anyone else."

'"Just name it, Dick," I invited him.

'"I'm asking you to promise that, should anything happen to me, you'll take care of Edith for me."

'My initial reaction to his request was to refuse it because of what my compliance might entail, so my response was slow in coming. Then, on hurried reflection, I considered that, because we were members of the same crew, it was likely that neither of us would survive if we were to be shot down.

'"OK Dick," I assured him. "You have my word on it," and we shook hands.

'Because it was nearing time for take-off, Dick gathered together his writing materials and left. I downed my beer and joined the others at the bar.'[4]

At RAF Waterbeach near Cambridge, where there was hardly a Nissen hut in sight because the station had been completed shortly before war was declared, crews on 514 Squadron in their red brick barracks awoke on the morning of 2 December and went to the ablutions where hot and cold water – such luxury – awaited them. An hour before take-off, time was spent in the mess eating the ops meal with its privileged eggs and some stressful hard-to-kill hours in the huts during which crews smoked, read magazines, talked or wrote letters, all the while keeping private fears to themselves.

When they looked later at Flying Orders, 27-year-old Australian Pilot Officer Noel William Faulkner Thackray's crew had varying emotions about the day ahead. They hoped that they would be listed for ops because, as Sergeant Edward L. Humes the navigator said, they felt that the more often they carried out a raid over enemy territory, the quicker they could complete their tour. None of them thought that they wouldn't complete their thirty operations, probably because on their first operation, to Biarritz on 19/20 November when they accompanied ten other Lancasters that were to drop mines in the harbour, no enemy aircraft was sighted, nor were they troubled by flak. Even though there was no sign of the other Lancasters that were supposed to accompany them they had flown on and on seemingly unnoticed. Humes knew that Berlin would be nowhere near as easy as Biarritz had been, but he believed that they were equal to any flying task allotted to them. Thursday, 2 December, however, was a date he would never forget and his nerves jangled for the whole of the day.

Nerves still 'jangling', Humes checked and re-checked every part of his pre-flight plan:

'This was the job I had been trained for during so many long months. What was more, I was responsible for the lives of seven others – four Australians and three Englishmen – or so I told myself. The youngest was 21 and the eldest 36. This was not quite the case as I discovered many, many years later, that Clive Banfield the flight engineer had falsified his age in order to leave a reserved occupation to fly. Jack Moulsdale who had started his flying training in Australia at the same time as Bill Thackray, but had not qualified as a pilot, was our bomb-aimer. 'Jock' Hughes the wireless-operator had become the fourth member of our crew. 'Clem' Hem was our Australian mid-upper gunner.'[5]

The 32-year-old Wing Commander Roderick Aeneas Chisholm DFC* was what he called 'an unobtrusive witness of the planning conference' for that night's raid on Berlin. Chisholm had only recently taken up his duties as second-in-command of 100 Bomber Support Group, which was so new that it had yet to be properly formed. The purpose of his visit to the 101 Squadron station at Ludford Magna that night was to learn the details of the plan of attack on Berlin and, more importantly, to acquaint himself with RAF radio-countermeasures, which his new command would soon be putting into practice over Germany. Chisholm was a fighter pilot by trade, having scored nine victories flying first on Beaufighters with 604 Squadron and then Mosquitoes on the FIU (Fighter Interception Unit), during which he had claimed two victories on bomber support duties over the Reich, his last victory taking place on 18/19 November.

Visits to Group headquarters and bomber stations conveyed more of the size of the command than did the order of battle in the operations room at the command headquarters and Chisholm began now to understand why it was that the frequent losses of thirty or more bombers, when spread over the many squadrons that made up Bomber Command, were not crippling:

'Considerate staff officers explained to me the more detailed 1 Group plan for an attack on Berlin, and at Ludford Magna I attended a briefing on the plan. A whistle, half in protest and half in jest, went up as the curtain was drawn aside, revealing to the crews the night's target and their route. I looked at those intent faces. They were ordinary-looking men. They must have come from all sorts of families and homes and have been to all sorts of schools, a group typical, I thought, of the Service. In these highly-trained crews brain was more important than muscle, and they were as expendable as the infantry of the first war; these men, too, had to 'go over the top', and it happened several times a week. Was this, I have since wondered, the end of a phase in warfare, the high-water mark in wastage restricted to experts?

'Did they realise how small were their chances if once seen by a fighter? I guessed that none knew that the exhausts of their Lancasters could be spotted from a mile and a half, and that they could be seen as silhouettes against the stars from nearly a mile away, while the fighter could be seen against the ground at only about a hundred yards. These were grim thoughts, and knowing full well the theoretical bias against the big bomber, I hoped that the facts would never be known by the crews, but would become more and more dominant in the moulding of tactics and die trend of planning. My feelings towards these men were of simple admiration, and later, when I had heard stories of the occasional superstitions which gave to some of them comfort and a feeling of greater security – a pilot's lucky pair of boots, the whip which another cracked before and after each operation, and the suicidal speciality of a third of flying well away from the bomber stream in which all the fighters were believed to be – my admiration was tinged with a mixture of sadness, pity and sentiment which is hard to describe.

On 83 Squadron at Wyton in 8 Group about 2 miles east of Huntingdon, deep in Pathfinder territory, an elderly civilian batman from Huntingdon awakened Canadian Flying Officer Thompson and his roommate, Flying Officer Maurice Kendall Chick, early. Thompson, born at New Westminster, British Columbia in 1920 and christened 'Walter' but who in later life liked to be called 'Punch', had joined the RCAF in 1941. After gaining 'his wings' he had been posted to Britain in March 1942. He flew his first operation to Stuttgart on 11 March 1943 with Wing Commander Guy Gibson VC in command of their Lancaster and by now had flown forty-six 'visual bombing' and 'back-Up', 'visual' and 'blind marker' operations.

'When the flight crews arrived in the mess,' recalled Chick, 'you got an idea from their general behaviour and attitude how long they would last. We would bet among ourselves – "Oh he'll make it" or "He won't make it." Sitting in a corner writing home was not the sort of thing the average chap did. There were too many things to do to worry about your mother. The young marrieds were the ones who suffered most. We just enjoyed ourselves in our free time. We loved flying. There were sadder times, if a crew didn't return. One night we lost three aeroplanes; twenty-one people. There was the ritual of moving their kit from the room. Not twenty-four hours later, or even less, a truck would come through the gates with the new crews to replace those lost. They would come into the Mess where those who had been on the Squadron for a month or two were considered old hands.

'I don't think we worried about it at the time. We had a job to do. Our role was flying aeroplanes to do whatever we could for the war effort. Of course, one never got to know people for any length of time. On the Squadron we knew that it was short-lived, that we would move on if we survived to the end of our tour. We sorted out our friends. The loners, the ones who sat writing letters home, these were the ones that didn't seem to last. The ones who enjoyed life, who seemed a bit juvenile at times, survived. My best friend on the Squadron survived with me. There were others that I knew very well who were killed. That was Mess life; Squadron life. It was an odd feeling – I could look back and think I was very hard, that people were hard, but they weren't really. It was a matter of accepting it. This is what happened in war.'[6]

Thompson and Chick soon found that ops were 'on'. Briefing was at 0400. The crew list showed a maximum effort. There was little doubt that the target would be Berlin; it had been Berlin at the last four briefings. The weather that morning was wet and overcast, but it began clearing later. At his High Wycombe headquarters Air Marshal Harris decided that the raid on the 'Big City' would go ahead, though most of the Halifaxes – about 210 aircraft – were withdrawn late that day because of fog, which was forming at their airfields in Yorkshire, leaving 458 Lancasters, 18 Mosquitoes and just 15 Halifaxes to be dispatched to the Reich capital:

'We assembled as usual in the briefing room, my crew and I sitting near the front of the room,' wrote Thompson, whose tenth op on Berlin would be as a 'Special Blind Marker'. 'The Station Commander walked in and the adjutant called us to attention. We stood as usual and he asked the adjutant to call the roll of captains, which he did and each captain responded for his crew. Then the curtain was pulled and without much comment the forecast of Berlin as the target was confirmed. I liked the route – straight in and straight out. To hell with all the usual dog-legs. The Station Commander told us who would be marking what.

'Our crew of course were to be "special blind markers" with our new H2S. I muttered to myself, "If the damned thing works." Then he told us the fuel load and the route-markers to be dropped by 156 Squadron, wished us a good trip and turned the briefing over to Squadron Leader Neal, the Intelligence Officer. Neal was an erudite man, not a member of air crew, whose face had been badly burned. His mouth was a gash set at 45 degrees to a piece of twisted flesh containing two holes for nostrils above which a pair of intelligent grey eyes looked out from under lids which had once been liquefied by flame before settling in their sockets. He told us the anticipated strength of the first and second Luftwaffe fighter divisions and in particular the strength and aircraft types of the Geschwader at Leeuwarden. We shouldn't meet much flak en route if we stayed on track; as for the defences of Berlin itself, he suggested that we probably knew them better than he did.

'The met briefing was next. It was given by a tall, slim man who hadn't a hair on his head. He was a flying officer in his early thirties but looked sixty. He said that there would be cloud over the North Sea, decreasing along the route until there was only thin stratus. Berlin itself should be clear, except for some ground haze and smoke. Icing would be encountered in cloud.

'The flying control officer then gave us our start-up times, marshalling instructions, take-off times, recognition colours, the forecast runway to be used and the altimeter setting. The navigators and bomb-aimers moved to their specialised briefing tables to determine flight plans and bomb settings and all the air crew then returned to the NCOs' and Officers' Messes for their flight meal. We had the usual bacon and eggs, the unheard-of luxury for ground staff and civilians. The conversation was casual, perhaps a little strained but nevertheless casual. We were joined by the Mosquito crews who would fly a diversionary raid, taking off an hour after we did and returning an hour earlier due to their great speed.

'We dressed in our room in our flying clothes. Chick had a small good luck doll called "Harry" which he customarily hung from his compass above his instrument panel. This night I hid it from him to see whether or not he was superstitious, but one look at his face as he anxiously searched our room convinced me that I should not cause him anxiety and I quickly "found" "Harry" for him. I put my loaded Smith and Wesson .38 as usual inside the blouse of my battledress. It was as much a talisman I suppose as Chick's doll. We set out to the crew-room where we picked up parachutes, escape kits, Mae West jackets and rations. Then it was a ride in a canvas-covered vehicle to the aircraft dispersals. "C-Charlie" was close to the main hangar and we got out of the vehicle to find the aircraft apparently serviceable; at least the ground crew said that it was. They had the battery cart and fire extinguisher already in position. We waited only a few minutes before getting in. Everyone on board was near the end of his second tour or on a third. Each knew his job well and there was no idle chatter.'[7]

At East Kirkby fourteen Lancasters on 57 Squadron were on the battle order. One of these was 'P-Peter' skippered by 29-year-old Flight Lieutenant Ernest Tansley. Born on 22 January 1914 at Upton Park, West Ham in 1930 he went to work as a clerk to the offices of Scrutton Ltd, a firm of shipping agents in Fenchurch Avenue, London. Being in a reserved occupation, Tansley was not obliged to enter the armed forces, but by early 1941 he had felt he could not stand on the sidelines any longer. He wanted to ensure a safe, happy future for his wife and young family so he enlisted in the RAF on 19 March. November 1943 had turned out to be a busy month and Tansley's crew was in the air on twenty-one occasions.

In a large house in Thundersley in Essex 3-and-a-half-year-old Anne Tansley's grandparents, Herbert and Elizabeth England, her mother Irene Florence who was expecting, and her brother Peter John who were staying with them were waiting for Ernest's next spell of leave. Crews were granted a week's leave every six weeks. Harris insisted on it.

On the night of 2/3 December Tansley had two new faces in the cockpit. The 20-year-old Sergeant Leonard ('Lennie') Charles Brown of Bermondsey, London was on his first trip with the crew as flight engineer and Pilot Officer Jack Proctor Dalton was going along as a 'second pilot' in order to gain operational experience before being given command of his own aircraft. He had only arrived on the squadron three days previously.

The five others were old hands. Pilot Officer Douglas Park, the 20-year-old navigator, was from Hull. Pilot Officer Ernest Harold Patrick, the 25-year-old air bomber, hailed from Southgate, Middlesex. Sergeant Ivor Francis Grove, the 20-year-old wireless-operator, was from Greet in Birmingham. Pilot Officer Roy Arthur Lewis, the 21-year-old air gunner, was a married man whose wife Ernestine Moya Lewis lived at their home in Sale, Cheshire. Flight Sergeant Harold Alexander Moad, the 23-year-old Canadian air gunner, was from Minnedosa in Manitoba. Flight Sergeant Jack Thomas, who had completed thirty ops after volunteering to fly the last six trips of his tour with Tansley, was at the flights to wave them off and give them the 'thumbs-up'. Tansley was the first to take off at 1619 hours. His estimated time of arrival at the target should make him the third to arrive.[8]

At Bardney Clayton Moore walked across the airfield and took up a position with what was known as 'The Press-On Gang' at the end of the runway in order to watch the squadron depart for the raid. 'As each of the heavily-laden Lancasters lined up with the runway and revved up, the assembled collection of WAAFs, ground-crew bods and off-duty air crew waved and cheered in the traditional manner. First of the twenty or so aircraft off was piloted by fellow Canadian Flight Lieutenant 'Mitch' Mitchell, with my old friends Plunket and Rogers manning the turrets of 'Johnny Walker', who bore the world-famous whisky logo emblazoned beneath the cockpit. Others that I recognised in the gathering gloom were Jack Dickinson, a native of my home town of Prince Albert, and the seemingly indestructible Knox and Trevena, gunners on Pilot Officer Argent's crew.[9] Another crew had 'borrowed' the '*Spirit of Russia*' for the night, but I couldn't recognise the crew as I watched my familiar old tail turret disappear down the runway and lift off into the night.

'At last 'C-Charlie' swung into position at the end of the runway. A green Aldis light winked from the nearby control caravan and the four Merlins roared as Pilot Officer Warwick unbridled the 8,000 horses in his charge. As 'C-Charlie' began to roll, I stepped forward from the rest and raised both thumbs as a gesture of good luck to the lone figure of Dick Jones seated in the Perspex dome of his turret atop the fuselage. He grinned and waved back at me as the aircraft pulled away and I watched the white tail light as it bounced along the runway before steadying and rising upwards. When the light was no longer in sight, I turned and walked back in the direction of the billets.'

Five press correspondents were to fly on this operation. Walter King of the *Sydney Morning Herald* would fly in 'G-George' on 467 Squadron RAAF at Waddington, as he recalled:

'The pilot of the crew was an Australian, Squadron Leader William Alexander Forbes, 'an old man at 23', whose parents live at Hornsby and his wife lives at Bundaberg. The flight engineer was Pilot Officer Frank Miller of Laidley near Brisbane. The others comprised two Scots, two Englishmen and a Canadian. They were doing their twenty-seventh operation together and their Lancaster 'G for George' its eleventh. It had not been scarred, not even scratched on its previous ten sorties, which were represented on the fuselage not by orthodox bomb replicas but by foaming mugs of beer.

'Why that symbol?' I had asked Sergeant 'Laurie' Parker of Bundaberg, one of the ground crew, when I was standing to board 'George'.

'Parker grinned. 'Trips to the "Land of Mugs" – big mugs,' he said, laconically.

'Typically the Aussie sense of humour that is lost on the rest of the world.'[10]

Norwegian poet, novelist and journalist Captain Johan Nordahl Brun Grieg of the Free Norwegian Army representing the *Daily Mail* and 40-year-old Australian Norman Stockton of Australian Associated Newspapers would fly with 460 Squadron RAAF. Grieg had escaped to England on board the same ship that carried the Norwegian Royal Family and the Norwegian National Gold Treasure. The Norwegian sought permission to take part in an RAF bombing raid on Germany in 1943 and was able to eventually achieve his goal through the assistance of Laurence Collier, Britain's minister to the Norwegian government in exile.

It was agreed that an American war correspondent would fly in a Lancaster on 50 Squadron at Skellingthorpe. Lowell Bennett, a 24-year-old American representing the International News Service, won the toss of the coin with fellow American correspondent William Warren Wade and would go on the trip. Bennett's

English wife was living with his parents in South Orange, New Jersey where she was expecting a second child. At first it was agreed that he would do the trip with the commanding officer, Wing Commander Robert McFarlane DFC and BAR. A Glaswegian, born on 12 July 1914, the son of a steel mill manager, he had worked as an organist and choirmaster in Glasgow before joining the RAFVR in April 1939. His crew included the observer Flight Lieutenant Les Rutherford, who recalled:

'Bennett was put in our crew room which crowded things a bit but it was only temporary. We became friendly and invited him out with us on one of our nights out in Lincoln. He soon became quite drunk. When he started firing a revolver in the air in the middle of the High Street we decided it was time to get him back to base! We were friendly with the Medical Officer so we rang him and he sent us an ambulance to get us back to base and get the American back to our room. McFarlane was at Group HQ and as we weren't on ops, Lowell would go with another crew captained by Flight Lieutenant Ian D. Bolton on 'B-Baker'. Before he went Lowell gave me a large envelope and asked me to make sure that if anything happened to him that this envelope would be sent to his paper.'[11]

At Woodhall Spa Edward R. Murrow, head of the CBS European Bureau in London, would fly in Lancaster 'D-Dog' on 619 Squadron piloted by 33-year-old Acting Wing Commander 'Jock' Abercromby DFC commanding the squadron, who before the war had been an apprentice at RAF Halton. Following the completion of his training as a pilot, 'Jock's first operational tour was on 50 Squadron where he eventually received the DFC in November 1942. Abercromby took part in the daylight raid on Le Creusot and one of the night raids on Genoa. In October 1942 he flew one of the aircraft detailed to attack Milan in daylight. Although faced with serious opposition he descended to within 100 feet before releasing his incendiaries on the target. His aircraft was hit many times and the rear gunner was mortally wounded.

While the USA was still neutral Murrow had become well-known in America for his broadcasts during the blitz and for his trademark introduction: 'This is London….' He was almost as famous for flying on operational aircraft. Some say he completed twenty-five operations. Now he was to record a commentary of the raid on Berlin for a broadcast on his American radio programme the following day.

Murrow would later tell his listeners: 'Yesterday afternoon the waiting was over. The weather was right; the target was to be the 'Big City'. The crew captains walked into the briefing room; looked at the maps and charts and sat down with their big celluloid pads on their knees.'

Murrow noticed that 'a big Canadian' [Flying Officer John Frank Bower MiD RCAF] 'with the slow, easy grin' had printed 'Berlin' at the top of his pad and then embellished it with a scroll. He and a red-headed English boy [Pilot Officer James Francis Ward] 'with the two weeks' old moustache' were the last to leave the room:

'The atmosphere was that of a school and a church. The weatherman gave us the weather. The pilots were reminded that Berlin is Germany's greatest centre of war production. The intelligence officer told us how many heavy and light ack-ack guns, how many searchlights we might expect to encounter. Then Jock the wing commander explained the system of markings, the kind of flare that would be used by the Pathfinders. He said that concentration was the secret of success in these raids, that as long as the aircraft stayed well bunched, they would protect each other.

'The captains of aircraft walked out.

'Late in the afternoon we went to the locker-room to draw parachutes, Mae Wests and all the rest. As we dressed, a couple of the Australians were whistling. Walking out to the bus that was to take us to the aircraft I heard the station loudspeakers announcing that that evening all personnel would be able to see a film, *Star Spangled Rhythm*, free!

'We went out and stood around a big, black, four-motored Lancaster, 'D-Dog'. A small station wagon delivered a vacuum flask of coffee, chewing gum, an orange and a bit of chocolate for each man. Up in that part of England the air hums and throbs with the sound of aircraft motors all day. But for half an hour before take-off the skies are dead silent and expectant. A lone hawk hovered over the airfield, absolutely still as he faced into the wind. Jack, the tail gunner, said: 'It would be nice if we could fly like that.'

'D-Dog' eased around the perimeter track to the end of the runway. We sat there for a moment, the green light flashed and we were rolling ten seconds ahead of schedule. The take-off was smooth as silk. The wheels came up and 'D-Dog' started the long climb. As we carne up through the clouds I looked right and left and counted fourteen black Lancasters climbing for the place where men must burn oxygen to live. The sun was going down and its red glow made rivers and lakes of fire on top of the clouds. Down to the southward the clouds piled up to form castles, battlements and whole cities, all tinged with red.

'Soon we were out over the North Sea. Dave, the navigator, asked Jock if he couldn't make a little more speed – we were nearly two minutes late. By this time we were all using oxygen. The talk on the intercom was brief and crisp. Everyone sounded relaxed. For a while the eight of us in our little world in exile moved over the sea. There was a quarter moon on the starboard beam. Jock's quiet voice came through the intercom: 'That'll be flak ahead.' We were approaching the enemy coast. The flak looked like a cigarette lighter in a dark room – one that won't light. Sparks but no flame. The sparks crackling just about level with the cloud tops. We flew steady and straight and soon the flak was directly below us.

'D-Dog' rocked a little from right to left but that wasn't caused by the flak. We were in the slipstream of other Lancasters ahead, and we were over the enemy coast.

'And then a strange thing happened. The aircraft seemed to grow smaller. Jack in the rear turret, Wally, the mid-upper gunner and 'Titch', the wireless-operator all seemed somehow to draw closer to Jock in the cockpit. It was as though each man's shoulder was against the others. The understanding was complete. The intercom came to life and 'Jock' said: 'Two aircraft on the port beam.'

'Jack in the tail said: 'Okay sir; they're Lancs.' The whole crew was a unit and wasn't wasting words.'

At Waterbeach Noel Thackray's crew and nine others on 514 Squadron had taken off successfully around five o'clock but three returned early. Edward Humes settled as soon as they were airborne but 'very few words were spoken during the flight; we were all on a knife-edge.'

'Little of note occurred on the outward leg and obviously my route planning had been OK.'

When out over the North Sea, 'Punch' Thompson levelled off the Lancaster and the gunners asked if they could test their guns:

'I gave the OK and listened to the muffled stutter of the six Brownings as they fired short bursts at a rate of 1,200 rounds per minute. They reported the guns and turrets operating well. This was nice to know as we had picked up a little ice. The outside air temperature was now bitterly cold at -60°C and there was danger of the guns freezing.'[12]

With no major diversions the bombers took the direct route across the North Sea and Holland and then on to the capital. Unexpected winds en route blew many aircraft off track and nullified the Pathfinders' efforts to make dead reckoning (DR) runs from Rathenow.

'The cloud below was ten-tenths,' said Ed Murrow. 'The blue-green jet of the exhaust licked back along the leading edge and there were other aircraft all around us. The whole great aerial armada was hurtling towards Berlin. We flew so for twenty minutes, when "Jock" looked up at a vapour trail curling across above us, remarking in a conversational tone that from the look of it he thought there was a fighter up there. Occasionally the angry red of ack-ack burst through the clouds but it was far away and we took only an academic interest. We were flying in the third wave. "Jock" asked Wally in the mid-upper turret and Jack in the rear turret if they were cold. They said they were all right and thanked him for asking. Even asked how I was and I said, "All right so far." The cloud was beginning to thin out. Up to the north we could see light and the flak began to liven up ahead of it.

'"Boz" the bomb-aimer crackled through on the intercom. "There's a battle going on, on the starboard beam." We couldn't see the aircraft but we could see the jets of red tracer being exchanged. Suddenly there was a burst of yellow flame and "Jock" remarked: "That's a fighter going down – note the position." The whole thing was interesting but remote. Dave the navigator who was sitting back with his maps charts and compasses said: "The attack ought to begin in exactly two minutes." We were still over the clouds. But suddenly those dirty grey clouds turned white. We were over the outer searchlight defences – the clouds below us were white and we were black. "D-Dog" seemed like a black bug on a white sheet. The flak began coming up but none of it close. We were still a long way from Berlin. I didn't realise just how far.

'Jock observed: "There's a kite on fire dead ahead." It was a great golden, slow-moving meteor slanting towards the earth. By this time we were about thirty miles from our target area in Berlin. That thirty miles was the longest flight I have ever made.

'"Dead on time, 'Boz'," the bomb-aimer reported. "Target indicators going down." The same moment the sky ahead was lit up by brilliant yellow flares. Off to starboard another kite went down in flames. The flares were sprouting all over the sky – reds and greens and yellows; and we were flying straight for the centre of the fireworks. "D-Dog" seemed to be standing still, the four propellers thrashing the air. But we didn't seem to be closing in. The cloud had cleared and off to starboard a Lanc was caught by at least 14 searchlight beams. We could see him twist and turn and finally break out. But still the whole thing had a quality of unreality about it. No one seemed to be shooting at us but it was getting lighter all the time. Suddenly a tremendous big blob of yellow light appeared dead ahead, another to the right and another to the left. We were flying straight for them.

'Jack pointed out to me the dummy fires and flares to right and left but we kept going in. Dead ahead there was a whole chain of red flares looking like stoplights. Another Lanc coned on our starboard beam; the lights seemed to be supporting it. Again we could see those little bubbles of coloured lead driving at it from two sides. The German fighters were at him.

'And then, with no warning at all, "D for Dog" was filled with an unhealthy white light; I was standing just behind "Jock" and could see the seams of the wings. His quiet Scots voice beat into my ears. "Steady, lads – we've been coned." His slender body lifted half out of the seat as he jammed the control column forward and to the left. We were going down.

'Jock was wearing woollen gloves with the fingers cut off. I could see his fingernails turn white as he gripped the wheel. And then I was on my knees, flat on the deck, for he had whipped the "Dog" back into a climbing turn. The knees should have been strong enough to support me but they weren't and the stomach seemed in some danger of letting me down, too. I picked myself up and looked out again. It seemed that one big searchlight, instead of being 20,000 feet below, was mounted right on the wingtip.

'"D for Dog" was corkscrewing. As we rolled down on the other side I began to see what was happening to Berlin.

'The clouds were gone and the sticks of incendiaries from yellow and started to flow to the preceding waves making the place look like a badly laid-out city with the street lights on. The small incendiaries were going down like a fistful of white rice thrown on a piece of black velvet. As Jock hauled the "Dog" up again I was thrown to the other side of the cockpit and there below were more incendiaries glowing white and then turning red. The cookies – the four 1,000lb high explosives – were bursting below, like great sunflowers gone mad. And then as we started down, still held in the lights, I remember that the "Dog" still had one of those cookies and a whole basket of incendiaries in his belly and the lights still held us. And I was very frightened.

'While Jock was flinging him about in the air he suddenly flung over the intercom: "Two aircraft on the port beam." I looked astern and saw Wally, the mid-upper gunner, whip his turret round to port and then looked up to see a single-engined fighter slide below us. The other aircraft was one of ours. Finally we were out of the cone, flying level. I looked down and the white fires had turned red; they were beginning to merge and spread. Just like butter does on a hot plate. Jock and "Boz", the bomb-aimer, began to discuss the target. The smoke was getting thick down below. "Boz" said he liked the two green flares on the ground almost dead ahead. He began calling his directions and just then a new bunch of big flares went down on the far side of the sea of flame and flare that seemed to be directly below us. He thought that would be a better aiming point. "Jock" agreed and we flew on.

The bomb doors were open. "Boz" called his directions: "Five left … five left." Then there was a gentle, confident upward thrust under my feet and "Boz" said, "Cookie gone." A few seconds later the incendiaries went and "D-Dog" seemed lighter and easier to handle.

'I thought I could make out the outline of streets below, this time all those patches of white on black had turned caught us but didn't hold us. Then through the intercom, "We're still carrying it." And Jock replied, "Is it a big one or a little one? I'm not sure – I'll check." More of those yellow flares came down and hung about us. I hadn't seen so much light since the day war began. Finally, the intercom announced that it was only a small container of incendiaries left and Jock remarked, "Well, it's hardly worth going back and doing another run-up for that." If there had been a good fat bundle left he would have gone back through that stuff and done it all again.

'I began to breathe and to reflect again – that all men would be brave if only they could leave their stomachs at home, when there was a tremendous whoomp, an unintelligible shout from the tail-gunner…. "D-Dog" shivered and lost altitude. I looked out the port side and there was a Lancaster that seemed close enough to touch; he had whipped straight under us – missed us by 25 to 50 feet. No one knew how much.

'The navigator sang out the new course and we were heading for home. "Jock" was doing what I had heard him tell his pilots to do so often – flying dead on course. He flew straight into a huge green searchlight and as he rammed the throttles home remarked, "We'll have a little trouble getting away from this one." And again "D-Dog" dived, climbed and twisted and was finally free. We flew level then and I looked on the port beam at the target area. There was a red, sullen, obscene glare – the fires seemed to have found each other … and we were heading home.

'For a little while it was smooth sailing – we saw more battles and then another plane in flames but no one could tell whether it was ours or theirs. We were still near the target. Dave, the navigator, said "Hold her steady skipper. I want to get an astral sight." And Jock held her steady. And the flak began coming up at us. It seemed to be very close. It was winking off both wings. But the "Dog" was steady. Finally, Dave said, "Okay, skipper, thank you very much" and a great orange blob of flak smacked up straight in front of us. Jock said, "I think they're shooting at us." (I had thought so for some time) and he began to throw "D for Dog" up, around and about again. When we were clear of the barrage I asked him how close the bursts were and he said, "Not very close. When they are really near you can smell 'em." That proved nothing; for I had been holding my breath.

'Jack sang out from the rear turret, said his oxygen was getting low, thought maybe the lead was frozen. "Titch", the radio-operator, went scrambling back with a new mask and a bottle of oxygen. Dave, the navigator, said, "We're crossing the coast." My mind went back to the time I had crossed that coast in 1938 in a plane that had taken off from Prague. Just ahead of me sat two refugees from Vienna – an old man and his wife. The co-pilot came back and told them that we were outside German territory. The old man reached out and grasped his wife's hand. The work that was done last night was a massive blow of retribution for all those who have fled from the sound of shots and blows on that stricken continent.'

Fiskerton had dispatched fourteen Lancasters on 49 Squadron and Warrant Officer Bob Petty and crew on 'J-Jig', who were on their seventeenth operation, would be one of those posted missing. 'J-Jig's rear gunner, Sergeant 'Ed' Smith, reported that his guns were u/s, but the crew still decided to press on. During the bombing run they were attacked by a Bf 110. Sergeant Owen Roberts in the top turret managed to hit the fighter's engine before one of his guns jammed. Continuing the bomb run, Owen spotted another Bf 110 just below them but when he tried to fire his guns, they were either jammed or out of ammunition. To add to their troubles, flak then struck the starboard inner engine which burst into flames immediately. Without hesitation Petty gave the bail-out order. Six members of the crew, including the second pilot, Sergeant A.M. Tucker, survived to become PoWs but the bomb-aimer Sergeant Bill Walker was killed along with 'Ed' Smith, who although seen to bail out, has no known grave. Owen landed in a tree and injured himself dropping 40 feet to the ground. It was freezing with snow on the ground. He lay there for sixteen hours before a German civilian, who himself had been a PoW in the first war, found him and called the Wehrmacht. Roberts was taken to the Hermann Goering Luftwaffe Hospital and well cared for.

Bombing was scattered owing to the incorrect forecasts, but some industrial areas were hit. As well as strong winds, the bomber force also had to contend with numerous fighters. There were gaps in the cloud covering the city; most of the bombing was scattered over a wide area of open country to the south. The German controllers had predicted Berlin as the target well in advance of the bombers' arrival and the enemy's running commentary began plotting the bombers from the neighbourhood of the Zuider Zee. At 1947 hours, nineteen minutes before zero hour, the JLOs announced that Berlin was the main objective. Many illuminated targets were provided for the night-fighters over the capital.

Back at Ludford, Wing Commander Roderick Chisholm was able to listen to some of the enemy fighter controller's orders and to get an idea of the reaction to the raid:

'Very early on all fighters were sent to Berlin, and I knew that some of those men I had seen at the briefing would soon be up against it. The German controller sounded calm and unhurried as he repeated mechanically with much guttural rolling of the Rs, 'Alle Dromedär-r-re nach Bär-r-e' – Dromedäre being the call sign of a certain group of squadrons and Bare being their code-name for Berlin. My blood ran cold; this was gruesome and depressing. The enemy would be waiting there in hordes, and I believed there would be disastrous losses.

'The broadcasting from this station of bogus instructions to enemy fighters, of reports of deterioration of weather and orders to land, had started some little time before and had been an immediate success. Confirmation of the success of this subterfuge came from the enemy controllers themselves, who became angry and as abusive as fishwives; they were answered back and, had it been possible to feel sorry for Nazis, one would have felt sorry for those fighter crews who had to listen.

'That night our 'spoof' was moderately successful. A bogus order from us was countered by the German controller telling his crews not to listen to the Englishman; the latter then countered by an almost word-perfect repetition of those instructions.

Identities became confused after a few such exchanges and, to annoy and upset the crews and further to add to the confusion, our broadcaster began an impassioned impersonation of Hitler. The tension broke and we laughed heartily.'[13]

At the beginning of the attack heavy flak was fired in a loose barrage up to 22,000 feet around the marker flares and was predicted at seen targets through gaps in the cloud. There were gaps in the cloud covering the city; most of the bombing was scattered over a wide area of open country to the south. Searchlights were active in great numbers and took every opportunity the weather offered for illuminating the bombers. After the raid had been in progress for half an hour and soon after the appearance of fighter flares the ceiling of the barrage was lowered and the flak decreased, although individual aircraft were heavily engaged when coned. Visibility was slightly hazy with a half-moon. There was 5 to 7/10ths cloud over the target and considerable fires and smoke up to 1,500 feet but little trouble from searchlights. There was heavy flak, fairly intense, decreasing as the attack progressed, and considerable fighter activity over the target. The bombing was scattered over south Berlin.

'Tame Boar' crews claimed forty kills; seven pilots of two 'Wild Boar' Gruppen (I. and II./JG 302) claiming another eight Viermots shot down over Berlin. At least thirty-two bombers went down in the main air battle that was concentrated in the target area. Only three Nachtjäger were lost in return fire.

At Schönwalde in the Spandau region of West Berlin Siegfried Wildenheim, aged 17 years 6 months, had every reason to be concerned. He lived at the family home in the small town of Trebbin about 25 miles south of the centre of Berlin. A few days earlier on 29 November, his grandmother had been very distressed because Siegfried's call-up papers had come through requiring him to go to Berlin for Work Service. He had left home on 1 December to report and that night he experienced his first air-raid when everyone had to take shelter in a bunker. It was only later that he learned of the Lancaster that had crashed that night, so nearly destroying his home in Trebbin.

The lone Lancaster was flying low, probably having already sustained earlier damage over the target area, when it was spotted near Trebbin and attacked by a night-fighter which came from the nearby Jüterbog airfield. It was a starry moonlit night. A searchlight, which was stationed in the neighbourhood, picked out the bomber first, quickly followed by two further searchlights and the Lancaster was caught in the cone. Next a flare appeared and the searchlights were switched off. When the night-fighter appeared, there was a short exchange of fire between both aircraft and then there followed an explosion in the Lancaster and a loud bang could be heard. Shortly after this, parts of the fuselage began falling away from the now blazing aircraft, along with the starboard wing and both engines. A gentleman who witnessed the combat said that despite the loss of two-thirds of the wing and engines, the flames emanating from the front of the aircraft and the other serious damage to the fuselage caused by the explosion, the pilot was still clearly flying his crippled Lancaster in an effort to land in a nearby field. In his words, 'It was an aeronautical miracle.'

Wreckage fell along the Luchstrasse and onto the small semi-detached houses that had been built there on the outskirts of Trebbin in 1934 but the skill of the pilot in landing his aircraft in the field ensured that they were not totally destroyed, thus avoiding any loss of life to the families who lived there. Part of the fuselage landed in the garden of the home of the main eye-witness. The roof and corner of the house where Siegfried Wildenheim lived with his family were struck by either the tail section or some other large part of the aircraft. Twin machine guns fell through the roof of another house and were left hanging in the kitchen ceiling. One wheel flew into the base of the fence and then into the house. One engine lay on an electricity pylon and the second engine was found on the road in the direction of the town, about 200 metres from the first.

The first crew member was found lying at the edge of a meadow by a small slope and he had suffered a head wound. He had been able to use his parachute and it is believed that he had probably survived for a short while and managed to walk to that spot. His boots and the legs of his trousers were singed. A second man, his parachute unopened, had fallen onto the Luchstrasse between two houses. Another young man whose parachute had not been used either was found on the borders of the gardens between two other houses. The rear gunner was still in his turret and had received bullet wounds in the chest. He was not burned because the fire had not reached as far as the tail of the aircraft. The pilot was still in the cockpit, in his seat and had been completely burned. He was not identified until exhumed by the RAF at the end of the war. Three men were found together in a field of rye. One of them had suffered an injury to the skull. When all eight members of the crew had been traced, two young Germans were sent out in a wagon to collect them. The men were gathered together and all were placed in the wagon and then taken to the wreckage where the rear gunner and the pilot lay dead. Here, all eight members of the crew were covered in one of the parachutes and then taken to the 'Old Cemetery' to await burial.

Two aircraft reported combats. One involved 'B-Baker' flown by 25-year-old Pilot Officer Garth Stewart Hughes, formerly a student at Sydney University, of Turramurra on the Upper North Shore of Sydney. 'B-Baker' was homeward bound at 2030 hours at 20,000 feet at 155 mph when it was badly 'shot up' in a stern attack from the port fine quarter, slightly down, by an Me 210. The one and only burst killed the 26-year-old Canadian rear gunner, Sergeant Leo Wilton, instantly. The mid-upper turret was put out of action and fires were started in the bomb racks and the inside fuselage which lasted about thirty seconds, setting light to Sergeant Moorhouse's clothing, compelling him to vacate the turret momentarily. The 210 broke away to starboard quarter up and made a second attack immediately from 400 yards. 'B-Baker' was effectively 'corkscrewed' to starboard on the instructions of the wireless-operator/air gunner controlling from the astrodome and the Me 210 was soon lost to sight. Attempts were made to extricate Wilton, whose turret was jammed with gun pointing starboard, but broken parts prevented effective use of the external rotation valve. Pilot Officer Hughes was killed on the Nuremberg raid on 30/31 March 1944.

Pilot Officer Noel Thackray's crew had no trouble in reaching the target area but when Edward Humes heard Jack Moulsdale say on the intercom 'Bomb-aimer to Skipper, target directly ahead', he was quite happy to listen to the observations of the crew, but he did not wish to look at the burning city.

As they turned on the course for home his pilot let out a horrendous cry: 'An aircraft was turning immediately ahead! Surely we were not going to end the trip by crashing into a friendly aircraft? In seconds the danger was over but I needed to work out a slight adjustment to our course. From my position I could see nothing but listened to the comments of the others. I was scared, the aircraft shook and rolled but this was simply because we were flying in the stream of other planes. Searchlights groped around the night sky and I could see these.'[14]

On Lancaster 'P-Peter' on 426 'Thunderbird' Squadron at Linton-on-Ouse, Warrant Officer Joseph Albert Roger Coulombe, better known as the 'Berlin Kid', who would fly a record twelve raids on Berlin, reported later:

'While over the target this aircraft was coned by 50 to 70 searchlights from 2024 to 2029 hours during which time we were attacked five times by enemy aircraft and damaged by flak. The mid-upper gunner, Sergeant Stan McKenzie first sighted a Ju 88 on the port quarter down at four hundred yards' range and gave combat manoeuvre corkscrew port. The fighter immediately broke off his attack. No exchange of fire by either aircraft. The second attack developed from the starboard quarter down and McKenzie saw the Ju 88 at four hundred yards, so he gave combat manoeuvre corkscrew starboard. Again the fighter immediately discontinued his attack and broke off at port beam down. There was no exchange of fire. The third attack came from the port quarter down at four hundred yards' range. Again McKenzie gave combat manoeuvre 'corkscrew port' and the enemy aircraft broke off his attack to starboard beam down.

'The fourth attack developed from the starboard quarter down at four hundred yards' range and McKenzie once again gave combat manoeuvre 'corkscrew starboard' and again the fighter discontinued his attack and broke away port beam down. The fifth and last attack developed from port quarter down at two hundred yards and McKenzie again ordered 'corkscrew port' and at the same time opened fire. The enemy fighter came in to sixty yards' range and broke away to port beam above, giving McKenzie a sitting target. Tracer appeared to enter the belly of the enemy aircraft; sparks and tracer were seen to ricochet off the fighter which dived steeply and was lost to view.

'During this attack our aircraft sustained damage to the port inner engine and the R/T was rendered u/s. The rear gunner was completely blinded by the blue master and other searchlights throughout these five attacks. During all these attacks an Fw 109 was sitting off at 1,000 yards dropping white fighter flares. Just as the Ju 88 opened fire on his last attack an Fw 190 was seen by the pilot and engineer off on the port bow up at four hundred yards coming in for an attack. The cannon fire from the 88 caused the Fw to break off his attack to the port beam and down at one hundred yards' range. He was not seen again. McKenzie claims this Ju 88 as a probable.'

Coulombe had instructed the crew to stand by to jump. A distress call was sent out and an SOS flashed on the light of the belly of the Lancaster. Immediately an airfield, which turned out to be a B-17 base 6 miles south-west of Attleborough in Norfolk, turned on the runway lights and the 'Berlin Kid' brought 'P-Peter' in with the crew braced for a crash-landing since only the starboard undercarriage wheel was down and locked as the port tyre, port outer tank and hydraulic system were damaged. The crew walked away from the crash-landing and Coulombe was commissioned and awarded the DFC for getting the bomber home. Two weeks later, returning from Berlin and encountering fog over eastern England, the 'Berlin Kid' took the gambling chance of flying totally 'blind' rather than ordering the crew to bail out. Once again his gamble would pay off.

Flight Sergeant Brian Edward George Soper, the 19-year-old flight engineer on Warrant Officer Arthur Rew's crew on 12 Squadron at Wickenby, recalled:

'On the way to Berlin we lost all the oil from the port inner engine and had to shut it down and feather it. The rear turret was 'U/S' and the starboard inner engine running hot. After shutting down the port inner, we lost several thousand feet. We were still losing height and very near to Hanover. It was decided that Berlin was still a long way off and if we got there, we wouldn't make it back. A suitable point was found near Hanover and the bombs released. With a lighter load we were able to maintain height and in spite of the return flak were routed for base. As we were damaged we kept a special lookout for night-fighters. Due to all the problems and only three engines, we arrived back a little early due to the shorter journey.'

In all, thirty-seven Lancasters were shot down by night-fighters. Fifty-three aircraft were damaged by flak. The Bomber Command ORS Report (No.481) said:

'Unexpected winds en route blew many aircraft off track and nullified the Pathfinders' efforts to make DR runs from Rathenow. Consequently there were gaps in the cloud covering the city; most of the bombing was scattered over a wide area of open country to the south. Six Lancaster IIs on 115 Squadron each dropped an 8,000lb blast bomb carried in the extra-large bomb bays of their aircraft on Berlin. Bad weather and other factors meant their effectiveness was not noted. (By the end of the war 115 would have the distinction of being the squadron with the most operational service, most losses by any one single unit and the most tonnage of explosives dropped.)

'At the beginning of the attack, heavy flak was fired in a loose barrage up to 22,000 feet around the marker flares and was predicted at seen targets through gaps in the cloud. Searchlights were active in great numbers and took every opportunity the weather offered for illuminating the bombers. After the raid had been in progress half an hour and soon after the appearance of fighter flares the ceiling of the barrage was lowered and the flak decreased, although individual aircraft were heavily engaged when coned. The running commentary began plotting the bombers from the neighbourhood of the Zuider Zee and announced that Berlin was the main objective at 1947 hours, nineteen minutes before zero hour. Many illuminated targets were provided for the fighters over the capital.'

'Tame Boar' crews claimed forty kills, seven pilots of two 'Wild Boar' Gruppen (I. and II./JG 302) claiming another eight Viermots shot down over Berlin. At least thirty-two bombers went down in the main air battle that was concentrated in the target area. It was a one-sided battle; only three Nachtjäger were lost in return fire.

The missing air crews were a mixture of young and old and several different nationalities, from different parts of the world and they all died equally violent deaths. However, what of the five press correspondents?

'D-Dog' on 619 Squadron flown by Jock Abercromby had begun to lose height over the North Sea 'We were over England's shore,' said Ed Murrow. 'The land was dark beneath us. Somewhere down there below American boys were probably bombing up Fortresses and Liberators getting ready for the day's work.

'We were over the home field; we called the control tower; and the calm, clear voice of an English girl replied, "Greetings 'D-Dog', you are a diverted to 'Mulebag'." We swung round, contacted "Mulebag", came in on the flare path, touched down very gently, ran along to the end of the runway and turned left and "Jock", the finest pilot in Bomber Command, said to the control tower, "'D-Dog' clear of runway."

Like Murrow, Walter King of the *Sydney Morning Herald* returned safely from Berlin, standing behind the armoured seat of 'G-George', and he too brought back a story of 'the fascinating and fantastic scene over Berlin…. Superb in the savage beauty of its light, but terrifying as a spectacle of devastation by explosive and burning, was the scene in a portion of Berlin as it appeared last night from a Lancaster of one of the Australian bomber squadrons in which I flew. Hundreds of searchlights probed the skies and coned several bombers. 'Scarecrow' flares soared up and burst into a cascade of light which turned night into day. Other flares broke into ominous red and green orbs and flak burst in angry blobs around us. The skies over the target were indeed in turmoil, but the target area itself was in even greater turmoil as 4,000lb bombs, 'cookies', smashed amid the built-up area and thousands of incendiaries cascaded down and took a hold among the blocks of buildings in fantastic alphabetical designs.

'Symbolic of the purpose of the attacks, one of the early strings of incendiaries flared up in an almost perfect 'V-for-Victory'. Other strings formed 'Is', 'Ts' and 'Ls'. The 'cookies' exploded in seemingly slow mushroom-like glows. They burned a dull red for some time and then died in plumes of smoke.

'The experienced crew brought 'George' efficiently and uneventfully past heavily defended areas on the way to the 'King of Targets'. Then the crux of the tense drama began. Cloud protected us practically the whole way. Then, ten miles from the target, it became wispy. Visibility was perfect over the target itself. But if the break in the clouds made the job easier for the bomb-aimers, it enabled the defenders to concentrate hundreds of searchlights and light and heavy flak against the raiders. The Germans used all their defensive devices but we saw one raider perfectly coned in searchlights without fighters attacking it or flak directed at it.

'George' was among the first waves of bombers over the target, which had been defined with remarkable clarity by the Pathfinder force a few minutes earlier with target-indicators of different colours. The bomb-aimers' particular objective stood out like beacons amid a confusion of colours. From the time we sighted them, about ten miles out, until we passed beyond them was the most exciting ten minutes through which I have lived. The two central figures in that brief period were Forbes and the bomb-aimer, Pilot Officer William Grime, of Ealing, London; two 'Bills' who co-operatively directed and instructed each other over the intercom phones.

'I stood behind the imperturbable Forbes and watched the fascinatingly fantastic scene over his shoulder.

'As soon as he sighted his target indicators, for which he was on the lookout, Forbes asked Grime whether he had seen them. Grime answered confidently in the affirmative and then gave the pilot a slight alteration of course, adding: 'You can weave a bit, Bill.'

'Bill Forbes weaved to lessen the danger from flak, but it was only for seconds. Then Forbes settled down to hold his plane to the level, undeviating run so essential for accurate bombing. Flak poured upwards, though none burst close enough to 'George' to threaten the crew's safety. But these were those few seconds which bomber crews dread and against which they must summon up all their courage, determination and imperturbability, a few seconds in which they never know whether the next flak burst is going to extinguish their life, smash their limbs, cripple their plane, or whether they will slip past the German gunners. The flak, to the uninitiated reporter, seemed desperately dangerous, but according to 'George's' veteran crew of youngsters, it 'wasn't much'. Whether heavy or light it failed to disturb 'George's' steady bombing run. Over the intercom from the bomb-aimer's compartment came Grime's calm voice: 'Bomb doors open'; magic words that thrill even the most hardened crews.

'Okay,' came back from Forbes.

'Seconds passed. Then, from Grime came the even more magic words, in his unruffled voice: '"Cookie" gone.' 'Okay,' came from the equally unruffled Forbes.

'I counted slowly to myself … one, two, three, four, five.

'Then Grime again spoke: 'Incendiaries gone.

'Okay,' came back from Forbes.

'We had delivered, free of charge, to Hitler and company, a 4,000lb building-blaster and morale-shaker and many fire-raisers.

'This was the climax of the flight.

'Almost four hours from base to target.

'Down below – four miles below – early comers had already started fires and our waves stoked them thoroughly. As they lightened 'George', I – the spare part on the plane – had the best opportunity to watch those fires increase in numbers and from a band seemingly join in an immense conflagration. Amidst them glowed 'cookies', angry explosions like boils on white flesh. Some billowed and grew in volume above the flames.

'Below 'George' another Lancaster nosed forward, silhouetted sinisterly against the flaming background like a shark in an aquarium pool.

'It was not without cost that the inferno in Berlin's heart was lit, three flak bursts seemed simultaneously to hit one Lancaster and it burst into flames. Another seemed to get into difficulties and later several parachutes could be seen floating down. For many miles beyond Berlin's outskirts the flames and their reflections in the sky could be seen. The later waves had done their work as efficiently as the early comers. All the bombing was completed in less than a quarter of an hour. Forbes' crew compelled my admiration with their thoroughness, confidence and attention to their duties.

'Typical of 'George' crew's keenness and efficiency was the work of the navigator, Pilot Officer James Robertson, a likable young Scot from Elgin, who, cooped up in a cramped compartment, poured over maps, made calculations and kept 'George' on the course and brought the aircraft to the right places at the right times. Another Scot, Sergeant 'Willie' McLeod of Ardrishaig (Argyllshire) tended the radio instruments with loving care and enlivened the intercom conversations with his broad accent.[15] One must not forget in telling this drama of the skies one other actor, 'G for George', who carried us without a hitch. Every crew which flies 'George' worships him. He bears a charmed life. His engines for seven hours last night did not miss a beat. The 5,000 horses in them gave unstintingly of their power. His body protected us in a temperature of -70F below. He gave us all the shelter and usefulness a good bomber should.

'If emphasis is given to the drama's climax, both the earlier and later acts had fascinating features.

'From the time Squadron Leader Forbes, having moved 'George' along the runway, asked 'All set? Okay, here we go' and without hesitation gathered taxiing speed and became smoothly airborne until wheels touched down, new and absorbing experiences jostled one another for this reporter.

'We set off with a sliver of the blood-red sun sitting prettily on top of a bank of slate-grey clouds.

'We soared up over lovely English fields and as we gained height 'George's' occupants busied themselves in the settling process.

'Forbes completed odds and ends of instructions and checking necessary for success.

'Everything was shipshape in five minutes.

'George' began a steady climb which was to take us into the high region in which the crew had been instructed to fly. There was little sensation of flying. 'George' was as steady as the deck of an ocean liner in a smooth sea.

'The moon shone on a weird and wonderful cloudland far below, like a crumpled snowfield.

'Now and again we saw other bombers; all, like 'George', pursuing height.

'The oxygen was turned on after half an hour and we wore masks like characters in a Wellsian fantasy. For six hours the crew was silently intent for long periods because Forbes, like all good skippers, dislikes intercom 'chatter', which some film producers have romanticised.

'Miller confided presently that the temperature was minus twenty degrees centigrade.

'The flight proceeded without incident until we crossed the coast into enemy-occupied country, where the first flak feebly challenged us, doing service in breaking the monotony, which is one of a bomber crew's most insidious enemies. The crew kept an anxious and intent watch against collision with other bombers in the cloud masses through which we passed. Occasionally they reported sighting other kites we knew to be bombers from dozens of stations linking up in the large attacking force – a real bombers' procession to Berlin. Orange-red flak bursts studded the clouds from time to time along the route, but it remained for a strongly defended area to provide the most remarkable spectacle of the outward journey. A thick cloudbank interposed itself between 'George' and the ground. Eighty or one hundred searchlights, ranged in rows with almost geometrical precision, probed through our protecting cover, but failed to penetrate it. The searchlights' crests seemed to squat on top of the clouds like large diamonds on a black cushion in a jeweller's shop. This area sent up more flak.

'We picked up markers which our Pathfinders had laid for us and saw the first of the lanes of red fighter flares which recently became a feature of Germany's aircraft defences. Soon after passing this strongly defended area our run into Berlin began. On our homeward journey, flak gave us a nasty three or four minutes with several bursts sufficiently close beneath 'George' to set it tossing resentfully. On the rest of the homeward trip it was sheer monotony, in complete cloud, until the last half-hour, in which we descended into clearer levels. Then came the thrill of the aerodrome's welcoming lights and after circling it several times to allow earlier arrivals to land, 'George' touched down as smoothly as it had left and at least I breathed a sigh of happy relief, despite the thrills of an experience I would never have missed.'

All the crews on the two Australian Lancaster squadrons had experiences similar to that of 'George', although one reported seeing six fighters simultaneously and on another the rear gunner was wounded by flak. All returned safely, although one very popular pilot caused anxiety when he was not reported for an hour. Australian Pilot Officer Colin Irwin Reynolds on 467 Squadron had been diverted to RAF Fiskerton. He would be KIA on Stettin on 5/6 January 1944. He was 31 years old.[16]

'When we went in for interrogation,' said Ed Murrow, 'I looked on the board and saw that the big, slow, smiling Canadian and the red-headed English boy with the two-week-old moustache hadn't made it. They were missing.'

Flying Officer James Bower and two of his crew on 'C-Charlie' were killed, the aircraft crashing into the Tegel, a heavily-wooded area near Berlin. Four of the crew survived and were taken prisoner. Pilot Officer James Ward and five of his crew were killed when 'N-Nuts' was hit by flak north of Magdeburg and burst into flames. As the crew prepared to bail out the Lancaster exploded. Sergeant G.W. Cross regained consciousness at 5,000 feet and landed safely, albeit with several broken ribs.

'There were four reporters on this operation,' said Murrow. 'Two of them didn't come back – two friends of mine, Norman Stockton of Australian Associated Newspapers and Lowell Bennett. There is something of a tradition amongst reporters that those who are prevented by circumstances from filing their stories will be covered by their colleagues. This has been my effort to do so. In the aircraft in which I flew, the men who flew and fought it poured into my ears their comments on fighters, flak and flares – in the same tones they would have used in reporting a host of daffodils. I have no doubt that Bennett and Stockton would have given you a better report of last night's activities.

'Berlin was a kind of orchestrated hell – a terrible symphony of light and flame. It isn't a pleasant kind of warfare. The men doing it speak of it as a job. Yesterday afternoon, when the tapes were stretched out on the big map all the way to Berlin and back again, a young pilot with old eyes said to me, 'I see we're working again tonight.' That's the frame of mind in which the job is being done. The job isn't pleasant – it's terribly tiring – men die in the sky while others are roasted alive in their cellars. Berlin last night wasn't a pretty sight. In about thirty-five minutes it was hit with about three times the amount of stuff that ever came down on London in a nightlong blitz. This is a calculated, remorseless campaign of destruction. Right now the mechanics are probably working on "D-Dog", getting him ready to fly again.'

At Skellingthorpe Flight Lieutenant Ian Bolton's Lancaster carrying Lowell Bennett was missing. 'B-Baker' had been attacked by two night-fighters which set the two starboard engines on fire. Bolton called: 'Okay boys, bail out. Sorry.' As they put on their parachutes Bolton said again: 'Hurry up boys – can't hold it much longer.' Bolton and his crew and Bennett began evacuating 'B-Baker', but two crew members were killed when it exploded. As Bennett floated down in his parachute, he recalled shouting to himself: 'You wanted a big story; well here it is.' Bennett again became a prisoner of the Germans. His editors first heard from him when he filed a dispatch 'from somewhere in Nazi Germany' saying he had eluded his captors and was writing a book of his experiences in longhand titled *Inside Nazi Europe*, which was picked up by the *Daily Express* who printed it under the heading 'I was in a Lancaster'. In May 1944 his editors heard from him saying that he was charged with espionage and sentenced to solitary confinement for the duration of the war. Bennett escaped twice more before being sent to Stalag Luft I, Barth, where he was reunited with Ian Bolton and Sergeant D.M. McCall, the wireless-operator. During his time in the camp Bennett was editor of the camp's underground newspaper, *PoW Wow*.[17]

At Binbrook, reporters who knew 460 Squadron RAAF had lost a total of five crews from twenty-five dispatched, including two that carried press correspondents, were waiting to interview crew members that had made it back, three of them limping home on three engines. Captain Johan Grieg was killed when 'Gardner's Flying Circus', the Lancaster captained by 28-year-old Flying Officer Alan Roy Mitchell of Devonport, Tasmania crashed close to Machnower See at Kleinmachnow between Potsdam and Berlin. Grieg and two of Mitchell's crew, all of whom perished, have no known grave. 'K-King', skippered by 27-year-old Pilot Officer James Herbert John English DFC, a native of Darlinghurst, Sydney and carrying Norman Stockton had exploded after an attack by a night-fighter. English, three of his crew members and Stockton were killed.

Group Captain 'Hughie' Edwards VC DSO DFC, the Binbrook station commander, was in the control tower personally bringing his crews in. Ron Douglas, a brash and aggressive young pilot who flew a first tour that included fourteen of the sixteen raids on Berlin during the winter of 1943–44, received his instructions as he made his approach. 'Cloud base 800 feet, visibility 1,200 feet.' However, he could not see anything and in the tension of the moment replied: 'Poke your head out and have another fucking look.' At interrogation afterwards, Edwards came up and said to him quietly: 'You'll have to watch your language, Douglas. Control is full of girls.'

About then, Douglas had acquired a very bright red, yellow and orange scarf on which a WAAF was embroidering the names of the targets his crew attacked. At briefing one night, Douglas laughed at something and Edwards quickly rounded on him. 'What are you laughing at, Douglas? And take that fucking scarf off. This isn't a flying club.'[18]

One of the skippers on 460 Squadron RAAF who was interviewed was 20-year-old Flying Officer Ronald Keith McIntyre of Mount Tyson, a Queenslander born in Allora on 24 February 1923 and a farmer prior to enlisting on 8 November 1941. He told reporters:

'There were blocks of searchlights; hundreds of them. They were trying to probe the clouds and the rear gunner saw two aircraft coned. The flak was pretty solid. The enemy seemed to be using the type that looks like hose-piping when it comes up. It gives you the impression that it is impossible to get through it but you do somehow, though we had one or two holes in the bomb doors.'

As a leading aircraftman McIntyre had trained in Canada and England under the Empire Air Training Scheme and was promoted to flying officer on 4 June 1943. He would die on the last raid of the year on Berlin on 29/30 December when his Lancaster exploded and crashed at Grossziethen. The Australian pilot and his crew of four Australians and two British airmen have no known graves.

During December the Australian squadron lost a total of eleven crews, all on operations on Berlin, four crews crashing on their return on the night of 16 December because of the appalling weather conditions that covered their base. In January and February 1944 460 Squadron RAAF would lose another fourteen crews; six on Berlin. By then the squadron was operating three flights, so the equivalent of the fighting force of the squadron had to be replaced in three months.[19]

Three Lancaster IIIs on 103 Squadron at Elsham Wolds, which carried out the most bombing raids in No. 1 Group and suffered the most losses in that group, also failed to return to Lincolnshire. The commanding officer left an account of the raid: 'A Lancaster exploded very fine on the port bow on the run-in to the target. It suddenly appeared – a huge ball of waves of fire rolling over each other and overtaking each other.' A surviving air gunner saw another Lancaster brush just above his head; he refused to fly ever again. Pilot Officer Arthur James Wakefield on 33-year-old Flying Officer Charles Peter Ready's crew was 42 years old. They were killed and the rest of the crew were lost without trace.

Another three missing Lancasters were on 12 Squadron at Wickenby. At Ludford Magna, 101 Squadron lost three Lancasters too. All eight members of Squadron Leader H.M. Robertson's crew survived to be taken prisoner. There were no survivors on the all-sergeant crew skippered by 22-year-old Laurence Victor Murrell or on the crew skippered by 31-year-old Flight Lieutenant George Albert James Frazer-Hollins DFC. The dead included Sergeant John J. Kelly, the American rear gunner who was laid to rest in the US Military Cemetery at Neuville-en-Condroz in the Belgian Ardennes. Hollins left a widow, Phyllis Lillian Frazer-Hollins of Old Woking, Surrey.

Wing Commander Roderick Chisholm, who had spent the night with the squadron at Ludford, did not allude to the three crews on 101 Squadron that died but he wrote later:

'Losses that night could not be called disastrous. Forty for Berlin was reckoned average. Bomber Command could take these losses. Other crews and other aircraft would be there to take off the next night. The Command was proud and defiant. Losses of thirty, forty or more aircraft per night, though tragic in individual thought and seemingly crippling to the newcomer, were accepted by the Command as a whole stoically and unflinchingly. Ranks were filled by the products of a vast training and industrial effort. New crews were ready to move into the front line and new aircraft were ready for them to fly; the battle was maintained. Bomber Command's war never flagged; it had been going on since the beginning, and our ejection from France had been the signal for its building to the present scale. Bombing under cover of the dark remained the only way in which we could hit the enemy from this country, and there had been no let-up. Bomber Command had good reason to be proud.'[20]

The 21-year-old Norwegian 1st Lieutenant Gunnar Høverstad piloted one of two Halifaxes on 35 'Madras' Squadron that failed to return to Graveley. They had been detailed to mark the target and had a Zeiss JKN camera on a special stand mounted in front of the H2S set with which to certify the aiming-point. On the way to Berlin the Halifax was hit by flak near Osnabrück and set on fire. The bomb doors jammed, preventing the release or even jettisoning of the bombs and markers. All of his crew including fellow Norwegian, Flight Sergeant Arne Storme the rear gunner, bailed out safely and were taken prisoner. Høverstad died on the aircraft. He was posthumously awarded the War Cross with Sword (the highest-ranking Norwegian gallantry award) for his heroic efforts on the night of 2/3 December.

The 83 Squadron Operations Record Book at Wyton stated: 'Night-fighters were very much in evidence as it was the well-worn straight in and out route but all our crews returned safely.' 'C-Charlie' was among the early ones back. It had set a record: six hours and ten minutes to Berlin and back; the average time on 'Punch' Thompson's other Berlin trips had been seven hours and forty-three minutes. At debriefing he told the station commander that the new H2S had not been working at the Dutch coast, 'but that when one got near the target it seemed to function properly.' He understood what he meant and turned without comment to the next crew being debriefed.

'The next night, December 3rd, we were scheduled to operate again, but there was a difference in this one. I had decided that it would be my last. I thought that the target would be Berlin. I was wrong. It was Leipzig. I didn't sleep at all the night following my last trip. For the first time in two and a half years I could permit my mind to think of a possible future but I felt a great sadness and kept hearing the powerful Merlins – they were throbbing – and they kept ringing in my ears, as they often did after an operation. Having decided to make it my last I sent a telegram to my mother that I was finished ops so that she could stop worrying for a while.'[21]

At Waterbeach crews on 514 Squadron reported at debriefing seeing fires from 120 miles away. There had been no word from 'J-Jig' skippered by Flight Lieutenant G.H.D. Hinde, a Rhodesian, which had been shot down by a night-fighter over Potsdam while approaching the target area, possibly by Leutnant Alfred Koerver of Stab.II/JG302 who claimed a Lancaster 25 kilometres west of Potsdam at 2011 hours. According to the Australian bomb-aimer, Flight Sergeant J.D. Alford, the port fin and rudder were shot away, port wing tank set on fire, undercarriage hydraulics damaged and there was possibly damage to the rear turret. The order to bail out was given by the skipper by intercom and lights were acknowledged by all except Sergeant Robert Curle, the 20-year-old rear gunner, who died on the aircraft.

Alford was first out. 'To the best of my knowledge all the crew with the possible exception of the rear gunner were still in the aircraft. At 19,000 feet the port wing was on fire and the aircraft was beginning to dive.' Hinde, who was blown out by the explosion of the aircraft, survived to be taken prisoner. Robert Curle's body was not recovered and he is commemorated on the Runnymede Memorial.[22]

'N-Nuts' captained by Flight Sergeant F.C.V. Steed was homeward bound at 20,000 feet at 165 mph when at 2023 hours Sergeant Sweet the mid-upper gunner reported a Bf 109 on the port beam at about 500 yards' range attacking another Lancaster. Shots were observed from the enemy aircraft but no return fire from the Lancaster. The enemy aircraft, however, appeared to break off the attack and passed over the gunner's aircraft from port to starboard beam and turning, closed range to 400 yards without attacking, when the mid-upper gunner opened fire and held it for two seconds, firing 100 rounds. Sergeant C.A. Forsythe, the Canadian rear gunner, did not open fire. The enemy aircraft immediately broke away on the port quarter down and was not seen again. Hits were claimed. At the time of combat, searchlight activity was slight and there was no predicted flak, track lights or flares. Visibility with the half-moon was good.

Noel Thackray's crew had made it home safely after bombing.

'In next to no time Jack was able to report the sighting of the enemy coast,' recalled Edward Humes, 'and a short time afterwards, the marvellous news that we had crossed the English coast. Soon we were over Waterbeach, home, safe and sound.

'Debriefing over, we returned to barracks and turned in. Sleep would not come as I lay thinking of the events of the day. I was not alone for the other crew members were also reliving the events of the night of our very first operation over Germany.'[23]

At about six o'clock the next morning, Clayton Moore was awakened by the sound of movement in the room, and turned on his pillow expecting to see Dick Jones. Instead he saw two men in the uniform of the Service Police and one of them was standing in front of Dick Jones's open locker.

'What the hell's going on?' barked the Canadian at the one wearing corporal's stripes. He quickly turned in his direction, obviously shaken by the tone of his outburst.

'I'm afraid your roommate's bought it, Sir,' he explained, 'and we've been sent to collect his kit and his personal belongings.'

'Moore sat up, trying frantically to rub the sleep from his eyes. 'This isn't real,' he thought to himself. 'I'm just having a bad dream, that's all.' However, the two SPs were still there when he again opened his eyes. 'You mean he's missing? – failed to return? – I want the details,' Moore demanded. 'I'm sorry sir, but we don't have the details. All I know is that we've been ordered to empty his locker. I suggest you contact the flight offices. There should be somebody there who can tell you what you want to know.'

'Once the SPs had completed their task and left, Moore got up and dressed while trying to collect his muddled thoughts. His first job was to inform the other members of the crew, then try to find out the truth of what had happened to Dick. When he finally contacted Bill Siddle in the officers' mess, he told him what had happened.

'I know, Clayton,' Siddle replied. 'The CO told me a few minutes ago. And he isn't missing, he's dead, I'm afraid.'

'The 20-year-old Pilot Officer Kenneth Edgar Warwick, who was from Ascot, and crew had crashed in fog, out of fuel at RAF Garnston, a satellite of RAF Ossington on the return. Clayton Moore stood at the telephone transfixed, unable to speak, unable to fully grasp the significance of what had been said. 'Not missing – dead. Only two survivors.'

'No, I'll do that later. Just you get your breakfast and get down to the flights. I'll see you there.'

'Moore found Dick Jones's pen, ink and writing tablet in a zip-up valise. Inside was the still-unfinished letter to Edith. The sight of this reminded him of the callous remark he had made when he found him writing it that evening and he was at once overcome by a feeling of shame and remorse for having said it. The crew had all developed the habit of thumbing their noses at the grim reaper, but his remark had been proved prophetic. The valise also contained a number of letters that Edith had sent her husband, plus some snapshots – one of a smiling and attractive young woman in a smart two-piece, the other showing her wearing a crisp nurse's uniform – together with a lock of blonde hair.

'Clayton Moore had lost a friend and a member of his crew in circumstances that could only be described as disastrous and he felt that he owed something to the memory of him. He decided that his first task would be to send the letters and snapshots in the valise back to Edith, together with a letter of condolences from himself and the other members of the crew. He resolved to write the letter that evening, but was at a loss as to how he should word it, not having had to write such a missive previously. Deciding on the content of the letter was to occupy his thoughts throughout most of the day.

'Dick Jones had asked his friend to take care of Edith should anything ever happen to him. Clayton Moore had agreed to his request and they had shaken hands on it. Although it was in no way legally binding, it was a gentlemen's agreement and he at once realized that his conscience would dictate his compliance, regardless of what the implications might be.

'Edith gave birth to Gloria Gwyneth, Dick's child. Clayton Moore and Edith married on 30 November 1946 and they had a son, Clifford Nelson.'[24]

Chapter Six

One Night in December

'I am not pressing you to fight the weather as well as the Germans, never forget that.'

Winston Churchill to Arthur Harris following the disastrous Berlin raid, 16/17 December 1943.

In Berlin German diarist Hans-Georg von Studnitz noted that 'Berlin has become one vast heap of rubble. One of the very few oases is the Hotel Adlon where one can still get a meal of sorts at lunchtime and where one comes across many acquaintances.' In the Adlon on Monday, 6 December von Studnitz met one of Germany's most famous night-fighter pilots. The 27-year-old Major Prinz Heinrich Alexander Ludwig Peter zu Sayn-Wittgenstein, descended from a famous Russian field marshal in the Napoleonic wars, was the leading night-fighting 'Experte' in the Nachtjagd with sixty-eight victories – twenty-three of them on the Eastern Front – and the holder of a Knight's Cross with Oak Leaves. Slim-built with a slender face and high forehead, his bearing was that of a confident, well-educated man of good family. Little else in life meant anything to him but service to his nation, but he would often speak of the agony he felt about having to kill people and how, whenever possible, he tried to hit the enemy plane in such a way that the crew could bail out. He had stayed with von Studnitz and his family during the attack on the night of Thursday 18/Friday, 19 November. Von Studnitz noticed how 'pale and haggard' he had looked:

'And like most young pilots, he was suffering from nervous strain; he has to take strong sleeping pills to get any sleep at all and even then he wakes up every half-hour. Wittgenstein says that because we are approaching full moon we shall probably be free of any major attack for the next ten days.'[1]

Sayn-Wittgenstein was proved correct. Due to an accumulation of adverse weather associated with the full moon, Bomber Command flew no major raids on German cities from the night of 4/5 December to the night of 15/16 December when even Mosquitoes were not sent to the 'Big City'.

On 7 December Harris declared that by 1 April 1944 he could bring about the collapse of Germany if he was able to launch 15,000 Lancaster sorties against Berlin and other vital cities. Meanwhile anxious families waited for news of their loved ones missing on recent raids. Three days after Harris's announcement a telegram delivered to 'The Poplars', a lovely old red brick, double-fronted Victorian house with masses of ground in Cedar Road, Thundersley brought the news that Flight Lieutenant Ernest Tansley's aircraft had been reported 'missing' following an attack on Berlin. In due course, Tansley's mother at Elm Park in Romford, Middlesex received a letter from the International Red Cross at 7 Belgrave Square, London telling her that up to the present, no news had been received about her son who was listed as 'missing, believed killed in action on 2nd December' but that all possible enquiries were still being made. The Red Cross added that Ernest Tansley's wife, as registered next of kin, would receive her first notification from the Air Ministry. This came much later, after a further official German report which was sent through the International Red Cross Committee at Geneva direct to the Air Ministry.

At Sunday lunchtime, 12 March 1944, 'everybody seemed to be in a bit of a flap', wrote Mrs Tansley's daughter Anne. That was the day 'Bobby', her new baby brother arrived. A few weeks later a letter from the Air Ministry confirmed that her father and all of his crew were now known to have lost their lives on 2 December 1943. They had been killed when their Lancaster was shot down on the return journey by a night-fighter at about 2300 hours, German time, over the small town of Trebbin:

'All Mum's hopes that he would return one day were shattered and she had to accept that her new baby son would never know his daddy. She was on her own now. It was at this time that she found the strength to write letters of condolence to the relatives of the young crew who had lost their lives alongside my father.'[2]

Gransden Lodge about 11 miles west of Cambridge, on the border with Bedfordshire, was home to 405 'Vancouver' Squadron RCAF. On Thursday, 16 December Canadian air gunner Sergeant William Francis Bill Bessent went to see his twin brother Henry and their mutual friend Gerald Lee Strang off on that night's raid on Berlin, the first to the 'Big City' for almost two weeks. When they were 2 years old the Bessent family had moved to Grande Prairie, a small town of only 1,645 people in north-west Alberta, to live on 101st Avenue, about eight blocks from 19-year-old Gerald Lee Strang. From the time they had been born in Windsor, Ontario Bill and Bob were never far apart, except when Bob went on his first bombing trip on 4 December to Leipzig. The twins' two pilots, 'Ed' Drew and 'Don' Patterson, had trained together in Canada at Penfield Ridge. Patterson already had a navigator, wireless-operator and rear gunner when he arrived in the UK. He chose Bill for his mid-upper gunner. Drew had chosen Bob Bessent as his mid-upper gunner. They so closely resembled each other that people would often get them mixed up.

Harold 'Sandy' Saunders, originally from McLennan, just outside Grande Prairie, and Claude Fitzpatrick, one of the ground crew, whose father, Jack Fitzpatrick, owned a saw mill business in Grande Prairie, were also posted to 405. Claude, who was older than the others at around 26, had got all the Grande Prairie boys together for a reunion. The twins, who joined the RCAF aged 17 in September 1942, and Gerald Strang had arrived at the PFF base in the winter of 1943. The billets were just ordinary single-storey Nissen huts. To keep warm in winter some of the airmen actually climbed up into the roof trusses and chopped out the wood to burn in the stove. Cold and wet made the station extremely muddy and Bill Bessent remembers wearing rubber boots a lot of the time.

Reginald John 'Sunshine' Lane, born in Victoria, British Columbia on 4 January 1920, the son of a Yorkshireman who had emigrated to Canada after the First World War, remembered the bitter conditions and the dreadful food that was the crews' lot at Gransden that winter:

'Coming back from a raid and we literally climb into a wet bed. The beds were as damp as could be – no heat – so that it was dreadful to get out of your flying gear and then crawl into a sticky bed. The food was bad; you couldn't get beer; if we wanted to have a party we literally had to go round the countryside and visit every brewery we could to see if we could steal a barrel of beer. Hard liquor was just not available. There may have been an allocation for the NAAFI or perhaps a bottle a week or something like that, for the whole mess; scotch or gin. Things were dreadful, clothing coupons had just about dried up – it was rough. It was in that environment that we launched ourselves into the Battle of Berlin.'[3]

Bob and Gerald Strang were dressing when Bill Bessent got to their hut and they had already had their briefing. It took some time for Bob Bessent and Gerald Strang to dress since they had to get their heated suits on. The trucks then came and took them away with their crews to the bombers. At this point, Bill Bessent said goodbye and went back to his billet. Little did he know that he would never see Bob and Gerald again.

On 61 Squadron at Skellingthorpe 23-year-old Flying Officer Bob West and his navigator Allen Beetch gave Sergeant Bernard 'Bunny' Clark the wireless-operator some good news. The crew was finally going to fly their first operation. It certainly beat spending most of an evening trying to get the stove in the billet alight with wet wood or having a very primitive bath on a mud-layered floor in the ablutions, which would leave 'Bunny' almost as dirty by the time he managed to get dressed. As was the usual routine, new arrivals were assigned a bed in one of the arctic corners of their hut. As the losses mounted one graduated to beds nearer the centre, until in the end they had a bed with their feet towards the stove.

The crew had been mooching about the base since their arrival a fortnight earlier. In between classes and cross-country flights over Lincolnshire they played poker and bridge, table-tennis and snooker, and skinned rabbits they caught in snares in the wood behind their hut. There were also odd trips to the 'Ritz' in Lincoln to see films like *The Four Feathers* and *Five Graves To Cairo* and having rissoles and chips and welsh rarebit, bread and butter and mince pies in Boots' cafe and then drinks before catching their crowded bus when the pubs closed at 10.00 pm. Miss it and they would have a 6-mile walk back to the Nissen huts and bed at eleven. On some evenings 'Bunny' Clark and Beetch would make the 2-mile journey to the nearest telephone box at Swanpool to make their whereabouts known to their respective 'Ball and Chains'!

Audrey Clark was always pleased to hear from her husband, or at least she seemed to be. She was a billeting officer in the Women's Volunteer Service and she and her 12-year-old son David shared the family home with many of the evacuees in Rushden, Northants. 'Bunny' Clark was 35 when he volunteered for the RAF in September 1941 and was nicknamed 'granddad' by his fellow crew members. Well-known as an amateur footballer and manager of Messrs Bignells boot factory at Raunds, he was an old boy of Wellingborough School. Only Bob West had broken the monotony, flying his 'second dickey' operation to Leipzig on 3 December.[4]

It was on 16 December that Sergeant Keith Parry, a 21-year-old Lancaster pilot on the squadron, who had flown only a couple of cross-country flights, made his 'second dickey' trip with a seasoned pilot and his crew. Parry wrote:

'Our normal routine on the squadron was, if not flying the night before, to report to the crew room at 9.30 in the morning. At ten o'clock the phone in the ops room would ring and the station would be connected to Bomber Command ops room on a command hook-up. The message would either be 'Stand Down', in which case the crews could bank on another twenty-four hours' respite, or 'Ops on tonight', usually accompanied by 'Maximum effort'; in which case everything and everybody would be airborne. The message would also give two pieces of vital information. Although the target for the night would not be revealed to the crews until briefing, the bomb load and fuel load for the aircraft would be given, so that the ground crews could start preparing the aircraft. Old hands at the game could then make a shrewd guess. A bomb load of 10,000lb mixed HE and incendiary plus 1,850 gallons of fuel usually spelt the 'Big City'. And so it was at 10 o'clock on the morning of 16 December. An hour later the Battle Order was published. My name was on it.

'As it was once again a maximum effort, all eighteen of 61 Squadron's crews were detailed. Under the list appeared the words: 'Sergeant Parry to report to Squadron Leader Moss at Main Briefing.' It also gave the time of the pre-flight meal, referred to by some as the 'Last Supper'. This was at 1300 hours and the Main Briefing was at 1430. As I read these words I feel my heartbeat quicken and was aware of a small cold lump forming in the pit of my stomach. It was like a leaden golf ball and was a sensation with which I was to become familiar over the coming months. It would last until I climbed into the aircraft and then – as I became absorbed in the routine of pre-start drill and checks and the Merlins coughed and spluttered into life – it would disappear, to be replaced by a feeling of cautious optimism. It was always the other blokes who got the chop: we were going to be all right.

'The briefing team took their positions on the platform and the Met man arrived – to be greeted with loud cheers and some quite original catcalls mostly advising him what to do with his charts. The Station Commander arrived, gave permission to smoke and we all lit up again. The Station Navigation Officer drew back the curtains and the target was revealed. Those who had bet on the 'Big City' were in the money. The red tape marking the route stretched across the North Sea, crossing the enemy coast near the Friesian Island of Texel and then crossed Holland and Germany straight to Berlin. This was known as the 'Straight' route. On leaving the target the tape turned northwards when the moon rose, crossed the Baltic coast between Lübeck and Rostock, then turned westward across Denmark towards the comparative safety of the North Sea on its way back to England. Some 1,300 miles in all; most of it over enemy territory and through one of the most efficient and determined air defence systems the world has ever seen.

'The attack [by 483 Lancasters and ten Mosquitoes; five more Mossies were to drop decoy flares south of the 'Big City'] would be in four waves and the whole force would pass over the target in twenty-five minutes. We were to be in the fourth and last wave. The weather for the trip would be fine, clear over the target. It was to be a cold night with a temperature of minus 50°C at 20,000 feet.

'On our return the UK would be misty, with frost on the ground, but the visibility was not expected to fall below three miles. Take-off time was 1630 and complete radio silence was in force. I left the briefing room with Flight Lieutenant Harvey who I would be flying with that night. Harvey was an Australian and on the squadron they had the reputation of being a bunch of tough nuts. They were engrossed in the maps and charts on the table in front of them, Harvey's dark blue battle dress contrasting with the light blue around him.'

Parry was unaware that a few weeks before, on the night of 26/27 November, Flight Lieutenant George Henry Harvey's crew had been one of the lucky ones who had returned safely from the raid on Berlin in thick fog over Lincolnshire. They had landed 'R-Roger' (JB116) at Catfoss and the aircraft was still parked there two days later awaiting a break in the weather when it was struck during a landing by a Beaufighter that hit the mid-upper turret area and broke it in two. Luckily, Canadian Pilot Officer Donald Frank Thomas, the Canadian mid-upper gunner from Merriton, Ontario, was not in the turret at the time! Unfortunately, a few days later, Sergeant Henry Alan Sheppard RAFVR, the bomb-aimer, died as a result of a road accident in Lincolnshire on 12 December.[5]

Squadron Leader 'Jimmy' Moss, Parry's flight commander, introduced him to Harvey's crew: 'This is Sergeant Parry – he will be flying with you on "R-Roger" [DV399] tonight.'

'Seven pairs of eyes looked up at me. Nobody spoke or smiled, except someone who muttered: "Jeez – not another Pommy sprog!"'

Harvey, who was 22 years old, was one of the more experienced pilots and was about halfway through his tour. Apart from Don Thomas, the rest of the crew consisted of 22-year-old Sergeant James Stuart Kennedy RAFVR, flight engineer; Sergeant Reginald Walter Carver RAFVR, the 22-year-old navigator; Sergeant Noel Stephen Joseph Meehan RAF, the 23-year-old wireless-operator; Sergeant Richard Stuart; and replacement bomb-aimer Flight Sergeant A.G. Leslie. Stuart was the younger son of Mr and Mrs R. Stuart of Gorse Farm, Astbury in Cheshire and a popular figure locally. Before enlisting in the RAF in 1940 he had been a keen footballer, once playing outside left for Congleton Town FC.

'After we had lost Henry Sheppard,' recalled Don Thomas, 'we had been offered a bomb-aimer whose crew had been lost while he was in hospital. For several reasons we did not want him. Another bomb-aimer asked to join us but when we discovered that he was a troublemaker whose own crew was anxious to get rid of him, we turned him down as well. Eventually, with the approval of the "Wingco" we decided to finish our tour using any bomb-aimer who was available. For eight months we had taken Harry for granted. We had found fault with him; even poked fun at him. Now he had been gone two days and we missed him. Leslie's crew had been lost while he was in hospital.'

After Harvey had introduced Parry to the crew he said, 'Get a chair and sit down'.

'I did as I was bid,' says Parry, 'and had to sit on the outside of the tightly knit group, as no-one moved to make room for me. I felt my lump get bigger and bigger and colder. I realised afterwards that their apparent animosity was not directed at me personally, but at the fact that I should be occupying their engineer's small, collapsible seat known as the 'Rumbold' seat after its inventor and usually referred to as the 'Rumble' seat. We were wished good luck, Harvey's crew feeling that we probably needed it. Back at the Squadron we donned our flying kit, had another smoke and then waited outside for the crew bus to take us out to the aircraft.'

In the misty twilight of a bitingly cold winter's afternoon RAF Station Bourn, 8 miles west of Cambridge, looked a very unattractive sight, typically constructed of many temporary buildings clustered in different dispersed sites around the airfield. Some 2,500 people lived and worked in this makeshift town, pieced together from concrete, corrugated iron and wood. The prevailing winds at the airfield were south-westerly so the Lancasters on 97 Squadron in the Pathfinder Force would take off using the shortest runway of all – NW-SE – which meant that just after becoming airborne they would pass over the villages of Highfields and Hardwick, close to St Mary's Church.

A local man, Bob Plane, recalled the Lancasters on 97 Squadron straining and labouring to gain height as they came directly over Hardwick:

'They used to come over the tops of the houses, laden with bombs and one would think, 'Please God, let them get over.' You would be sitting there with a cup of tea and when they had gone over the saucer was full of tea and the cup was only half full because of the vibrations. It was a hell of a noise'.

Canadian Warrant Officer Robert Douglas Curtis of Nanaimo, British Columbia was the rear gunner on Lancaster 'X-X-ray' captained by Pilot Officer 'Jimmy' Pymar Billing, a Scot. Doug Curtis remembered that 16 December started out much the same as any other day:

'Our crew crawled out of the sack in mid-morning and made our way to the mess. A quick look at the board told us that we were on for later that night. We'd had a good long lay-off of two weeks as a result of problems encountered on a trip to Berlin on 2 December. For that matter we had not even seen the inside of a Lancaster since that trip. It was unfortunate in a way that our layabout could not have lasted one more day as the op that we were up for turned out to be one of the most hair-raising of the war. Only the raid on Nuremberg would prove to be a bigger disaster for the Air Force. 97 Squadron had scheduled twenty-one crews for this target, which we learned at briefing was to be Berlin. The very name Berlin could raise the hair on the back of your neck.'

Flight Sergeant Fred White, the wireless-operator on 'U-Uncle' on 'B' Flight skippered by Flight Lieutenant (later Squadron Leader) Peter de Wesselow, agreed with this sentiment: 'At the briefings, when Berlin was announced as the "Target for Tonight" you could see all the heads drop. We hated it.' Fred had joined up in December 1940 at the age of 20:

'I had been working in the shoe trade in Kettering before then, but decided to join up because I wanted to join the RAF as flight crew and you had to volunteer to get into that. My first op was on 29th July 1943 and was a raid on Hamburg. We were caught in a searchlight cone and it took us about eight minutes to get out. It might not sound long, but when you are caught in the searchlights over the target, it felt a very long time indeed. The squadron had lost the last four 'U' planes in successive raids. We made it back, but with very heavy shrapnel damage.'

In total Fred White would fly thirteen raids on Berlin with Charles Peter Crauford de Wesselow, a surgeon's son of White Russian origins who had re-mustered from the Brigade of Guards and who spoke several languages fluently. In November 1942 he and his crew had force-landed in Portugal in a Blenheim and were interned until January 1943. The precise, immaculate de Wesselow collected antique glass and could call on a rower's physique for throwing a Lancaster around the sky. In October 1944 Squadron Leader de Wesselow would contact Flight Sergeant Fred White asking if he wanted to go back on ops for a second tour. Fred White leaped at the chance:

'We were assigned to 635 Squadron at Downham Market and in February 1945 our plane was the Master Bomber[6] on the Dresden raid. It took us eight hours and fifty minutes; we had to circle the target for about twenty minutes showing the other planes where to drop their bombs. I flew 68 operations in all during the war and had the same pilot and flight engineer throughout.'

Doug Curtis further recalled that nothing was mentioned at briefing that would lead one to believe this trip would be any worse than any of the four previous jaunts that he had made to Berlin:

'In retrospect we should have had at least an inkling that all was 'not right in Denmark' as our Met man spent an inordinate amount of time detailing the various weather conditions that we would encounter, not so much on the way to the target but rather that there may be fog on our return. However, it was not forecast until hours after our return. What we didn't know was that the Met people had apparently suggested, as they could not be certain what conditions might be like six hours or so hence, the raid should be scrubbed but off we went. With hindsight it was determined that there were a number of factors that would impact on this night's effort. In addition to the possible fog hazard, there was also a full moon. And, as if that were not enough, our route was a straight line directly to Berlin. No attempt was made to try and bluff Jerry into thinking that we had some other target in mind.'[7]

Sergeant Arthur Tindall, the wireless-operator on 'T-Tommy' on 97 Squadron skippered by Squadron Leader Eric Frank Cawdery, recalled: 'The Met Officer said that the weather would close in by the early hours of the following morning and he anticipated the raid being cancelled. In the event it wasn't – with disastrous results.' Cawdery was a pre-war pilot of about 31 years of age; most of his contemporaries were either dead or had already finished their tours. His crew, all youngsters of 19 to 21 years old, would get joshed for the age of their skipper: 'What on earth are you flying with an old man like that for? What right has he to still be alive?' He and his crew would be among the few who would survive their Pathfinder tour.

The mid-upper gunner, Sergeant James Harvey McGregor, would be killed on 31 May 1944 in an air crash at OTU Chipping Warden. The navigator, Sergeant Ken Swale, would die alongside his pilot Peter Drane in a 139 Squadron Mosquito on 15 January 1945.[8]

Cawdery was one of four Lancaster skippers who each carried a 'second dickey' to gain experience. Flight Lieutenant Ernest Sumner Clarke, who had been the crew's instructor at 14 OUT, would share the controls of 'T-Tommy' with Cawdery. Clarke had come to 97 Squadron to do his second tour – as was customary – and as this was his first op since leaving the OTU.

On 'E-Easy' the Australian skipper Flight Lieutenant Jeffrey W. Pelletier was accompanied in the cockpit by Flying Officer Leslie Henson. On 'Q-Queenie' 22-year-old Flight Lieutenant David James Brill, son of Squadron Leader and Mrs Claude Cecil Brill of Corsham, Wiltshire was accompanied up front by 32-year-old

Flight Lieutenant Rowland Ernest Handley DFM. Having completed several trips on 'Wimpys' in the Western Desert, Handley had joined 97 Squadron on 1 December. His wife Hilda Cecilia lived in Southend-on-Sea in Essex. Due to illness, Brill's regular navigator, Flight Lieutenant Arthur Weston, had been replaced by 24-year-old Australian Flying Officer Norman Gregor McIntyre, a clerk from Cairns, Queensland prior to enlisting in 1941. 'Mac' was married to Maud Eileen Daphne McIntyre of Wandsworth in London. The crew's 21-year-old Canadian mid-upper gunner, Flying Officer Gordon James Little was born on 30 October 1922 in Port Arthur (now Thunder Bay) in Ontario, the family moving later to Lorain, Ohio in the United States where his mother and father now lived. Sergeant John Stone was the flight engineer. Pilot Officer Robert Butler, the 20-year-old air bomber was from Stafford. Sergeant Harry Chappell, the 23-year-old wireless air gunner, came from Southey, Yorkshire. Flight Sergeant Ernest John Battle, the 22-year-old Australian rear gunner hailed from Rose Bay, New South Wales.

On 'V-Victor' Flight Lieutenant (later Squadron Leader) Charles Blundell Owen was flying his first trip on 97 Squadron in his own aircraft but not with his own crew. His 'second dickey' was a complete 'sprog' but the neophyte must have been heartened to learn that they were old hands, having flown several ops including three on Berlin. On 2 January on the way home across France they had been jumped badly by a fighter. Both gunners were wounded, the rear gunner seriously, and the starboard outer engine caught fire. Owen wrote:

'... found it impossible either to extinguish fire or feather prop and had to have rudder tied by engineer to maintain straight flight, as the rudder trimmers had been shot away. Limped into Tangmere and swung off runway on landing due to starboard tyre being holed by cannon shell. End of V-Victor I.'

'P-Peter' was skippered by Squadron Leader Ernie Deverill DFC DFM who was flying his first raid of his third tour. Deverill, born in Gillingham, Kent was known as 'The Devil Deverill' at Bourn because of his utter contempt for enemy fighters and anti-aircraft defences. On 17 August 1942 he had flown the infamous Augsburg daylight raid which involved twelve Lancasters flying in broad daylight at 25 to 30 feet all the way across occupied Europe to Augsburg, 500 miles into Germany. The raid demanded an immensely high degree of courage, navigational accuracy and flying skills, and despite heavy losses was a PR triumph. It was possibly the most audacious Bomber Command operation of the war and was only surpassed in RAF folklore by the more famous 'Dam Busters' raid in May 1943. Deverill's crew consisted of flight engineer, Flight Sergeant Alexander Russell; navigator, Pilot Officer John Thomas Brown from Belfast; bomb-aimer, Flight Sergeant Francis Roy Farr from Windsor; wireless-operator, Flight Sergeant Ralph Crossgrove, a 25-year-old New Zealander; mid-upper gunner Warrant Officer James Benbow who was older than the average crew member having been born in 1909; and rear gunner, Warrant Officer Donald Jamieson Penfold from Worthing.

'K-King' was skippered by 23-year-old Flying Officer Ted Thackway. Born on 10 January 1920, he grew up in Bilton, a northern suburb of Harrogate in Yorkshire. His younger brother Jim was serving in the RAF on ground-crew duties. Ted and Jim were brought up by their mother Elsie who worked as a seamstress at Marshall and Snelgrove in Harrogate almost entirely on her own, as her husband George was something of a wanderer. In June 1939 at the age of 19, Ted signed up with the RAF for six years, beginning as an aircraft hand/flight mechanic, but such was his natural ability that he soon transferred to pilot training and became an officer. Ted was even-tempered, slow to anger and very self-controlled. At the same time he was always ready to see the funny side of things. At the same time he was equable, likeable and easy-going. At a height of 6 feet, he was by far the tallest man in the crew.

Like his skipper, Jack Powell the 31-year-old navigator came from Yorkshire. Standing 5 feet 9 inches tall with brown hair, blue eyes and a thoughtful, serious and determined face, he had spent most of his life in the large manufacturing town of Wakefield. He came from a very poor family but at some stage money became available which permitted him to escape the usual fate of gifted working-class boys, for instead of having to leave school early he was able to continue his education. He became a chartered accountant working in local government, was regarded as a high-flyer and would probably have ended up as a county council treasurer. With his independence assured, he was able to go ahead and marry his long-time sweetheart Agnes. They made a most handsome couple when they married on Christmas Eve 1937. When the war began, Jack was in a reserved occupation, quite safe from danger, but after a long struggle with his conscience he told Agnes he was going to volunteer; he did not want other people to fight his battles on his behalf. Poor Agnes found it very hard to accept his decision. Jack joined the RAF in 1941 and became a first-class navigator, with much of his training taking place overseas. Agnes moved back to her family in Wakefield, taking work in a munitions factory to help the war effort.

George Grundy, the 21-year-old flight engineer, came from a poor working-class family in Eccleshill, a suburb of Bradford, about 12 miles west of Harrogate. Dark-haired with grey eyes and a cheerful smiling face, George was a good-looking fellow. At 5 feet 5 inches though, he was no taller than Leslie Laver, the 20-year-old rear gunner. Leslie was born at home at 6 Calmington Road in the poor, densely-built streets of south London between the Elephant and Castle and Peckham. He had three brothers and four sisters and the family was extremely poor, yet they were all quite happy together. Leslie left school early, between 14 and 15 years of age, and began work as a milkman. He joined the RAF just before his 19th birthday but was not called to the Volunteer Reserve until 22 March 1943. 'Sandy' Grant, the bomb-aimer, was a temporary flying officer. Born in 1920, his full name was Leslie Kenneth Alexander, but the crew always called him 'Sandy', which both reflected his hair colour and usefully distinguished him from the other Leslie on the crew. He was a small man, slight and short with reddish Celtic colouring and a little moustache. His father was Canadian; his mother Scottish. His early childhood had been spent in Princeton, British Columbia, but at some stage the family had moved to Vancouver. At the age of 18 'Sandy' joined the Royal Canadian Signal Corps, but after six months he took up the occupation of painter and interior decorator at the Ritz Apartment Hotel. He finally won his Observer Badge on 19 March 1943 and then embarked for England and joined Ted's crew.

At the outbreak of war on 3 September 1939 Joe Mack the wireless-operator was 17 years old. He had left school three months earlier and was then on a business course, prior to officially joining the prosperous and successful family company in April 1940. This was a large imports firm specializing in tobacco. The prospect of being a tobacco merchant had never filled Joe with any degree of enthusiasm; he wanted to have a career in music, for which he had a most exceptional ability, but he lacked the will to stand up to his practical father. Shortly after his 19th birthday, Joe joined the RAF Volunteer Reserves and began training as a navigator, but was re-trained as a wireless-operator. He and Tony Lawrence, the 20-year-old mid-upper gunner, were very close friends, probably because they came from very similar backgrounds. Joe was very musical while Tony was very artistic; neither was in the least bit academic and both came from prosperous middle-class families in business. By the time he joined the RAF Tony was a slim, tall and dramatically good-looking young man with auburn hair and blue-grey eyes.[9]

Squadron Leader Joe Northrop was neither musical nor artistic and he was the least bit academic but the former 'Trenchard Brat', who had joined the RAF as a Halton apprentice in 1929 at the age of 16, became in turn an aircraftsman, soon plying his trade as an engineer at the newly-completed Cranwell Staff College, and by the time war began he was a fully-qualified pilot to boot. A tour of flying on radio-countermeasures against the Luftwaffe beam systems was followed by special bombing operations against the German battleships in Brest, flying Stirlings on Nos 7 and 15 Squadrons. By 1944 at the age of 31 he was one of the finest pilots in the RAF where his wise head on 83 Squadron at Wyton prevailed on more than one occasion and was evident on the night of 16 December.

'Europe's a very funny place to operate over,' he would later write. 'The weather usually comes over from the west and hits us first in this country and then it carries on and either swings up a bit towards Norway or swings down a bit towards the Mediterranean. We had a fairly big cyclone centred over Europe with cold weather which created a fog every evening as soon as dusk fell. By six or seven o'clock in the evening you'd got fairly thick fog. You were in for it.

'Well, when the whole of England is covered with that and you've got say thirty aircraft a station to land – if you've sent thirty aircraft off, you want them back. But to get them down was practically impossible.[10]

'As the crews trooped yet again into the operational briefing room, already it was evident that we were in for another foggy night and the odds were already being laid against take-off by the squadron bookmaker. This time, however, he was in for a surprise! As the curtains covering the wall target map and route were drawn aside, the usual noisy outburst from the assembled crews confirmed that Berlin was once again the target.

'The hubbub died down as the squadron commander (Group Captain John H. Searby DSO DFC) called for order and waved a signal form in the air. "I've just received this signal from the Commander-in-Chief," he said; "'Butch' wants you all to know that the only reason you haven't been going to the 'Big City' of late is that he's been waiting for a night when the weather is so bad that all the German fighters are grounded and so give you all an easy trip. Tonight's the night for sure, so you'll soon be on your way. However, he wants to assure you all that you won't always have it this easy."

'The crews' tense expressions dissolved amid roars of laughter at the very thought of the tough C-in-C sending such a message and in a more relaxed atmosphere we settled down to the more serious business of briefing. All, that is, except for the station commander (New Zealander, Group Captain Lancelot Michael Edworthy Jarman DFC, born Christchurch, 17 August 1907) seated in the front row; a stickler for Service procedure and hardly noted for his sense of humour. For the rest of the briefing he sat deep in thought, no doubt wondering why he had not been the first to get a copy of the mythical signal. Such "jollying" of the crews certainly helped to relieve tension, particularly at this period as the squadron was going through a bad patch.

'Briefing was soon over. The met officer had painted a gloomy picture of fog obscuring the country and with no diversion airfields available by the time of our return, the general attitude was one of "If we're going let's get on with it – we might even get back then before the fog really clamps down." Indeed, by now little enough time remained to hastily swallow operational meals in the messes and get along to the aircrew changing rooms to don flying kit and draw out personal parachutes. The short December day was rapidly drawing to a close and already the chill in the air and the clear skies indicated that radiation fog would be forming only too quickly after dark.

'By the time we had carried our heavy parachutes and dinghy packs out of the building the aircrew buses were waiting to take us out to the dispersal area, and we piled on board the first one complete as a crew. Our bus was soon filled to capacity and it then trundled off around the peri-track dropping off each crew close to the aircraft they were flying, the aircraft letter being announced at each dispersal pan. The crews waddled out of the bus looking like overgrown teddy bears in a weird and wonderful assortment of flying kit to the accompaniment of a chorus of well wishes from those remaining. The superstitious ones clutched or wore their personal good luck charms while others, particularly the Canadian contingents, affected the tougher "Wild West" style with .38 Smith and Wesson revolvers or murderous-looking Bowie knives tucked in the tops of their flying boots.

'Soon the driver called out "F-Freddie" and we bundled out of the bus giving the thumbs-up sign to start pre-flight checks on our aircraft; this was standing on the pan well down on its undercarriage legs with the weight of the high-octane fuel and the five x 2,000lb HC (Heavy Capacity) bomb load pressing down on them. From now on there was no time to think of anything other than our respective jobs as part of the crew and the prime necessity of getting Freddie airborne on time. Fortunately there were no snags and the crew soon settled down in their stations and checked-out on the intercom. The engines were started and, maintaining radio silence, the chocks were taken away from the wheels and we moved out to take our place in the line of aircraft taxiing towards the runway holding-point. Each aircraft took off in turn on receiving a steady green from the runway controller in his caravan, and in a very short time we were at the head of the queue. I flashed the aircraft letter in Morse on the downward ident' lights and got a steady green in reply. Then turning smartly on to the runway, I lined up the compass and set the directional indicator, opened up the Merlin engines against the brakes until they were running evenly, then released the control and started the take-off. After some juggling with the throttles to keep in a straight path the aircraft began to gather speed, the tail came up and the controls began to respond. I eased the control column back as we began to run out of runway and we were on our way.[11]

'Flying to Berlin some pilots took the view they should get in and out of the target as quickly as possible. "Be the first one home." That way there'd be less chance of getting hit. They'd charge into the target, getting all they could out of the engines and to hell with whoever used the aircraft after them. They also knew that with lots of planes being damaged and others running out of petrol there'd be hardly any airfields to land on. We always knew who they were because they'd get home about an hour before anyone else. Sensible and reasonable pilots, and I regarded myself as one, would be careful how they used the engines and would take indirect routes, so they arrived back later. I always tried to fly so that there would be about two hours of petrol left when I got back to England. I flew around for twenty minutes and then came in. An experienced pilot would bide his time: he was safe while he was up there.'[12]

At Waltham 5 miles south of Grimsby 21-year-old Gilbert Charles Denman's all-sergeant crew was given 'F-Freddie' to fly as part of 100 Squadron's contribution of seventeen Lancasters. During the early 1930s Waltham Grange aerodrome was a small civilian airfield. After the former grass airfield was expanded to support a bomber squadron it became an extension of nearby RAF Binbrook. Known to all those that served at this typically remote outpost in Lincolnshire as Waltham after the nearby village, the first operational sortie from here for 100 Squadron was on 4/5 March 1943 when the squadron's Lancaster bombers were sent on mine-laying sorties along the coasts of occupied Europe. Two Lancasters were lost. Probably to avoid the growing confusion with RAF White Waltham near Maidenhead, the station became RAF Grimsby in September 1943. No matter. For an RAF airman like 19-year-old Alfred Henry Johnson who was brought up in the equally flat farming fields of Norfolk and was now flight engineer on Denman's crew, it was simply a 'home from home'.

Alfie, or 'Yonker' as he was known on the crew, had been born on 17 August 1924 and he lived at the family home at Wayford on the River Ant close to the idyllic Norfolk Broads. At Stalham Primary he began flying model aircraft propelled by rubber bands. In 1938 at the age of 14 he had left school, the normal leaving age at that time, to commence an apprenticeship at a local garage. On 27 December 1942, just four months after his 18th birthday Alfie was called up for service in the RAF. In a letter to his parents, Alfred Henry and Lucy Johnson, he wrote: 'the flight engineer's job is quite interesting, but boy! It's bloody hot on ops, especially over Leipzig and Berlin. I'll be jolly glad when this mess has been cleared up so that I can come home, get married and settle down.' Sadly, he was destined only to serve his country ten days short of just one year. His operational flying, which began with an op to Leipzig on 22 November 1943, would last approximately two months. It was packed full of incident. On one of their two trips to Leipzig Lancaster 'H-Harry' developed engine faults. Then on another raid flying in the same Lancaster, while en route to Berlin, they had to abort the operation because of oxygen problems, returning to make an unscheduled touchdown at Binbrook. The crew got in their fourth operation before the squadron was 'stood down'.

They were to be led by their new Commanding Officer David Holford DSO DFC* who, at the age of 22 had finished his second tour, a total of sixty operations,[13] and was on his third tour. David Holford was born in Kingston upon Thames in 1921. Holford had been awarded the DFC at 18 and the DSO at 21 for his leadership in attacks on the Scharnhorst and Gneisenau. On first impressions Holford appeared smallish in stature, softly-spoken and inconspicuous among the more animated, exuberant personalities but he was charismatic; a devil-may-care person determined to dissipate frustrations. He went out of his way to help crews having trouble reaching operational standards, but no condemnation of them escaped his lips. Green crews from OTUs, the pilots especially, were inspired by Holford's talks. For before them was living proof that with luck and a degree of skill, survival was possible.[14] On operations he had one idiosyncrasy. After the normal 'All set boys? Here we go!' he would sing, 'I've got spurs that jingle, jangle, jingle as we ride merrily along' until 'Wheels up!' was ordered.

David and Joan Audrey Holford, a WAAF intelligence officer at Elsham Wolds, had been married only a matter of weeks and were staying at the Ship Hotel in Grimsby. Also staying at the hotel at the same time were Wing Commander James Johnson Bennett DFC* and his wife. 'Jimmy' Bennett, with two tours behind him, had arrived at Waltham three weeks earlier to form 550 Squadron, which was due to move to North Killingholme on the southern bank of the Humber Estuary north-west of Grimsby in the New Year. He had earned his DFC as a flight lieutenant captaining one of the aircraft which attacked the seaplane base at Sylt on the night of 19/20 March 1940 when, in spite of being held and dazzled by searchlights, he descended to 1,000 feet over the base and pressed home his attacks at this low altitude under heavy anti-aircraft fire, causing an outbreak of fire. A bar to his DFC had followed on 26 June 1942 on 144 Squadron Air Force. In part the citation stated that:

'Since being awarded the DFC Wing Commander Bennett has completed many operational sorties. In July 1941 he led a flight in the first daylight attack against enemy battle cruisers at Brest. Despite the severe damage which his aircraft sustained through anti-aircraft fire, he continued to lead his formation over the target and returned to base safely. Wing Commander Bennett has set a magnificent example as a pilot.'

Wing Commander Bennett chose to fly with Squadron Leader G.D. 'Bluey' Graham and his crew on the Berlin trip. Holford would pilot 'N-Nuts'.

A three-quarter moon would appear later in the night so the earliest possible take-off time was set for just after 1600 hours. At Elsham Wolds at around 1630 hours along a lane just wide enough for a truck and a ditch each side Marie Harris, an ATS driver from the ack-ack site at Goxhill Haven, was driving a load of stores to a site in the Guy truck, which had an open front and canvas-covered back:

'Coming up to a farm on my right,' she recalled, 'it was very low cloud and the Lancasters were taking off into the circles, up and away, as I looked up and raised my right arm in a salute. They were so low and so near I felt I could nearly touch them. One went into low cloud and I was thinking it's a wonder they don't crash, they are so close together, when in a split second as it came out of the cloud, God, it was a head-on crash with another Lancaster; one almighty explosion and all Hell was let loose. It was awful. I couldn't believe what had happened practically over my head, just over the farmer's field. I was so stunned, streaks of fire shooting all over the road and my truck. I pulled on the brakes and jumped in the ditch but only for five minutes thinking some of the crew could be saved, so I ran up past the farmer's house, bits and pieces flying all over, just passing a barn and someone caught hold of me from behind and wouldn't let go, kept saying, "No Lass, no Lass, there'll be nothing." It was the old farmer.

'In no time at all the fire engines etc were arriving,' continues Marie. 'I pulled myself together and went back to my truck in a daze and drove onto the site, still couldn't believe what had happened. When I pulled up at the guard room I was just rooted to my seat and couldn't stop crying, thinking of the "Bobs", "Alecs" and "Bills" – whoever – just blown to bits. It was awful. The guard called the sergeant, who took one look at my truck with all the bits and pieces and burns on the canvas and said "she must have been under it." They took me into the mess and gave me a hot mug of strong tea and twenty minutes by the round stove (they were really kind). I felt better and had to get on with it, so back to Goxhill. On arriving our MT Officer was concerned. Did I need to go to the MO? No Sir, I'll be OK but when I went to bed I couldn't shut my eyes. This terrific explosion flashed before me every time. I was like this for quite a few nights.'[15]

The 24-year-old Flight Sergeant Frederick Roy Scott from Cabramatta, NSW and crew on 576 Squadron who were on their first operation had been among the first to take off. They were soon followed by 22-year-old Flight Sergeant Valentine 'Val' Richter of Chingford, Essex and crew on 103 Squadron who were flying their third operation. This was a scratch crew made up from members of both 103 and 576 Squadrons, an unusual occurrence. As Richter took off and climbed away, Scott's Lancaster appeared out of the clouds flying directly towards them. A collision was inevitable and the machines crashed head-on just outside the village of Ulceby and wreckage fell over a wide area. There were no survivors on either crew. Among the dead was Sergeant Stanley Victor Cull, the flight engineer on Scott's crew. At 18 years of age, he was among the youngest air crew members in Bomber Command to lose his life on operations.

At Waltham Squadron Leader 'Bluey' Graham's take-off was early, about 4.30 in the afternoon. 'And even then visibility wasn't very good and it was plain we were not going to be in for a very pleasant journey,' wrote Bennett. No. 550 Squadron was putting up fifteen Lancasters but ED730 would return early when the WT/RT and DR compass and the Sperry panel went unserviceable and a coolant leak on the port outer caused overheating. In all, 483 Lancasters and 10 Mosquitoes were detailed to carry out the attack on the 'Big City' using the bomber route leading directly to Berlin across Holland and northern Germany. No major diversions would be flown but a further five Mosquitoes would drop decoy fighter flares south of Berlin. On the return flight the Lancasters would take a northerly route over Denmark.

Sergeant 'Gil' Denman's crew took off fifteen minutes after Graham for their fifth operation. For one 100 Squadron crew there was more than the usual apprehension as they would finish their first tour if they successfully completed this trip, but as Pilot Officer Johnny Stow sat in 'K-King' with its engines running up in readiness to taxi out, the 'Gee' set went unserviceable. After breaking radio silence to relay this problem a few minutes later the radar van came tearing along the perimeter track dodging taxiing Lancasters to arrive at the dispersal with a replacement set. It was very quickly installed and tested and Stow was on his way.[16]

Bob West's crew on 61 Squadron at 'Skelly' had been given 'Y-Yorker' for the operation. After their ops meal of egg and bacon, bread and butter and coffee in the mess, Bill Warburton, the flight engineer, Lloyd Cuming, the Canadian bomb-aimer and 'Bunny' Clark had dashed off to change into long underwear. Phil Brander, the Australian air gunner, collected coffee and oranges and they had been transported back to the crew room and final briefing, then out to the aircraft with half an hour to go to zero. All excited, the engines were revved up and down the taxi path with a full load of a 'cookie' and incendiaries and 'nickels'.[17]

There was quite a crowd to cheer the Lancasters off and then off they went at 1840, climbing up and up, the 'Monica' device packing up on one side. 'Bunny' Clark went back to check up and found the fuselage door open. The wind pressure was terrific so he could only just close the door but could not fasten it. Bill Warburton tied up the door with a piece of rope. Bunny managed to get the 'Monica' set on the go and everything seemed 'grand' with first contact with base. Next thing they were over the enemy coast near Amsterdam amid 'tons' of cloud and some flak bursting and on to Berlin at about 21,000 feet.[18]

At 1700 hours 'R-Roger' skippered by George Harvey lifted off with a full load of fuel and bombs with Sergeant Keith Parry the 'second dickey' standing behind Jimmy Kennedy the flight engineer. He remembered Parry and Leslie sitting with them at briefing, riding out to the aircraft in the van, sitting again drawn and tired while the crew was debriefed, but had no clear picture of their faces. Nor could he remember, except for a single shouted word by the bomb-aimer, either man saying anything while they were airborne.

At altitude the crews found cloud base at 2,000 feet persisting to 18,000 feet, but there were no icing problems.

'We had "X-X-ray" airborne at 1650 hours,' recalled Doug Curtis, 'and headed to the assembly point over the North Sea. As we came through the cloud layer we beheld a beautiful sight as the sun was slowly sinking into the multi-coloured clouds directly behind us. As the minutes passed, it began to grow darker. It was a comforting thought to watch the hundreds of aircraft slowly making their way through the clouds reaching for operating altitude. It was dark as we reached the enemy coastline and it soon became obvious that the welcome mat was out for us. The enemy fighters quickly determined our flight path and began to lay down a string of flares which reached eventually all the way to Berlin. A dozen or more bombers were shot down even before we crossed into Germany. Fighters followed us all the way to the target where more were waiting to take over. Flight Lieutenant Pelletier was attacked by a Ju 88 which his gunners beat off and were able to claim one damaged.'

'The Dutch coast when we reached it,' wrote Don Thomas, 'lay beneath 10/10ths cloud. Crossing in we were greeted by the usual flurry of light and heavy flak; most of the shells bursting wide or beneath us. One shell flashed nearer than the rest but still too far away to be dangerous. I heard a click. Above the roar of the engines it sounded no louder than a spring-loaded catch snapping home when a door is gently closed.

'The cumulative effect of operational flying was beginning to tell and for the past two or three weeks, I had been having a bout of nerves. It was something that I could handle by myself but now, when I flew, it was as if I flew on springs. For one thing I began listening to the engines. If their rhythm changed I knew it; if an engine emitted a snort or a growl or an unusually large gush of sparks, I worried and fretted until the sound and the spark flow was back to normal. Let a wing drop three feet and my built-in gyroscope took over and I found myself leaning to the opposite side of to counteract the tilt. Several times I was on the verge of telling George how to fly his aeroplane – but I never actually did. The pilot and the engineer had their knobs and gauges and charts to tell them when something was wrong: I didn't need them. That was why I knew, almost before anything else, that we were losing our starboard outer engine.

'At first it was only the thin, high-pitched scream of an engine out of synchronisation. Then flames and a thick shower of sparks blew out from behind the spinner and from the exhaust stacks of the engine alternatively slowed then over-revved.

'Starboard outer running wild! Temperature going off the clock!' the engineer shouted.

'Feather it then.'

'"Ken" Kennedy shut the fuel cock, rammed open the throttle to burn up excess fuel and then closed it and jabbed at the feathering button. The flames flickered and died down and the sparks ceased. But the propeller, the blades flat against the line of flight and creating a tremendous drag, continued to windmill aimlessly.

'It won't feather!'

'Keep on trying,' said George.

'Eventually the blades were turned until they presented a knife edge and the propeller stood motionless. We were perhaps thirty miles inside Germany and we were still heading for Berlin. The ship had lost too much altitude – was still slowly dropping – and I expected to hear George order the load jettisoned then ask for a course home.

'How much height did we lose?' George asked.

'We're down to 16,000 feet,' replied the engineer.

'Jettison and turn back,' said Dick from the rear turret.

'No, we've come this far. We'll go on. "Ken", how high will we be when we cross Berlin?'

'I figure we will hit the ground about ten miles short of it.'

'There was a long pause. George seemed to be thinking it over. Finally he said, "OK, we'll drop the 'cookie' and go on with the rest."

'Ahead and slightly to port an anti-aircraft battery was firing as fast as the loaders could ram shells into the breeches of their guns. George altered course towards the flashes.

'Bomb-aimer; line up on those guns,' he said.

'The bomb doors opened; our leaflets blew back in a cloud and the outhouses of rural Germany were supplied with paper for months. The 4,000-pounder went down. It was the only time we were ever certain we'd seen our bomb explode. We missed the gun flashes by at least two miles but the battery ceased firing.

'Although he had never been particularly fond of Harry, Dick then said, "Old Harry wouldn't have missed it."

'Powered by the failed engine, the mid-upper turret was out. It would not rotate and the guns could be neither elevated nor depressed. And, although an electric solenoid released the breech blocks, the circuit had fused and the guns would not fire. As quickly as three pairs of thick gloves would permit, I sorted through my bag of tools and with a screwdriver removed two previously loosened bolts so that the guns, still yoked together, could be raised or lowered manually. Next I passed a four-foot length of parachute cord through a wire ring that I had fastened to the top of my right boot and then snapped the clips on each end of the cord into holes I had had drilled in the outside seat release of each gun. Finally I engaged the handle so that the turret could be hand-cranked horizontally.

'I didn't expect to shoot anything down; at best I hoped that my tracer would give an attacking fighter something to think about. For now, by grasping the extension at the rear of the left gun with my left hand and cranking with my right, the turret could be revolved and the guns moved up and down. Kicking back and down with my right foot would tighten the cord, pull down the seats and fire the guns. It was a "Rube" Goldberg affair, slow and awkward to manipulate; it was dangerous for with the mechanism that prevented the guns firing when a part of the aeroplane was in the line of fire out of action I could, if not careful, shoot holes in the wings or in the tail or in the back of Dick's head. I fired a burst over the side; the system worked.

'We had crossed Holland with the first wave but with our speed reduced by approximately seven mph, we had dropped back and now approached the defences with the last. And we had lost another 1,500 feet. But tonight, with Roman Candles of light flak sputtering up to 12,000 and heavy flak and fighters tearing at the pack a mile above us, we sailed unmolested across Berlin somewhere in between.'

Berlin was cloud-covered but the Pathfinder sky-marking was reasonably accurate. Squadron Leader D. Miller DSO DFC, born in Auckland on 12 November 1917, who had been a clerk before joining the RNZAF in July 1940, was one of the first of the Main Force to arrive. He said that the fighters were active along the route. 'The cloud was keeping the searchlights down and they did not bother us at all as we made our bombing run, although we were so early in the attack. The fires had got going even then. It was an ideal night from our point of view.'

Bob West's crew on 'Y-Yorker' appeared to be well on time and in the stream in between Bremen and Hanover, right on the markers and bang on track. The target had come up right on time. Frank Langley the air gunner called on intercom to say that he had trouble with the oxygen and was feeling awful. West asked him to hang on until they were off the target if possible and on they went. Lloyd Cuming espied the target markers and West flew 'Yorker' level on to them and 'Zump! Bombs Gone!' There was an 'Ok' from Cuming. 'Bunny' Clark's thoughts as he felt the floor of the aircraft jerk when the 'cookie' went were 'take that one and those and share between you!'[19]

Keith Parry wrote: 'we could see the target markers now – reds and greens cascading down onto the aiming point. Incendiaries from the leading wave followed them and soon a pool of fire developed on the ground, speckled with the bright flashes of exploding HE. A few miles in front of us and above an aircraft blew up with a brilliant red and orange flash. Harvey gave no sign that he had seen these things: he was concentrating on the instrument panel and holding the aircraft rock-steady as the target came into the range of the bombsight. "Steady, steady," said the bomb-aimer. Searchlights flicked onto us and a light flak battery opened up. The red balls of the tracer shells rose slowly and gracefully from the ground, gathering speed as they got nearer. They flashed past, just to our starboard. Above us the defences had established a box barrage over the approach and the sky was thick with the black puffs of bursting shells, easily visible in the light from the target. "Left, left," said the bomb-aimer and Harvey jinked the aircraft accordingly. "Steadeee, steadeee." If twenty-four hours was a long time in Bomber Command, I now realised that a minute was forever on the bombing run. There were still some seven or eight minutes to the release point. We lost the searchlights, but more light flak whizzed past us, not so close this time: they were firing at random.

'"Twenty-eight fifty," said Harvey and I put the revs up. The target inched its way down the bomb sight. The bomb-aimer's voice became more strident as we neared the release point. Under Harvey's hands the aircraft flew as though it were on rails: the air speed, height and heading were all dead steady; he had shut his mind to what was going on around us. "Bomb doors open!" said the bomb-aimer. "We're nearly there. Steady – steady – steady" – his voice was rising to a crescendo – "Bombs gone!" The release arm known as the "Mickey Mouse" started its semi-circular journey round the contact points, one for each bomb station. The bombs were thus released in a pre-determined order, so that the trim of the aircraft was preserved. The Lancaster soared and shook itself, like a big black Labrador coming out of the water.

'With the aircraft 10,000lb lighter we all knew we now had a fighting chance. Harvey still held the aircraft steady, waiting twenty more seconds for the photo-flash to go off. This ensured that we took back a photograph of the target at our release point. I looked over my side of the aircraft at the sea of fire underneath us. The long straight black line running through the middle of it was the Unter den Linden. I thought of the burning streets of East London in 1940, of the carnage I had seen outside Liverpool Street station when a bomb had dropped on a rush-hour queue. There was no compassion in my heart for those on the ground below. Rather, I heard Harris's voice: "You have sown the wind, but you will reap the whirlwind. For every bomb you drop on London, we shall repay you ten-fold." We were the whirlwind, riding high above them, over Hitler's Chancellery at the heart of the Third Reich. I wondered if he was getting the message.'

'Our incendiaries carpeted the burning city,' says Don Thomas, 'and we were on our way out when above and ahead of us, in a sky torn by bursting shells and thick with drifting pink flask clouds, a Lancaster exploded. A full minute later I reported that a piece of aluminium about two feet long and rolled by the explosion into the shape of an ancient scroll, had glanced from our starboard wing. No one believed me. But in the morning the dent was there and a shiny area where the paint on our wing had been flaked off. And, had George not seen it too, the crew would never have believed that while we were on our bombing run a slowly tumbling 4,000-pounder had missed our port wingtip by 50 feet. Had it hit us, both Lancaster and crew should, in a split second, have been transformed into four engines and scraps of dural [duralumin] and skin raining down into the streets of Berlin.'

Large-scale jamming of German radio and radar was carried out. First Jagdkorps VHF was jammed by bell sounds, R/T traffic was rendered almost impossible and Korps heavy frequency was jammed by quotations from Hitler's speeches. Korps alternate frequency and Division frequencies also were strongly jammed and there was a very sudden jamming of the Soldatenrundfunksender (Forces Broadcasting Station) 'Anne Marie' by continuous sound from a strong British jamming station. However, since the coast of Holland, from where they flew direct to the target with no major diversions, the bomber crews found that the German controllers had plotted their arrival with great accuracy. German radar had begun picking up 'J' beams from 1800 hours and the assembly of the RAF formations, their leaving England and approach were all plotted correctly by H2S bearings. Mosquito 'spoof' attacks on Kassel and Hanover were clearly recognized as such.

Although the attack was scheduled to last only fourteen minutes, in the hope of preventing outlying fighter units from responding in time, that degree of concentration was not achieved. Bombers were over Berlin for ninety minutes. However, widespread mist and fog at 150 to 300 feet in the North German plains reduced the overall effectiveness of the fighter defence and twenty-three aircraft, mostly Bf 110s, with short endurance, had to abandon their sorties prematurely as there was no possibility for landing in the Berlin area owing to ground mists. Only crack night-fighter crews were sent aloft to intercept the bombers and these were guided in to the bomber stream throughout the approach to the target. The 30 night-fighters engaged in 'Objektnachtjagd' ('Target Area Night Fighting'), 28 for 'Zähme Sau' and 34 for 'Himmelbett' (over Jutland) claimed 18 to 20 bombers. 'Wilde Sau' night-fighters and flak claimed another five to seven. All told, twenty-three RAF bombers were shot down over the Netherlands and Germany.

'We left the revs at 2,850 and cleared the target, climbing slowly,' wrote Keith Parry. 'We would be able to maintain at least 12,000 feet now, which would keep us clear of the light flak defences. We turned to a north-westerly heading and started off across the north German plain towards the Baltic coast, which we would cross between Rostock and Lübeck. The light from the target faded astern of us and we were soon concealed again in the false security of the velvety blackness. The stars were more easily visible now and we could clearly see the "Great Bear". Harvey reminded me how, by using it as a guide, the Pole Star could be found and identified. "That little joker is the best compass there is," he said. Months later this advice was to save the lives of myself and my crew on a particularly fraught occasion off the Danish coast. But it was quiet now. We had been able to reduce the power setting on our three Merlins to 2,500 rpm and they were singing along beautifully.

'As we neared the coast we could see that the defences of both Rostock and Lübeck were active, indicating that stragglers in the first waves had strayed over them. Harvey aimed at the black gap between them and we passed serenely out into the Baltic, soon turning onto a westerly heading which would take us north of Kiel on our way to the North Sea. Harvey put "George" – the automatic pilot – in.

I found my thermos flask and we had a cup of coffee. It tasted like nectar. We put the thermos away and concentrated on the next task, which was to cross the Danish-German border. The navigator said: "Ten minutes to the coast."

'We were flying over an area notorious for night-fighters – there were several airfields in the vicinity. To our left, searchlights and flak shattered the blackness. "That's Kiel," said Harvey. Our track would take us over the island of Sylt, on which there were at least two night-fighter airfields. I began to wonder if it was going to be as difficult to get out of Germany as it had been to get in.'

'We had flown on unmolested,' says Keith Parry, 'and soon crossed the coast out into the comparative safety of the North Sea. We now had 200 miles of water to cross before we would see the Lincolnshire coast. We eased the revs back to 2,350 and started a slow descent. After half an hour or so we passed through 10,000 feet and were able to take our oxygen masks off. The coffee went round again and the tension subsided. There was no need now to maintain radio silence and the wireless-operator was busy trying to contact HQ 5 Group to get a met forecast for landing at "Skelly". We still searched and quartered the sky, but with any luck all aircraft would be friendly. Someone sang *The Wild Colonial Boy* and they all joined in the chorus. "Ned" Kelly, I thought, would be proud of them.'

Squadron Leader Joe Northrop had headed towards the North Sea on his first course, climbing to reach his operational height of 20,000 feet before the Dutch coast. 'Aircraft could be seen all around us in the still-light skies above the now dark ground of East Anglia, all with the same purpose in mind. Looking down at the patches of grey mist and fog already forming above the dark earth I could not help wondering what it would be like in seven or eight hours' time if and when we came back. By the time the Dutch coast was reached we were cruising at operational height above a thick woolly blanket of greyness stretching as far as the eye could see. Although a sharp lookout was kept for fighters none were seen as they were undoubtedly grounded by the weather at the airfields in the Low Countries controlled by the GCI centres. We pressed on over Germany, checking the route-markers as they were placed by earlier PFF aircraft, as though on a navigational exercise; and still no sign of the enemy other than sporadic bursts of flak and occasional glows from searchlights appearing in the murk below as the odd aircraft strayed off course and passed too close to a defended area.'

Time began to drag a little until, with thirty minutes to go to H-hour on target, H2S set operator Frank Foster came forward to switch on the bombsight and so ensure that the gyros would stabilize in good time before the bombing run:

'From now on the run-in seemed endless sitting on top of the five 2,000lb HC bombs and TIs nestling in the bomb bay, the greasy black puffs of exploding shells all around – any one of which could well deliver us to Kingdom Come in a single flash. For what seemed an eternity we stuck rigidly to the heading, correcting as necessary on Foster's instructions, until at last the welcome 'Bombs gone' came over the earphones, accompanied by the familiar lurch upwards of the aircraft now free of its 5-ton load of high explosive.

'I held the aircraft on its last heading to make sure of a photo-flash picture of the aiming-point on the ground and then dived to port out of the target area to get away from the forest of greasy black puffs of smoke that still came up all around us. After a while we were clear of the defences.

'Now silhouetted against a sky lit up blood-red from the reflected glow of the fires raging in Berlin, I headed for home on Charlie Burdett's course. Feeling naked and exposed in the clear night at altitude, and apprehensive of what was yet in store for us on return, I ordered boost and revs reduced to a minimum and trimmed the aircraft to fly for maximum endurance and thereby conserve fuel.

'As it turned out the trip back proved as uneventful and devoid of enemy action as the outward flight; although some reflected searchlight glow and bursts of heavy flak appeared at intervals through the grey cotton wool mass below us, there was still no sign of any Luftwaffe night-fighters as we ploughed westwards.'[20]

Eric Stephenson on Flight Lieutenant Ralph Allen's crew on 'P-Peter' on 207 Squadron at Spilsby recalled. 'Our flight engineer, Maxwell Millward was not able to fly with us. 'Mike', as he was always called, was the oldest member of the crew and we had all clicked with him straight away. He had been a fitter before graduating to aircrew and really knew his stuff and was very good. Instead we had a substitute, Sergeant Derrick Peppal.

'The trip had a fateful feel to it from fairly early on because the route we were ordered to fly went directly to Berlin across Holland and northern Germany, without any significant diversions. I read later that the German controllers were able to plot our course with great accuracy and so directed a lot of fighters up at us from the moment we crossed the Dutch coast. Our aircraft alone was attacked twice by German night-fighters on the way to the target. In fact Joe Brindle the bomb-aimer said that the rear gunner, Bob Stone, a good-natured Canadian and most popular member of the crew, had set one of our attackers on fire and caused it to blow up below our aircraft, but we never had this confirmed.

'The target was in the south-west suburbs of Berlin, so we did not have any trouble getting to it. I forget what it was that we were supposed to be hitting, but we were always a bit cynical about this anyway. Bomber Command made no bones about the fact that we were doing area bombing, because there was no other way at night. Often we did not even see the ground, so inevitably we were doing area bombing rather than precision attacks. Berlin was covered by cloud but the Pathfinder Force had developed a technique called sky-marking, which involved dropping flares which burned above the clouds and we just had to bomb the flares. The Pathfinders had done their job pretty well and we got away our big 'cookie' bomb, as well as several hundred incendiaries, with reasonable accuracy. Bear in mind that a 'cookie' was 4,000lb of high explosive and when it went down it made a hell of a hole wherever it landed.

'Because we were in the third stream for this operation, we had been tasked to photograph the pattern of explosions with an infra-red camera that we were using for the first time that night. We were under strict instructions to fly straight and level over the target for twenty-nine seconds after we had released our load, in order to take pictures of the tail end of the raid. This meant we were highly vulnerable, because we could not corkscrew or take any of the usual evasive action meant to throw off enemy fighters. Moreover, the Germans had a trick of putting huge quantities of searchlights into thick cloud, because that lit up the cloud and made an aircraft passing through it as obvious as a fly walking across a sheet of white paper. Of course, the fighters would have no trouble at all in seeing us either.

'We were still completing our photographic task when all of a sudden I heard the voice of Derrick Peppal the flight engineer say on the intercom, 'Christ, predicted....' There was also a 'beep, beep, beep' sounding over the intercom as he shouted, which came from a device called 'Fishpond' warning there was an aircraft underneath us. This warning came too late because right at that moment all hell broke loose around me. My instrument panel disintegrated and I got a gash on the forehead from a flying piece of metal that left me momentarily dazed. I then realised that everything was very bright for what was supposed to be a dark midwinter night over Berlin. When I pulled back the curtain that separated me from the front part of the flight deck I saw the port wing was on fire. Having several hundred gallons of 90-octane petrol burning just a few feet away from me seemed to be an occasion requiring rapid action, although I am not a person normally given to that.

'It was then that I saw the skipper and the engineer had their chutes on and were heading forward down the small stairs into the bomb-aimer's compartment. The skipper waved to me, indicating that I should follow them; he told me afterwards that the intercom had all been wrecked.

'The controls were wobbling backwards and forwards in a crazy fashion and the aircraft was in a flat spiral dive, probably in what was known as a 'falling leaf'. So I went back to the navigator position and clipped my parachute pack onto my harness. Just then the rear gunner called the skipper on his intercom to say his turret was jammed. I realised I was still in contact with him because I was wearing my helmet and headset and before disconnecting it I told the gunner to use the turning handle and to bail out quickly. It was then that I noticed that the wireless-operator was still sitting calmly at his radio. I thumped him on the shoulder, pointing to my 'chute and indicating for him to go forward as I called 'Bail out!' over the noise of the engines. He told me afterwards that he had no idea of what was going on and probably would not have got out if I had not told him.

'All of this took a few seconds only. Then I nipped towards the nose of the aircraft, leapt down the small steps and dived headfirst through the open escape hatch and into the cold night air. I rolled on my back as I had done so many times in diving from the edge of swimming pools, counting to five before pulling on the ripcord. It was a chest type 'chute and because I had always placed it on my chest in such a way that the D-ring was on the right I knew exactly where to find the ripcord. When I felt the opening shock of the parachute between my legs I looked up and initially I was horrified that the canopy seemed so small. I thought it had been ripped off until I realised that it was so far above my head because the shrouds were about thirty feet long. We had never done a jump before, just practised landings by swinging down on harnesses hanging from a beam, so I did not even know how to steer a parachute properly. After I pulled on the risers and the 'chute responded, I felt much better.

'The complete and utter quiet that I experienced at that point was astonishing. Of our burning Lancaster there was no sign and because we had been at the end of the raid the other bombers were now gone too. The only reminder of the war going on was little puffs of reddish light coming up from the ground, which I took to be light ack-ack shells or something. What they were aiming at, I had no idea. Of course, if I turned around in my harness there was a very vivid reminder behind me in the form of the burning city, but even so it was all terribly silent and quite extraordinary. Some distance below me I could see one or two parachutes of other members going down. They seemed a long way off and I appeared to be drifting even further from them. Luckily the prevailing winds were taking us all away from fires in the target area. I guessed we were going to come down in one of the outer suburbs a good distance from central Berlin.

'Even in my slightly dazed state, I was engrossed in the picture laid out in front of me, which was so beautiful in a bizarre sort of way. I also found myself wondering how I was going to explain all this to Freda. I thought, 'Just two weeks before our wedding, she'll be livid!' Gradually I became conscious of snow-covered ground coming up at me, but I did not even see the church steeple that snagged my parachute and sent me crashing into the wall of the building, giving me another crack on the head and knocking me unconscious. When I came to sometime later, I found I was hanging alongside a clock face about thirty or forty feet above the ground. I could not see what time the clock was showing because I was hard up against the wall but my wrist watch was stopped at 8.21, probably from the force of impact. I could hear the mechanism grinding away inside the tower and every now and again there was a loud clunk as the clock tried to chime. The Germans had obviously taken the clappers out, just as had been done back in England with clocks. It made a lot of noise and it bothered me. It occurred to me what a thorough mess I had made of our wedding plans by turning up at the wrong church on the wrong day and in the wrong town.

'There were now people on the ground shining torches up at me, including a tall man wearing a strange orange helmet who called, 'Are you English or American?' I think I replied to the effect that of course I was English; Americans did not fly at night. I have no idea how I was lifted down from the steeple because by then I had lapsed back into unconsciousness again. I came to lying on my back on a table looking up at my skipper while a man whom I later found was a German doctor stitched up my head. I heard from Ralph that his 'chute had also got snagged, in a tree in the backyard of a German house. Joe Brindle was also there, after landing on the edge of a lake.

'We were then taken to a hospital in Berlin, or certainly near Berlin and put into what had been a maternity wing, presumably until the raids got so bad that the patients were evacuated elsewhere. While at the hospital we also met up with the other survivors from our crew. Six of us had managed to escape using our Irving parachutes. Sadly, neither of our two gunners, Sergeant Bob Stone and Sergeant Ernest John 'Taff' Takle, a lad from South Wales with a dry sense of humour, had got out.[21] It appeared that the latter had most likely been killed when our bomber was attacked from below, probably by a Messerschmitt 110 or 210 armed with upward-firing cannon.'[22]

Four Lancasters on 7 Squadron PFF failed to return to Oakington. Shortly after crossing the Dutch coast 'D-Dog' piloted by 23-year-old Flying Officer Francis William Rush of Battery Point, Tasmania was attacked 12 kilometres from Alkmaar at 1815 hours by a Leutnant Heinz Rolland piloting a Bf 110G-4 from Bergen airfield. It was Rolland's ninth victory. 'D-Dog's engineer, Sergeant John Stuart Ogg, bailed out just in time, the Lancaster exploding shortly after he had opened his parachute. 'D-Dog' came down in the Schermer polder behind the farm called 'Wait and See' near Stompetoren/Oterleek. On landing Ogg could not find any of the others. He was found by a farmer who took him to Broek where he was given civilian clothes and a Dutch identity card. Remaining at Broek until after Christmas he was sent to Amsterdam in the New Year but an unsuccessful attempt to put him on his way to Lisbon resulted in him remaining where he was for a whole year. In March 1945 he went to Swiendrecht hoping to cross the Bies Bose into Brabant but some airmen had been captured the night before and so it was cancelled. Ogg remained in Rotterdam until the liberation and only after his return to England did he learn why he had found none of his crew. They had all died that night seventeen months earlier. On 8 January 1944 the body of air gunner Sergeant William Robert Buntain was found in a marsh near a farm. He had been on his first flight.

At around 1845 hours 'K-King' captained by New Zealand Flight Lieutenant John Russell Petrie DFC was shot down with no survivors west of Cloppenburg by Oberleutnant Dietrich 'Dieter' Schmidt for his ninth victory. Born in Foxton on 11 August 1917, Petrie had been a labourer before joining the RNZAF in July 1941. 'J-Jig' captained by Australian Pilot Officer Geoffrey Tyler crashed at Wilsum in Germany. Tyler and three of the crew were killed. The two survivors were taken into captivity. 'L-London' piloted by Australian Warrant Officer Wallace Arthur Watson which crashed on Bangma's farm at Follega with no survivors was the first of four victories this night credited to Oberleutnant Heinz-Wolfgang Schnaufer, Staffelkapitän, 12./NJG1.

'Das Nachtgespenst' ('The Bogeyman') and 'The ghost of St. Trond', as he was known, had taken off from Leeuwarden in a 'Schräge Musik'-equipped Bf 110 with his radar-operator Unteroffizier Fritz Rumpelhardt and braved low cloud and icing up to 15,000 feet to seek out the four Lancasters over Friesland Province with the aid of the ground controller in the night-fighter box 'Eisbär' ('Polar Bear') at Sondel in northern Holland. Schnaufer's second victim was a 101 Squadron 'ABC' ('Airborne Cigar') Lancaster piloted by Canadian Flight Lieutenant Ronald Ernest MacFarlane DFM, which exploded over Banco polder. His third victory was 'O-Orange', a 49 Squadron Lancaster flown by Flying Officer Gordon Lennox Ratcliffe, who was on his first operation, which crashed at Sonnega. Both Lancasters went down with their crews.

Schnaufer's fourth victim, 19,700 feet south of Leeuwarden, was 'N-Nuts' on 432 'Leaside' Squadron RCAF at East Moor flown by 22-year-old American Flying Officer William Charles Fisher who was from Independence in Jackson County, Missouri. His wife was eight months' pregnant at this time. Flight Sergeant Herbert Turner, his 24-year-old rear gunner, spotted the Bf 110 and Fisher corkscrewed violently, almost shaking off their pursuer, but Schnaufer holed the petrol tanks and the Lancaster flew over Leeuwarden trailing a sheet of flame to crash between Wijtgaard and Weidum a few kilometres south of Leeuwarden where it disintegrated on impact with the ground and the bomb-load exploded. Only Sergeant Owen Donald Lewis, the 23-year-old second pilot survived and he was taken prisoner. Among the dead were the 19-year-old flight engineer Sergeant Raymond Hughes and Flight

Sergeant Thomas Walter Pragnell, the 22-year-old air bomber of Northampton whose twin brother Jack was also a bomb-aimer in Bomber Command.

Schnaufer had to make five attempts to land back at Leeuwarden and then only by a fortuitous hole in the cloud. These four victories took Schnaufer's total to forty victories. Only three German aircraft were lost this night.

The Lancasters were able to shake off the opposition on the return flight by taking a more northerly route via Denmark. Some crews reported that they had met little opposition and described the raid as quite uneventful. This was thought to be very unusual for Berlin. Widespread mist and fog at 150 to 300 feet in the north German plains reduced the overall effectiveness of the fighter defence and twenty-three aircraft, mostly Bf 110s, had to abandon their sorties prematurely. On the Berlin attack, 10 Lancasters were shot down inbound to the target by fighters, 5 fell to flak in the target area, 4 more were due to collisions in the target area and 6 more that went missing took the losses to 25. Sergeant John Walter Hinde, the 20-year-old pilot on 'N-Nuts' on 57 Squadron, ditched his Lancaster in the North Sea on return. Only the wireless-operator Flight Sergeant G. Hurley survived after drifting at sea for thirty-eight hours and being picked up by the Royal Navy minesweeper HMS *Typhoon*.

Five aircraft were lost on the diversionary operation and six Halifaxes on SOE (Special Operations Executive) operations were lost on their return to England due to fog-bound airfields. One crashed in the vicinity of Spilsby. Three crashed into the sea off Felixstowe and Harwich. A fifth crashed into trees attempting to land in fog at RAF Woodbridge and another, which was diverted due to poor weather conditions, hit a wooden pylon near the airfield and crash-landed on a mudbank in the River Debden off Bawdsey.

Worse was to follow.

Chapter Seven

A Hymn for the Haunted

'We roared across the wet, dripping roofs of a small village almost knocking the chimneys from the peaks. A window shade thrown suddenly up revealed behind it a lighted room, a brass bed and someone sitting bolt upright in the bed.'

Canadian Pilot Officer Donald Frank Thomas,
mid-upper gunner on 'R-Roger', 61 Squadron.

Over the North Sea on the return from Berlin on 16/17 December, Pilot Officer Johnny Stow's wireless-operator on 'K-King' received a message which said that cloud was down to 500 feet over Waltham. They were then flying in cloud at 20,000 feet or thereabouts, but were slowly letting down which was a bit tricky because the altimeter was playing up. The needle, indicating feet calibrated in hundreds, kept sticking at 500 as it unwound but the thousands hand was working well. This meant that the accuracy between the thousands could not be relied upon and with cloud base so low over Waltham this would cause quite a problem. Stow had instructed his wireless-operator not to wind in the trailing aerial. This was suspended 40 to 50 feet below the aircraft. The wireless-operator was also told to report the fact as soon as it was lost. This would give some warning if they were still in cloud and unable to see the ground. However, the Lancaster came out of cloud at approximately 700 feet and the crew were just able to make out the sea below. As they crossed the coast it was possible for them to pick up Waltham's flashing beacon. Circling the airfield at about 500 feet and as they approached, the wireless-operator yelled out that the aerial had gone but Stow had the runway lined up and with visibility good below 500 feet, control cleared him to land.

Thus Stow and his crew finished their first tour totally unaware of the tragedy that was unfolding around them, which, when the situation became fully known, subdued the whole squadron for quite some time. One of Stow's colleagues told him a few days later that another pilot had been complaining that some 'blasted idiot' had forgotten to wind in his trailing aerial which had become wrapped around his tail unit. Johnny would bomb Berlin thirteen times before ending his tour on the night of 16 December. The award of the DFC followed and after a year as a 'screened' instructor he transferred to Mosquitoes.[1]

Wing Commander 'Jimmy' Bennett recalled: 'There was no high cloud and at times we could see dozens of aircraft around us. The clouds below cleared slightly over the city, we dropped our bombs and got away again. There was some fighter activity but we were not bothered. Coming back the cloud started to increase again and it was clear that by the time we reached England it would be almost right down to the deck. 'Bluey' decided to come down through the cloud over the North Sea. In conditions like that it was always wise practice. Lincolnshire may have been fairly flat, but other places weren't and there were always a few of what we called 'stuffed clouds' around, clouds which contained something hard, like a hill. We dropped down into the mist but 'Bluey' picked up the outer circle of sodium lights at Waltham, stuck his port wing on them and followed them round until he found the funnel and put her down. We rolled along the runway to the far hedge and we were already aware that planes were coming down all around us, landing at the first opportunity, so we decided it would be a lot safer to leave the aircraft where it was and walk the rest of the way.'

It was said that at Waltham, fifteen Lancasters were circling the airfield at the same time, each awaiting its turn to land:

'As we headed across the airfield,' continues 'Jimmy' Bennett, 'I looked up and saw the red starboard wing-tip light of a Lancaster and I remember thinking that it shouldn't be there. The rule was to go round in the other direction. Then there was an almighty crash and a Lancaster hit the ground. When we got to the debriefing room, Nick Carter (the station commander at Waltham) told me what was happening and asked me to go with him to a village somewhere just outside Louth to help him sort out some of the mess from that night. When we arrived we found one of those wartime wooden buildings which were in the charge of an Irish nursing sister and she had had to turn it into a temporary mortuary. The crash crews were going all around North Lincolnshire and there must have been the bodies of forty or fifty lads laid out in there, down both sides of the room, all covered in service blankets. It was a terrible sight, a sight I will never forget. It was impossible to recognise some of them. All we had to go by was their identity discs.'[2]

Four Lancasters on 100 Squadron had crashed. 'H-Harry' flown by 24-year-old Flying Officer Robert Laval Proudfoot came down at Hatcliffe Top near Barnoldby-le-Beck, a small Lincolnshire village close to the Waltham airfield. Proudfoot and three of the crew were killed. The pilot left a widow, Mary Willmott Proudfoot of Brentwood. The three other members of his crew were severely injured and were taken to Grimsby Hospital.

'Q-Queenie' piloted by 21-year-old Flight Sergeant Allen James Kevis and 'F-Freddie' flown by Sergeant Gilbert Denman collided and exploded in a fireball over the village of Waithe 1 mile south of Waltham airfield at 0040 hours. Kevis and his crew perished only a few yards from Waithe House Farm where the occupants had a very narrow escape and were greatly shocked by the horrific scene that confronted them in the early hours of that morning. The rear turret had been severed from the main fuselage and still contained the body of Sergeant Thomas Edward Cain. This was the second tragedy to befall the Kevis family. Allen's 28-year-old brother Lieutenant Leslie William Kevis had been killed on the trawler HMS *Northern Princess* on 7 March 1942.

It was said that Bomber Command air crews had an average life expectancy of about six weeks, but for many like 19-year-old 'Yonker' Johnson it was much less. He would not be coming home, getting married and settling down. 'Gil' Denman, Ivan A. Redman, Hubert L. Blackwell, James William Christmas and Raymond G. Read were killed instantly when their Lancaster fell approximately half a mile away on land belonging to the Grainsby estate, only 50 yards from the Parish Church of St Nicholas. The seventh airman, Sergeant Clarence Burdett Wallace, the 20-year-old rear gunner of Stony Beach, Saskatchewan survived the impact. According to eye-witness accounts Wallace was rescued by an unknown man and was made comfortable and offered a cigarette. At that time it was not apparent just how serious his injuries were. He would die of them in hospital on 8 January 1944.

Wing Commander David Holford piloting 'N-Nuts' had nursed his badly-damaged Lancaster back, but chose to remain airborne until less experienced crews had landed. Having diverted from Waltham to Kelstern near Louth, he made his approach. 'N-Nuts' clipped a small hill and crashed. Holford was thrown from the cockpit, suffering two broken ankles. He was not found until dawn, after lying in the snow, by which time he was dead. Four of his crew also died. Later that day 'Jimmy' Bennett and his wife had the terrible responsibility of breaking the news to David Holford's wife that her husband was dead.

Eric Jones on 49 Squadron had experienced brushes with electrical thunderstorms on a few occasions, but well into the homeward journey he ran into dense cloud:

'I tried to get above it,' he wrote later, 'but with no success. Initially, it was fairly smooth going and I was, by now, quite accustomed to such flying conditions. But the going got rougher with the aircraft becoming difficult to hold on a steady course and we were flying into the heart of an electrical storm. I knew that the cloud tops would be well above the capacity of the Lanc and that the cloud base could be as low as six hundred feet. We didn't know whether it thinned out to the right or to the left so the only thing to do was to keep going until we flew out of it. We then experienced St. Elmo's fire and this occurs when the whole aircraft becomes charged with static electricity. The propellers become giant Catherine wheels and every bit of Perspex in the plane (all the windows) are framed in a blue flashing light. A scaring but fantastic experience. I had never seen anything like it before. In these conditions it was nothing for the plane suddenly to lose a few hundred feet and regain them just as quickly.

'We must have passed through a series of these storms without realising it; we were in cloud for what seemed like "forever". Ken eventually said that we were over the North Sea and should start dropping off height. This was a relief because I don't recall any icing up and to get to lower levels would help eliminate this further hazard. Once again there was no time for ration-eating and smoking over the North Sea – it was going to take all my concentration to get us all safely back to Fiskerton. I was well aware that the safety height over Lincolnshire was 1,500 feet (the height to which one could safely descend in cloud) and to break cloud below this height without knowing one's exact position was asking for trouble. So I was back with Ken Blackham my navigator and his 'Gee' fixes. When he said we were over the coast I continued to lose height below 1,500 feet. I was very conscious that Lincoln cathedral must be at least five hundred feet above sea level so I was putting implicit faith, once again, in Ken's navigational skills. Suddenly, we were out of the cloud and very low with perfect visibility and the 'Drem' systems of Lincolnshire's airfields, for miles around, formed a very welcoming scene. Sometime after debriefing, we heard of reports coming in of engines freezing up and only restarting when the aircraft reached the warmer air levels at lower altitudes.'[3]

At Bardney there was no word from 'B-Beer' on 9 Squadron piloted by 21-year-old Scottish Pilot Officer Ian Black of Aberdeen or 'Y-Yorker' flown by 20-year-old

Pilot Officer Richard Anthony Bayldon of Hove. Ian Black had taken 'B-Beer' off at 1647 hours and was last heard by Bardney Control calling on W/T at 2348 hours. The Lancaster lay smashed to pieces at Salzbergen a few kilometres north-west of Rheine with all seven crew dead. Bayldon, who had taken off four minutes before Black, had crashed at Eberswalde-Finow, 43 kilometres north-east of Berlin. All seven crew including Sergeant Raymond John Baroni, the 21-year-old Canadian mid-upper gunner born in Winnipeg, lay dead in or around the aircraft.

When the *Los Angeles Times* hit the streets back home in California there would be no mention of Baroni whose parents lived in Glendale, or of other Americans on the raid, yet; but banner headlines proclaimed: 'The attack was described in Berlin as a terror attack on a considerable scale. Well-informed circles point out that it was carried out in poor visibility. Residential quarters in the capital were hit.'

The *New York Times* reported that 'immediately after the attack Berlin broadcast a talk for overseas listeners', saying: 'The enemy will never destroy the Berlin population's will to win. Factories in Germany are working full blast to produce weapons of retaliation, which will come.'

On 619 Squadron Flight Lieutenant Anthony Herbert Tomlin DFC and Flight Sergeant Albert Edward Brookes his flight engineer were decorated for bringing their badly-damaged Lancaster home to Woodhall Spa. When nearing the target area 'F for Freddie' was attacked by fighters and one of the starboard engines was put out of action and it caught fire. Quick work by Brookes extinguished the flames and, although much height had been lost, Tomlin flew on to the target and bombed it. On the return flight Brookes displayed great engineering skill and his efforts proved of material assistance to his pilot in his endeavour to reach England. On reaching Woodhall, a second engine failed but Tomlin effected a successful crash-landing without injury to any of his crew. The citations for a bar to Tomlin's DFC and a DFM for Brookes said 'the pilot displayed outstanding determination and devotion to duty and that Brookes had displayed similar qualities and proved himself a valuable member of aircraft crew.'

Another crew which narrowly escaped joining the casualties that night was one on a 101 Squadron Lancaster at Ludford Magna in 1 Group. 'Len' Brooks, the rear gunner on a Lancaster flown by Sergeant Walter Evans, remembers that they were diverted to Driffield because of the bad weather. Over East Yorkshire they were picking up R/T messages from Driffield, Dishforth and Catfoss but could see no lights through the murk. Then Catfoss offered to put a light up for them. 'They realised we were very low and put the beam almost parallel to the ground right on us,' wrote Brooks. 'I remember feeling the power go on, the nose lift and suddenly I saw under the turret chicken huts, a garden shed and finally chimney pots flashing by. That light had saved us.'[4]

The worst-hit station in 6 Group RCAF in the Tyne Valley and North Yorkshire was Linton-on-Ouse where 426 'Thunderbird' Squadron lost four Lancasters and 408 'Goose' Squadron two. On 426 Squadron 'Y-Yorker' was shot down by a night-fighter and crashed at Hoya, Hanover and 'V-Victor' crashed at Lake Asan near Urshult in southern Sweden. The crew was interned. The crew on Lancaster DS837 piloted by 29-year-old Squadron Leader Thomas Matthew Kneale, born in Woodstock, Ontario had bombed the target and were well on their way to returning to Linton-on-Ouse, having set out from there at 1630 hours. He was the commander of 'B' Flight's seventeenth operation. The main part of the crew had flown operational flights in the Wellington before converting to fly the Lancaster and then all had flown at least fourteen operational flights on the Lancaster. During the flight the 'Gee' navigation system had stopped working. As they neared home they contacted the tower and were informed that the Linton beam transmitting equipment was unserviceable so the crew had switched to following the nearest to Linton which was East Moor airfield's beam. At 2345 hours the aircraft was flown into Yearsley village on top of a hill on the western edge of the Howardian Hills.

The crash investigation suggested that a minor error in setting the altimeter's pressure setting could have given the pilot a false reading of his actual height and combined with flying in thick fog the crew would probably have been unaware of the problem until they struck the ground possibly after leaving the beam to make a turn. Given the poor weather it is also probable that they were unaware that they were over rising ground to the east of their base, higher than that they would have been expecting over the Vale of York. Only air gunner Sergeant Gordon Charles 'Charley' Fortier, born in Montreal on 9 February 1924, survived.

Four crew on the Lancaster flown by 20-year-old Warrant Officer2 Reginald Donald Stewart of Cochrane, Ontario were killed outright when the aircraft crashed near Northlands Farm, Hunsingore in Yorkshire. Stewart had flown two 'second dickey' trips to Berlin and completed one operation in October when he had returned with technical problems. On 24 February Sergeant Duncan Stewart, the 20-year-old air gunner, died as a result of his injuries at Northallerton Hospital. The other air gunner, Sergeant Donald Sinclair Jamieson, born on 2 June 1924 in Winnipeg, Manitoba who was also injured, returned to operations at the end of January 1944. On 5 March the Lancaster he was flying on was being flown on an air test combined with a sea search of the area of North Sea off Bridlington when it hit the water and ended up being ditched. One member of the crew died. Jamieson and the other five members were rescued. On the night of 28/29 June he was flying on a Halifax on the operation on Metz, France when the aircraft was badly damaged by a night-fighter. All the crew bailed out and survived, with some managing to evade capture. Jamieson and Flying Officer Hugh Waldie Birnie, the 22-year-old navigator, were eventually caught in August 1943 but were handed over to the Gestapo at Pont-l'Évêque. Both the Canadians were taken by SS guards Harold Heyns and Herbert Koch who murdered them on either 21 or 22 August prior to an Allied advance that took the area. Jamieson and Birnie have no known grave.

On 408 'Goose' Squadron 'E-Edward', which was flown by 22-year-old Flying Officer William John Maitland DFM of Vancouver, British Columbia who was flying his first sortie of his second tour, was shot down at Heyrothsberge in Germany. There were no survivors. At 2330 hours Lancaster 'C-Charlie', better known to the crew as 'The Countess', hit a wall and outbuildings at Silver Hill 10 miles north-east of Thirsk between the villages of Boltby and Hawnby on the North York Moors. The pilot, 25-year-old Flying Officer Russell Stanley Clark of Ericsson, British Columbia and two of his crew initially survived the crash with four others killed but Clark succumbed to his injuries on 21 December. He was on his eighth trip of his second tour.

On 432 'Leaside' Squadron RCAF at East Moor two Lancasters had been shot down. 'E-Edward', which had a crew of eight and was skippered by Canadian Flying Officer Hubert Baker Hatfield, was hit by flak on the port side of the aircraft on approach to the target bombing-point. His Canadian navigator, Flying Officer Joseph Layton Higgs RAFVR, was to recall later:

'We soon found that we had lost that tank of petrol. We never carried very much extra fuel as the load was for bombs not fuel. We bombed our target and turned north for the coast and reaching the Baltic and before turning for home I had to rapidly calculate if we could make it with the fuel on board. We calculated that as we had a direct route home and would be going downhill in effect and the winds were not overly strong, we probably could get back to England with possibly fifteen minutes' fuel left. The alternative was to proceed on our northerly course and land in Stockholm, the lights of the city we could see on the horizon. It was a tough decision but everyone agreed in the end to try for home.

'It was an uneventful trip back other than continually checking on the fuel and distance situation. The target to base distance on this route was about seven hundred miles and it would normally take four and a half to five hours to complete the trip. On approach to the English coast we could see a layer of cloud, the top about five thousand feet and no idea how deep but we soon found out. We called the station requesting emergency landing due to low fuel. They advised to approach carefully as the cloud deck was only about two hundred feet. We eased our way down on the advising heading and we still could not see the flare path and pulled up into the clouds. The station then vectored us to Leeming as they said the cloud deck was better. We proceeded on instructions and broke through the clouds again and at about two hundred we saw the flare path for a few seconds and then the cloud lowered again. We were now practically on air in the fuel tanks and decided the best thing was to climb to five thousand feet, set a course for the North Sea and bail out.

'On reaching our height we were in clear moonlight and we started the bail-out procedure. Sergeant Bill Poole our RAF wireless-operator was first out of the aircraft followed by Flight Lieutenant John Allen who was with us on this operation as second pilot. Poole apparently went out of the front escape hatch the wrong way facing aft and he hit his neck on the edge of the hatch. Seeing this, Allen immediately caught Poole and pulled his ripcord otherwise he would never have made it. Alfred Phillips our flight engineer and the bomb-aimer George Smith went next and the gunners, Sergeant Robert Hutchinson RAFVR and Flight Sergeant Alexander McGregor RCAF left by the rear exit. I went through the hatch next and was followed by Hatfield.

'I watched our Lancaster flying alone but it seemed to be climbing and then it tilted over and went down into the clouds. My 'chute opened with a snap that startled me and I breathed a prayer as I too went into the clouds and started to swing and sway pulling on the shroud lines, to correct this or make it worse I could not tell. But I was aware that the land was rushing towards me and I kept looking down hoping to see something. Finally I noticed two dark stripes and my mind immediately thought 'Oh great' a river, but the next second I hit the middle of a field with a crash twisting my ankle. I was down and alive.

'Hatfield had broken his leg after landing in a small village. Poole was in bad shape and they said he would be in the hospital for some time. The rest of the crew seemed to survive without any major injuries. That was the end of our crew.'[5]

Three Lancasters on 460 Squadron RAAF did not make it back to Binbrook. Faced with difficulties, Australian Warrant Officer M. Stafford's crew had voted to attempt to make it home because of the impending fatherhood of the 23-year-old rear gunner Pilot Officer Hedley Howard Garment, who was from Ruislip. When the Lancaster crashed at Normenby in Lincolnshire, he was the only member of the crew to be killed.

Flight Sergeant Kenneth James Godwin, born in Bexley in southern Sydney on 14 October 1921, flew JB704 to Berlin and back that night. Growing up in Sydney's southern suburbs, on leaving school Ken Godwin first worked as a telegraph messenger, then as an assistant customer shipping clerk, before becoming a junior porter with the New South Wales Government Railways. At the outbreak of war in September 1939 Godwin was initially hesitant to enlist, telling a sister he would wait until 'the enemy comes along here' but in August 1941, after the death of his father that March, the 19-year-old Godwin enlisted in the Royal Australian Air Force. In the second half of 1942 he wrote to his mother about the joys of flying. 'There is nothing to be compared with it, the thrills and spills,' he wrote: 'I simply love to do aerobatics at about 400 miles an hour, first you're upside down, then on your head and the next thing you know you are on your ass again.' In July 1942 Godwin qualified as a pilot and four months later sailed to Britain. After several months in various units he was posted in October 1943 to 460 Squadron.

Despite having to feather an engine outbound over the Dutch coast Godwin continued on three at the reduced altitude of 17,000 feet to bomb Berlin. Returning short of fuel and unable to see the runway through the fog as he approached Binbrook he proposed climbing to a higher altitude so his crew could bail out, but was told to descend to a break in the clouds at 500 feet. Instead, the Lancaster crashed a few fields short of the runway, wrecking the aircraft and all but one of the crew was injured. Godwin did not fly again until late January 1943, when he was commissioned as a pilot officer. His luck would finally run out on his eighth operation on the night of 19/20 February 1944 when he and his crew were shot down by a night-fighter in the attack on Leipzig. As the Lancaster went into a dive Godwin ordered the crew to bail out. The bomb-aimer, Flight Sergeant Vern Dellit, managed to parachute safely and became a prisoner of war. He afterwards described his aircraft as 'a mass of flames heading earthward'. Witnesses on the ground later described seeing the Lancaster explode in the air and again as it crashed into Steinhudermeer Lake in Lower Saxony. Godwin and four of his crew were killed. Only Dellit and the navigator survived. Godwin's body was never recovered. He was 22 years old.

The Lancaster piloted by Flying Officer Francis Archibald Randall, a pre-war science student at the University of Sydney, returned after being damaged over Berlin. On 3/4 September Archie had crash-landed his aircraft after being shot up by a night-fighter over Berlin and eventually made a home run after escaping from Sweden. After trying for forty-five minutes to land at Binbrook, Randall radioed Binbrook to say that he had clipped a tree. Shortly afterwards the Lancaster crashed into a wood 10 miles south of the airfield runway near Market Stainton, south-west of Louth, and detonated an ammunition dump, killing everyone on the crew. Randall had learned just before the raid that he had been awarded the DFC. The flight engineer on the otherwise all-Aussie crew was 21-year-old ex-Halton apprentice Sergeant John Jack McKenzie who, despite his Scottish surname inherited from his father, had been brought up in Pembroke Dock, Wales, his mother's home town. His mother, uncle and two younger brothers had been killed in a German air-raid on the town during the early hours of 12 May 1941 and Jack wanted revenge.

Flight Sergeant (later Flight Lieutenant) L.H. Richards, the English navigator on 'D-Donald' on 460 Squadron, recalling his own feelings before and after a raid, surprised him:

'I have always been a coward and was very nervous before every operation. When an operation was scrubbed I was delighted. I dreaded, before each trip, how I would react if we got shot-up or in difficulties and my nerves were as taut as a bowstring throughout every operation. However, when we did meet trouble, to my absolute amazement, my stomach froze but I was as calm as could be, calmer than at any time throughout my tour of operations. I worked like the devil to get us back on course with what instruments were left. When we finally arrived over an airfield in England, the calmness left me and the fear returned. I was quite terrified at the thought of a crash landing and yet I had every confidence that our pilot would manage it. There was such a strange and unreal feeling of fear and confidence. Throughout our whole tour of operations I was pretty certain that we would be killed.

'All my fear and nerves were unfounded. Each operation was as uneventful as a cross-country training flight. But there was no comfort in that, I still died thirty deaths just down to cowardice. I suppose I simply couldn't see us surviving when others were not. Towards the end, say from about twenty-five operations onwards, I began to see that there was a chance that I would survive a tour. That made each operation more of a nerve-wracking experience than ever. I used to calculate the days it would take to complete the remaining operations and to say to myself if I live for just another two weeks I will live forever. Obviously I kept all this from the crew. They had great faith in my ability as a navigator and thought that this and the skill of our pilot would help get us through the tour. I think it was just luck, but the leadership of our pilot throughout was a tremendous example to each member of the crew.'

Richards' nervousness might have been a result of a crash on 22 October 1943 when his crew's Lancaster had crash-landed at Elsham on return from Kassel and was damaged beyond repair. None of Flight Lieutenant J.H. Clark's crew, including the rear gunner, Pilot Officer Roberts C. Dunstan, was injured. Dunstan had served as a sapper in the 2/8th Field Company, Royal Australian Engineers, until he was wounded on 25 May 1942 in the right knee by shrapnel from Italian artillery as Australian and British forces prepared to attack Tobruk. His right leg was eventually amputated and he was evacuated to Australia and discharged from the army aged only 18. After a brief period of inactivity he applied for air crew training in the RAAF. He was eventually selected for training as a gunner. He left Sydney for England on 24 August 1942 and was posted for operational duty as a tail gunner to 460 Squadron RAAF. He would take his crutches with him in the air and when he had to go aft would crawl there on one leg. He was commissioned as a pilot officer, awarded the DSO and completed his tour of thirty bombing operations on 3/4 November 1943, the day before his 21st birthday.

W.R.P. Perry on 106 Squadron at Metheringham shared Richards' apprehension: 'Going into the briefing room one rare sunny afternoon, the window was open. We were amazed (and shaken) when three Irish workmen (the airfield was still being completed) looked through the window and commented on 'them pretty red ribbons on that map'! They led straight to Berlin! We were not sorry when Command 'scrubbed' the op later in the day.'

On 101 Squadron, 20-year-old Pilot Officer Norman Maylin Cooper of Letchworth, Hertfordshire had taken his Lancaster off from Ludford Magna airfield around 1630 hours. On their return the crew tried to find somewhere to land as thick fog was down to ground level over most of the area of Lincolnshire and Yorkshire. Cooper was diverted north to land at Holme-on-Spalding-Moor but the aircraft crashed at 0027 hours near Howden, between Selby and Goole in East Yorkshire. It appears to have flown into the ground to the north of the village of Eastrington where it broke up. Five of the crew and the special operator were killed. Only the two air gunners survived.

On 625 Squadron at Kelstern 'A-Apple' flown by Second Lieutenant A.E. Woolley USAAF crashed into the side of a hill near Gayton-le-Wold in Lincolnshire. Two of the crew died and the injured American pilot and his four injured crew members were taken to Louth County Hospital. 'B-Baker' is believed to have crashed at Wetschen near Diepholz.

'R-Roger' was down to the last 300 gallons of fuel by the time the crew reached the coast of Lincolnshire:

'The met reports were not good,' wrote Keith Parry. 'Several bases in north Lincolnshire were closed, as were some of the fields in Yorkshire, the home of the Halifax force. We still hadn't got a forecast for "Skelly". Finally it came through: it said "clear sky, visibility 3,000 yards and frost on the runway". We were flying level at 4,000 feet with the Merlins still at 2,350, trying to save as much fuel as possible. No wife or lover was ever handled with as much care and consideration as those three engines.'

'We reached the coast without incident but well behind the rest,' wrote Don Thomas, the mid-upper gunner. 'We were far lower than we would have liked. George Harvey put the nose down and with the three good engines screaming in protest we dove out. Not a shot was fired at us. Now only the North Sea stretched between us and home. For our return Met at briefing had promised brief fog patches in low-lying areas and scattered cloud. Base, they said, would remain clear until 0200. Instead we arrived over England to find our aerodromes shrouded in fog and rain and low cloud so thick and seemingly impenetrable that from the air it looked as though the entire country had submerged beneath a vast 2,000-foot layer of curdled cream.'

'Our first sight of the coast,' wrote Keith Parry, 'was a searchlight battery, friendly of course, waving from side to side to show the returning bomber fleet the way home. It was a pleasant sight. Harvey put the navigation lights on and soon we could see the lights of other aircraft appearing out of the darkness. He contacted

"Skelly" on the VHF and, because we were on three engines, we were given a priority landing. This meant that we could join the circuit straight away without having to descend through the stack. The fuel was down to less than eighty gallons each side. We were at 2,000 feet now and could not see the ground: it was hidden beneath a bluish haze, with white patches here and there. "Blast," said Harvey. "It's fogging in." We saw an airfield beacon; it was Fiskerton: we would soon be home.'

'Reg Carver had fixed our position on the English coast with "Gee",' says Don Thomas. 'We were 25 miles north of where we should have been. As George altered course for base, inland and to the north-west the clouds glowed suddenly red as a bomber went in. A mile from the first, another crashed and exploded. Later we learned that the two aircraft had collided over their own aerodrome and that there were no survivors.

'Presently, from his curtained compartment, the navigator announced: "You should see base in five minutes." Then, when the five minutes had elapsed, "You should see base now."

'We had enough faith in Reg to know that it was there. But, except for the featureless plain of white that stretched out beneath us for as far as we could see in every direction, a solitary Lancaster down low searching and probing to find a way through and a rapidly fading oval of pink near the coast that marked the remains of yet another crashed bomber, we could see nothing at all.

'Then, out from the between the guns in the rear turret and looking like a lead half-dollar lying at the bottom of a murky well, slid the faint grey disc of the Skellingthorpe searchlight.

'George called the tower and a WAAF's crisp voice came up: "Hello 'Carlight R-Roger', 'Biddy' calling. Ceiling at base 200 feet, visibility 300 yards. Orbit at 2,500. Your turn to land is number three."

'Five minutes later we were diverted to an aerodrome miles to the north-east. But we had flown in from that direction over dense cloud and we were certain that the diversion would be cancelled. Almost immediately it was. Then the mists lifted and Einarson got down and a Lanc from 50 Squadron, before they again rolled across the field even thicker than before.

'For thirty minutes more, while the needles of the fuel gauges backed steadily towards the bottom line, control held us in the circuit waiting for the cloud to break up. But ours was not the only Lancaster still airborne, for over Waddington nav lights still patrolled and stray aircraft, lost and uncertain what to do, sometimes fell in with us for a few orbits and then wandered away to try their luck somewhere else. From the starboard beam, a Lanc eased in, an Aldis lamp in its front turret blinking a message that we could not read. "Skellingthorpe" our bomb-aimer returned and the stranger banked away.

'In contrast to the usual post-op clamour, the R/T was silent and we assumed that all of the station kites were already down or had landed elsewhere. Then Fitch and about two minutes later, Cunningham, hedge-hopped in from the coast and got in safely.

'From the rear turret Dick said: "They got down OK George. Balls to control; it's our neck. You should have flown east, come down over the sea and then tried to come back under this stuff. Balls to control."

'"Now don't you start. We were told to stay in the circuit and we did," George said. He was not the man to do anything against orders.

'"It's too late anyway," the engineer added. "We haven't the fuel."

'"How long do we have?" asked George.

'"About twenty minutes."

'"Well," said George, "we have to do something now. We can go up another couple of thousand, head her towards the sea and jump or we can ease her down slow and flat and hope we break clear before we hit the ground."

'There was an uncomfortable silence while everyone waited for someone else to speak first. Then Dick voted to jump and "Ginger" [Sergeant Noel Stephen Joseph Meehan, the wireless-operator] and an unfamiliar voice that was either the bomb-aimer or the second pilot. George was unwilling to lose another aeroplane and Reg, as always, went along with George. Ken remained silent; reluctantly I joined the jumpers. I had always wondered what it would be like to bail out. The idea had never particularly frightened me but if I had to go I would have preferred it being in my own time and in broad daylight.

'"All right skipper; we'll stay with you," somebody said. It had to be Ken.

'"That's settled then; we'll try to get down."

'It wasn't settled at all but there wasn't much that I could do about it. As George explained the situation to the ground and in reply was told to try a single let down but to pull up if still in cloud at five hundred feet, I refastened the belts and straps and wires that I had disconnected in preparation for bailing out.

'With the engineer calling out the height – the changed barometric pressure was almost certainly giving a false reading to the altimeter – George throttled back and eased the Lancaster down until we were skimming along the cloud tops. Then the wings submerged and the fuselage and for a moment the mid-upper turret and the tips of the rudders were all that remained above the surface. It was like cruising in the conning tower of a midget sub. Then the turret too went under.

'I cranked around to face the front. Braced my knees against the ammunition boxes and waited, eyes straining out and down for a first glimpse of the ground that might be brief and final. Settling down into thick cloud was far more terrifying than climbing up through it. Climbing up you knew that you must eventually break clear – and you had thousands of feet to do it. Going down you could go only so far.

'At 400 feet, still in mist and rain, George shouted, "Throttles!" The engines screamed, he hauled back on the controls and we shot up into the clear.

'Five times George nosed down into that sea of cotton wool and five times, the last time with the bomb-aimer screaming, "Trees!" at the top of his voice, he pulled up at the last moment.

'I don't know who first saw the hole; it might have been the second pilot. It began as an elongated smudge, no more than a dark crayon stroke drawn across the smooth white surface of the cloud fifteen miles north of us. George swung towards it. As we flew closer it began to take shape; now we could see that it was perfectly round, about half a mile in diameter and that it looked like a steam bubble in a huge kettle of porridge. And we could also see that the edges were folding in and that it was closing up.

'Other crews too had seen it and navigation lights turned and raced north. With aircraft converging from a half dozen aerodromes in the area, I thought that there might be one unholy bang when everyone arrived over the hole at the same time. But we got there first. We popped down through and I could almost hear the clouds bang shut behind us.

'But we weren't much better off for now it was pitch dark and we were in heavy rain. A spray of water drove through the circular ventilation ports in my turret and ran down my neck. I closed the ports but the Perspex misted over and I had to twist them open again.

'George made a flat turn to the south-west. From not more than 150 feet I looked down into fenced back yards and at rows of soggy laundry. Roads, fields, roofs, trees, flashed by. For a while we followed a road and then turned off to follow a line of railroad tracks that Reg thought led to Lincoln. Then the tracks ended or we lost them.

'We roared across the wet, dripping roofs of a small village almost knocking the chimneys from the peaks. A window shade thrown suddenly up revealed behind it a lighted room, a brass bed and someone sitting bolt upright in the bed. The village left behind, mist closed momentarily around us as George pulled up to hurdle a raised canal bank and then dropped down on the other side.

'"How's the fuel?" I heard him ask.

'"We ran out five minutes ago," Ken answered.

'Ahead was a solid-looking wall of white. There was no going under it for it hung down and merged with the ground. We hurtled into it. I had never known cloud to be so dense; even the wingtip lights were blotted out. And in the utter blackness I could see that the metal cowlings of the engines were glowing red hot. In sixty seconds we were through and someone shouted, "Hell, that wasn't cloud; that was snow!" Another flurry loomed up but George edged around it.

'And then we were diagonally across a lighted runway. To starboard and if anything slightly above us, I saw the lighted windows of the control tower and three people, one of them a WAAF for I could see her fluffed-out hair, standing and looking down at us.

'"That I take it was Wickenby. Skipper, turn about fifteen degrees starboard."

'Reg, having no use now for his chart, had left his table and was standing behind the engineer trying to map-read. His calmness was surprising. I think that he had forgotten that Lincoln Cathedral sat perched on its high hill somewhere ahead of us. I hadn't. Neither apparently had Dick.

'"Don't forget Lincoln bloody cathedral and that damn hill," he said. He occupied the most unenviable position of all for, riding backwards, he could hear the shouted warning about trees, buildings and hills but he could see them only when they were safely behind us.

'"Dick, I do wish you wouldn't swear in every sentence. I know about the Cathedral," George said quietly.

'"Yes George."

'We passed over a brightly glowing white light. Ahead was another; beyond that a third and a fourth.

'"We're in somebody's circuit," Reg said. "It should be Skellingthorpe."

'George called control. "Hello 'Biddy'! Hello 'Biddy'! This is 'Carlight R-Roger'. We are somewhere north of the field. Do you hear us? Over."

'There was a pause and then "Affirmative 'R-Roger'. We hear you on bearing three-four-zero."

'"Thank you 'Biddy'. We are at a hundred and fifty feet on finals. We are on three engines and low on fuel. Coming straight in."

'"Pancake 'R-Roger'. Pancake." The reply was immediate.

'Using the circuit lights as stepping stones, we picked our way around to the landing funnel and turned in. But for some reason George had trouble lining up with the runway and as we settled down I could see the flarepath drift from starboard to port.

'"Overshooting!" George shouted. "Full throttle! Flaps and wheels up!"

'As the Lancaster staggered along the runway barely above stalling but slowly picking up flying speed, Ken said quietly: "I don't think you can go around again. Better land this time."

'George again picked up the Drem lights and swung port. Below us something was burning on the ground with a white glare. It looked like a four-pound incendiary.

'I tried to remember what lay beneath us; what we would hit if the engines – or even a single remaining engine – should suddenly stop. But all that I could think of was our ground crew waiting huddled around the fire in their little shack. Probably they could hear us overhead but they could not know who it was. Poor sods; their night watch was nearly over. In a few minutes they would know whether they had to tie down DV399 and in the morning stencil a yellow bomb on her black nose – or break in a new aeroplane and crew.'

'Harvey called for 15° of flap, wheels down and 2,850 rpm,' recalled Keith Parry. 'We followed the Drem and it led us to the funnel. Left into the funnel, 30° of flap and the flare path came into view. We were in a double green, just right for a three-engined landing. In the threshold Harvey said, "Your throttles – slow cut", and I eased them back. The Merlins coughed and spluttered as the power came off. The big smooth Palmer tyres kissed the runway and we were down. It was perfect.'

To 'Don' Thomas it was as if the landing was on glass: 'Only when the tail dropped and we began to rumble along the uneven concrete did we know we were down. At the end of the runway an airman, his black rubber raincoat shining wet, waved us to the left with a red-lensed flashlight. A van, a large illuminated board painted in diagonal black and yellow stripes fixed to its rear bumper, waited to guide us to our dispersal. Although it was unlikely that anyone else would be landing behind us, George reported to control: 'Roger clear of runway.'

'And then the remaining starboard engine stopped. It just belched a long tongue of flame and a cloud of white smoke from its exhaust stacks, kicked the prop back once and stopped dead.

'That's cutting it fine! That's cutting it too bloody fine!' the engineer said.

'George shut down the port engines. 'That's it! They can tow it the rest of the way,' he said.

'To an airman there is no greater silence than when, after a long difficult flight the engines are closed down. For at least a full minute we sat there, the 'plane rocking gently in the strong wind that blew across the airfield, the only sound the rain beating down on the wings and fuselage and the mild crackling from the slowly cooling Merlins. Then belts were unbuckled, loose gear stowed away in bags, guns unloaded, 'chutes taken from storage and the crew began moving stiffly and noisily towards the rear exit. Just being able to stand up after so many hours in one position was wonderful. When I dropped down into the fuselage I felt dizzy and staggered a little; my legs and lower body were numb. But I was the first one out of the aircraft and I waited by the tail for the others.

'Like the bad penny,' I said when they joined me.

'They did not answer. Deafened by the eight-hour roar of the engines and with their minds filled with the fresh memory of the flight, they might not have heard me. It had been our twentieth operation as a crew.

'We had been airborne for eight hours and ten minutes,' recalled Keith Parry. 'We turned off at the end of the runway and came to a halt. I shut down the port outer and we taxied slowly back to dispersal on the inboards. Harvey swung the aircraft round onto our pan, the marshaller held his wand across his throat and we shut down the two remaining engines. As the propellers came to a standstill, the silence was shattering. We sat there for a few seconds trying to adjust to it and then climbed slowly and stiffly from our seats, made our way down along the fuselage and out onto the concrete of the pan. It felt firm and good beneath my feet.'

Once over the North Sea Joe Northrop had brought 'F-Freddie' down below oxygen level:

'Navigator Charlie Burdett passed me the last of the coffee from the crew thermos and lit me an illegal cigarette; it tasted good. We crossed the English coast seen on the H2S scope and wireless-operator Gerry Hoey identified. We shook off more height as we headed over home territory for base and I switched on the beam approach set to check that it was functioning. It was a relief to hear the old familiar Morse signals coming through loud and clear as there was no sign of a break in the grey mass below in any direction, and the beam was our only let-down aid.

'The only facilities available to bomber crews in really bad weather, apart from a few homing and navigational aids, were the standard Beam approach installations used at base airfields separately or in emergency, in conjunction with the FIDO [Fog Investigation and Dispersal Operation] equipment installed on the emergency landing strips on the coast at Woodbridge, Manston and Carnaby. Many of the wartime bomber pilots had little more than a few hundred flying hours experience; on operations they had to fly long distances at night and in bad weather, much further than most pilots ever flew before the war, and also suffer enemy attacks, cold and discomfort, fatigue and fear as a matter of routine. For example, after one of the earlier attacks on Berlin in November half the squadron air gunners were out of action with frostbitten faces, fingers and toes; the next night we had to borrow half-trained gunners from the training units to make up the crews. Later on, electrically-heated flying kit became available for gunners.

'Pilots too had their problems. Although every opportunity was taken to practise SBA approaches during air tests or practises in Oxfords, or in simulation on the Link trainer, the lengthy process of homing on the 'cone of silence' over the transmitter and flying accurate procedure patterns required a high standard of skill and no little experience. Not only that, but as many as twenty or thirty aircraft might have to get down using the beam in the space of an hour or so before they ran out of fuel. On such a night, a single pilot unable to cope could play havoc with the stacking and positioning of other aircraft in the circuit. These thoughts ran through my mind as we approached Wyton airfield, at which stage Flying Control passed routine landing information and instructed us to join the stack of Lancasters already milling around above the overcast. Due to the economies in fuel consumption achieved on the return flight we had a fair amount of fuel in reserve and a plan for landing. I intended to start my approach on SBA well above the fog layer, the top of which was around 1,200 feet; then, with all cockpit checks done except for final flap, I would be able to concentrate on flying the aircraft accurately on a straight approach and let-down.

'The stack of aircraft dwindled slowly until at last I was given No 1 to land. At this time Control warned me to watch out for an unidentified aircraft in the circuit attempting to land visually. I acknowledged and alerted the crew to keep their eyes peeled as I flew the aircraft well out from the outer marker beacon, carrying out landing checks on the way and started a procedure turn to bring the aircraft on a straight approach to the main runway. When lined up in the centre of the beam I let down the aircraft into the rather turbulent upper layer of fog and mist at a constant rate of descent until the altimeter read six hundred feet, at which stage I applied power to maintain height until the outer marker signal was heard. I then continued to descend keeping in the centre of the beam and listening for the inner marker signal. At this moment, with the altimeter showing around 200 feet, we received the full impact of the slipstream of another aircraft which suddenly crossed our path from the port side in a steep turn, its port wingtip almost scraping the mid-upper turret and nearly causing the gunner to throw a fit.

'Our aircraft plunged madly and lost height (we found afterwards that it had actually ploughed through the upper branches of some trees in the area) and I slammed the throttles fully open to emergency boost to keep us from hitting the ground. For what seemed ages 'Freddie' literally hung on its props: then, as the engineer retracted the undercarriage and the speed began to build up, it started to climb through the murk to temporary safety, bearing one very shattered crew aloft.

'Once above the fog I called Control and let them know in no uncertain terms what had happened. They replied that an unidentified aircraft had just crashed near the funnel and was on fire. It was later found to be an aircraft of my flight ['K-King', flown by 21-year-old Australian Pilot Officer Francis Eric McLean, fated to be killed on a trip to Brest on 14 August 1944 while still with 83 Squadron] who, after sustaining flak damage over the target that had put all his communications equipment out of action, had been trying to land visually. During what must have been his final despairing attempt he had flown the aircraft into the ground and almost taken us along with him.

'K-King' clipped a tree and eventually came down in a ploughed field before careering towards a brick wall with a ditch in front of it. The ensuing collision sent the Lancaster's four engines spinning in all directions, shattered the fuselage in three parts and ripped the wings away from the fuselage. Then the wreck caught fire, triggering explosions of ammunition, signal cartridges and petrol. McLean later commented that the bomber's biggest remaining piece 'could fit snugly within the confines of a billiard table'.[6]

'Safe for the moment at least, I turned back on the beam to take us on a reciprocal course over Wyton. The airfield was now identifiable by the flickering red glow of an aircraft burning on the ground seen through the murk.

'At this moment, hearing my engines no doubt, Control called me up again to ask for my fuel state. I replied that although I had a good hour's endurance in hand, in the light of what had happened I hadn't the least intention of attempting another landing until all other aircraft were out of the way and the circuit was clear of hazards. With that I broke off contact and stayed in the clear atmosphere around 5,000 feet to practise simulated let-downs on the beam for a while. After half an hour or so, having simmered down to some extent, I called up Control again, much to the relief of the controller. He then informed me that I was the only pilot in the group still airborne and gave me No. 1 to land. I looked at my watch and calculated that we had been in the air for just on eight hours as against our estimated time of flight of around seven; it was obviously time to land.

'Once again we repeated the landing procedure up to the point over the inner marker which had almost proved fatal for us, and carried on with the descent from there, still entirely on instruments and keeping our fingers crossed. The engineer and the navigator, who were both standing up and peering ahead, saw the first of the runway lights flash under the port wheel simultaneously and yelled out. I pulled everything back, prayed, and 'Freddie' sank gently down through the last few feet, to touch down with one wheel on the runway and one off.

'What matter – we were down in one piece.'[7]

Flight Sergeant Tony Lindsay, 'King's New Zealand navigator was thrown 50 feet in front of the aircraft. He was badly burned about the face and sustained a broken arm and a broken ankle. Yet despite these injuries he dragged himself back to the wreckage, where he braved both the intense heat and blazing petrol in order to help extricate Flight Sergeant Vincent Gregory Tankard, the 23-year-old Australian bomb-aimer, and the flight engineer who were trapped and seriously injured. Lindsay then helped move them to safety, a feat that later saw him awarded the BEM. Unfortunately, Sergeant Charles Clifford Reid and Vincent Tankard died of their injuries during the morning of the 17th in Ely Hospital. Tankard was due to marry his English girlfriend later that week. Flight Lieutenant McLean DFC and his crew were killed on a daylight raid on Brest eight months later, on 14 August 1944. Tony Lindsay returned to flying duties on 635 Squadron, completed thirty operations and flew with Peter de Wesselow, Master Bomber on the Dresden raid in February 1945.

No. 1, 6 and 8 Groups were particularly badly affected by the bad weather and those who made it home did so by the skin of their teeth. No. 1 Group south of the Humber in north Lincolnshire had lost thirteen aircraft. Near Diepholz ED411 and crew on 166 Squadron at Kirmington were shot down by Feldwebel Rudolf Frank of 6./NJG 3, flying a Ju 88 C-6. The pilot, 22-year-old Flight Lieutenant Peter Walter Robert Pollett, a law graduate before enlistment, had only just received his promotion a few days before on 27 November. The crew was on only their ninth operation.

Another two Lancasters and fourteen men on 166 Squadron were lost when the returning bombers found North Lincolnshire shrouded in low cloud and fog. It was a minute before midnight when Lancaster 'N-Nan' in the hands of 22-year-old Sergeant Stanley F. Miller of Scarborough emerged from low cloud just north of Caistor at the end of an eight-hour round trip from Kirmington. A month earlier, on 18/19 November, the crew's first operation to Berlin must have been one of the most dramatic combat baptisms for any crew on their first operation. After bombing successfully through cloud before turning for home, their Lancaster was hit by radar-directed flak which damaged the port wing and rear turret and they were then attacked by a formation of eight Ju 88s but had managed to reach the temporary safety of cloud before they were attacked again fifteen minutes later as they came up through overcast. Now, as Fred Miller pierced the murk over Lincolnshire there was barely time to register what was happening before the Lancaster struck high ground. When rescuers arrived they found no survivors. Miller, who had been married for barely four months, was buried in his home town.

'S-Sugar' piloted by 23-year-old Sergeant Arthur Edward Brown of Ipswich, Suffolk had outrun the German night-fighters, but on return crashed in open land near Little Walk Farm at Thornton Curtiss between Elsham and Goxhill. All seven crew were killed.

In 8 Group five Lancasters on 405 'Vancouver' Squadron RCAF managed to land back at Gransden Lodge. Last to land was Reg Lane who used the beam, but even taxiing was difficult because the visibility was so poor. He groped his way round the airfield until he knew that he was in the vicinity of the control tower and then shut down his engines. Furious, he ran up into the control tower and said: 'For Christ's sake, why haven't you diverted everybody – what's wrong with you? For crying out loud, we shouldn't be landing here; we're going to have crashes all over the place!' Lane told them that he had 'only just made it'. 'I'm sorry sir,' said the controller. 'There isn't a base open in England; this is right across the country.' Lane said: 'Oh my God, my God! Well, I didn't know what the hell to do; there was nothing I could do.'[8]

Five aircraft were sent to Graveley near Cambridge, where it was thought that the newly-equipped FIDO equipment would help them and two aircraft were sent to Marham where the cloud base was slightly higher. At 0050 hours 'D-Donald' piloted by 26-year-old Canadian Flying Officer Burus Alexander McLennan, who was on his seventeenth trip, crashed in a potato field at Ingle's Farm just outside the village of Yelling near Ely after the Lancaster ran out of petrol while attempting a second landing at Graveley. Rear gunner Warrant Officer2 S.H. Clair Nutting DFM who was on his forty-fifth and final trip was the only crew member to survive the crash. His pilot, rushed to hospital barely alive, died of his injuries at 8.10 am on 17 December. Left to mourn his memory were his mother, his sister Mrs Ruth Morrison of Victoria and a nephew, Burns Morrison.

At 2358 hours 'O-Oboe' captained by 25-year-old Flight Lieutenant William Cosmo Allan of Toronto crashed 2 miles south-east of Graveley. Three men on his crew including Sergeant Gerald Strang were killed and the rest injured. Allan died of his injuries in hospital in Oxford on 28 December. At 0225 it was reported that 'R-Robert' had crashed near Marham and that four of the crew including Bob Bessent – not yet 19 – and 'Sandy' Saunders were killed and Flying Officer 'Ed' Drew was seriously injured. Only Sergeant L. McCrae was uninjured.

In the early hours of 17 December Bill Bessent was told about the crash and the tragic news that his twin brother and Gerald Strang had both been killed. Their funerals and those of the other 405 Squadron men who had died took place at Cambridge City Cemetery on 22 December. On 24 December Bill flew his first and only op on 405 Squadron. The op was to Berlin. Before going on that trip he was called into Group Captain Johnny Fauquier's office and asked if he was ready to fly so soon after the funeral. 'If his crew was flying, he'd be flying with them,' he said. Bill and the crew were posted to 426 Squadron at Linton-on-Ouse after that first trip where they completed their tour on 11 August 1944.

'Q-Queenie' flown by 22-year-old Flight Lieutenant David Brill of Corsham, Wiltshire was the only Lancaster on 97 Squadron to fall over enemy territory that night, all eight men being killed. Arthur William Weston, who had missed this operation due to illness, was killed on 10 May 1944. However, as Doug Curtis on 97 Squadron says:

'The worst part of this night's horror was waiting for us back in England. It was obvious as soon as we neared the coast of England that we were in trouble. A blanket of fog extended as far as the eye could see. The whole country was covered. The only clear airfields were too far away for anyone to reach as most aircraft were almost out of fuel. Aircraft began to stack up over the area that they assumed was base and waited for instruction from the ground. We were number three or four so were told to orbit and wait our turn. Preference was given to those with wounded on board or those about to run out of fuel.

'While orbiting we listened in to two of our crews, Pilot Officer 'Smitty' Smith and Flying Officer Mooney DFM, who had pushed their fuel to the limit and now had no option but to point toward the North Sea and jump for it. All fourteen landed safely and were soon rounded up by the Home Guard.'

'Y-Yorker' and the crew skippered by 'Smitty' Smith, who was on his first operation, bailed out after running short on fuel and the aircraft came down close to the North Sea at Iken Common near Sudbourne, Suffolk on land that had been requisitioned for tank training. Mooney and the crew on 'S-Sugar' bailed out safely over Ely and Wyton, the aircraft finally going down in the North Sea. A fortnight later, on New Year's Day, Mooney's crew was killed when their aircraft was hit by flak near Aachen on the trip to Berlin.

'As for us,' said Doug Curtis, 'we could do nothing but continue to orbit until at last we heard the welcome words, "'X-X-ray', you may pancake." We prayed that we could do just that. "Jimmy" began a very slow, painful let-down. Navigator "Mort" Moriarty read off the elevation as we kept dropping while the rest of us peered through the muck hoping to see the ground or anything recognisable before it hit us too hard. It was like sitting in a giant ball of cotton batting. Even though "Mort" was calling off the altitude, we all knew that it didn't take much of a variance to put us into the turf but it gave him something to do. After what seemed like an eternity as we got closer to being either down or dead, "Jimmy" spotted the deck and dropped the kite straight down with a hell of a wallop. We were down but rolling into Lord knows what. "X-X-ray" bounced violently so we knew that we were not on tarmac; it felt more like a ploughed field. At last we came to a halt and in less time than it takes to tell we were out on the ground alive, something that only a short time before we felt might not come to pass. It took several minutes for the thought to sink in that we had actually come through that pea soup and were standing on terra firma.

'We soon became aware of two reddish glows reflecting on the fog that we assumed were prangs and in fact they were. Suddenly a Lanc roared directly over our heads, so close that we were able to make out his starboard green as it dipped, hit the ground and cartwheeled off into the fog in a flash of flame. You knew in that split second that seven men had died. There but for the grace of God go I. After a short while we made out a slight glow moving in our direction. All seven of us blew on our whistles to direct the truck our way. We were so relieved at arriving back in one piece that we hopped on board not really caring where we ended up. A few moments later the WAAF driver dropped us off at the interrogation room. She must have had a built-in compass to be able to navigate in those conditions.'

It was just before midnight when Charles Owen and the crew of 'V-Victor' arrived over Bourn. He wrote later that

'the target was clear and we could see fires burning from an attack on the previous night. Hundreds of searchlights and very heavy flak, firing mainly into the cones.... Flew over Hanover by mistake on return journey and was coned for seven minutes; lost height from 20,000 to 13,000 feet during evasive action.... Several holes in starboard wing and roof of cockpit and the bomb-aimer wounded slightly in the leg.... Also attacked by fighter when coned, but only damage was six inches knocked off one blade of the starboard outer prop.'

In classic understatement, he said that 'the trip generally "was quieter than usual – 10/10ths cloud over target and rather less flak than usual"! But on the long trip back all the aircraft's navigation aids had stopped working.' The navigator, Bill Shires, recalled:

'We had a radio receiver, but no transmitter, so we couldn't ask for a course. I got 'Dougie' Knowles, the wireless-operator to turn the D/F aerial round so it was facing forward and we homed in on one of the transmitters, which luckily was not jammed. Charles Owen had been a flying instructor and he was good at side-slipping so we side-slipped in and still landed way up the runway, but fine.'

'Tom' Leak the bomb-aimer, who at 30 was the old man of the crew, recalled: 'Tension was beginning to build up and cloud base beginning to drop and we began to wonder if we ever would land. Then eventually one aircraft got down, but the runway wasn't cleared. By this time our pilot was getting anxious and we were also wondering about the position of the petrol. So he said, 'Well, look, lads, I'm going to land.' Bill Shires got very concerned and said, 'If you land without permission, this could be a court-martial.'

'Yes, and if we don't try to land it could be a coffin for us,' said Owen.

'So the navigator called out again; he said: 'But the runway's not clear, there's an aircraft still on the runway.'

'Oh well,' Charles Owen said, 'we'll have to take that chance.'

'The pilot realised that this was a desperate position and that if we didn't do something we never would get down. Meanwhile, all the other aircraft were circling around and he came down low and we could just see one or two of the perimeter lights at a time, but it was very difficult to see much. And he came in and Sergeant

D.E. Lacey the flight engineer helped him to try and pick out the flare path and we landed with a terrific bump and shot up in the air, but it was the best landing we ever made.'

Charles Owen's entry in his log book reads: 'Homed on to base on SBA, breaking cloud at 250 feet to find fog, rain and visibility about three hundred yards and deteriorating. R/T then packed up, so after circling for ten minutes at 200 feet landed without permission in appalling conditions. Six other aircraft landed at base, three landed away, three crews bailed out when they ran out fuel, four crashed when trying to land and one was missing. Quite a night.'[9]

In fact only eight landed safely back at Bourn. Five made it down after being diverted to other airfields, five crashed and two crews bailed out when they ran out of fuel. Twenty-eight men lost their lives on English soil and four more were so severely injured that they never flew again.

'F for Freddie' piloted by 27-year-old Squadron Leader Donald Forbes MacKenzie DFC, a small reserved Scot, crashed at Two Pots Farm opposite the main entrance to Bourn airfield on the main Bedford to Cambridge road. MacKenzie and Pilot Officer John Towler Pratt DFM, the 22-year-old married flight engineer were killed. John Pratt had joined the RAF in 1939. Prior to this he assisted his father who farmed at Gisburn before going to Clitheroe and becoming a cattle and poultry dealer. Flying Officer William Alfred Colson DFM, the 28-year-old bomb-aimer who had flown a full tour on Whitleys and another on Wellingtons and Lancasters, died standing in for Ivor Glynn Stephens, the crew's usual bomb-aimer. 'Willy' Colson had been a bricklayer before the war. On an earlier operation his aircraft had been blown onto its back by a flak shell. During the inverted dive that followed he rendered invaluable assistance to the pilot in righting the machine, for which he was awarded the DFM. He left a wife and two small children.

Navigator Flight Sergeant Robert Marshall and rear gunner Flight Sergeant Keith Kirby, who were seriously injured, wireless-operator Flight Sergeant Tony Hunter and the mid-upper gunner Flight Sergeant William Robert Lang, both injured, were taken to hospital or to the station sick quarters. The medical officer diagnosed that Marshall had a fractured tibia and fibula and shock, and Keith Kirby had internal injuries and shock. Hunter had lacerations of the scalp and Lang abrasions and lacerations of the face. The fractures were splinted and the burns and lacerations dressed, but as soon as possible Lang, Marshall and Hunter were sent on to Addenbrooke's Hospital in Cambridge in one of the station's ambulances. Kirby, because of his injuries, was taken to the specialist RAF hospital at Ely, where he was found to be suffering from a fractured spine.

Flying blind over Bourn, Flying Officer Ted Thackway looked for a familiar spot to crash-land. Circling round and round at 0042 hours a dull glow could be seen. A Lancaster had just crashed on the edge of the airfield. It was MacKenzie's burning aircraft. 'K-King' was flying at 110 mph and was now down to just 50 feet. Visibility was around 150 yards. Then as 'K-King' got lower and lower the thick mist seemed to part slightly and almost immediately they flew through a hedge and made a perfect landing in a field near Highland Farm to the east of the airfield, but as the Lancaster thundered across the rough ground the undercarriage collapsed. 'K-King' broke apart and caught fire. Two crew were killed instantly.

Just at that moment, Sergeant Sidney Mathews, the flight mechanic on 'K-King's ground crew, was sneaking back to base on his bicycle after an illicit night in Cambridge with his girlfriend. He heard a terrific noise and a glow from several fires. Throwing down his bicycle, he jumped over a gate and stared at the horrific scene before him. Suddenly from out of the flames appeared Leslie Laver with just small cuts and abrasions. The rear gunner was in shock, but he and Sidney Mathews went back to rescue Joe Mack who had lost consciousness and was trapped in the shattered fuselage. The fire spread to a link of .303 ammunition and it began to detonate. One round smacked into Mack's arm, breaking it before exiting cleanly out the other side. It was enough to snap him back into the land of the living and he felt the metal all around him heating up and flurries of small white-hot sparks settling on his face. The next thing Mack remembered was being pulled out by Leslie Laver and Sidney Mathews. They then went back for Ted Thackway. He was a big man and they had considerable difficulty in extricating him from the burning Lancaster, but they eventually succeeded and they laid him down near a hedge. Unfortunately, he had suffered appalling injuries and he died while cradled in Sidney Mathews' arms.

Sitting down next to Ted Thackway's limp body Leslie Laver persuaded Joe Mack to have a morphine shot from the medical kit he had just salvaged from the wreckage. Sidney now suggested that he should summon help immediately and he ran off into the fog to find his discarded bicycle. Just over an hour after the crash had occurred he could hear voices in the gloom and he led them to the scene of the crash.[10] George Grundy, Jack Powell, Tony Lawrence and 'Sandy' Grant lay dead in the wreckage. Joe Mack never returned to operational flying. Leslie Laver was grounded for a month and then on 14/15 January he lost his life on the trip to Brunswick when flying for the first time with another crew skippered by Flight Lieutenant Kenneth Munro Steven DFC. Sidney Mathews was subsequently awarded the British Empire Medal for his brave actions in rescuing crew members on 'K-King'.

'Ernie' Deverill piloting 'P-Peter' crashed at Graveley after asking, 'Can I have a crack at your FIDO?' Warrant Officer James Benbow DFM, the mid-upper gunner, was the only survivor. He was taken to Ely RAF hospital suffering from second-degree burns to his face and hands and a fractured tibia and fibula and was then admitted to East Grinstead for further treatment as one of Sir Archibald McIndoe's 'guinea pigs'. He was not discharged until April 1945 pending the imminent birth of his son Peter. McIndoe asked Benbow to return later for further surgery, but he never did; he never fully recovered from the effects of his severely broken leg and needed a built-up shoe. 'Ernie' Deverill, a veteran of more than 100 operations, was posthumously awarded the Air Force Cross. He is buried in the churchyard in the Norfolk village where he married in the summer of 1940. He left a widow, Joyce (Burgis) of North Farm, Docking. Joyce never remarried.

Australian Flight Sergeant Ian MacDonald Scott and crew on 'C-Charlie' crashed near Papworth St. Agnes more than a mile from the airfield, all being killed. It was the 20-year-old Australian pilot's second operation. Navigator Flight Sergeant Samuel Joseph Peek had replaced Flight Sergeant Pinkney on the Berlin flight this night. Three-quarters of an hour later at just past midnight 'R-Roger' captained by

Pilot Officer James Kirkwood crashed into Hayley Wood close to the perimeter of Gransden Lodge airfield in deserted farmland during an attempt to land there, where conditions were no better than at Bourn, and was not discovered until quarter to eight on the Friday morning, with the entire crew dead around or inside it. They had only been posted from 207 Squadron to the Pathfinders on 27 November. During the evening of 17 December Kirkwood's wife Margaret, living with their young son (also James) in Kilwinning in Ayrshire, Scotland, the town where James, born in 1915, had spent much of his youth, received the dreaded telegram notifying her that he had been killed on operations. James was posthumously awarded the Distinguished Flying Cross and Margaret went to Buckingham Palace to receive it from the king on 5 March 1945.

All told on 17 December 97 Squadron lost seven Lancasters in crashes with twenty-eight men killed and seven injured. The losses could have been even higher. Flight Lieutenant Jeff Pelletier's crew on 'U-Uncle' had managed to fend off an attacking Ju 88 at 1853 hours and get back to Bourn without a scratch. They landed back at 0005 hours. The skipper and his crew were welcomed by Squadron Leader Eric Cawdery's crew on 'T-Tommy' on their entrance to the 'B' Flight debriefing room, sharing a mutual delight in having survived. Sergeant Arthur Tindall recalled that it was the crew's longest trip ever to Berlin. 'By the time we landed at Bourn we were airborne for seven hours 45 minutes compared with usual Berlin raids of six to six and a half hours.' It was 0035 hours when the crew landed after their third attempt. Cawdery had handed Flight Lieutenant Ernest Clarke control sometime before the end of the trip so that he could get some practice. Clarke muffed the first two attempts to land using SBA (Standard Beam Approach) and then offered to let Cawdery take over the controls. Cawdery, with supreme coolness of nerve, replied 'No, you've got the practice in now' and at his last attempt Clarke landed the Lancaster without mishap. 'The following morning,' says Tindall, 'our ground crew said that we had less than fifty gallons of petrol. In other words, we were lucky to have made it.'[11]

The crew on 'N-Nan' flown by 20-year-old Flight Sergeant William Darby Coates had a close call over Berlin at 19,500 feet when incendiaries dropped from an aircraft above hit the port wing, front turret and amidships and set the Lancaster on fire. The crew was ordered to put on their parachutes as Coates put 'N-Nan' into a dive in an attempt to dislodge the burning incendiaries. This action toppled the DR compass, upsetting all the instruments connected to it. However, the fires were extinguished and they climbed back up to 21,000 feet. Some while later 'Nan' was hit by flak which damaged the propeller tips of the starboard inner engine. One of the tips went through the fuselage cutting the hydraulic pipelines and another piece damaged the tailplane. The starboard outer engine was also hit and with power lost in both motors on the starboard side, they had to be closed down.

Still 20 miles from the Danish coast and losing height, the captain ordered everyone to take up ditching positions while the wireless-operator Sergeant Bill Chapman sent out an SOS. This call was eventually cancelled after Coates and his Welsh flight engineer, Bertram Horace Nicholas, managed to coax 'Nan' into maintaining a height of 5,000 feet if they flew at a steady speed of 120 knots. On arriving in the vicinity of Bourn, Coates found weather conditions which made it impossible to land so he was diverted to Marham, who in turn sent him to the FIDO airfield at Downham Market where the cloud base was down to 400 feet and visibility bad. Nevertheless, Coates made a perfect landing using the emergency air system for lowering the wheels. For his devotion to duty and superb captaincy he was awarded the DFM.

Flight Lieutenant Charles Thomas Wilson got 'Z-Zebra' down at ten minutes to midnight, but was too far down the runway and it seemed he would not avoid a collision. In desperation he swung the aircraft to one side but relief was only temporary. Finally, as the engines roared and the tyres squealed in protest the Lancaster struck a transformer violently, sideways on, the point of impact being just above the tail wheel. The rear gunner, Flight Sergeant Horace John Pleydell, narrowly escaped injury when the tail section was ripped off on the port side and twisted back at right angles to the main fuselage. By the time the aircraft had finally jolted to a halt, Pleydell had decided that enough was enough. In his hurry to get out of the Lancaster, no doubt thinking with good reason that it was likely to catch fire, he used his axe to hack his way out of the gun turret.

The crew was lost without trace on 29 January 1944 on Berlin and they are commemorated at Runnymede. Charles Wilson, who was aged 33 at the time of his death, was awarded a posthumous DFC, which was accepted at Buckingham Palace by his mother Alice, his widow and his daughter Christine. The 33-year-old navigator, Flight Lieutenant George Wilson Syme Borthwick, also died. His DFC award was gazetted posthumously on 11 February 1944.

As 'Jimmy' Billing's crew entered the interrogation room, two other crews, none of whom they recognized, were being interrogated:

'We assumed that they had touched down at Bourn,' wrote Doug Curtis, 'and you can imagine our surprise when we were told that we were the visitors, having landed at Graveley. After that flight we would have been happy to have landed anywhere. Graveley had had a full list out that night and were not against taking in the odd stray. As a matter of fact three of our crews managed to touch down at Graveley and were bloody glad to have done so. Following our session with the intelligence officer we were pointed toward our eggs and bacon and a spare cot where we were able to log a much-needed forty winks. Later in the morning we were given a few gallons of fuel and made our way back to Bourn. There we were apprised of just how costly the raid had been. Our squadron had taken a dreadful beating. We suffered the highest losses with 28 killed and seven injured, plus Brill's crew lost over the continent. To all of those involved it will always be remembered as "Black Thursday".'

At Skellingthorpe Bob West and 'Yorker's crew on 61 Squadron had got away from Berlin and had just missed Rostock before flying on, across Denmark and out over the North Sea. There had been lots of flak on the Danish coast, but although Bob had come down several thousand feet to help Frank Langley who was suffering with oxygen problems they dived through the barrage without a scratch and Langley gradually returned to normal except that his electrical suit did not work and he was very cold. They carried on until just off the coast near Cromer where the cloud was only 700 feet high so West remained higher until they got back to Skellingthorpe. Base gave them the No. 7 position and they came in to make a 'wizard' landing at about 1239 hours. 'Yorker's ground crew cheered them in and the crew soon got down to breakfast after interrogation, eventually getting into bed at 2.45 am. They would sleep soundly until 1215, have lunch and clean up the inside of 'Yorker' before Allen Beetch and 'Bunny' Clark caught the bus for Lincoln. They had some Welsh rarebit and chips in Boots' café before going to see the film *Bataan* at the Ritz, which 'Bunny' Clark felt was 'quite a bloodthirsty picture'!

Keith Parry joined George Harvey's crew who had moved away from the aircraft and stood in a group, waiting for the crew bus. He was included in the banter and the cigarettes, conscious of the fact that he was now a fully paid-up member of this strange fraternity whose life expectancy revolved around a ten o'clock phone call.

'The bus pulled into the pan and we climbed aboard. It was a Dodge, dimly lit inside with three small blue lights. The air was thick with cigarette smoke, the tips glowing in the gloom, in which the faces were barely recognisable. We were greeted with a great deal of ribaldry, mostly to do with the lengths some people would go to get a priority landing. We drove off to debriefing. Just inside the door of the debriefing room were two or three large urns of tea and coffee and the rum bottle – or rather, several rum bottles. Every British serviceman is, by tradition, entitled to a rum issue before going into action. In the RAF the rum ration is issued after the action, when the crews are safely on the ground. There were ten or so debriefing tables, their number limited by the number of debriefing teams available. We stood around, drinking our rum and coffee and exhilarating in our safe return and the thought of a probable day off. The noise in the room was considerable, everyone talking at once, the aircrew talking at the top of their voices, their hearing deadened by eight hours of engine roar.

'When interrogation was over George left for the officers' mess,' wrote 'Don' Thomas. 'I pulled an old leather jacket over my tunic and ate with the crew.

'After breakfast, as we left the mess hall and began the long trudge to our respective billets, a car stopped beside us. The window on the driver's side rolled down and a familiar head poked out.

'It was Wing Commander Stidolph DFC.[12]

'"Hop in boys; I'll drive you to your digs."

'"All of us?"

'"Certainly, all of you."

'Somehow we packed into the tiny Hillman. It wasn't often that a junior officer and six NCOs went motoring with their squadron commander. But I thought, "Oh! Oh! He's going to say something about my eating in the Sergeants' Mess or about the 'Big Aircrew Strike'. I put it down to the rain and the darkness of the night when he didn't."

'"Went to Berlin on three engines, eh?" the "Wingco" said. "We were beginning to worry about your lot. Everyone else had landed or was accounted for. Our kites were scattered from hell to breakfast but thank God they all got down somewhere. Can you beat that? Every last one got down OK."

'I began to warm to Stidolph. Seeing him for the first time as a decent human being and not the stern disciplinarian that he had to be as squadron commander.

'"Oh don't worry about us; we'll always come back," I said, and at that moment I sincerely believed that we would.

'"Was that you who parted the trees?" the "Wingco" asked, nodding towards the tall poplars that grew in a row near our sleeping quarters. "When we heard your engines and then saw your 'nav' lights coming up the road from Lincoln, we expected to hear one hell of a crash."

'"So did we," I said.

'It was a short walk to my room and we left the car together. Before I started off, Dick, who had been utterly speechless in the car, said: "You know, I hope George gets a medal for this." He paused for a moment and then added, "I want to tell him exactly where he can put it."'

Keith Parry went to sleep feeling that he had earned his day's pay of 13 shillings and sixpence [67½ pence]. 'Don' Thomas lay between damp sheets and sleep was a long time coming and of short duration when it did:

'At 1010 I was up and at noon, shaved and cleaned up. I waited, leafing through a magazine in the mess to have lunch with George. Nearby, one of the replacement crews who had arrived to make up the squadron losses of 26th November were talking about last night's op. Apparently they had not been on it.

'They say they lost twenty-five kites over Germany and another twenty-nine [plus two Stirlings returning from mine-laying operations] crashed in Britain,' the navigator, a slight, fair-haired boy was saying. 'They say 130 aircrew were killed in the UK alone.'

'My God! That's 54 kites; about 12%. That works out to eight ops and you're out,' said the pilot.

'Their conversation was none of my business and ordinarily I would have said nothing. But I thought back to our own first two or three confused weeks on the squadron. 'It was an unusual op. Met was all wrong. They aren't all that bad,' I said. The look of relief on their faces made me glad that I had spoken up.

'George, when he entered, looked more thoughtful than usual and I wondered if the 'Wingco' had had a few words with him but it wasn't that. 'You remember that incendiary we saw burning north of the airfield?' he said, settling in the chair next to mine. 'Well, we dropped it. They turned out the station fire brigade to put it out. Biggest flap around here for months.'

'I looked at him, wondering what on earth he was talking about.

'Well, when that Lanc above us dropped the "cookie" that just missed us, his incendiaries went down at the same time – and our port wing caught three of them. Luckily they fell flat and didn't ignite for two of them went through into a tank. The third lodged in the wheel and then fell out when we lowered the wheels to land.'

Harvey's crew had survived their brush with death, but six of them had used up all of their nine lives and would not see out the month.

It was probable that in the crashes on 16/17 December air crew casualties were 148 killed, 39 injured and 6 presumed lost at sea.

Phyllis 'Pip' Beck, a WAAF radio telephone operator in Flying Control at Dunholme Lodge whose birthday fell on 16 December, wrote:

'I thought it was tragic that crews should get back to this country only to become casualties here, but it was all too common. It was a very saddening thing and there was nothing anyone could do. The routine was always the same. Stack them up, bring them in…. We might overhear a conversation between the CO and the flying control officer. 'So-and-so's very late. Doesn't look good. If we don't hear something soon, I suppose that's it.'

'The aircrews knew what the chances were and the war had to go on. It was no good waiting up and biting your nails. You'd never cope if you did that. And at eighteen, one recovers quickly.'[13]

Like everyone else, Flight Sergeant 'Tom' Forster, the 32-year-old navigator on Pilot Officer Brian Lydon's crew on 103 Squadron at Elsham Wolds, would never forget 16 December. 'Nearly all the Berlin raids were of long duration, the shortest six hours five minutes; the longest eight hours fifty. It depended upon the route and the met conditions. Usually because of the prevailing westerly winds it was far quicker getting to the target than returning to base. Aircraft were landing all over the place. One of our Aussie crews went to Wickenby and we were ordered to divert as well. But Brian decided to land at Elsham and we came in through a gap in the clouds. In the shower room the following morning the various crews were discussing how they had got down. Brian asked an Australian skipper how he had made it and he replied, in his down-under brogue: 'Jesus Christ brought me in.'

The night of 16/17 was a hymn for the haunted for Bomber Command and for relatives who received the dreaded telegrams announcing that their loved ones had died 'on ops'. After 'Black Thursday' the terrible task of sending twenty-eight letters to the bereaved families on 97 Squadron befell Squadron Leader Charles McKenzie Dunnicliffe DFC. The acting commanding officer had only taken over from Group Captain Neville H. Fresson DFC on 15 December when Fresson was posted to RAF Snaith near the town of Selby, 20 miles south of York.[14] Dunnicliffe then had a further eight letters to send to the families of the Brill crew who were missing and later confirmed as all killed over Berlin.

The raid on Berlin had no identifiable aiming-point but the central and eastern districts were hit more than other areas. Most of the bombing hit housing and the damage to the Berlin railway system was extensive. A thousand wagon-loads of war matériel destined for the Eastern Front were held up for six days. The National Theatre and the building housing Germany's military and political archives were both destroyed. By this date more than a quarter of Berlin's total living accommodation was declared unusable. In all, 545 people had been killed, 796 injured and 160 were missing. Many of them died when the train in which they were travelling was bombed at the Halensee Station.

Hans-Georg von Studnitz had escaped by a hair's breadth from being bombed out for the second time when in a twenty-minute spell he had counted twenty explosions in the immediate vicinity, which had caused his deeply-dug trench to rock. His neighbours, the Schmitz family, who had installed themselves in the shelter in wickerwork chairs, had begun to pray aloud, which helped everyone to keep calm. When the noise had subsided a little, von Studnitz had clambered back to the surface to find the whole neighbourhood ablaze.

A few days later the weather finally cleared, making possible the first photographic reconnaissance of Berlin since the battle had begun. Analysis of the photos brought back by a Spitfire whose pilot made four runs over the capital on the 21st and others taken the day before revealed that damage was 'widespread and severe':

'The area in which the greatest havoc is seen, due almost entirely to fire, stretches from the east side of the central district of Berlin to Charlottenburg in the north-west and Wilmersdorf in the south-west and covers an area of nearly eight square miles. There is also severe damage in the important industrial districts of Reinckendorf and Spandau.'

In fact, little industrial damage was caused. An examination of the statistical analysis of damage showed that over 125 net acres of business and residential property had been affected in the fully built-up and 50 per cent to 70 per cent built-up areas and that over 60 per cent of the buildings in the Tiergarten district alone had been destroyed. Very substantial figures were also given for Charlottenburg, Mitte, Schöneberg, Wedding, Wilmersdorf and Reinckendorf.

Feldwebel Friedrich 'Fritz' Ostheimer, who had recently joined Major Heinrich Prinz zu Sayn-Wittgenstein as his replacement bordfunker, wrote:

'At this time large parts of Berlin had been heavily damaged. Entire streets were in ruins. It was an unimaginable sight.

'I had once experienced a night attack on the city from the ground. I was in an underground station with many others, the earth shook with each explosion, women and children screamed and smoke billowed through the place. Anyone who did not feel fear and horror would have had a heart of stone.'

Chapter Eight

'We won't be home for Christmas; we know that very well'

'...over Berlin I looked down into the flames and thought: "How many kids down there are not going to see Christmas Day?"'

Flight Sergeant 'Charlie' Kaye, a navigator on 101 Squadron.

In early December 1943 Major Prinz zu Sayn-Wittgenstein and his crew were transferred from Deelen in Holland with their aircraft to Erprobungsstelle (E-Stelle) Rechlin on the Mürlitzsee, where a new night-fighter experimental unit was to be established. 'This came as a surprise for Unteroffizier Kurt Matzuleit our flight engineer and me,' recalled 'Fritz' Ostheimer. 'Within a few hours we were torn from the circle of our comrades. In Rechlin we knew no-one and frequently sat unhappily around. Most of the time, Prinz Wittgenstein was away at meetings at the Air Ministry in Berlin. Our job was to keep the machine in constant readiness. There was no night-fighter unit stationed at Rechlin. It often took me hours to obtain the operational data for radio and navigation by telephone. For accommodation we had railway carriages with sleeping facilities.

'During our three weeks in Rechlin we flew some sorties over Berlin. Kurt and I had a small room in flying control at our disposal. During reported attacks we waited there for possible orders. One evening it looked as if Berlin might be the target for the bomber stream. Prinz Wittgenstein had already reported our imminent take-off. We climbed on a south-easterly course in the direction of Berlin. The distance Rechlin-Berlin is about 100 kilometres. The speaker in the so-called Reichsjägerwelle (Reich fighter frequency) gave a running commentary of position, course and height of the enemy bombers. Their code-word was 'Dicke Autos' ('Fat Cars'). This kept all the airborne fighters constantly informed. Meanwhile Berlin had been recognized as being the target and the Reichsjägerwelle gave the order: "Everything to Bär ('Bear'), everything to Bär!" Meanwhile we had reached the height of the bombers at about 7,000 metres. We entered the bomber stream on a south-easterly course. The radar was switched on and we observed the air space around us as far as the visibility allowed.

'I soon had my first target on my screen. I passed the required changes of course to the pilot on the intercom. We were closing in on our target. "Straight ahead; a little higher!" Very quickly we had reached the heavily laden four-engined one. It was, as nearly always, a Lancaster. Prinz Wittgenstein set it on fire with a single burst from the 'Schräge Musik' cannon and the enemy went down.

'Ahead of us the first beams of the searchlights were searching the night sky. The fire of the flak defences intensified and as a signal for the attack the British Pathfinders dropped target indicators for the approaching bombers. And again I had a target on my screen. The distance to the enemy bomber decreased quickly. By this difference in speed alone we could see that it must be an enemy bomber. But suddenly the closing speed became very high indeed and I could only call out on the intercom: "Down, down, the machine is coming straight at us!" A moment later a shadow passed above us in the opposite direction. We just felt the slipstream and the aircraft, probably another Lancaster, had disappeared into the night. The three of us sat rigid in our seats and we only relaxed when Kurt said, "That was close!" Once more we had been lucky.

'Now for the next target. The approach was almost complete and both the pilot and engineer could recognize the aircraft. Then suddenly the starboard engine began to shake, the propeller revolutions quickly decreased and finally stopped completely.'

Prinz Wittgenstein managed to reach Rechlin and make a perfect landing. As the machine rumbled over the runway, Ostheimer felt a great relief:

'We praised our pilot very highly of course and Kurt and I thought that we had earned some relaxation. Prinz Wittgenstein was a tall, good-looking officer with a fine, reserved and disciplined personality. As a night-fighter he did his utmost, shunned no danger and never considered his own life.

'After a few days the engine had been changed and our machine was again ready for action. Prinz Wittgenstein was impatient again. At the next approach of enemy bombers – Berlin was the target again – we were once more in the air. The weather was good for a change. There was a slight layer of haze at medium altitude, above that the sky was clear. I tuned in to the Reichsjägerwelle and so we were kept well informed about the general situation. Everything was pointing to another attack on the Reich capital.

'Back to our operation; we had meanwhile reached the altitude of the bomber stream and entered, like the Lancasters, the flak barrage over the city. British Pathfinders – we called them 'Master of Ceremonies' – had already dropped markers. The scene over the city was almost impossible to describe. The searchlights illuminated the haze layer over the city, making it look like an illuminated frosted glass screen, above which the sky was very light. One could make out the approaching bombers as if it were daylight. It was a unique sight.

'Prinz Wittgenstein put the aircraft into a slight bank. At this moment we did not know where to make a start. But the decision was suddenly taken from us, as tracer flew past our machine. Wittgenstein put the machine into a steep turn and dived. As we went downwards I could see the Lancaster flying obliquely above us and its mid-upper gunner who was firing at us with his twin guns. Fortunately his aim had not been very good. We had got a few hits but the engines kept running and the crew was unhurt. We went off to one side into the dark, keeping the Lancaster just in sight.

'We now continued parallel to the bomber for a while. The darker it got around us, the closer we moved towards the enemy machine. As the light from the searchlights decreased and the fires which the attack of the enemy had started lay behind us, we were well closed up to the bomber. The Lancaster was now flying above us, suspecting nothing. Perhaps the crew was relieved to have survived the attack and to be on their way home. But we, intent on the hunt, sat in our cockpit with our eyes staring upward, hoping that we had not been detected.

'Prinz Wittgenstein placed our Ju still closer to the huge shadow above us, took careful aim and fired with the 'Schräge Musik'. The tracer of the 2cm shells bored into the wing between the engines and set the fuel tanks on fire. We swung immediately to one side and watched the burning Lancaster, which continued on its course for quite a while. Whether the crew had been able to bail out we could not tell. They had certainly had enough time. The bomber exploded in a bright flash and fell disintegrating to earth. I got good contact with our D/F station right away. We flew without any problems to Rechlin and landed there.'

During his time on 57 Squadron at Scampton, from his place in a corner of a corrugated-iron Nissen hut with beds for a dozen officers, Pilot Officer Harold Chadwick had seen every other bed change ownership at least twice as the occupants went missing on ops. It was the duty of each WAAF batwoman to look after the domestic welfare of two junior officers. Harold felt sorry for these women, often 'motherly' types who, with tears in their eyes, collected up a small bundle of possessions belonging to yet another of 'their officers' who would not be coming back.

Chadwick's baptism of fire had been on the night of 3/4 September on Berlin when he and the other neophyte members of Sergeant Arthur Fearn's crew witnessed some of the twenty-two Lancasters being shot from the sky. Arthur was grey-haired and in his 30s with a wife and family to go home to. Chadwick thought that he 'looked steady and reliable' but concluded that there was little hope of completing more than one or two such trips.

Chadwick had been born on 14 September 1922 in Nottingham. Later the family moved to Uttoxeter. His father, a First World War veteran, had transferred from the cavalry to the RFC and he flew as a scout pilot, flying Spads, Bristol Fighters, Sopwith Triplanes and SE5s over the Western Front and was shot down on a couple of occasions. Young Harold had always admired his father's exploits in the air and was determined to become a fighter pilot himself. After leaving school he went to work in Woolworths as a trainee manager. Harold did not like routine and as soon as he turned 18 he volunteered for flying duties with the RAF. He was accepted but in Canada he was 'washed out' of pilot training because every time he took to the air he had thrown up. He re-mustered as a 'Nav/B': essentially a bomb-aimer with a working knowledge of navigation.

Unfortunately, Chadwick's air sickness and nasal bleeding never left him. When returning from an operation over Germany he would be plagued with the stench of his own vomit, while his oxygen mask would be slimy with blood, yet, lying alone in the dark isolation of the front compartment of a Lancaster he was able to conceal his suffering from the rest of the crew.[1]

Having got over the shock of their awful baptism over Berlin, Arthur Fearn's crew survived those terrible winter nights, although death was always close at hand. Returning from one raid in the early hours of the morning, when they climbed wearily from their Lancaster they noticed the station ambulance drawn up beside one of the squadron's aircraft. A blood-stained figure was being lifted into the back of the vehicle. On inquiry Harold was told that it was the bomb-aimer who had been killed by flak. A fragment of metal had entered below his chin, spiralled up through his skull and sliced off the top of his head. Harold wandered round to the nose of the Lancaster and looked up. There was a hole no bigger than a 2 shilling (10 pence) piece.

They would complete nine raids on the 'Big City'. It should have been ten. On the night they 'boomeranged' they were flying across the North Sea, still climbing steadily, when the Lancaster was attacked by a Ju 88 night-fighter and the starboard outer engine set on fire. Arthur threw the bomber all over the sky while his two gunners replied as best they could with their Brownings. For some reason the German broke off his attack and disappeared into the night. Although the crew managed to get the fire under control, their aircraft was in no shape to continue the long journey to Berlin. After some argument Harold persuaded his skipper to press on and drop their load on Heligoland. Over the island the enemy opened up at them with everything they had, so Harold aimed at the gun flashes. After the line-overlap photographs had been developed and examined the crew were credited with their op.[2]

Harold had a high regard for Sergeant Howard Dewar, the Canadian rear gunner, a tough ex-lumberjack, who seemed to be without fear. He and the mid-upper gunner Wilson Williams had saved the crew from disaster on at least two occasions. Then one night, on yet another trip to Berlin, an extraordinary thing happened. They were approaching the target when they were attacked by a Bf 109. Arthur went into his usual corkscrewing routine to try to throw the German off his tail. During this manoeuvre the crew temporarily lost communication with each other. Nevertheless the fighter was foiled and they went on to bomb the 'Big City'. As they set course for home, the skipper, as usual, called up each crew member in turn to ask if they were all right. Everyone replied except Howard. After several unsuccessful attempts to get an answer, Jack Baker the wireless-operator went along the fuselage to investigate. To his astonishment, Jack found the rear turret empty; Howard had bailed out over Berlin! Dennis Pearson, a West Indian, took over the tail gunner's job and remained in Arthur's crew until the completion of operations, as did all the other NCOs, including Harry 'Johnny' Johnson as navigator and Trevor Davies, the recently-promoted flight engineer.[3]

On the night of Thursday 23/Friday, 24 December the Main Force Halifaxes were rested once more and only seven 'Hallys' accompanied the 364 Lancasters to the 'Big City'. Twelve 'Oboe' Mosquitoes were to raid Aachen and then to carry on to a second site to route-mark Berlin for the heavies. Originally planned for a late-afternoon take-off, a forecast of worsening weather over the bomber stations caused the raid to be put back by seven hours to allow the heavies a return in daylight.

Sergeant Arthur Tindall on Squadron Leader Frank Cawdery's crew on 97 Squadron at Bourn wrote: 'Another early take off – 0020.' At Wickenby two Lancasters on 12 Squadron collided while taxiing. A 7 Squadron Lancaster at Oakington crashed out of control and there were injuries to all of the crew skippered by Pilot Officer H.C.W. Williams, a New Zealander. With aircraft loaned from 100 Squadron, at Waltham (Grimsby), seventeen Lancasters and crews on 550 Squadron were briefed for operations and to attack targets in Berlin.

Over base at 0003 hours at 15,000 feet 24-year-old Flying Officer James Gilmour ('Gil') Bryson who was from Gretna in Scotland was forced to return early when his rear turret went unserviceable. The crew had joined the squadron on its formation at Grimsby on 25 November 1943, having transferred from 12 Squadron where they had begun operations on 3 September. At 0030 hours shortly after take-off from Grimsby 'George Squared'[4] on 550 Squadron skippered by 21-year-old Sergeant Hubert Frederick John Woods and a 100 Squadron Lancaster flown by 21-year-old Flight Sergeant William Richard Cooper were involved in a collision over Lincolnshire and they crashed near Fulstow, 6 miles north of Louth. All fourteen crew members including Woods' 19-year-old rear gunner, Sergeant John McConnell from Motherwell, were killed.

On 101 Squadron soon after take-off from Ludford Magna one of the navigational aids on the Lancaster skippered by Squadron Leader Joseph Finlay Marshall AFC caught fire and the aircraft quickly filled with smoke, but the skipper's prompt fire-fighting instructions were acted upon with efficiency and the flames were extinguished. Despite the loss of equipment and after ensuring that no member of the crew had suffered any ill effect, Marshall went on to complete the sortie. Soon after take-off one of the engines on another Lancaster on the same squadron skippered by Flight Lieutenant Alan Lansdale Lazenby, born in 1915 at Guisborough, became defective and began emitting smoke and a long flame from the exhaust. In spite of this Lazenby continued his flight to Berlin which, despite difficulty in gaining height, he successfully attacked. When crossing the North Sea on the return flight it was evident that to complete the sortie the petrol supply would have to be carefully governed. By skilfully using his engines, however, Lazenby succeeded in reaching base. He received a DFC in 1944 when, on the night of 2/3 January, Lazenby was killed on Berlin.

At West Raynham in Norfolk 141 Squadron in 100 (Special Duties, later Bomber Support) Group was still going it alone on the 'Serrate' beat and managed only three Beaufighter VIFs for the night's operation. 'Serrate', a radar detection and homing device, had first been used by 141 Squadron Beaufighter F.VIs on 14 June 1943 to 'home' onto the radar impulses emitted by the FuG Lichtenstein (AI) radars in the 490 megacycles band but only worked when the Li sets were active. One Beaufighter was forced to abort and a second was never seen again. The third Beaufighter, flown by 24-year-old Flight Lieutenant Howard Kelsey and Pilot Officer Edward M. 'Smitty' Smith DFM who were seeking their fourth confirmed victory of the war returned to base with a claim for a Ju 88 flown by Oberleutnant Lenz Finster, the Staffelkapitän. Their victory was the fourth they had chalked up since joining the squadron and the first in 100 Group.

The raid was the sixth trip to the 'Big City' for Brian Soper, flight engineer on Warrant Officer Arthur Rew's crew on 12 Squadron. He recalls:

'We were approaching the target and getting lined up for the bomb run. I was helping the gunners to look out for fighters. Suddenly, above, to my right, came a Halifax, diving and weaving across us. It came within a few feet of us and must have been taking evasive action against a night-fighter. It looked near enough to touch!

Remember of course that all around us, apart from the target, was total blackness. I just happened to be looking that way. I shouted and tried to help the pilot push the control column forward. Any action would have been too late anyway. Of course it missed and when we recovered we just got back on course and carried on with the bomb run. We all agreed it was probably our closest encounter. There were of course many other close calls.'

On the afternoon of 23 December Siddle's crew discovered that they were on that night's battle order to fly their first trip to the 'Big City':

'Berlin, together with Essen and the industrial towns of the Ruhr was looked upon by most crews as the ultimate test of one's nerve and skill because of the strength of the defences,' wrote Clayton Moore. 'The "Big City" differed from the Ruhr targets in just one respect. A trip to Essen or Cologne, although it could prove hectic in terms of the opposition to be met, usually lasted little more than four hours, of which about ninety minutes would be spent in enemy air space. Berlin, being inside Germany, demanded long hours of concentration, alertness and the suffering of severe cold on the part of the crews involved. In addition to the heated reception one could expect from the city's considerable defences, there was always the guarantee that the fighters would be in close attendance for most of the six or more hours spent over Germany and the occupied areas of Western Europe.

'Despite the trepidation I felt at being ordered to visit Berlin for the first time, the outward flight passed without incident. The presence of fighters within the stream was savagely demonstrated by the number of bombers that I saw spiralling down in flames along the route to the target. The fearsome spectacle of a fully-laden bomber meeting such a fate was one never to be forgotten. The slow, agonizing, downward spinning flame-engulfed hulk; the pieces breaking away; the holocaust when it hit the ground. I observed and reported six such disasters during our flight to the target.

'On reaching Berlin, we found the city to be almost totally blanketed in cloud, which was effectively illuminated by the searchlights beneath it. This presented the area as a sheet of opaque Perspex across which the bombers could be clearly seen as they crawled like army ants across the brightly lit cloud tops. The gunners were sending up a box barrage and I saw a couple of single-engined fighters lurking beneath us as we began our bombing run.'[5]

The German controllers made an early identification of Berlin as the probable target; their single-engined fighters were gathered over the city by zero hour and other fighters arrived a few minutes later. Bomber crews noticed that flak over the target was unusually restrained, with the German fighters obviously being given priority. The target was again cloud-covered and the Pathfinders carried out sky-marking, but many of the Main Force crews aimed their bombs through the cloud at the glow of eleven major fires still burning from the previous night to cause much further destruction in Berlin. The heaviest bombing was in the southern and south-eastern districts, but many bombs also fell to the east of the city. Approximately 1,400 to 1,500 people were killed and more than 10,000 more were bombed out.

Losses were not as heavy as on recent raids, partly because German night-fighters encountered difficulty with cloud covering the Berlin area which grounded several night-fighters and partly because the German controller was temporarily deceived by the Mosquito diversion at Leipzig. A strong countermeasure presence with false instructions being broadcast from England severely disrupted the JLO who was giving the 'running commentary'. The Germans had started using a female commentator, but this was promptly countered by a female voice from England ordering the German pilots to land because of fog at their bases. 'Spoof' fighter flares dropped by Mosquitoes north of the bomber stream also caused some diversion of Nachtjagd effort. At the target there were no fighters and few searchlights because of scattered cloud, but only eleven of the thirty-nine Blind Markers released their markers mainly because of H2S failures. Just one other aircraft was able to drop its eleven Green TIs and these landed 6 miles away. Most of the Main Force had bombed by the time the PFF backers-up could get their markers away and mainly the bombing was in the suburbs of the German capital.

The main force of fighters only appeared in the target area at the end of the raid and could not catch the main bomber stream. Fifteen Lancasters in all were lost. Two of these were shot down on the run-up to the capital and two more were shot down over the target. On 207 Squadron 'J-Johnny' skippered by 21-year-old Pilot Officer Gordon Edward Moulton-Barrett who was on his seventeenth operation and his seventh on Berlin, was shot down after bombing to crash at Luckenwalde, south-south-west of the capital. His father, Edward Selwyn Moulton-Barrett, had been a First World War Camel pilot and in 1941 had formed the Merchant Ship Fighter Unit (MSFU) whereby Hurricane fighters were catapulted from merchant ships on the Atlantic runs and on voyages to Russia, Gibraltar and the Mediterranean. Gordon and five of his crew scrambled to safety and were taken prisoner. His 20-year-old rear gunner Sergeant David Oswald Davies, who had been drafted into the crew as a replacement for the regular gunner who was suffering from a bad cold, was killed.

Harold Chadwick on Arthur Fearn's crew had just got his bombs away when he saw another Lancaster just above on the port side with its two port engines on fire and the rear door on the starboard side of the fuselage wide open. As he watched, three of the crew members appeared at the door and then jumped out into the night. Chadwick saw their parachutes open and they floated down into the flames below. Then, with four of the crew injured, trapped or dead inside, the stricken bomber plunged in an ever-steepening dive into the target. The aircraft was probably 'Nulli Secundus' ('Second To None') on 576 Squadron at Elsham Wolds, a veteran of more than seventy operations when it was lost. 'As this was almost Christmas Eve,' wrote Harold Chadwick, 'we had a very sad flight back to base, thinking about that unfortunate crew, with the pilot diving down away to port trying to keep his aircraft level enough for his crew to abandon it.'[6]

Oberleutnant Paul Zorner picked up 'Nulli Secundus' flying at 16,500 feet and shot the bomber down for the first of his three victories this night. Paul Anton Guido Zorner had been born Paul Zloch on 31 March 1920 and he had left school in 1938 to pursue a military career. He had been accepted by the Luftwaffe as a Fahnenjunker (officer candidate) in October 1938. By 20 March 1944 he had thirty-five confirmed night victories.

'Nulli Secundus' went down in a steep dive and plunged burning into the clouds to crash east of Giessen. The skipper, Pilot Officer Richard Lloyd Hughes and three of his crew died on the aircraft. The navigator Sergeant Jack Woodruff, air bomber Sergeant Donald A.H. Morris and rear gunner Sergeant Frank H. Lanxon were blown out of the aircraft over Hanover. Donald had worked as a fire-watcher in London before volunteering for the RAF in 1941. He recalled that his crew did 'everything together' and when they were not flying 'they were boozing!' Donald landed in a tree and the two others landed nearby. There was deep snow on the ground. Once Woodruff and Lanxon released Morris from the tree it became apparent that he had injured his leg and that he could not walk very far, but his two companions refused to leave him and make their escape. The three men remained at large for about twenty-four hours before they gave themselves up to a local woodcutter in a forest near where they had landed. Unable to walk, Donald was transported to a police station in a goat cart. The three prisoners were held overnight before the Luftwaffe came to collect them.

Donald Morris's parents were informed that he was 'missing on operations' by telegram on Christmas Day. They had no further news of their only child until they received a Red Cross postcard from him in PoW camp in April 1944.[7] Sergeant Francis E.A. Rivett, the mid-upper gunner, and Sergeant John Philip Gray the wireless-operator were only 19 years of age. The telegram delivered to John Gray's parents in Bristol was opened on Christmas morning.[8]

After claiming his first victory of the night Oberleutnant Paul Zorner had lost contact with the bomber stream and, almost out of fuel, he landed at Gütersloh, refuelled and took off again forty minutes later. By now the bombers were returning from Berlin and Zorner's radar-operator picked up a contact at 18,900 feet. It was 'X-X-ray', a 44 ('Rhodesia') Squadron Lancaster flown by Sergeant Roy Ladbrooke Hands. Zorner hit the Lancaster in the right wing and it spiralled down into cloud. He saw an explosion. There were no survivors. Eleven minutes later Zorner's radar-operator picked up another contact at 18,300 feet. It was 'L-London', a 50 Squadron Lancaster flown by 21-year-old Flying Officer Derrick Wilson Herbert. Zorner twice carried out attacks on the bomber and a fire started in the right wing. Then the wing exploded and a few seconds later the aircraft went down with all the crew trapped inside. Zorner flew back to Lüneburg to log claims for his seventeenth, eighteenth and nineteenth Viermots.

The entire night-fighter force could claim only eleven successes at a cost of six of their own aircraft lost. It is likely that 'B-Baker' on 514 Squadron skippered by 26-year-old Australian Pilot Officer Kenneth George Whitting was attacked by Oberfeldwebel Walter Mackens or Oberleutnant Hans-Heinz Augenstein, both of these unidentified claims being in the Frankfurt area. Australian Flight Sergeant J.E. Maloney, the mid-upper gunner, was the only survivor. Two Lancasters were claimed by Oberfeldwebel Karl-Heinz Scherfling.

A Ju 88C-6 night-fighter piloted by Oberfeldwebel Rudolf Frank from Lüneburg which was shot down over Berlin was probably downed by Australian Warrant Officer Harry Stanley Fidge, rear gunner on the 514 Squadron Lancaster skippered by 22-year-old Flight Lieutenant Leonard John Kingwell from Southgate, Middlesex; a tall fellow with a memorable dry humour. Fidge's fellow crew members had spotted the Junkers coming towards them and about to pass overhead. They warned the Australian and he gave it a quick burst as it passed over him and the Junkers went down in flames. Frank and Unteroffizier Hans-Georg Schierholz, the bordfunker, had twice bailed out before. Schierholz put his foot on the stomach of the bordmechaniker who had frozen, clinging on, unwilling to go, and pushed him out and then bailed out himself. Frank put the aircraft onto automatic before he went out. Schierholz, who bailed out 4 times in all during his 212 combat sorties, assisted in 57 aerial victories on the crews of Oberfeldwebel Frank and Major Werner Husemann. Kingwell's crew was shot down on Leipzig on 19/20 February 1944. All eight crew members including Harry Fidge were killed. On the night of 26/27 April 1944 Rudolf Frank claimed his forty-fifth and final victory before he and his crew were hit by debris from their victim. Frank and Oberfeldwebels Schierholz and Schneider crashed to their deaths.

In his rear turret on the '*Spirit of Russia*' Clayton Moore was relieved when at last the bombs were gone and they had taken their 'worthless picture' of the cloud cover before turning north into the night:

'Suddenly the gathering darkness glowed red as another Lancaster stopped one a few hundred feet above us and began its death dive. The skipper took immediate evasive action, throwing us into a steep dive to port. But the stricken Lanc followed us. Bill asked me for instructions on its location and what further action to take in order to avoid a collision. I watched and waited, unable to decide on which way we should go. The doomed aircraft was obviously out of control and it was difficult to predict which direction it would take next. The port wing was blazing furiously; also a large section of the fuselage aft of the wing. It was directly behind us and getting uncomfortably close despite our dive and I could make out details of it as it began to break up about a hundred yards astern.

'Fearing the danger of the aircraft exploding, I realised the need for immediate action on my part if we were to avoid being brought down with it. 'Level out to starboard, NOW!' I shouted into my microphone, having detected a slight course alteration to port by the stricken bomber as it continued its death throes. Even as I spoke, the fire in the after part of the fuselage flared and I could clearly see inside the cockpit two dark figures silhouetted against the flames as they struggled to make their escape. The '*Spirit of Russia*' winged over to starboard at once and I fought against the forces of gravity in order to stand up and watch the wretched Lancaster as it disappeared from sight beneath my turret. As we began to level out, the falling aircraft again came into view, permitting me to see that the port wing had broken free, leaving the still burning fuselage to spin drunkenly downwards. Once clear of the danger, we resumed course, while I watched the ill-fated Lanc continue its downward plunge. The fire had spread from the fuselage to the starboard wing by this time and more bits were beginning to break off, but I didn't see any parachutes come out, nor had I been able to read the aircraft's markings. 'Poor devils,' I thought as I watched it strike the ground far below us; 'there but for the grace of God go us!' Four hours later, we touched down at Bardney. Although the Battle of Berlin was proving quite costly to the hard-pressed aircrews of Bomber Command and the Pathfinders, 9 Squadron suffered no losses on the trip.'[9]

Bomber losses could have been higher but despite heavy damage to 'T-Tommy' Squadron Leader Frank Cawdery managed to reach Bourn safely. The Lancaster was attacked by a Ju 88 on no fewer than eight occasions and with all guns in the Lancaster frozen. One engine was knocked out, the aircraft damaged and Cawdery himself was fortunate when a bullet hit the heel of his flying boot. He put Tommy into a power dive from 18,000 to 6,000 feet to finally shake off the enemy fighter but soon afterwards a second engine began to falter and had to be shut down. 'Tommy' was landed at Bourn, although unbeknown to the crew the starboard tyre had been punctured and pulled the aircraft to the right, eventually finishing up off the runway. As Arthur Tindall recalls, the aircraft was written off. After debriefing it was between nine and ten o'clock before the crew got to bed, only to be awoken because it was Christmas Eve and so they set off to Cambridge for drinks in the pub.[10]

George Lang's crew on 'C-Charlie' on 57 Squadron returned to East Kirkby on two engines. After losing two of the engines the Canadian skipper had asked his crew if they had wanted to bail out. 'Geoff' King said: 'Let's go on – I didn't fancy being a PoW and another thing: it is obvious some of our men were killed by Germans if they did bail out. And could you blame them, when you consider what we did to their cities?'[11]

On 550 Squadron there was no news after take-off of the Lancaster skippered by 27-year-old Australian Pilot Officer Donald Campbell Dripps who had made twenty-nine trips. He had been a textile worker before enlistment in 1941. He left a widow, Beryl Violet of East Coburg, Victoria. All the crew, including the 18-year-old flight engineer Sergeant James Clark Scott, were lost without trace. In all twelve Lancasters on 550 Squadron returned, though the aircraft piloted by Flight Sergeant R.E. Oliver only just made it back after it was attacked by a Ju 88 at 500 yards astern when the rear gunner Sergeant W. Russell opened fire and a Bf 109 at 300 feet above which then opened fire. Oliver evaded, the enemy aircraft were lost to view and the Lancaster returned on three engines after the starboard inner caught fire during the bombing run.

This was the first time that Flight Sergeant Charlie Kaye, the Liverpudlian navigator on Australian Flight Sergeant Norman Marsh's Lancaster on 101 Squadron, had an uneasy conscience:

'I had seen the extensive damage in Liverpool where a lot of children had been killed. As we were running into the target over Berlin I looked down into the flames and thought: 'How many kids down there are not going to see Christmas Day?' This made me feel just a bit uneasy. The only way I could reassure myself that we were doing the right thing was by thinking of what had happened to Liverpool and of course, this was all-out war.'[12]

Flight Sergeant Elmer John Trotter DFM on 101 Squadron was flying a Lancaster on his fourth operational sortie, all to Berlin. An American by birth, born on 23 February 1923 in Santa Cruz, California, Trotter's home now was in Tuberose, Saskatchewan where he had earned a living as a farmer before enlisting on 1 September 1941. His Lancaster was hit by AA fire after releasing its bombs and thrown completely out of control and into a dive. Trotter ordered the crew to put on their parachutes while he struggled to regain control. With great skill he managed to do this, only to find he had scarcely any aileron control and no trimmers. His starboard mainplane had been shot to pieces aft of the rear spar and there were three large holes inboard, between the two starboard engines. To add to this, his mid-upper turret and compass were put out of action. As he left the target and tried to gain height, the Lancaster was attacked by a fighter which Trotter evaded, though not before the port outer engine was damaged. On their way back to base Trotter again ran into flak, but avoided being hit and eventually made a safe landing. He received an immediate DFC.

The Canadian Group's contribution to the raid was only twenty-six aircraft, of which nineteen took off and three returned early. No. 6 Group lost a Lancaster II on 408 Squadron on the raid. Just after midnight Halifax LL629 on 426 'Thunderbird' Squadron, which had been damaged by flak over Berlin knocking out the starboard outer engine and the aircraft's 'Gee' navigation system, flew into high ground at 0030 hours near High Mowthorpe Farm, south-east of North Grimston, where it reportedly cartwheeled on impact and ended up on its back. The 26-year-old air bomber, Flying Officer George Lawrence Huffman of Winnipeg, Manitoba and the 20-year-old rear gunner, Flight Sergeant Clarence Delrose Manders of West Kildonan, Winnipeg, were killed. The skipper, Pilot Officer David R. DeBloome of Windsor, Ontario and his flight engineer, Sergeant Frederick Cameron Borst of Southampton, Hampshire were injured. The mid-upper gunner, Flight Sergeant Willard Graham Martin of Westville, Nova Scotia and Flight Lieutenant James Barry Cleveland of Toronto, 426 Squadron's senior navigation officer who was coming to the end of his tour, were seriously injured. The wireless-operator, Sergeant William Henry McGarrighan of Rawtenstall, Lancashire, who was slightly injured, was later Mentioned in Dispatches for having the 'courage and presence of mind' to rescue a number of his crew. He was directly responsible for the death toll in the crash not being higher.

A second MiD awarded this night went to Warrant Officer Edward Sydney Ellis, captain of Lancaster III 'B-Bertie' on 625 Squadron at Kelstern. Apart from Sergeant Arthur Boud, navigator, the crew was made up of 'sprogs' on their first op. 'Bertie' was hit by flak near Berlin and the rear turret damaged but they went on to drop their bombs and as they did so were attacked by a night-fighter, and Sergeant W.G. Jones, mid-upper gunner, and Sergeant D.G. Wightman, rear gunner, were injured by cannon shell fragments. The aircraft by now had no hydraulics and no intercom, the bomb doors were jammed open and there was considerable damage to the wings and fuselage, but Ellis managed to get the Lancaster and his crew back to England. As fuel was short, a landing was made at Bardney, using the emergency method of lowering the undercarriage without flaps and on flat tyres. The aircraft nosed over on landing but tipped back again and no further injuries were sustained by the crew. Arthur Boud recalled, 'Great welcome back at squadron; felt a hero.' Boud later received the DFM at Buckingham Palace. Both gunners were taken to RAF Station Hospital Rauceby.[13]

A 100 Squadron Lancaster, 'S-Sugar', piloted by Flight Lieutenant K.A. Major was involved in an incident that almost had disastrous results for the town of Grimsby. (Seven days earlier the crew had met with very strong opposition, but had pressed on to make a successful attack on Berlin.) On returning to base, Major was able to make a safe landing despite the very low cloud, finding themselves to be the first crew to return and they had witnessed the collision between the two Lancasters over Waithe. 'S-Sugar' had become airborne and was shaking quite noticeably and there then followed a thump which was felt by all the crew. It seemed to be localized near the mid-upper turret in which Sergeant R.A. Creamer was sitting.

Immediately he informed his skipper and climbed out of the turret to investigate. Looking down into the bomb bay through the inspection panel, he saw that the 4,000lb 'cookie' had broken away from its supports and was wallowing about in the bottom of the bomb bay with only the doors, which had opened slightly, holding it in. He reported the predicament to his pilot, who then made for the North Sea with all possible haste, hoping that the bomb would not break away from the aircraft and fall on Grimsby, over which they were now flying. Thankfully they reached the North Sea safely and managed to jettison the errant bomb successfully from 3,000 feet, returning to land at Waltham to find that considerable damage had been done to the bomb bay doors and the hydraulic system. The drama had lasted about fifteen minutes.

At Skellingthorpe Sergeant Keith Parry was now fully qualified and he and his crew had been allocated their own aircraft, which carried the squadron letter 'Z'. It was known as 'Zeke' after a cartoon character popular at the time:

'We flew "Zeke" to Frankfurt on 20th December and to the "Big City" on the twenty-third,' he wrote. 'Apart from the barrage over the target, both trips were uneventful and we returned unscathed. A total of 57 aircraft were lost on these two operations. There was a dance in the Sergeants' Mess on Christmas Eve, well attended by all the WAAFs and local ladies and what with one thing and another it turned out to be one of the best Christmases I can remember.'

All around the world the war continued, with few interruptions in the fighting. Nevertheless, wherever it was possible, there were many who did their best to mark Christmas Day with some form of celebration. On the fighting fronts Germany still felt secure behind the Atlantic wall but behind the wire, the other battle – for survival – went on. Bombs dropped by RAF Bomber Command and Eighth Air Force four-engined bombers sometimes caused explosions that were audible in Luftwaffe PoW camps in the Reich and helped fuel the fires of German discontent. Though spirits soared with each and every Luftangriff (air-raid), the thousands of RAF and Commonwealth airmen and American 'fly-boys', knowing they wouldn't, in the words of the song, *I'll Be Home For Christmas* instead sang 'We won't be home for Christmas; we know that very well'. Even if it seemed inevitable to many that the war would eventually be won by the Allies, it wasn't going to happen until many more had died in many different parts of the world.

Chapter Nine

'After Every December Comes Always a May'

'The havoc wreaked on Berlin was not only on industrial and commercial buildings, public utilities and transportation services which bore the brunt of the attacks, but also on more than two hundred state or public buildings. Fire services from as far as Frankfurt had to be called upon to help extinguish the fires. Some Berliners who marched through the devastated thoroughfares of their war-torn capital paraded banners bearing the words 'You may break our walls but not our hearts'. Others stoically sang Nach jedem Dezember kommt immer ein Mai *– After every December comes always a May.'*

A most popular song of the day that was to prove prophetic.

In England on Christmas morning the bomber crews were warned for operations that night but the order was cancelled a half-hour later and they were stood down. Joy was unbridled. Officers donned aprons and served the erks with Christmas dinner in the time-honoured custom as Sergeant Edward Humes on 514 Squadron recalled:

'Christmas Day was an occasion when senior ranks showed their appreciation for the work done by ground staff by serving the midday meal. The Australian members had saved a good portion of their parcels from home to pass on as thanks to our own ground crew. Fruit cake, chocolate bars, tinned fruit and all manner of goods which were hard, almost impossible to obtain in England, were eagerly accepted. Life returned to normal the following day. Christmas 1943 was very cold indeed and all personnel not engaged in other duties were ordered to assist in removing snow from the runways. All hands were called out to help clear the runways and it was an amazing sight to see hundreds of airmen, aircrew and some WAAFs shovelling away until well into dusk to free the main runway. Surely ops would not take place that night. After all the hard work, the 'Stand Down' was given.'

Throughout December 1943, January, February and March 1944 Noel Thackray's crew continued operational flying and their last Christmas became a dim and distant memory. Six of them would never see another. Their luck finally ran out on 11 April when their Lancaster was shot down on Aachen. Humes was the only survivor and he was taken prisoner.

The battle order was not posted again until the night of Wednesday 29/Thursday, 30 December. In all, 712 aircraft (457 Lancasters, 252 Halifaxes and 3 Mosquitoes) were detailed to bomb Berlin, the ninety-fourth time since 1940 that the 'Big City' would endure an RAF bombing raid. At the 1 Group aerodrome at Elsham

Wolds, Sergeant Ben Frazier, *Yank* staff correspondent, boarded 'V-Victor' on 576 Squadron for the operation to the 'Big City' with Flying Officer Gomer S. 'Taff' Morgan and his crew.[1]

Frazier wrote: 'England. A small village lay tucked away in the fold of a valley just below the high, windswept, bleak plateau where a Lancaster bomber station was situated. Housewives were busy in the kitchen preparing food and the men had left their ploughing to come in for the noon-day meal. In the lichen-covered Gothic Church, the minister's wife was arranging decorations and placing on the altar freshly-cut chrysanthemums that had managed to escape the north winds and were still blooming in December. The placidness of the village life was in sharp contrast to the bustling activity at the airfield. It seemed as remote from war as any hamlet could possibly be, although the provident farmers, living so close to an obvious military target had wisely provided themselves with shelter trenches at the edge of each ploughed field. Nevertheless, the name of this quiet, lovely village had spread far. By borrowing it, the bomber station had made it one to strike terror into the heart of the Nazi High Command.

'At the airfield, 'Victor's crew lounged around 'B' Flight's Office waiting to see if operations were on. They kept looking up into the sky as if trying to guess what the weather was going to be like. Some of the men chuckled. '"Papa" Harris [Air Chief Marshal Harris, chief of Bomber Command] is so set on writing off the "Big City" that he hardly even notices the weather,' one of them said. 'The last time, there were kites stooging around all over the place. The met boobed that one.'

'It was a strange new language. What the airmen were saying was that the last time out the meteorological men had given a wrong steer on the weather and the planes had been flying all over looking for the field on the return trip.

'Victor's captain came back from the operations room with the news that there would be ops. That settled the discussion. You seemed to be aware, without noticing anything in particular, of a kind of tension that gripped the men; like they were pulling in their belts a notch or two to get set for the job ahead.

'And with the news, everybody got busy – the aircrews, the ground crews, the mechanics, the WAAFs, the cooks. The ships already had a basic bomb and fuel load on board and the additional loads were sent out in ammunition trailers and fuel trucks. The perimeter track lost its usually deserted appearance and looked like a well-travelled highway, with trucks and trailers, buses and bicycles hurrying out to the dispersal points. It was just like the preparation at any bomber base before taking off for enemy territory – but going over the 'Big City' was something different. These men had been there before. They knew what to expect.

'In the equipment room, June, the pint-size WAAF in battledress, was an incongruous note. Over a counter as high as her chin, she flung parachutes, harnesses and Mae Wests. The crew grabbed them and lugged them out to the ships. You kept thinking they ought to be able to get somebody a little bigger for the job she was handling.

'In the briefing room, the met officer gave the weather report and the forecast over enemy territory. There would be considerable cloud over the target. The men grinned. An operations officer gave a talk on the trip. The route was outlined on a large map of Germany on the front wall. It looked ominously long on the large-scale map. He pointed out where the ground defences were supposed to be strong and where fighter opposition might be expected. He gave the time when the various phases should be over the target. He explained where the 'spoof' attacks were to be made and the time. He told the men what kinds of flares and other markers the Pathfinders would drop. There was the usual business of routine instructions, statistics and tactics to be used. The Group Captain gave a pep talk on the progress of the Battle of Berlin. And all the while, that tape marking the route stared you in the face and seemed to grow longer and longer.

'Outside it was hazy and growing more so. But this was nothing new. The men were convinced that the weather was always at its most variable and it's dampest and it's haziest over their field. What could you expect? Ops would probably be scrubbed after all. Hell of a note.

'In the fading light the planes were silhouetted against the sky. They looked, on the ground, slightly hunched and menacing like hawks. Seeing them there, in the half-light you would never guess how easy and graceful they are in flight. Nor would you realise when you see them soaring off the runway, what an immense load they take up with them. It is only when you see the open bomb bay on the ground, that you get some idea of a Lancaster's destructive power. The open bomb bay seems like a small hangar. The 4,000lb blockbuster in place looks like a kitten curled up in a large bed. It is a sobering sight.

'In the evening some of the men tried to catch a few winks; most of them just sat around talking. The operational meal followed. It was only a snack, but it was the last solid food any one would get until the fresh egg and bacon breakfast which has become a ritual for the proper ending of a successful mission.

'There was still some time to wait before take-off so 'Victor's crew sat around the ground crew's hut near the dispersal point, warming themselves by the stove or chewing the rag with the ground crew. The 'Wingco' came around to make a last minute check-up. The medical officer looked everyone over. The engineer officer checked the engines.'

On 427 'Lion' Squadron RCAF at Leeming one of the Halifaxes on the ops board for that night, 'W-Willie', the Flight Commander 29-year-old Squadron Leader 'Turkey' Laird's aircraft, was being taken by 27-year-old Pilot Officer 'Deeg' Deegan's crew on their third op to the 'Big City'.[2]

The rear gunner, Flight Sergeant Philip Alfred Dubois, the youngest member of the crew who was only 19 at the time, recalled:

'Willie' was a replacement for our beloved 'Y-York', mostly referred to as '*Yehudi, the Gremlin*', which was painted on the nose. Our crew had been on a week's operational leave. The date was 22nd December. Several of us had arranged to catch the 3.30 pm train from King's Cross to York where we had a few pints before catching the milk train to Leeming. None of us were feeling too much pain when we passed through the main gate. There was an aircraft coming in to land. I made a remark that 'the bastard is going to prang'. We were even betting ten bob one way or the other. We then heard a bank, a crash and a screech, which tended to sober us up; especially the next morning when we discovered it was our beloved 'Y-York'.

A new Canadian pilot on the squadron, 20-year-old Flight Sergeant 'Rex' Alexander Clibbery who was from Regina, Saskatchewan was returning from a 'Bullseye' bombing exercise and forgot to lower the undercarriage:

'He badly bent our aircraft and it never flew on ops again,' recalled Philip Dubois. '"*Yehudi*" was a Halifax V. By the time she was repaired we had converted to Halifax IIIs. [The Mk III was the first Halifax to change from the Merlin to Hercules engines.] At the briefing 'Rex' was our 'second dickey' for the Berlin trip. There were no hard feelings about him pranging our kite and 'Rex' turned out to be a real Squadron character.'

Robert Cyril Deegan was born in Smiths Falls at Lanark in Ontario. He would be making his fifteenth operational trip. Flight Sergeant Cecil Axford, the 21-year-old Canadian navigator on the crew, was from Hamilton, Ontario where he had worked as a boilermaker's apprentice. He had officially 'claimed' his brother, Sergeant Wilfred Valentine Axford, a ground crew member who was transferred to Leeming.

'Actually, it was harrowing having him around,' wrote 'Wilf', 'because every time he went out on an op I would worry like crazy until he finally made it back to base. One night the squadron bombed Milan. My brother's plane lost an engine on the way down. Realising that they couldn't make it over the Alps to come back, they flew down to Bone, North Africa. At first they didn't know if they had landed in enemy territory or not. They were just about to destroy their aircraft when some Americans came running up and told them where they were. His crew actually stayed at Bone for a month until their received a new engine. When the crew came back to England the plane was loaded down with bananas and oranges they had purchased, along with some scotch, which was dirt cheap down there – only ten shillings a bottle. There was quite a celebration the night they came back.'[3]

At Skellingthorpe Pilot Officer Michael Beetham and his Lancaster crew was one of fifteen on 50 Squadron called to the Nissen-hutted briefing room at 1400 hours:

'The Squadron commander pulled back the curtain over the map and revealed the target – Berlin. We swallowed a little. For me and my crew it was only our seventh trip and this would be our fourth to the 'Big City'; the Battle of Berlin was clearly on. Seven hundred Lancasters and Halifaxes from the Command would attack in five waves – all phased through the target in twenty minutes to saturate the defences. Mosquitoes would carry out diversionary attacks on Magdeburg and Leipzig. We were to feint towards Leipzig and then turn north to Berlin at the last minute. The met man told us there would be heavy cloud over most of Germany, widespread fog and poor visibility. Hopefully, that would restrict their fighters. Our bases were forecast to be fine for return. That was a relief, for on our last trip to Berlin we returned to fog-bound bases and only got down in Yorkshire with difficulty. Out to aircraft dispersal at 1600 hours for a final check of everything. We had our brand-new Lancaster 'B-Bertie' with the latest paddle-bladed propellers air-tested that morning and this was our first trip in it. Take-off at 1700 hours. All fifteen aircraft taxied out in turn and there was a good crowd as usual beside the runway controller's caravan to see us off.'

At Elsham Wolds

'the minutes crept by until at last the time came to get into the planes,' wrote Ben Frazier. 'The deep stillness of the night was awakened by the motors revving up; one after another until each one was lost in the general roar. The crews scrambled into the planes and took their places. The great ships were guided out of their dispersal areas by the ground crews who gave a final wave as the Lancs moved off slowly down the perimeter track. They appeared more menacing than ever creeping along in the dark with their motors roaring. One by one they turned onto the runway and noisily vanished into the night.

'From now on, until they would return, the members of "Victor"'s crew were a little world in themselves, alone and yet not alone. For all around them were other similar little worlds, hundreds of them with a population of seven, hurtling through space, lightly – huge animated ammunition dumps. For its safety, each little world depended utterly and completely on its members – and a large dash of luck.

'There was not much conversation over the intercom. When you're flying without running lights on a definite course and surrounded by several hundred other bombers, you have not time for any pleasantries. The navigator was busy checking the air speed and any possible drift. Almost everyone else kept a look out for other aircraft, both friend and foe. A friendly aircraft is almost as dangerous as an enemy plane, for if two blockbusters meet in mid-air, the pieces that are left are very small indeed.

'Occasionally the ship jolted from the slipstream of some unseen aircraft ahead and frequently others overhauled "Victor", passing by to port and starboard, above and below. "Victor" gained altitude very easily for maximum ceiling. She was a veteran of over fifty ops and had the DFC painted on her port bow to celebrate the fiftieth, but she had the vitality of a youngster. "Blondie" [Sergeant J.R. O'Hanlon], the wireless-operator, broke the silence. "'Taff', the W/T has gone u/s."

'The wireless is not used except in an emergency such as ditching, but it is nice to know it's there. We went on. Occasionally "Taff", the pilot, would call into the intercom, "Bob [Sergeant C.E. Shilling, the rear gunner], are you OK?" There would be a silence for a moment while he fumbled to turn on his intercom, until you wondered if he had frozen back there. Then he'd sing out, "OK, 'Taff'." He and the mid-upper gunner [Sergeant A. Newman, standing in for Sergeant Stan S. Greenwood] were the only two outside the heated cabin. Inside the cabin it was warm and snug. You didn't even need gloves. "Jock" [Flight Lieutenant Edward McPhee Graham DFC], the navigator, wore no flying gear, just the Air Force battledress.[4]

'Up ahead the Pathfinder boys dropped the first route-markers, flak shot up into the air and the men knew that "Victor" was approaching the Dutch coast. An enormous burst of flame lit up the night off to port. "Scarecrow to starboard," the mid-upper reported on the intercom. Jerry intended the "scarecrow" to look like a burning plane but it did not take long to see that it was not.[5]

'"Jock"'s Scots accent came over the intercom: "'Taff', we're eleven minutes late." "OK, we'll increase speed." The engineer [21-year-old Flying Officer John Ross "Jock" Mearns] pushed up the throttles. Everything was black again below. Occasionally there was a small burst of flak here and there.

'"Plane to starboard below!"

'"OK, it's a Lanc." As "Victor" passed it you could see the bluish flame from the exhausts lighting the aircraft below in a weird ghostly manner. It was unpleasant to realise that our own exhausts made "Victor" just as obvious as the other plane.

'Away off the port bow, a glow became visible. It looked like the moon but it was the first big German searchlight belt, encompassing many cities. The beams were imprisoned under cloud.[6]

'"That will be Happy Valley," "Jock" said. Another route-marker appeared ahead.

'"Tell me when we're over it," the navigator replied. Shortly the bomb-aimer said, "We're bang over it now."

'"OK 'Digger'."'

Pilot Officer Neil Allason 'Digger' Lambell DFC of Gulargambone, NSW was a grazier, born at Greenwich, NSW on 27 January 1922. Lambell would take part in eleven sorties against Berlin, the first two before the end of November 1943. During the latter attack on the 'Big City' on 23/24 November he was hit on the face by a piece of shrapnel while making his bombing run but, undeterred, he released his bombs at the correct time and it was not until his aircraft landed at base that other members of the crew realized he had been injured. Lambell's nose was substantially damaged and restorative surgery was undertaken by pioneer plastic surgeon Dr Archibald McIndoe.

'"Taff", we're nine minutes late.' The navigator took a couple of astro sights to get a fix. From this he could determine the wind and the drift of the plane.

'Another searchlight belt showed up to starboard. It was enormous, running for miles and miles. It was all imprisoned under the cloud but it was an evil-looking sight just the same.[7] The top of the clouds shone with millions of moving spots, like so many restless glow worms, but the impression was much more sinister – like some kind of luminous octopus. The tentacle-like beams groped about seeking some hole in the cloud, some way of clutching at you as you passed by protected by the darkness. The continuous motion of the searchlights caused a ripple effect on the clouds, giving them an agitated, angry, frustrated appearance. Once in a while one found a rift and shot its light high into the sky. Flak came up sparkling and twinkling through this luminous blanket. 'Victor' jolted violently from close bursts, but was untouched. It passed another Lanc, which was clearly silhouetted against the floodlit clouds.

'Another leg of the trip was completed. The navigator gave the new course over the intercom and added, 'Seven minutes late.'

'OK Mack.'

'"Jock", make it 165.'[8]

'Victor' passed plane after plane and occasionally jolted in the slipstream of others. A third searchlight belt showed up, this one free of cloud. It was a huge wall of light and looked far more impenetrable than a mountain. It seemed inconceivable than any plane could pass through and reach the opposite side. You thanked your lucky stars that this was not the target. To fly out of the protecting darkness into the blaze of light would be a test of courage you would rather not have to face.

'Nevertheless, there were some facing it right now. The flak opened up and the searchlights waved madly about. It was a diversionary attack, the 'spoof'. You watched in a detached, remote sort of way. It seemed very far away and did not seem to concern you at all. Until suddenly, one beam which had been vertical, slanted down and started to pursue 'Victor' and you realised that it did concern you very intimately. The seconds ticked by as the beam overtook the plane. But it passed harmlessly overhead and groped impotently in the darkness beyond.

'Four minutes late,' 'Jock' called over the intercom.

'The target itself, the 'Big City', came into view like a luminous patch dead ahead. It was largely hidden by cloud and showed few searchlights. It seemed so much less formidable than the mountain of light just behind, that it came as a sort of anticlimax. Surely, you felt, this cannot be the 'Big City', the nerve-centre of Europe's evil genius.

'It was quiet. There was no flak as yet, no flares and just the handful of searchlights. You tried to imagine what it was like on the ground there. The sirens would be about to sound; the ack-ack batteries would be standing ready, the searchlights already manned. You wondered if the people were in shelters.

'But it was too much of an effort. It was too remote. Your problems were flak, fighters, searchlights and whether you were on the course and on time. What happened below was an entirely different problem, which had nothing to do with you. What happened below might just as well be happening on Mars. 'Victor's own little world simply hovering off this planet and leading a life of its own.

'Ever so slowly 'Victor' crept up on the target. The two worlds were coming inevitably together. But it still had the quality of unreality. It was like a dream where you were hurrying somewhere and yet cannot move at all. Nevertheless, 'Victor' was passing plane after plane and jolted in somebody's slipstream now and again. The other Lancs looked ominous bearing down on the target, breathing out blue flame as they approached.

'The minute of the attack and still the target was quiet. One more minute ticked by – still quiet. The engineer opened up the throttles to maximum speed and increased the oxygen supply. Still quiet. The whole attack was a minute or two late. Winds, probably. Suddenly the whole city opened up. The flak poured up through the clouds. It came in a myriad of little lights. It poured up in a stream of red, as if shaken from a hose. It would be impossible to miss such a brilliantly marked objective. Bright flashes started going off under the clouds. That would be the 'cookies' from the planes ahead. 'Victor' started the bombing run. The bomb-aimer called the course now.

'Left, left.... Steady now.... Right a bit.... Steady ... steady... "cookie" gone!' 'Victor' shot upward slightly. 'Steady.... Incendiaries gone...' 'V for Victor' surged again ever so slightly.

'Stand by "Taff";' it was the voice of Bob, the tail-gunner: 'Fighter.'

'Instantly the pilot sent 'Victor' over to starboard and rushed headlong downward. A stream of red tracer whipped out of the dark, past the rear turret and on past the wing-tip, missing by what seemed inches. A second later the fighter itself shot past after the tracer, a vague dark blur against the night sky.

'Me 109,' Bob said calmly.

'Victor' squirmed and corkscrewed over the sky of Berlin. You wondered how it could be possible to avoid all the other planes that were over the city. But the fighter was shaken off and 'Victor' came back to a normal course again.

'Down below through rifts in the cloud, you could see that Berlin was burning. The bright, white flame of the incendiaries showed up as a carpet of light, always growing. And flash after flash went off as the blockbusters fell. The dark, black shapes of many Lancasters could be seen all over the sky, against the brilliant clouds below. They were like small insects crawling over a great glass window. It did not seem possible that these tiny black dots could be the cause of the destruction which was going on below. The insects crawled to the edge of the light and disappeared into the darkness beyond. They had passed safely through the target, 'Victor' close behind.

'Shortly the course was set for the return and Berlin was visible for many miles on the port quarter. The attack was over now. It took only fifteen minutes. The ack-ack was silent. There was no flak flashing over the city, but the city was brighter than ever. The clouds were getting a reddish tinge, which showed that the fires had caught hold below.

'And so, the capital of Nazism dropped astern, obscuring the rising moon by its flames. The Government which came into power by deliberately setting fire to its chamber of representatives, the Government which first used wholesale bombing and boasted of it, was now perishing in fires far more devastating than any it ever devised. It was perishing to a fire music never dreamed of by Wagner.

'But it was impossible to connect 'Victor' with the death struggles of Berlin. There was no time for contemplation.

'Stand by, Ju 88 starboard – corkscrew,' came 'Bob's voice. Again with lightning speed, the pilot put 'Victor' over and dived out of the way. The Ju 88's tracers missed us and shot down another Lanc which had not been so fortunate.'

It took Pilot Officer Mike Beetham three and a quarter hours to reach Berlin: 'We climbed to cross the Dutch coast at 1,900 feet and then gradually got to maximum height around 20-21,000 feet. Our route was north of the Ruhr and then south-east past Osnabrück and Hanover towards Leipzig.... A sharp turn north twenty miles short of Leipzig with the diversionary aircraft heading straight on – hopefully the fighter controllers would be fooled. [A long approach from the south, passing south of the Ruhr and then within 20 miles of Leipzig, together with diversions by Mosquitoes at Düsseldorf, Leipzig and Magdeburg and RCM sorties caused the German controller great difficulties and there were few fighters over Berlin. Bad weather on the outward route also kept down the number of German fighters finding the bomber stream.] The final run up north of Berlin. We were in the third wave. Much more activity now, with searchlights trying to penetrate the cloud and pick up the bombers ahead of us. Plenty of flak as we approached the target but not really close. No sign of fighters. Some turbulence from the slipstream of other bombers – always a bit disconcerting.

'Wanganui' marker flares ahead were going down on time. We would be bombing blind. The markers were well concentrated and a good glow of fires started by the aircraft attacking ahead of us showed through the cloud.

'Straight and level now with two minutes to go and bomb doors open. Bomb-aimer called 'Bombs gone' on the middle of the markers. We felt the 4,000lb 'cookie' go and then the canisters of incendiaries – always a relief to have them away and the bomb doors closed again.[9] We flew right across Berlin and out well to the north before turning for home. Navigator said four hours to go.... A long haul to the Dutch coast; we eventually crossed but didn't relax – you could get caught by fighters over the North Sea.'

Berlin was again covered by 10/10th's cloud. The heaviest bombing was in the southern and south-eastern districts but many bombs also fell to the east of the capital. No. 6 Group records declared: 'Bright red glow visible on cloud and several explosions were seen.' All told 388 houses and other mixed property were destroyed; 182 people were killed, more than 600 were injured and another 10,000 were bombed out. By now it was estimated that 25 per cent of Berlin's accommodations were uninhabitable.

After bombing 'Ben' Frazier described 'Victor's route home as 'uneventful': 'Crossing the North Sea, 'Victor' went into a gentle incline towards home base, as if by a sort of homing instinct. The searchlights of England sent out a greeting of welcome. For miles along the coast they stood almost evenly spaced, vertical sentries guarding the island. Then they started waving downwards in the direction of the nearest airfield. No doubt they were helping home a damaged bomber. How different they were from the menacing tentacles over the German cities. 'Victor' arrived over the home field. The wireless-operator called base over his repaired equipment. He said simply: 'V-Victor.'

'The clear voice of a girl came pleasantly over the intercom, '"V for Victor", prepare to pancake.' The short businesslike message in service slang was a wonderful welcome home. 'Victor' circled the field, losing altitude.

'"Victor" in funnels.'

'"V-Victor", pancake,' the girl's voice said. 'Victor' touched down, ran down the flarepath and turned off on the perimeter track.

'"V-Victor" clear of flarepath.' The ground crew met 'Victor' and acted as a guide back into the dispersal area.

'How was it?'

'Piece of cake,' someone said. The crew got out, collected their gear, the parachutes, Mae Wests, the navigator's bag, the guns, etc. and then, as one man, lit up cigarettes. The pilot walked around the plane looking for any damage. There was one small hole through the aileron but it was too dark to see it then. The bus arrived and the crew clambered in with all the gear and were taken back to the locker room. June was there and gathered all the stuff over the counter and staggered away, lost from sight under a mound of yellow suits and Mae Wests. Then back to the briefing room where a cup of hot tea with rum in it was waiting. Each captain signed his name on the board as he came in. Crew by crew, the men went into the Intelligence room, carrying their spiked tea with them. There were packages of cigarettes on the table and everyone chain-smoked, lighting up from the butt of the previous one. The Intelligence Officer asked brief questions and the replies were brief such as 'The heavy flak was light and the light flak heavy.' It was over in a very few minutes and you went back to the briefing room and bantered over the trip with the other crews. No trouble, any of them, but there were gaps in the list of captains chalked on the board.

'It's like that,' the 'Wingco' remarked. 'In night flying, you usually get back intact, or you don't get back at all. If you get coned, or a fighter sees you before you see it, then very often you've had it, but if somebody else gets coned then it's that much easier for you.'

'You thought of the other Lancaster the Ju 88 got with the same burst that missed 'Victor'. And you lit another cigarette. The first signs of dawn were coming over the field now and off in the distance, on the bleak, windswept, little knoll, 'Victor' stood guard over the empty dispersal points from which other men and ships had gone out a short while before. '… If somebody else gets coned then it's that much easier for you.'

'Ben' Frazier was not the only American national flying this night. On 207 Squadron at Spilsby 'T-Tommy' was flown by 22-year-old First Lieutenant Frank B. Solomon USAAF of Lincoln County, Maine. The 23-year-old Flying Officer Willis A. DeBardeleben USAAF, born on 25 January 1920 at Lake Charles, Calsasieu Parish in Louisiana, was his wireless-operator. They also carried a 'passenger', Sergeant F. Collis, who was flying his first operation as 'second dickey'. Collis observed that the two Americans 'flew in a manner which would have raised a few eyebrows in the RAF. After take-off they argued about everything that should have been mutually accepted, such as which course to take, at what height and this was the pattern throughout the flight. We had an adventurous trip, which I thought was the norm, because it was my first op. And I thought it would be my last. It was only by the Grace of God that we got back.'[10]

It was actually Solomon's twenty-fourth trip and he was due to complete his tour with the USAAF, but all of 'T-Tommy's crew were killed on the next Berlin trip:

'This time the route home was north of the Ruhr and the flight time was seven hours and five minutes,' wrote Sergeant Keith Parry on 61 Squadron at Skellingthorpe. 'Again, apart from the target, we had an easy ride. Not so for George Harvey, whom I had flown my first trip with for this was the night his luck ran out. On my return I stood in the ops room and stared at the blank space on the ops board where his landing time should have been. I couldn't believe it. I hung around until his endurance had expired and I knew he must be down somewhere. There was no news of him diverting and "MISSING" was chalked up on the board opposite his name. I went back to the Mess with a heavy heart. I never did hear what happened to them: they just disappeared, with all the others, into that black void on the other side of the North Sea, which was gobbling up men and machines with increasing ferocity. The next day, Harvey's name had been erased from the board in "Jimmy" Moss's office.'[11]

George Harvey was once again piloting DV399. He and some of his crew were on their twenty-second operation of their tour, which included seven trips to the 'Big City'. On approaching Berlin the Lancaster was, without warning, suddenly coned by searchlights and subjected to intense flak. Receiving a direct hit 'R-Roger' burst into flames. Pilot Officer Don Thomas was thrown across his turret, his oxygen tube twisting around his throat and strangling him. His clothing and parachute were on fire. Tearing off his helmet, he struggled through the smoke and flames. George Harvey had given the order to bail out, but Thomas was only half-conscious through lack of oxygen and on the verge of collapsing. Then he saw Dick Stuart waving to him and pointing to the escape hatch and the sight caused him to take fresh heart, crawl to the hatch and bail out. Dick Stuart was quite fit and unharmed and could have followed him out. 'He must,' said Thomas, 'have gone back to help the other members of the crew.'

The aircraft exploded shortly afterwards. Don Thomas's parachute was badly burned; consequently descending at such speed, that on landing, his body was driven a foot deep into the earth, his spine damaged, ankle broken and his face terribly burned. After recovering consciousness he blew his whistle to attract help. Civilians who came to him kicked him savagely. He was later tortured in an attempt to make him divulge information concerning the object of the raid. Eventually he was taken to hospital, treated and sent into captivity. There were no other survivors on 'R-Roger', the others being laid to rest in the Berlin War Cemetery. Flight Sergeant Kenneth Prouten was the unlucky bomb-aimer on this occasion. He was 20 years old.

Mike Beetham landed safely back at Skellingthorpe at around half-past midnight as a wedge of high pressure moved east over the British Isles and the overnight fog in the east and south-east started to lift.

'At debriefing we reported a quiet and uneventful trip – for Berlin. Just one aircraft lost on our squadron – not bad for such a tough target and looked like it had been a good attack. And so to our bacon and eggs and bed at 0200 hours. Next morning at Skellingthorpe I reported to the flight at 10.00 hours to see whether ops were on that night. The Flight Commander said, 'So you had a quiet trip last night?'

'Yes,' I replied. 'Fairly uneventful.'

'Come with me,' he said.

'We drove out to the flight dispersal and to my aircraft.... Two of my ground crew were on top of the starboard wing. I was staggered to see a large hole through the starboard wing outer fuel tank – a clear gash through it. 'What have you done to our new aircraft?' asked my corporal airframe fitter. 'We are going to have to change the wing.' We had collected an incendiary from another Lancaster above us over the target – the outline was clearly visible through the wing. 'Didn't you really feel anything over the target?' queried the flight commander. 'No,' I said. 'Some usual turbulence from the slipstream of other aircraft and some flak but not close enough to worry.' I thanked my lucky stars we always used the outer wing fuel first so the tank would have been empty and purged with nitrogen well before the target – and I wondered how close had been the rest of the bomb load.'

At Kirmington, which had thirteen Lancasters operating, 166 Squadron had almost given up all hope of seeing 'X-X-ray' and Pilot Officer Joe Horsley's crew again but then a message was received giving an ETA, which unbelievably was two hours after everyone else. 'X-X-ray' had developed engine trouble on the outward trip after crossing the Dutch coast but Horsley continued on to the target with the starboard engine feathered. Over the target he had difficulty in getting the bomb doors open, but managed to jettison the 'cookie' on his second run. The bomb-aimer then reported that the incendiaries would not release. 'X-X-ray' was hit by flak and the port-outer engine caught fire. The fire was extinguished and the engine was feathered. By now, 'X-ray' was down to 5,000 feet and outside the target area. The artificial horizon and directional gyro were u/s and the aircraft was now flying on one starboard and one port engine.

When crossing the Dutch coast at low level on return, searchlights attempted to cone the aircraft, but the gunners discouraged them by firing at them. Horsley brought 'X-X-ray' in to a safe landing on the two remaining engines and as he touched down, the third engine cut. When the engineer officer checked his remaining fuel supply, he couldn't find any. This remarkable performance earned Horsley and his 20-year-old navigator, Pilot Officer Kenneth Frank Cornwell, immediate DFCs. Their luck ran out, however, on 28/29 January on another Berlin raid when 'Z-Zebra' was shot down and crashed at Fretzdorf with no survivors.

At the bomber airfields in the early hours of that Thursday morning the word was that Berlin's defences had been hampered by Bomber Command's tactics and bad weather, resulting in relatively 'low' losses overall. A long approach route from the south, passing south of the Ruhr and then within 20 miles of Leipzig together with Mosquito diversions at Düsseldorf, Leipzig and Magdeburg, caused the German controller great difficulties and there were few fighters over Berlin. Bad weather on the outward route also kept down the number of German fighters finding the bomber stream. The alarm in Berlin sounded at 7.23 pm and the all-clear came at 8.56. A total of just over 2,314 tons of bombs and incendiaries were dropped causing 151 casualties and 514 injured with a further 100,000 made homeless. Preliminary evidence revealed that extensive damage was caused to the area around the Tiergarten and in the government district. Eight industrial targets were also destroyed, thirty more severely damaged and twenty-seven slightly damaged. Seven military installations were destroyed with another twenty-four damaged.

The raid was Clayton Moore's thirteenth trip on 9 Squadron: 'We again took off in '*Spirit of Russia*'. It proved to be reasonably trouble-free, despite the feeling of fear born of superstition that stayed with me throughout the flight. Again, all of the Squadron crews returned safely, thus indicating the degree of efficiency attributable to the squadron's air and ground crews. However, command's tally amounted to twenty aircraft lost, which was about the going rate for such a raid, but the overall trend was moving steadily upwards.'[12]

'Low' the RAF losses might have been (more than 100 aircraft were damaged), but each of the 11 Lancasters and 9 Halifaxes that failed to return was an individual tragedy that greatly affected all and sundry, and as for 217 missing airmen there would be no more flying in this world, for the duration or forever. Then there were the dead and wounded on the bombers that did return. In 6 Group thirty-nine Lancasters on 408, 426 and 432 Squadrons and ninety Halifaxes on 419, 427, 428, 429, 431 and 434 Squadrons were over the target at between 18,000 and 24,000 feet, releasing 300,000lb of high explosives and 432,000lb of incendiaries. On 434 'Bluenose' Squadron RCAF Pilot Officer Robert Alexander Pratt's Halifax was hit by flak and a night-fighter outbound. The starboard inner engine was damaged and caught fire and both outers were damaged. Pratt was slightly injured in the leg, but Sergeant Albert Bostock the RAF flight engineer was killed instantly while taking astro shots. Canadian Sergeant John Gordon Stinson, who was on his first operation as second pilot, took over, went to the target and bombed it while Sergeant Samson, the bomb-aimer, took over the flight engineer's duties. Stinson brought the damaged Halifax back to a safe landing at Woodbridge where at least sixty-five holes were counted throughout the fuselage. He and Samson were later commissioned and awarded DFCs.

On 408 'Goose' Squadron 24-year-old Canadian Flight Lieutenant Walter Torrence Wilton and his Lancaster crew failed to return, the forty-second victory for Oberleutnant Heinz-Wolfgang Schnaufer and his second of the night. Two Halifax crews, one skippered by Canadian Flight Sergeant R.L. Thompson on 419 'Moose' Squadron and the other by Canadian Flight Lieutenant Jack Norrin Nelson on 431 'Iroquois' Squadron, also failed to return. Thompson had taken 'Y-Yorker' off from Middleton St George at approximately 1648 hours. Somewhere near the target mechanical problems were believed to have caused the outer port engine to lose power and then start a fire on the port wing spreading across to the inner engine and moving towards the fuselage. Orders were given to bail out. All the crew safely bailed out and the crew was rounded up by the German patrols in the area and became PoWs for the rest of the war. There were no survivors from Nelson's crew.

'W-Willie' on 427 'Lion' Squadron RCAF had taken off at 2000 hours: 'The crew was well into Germany when, in the area of Hanover,' recalled Flight Sergeant 'Phil' Dubois, 'our mid-upper gunner Johnny Gibbs told me there was another Halifax on our port beam. It was slightly above us and flying slightly to starboard. We could both see that there was no fear of collision. When it was directly above us our flight engineer looked up through the astrodome and yelled, "DIVE!" We were at 18,000 feet. Deegan pulled up at 14,000 feet. The constant speed unit in the port outer went U/S. "Deeg" managed to feather it, but we were unable to gain altitude. By then we were well behind the bomber stream and had no desire to fly over Berlin at 14,000 feet by ourselves so decided to jettison our bombs live and return to base. There was a very large explosion when our 2,000lb bomb exploded.

'Soon after we set course for the Dutch coast the red fighter flares started dropping. At this stage of the war the fighter boxes were being manned by inexperienced crews, the experienced crews attempting to and quite successful in intercepting the bomber stream with their "Zahme Sau" or "Tame Boar" method. We did have one night-fighter come within six hundred yards of us. I gave evasive action. The fighter had his navigation lights on. This was not an uncommon practice with German night-fighters. While the gunner's attention was drawn to the fighter with its "nav" lights on, another one came in from a different direction and shot you down; however, this was not the case. We were throwing "Window" out like mad to confuse the radar. I think it was an inexperienced pilot confused by the "Window".

'As we approached the Dutch coast we were unable to maintain altitude on three engines and were down to 10,000 feet. At this time the starboard engine sprung a glycol leak and had to be feathered to maintain altitude. It then became a comedy of errors.

'We had enough "Window" for the trip to Berlin and back. Our flight engineer, "Clem" Corbiell, in an effort to lighten our load opened one of the top escape hatches and started throwing out whole unopened bundles of "Window". The first one struck the mid-upper turret, giving "Johnnie" quite a scare. He then commenced throwing them out either side and in the darkness not knowing that he had severed both the pilot's sending and receiving aerials which ran from the radio loop to both rear tailplanes.

'Jim Smith, our radio-operator was busy sending out SOSs. Of course he was not on intercom so he did not know what was going on. We still had the incendiary containers. To lighten the load further the bomb doors were opened and Bob Anderson, our bomb-aimer, jettisoned the incendiary containers. In doing so he lopped off the trailing aerial. "Smitty" managed to locate his spare trailing aerial which had come loose from its mooring in our dive and was buried in the nose under piles of open "Window" that had ended up in the nose when Deegan had pulled out of the dive. He managed to splice it on to what was left of his trailing aerial and continued sending SOSs. By this time we were down to 5,000 feet over the North Sea. The port inner engine had overheated so much that it had burnt off the exhaust manifolds, or flame dampeners, only developing about one-half power and was trailing an exhaust flame about fifteen to twenty feet behind. "Johnnie" said he could read a newspaper in the mid-upper turret. We never considered removing the guns as we did not know if we were being tracked by a German fighter.

'By the time we were halfway across the North Sea we were at 5,000 feet and staggering through the air at 110 mph, just above stalling speed. I had no desire to ditch in the North Sea at night in the middle of winter. "Smitty" had managed to splice in the pilot's sending aerial onto his trailing aerial, but not the receiving aerial. Deegan was calling "Darkie", but not receiving an answer.

'We were down to 1,000 feet when the English east coast was sighted. The skipper told me to come out of my rear turret to the rest position as we may have to bail out. I was just over six feet tall and had difficulty getting out of the turret. I certainly preferred bailing out rather than ditching in the North Sea.

'When I plugged into the intercom in the rest position, I heard US Army Station Bungay [a US Eighth Air Force Liberator base at Flixton just outside the Suffolk market town] answering our distress call. "Clem" was trying to pump down the undercarriage, but was quite exhausted from trying to lighten the aircraft. He told me years later that a big hand came over his shoulder and in a few strokes finished the job. He said, "That was your hand 'Phil'."

'Bungay turned on its lights and fortunately, we were lined up with the runway as the port inner packed up on the way in. "Deeg" made a successful one-engine landing. We had no brakes, consequently we ran off the end of the runway, but no one was injured.'

Throughout eastern England as the ETAs on the missing aircraft came and went, ground crews, WAAFs and airmen waited more in hope than expectation for news. Australian Flight Sergeant (later Flying Officer) George Martin Burcher on 10 Squadron had the starboard outer engine of his Halifax hit by flak two minutes from Berlin, but carried on into the target area where two incendiary bombs struck the starboard fuselage side which cut the leads to the instrument gauges while the other bomb crashed through the starboard flaps. On operations Burcher would wear a sheepskin vest supplied by the Australian Comforts Fund. Painted on the back of the vest was the word 'Australia', along with a picture of 'Mickey Mouse' and an RAAF logo inside a map of Australia. On the return journey a 2,000-pounder was discovered hung up in the bomb bay. It could not be released in the normal way so Pilot Officer Barry Ward, the Australian bomb-aimer, tried to release it manually, which he did after one and a half hours. Shortly after crossing the Norfolk coast the port inner engine failed completely and Burcher made an emergency landing at the grass airfield at RAF Swanton Morley.

For his action Burcher was awarded a DFM on 11 February 1944. A Distinguished Flying Cross followed on 14 July 1944 for being 'a most outstanding captain whose fighting qualities and personal courage have greatly inspired his crews.' He returned to Australia in June 1945, taking up a staff position at Tocumwal, later flying repatriated prisoners of war home from Manila.

Another Australian, Pilot Officer Stanley James Ireland, a 30-year-old pilot from Glebe, New South Wales on 460 Squadron RAAF took 'N for Nancy' off from Binbrook at 1703 hours for the raid on Berlin on 29 December 1943. The 'Big City' was successfully bombed but on the return flight at 2230 hours 'Nancy' was attacked by a night-fighter over Aachen and it crashed in nearby Kerkrade in the courtyard of the monastery of the friars of Sint Franciscus in Kerkrade- Bleijerheide with the loss of Stan Ireland and five crew. Only Flight Sergeant Francis John Seery, the 21-year-old bomb-aimer, survived. He spent the rest of the conflict as a prisoner of war at Stalag IVD near Torgau by the River Elbe.

Frank Seery wrote: 'In my understanding we crossed the German/Dutch frontier much further north than Aachen. Our prescribed track that night also coincided with my understanding. The quiet of our night was rudely shattered by what appeared to be a single shot which hit the nose of our plane. Stan called out 'It's a fighter' and dived the plane to port. While in that dive we were hit by a massive fusillade of shells. Four of the crew were killed immediately, the four engines destroyed and the plane set ablaze. Somehow Stan righted the plane, which was now on a southerly course. As I ditched the escape hatch, the slipstream caught and twisted it, jamming it in the hatch opening. My kicking of the hatch proved futile, until I got the flight engineer to join me. A couple of united kicks and the hatch flew out, followed rapidly by me, as the flight engineer raced back to collect the pilot. Unfortunately, Stan and Bill Squire didn't have a chance to follow me as the aircraft exploded a few seconds after my exit. It was a tragedy that but for the hold-up with the hatch, the three of us could possibly have escaped. Our track home that night would not have taken us anywhere near Cologne or the Aachen area, but Stan's righting of the plane, after his dive to port, would have set us on the way. Stan's only concern, of course, was to hold the plane as steadily as he could until the three of us were able to escape from it.

'When I landed in Holland my great hope was that Stan and Bill were blown clear in the explosion, but, unfortunately, they were both killed by it. '

Sergeant William Albert Henry Squire, the 19-year-old flight engineer, came from Tottenham, Middlesex. Pilot Officer Ambrose E. Blight, the 29-year-old navigator, left a widow, Patricia Collier Blight of Rose Bay, New South Wales. The others who died were the two air gunners, 21-year-old Sergeant Reginald James Poulter and 20-year-old Flight Sergeant Maxwell Hope Squires who came from Tamworth, New South Wales, and Sergeant Cyril Seddon, the 22-year-old wireless-operator who was from Ormskirk in Lancashire. All six bodies were buried in temporary graves in the grounds of the monastery. Their last internment was at the Reichswald Forest War Cemetery at Kleve.

At Waterbeach in Cambridgeshire nineteen Lancasters on 514 Squadron were detailed for bombing operations, of which two failed to take off. The only word from Canadian Flying Officer Louis 'Lou' Greenburgh and the crew of 'S-Sugar' had been a short radio message saying they were going to ditch. Greenburgh, a Canadian Jew, was born at Winnipeg in March 1916. His parents separated shortly after his birth. In 1928 Louis attended St. John's Technical High School but in 1933 he was expelled after appropriating the answers to an exam. That same year he left home and rode the rails, ending up at Vancouver, British Columbia where he worked at a variety of jobs including construction of the Big Bend Highway at Revelstoke and as a store clerk at Victoria. He later lived at Edmonton, Alberta and Usula, Ontario before ending up at Regina, Saskatchewan. There he was involved in the Regina Riots and served jail time in 1935. Upon release, in 1937 he went overseas to England with aspirations of becoming a pilot but he was accepted as a flight mechanic. He married Patty Violet 'Pat' Hamling at the Shire Hall in Cambridge on 25 September 1941. Not content with maintenance and having always longed to be a fighter pilot, Louis trained arduously and in 1942 received his wings and commission.

The Berlin raid was Greenburgh's first operation and almost his last. Near Meppen at 1815 hours he was at 20,000 feet and flying at 155 mph when Colin 'Connie' Drake, Greenburgh's Australian rear gunner saw the exhaust of a Ju 88 on the port quarter down at a range of about 700 yards, closing in. At 400 yards' range on port quarter down the night-fighter opened fire on the Lancaster. Drake gave the order to corkscrew to port while returning the enemy aircraft's fire with a very long and almost uninterrupted burst of six seconds as the Ju 88 closed in slowly passing under the Lancaster and finally breaking away on the starboard quarter down.

Sergeant Fred Carey the mid-upper gunner did not see the enemy aircraft, but fired some short bursts in the direction of 'Connie' Drake's trace. In the corkscrew Drake saw what appeared to be a rocket projectile fired at the Lancaster from the Ju 88 and 'Lou' Greenburgh and his wireless-operator, 19-year-old Gordon 'Strommy' Stromberg saw an orange glow or explosion close under the Lancaster's port wing. Greenburgh's strenuous efforts to corkscrew his way out of trouble paid dividends and the Ju 88 was shaken off, though petrol was now leaking from the damaged fuel tanks. He decided to carry on and drop his 4,000-pounder, 24 x 30lb incendiaries, 54 x 4lb incendiaries and 90 x 4lb incendiaries on Berlin. All the route-markers on the way to the target were seen in the correct positions and were effective and 'Lou's navigator, Sergeant Patrick G. Butler had little difficulty in finding the target. Fires were large and could be seen from 70 miles. At the target there was 10/10 cloud well below but at 19,000 feet Sergeant 'Don' L. Bament the Australian air bomber aimed 'S-Sugar's bomb load in the centre of about a dozen concentrated red and green sky-markers.

On the return leg near the site of the first attack at 2200 hours at 175 mph at 21,000 feet, Fred Carey reported a bright yellow flare about half a mile to starboard and identified a Ju 88 climbing on the fine starboard quarter level, not firing but manoeuvring for attack at a range of 200 yards. Carey immediately gave the order to corkscrew to starboard and he and 'Connie' Drake, who also sighted the enemy aircraft, simultaneously fired on the enemy aircraft while Greenburgh once again threw the Lancaster into a corkscrew. Carey fired three very short bursts and 'Connie' Drake fired a large number of short bursts, many of which appeared to be hitting the Ju 88. As the night-fighter broke away to starboard quarter up, 'Connie' Drake saw it wobble as if out of control and Carey saw a red glow in the centre of the fuselage as it broke away, seemingly out of control and it was claimed as probably destroyed. Three twin-engine night-fighters were lost on the evening and it is possible that Carey and Drake had accounted for one of these. Ten '4-mots' in total were claimed by nine Nachtjäger; a Halifax and a Lancaster being claimed by Oberleutnant (later Major) Heinz-Wolfgang Schnaufer.

The defenders of the Reich had not yet finished with 'S-Sugar' and her crew, however. While in the Enkhuizen area a quarter of an hour later, at height of 17,000 feet 'Connie' Drake reported and identified a Ju 88 on the starboard quarter up at a range of 400 yards, closing in and firing. The night-fighter was piloted by 25-year-old Oberfeldwebel Karl-Heinz Scherfling, who was seeking his twenty-sixth abschuss ('kill'). Drake ordered 'corkscrew starboard' and Carey saw the Ju 88 just after the dive had commenced. Both gunners opened fire simultaneously when the Junkers was at a range of 300 yards. Scherfling broke away to port quarter up, repeated a similar attack from there to starboard quarter and again a similar attack from starboard to port quarter. During each of these attacks Carey was firing a series of short bursts at the Ju 88 and Drake a long burst. In the three engagements Carey had fired 500 rounds and Drake 1,240.

Eventually Greenburgh managed to make good his escape. The damage was done, however, and the flight engineer Sergeant Les Weddle told his skipper that they had lost too much fuel and could never reach England. 'Strommy' Stromberg managed to transmit a message to Waterbeach before 'Lou' ordered the crew to bail out, 'but,' he says, 'they decided to stick with me and the ship and I didn't intend to bail out over Germany with a name like Greenburgh.

'Coming back, a hundred miles away from England, I found that I had four dead engines and we fell like a rock. I knew we would all be dead in a few minutes. The altimeter unwound fast. I couldn't see a thing; everything was black. When the altimeter registered zero I heaved back on the wheel. The bomber hit a wave, nosedived into the heavy sea and broke in two. I was knocked cold. The crew was in forward crash positions and jumped into the half-inflated dinghy. Two of them pulled me out of the water-filled cockpit.

'That night was sheer hell. The waves tossed the dinghy all over the place and by the next day we were completely exhausted and felt helpless. Sergeant "Paddy" Butler said he intended to join the navy to see the world. "Strommy" Stromberg the wireless-operator said, "So you joined 'Lou's crew and you'll see the next world."

'Hours later, the dinghy was half-filled with water and leaking. "Connie" Drake saw a flicker in the sky. I shot off our last Very cartridge. The flicker turned out to be a Lancaster.'

At first light that morning Wing Commander Arthur James Sampson DFC refused to leave his crew without hope of rescue. Assembling a scratch crew he flew back along the return route. Seventy miles off the Norfolk coast, on the first leg of the search, a Very light was seen and a dinghy in which there appeared to be six men was shortly afterwards sighted. This was kept in sight for three hours during which time other aircraft on ASR duties appeared and remained on the scene. A second dinghy and packages of warm clothing were dropped. As one of the packages was being hauled into the dinghy it fell on 'Connie' Drake's foot. Finally, a rescue launch appeared in the vicinity and was guided to the dinghy and all the occupants were taken on board. This was the first known case of a 'ditching' on 514 Squadron and the circumstances of the rescue 'caused great satisfaction'. The crew was admitted to the Royal Navy hospital at Great Yarmouth at 9 o'clock that night. They had been fifteen hours afloat. The Lancaster itself was observed still afloat, after nearly twelve hours in the sea. Butler had received a nasty bang on the head when the Lancaster had hit the sea, but apart from that and 'Connie' Drake's injured foot, all were in remarkably good shape. While Drake remained in the sick bay for a further week the rest of the crew enjoyed a long leave, tradition being one day off for every hour in 'the drink'. They rejoined the squadron during the last week of January 1944.[13] Greenburgh was rewarded with the DFC on 14 March for his gallantry. This was not the last time his exploits would feature in the annals of the history of 514 Squadron.

At Leeming news had been received that 'Deeg' Deegan's crew had got down safely at Bungay. 'Later in the day,' recalled 'Phil' Dubois, 'the CO and the Engineering Officer flew down in an Oxford. The EO said, "four new engines". They took our navigator and Skipper back with them. That night the remainder of the crew headed into Norwich where "Rex" Clibbery entertained our gracious "Yank" hosts by singing many songs including "*We were Flying Fuckin' Fortresses at 40,000 feet*". The next day we were given railway passes to return to base. We got as far as Peterborough and "Rex" said there was no way he was going to spend New Year's Eve on a bloody train. We booked into a hotel and spent the night in a pub. "Clem" said we had a good time and were invited to a house party after the pub closed. After a few pints of beer my recollection was very hazy.'

'Deeg' lauded the work and co-operation of everyone concerned including his second pilot 'Rex' Clibbery and particularly praised the work of the 19-year-old wireless-operator Flight Sergeant James Albert Smith and the 23-year-old Canadian flight engineer Sergeant Joseph Clement Aloysius Corbiell. Acting Squadron Leader Bob Deegan was awarded the DFC on 13 October 1944. He survived the war. Both Clibbery and his mid-upper gunner Sergeant Robert E. Qualle received the DFM for their actions on Magdeburg on the night of 21 January 1944. On 10/11 May Warrant Officer2 'Rex' Clibbery's Halifax was badly shot about by a night-fighter while on an operation to Ghent and he was forced to land at Woodbridge where the aircraft was so badly damaged it was classified as beyond repair.

'Deeg's erstwhile navigator, Cecil Axford, had been posted to 420 'Snowy Owl' Squadron at Tholthorpe where he finished his tour. 'He had wired to go home to Canada,' recalled 'Wilf' Axford, 'but on the very next op on 12th August a navigator had taken sick, so my brother went along. It was just a short trip to France; however, the 'plane was hit by flak and my brother was the only one who died.'[14]

At Witchford on Friday, 31 December *Bang On*, the 115 Squadron newsletter, said: 'Have patience chaps, the 'Happy Valley' is still there. Berlin it must be until the place is wiped out. It is the HQ of nearly everything that matters to Germany: armaments, engineering, food stuffs … administration. Berlin is the 'London of Germany'. Until Berlin is 'Hamburged', 'Jerry's mainspring is wound up.

'Considerable damage has been inflicted in the Tiergarten area and in Berlin's Whitehall in the central district where over one-third of the inhabitants and the largest part of the machinery of government have been driven from the capital. If the corresponding area of London had been bombed as Berlin had been the government buildings in Whitehall would have suffered severely. The Treasury largely destroyed, the Foreign Office partially gutted, Scotland Yard would be soot black and ruined, the Ministry of Transport also. Downing Street would not have escaped, the Cabinet Offices at No. 10 would be roofless and fire would have destroyed No. 11. Many other well-known landmarks in central London would have disappeared such as the British Museum Library and the University would have been damaged, the Albert Hall and Drury Lane smouldering wrecks, office blocks like Shell Mex House and Bush House burnt out; the Ritz Hotel destroyed and the Savoy damaged by fire; the Café Royal would have been gutted from roof to basement. Hardly an embassy or legation would have escaped. Railway stations such as Euston, Victoria and King's Cross would either be gutted or severely damaged by fire.'

At year's end the greatest devastation in Berlin extended over an area of 8 square miles from the east side of the central district to Charlottenburg on the north-west and to Wilmersdorf on the south-west. The eight major attacks delivered during November and December, involving 3,646 successful sorties and a bomb weight of 14,000 tons, had wrought enormous damage over a wide area of the city. No less than ninety-eight industrial concerns had suffered varying degrees of destruction including many factories engaged in the manufacture of aircraft engines and components, electrical and wireless equipment and a whole range of products essential to the German war effort. In addition rail and road communications, public utilities, ministerial and public buildings and military installations had all sustained appreciable damage. Devastation, as confirmed by day photographic cover, extended over an area of 2,757 acres representing approximately 20 per cent of the fully built-up zones. The aircraft firms of BMW, Argus Motoren (a manufacturing firm known for their series of small inverted-V engines and the As 014 pulsejet for the V-1 flying bomb), Dornier and Heinkel had all been hit. The total of aircraft missing from these operations was 183.

Some considered this figure 'small for Berlin', but these were early days. With the turn of the year the situation would change markedly as the Germans put forth everything they had in terms of night-fighters and by the end of March the North German Plain was to be littered with the bones of burned-out Lancasters, Halifaxes and Stirlings.[15]

Chapter Ten

Unhappy Hogmanay

'This Battle (Berlin) was indeed the bitterest part of the war for me – I thought that the backbone of the Pathfinder Force was really broken.'

'Pathfinder' Bennett.

On Saturday, 1 January 1944 Ursula von Kardorff got out her journal, which had become 'a diary of a nightmare'. The year 1943 had been the worst of her life. Her brother Jurgen, one of her two brothers fighting at the front, had been killed. Because of the raids, people were rendered homeless by bombing, so that the Germans now wandered around as homeless as the Jews, loaded down with the same kinds of sacks and bundles. At least it relieved one of some of one's guilt and that was a comfort.

'This must be a better year,' she wrote in her diary as a motto. 'If only the war could end this year and we could be freed from that monster Hitler I should never ask for another thing for the rest of my life. Last night I saw Barchen home at two in the morning because she was too frightened to be alone in the subway which leads from the Savignyplatz station, where a man was shot dead before her very eyes a few days ago. We said goodbye by the light of our torches and I was walking home alone when suddenly a ruined house collapsed, just behind me, with a terrifying crash. My hat was blown off and if it had happened a second earlier I should have been buried. All the same I was not at all frightened, I don't know why. I imagine that the climax of the war will be reached in the spring and that if we here in Germany do not do something soon to change the situation radically we shall be finished by the autumn. By then the Russians will be here.'[1]

At Waddington the first day of the New Year began as a very quiet and wintry Saturday morning with personnel either exhausted from the recent trips to Berlin or hung over from the New Year's Eve fancy dress dance that had been held in the mess the night before. However, things would not stay quiet for long because that night the 'Big City' was on the battle order again, for the ninth time that winter.

For Flying Officer John Chatterton DFC and crew on 'Y-Yorker' on 44 ('Rhodesia') Squadron at Dunholme Lodge it was the eighth operational trip and fifth to Berlin (their first operational flight to Germany had been Berlin on 18/19 November). The two Scots on the crew were disgusted. They considered that there were better ways of celebrating Hogmanay. 'We were definitely a bit weary, both in mind and body,' wrote Chatterton. However, while the target on the weekend of 1/2 January was not unexpected, the overworked ground crews at every aerodrome in Bomber Command had their work cut out getting the requisite number of aircraft operational. At Waddington 463 and 467 Squadrons, for instance, had only ten Lancasters each that were serviceable after the two recent raids on the 'Big City'.

Another pressing problem was that some of the recent replacement air crews would not be ready in time. Two new crews on 467 Squadron that had just arrived were not on the battle order. One of these crews was led by the quiet but highly-experienced Australian Squadron Leader Donald Philip Smeed Smith, better known as 'Phil'. Born on 13 March 1917, he was an industrial chemist working in the sugar industry when he joined the RAAF in 1940. In England he completed his first tour of operations flying Wellingtons from Elsham Wolds on 103 Squadron and had followed this with almost a year and a half instructing at an Operational Training Unit in the Cotswolds.

Smith had some additional administration to attend to, having been selected to replace the outgoing Flight Lieutenant Bill Forbes as Officer Commanding 'A' Flight and so he and his crew were stood down. Yet Flight Sergeant James Mudie, the other new crew's 21-year-old skipper, was anxious to 'get cracking'. Born in Dundee, Scotland on 20 May 1922, his family emigrated to Dalkeith, Nedlands in Western Australia. Mudie had enlisted in the RAAF when he was living in Perth. He would join 30-year-old Flight Sergeant Leo Braham Patkin's crew as a 'second dickey' on 'M-Mother' for the Berlin trip while his crew settled into their new surroundings. Patkin had been born in Melbourne on 28 September 1913 and was married.

At Waltham (Grimsby) a dozen Lancasters were on the 550 Squadron battle order. 'T-Squared' was skippered by Flying Officer 'Gil' Bryson. Their last two trips had been to the 'Big City' before they had received two days of rest:

'That Saturday evening,' recalled wireless-operator Sergeant Jim Donnan, 'we were engaged in routine pre-operational checks and testing of our equipment prior to the main briefing, which commenced in a tense atmosphere. When the curtain was drawn aside exposing the operational map, the target was Berlin for the third consecutive time, only this time our route to the "Big City" was almost directly from the Dutch coast across an area which was becoming increasingly dangerous because of night-fighter activity.'

The original take-off time was planned for mid-evening but deteriorating weather conditions delayed take-off for several hours. It was therefore difficult during this period for crews, keyed-up but weary after the two punishing trips recently to Berlin, to relax. At Metheringham 21-year-old Pilot Officer Dick Starkey and two other Lancaster pilots on 106 Squadron, Pilot Officers Fred Garnett (21) and 27-year-old Edwin Ted Holbourn, who had reported at the normal time, cycled back in the blackout to the mess and played table-tennis to kill time. Holbourn, who was from Hounslow in Middlesex, had been a railway guard before enlisting. On 16 December 1939 he had married Hilda May Cushing.

Dick Starkey was a former pit office worker from Barnsley who had wanted to give the enemy 'a taste of their own medicine' after watching the Germans' two-night blitz on Sheffield earlier in the war. His navigator Colin Roberts was also from the 'steel city'. Starkey had received his commission two hours before the crew's first operation, to Leipzig, on 20 October 1943 and their second, to Berlin, had followed at the commencement of the Battle of Berlin in November. On stand-down on foggy and cold drizzly nights in the middle of the 'Berlin Season' survival was the topic of conversation among the six officers in Starkey's Nissen hut on the edge of the Fens. The three pilots more or less accepted what would be their fate because of extreme odds against their survival, having to try to control the aircraft while the crew bailed out. The bomb-aimer and navigator in that hut were shot down, but Starkey and the two other pilots had so far lived a charmed life.[2]

As New Year's Day was drawing to a close 421 Lancaster crews throughout eastern England prepared for take-off. At Metheringham at one minute to midnight Canadian Squadron Leader Albert Robinson Dunn led fifteen Lancasters on 106 Squadron off into the night sky.[3]

At Wickenby Lancasters on 12 Squadron began lurching slowly out of their dispersals within sight of Lincoln Cathedral, 11 miles to the south-west as the crow flies.

On 'C-Charlie' Pilot Officer K.L. West checked on each of the other six crew members in turn:

'OK engineer, it's 2358 hours and we're ready to start up.'

'OK Skip, ground/flight switch to ground, trolley acc is plugged in, engine controls set, fuel OK.'

'Right, start up number one.' The big prop turned slowly with a whining noise, it kicked and with a cloud of exhaust smoke burst into life with a deep-throated roar. Number two, three and four were running now, all gauges OK.

'Ground/flight, switch to "flight": set engines to 1,200 rpm to warm up.'

Sergeant R.H. Pearce, the flight engineer, was sitting next to the pilot on a fold-down seat, thereby enabling him to assist him with some of the controls during take-off and landing. His station was equipped with a panel which enabled him to monitor the engines and the various hydraulic systems and to transfer fuel from one tank to another.

Sergeant Ken Apps, the mid-upper gunner, and Vernon Archie Panniers, the 27-year-old rear gunner checked the movements of their turrets. In the radio compartment on the port side of the aircraft, as well as operating the wireless equipment 21-year-old Sergeant Dennis Leslie Smith was also required to act as an air gunner in an emergency, to discharge 'Window'. He was also responsible for monitoring the 'Monica' or 'Fishpond' equipment.

At his station on the port side of the aircraft, behind the pilot and flight engineer and in front of the wireless-operator's station, Warrant Officer E.A. Walters, the Canadian navigator, sat with a large chart table in front of him and checked the 'Gee' and the compass etc. Bomb-aimer Sergeant E. Waterhouse checked his Mk XIV bomb sight. While his station was in the nose of the aircraft, he would spend the bulk of the flight seated beside the navigator so that he could provide fixes, weather reports etc. to assist the navigation process.

All the crew were working like clockwork now, going though the actions in which they had been well trained. With the work in hand, they could feel their confidence building and the butterflies being flushed out.

West set each engine to 1,500 rpm and checked magnetos, opening up all four engines in turn to zero boost and checking the superchargers and the constant speed units. He received a good luck wave back as he throttled back to 1,200 rpm and the aircraft trundled forward, making one last check on intercom:

'Pilot to rear gunner, all OK?'

'Rear gunner OK Skip.'

'Mid-upper OK?'

'OK Skipper', and so on checking on all the crew in turn once again, a procedure that would be carried out over and over again during the trip.

'Right chaps, we are ready to taxi.' West gave thumbs-up to the ground crew and waved the chocks away.

Each Lancaster was marshalled by an airman walking backwards, beckoning hands above his head. As West swung 'C-Charlie' onto the perimeter track the marshaller turned and ran for the grass, out of 'Charlie's path. He stood holding up his thumbs as the bomber lumbered past and then bent over, clasping his cap to his head, as the slipstream of the four propellers washed over him. The light was beginning to fade and other Lancasters were starting to roll along the perimeter track, big and black with their navigation lights on, towards the take-off point. The Lancaster moved warily along the taxiway, rudders swinging, brakes squealing and as it passed by another Lancaster pilot saw the mid-upper gunner's face behind his gun barrels. He put a thumb up and saw his gloved hand wave in reply.

'Last one back buys the beers' had been the mid-upper gunner's bet with the pilot's crew as they were leaving the briefing. 'Don't forget, I'll have your ration tomorrow night because you won't bloody well be coming back,' was the response!

'Charlie' was ready to take its place in the queue for take-off, the usual group of well-wishers gathered by the signals hut at the end of the runway. All ranks, officers, airmen and WAAFs, all with friends and loved ones taking off into the evening sky, perhaps never to be seen again. All had learned to steel themselves and put on a cheerful smile and a wave to give the crews confidence and they repeated this performance night after night.[4]

Before West reached the runway he called up the crew to say that they had an overheated engine. 'After a quick vote,' wrote Ken Apps, 'the crew decided to cross fingers and get the old lady off the ground as quickly as possible.'[5]

West closed the cabin window and instructed Panniers: 'Turret to port, Archie.' After a thumbs-up signal to the spectators he advanced the throttles with the brakes on, released the brakes slowly, advanced the throttles further as the Lanc surged forward, began to pedal the rudder controls with both legs, took his right hand off the throttles so that both hands could grip the control column, and saying 'Okay flight engineer, through the gates', Pearce would push the throttles to their furthest extent, West would ease back the column and the bomber would become airborne. During this procedure it was the bomb-aimer's job to watch the engineer's panel where, among other instruments, there were four small sockets in a row. If the lights in any of these sockets glowed red it meant that the engineer had about fifteen seconds in which to switch over the petrol cocks before an engine cut from fuel starvation.

'C-Charlie' got airborne but the crew's troubles were far from over, as Ken Apps recalled:

'As we climbed over the aerodrome the guns started firing on their own and there were tracers flying everywhere; this was due to a short in the electrics. Archie Panniers and I quickly dismantled the Brownings, therefore leaving the plane with no armament at all – and still, the young, motley crew decided to press on towards the target.'

The delay caused by the weather also caused a change to the route, which was originally planned as a wide northerly approach over Denmark and the Baltic and a long southerly withdrawal south of the Ruhr and over Belgium. The late take-offs would not allow enough hours of darkness for this long flight and the bombers were ordered to fly to Berlin on the much-used direct route across Holland. In an attempt to try to draw defenders away from the attack on Berlin, a total of twenty-three Mosquitoes were detailed to make precision raids on Witten, Duisburg, Bristellerie and Cologne, eleven OTU Wellington sorties would scatter propaganda leaflets over France and a diversionary force of fifteen more Mosquitoes were to harass Hamburg. Six bombers were detailed to fly RCM sorties.[6]

The sky was dark and overcast as the bombers flew through layers of broken cloud, climbing to their operational height, heading east over the North Sea. John Chatterton had taken his 'ancient Y-Yorker' off from Dunholme Lodge at 2300 hours on this murky night:

'The start was not auspicious!' wrote Chatterton. 'As we left the English coast, in cloud, a shot from "friendly forces" (could it be the Navy again?) shattered the Perspex above my head, nicked the helmet and put me in a daze for the next hour or so as we ploughed through layers of cloud to the target.'

Brian Rew's crew on 12 Squadron at Wickenby had flown a total of eight successful trips to Berlin. This would be their ninth, but about one and a half hours into the flight, Rew's crew were recalled by W/T. The HE bombs were jettisoned at sea and the incendiaries brought back. Other aborting crews had not even taken off. At Ludford Magna Lancasters ran off the perimeter track and prevented three ABC aircraft from taking off. At Graveley two Pathfinders on 35 Squadron were also prevented from taxiing out to take off. On 550 Squadron two Lancasters had returned to Grimsby early. As the ten remaining crews approached the Dutch coast they could see that the anti-aircraft defences were very active and men like Jim Donnan on 'T-Squared' became alert to the dangers ahead:

'Flying over Germany, occasional bursts of flak and flashes lit up the thick, unbroken cloud along the route. While searching the night-fighter waveband I was aware of considerable activity by the German control. We found it necessary to keep a sharp look out even though our trip had been uneventful so far.'

After celebrating the incoming New Year and her birthday at Schlöss Königswart with champagne and jam puffs, 'Missie' Vassiltchikov had caught the midnight train from the spa town of Marienbad in West Bohemia for Berlin. She hoped that by taking the late train she would avoid the now almost nightly raid and arrive in the city early on Sunday. However, her train was, as usual, late and she was not to know that the operation was shifted to the early morning hours so as to avoid raiding by moonlight. The passengers sat for an hour in the freezing station. It was snowing hard. Just as the train was pulling in, the sirens sounded. The lights went out and 'Missie' climbed into the wrong carriage; it was full of sleeping soldiers returning from the Balkans in various states of disarray, most of them with beards several weeks old. Later on the female train controller told 'Missie' to change carriages, but as planes were still flying overhead she chose to remain under the protection of 'the brave boys in blue'.

'Missie' worried about her mother having to drive back to Königswart during a raid. She was also worried about herself as, with snow on the ground, her train was far more visible. However, the Allied planes were apparently heading for a more important target and the train reached Leipzig safely, just in time to make her connection, but when the train reached the outskirts of Berlin the passengers were held up for another four and a half hours. Many tracks were torn up and trains had to wait their turn. Some of the passengers got hysterical, climbed out through the windows and took off on foot.

'Missie' stayed in her seat and reached Anhalter Bahnhof at 3 o'clock on Sunday afternoon, found a bus still running and headed for the Woyrschstrasse. As far as she could see, Berlin had not changed much since her departure five weeks earlier, but things had been cleaned up a bit and the streets swept clear of debris. Her neighbourhood looked worse than the others she passed through. She went through her house with her cook. It was a dreary sight with the windows now gaping holes. 'Missie' deposited the turkey and wine she had brought from Königswart, restored herself slightly with some soup and took the train out to Potsdam.[7]

The 'Big City' was completely cloud-covered, the tops of the clouds varying from 10,000 to 18,000 feet, and many crews found a further layer above so they instead bombed cascading skymarker flares dropped by the Pathfinder Force. Furthermore, the accuracy of the sky-marking soon deteriorated as eight marker aircraft had already been lost and another exploded when hit on its marking run.

The first of these to go down on the way to the target was 'A-Apple' piloted by Wing Commander 'Jock' Abercromby DFC* who had received the Bar to his DFC in recognition of his efforts on the raid on 2/3 December while on 619 Squadron before taking command of 83 PFF Squadron. Abercromby's order banning weaving or banking gently over enemy territory probably contributed to 'A-Apple's downfall. An unseen night-fighter, probably flown by Leutnant Wendelin Breukel, set the aircraft on fire at Lutten north-east of Vechta.

The 19-year-old flight engineer Sergeant Lionel H. Lewis, who was the only survivor, wrote:

'We reached our operational height of 21,000 feet and Wing Commander Abercromby engaged the auto pilot and we were flying straight and level on a very predictable course. In quite a short time we saw the whole sky lit up like a cauldron. Twice this happened and the pilot requested the navigator to log that it was aircraft blowing up. We had no warning when the aircraft gave a lurch and went into a steep dive and I could see a glow coming from the bomb bay area. The order came to abandon the aircraft. I grabbed my parachute and put it on, removed my helmet and oxygen mask and remember putting my hands on the cushion to get at the escape hatch but I did not make it.

'There were vivid colours and an explosion. When I came to, I was falling through the air, on my back, spinning round and round. I pulled the parachute release and the handle and cable just came away and nothing happened. I got my fingers under the flap and pulled at the press studs and the parachute opened with such a jerk that I passed out again. I came to and felt very cold and found that my flying boots had gone. I came down amongst fir trees and the parachute caught up and I was swinging six feet off the ground. I released the harness and fell to the ground. The feeling of utter loneliness and wondering what to do next is something I will never forget. I was not injured, only superficial wounds to my head and hands and very heavy bruising down my left side.

'It was too dark to move around so I sat down and cut up my Mae West and parachute to make some footwear.

'As soon as it was light I started to head towards Holland. I'd found bits of newspaper with Bremen on, so had some idea where I was. Lots of aircraft debris was scattered around, one section was the nose, forward of the bomb bay, with the escape hatch intact.

'I stayed in the trees which gave very good cover; at one clearing I saw a farmer looking at one of our engines that had fallen into his field. Late that afternoon, having walked some distance I heard voices. I got back in the trees and thought I was well hidden, but the next thing I remember was being confronted by the biggest German shepherd dog I have ever seen, followed by a Wehrmacht and five civilians who each searched me and asked where I had come down and where was my parachute. They took me to a house and sat me in a room and gave me a piece of hard brown bread and a glass of Schnapps. The entire population then came to view this RAF man.

'I was later collected by two servicemen in a Volkswagen and taken to an army camp and put in a cell, prior to my wounds being treated by nuns in a small hospital. The Doctor called me 'baby killer, murderer, terror flier' and I was glad when a Wehrmacht feldwebel collected me and I was taken by rail to Bremen and then to Dulag Luft at Frankfurt for interrogation etc. With a number of other prisoners we were taken in cattle trucks on a long tiring journey, stopping at night in sidings because of bombing raids to Stalag Luft IVB at Mühlburg/Elbe.'[8]

Worst hit was 156 Squadron PFF at Warboys which readied eighteen Lancasters for the operation but four did not take off and one returned early. Of the remaining thirteen, four aircraft failed to return, all of their crews being killed. 'L-London' was flown by Squadron Leader Rowland Eden Fawcett DFC, a 26-year-old Canadian who had joined the RAF in the 1930s. In 1941 he had been shot down near Tobruk in a Lysander. Now on his third tour, Berlin was his sixty-ninth operation. He and his crew were lost without trace. 'R-Robert' flown by Flying Officer Thomas Docherty, 'X-X-ray' captained by 23-year-old Squadron Leader Robert George Falconar Stewart DFC and 'D-Dog' skippered by 22-year-old Pilot Officer Gerald Peter Robert Bond DFC of Bournemouth, Hampshire were the three others that were lost.

'K-King', one of two Lancasters on 405 'Vancouver' Squadron was shot down by a night-fighter flown by Leutnant Friedrich Potthast. Canadian Flying Officer Thomas Henry Donnelly DFM who was on his second tour of operations and his crew were buried on 5 January in Oud Schoonebeek General Cemetery not far from where the Lancaster crashed. 'R-Robert' piloted by 22-year-old Canadian Flying Officer Allan Paul Campbell crashed in France returning from Berlin. Only two of the crew survived and they were taken into captivity.

Out of twenty Lancasters on 7 Squadron that took off from Oakington, thirteen located and attacked the target. The loss of 'A-Apple' which crashed at Ramsel cost the lives of all on 27-year-old Squadron Leader Harold Royston Jaggard's crew. New Zealand Flight Lieutenant L.C. Kingsbury DFC piloting 'V-Victor', born in Christchurch on 25 May 1916, had joined the RAF in December 1938 before transferring to the RNZAF. He had survived many hazardous trips, but his luck now failed him. With one engine out of action and the port mainplane damaged by flak during the outward flight, he had pressed on through ice-laden clouds to drop his bombs, but over Berlin 'Victor', unable to maintain sufficient height, was hit again. It began to go down, completely out of control. Kingsbury was the last to leave the crippled bomber and his parachute had barely opened before he hit the ground. On regaining consciousness some hours later he found himself lying in slushy snow in a clearing in a lonely wood. His left leg was broken but he managed to crawl to the edge of the wood and find two forked branches to use as crutches. Finally he hobbled to a roadside where, after being ignored by several passers-by, he was finally found by a German policeman. All his crew survived and they too were taken prisoner.[9]

The host of bombers, averaging twelve per minute over the target, scattered around 1,200 tons of bombs, mainly in the southern parts of the city. A large number of bombs fell on the Grunewald, an extensive wooded area in the south-west of the capital. Little damage was caused and casualties were few.[10] The diversionary raid to Hamburg failed to have the desired effect. German fighter controllers were 'never in doubt as to the identity of the main objective' and German night-fighter pilots claimed twenty-seven victories this night, though the Air Ministry in London later announced that 'only isolated German night-fighters appeared over Berlin itself during the raid and during the outbound and return flights the bombers were attacked by only a few enemy aircraft, two of which positively were shot down.[11] Only twenty-eight bombers were lost on the night operations, an exceptionally low figure.'[12]

Lieutenant 'Nick' Knilans, the American pilot on 619 Squadron, might have disagreed with the official version. He had to make a sudden dive under about ten Bf 109s that suddenly appeared out of the darkness right over the target. 'Don't shoot,' he shouted at his gunners, 'they're not bothering us, don't attract their attention.' The two night-fighters that were shot down were claimed by the gunners on a Lancaster on 626 Squadron west of Hanover at 0223 hours. One attacked the bomber four times before it was hit and fell away in flames and exploded beneath the clouds. Another fighter claim was a Ju 88 destroyed by the gunners on a 7 Squadron Lancaster while making its third pass at them.[13]

'Gil' Bryson's wireless-operator, Jim Donnan on 'T-Squared' on 550 Squadron, wrote: 'Our navigator, Sergeant Thomas 'Rocky' Roxby had called for a slight change in course for the final leg to Berlin as we reached a position between Hanover and Bremen. It was almost immediately afterwards that a series of thuds vibrated through the floor and the aircraft seemed to bank away to starboard. I leapt up from my seat to the astrodome where I could see the starboard engines were on fire. As I switched over from radio to intercom I saw that a fire had started under the navigator's table on the floor just behind the pilot. It was soon burning fiercely. Bryson gave the order to abandon the aircraft.... Grasping the release handle on my parachute I prepared to jump but I must have lost consciousness, as I have no recollection of what happened next or how I left the plane. When I regained consciousness, my parachute was already open and I was floating in pitch darkness, very cold and my feet were freezing.'

Jim Donnan landed on soft ground in an open space. He remained at large for the next twenty-four hours, but when he asked some German civilians for some food and drink he was taken into custody.

'T-Squared' crashed between Holtrup and Schweringen and blew up with its full bomb load, including a 'cookie', in a deafening explosion. The 15-year-old Friedrich Deike and 16-year-old Heinrich Eickhoff living in Holtrup would never forget that New Year's evening of 1944. There was an air-raid alarm and Eickhoff had just returned home from a party in Sebbenhausen. 'It was a soggy, cold night when the sirens started to shriek. Suddenly there was a loud explosion like I have never heard. Outside it was as clear as day and there was fire everywhere. In the cellar the preserves fell from the shelves. Immediately the word spread around that a bomber had crashed and exploded and some airmen had bailed out by parachute.'

Friedrich Deike said that when his father looked out, he suddenly stared at a sea of fire. 'The deafening explosion blew open doors, plaster fell from the walls, windows shattered and roofs were ripped off…. The bomber was blown into thousands of pieces. The four motors were found hundreds of metres away in a field near Schweringen. The crash place was turned into a deep crater.'

Bryson and his navigator 'Rocky' Roxby had been trapped in the cockpit and were killed in the crash. Flight Sergeant Paul Evans the bomb-aimer and Sergeant 'Don' Fadden, flight engineer, had a very lucky escape. They were in the nose section when the aircraft suddenly dived, pinning them down with the centrifugal forces. They were released when an explosion blew off the front of the nose section, enabling them to escape by parachute just before the bomber crashed. Sergeants Jack Sawkins, the mid-upper gunner, and 'Taff' Gundry, the rear gunner, also survived. Most probably Bryson's Lancaster was the third of six victories attributed to Major Heinrich Prinz zu Sayn-Wittgenstein who that same day had become Kommodore of NJG2.

Flying a Ju 88C-6 with Feldwebel Friedrich 'Fritz' Ostheimer his bordfunker and Unteroffizier Kurt Matzuleit the bordmechaniker, the Prinz destroyed six Lancasters in quick succession using SN-2 radar and 'Schräge Musik'. Wittgenstein's fifth victory was 'A-Apple' on 9 Squadron flown by newly-promoted Flying Officer Geoffrey Ward, who had been at the controls of 'N-Nuts' when it crashed returning from Berlin on 24 November. This time there were no survivors. Among the dead was 19-year-old mid-upper gunner Sergeant Norman Frederick Dixon of Old Balderton. Sergeant George Bedwell, the 24-year-old wireless-operator, left a widow Joan Louisa and two children in Saxmundham, Suffolk. The only Canadian on the crew, Warrant Officer2 Willard Lawrence Doran, the 21-year-old rear gunner, was from Edmonton, Alberta. Ward was an accomplished pianist and his tuneful renditions in the mess would be sadly missed. Bedwell was a member of an RAF band who wrote his own music and, like his skipper, played the piano. He had planned a career in music after the war.[14]

No word was received from two 'Airborne Cigar' radar-jamming Lancasters on 101 Squadron at Ludford Magna. The 22-year old Squadron Leader Ian Robertson DFC and crew on 'Z for Zebra' were lost without trace. Pilot Officer Bill Parker, the usual special operator on the crew, who had just been commissioned, had left for London to collect his officer's uniform and had arrived back to find himself on the battle order but in order to let him settle into the mess, it was agreed that Flying Officer Alfred Herbert Duringer DFC DFM would take his place. The 31-year-old special operator asked Parker if he would look after his fiancée, WAAF Section Officer Pleasance Anne Knatchbull-Hugessen, while he was gone. Parker said that he would. Robertson and six of his crew were commemorated on the Runnymede Memorial and Technical Sergeant Ereil Jones USAAF, the American rear gunner, is perpetuated on the Wall of the Missing at Madingley Cemetery just outside Cambridge.

'V for Victor' flown by Pilot Officer Derrick J. Bell went down in Belgium. Bell, who was from Nottingham, had joined up in August 1941 and had done most of his training in California. He was on his seventh operation:

'We got in a muddle,' wrote Bell later. 'The navigator went a bit wrong and we arrived over Berlin late. I can vividly remember as we flew up to it, there were two layers of cloud; there was one below us and one above and it was weird, as though you were flying along an illuminated corridor. As far as we knew we were the only ones there, as we were terribly late. So we bombed on what we hoped was the target. There was nothing to aim at. I actually couldn't see the flames but could see the glow on the clouds where the fires were. The Pathfinder markers had disappeared; we were as late as that.'

Bell flew back fairly uneventfully until at 0546 hours over Belgium, 'V-Victor's crew was completely surprised by an attack by a Bf 110 flown by Major Wilhelm Herget who attacked from below. This victory, at Grandrieu, south of Beaumont, was recorded as his sixty-first abschuss:

'The first thing I knew about it,' says Bell, 'Larry Somers, the 19-year-old engineer, said, "Oh, something's hit us" and the next thing the starboard wing was in flames. I don't know what it was that hit us, but I think it must have been a fighter. I discovered later that the Me 110 might have had upward-pointing guns. None of us bailed out. I honestly think that four of us were the luckiest people alive. The Lanc went out of control; we just lost it and I can remember as plain as anything saying "we've had it boys", or trying to say it. Then I knew nothing until I woke up in mid-air. The Lanc had obviously blown to pieces. The crew at the front of the aircraft had been thrown out; four of us woke up in mid-air just in time to pull our 'chutes. I had only got mine on one hook as that was all the time I'd had to put it on. Anyway it worked.'[15]

Derrick Bell, his bomb-aimer First Lieutenant M.H. Albert USAAF and the wireless-operator Sergeant E.H. Harris were taken prisoner. The navigator, Sergeant H.W. Bailey, evaded capture. Sergeants Laurence Frazer Somers and George Christie Connon, the 20-year old special operator, and the 18-year-old Canadian mid-upper gunner, Flying Officer 'Frank' Joseph Zubic of London, Ontario were killed. So, too, was the 23-year-old rear gunner, Flying Officer William Edward Suddick DFC of Toronto, who, agonizingly, was on his eighty-ninth operation. They were each laid to rest in Grosselies Communal Cemetery. Major Wilhelm Herget became one of the leading Nachtjagd 'Experten', finishing the war with seventy-three victories.

On 207 Squadron, two Lancasters failed to return to Spilsby. 'L-London' and 29-year-old Pilot Officer William John Bottrell's crew was lost without trace. 'T-Tommy' flown by First Lieutenant Frank B. Solomon USAAF who had taken Sergeant F. Collis to Berlin on his 'second dickey' trip on 29 December crashed in the vicinity of the Daimler Benz works at Genshagen, where all the crew were initially buried. Their 'second dickey' on this occasion was Flight Sergeant Leonard David Gosney, a 21-year-old, chunky, irrepressible Canadian and the joker in the pack in his crew's sleeping quarters, who was laid to rest in the Berlin War Cemetery. Solomon and Flying Officer Willis DeBardeleben were re-interred at the US Cemetery at Neuville-en-Cordon in Belgium in October 1947.

On returning to England two Lancasters crashed trying to land back at Witchford and Grimsby. 'E-Edward' on 115 Squadron piloted by 22-year-old Flight Sergeant Robert Edward Chantler force-landed at Stretham, 4 miles south-south-west of Ely at 0739 hours. There were no injuries. (This crew were killed on 22/23 April when their Lancaster was shot down by flak on the Düsseldorf operation.)

'R-Robert' on 550 Squadron crashed at Whaphole Drove 8 miles south-east of Spalding in Lincolnshire at 0708 hours. Everyone on 22-year-old Flying Officer Roger Hanson Mawle's crew died. Among the dead was the flight engineer, Sergeant Patrick Peter O'Meara from the Irish Republic. Born in 1915 in Tipperary, Southern Ireland, O'Meara was married and had four sons. He moved to England to train as an airline pilot and when war broke out he joined the RAF. After his death his wife and family moved back to Tipperary to be nearer her family.

The Belgian navigator, Flying Officer Georges Marie Ghislain de Menten de Horne, born in Brussels on 5 May 1913, was the son of a Belgian count and had a brother Eric and sister Odette and a cousin, Ghislaine. Eric de Horne was active in the Belgian Resistance but in February 1943 the group was discovered by the German Intelligence services. He was captured, imprisoned and on 20 October he was executed in Brussels. After his execution at the shooting range, he was buried there. In a period of a little over two months the family lost both sons to the war. Ghislaine de Menten de Horne, who also worked for the Resistance, was twice arrested by the Gestapo, but managed to talk her way to release and survived the war. Once the war was over she married a British agent and she came to England. She was awarded a number of medals by the Belgian and British governments. Before the war she had been an artist and post-war took up painting again.

Twenty aircraft had left Waddington, but only eighteen returned. Both absent crews were on 467 Squadron. Pilot Officer Ross Stanford, who had run short of fuel and diverted to Ford, finally arrived at Waddington late on Sunday, but Leo Patkin never returned. 'M-Mother' was most likely Prinz Sayn-Wittgenstein's third kill of the night, which he set on fire with a single burst. The Lancaster flew on for a few moments before plunging down and crashing in flames at 0230 in a field at Altmerdingsen near Hanover. The aircraft exploded so violently on impact that roofs and windows of nearby houses were shattered and the crater caused was approximately 25 yards in diameter. There were no survivors of the crew. Patkin left a widow, Claire of South Tarra, Victoria. The 28-year-old air gunner, Flight Sergeant William Donald Blackwell, one of the three other Australians on the crew, was married to Gladys Muriel.[16]

The loss of the 'second dickey' meant that James Mudie's crew were now 'headless'. They would be posted back to a Heavy Conversion Unit a week later.

Pilot Officer Dick Starkey had landed back at Metheringham at 6.00 am after what was another harrowing raid:

'As the crews came into the Interrogation Room our main question was 'Is everybody back?' If not the flare-path was left on for a time until news was received that missing aircraft had been forced to land elsewhere or no further communication was received from them when the lights of the flare-path would be turned off. No further news was received from the aircraft of my table-tennis partners who had failed to return and as I cycled from the airfield to the mess the flare-path was turned off. After I had breakfast I looked in the ante room and there on the table were the bats and balls as we had left them before they flew off into eternity.'[17]

Pilot Officer West's crew on 12 Squadron were also never to be seen again. The adjutant's thoughts would have already turned to removing the crew's kit and personal belongings from their lockers and cataloguing them, returning their kit to the stores and sending their personal belongings to the RAF Central Repository at Colnbrook, Slough. The commanding officer's onerous task the next day would be to send a 'missing, believed killed' telegram to the next of kin once their fate was known. Letters would follow over the following weeks or months or even years, once identification and the location of the grave sites had been ascertained through 'channels'.

'When "C-Charlie" came up to the Dutch coast the navigator said that the "Gee" box had gone U/S,' says Ken Apps, 'so the crew had no homing device. Still, this didn't deter us. With that expensive load in the belly, it was on to Berlin or bust. We didn't believe in dumping in the sea.

'We reached the target and released our bombs. It made us a total of twenty-four sorties, so we thought: home now to a tot of rum, eggs and bacon and a nice long sleep, but it was not to be. Turning south, leaving the target, we felt both lucky and on top of the world but, suddenly, the engineer called to say that our petrol was disappearing at a staggering rate. Thank goodness we had our reserve to get us to the North Sea. Wrong! When he switched over, this went just as quickly. Those four Merlins just went silent and, at 20,000 feet if you haven't any power, the old lady decides to put her nose down and find terra firma pretty quickly.

'The order came to bail out, so on with the emergency oxygen bottle and into the fuselage to get the parachute, only to find Archie Panniers out of his turret, staggering around with no oxygen. I dragged him up to the side hatch, put the rip-cord in his fist, doubled him up and pushed him out. He got down safely. I then jumped myself. I was on my own at four o'clock in the morning.

'It was a long and silent journey down, so many things to think about. What was going to happen to me?'[18]

All except Dennis Smith, who was wounded in the aircraft, made it safely to the ground and everyone was soon captured. Dennis was found by the Germans still attached to his parachute, but his head had been severed, probably as a result of him hitting the tail rudder. 'C-Charlie', meanwhile, was found almost intact at Taunusstein, Wingsbach near Wiesbaden after landing wheels-down and incurring damage to the right main wheel. The Lancaster was put back to airworthy condition over a period of six months in the Lufthansa workshops at Travemünde on the Baltic coast and was to be flown by Hans Werner Lerche, a German test pilot, but before he could study it more closely, on 6 June 1944 he received the message that the Allies had invaded.

On 432 'Leaside' Squadron, Pilot Officer 'Tom' Benson Spink had taken his Lancaster off from East Moor at 0030 hours, the aircraft's seventh operational flight and Spink's ninth. The Lancaster carried the nose art '*Bobby Boy*', named in honour of 'Tom' Spink's young son. Born in Vancouver in 1919, Spink had enlisted there on 26 June 1941. The flight proved uneventful until the return leg at around 0730 hours. While they were over Calais he discovered that the throttle on the port inner engine had jammed at cruising power.

On arrival at East Moor a landing was attempted with three engines throttled back and the port inner jammed on a much higher power setting. The Lancaster overshot the first attempt at landing and Spink applied power and went around for another attempt. On the second approach the Lancaster touched down safely, but because the port inner could not be throttled back the aircraft swung off the runway and across the grass, narrowly missing flying control before being brought to a halt on an empty dispersal pan at the northern end of the airfield. '*Bobby Boy*' sustained some minor damage on the way. The crew were then debriefed and crawled into bed by 1030 hours, only to be awakened at 1700 hours. They were stunned to learn that they and the rest of Bomber Command were to return to Berlin that night.

Chapter Eleven

Berlin Back to Back

'Berlin has been blasted again. Nine RCAF squadrons helped carry the 2,300 tons which smashed the German capital Thursday night. So, Berlin will be destroyed, beaten into the dust, a thing despised. The thrill, the sheer delight, which news of the Canadians contributes to these raids sends through the nation each time it is repeated comes not from the satisfaction of destroying. It resides in the pride which all their people have in the courage and stern idealism of the young men of the RCAF.'

The Toronto *Globe and Mail* report on the raid on Berlin on Thursday 20/Friday, 21 January 1944.

Fatigue mixed with anger caused severe rumblings and ructions at briefings on most all stations in Bomber Command on Sunday afternoon, 2 January 1944 but there were those like Sergeant Ted Cachart, the wireless-operator on 'N for Nan' on 49 Squadron at Fiskerton, who regarded each operation as 'something very special'. 'It was never, 'Oh we're on ops' said in a gloomy tone, it was always: 'Hey, we're on ops tonight!' The adrenaline kicked in as you thought about the target, the number of night-fighters and if there would be heavy flak and searchlights. It was incredibly exciting. It started with our regular WAAF driver 'Dot' Everett who drove us to 'Nan' or 'Nancy Pants' as 'Dot' renamed her after the mascot doll she had made for us. 'Nan' was a brand-new Lancaster, only three days old.'

Ted was born on 15 June 1925 in Gorleston-on-Sea in Norfolk, one of five children to Benjamin and Dorothy Cachart. Mr Cachart was a former RSM and First World War veteran who studied to be a chartered accountant. Newly-qualified, the Cachart family moved to Wealdstone and eventually Pinner. After leaving school, Ted attended the City of Westminster Catering College in Vincent Square, but there was a war on and his older brothers were already in the army and his sister was joining the WAAF. He was dissuaded from joining the army by his brothers:

'I wanted to join the RAF rather than be conscripted into the army or navy, as it seemed the best option to me. It also appealed as the RAF were known as the Brylcreem boys in those days and believed to be more attractive to the young ladies. There was a poster that showed a young woman kissing an airman and a queue of young women waiting to kiss him. The slogan read: 'The girls will queue for the boys in blue' and I wanted to be a boy in blue!

'In 1941, although only 15 years of age, I went to this local Recruiting Office where I was told I could not volunteer until I was 17 and a quarter, with my parents' consent. I took the forms home and asked my father and a priest to sign them, telling them: 'It's just to make sure I get into the RAF.' No lies passed my young lips! I sent the signed forms off, having entered my birth year as 1923 rather than

1925. In April I attended a medical examination board at Edgware Hospital and was passed as A1. In May I was told to report to Oxford University where, with others, I took a written exam, followed by an interview with the Air Crew Selection Board. Only too aware of my young age I declined to train as a pilot and trained as a wireless-operator/air gunner. I was then sworn in and on 13 May 1941, a month before my 16th birthday, I became a member of the RAF.

'I turned 16 in June and received my call-up papers in October. My father was quite annoyed, but when I told him I knew he had joined the army under-age in the First World War, he accepted and said 'OK, but I'll bet you will want me to get you out before Christmas comes.'

However, Ted completed his training in wireless and gunnery and promoted to sergeant had proudly sewed on an air gunner's brevet and three stripes. He was sure he swaggered home for ten days' leave.

Further training followed when Ted joined Canadian Flying Officer J.E.M. 'Johnny' Young's crew. Fellow Canadian Pilot Officer Jack Scott was the navigator, Pilot Officer Les Orchard was the bomb-aimer, Sergeant 'Len' Crossman the rear gunner, Flight Sergeant Allen Vidow was flight engineer and Australian Sergeant 'Spud' Mahony the mid-upper gunner. As a group they would sleep, eat and play together. They were no longer individuals, they were a unit. It was quite natural to go to the cinema together where they would sit all seven in a row. It made them confident that each person would do their job to the best of their ability.

Flying Officer Victor Lane Cole's crew on 106 Squadron, one of the 'gen crews' at Syerston, having flown twenty-five trips since their first on 9 July 1943, were 'on' again after their eight-hour trip to the 'Big City'. 'Vic' Cole came from Farnham in Surrey and had been employed by Shell before the war. Flying Officer Harold 'Johnny' Johnson, the 26-year-old air bomber, had been born in Stepney where his father was a cycle-maker and plumber for the London County Council and had joined the Metropolitan Police in 1937. PC Johnson and another constable tried to enlist as pilot trainees and fight in the Spanish Civil War, which they thought would be over by the time they had completed training, but news of their proposed venture reached Sir Philip Game, the Police Commissioner, and they were summoned to Scotland Yard where they were suitably admonished. Game was ready to discharge them but they remained in the force.

When war was declared in September 1939 Johnny was stationed at Rochester Row Police station. He could not volunteer for the RAF because the police force was a 'reserved occupation' and on Saturday, 24 August 1940 he was on duty in Downing Street when the first raid on London took place. At the start of the blitz he was walking the beat at Woolwich when German bombers carried out two separate raids, one in the afternoon and a second at night. The dockland area and all adjacent buildings were destroyed. Finally, in 1942, when policemen could be considered for air crew, Johnny was selected for pilot training. The medical was at the Recruiting Centre at Lord's Cricket ground in the famous Long Bar with its trophies. All the recruits stood in line and were ordered 'shirts up – trousers down' as the MO stood ready with a stick. Suddenly a Cockney voice bawled out, ''Arry, if he gives you that bloody cup, you've won!'

Johnny went to Canada for pilot training, but eventually washed out because he could not judge height during landings and he retrained as a bomb-aimer. He crewed up at 19 OTU Kinloss and soon formed the opinion that there was not a better pilot anywhere than 'Vic' Cole. "'Vic' always went in as high as he could and would then glide the Lancaster home. Nine times out of ten we would be first back.' The rest of the crew included Alfie Bristow the navigator, Bill Haig the WOp/AG, Eddie McColn, the 'excellent' flight engineer, and Malcolm 'Parky' Parkinson, the always alert rear gunner.

Only 383 Lancasters and 9 Halifaxes on 35 (PFF) Squadron already equipped with the improved B.Mk III version would start for Berlin. At some airfields getting a requisite number of aircraft available had proved impossible. At Waddington, for instance, some air tests were flown during the day to check the aircraft over, but only eight from each squadron were ready for take-off in time. At Fiskerton, 49 Squadron had managed to get twelve Lancasters airborne from the thirteen detailed. They included 'S-Sugar' piloted by Flight Lieutenant Cecil John Edward Palmer who were on their eleventh operation. The navigator Flying Officer George Thomas Young was the old man of the crew at 31. Flying Officer Ronald Stobo the air bomber was 21 years old. Sergeant Philip Otley 'Lofty' Camm, the flight engineer, was 23. The rear gunner, Derek Prusher, was the youngest member on the crew at just 18 years old. Sergeant Douglas Demas Russell Dallaway, the mid-upper gunner, born 1923 in Sedlescombe, East Sussex, was known as 'Nibs'. Sergeant Henry 'Mickey' Conrad was the crew's 22-year-old wireless-operator. On 20/21 October they had had a close shave near Berlin on the trip to Leipzig and were lucky to make it home. It would prove to be but a reprieve.

At Binbrook 28-year-old Australian Flight Lieutenant Barrington Armitage Knyvett DFC on 460 Squadron RAAF who was from Leadville, NSW took Lancaster 'T-Tommy' off at 2330 hours, completed a half circuit and then dived into the ground six minutes later a quarter of a mile east of Binbrook village, killing all seven crew. Over the North Sea a recall signal was picked up and half an hour later the recall was cancelled, but fifteen bombers had already chosen to abort. In fact the original recall was for the twenty-six Wellingtons of the mine-laying operation. In all, sixty bombers turned back before the enemy coast was reached.

The weather was foul throughout and cloud contained icing and static electricity up to 30,000 feet but clearer conditions were expected at Berlin. A dozen Mosquitoes were detailed to attack the 'Big City' four minutes before the attack began and then forty minutes after the Main Force bombing. A long, evasive route was originally planned but this was changed to an almost straight in, straight out route with just a small 'dog-leg' at the end of it just beyond Bremen to allow the formation to fly into Berlin from the north-west, to take advantage of a strong following wind from that direction. Save for a small force of Wellingtons, mine-laying in the Frisians and off French ports, there were no diversionary operations to hopefully draw the enemy fighters away from the Main Force.

On approaching the final turning-point 60 miles north of Berlin the bomber crews were made well aware of the presence of night-fighters by the lanes of flares in the sky. For the first time in their eight operations the 'Fishpond' radar screen on 'Nancy Pants' was functioning well. It was Ted Cachart's task to work the set. He reported a large number of 'blips' reflected from the aircraft below them. A number of these were heading in the direction of the final turning-point but with the majority heading towards the target. The Australian top turret gunner, Sergeant Allan 'Spud' Mahony, keeping a watchful eye out for fighters as many combats had already been sighted, had requested that Johnny Young gently roll the Lancaster so as to give the gunners some vertical vision. 'We were skimming through hazy cloud,' 'Spud' recalled. 'Johnny Young had just lowered the starboard wing when in a split second I saw another Lancaster heading straight towards us. Before I could yell a warning, the oncoming Lancaster's cockpit struck our starboard wing between the two engines.'

As he looked from the astrodome Ted Cachart saw part of his aircraft disappear: 'In the collision I lost my helmet and oxygen mask and at that height, if you're lucky, you have about two minutes before you pass out through lack of oxygen. I worked my way along the darkened fuselage and saw both gunners standing at the open door. I couldn't talk to them and don't remember if they gave me the thumbs-up to bail out. I do know I sat on the steps and rolled out. I don't remember pulling the ripcord; I just remember descending in the 'chute. I could have been court-martialled for having abandoned the aircraft without permission. At that moment I was more concerned to see the aircraft fly away into the clouds, perhaps back home, than what lay ahead of me in Germany below.'

It is most probable that 'S-Sugar' was the Lancaster that was in collision with 'N-Nan' because if slightly ahead of 'Nan' it would have changed course and headed back across the track of the oncoming tail-enders. 'Sugar' and 'Nan' and the others on 49 Squadron were in the last wave.

Everyone on 'N-Nan' survived to be taken prisoner. 'Spud' Mahony landed in a 30 feet-high tree after releasing his harness and attempting to climb down, fell and injured his back. It was never reset properly and he had to wear a support harness for the rest of his life. The skipper, who was last to leave, dislocated his shoulder on landing. All seven crew members on Flight Lieutenant Cecil Palmer's crew were killed. Sergeant 'Mickey' Conrad had been married for just two months.

The Pathfinders were punctual and dropped their TIs and sky-markers in a better-than-average concentration. Ground markers were unobserved owing to cloud conditions and sky-markers were the objective of a considerable volume of light flak. Heavy flak in barrage form was 'moderate'.

All was for naught, however. Just 311 bombers struggled to reach Berlin where the bombing was spread with no concentrated fires developing. Losses at Warboys rose to nine PFF aircraft in two nights when five more Lancasters on 156 Squadron failed to return. 'T-Tommy' flown by 23-year-old Flying Officer Charles Gordon Cairns DFM crashed at Riesdorf on what was the pilot's forty-seventh sortie. All seven crew including Technical Sergeant Jack E. Haywood USAAF died. 'V-Victor' captained by 23-year-old Pilot Officer John Donald Range Cromarty was lost without trace. 'J-Jig' flown by 20-year-old Pilot Officer James Borland DFC which was lost without trace was presumed to have crashed in the target area. 'O for Orange' flown by 24-year-old Flight Lieutenant James Clarence Ralph DFM of Mount Eden, Auckland City also disappeared with all seven crew. Near Bremen 'C-Charlie' flown by 20-year-old Sergeant Alan Douglas Barnes was attacked from the port quarter by a night-fighter. The Lancaster entered into a steep dive and was partially abandoned by four of the crew, who were captured and taken into captivity. Barnes, his navigator, 17-year-old Sergeant Ronald Victor Hillman, and the rear gunner, Sergeant Arthur John Hackett died.

At Wyton 83 PFF Squadron lost three Lancasters and their crews. 'J-Johnny' skippered by 20-year-old Canadian Pilot Officer Fred Allcroft DFC was the first of the H2S Mk III aircraft to be lost. Flying Officer Alec William Blakeman DFC, the 30-year-old navigator, was on his fiftieth operation. He left a widow, Gertrude Ellen of Stafford. 'Q-Queenie' skippered by 30-year-old Flight Lieutenant Lindsay Will Munro MiD, a New Zealander, crashed at Zehrensdorf a few kilometres south-east of Zossen. Munro had previously completed a tour on 103 Squadron in 1941. He left a widow, Vera Munro of Broadway, Worcestershire. 'F-Freddie' flown by 23-year-old Canadian Pilot Officer Ernest Blair Stiles of Apohaqui, New Brunswick crashed at Blankenburg.

The Canadian 6 Group dispatched twenty-eight bombers, four returning early and three lost. Two of the missing Lancaster IIs were from Linton-on-Ouse. On 426 'Thunderbird' Squadron RCAF 21-year-old Pilot Officer Charles Anthony Griffiths of Selkirk, Manitoba and five crew members on 'M-Mike' were killed.

On 'G-George' on 408 'Goose' Squadron RCAF 20-year-old Flight Sergeant Donald Ernest Hilker of Red Willow, Alberta and crew failed to return. Hilker's rear gunner, Warrant Officer S.R. Sweetzir remembered Berlin as a 'blazing hellhole: flak and rocket fire of all shapes and sizes.' Half a minute after the Lancaster's bombs fell away an Me 210 attacked from starboard, setting the wing on fire. Hilker gave the order to jump. A minute later the fire went out. The skipper cancelled the bail-out order. Then the fighter attacked again and within moments the wing was burning once more. Sweetzir returned the fighter's fire and saw flames in the Messerschmitt's port engine. Hilker again ordered the crew to abandon the aircraft. Sweetzir did not hear the order, but he scrambled out of his turret anyway because burning oil had appeared on the floor beneath his feet. He squeezed through the narrow aperture, going forward to the door beside the tail. There he encountered Sergeant Hubert James Mouland, the mid-upper gunner who, although he wore his parachute, was disinclined to jump. Sweetzir took hold of his harness and told him to hurry up. There was little time, he yelled. He was right. The aircraft blew up. Sweetzir lost consciousness, coming to on the ground. His parachute had somehow opened without his assistance. The Germans captured him and four others on the crew, including the flight engineer, the only RAF member on the otherwise all-Canadian crew. Hilker and Mouland died in the aircraft.

On 432 'Leaside' Squadron at East Moor Flight Lieutenant John Allardyce Allen of Brantford, Ontario, a 23-year-old veteran pilot on the eighth trip of his second tour, was lost together with his crew when 'Y-Yorker' went down. The pilot left a widow, Honor Mary Allen of Paddington in London. For the second night running 'U-Uncle' on the 'Leaside' Squadron flown by 22-year-old Pilot Officer James Alexander Jim McIntosh was attacked by a night-fighter shortly after dropping the bomb load, just after he turned for home. McIntosh, born and raised on the family farm in the 'Big Eddy' part of Revelstoke, British Columbia had been a locomotive fireman with the Canadian Pacific Railway before joining up. He could drive a train and pilot a plane before he could drive a car. His crusty exterior disguised a very warm heart. Sergeant Leo Bandle, the rear gunner who was from Tilbury, Ontario spotted a Bf 110, which opened fire. The same instant he and Sergeant Andrew F. De Dauw, the mid-upper gunner, returned fire at 100 yards range, loosing off 500 rounds without taking their thumbs off the firing buttons. The enemy's port engine caught fire just as he broke away. He went into a succession of dives and half-hearted pull-outs, finally spinning out of control until lost to view.

'Cannon shells hit our aircraft like sledge-hammers,' recalled McIntosh. 'Hits were scored on the 110's port engine and cockpit and the fighter went down, burning fiercely. All this happened within five seconds. Meanwhile my control column had been slammed forward (the elevator had been hit), putting the aircraft into a near-vertical dive. By putting both feet on the instrument panel, one arm around the control column and the other hand on the elevator trim, then hauling back with every ounce of strength while trimming fully nose-up, I managed to pull out of the dive at about 10,000 feet (13,000 feet below bombing height). My compasses were unserviceable, the rudder controls had jammed and I could get very little response from the elevators. I still had to wrap both arms around the control column to maintain height.

'We were now far behind the rest of the bombers and our only hope was to stay in the cloud-tops and take our chances with the severe icing we were encountering. Fighter flares kept dropping all around us and the flak positions en route were bursting their stuff at our height but the fighters couldn't see us in that cloud. Pilot Officer Alex Small, my navigator, who was from Morris, Manitoba, took astro fixes and kept us away as much as possible from defended areas. We had been losing a lot of fuel from the starboard inner tank but enough remained to take us to Woodbridge. About 70 miles out to sea I let down through cloud, experiencing severe icing and then I broke through. The aircraft was now becoming very sluggish and only with difficulty was I able to hold height. I detailed the crew to throw out all our unnecessary equipment and to chop out everything they could. This considerably lightened the aircraft and made it easier to control.

'I then ordered the crew to stand by for ditching, just in case. The navigator headed me straight for Woodbridge on "Gee". I used all the runway and felt the kite touch down on our port wheel. It rolled along until the speed dropped to about 30 mph and then I settled down more on the side of the starboard wheel, did half a ground-loop and stopped. I shut down the engines, got out and took a look. Both starboard engine nacelles were gone; the hydraulics were smashed and twisted; two large tears were in the starboard wing near the dinghy stowage: the dinghy was hanging out; the starboard fuel jettison sack was hanging out; the tail-plane was riddled with cannon and gunfire; the fuselage had five cannon holes through it (three of the shells had burst inside, near the navigator); there were two cannon holes in the rear turret (one of these shells had whistled almost the entire length of the fuselage before exploding); there were hundreds of holes of all sizes in the kite; every prop blade had at least one hole in it, one being split down the middle; the starboard outer oil tank was riddled and the starboard tyre was blown clean off. But nobody was injured. It had been a good trip until we were attacked by the fighter.'

McIntosh was awarded the DFC for this action.

Pilot Officer 'Tom' Spink, who had brought his misbehaving Lancaster back from Berlin the night before, also had an encounter with a night-fighter. He reported:

'On the way in to the target an enemy aircraft opened fire from ahead, slightly to starboard and about three hundred yards above. I immediately made a diving turn to starboard and the attack was broken off. A second attack to port was attempted by the enemy aircraft after we resumed our original course. This attack was not carried out as I immediately took evasive action.'

Spink put his aircraft into a steep dive for 6,000 feet before he eventually levelled out. About fifteen minutes later when the crew was certain they had lost the enemy aircraft the navigator, Canadian Pilot Officer Gerald Irwin Phillips, reported his oxygen had been cut off. The engineer Sergeant John Albert Banks reported a bullet through the instrument panel which damaged the oxygen regulator causing a leakage which he estimated would cause total loss of oxygen in approximately three-quarters of an hour. The bomb-aimer reported the electrical bomb release u/s and Canadian Flight Sergeants Donald Ryan and W.R. Leadley, the mid-upper and rear gunners respectively, reported several holes through the rear of the fuselage and tail.

By this time Gerald Phillips estimated they were one hour from the target. Having arranged with the bomb-aimer to release the 4,000lb bomb manually over the target and to collect all the oxygen bottles and bring them to the navigator, Spink decided to carry on and hope their oxygen supply would last until reaching the target. Phillips then made a splendid job of navigating to the target, although they were flying through 10/10ths cloud in freezing conditions with static lightning flashing on the windscreen. While over the target they then realized that the electrics had also been damaged and this prevented the bombs being released electrically. They were later dropped after being released by hand. On the return leg Spink was hand-fed oxygen by the flight engineer Sergeant John Albert Banks from a hand bottle and Spink made a landing at Coleby Grange. It was then discovered that the photo-flash had been rolling around the aircraft, making a hole in the floor. 'Tom' Spink was awarded a well-deserved DFC, but he declined to accept it. It was posted to him in Canada in March 1949.

Pilot Officer Edward Charles Weatherstone on 50 Squadron, who had hit an RAF van on landing back from Berlin on 26/27 November, was on the way home when a Focke-Wulf 190 and a Ju 88 were seen. He immediately started to corkscrew and Sergeant H.J. Lineham and Flight Sergeant Ralph Adey Cuthbert Collingwood opened fire and continued to fire while the 190 flew out and above to 600 yards on the starboard side. Many hits were scored on the fighter and it broke off its attack. The Ju 88 then commenced its attack, the gunners hitting this also. Then both fighters joined up some distance to port where the gunners continued to fire at them until they were lost to sight, but both were claimed as damaged.

Another Lancaster on 50 Squadron flown by Flight Lieutenant Short was on the homeward journey when his bomb-aimer, Pilot Officer Kenneth William Odgers who was manning the front turret, sighted two lights approaching fast, below on the port bow at 600 yards. He identified it as a twin-engined aircraft and opened fire with long bursts of 250 rounds. The fighter did not attack but maintained its course and was lost to starboard.

On reaching Berlin John Chatterton piloted 'Y-Yorker' over the cloud blanketed city, which was lively with flak and fighters. 'Once again we were lucky and having bombed, passed through unscathed, although there was one heart-stopping moment when the great radial engine of a roaming Fw 190 swept head-on a few feet over the cockpit.' However, the jagged hole in the canopy of their Lancaster was beginning to cause a few problems as Chatterton turned for home.

'More Perspex vibrated free and the topographical maps 'borrowed' from the bomb-aimer to bridge the gap had been sucked out into the night, souvenirs for some German boy. It did nothing for the cabin heating and I was glad I had put on all three pairs of gloves for a change. The draught tugged at the 'nav's black-out curtain, letting out streaks of light which interfered with our night vision in the cockpit and he was struggling to keep his charts on the table and searching for missing 'flimsies' in a whirl of strips of 'Window' and loose 'nickels'. The latter were propaganda leaflets which were meant to persuade their German readers of the folly of war, but which more probably were received gleefully to help solve the paper shortage in a more earthy fashion.

'Running for home we re-entered the cloud barrier. Cloud was heaped upon cloud, up to 28,000 feet, according to the Met man at briefing. He had said nothing about thunderstorms but mentioned a 'bit of static', which startled us by appearing as 'St. Elmo's fire', frightening but harmless, eerie blue lights making circles round the four props and streaking across the Perspex of the astrodome and gun turrets. This was just the element's curtain-raiser; the next act was a sudden and nasty bout of icing which stiffened the controls, made the engines cough and sent bits of ice from the props rattling on the fuselage. Ken, the flight engineer, cleared the engines by selecting 'Hot Air' and I put the nose down to get into warmer air. Alarmingly, the airspeed did not increase; the pitot head was frozen, so I had to carefully watch the climb and descent needle to avoid getting out of control. Then to cap it all we were hurled over sideways by a lightning strike and instead of being surrounded by a comforting array of luminous dials, the instrument panel registered instant chaos. The gyros of the artificial Horizon and Direction Indicator lay toppled and useless, the DR compass was dead, never to return and the standby P4 compass by my left knee wallowed aimlessly.

'With no visible outside world to aid stability I was frozen with panic and the aircraft was plunging headlong to destruction, when by some miracle I heard the nasal twang of my old bush pilot instructor in Arizona – 'Now boy! We've toppled all the new-fangled instruments and we'll have to rely on the basics – what are they?' Needle – ball and airspeed! With an effort I pulled myself together and using the turn and bank indicator, climb and descent needle and the thawed-out altimeter finally got 'Y-Yorker' straightened out again. In the warmer air, the airspeed indicator revived, showing over 300 mph and I was very thankful that my farm-boy's muscles (fortified by long hours of muck-spreading) were able to ease her out of the dive.

'The intercom was dead and I looked round for Ken who had been pinned to the floor by 'G' forces while checking his fuel gauges. He lifted the earpiece of my helmet and shouted, 'All the electrics are off. I'll go back and sort it out.' I applauded his confidence and set myself to fly straight and level in the unfriendly dark, hoping the compass would settle down. Eureka: there was a faint lightening in the gloom ahead and suddenly we burst out of the cloud into glorious starlight. What a marvellous relief; the real, tangible world again! Where were we heading? I looked round for Polaris and found him behind us instead of on our right where he ought to have been. I used him to zero the now settled directional gyro and was able to steer west for home while Jack the navigator used his sextant for an astro fix. He worked swiftly and got a couple of these which showed us well south of track heading for the Atlantic Ocean.

'I altered course on the dubious P4 compass while Ken and the wireless-operator with the help of bits of wire got some of the electrics and the intercom working again, but the W/T set and 'Gee' box were burnt out beyond repair. The lost 'Gee' box meant that Jack would not be able to get any radar fixes as we neared home and the wrecked W/T meant that the wireless-operator could not receive the half-hourly broadcasts with vital information about weather at home and possible diversions. After a long, cold, weary time on instruments I was dog-tired and not very confident when Jack said we had reached the Dutch coast but a few desultory bursts of flak confirmed this and sharpened me up for a bit. Safely out to sea, I let down to just below the cloud base with the altimeter reading 1,000 feet and still in inky blackness.

'Jack was saying in the confident way that navigators do, even when they've been on dead reckoning for the last two hours, 'ETA Norfolk coast in five minutes; can you see anything down there Scotty?' The bomb-aimer's reply was an anguished yell, 'Pull up Johnny!' as, out of the darkness ahead a single searchlight sprang up, illuminating the cloud base and showing the sea heaving menacingly just a few feet below us. Wide awake, I yanked 'Y-Yorker' up to the cloud base again until I recovered my wits once more. Surely, the crew deserved a pilot less careless than this! But if only the wireless-operator had received those vital broadcasts the adjusted altimeter would have indicated how dangerously low we were.

'The coastal searchlight now lay horizontally, pointing to an unknown airfield, so I used the distress call 'Darkie' (less urgent than 'Mayday') to find out that it was Little Snoring (just the place for a sleepy pilot),[1] and they gave us a QDM (course to steer) for Dunholme Lodge, our base near Lincoln, omitting to tell us it was closed.

'I thankfully extricated myself from the mesh of weaving navigation lights of other diverted aircraft while Jack drew a reciprocal on his chart to find out where we had been and wished longingly for the local maps lost through the roof. The visibility got worse as we crossed the Wash but 'Scotty' picked out the practice target at Wainfleet a few hundred feet below. Lincolnshire at last! So I tried to call Dunholme on the RT and at the third attempt heard faintly 'Hello "Y-Yorker" – regret base is closed, land at Spilsby.' No problem, I had been to school at Spilsby! So I turned right and with permission to land was groping round the circle of Drem lights trying to find the funnel leading to the runway when Ken reminded me we hadn't put the wheels down. Heaven forgive me – forgotten the landing drills! Down came the wheels, but a red light showed one was not securely locked. Ken pulled the 'Emergency Air' lever but no better.

'While all this was happening Spilsby also closed down and sent us to Coningsby where we finally landed after giving way to another aircraft from our squadron,

Pilot Officer Lyford on three engines. The red light still gleamed reproachfully as we held our breath and touched down but thankfully the undercarriage held firm. As we switched off, the 'nav' said for all of us: 'Well that was a trip full of interesting incidents and not one of them due to Hitler!' The WOP, extremely frustrated without his wireless, burst out, 'It was a bloody German thunderstorm that wrecked my set!' Jack replied: 'They told you when you joined, it would be Per ardua ad astra!' I said: 'Thanks to the navigator it's been "Per Astra ad Coningsby"!'

'As the crew gathered their gear and stumbled down the fuselage to the rear door, I unplugged my intercom and eased the helmet off my sore head and Merlin-numbed ears. I opened the side window to the Lincolnshire dawn. It was blessedly still, the only sounds the tinkling noise of cooling engines and somewhere below the muted murmur of Ken telling the ground sergeant about the undercart. The fresh air was cool on my cheek and tasted good – I was very glad to be home.'

So too were 'Vic' Cole and the crew on 106 Squadron, who only made it back to Syerston by the skin of their teeth.

'On approaching Hanover,' recalls Johnny Johnson, 'with the cloud we were in thinning, "Parky" Parkinson ordered "Vic" to "corkscrew starboard". Without hesitation he carried out this operation but not before all hell broke out. We were under attack by an Me 110, which had come out of the cloud with us and was underneath us. We were an easy target and he opened fire with his "Schräge Musik" guns. He missed the bombs but we were holed everywhere and one or more shells must have hit the No. 2 tank in the port wing. The jettison toggle dropped out and so did all the petrol but there was no fire. Next "Vic" called out "Prepare to abandon aircraft – I can't get this bastard out of the dive." I jettisoned the escape hatch but the "G" force took over and I could not move. I knew that I was going to die and in that terrifying moment I had a vision of my Mum and Dad together with Enid, my WAAF bride-to-be. Enid was in charge of the Officers' Mess at Syerston and I always received large helpings of eggs and bacon! We were circling to such a degree that we were more or less transfixed but as a last resort "Vic" put the auto-pilot in and it pulled the aircraft out and his corkscrew tactics lost the Me 110. We slowly levelled out at 6,000 feet before beginning a slow climb and "Vic" ordered the bombs to be jettisoned. I said "No – we've got a 4,000lb 'cookie' on board" and we were too low. I would take a chance on 8,000 feet but I was not about to do so at 6,000 feet. We finally dropped the "cookie" and the rest of the bombs at 10,000 feet and I had remembered to fuse them.

'Next "Parky" Parkinson called out, "Skipper we're on fire at the back." The WOp/AG was belting out "Mayday, Mayday". I got a fire extinguisher and climbed over the main spar but there was no smoke and the interior light was on. I could see that the rear door was open. John Harding the mid-upper gunner had bailed out! We found out much later that he broke his ankle on landing and was captured. Eddie McColn estimated that we had less than an even chance of making it back to base but "Vic" decided to try and get us home.

'Alfie Bristow quickly assessed a heading for base and I went up into the mid-upper turret as "Vic" knew we would probably be attacked on the way home. We came back fairly low over the North Sea. We couldn't afford to ditch because the back door was open, all the hatches were gone and we were full of holes. Everything was wide open for water to come in. We were very fortunate that we were not attacked again. "Vic" flew very carefully, hit the Lincolnshire coast and flew straight to Syerston. We landed and as we taxied off the runway all four engines stopped! The first to get to us were our overworked, underpaid, seldom mentioned ground crew – God bless them – with the blood wagon not far behind. But we didn't need him.

'Next day the station commander sent for "Vic" and he wanted to know why he hadn't continued to the target! At that moment the engineering officer came in and told the Group Captain that our Lancaster had been SOC – it had a broken back.'

'Vic' Cole's crew completed their tour with a trip to Magdeburg on 21/22 January. Johnny Johnson married Enid Thorpe, who was from Norwich, on 28 March 1944. However, he had not asked his station commander's permission to marry and he threatened Johnny with a court martial. Apparently an officer marrying a corporal was not 'the done thing'. Johnny fought his corner and said that he could give him his discharge papers because the Met Police would welcome him back with open arms. Instead, having completed twenty-eight ops and his first tour he was posted south to Skellingthorpe where he flew further ops on 61 Squadron. Enid was posted north.

An eerie silence hung over Waddington around the time the crews were due back from Berlin on the morning of Monday, 3 January. A quick look outside confirmed that thick fog had settled on the aerodrome and it was soon established that all aircraft returning from Berlin had been diverted to other bases. By midday, all but two of the diverted aircraft had returned to Waddington, but there was one still outstanding.

On 463 Squadron 20-year-old Flight Sergeant Jack Weatherill and crew on 'D-Dog' would not be coming back. They had been hit by unidentified flak, causing the bomb load to explode and had gone down over the Ijsselmeer in Holland. Weatherill and his crew were killed in the explosion. Sergeant Colin Hemingway, the 25-year-old Australian rear gunner, was discovered weeks later at considerable distance in the bottom of a ditch, after which he was buried with the other crew members in Vollenhove. Three of the crew have no known graves.

Over the midday news the number of aircraft lost was given as twenty-eight but by the 1830 hours' broadcast it had been reduced to twenty-seven. Most of the bomber casualties were in the Berlin area and included ten Pathfinder aircraft.

Some bomber crews continued to defy the odds stacked against them, even though many took part in not just one or two but several trips to the 'Big City' and equally tough targets in between, at the end of which they were very tired indeed. Flight Lieutenant Aubrey Howell, a pilot on 115 Squadron at Witchford near Ely recalled:

'During the past six weeks we had completed nine nerve-sapping operations to the 'Big City' (and one to Leipzig and Frankfurt) culminating in consecutive flights on the 1st and 2nd of January 1944. On the first one of these we were nearly chopped out of the sky by a Halifax diving down out of nowhere. We just did not see each other and he missed us by only a yard or two. After bombing I opened up the throttles and came back at a high rate of knots and very high petrol consumption; we didn't have a lot left in the tanks when we got back to dispersal. On the next we had to climb through a lot of cloud with icing conditions and we did not see much of the target, we just bombed on the Pathfinder flare markers and got the hell out of there as fast as we could. We saw a lot of fighters but they were busy with other Lancs not as fortunate as us and we belted for home. They were all long, cold and tough, tiring trips during which we could not relax for a moment because of the increased use of enemy fighters and of course Berlin was one of the most heavily defended targets in Germany.

'Berlin trips meant a bit extra to the mid-upper gunner 'Tommy' Thomson and myself; both being Londoners, our families had had to put up with month after month of sleeping in air-raid shelters, windows and doors being blown in and neighbours and friends killed by our German counterparts in the Luftwaffe. Bomber Command losses became very heavy indeed and many of our good friends and comrades failed to return. It was generally considered at this phase of the Bomber offensive that only approximately one-third of Bomber Command crews finished a tour of thirty ops; two-thirds 'got the chop'. It took us between six and seven hours to complete each of these trips and most of that time we were vulnerable over enemy territory with the odds stacked against us, with no easy route to the 'Big City'.

After the 2/3 January raid there was one night of rest and the night following another 'stand down' as mainly Stirlings and a dozen Mosquitoes and eleven Lancasters bombed two flying bomb sites in France. Then, on the night of Wednesday 5/Thursday, 6 January 348 Lancasters and 10 Halifaxes raided Stettin. Thirteen Mosquitoes raiding Berlin kept most of the German night-fighters away from the Main Force attack, which lost sixteen heavies. One of those that failed to return was a 626 Squadron Lancaster at Wickenby coded UM-T2 or 'Tommy 2', as it was more familiarly known, which was piloted by Australian Flight Lieutenant William Noel Belford. Born on 5 November 1920 at Taree, New South Wales, Noel had worked as a clerk for the state bank before enlistment in October 1941 and he had a fiancée waiting for him at home. His rear gunner, fellow Australian Flight Sergeant Robert Gould, a 32-year-old former railway employee from Nannine, Western Australia had married Ivy Frances of Geraldton.

Just before 0400 hours the air bomber, 22-year-old Sergeant John Cottis Lee, had dropped his bombs and incendiaries on the centre of the markers and Belford turned for home. It was some hours later when the mid-upper gunner, Sergeant Hugh Harrison Mewburn, asked how it could be that the Pole Star lay astern if they were flying west? Flight Sergeant Arthur J.P. Lee, the 22-year-old navigator, a Londoner who was an office worker before the war, realized that the gyro compass was u/s and that they had been flying in the arc of an enormous circle. Belford and the flight engineer Sergeant Harry Hill were not alone in knowing that they would not have enough fuel to make it back. Sergeant 'Tommy' S. Trinder the WOp/AG began sending out distress calls on his radio. Shortly before 1000 hours, after several dummy runs, Belford ditched 'Tommy 2' across the troughs in the heavy swell 60 miles off Withernsea, Yorkshire using the wave crests to slow the aircraft down. All the crew managed to scramble into their dinghy and were afloat in the open sea until they were eventually rescued by an RML (Rescue Motor Launch) which put them ashore at Great Yarmouth at noon on Friday the 7th.

The next major bombing effort was on Friday 14/Saturday, 15 January when 498 bombers set out for Brunswick but most of the attack fell either in the countryside or in Wolfenbüttel and other small towns and villages well to the south of the city and 42 Lancasters including 5 on 156 Squadron were shot down. Nachtjagd, operating 'Tame Boar' freelance or Pursuit Night-Fighting tactics to excellent advantage, seemed to have rendered 'Window' counter-productive. From the 15th to Wednesday the 19th there was little doing on the bases as the weather was not behaving well and it was a case of 'more of nothing', so wrote Flying Officer Alan McDonald, the officer who had the job to compile the 467 Squadron ORB on 18 January. Even the Mosquitoes left Germany alone.

At Waddington it was foggy on Saturday and foggy with frost on Sunday. It cleared up a bit on Monday morning before the weather closed in again in the afternoon, there was a low cloud base on Tuesday and then it was very wet and miserable on Wednesday. Even so, 'Phil' Smith wrote to his mother on Saturday that the winter hadn't been, in his opinion, particularly bad; 'but there is still plenty of time I suppose.'

Having been in England since August 1941, this was 'Phil' Smith's third British winter. As he sat down to write his weekly letter home (albeit six days late), he was clearly of the opinion that, while the weather had prevented much happening in terms of operations while he had been at Waddington, he had seen worse before. He was, however, quite impressed with the food that the RAF fed him and credited it with his quick recovery from a mild cold he had suffered the previous week.

Smith's short, stocky rear gunner, Flight Sergeant Gilbert Firth Pate, who had a brief flirtation with becoming a jockey as a teenager until his father put a stop to his ambition, also took the opportunity to write a couple of letters home. He got one off to his mother on Sunday to thank her for a recently-received parcel. He was also getting regular parcels from his father, usually containing a newspaper or a *Bulletin* magazine. Once he'd finished with the periodicals, he would forward them on to his uncle Herbert who lived in Padiham in Lancashire.

It began to snow on Monday afternoon. For the Australians on the station this was a great novelty, many of them never having seen snow before. With training flights planned for later in the evening, the ground crew were given shovels and told to clear the runway of the falling white stuff. Given the poor weather, many airmen found the time to write home a quick letter or two. Dale Johnston wrote to his father. He knew that he was getting closer to going into battle and sought to reassure his family:

'Perhaps next week we will be going on ops, but don't worry, there is nothing to panic about. I firmly believe that in these times, if a fellow has got to go, he will. If your number is up, then you are for it. The rest of the crew and me are all anxious to get into it, especially with the new skipper.'

The straight-in, straight-out routes, which had so often characterized raids on Berlin were abandoned on the night of Thursday 20/Friday, 21 January when 769 Halifaxes and Lancasters returned to the 'Big City'. Early fog cleared at Waddington by mid-morning, so the flag was run up over the 463 Squadron 'A' flight office to signify that war was on for that night. No. 463 Squadron RAAF had eleven crews detailed for the night's operation, including Wing Commander Rollo Kingsford-Smith, who arrived back from Acklington just in time for briefing. With the surname of one of Australia's pioneer aviators, it was almost inevitable that Rollo would join the RAAF, becoming one of Australia's most decorated aviators and post-war becoming the chief executive and later chairman of Hawker de Havilland Pty Ltd. Even so, Rollo, who was born on 14 July 1919 in Northwood, wanted to become a doctor rather than a pilot, even after taking his first flight as a boy in a converted First World War fighter plane flown by his uncle, the pioneer aviator Sir Charles Kingsford Smith. The male Smiths all had Kingsford as their second names; the RAAF gave Rollo and his two brothers, who also served, the hyphen. In September 1943 Squadron Leader Rollo Kingsford-Smith became a flight commander on 467 Squadron RAAF. His first flight in command of the squadron was to Kassel, a well-defended city in Germany, on 3/4 October. He recalled: 'It was a cauldron of hell, magnificent, awesome and we had to fly into it and through it. It scared all the self-confidence out of me. I remembered how to pray.' In November he was promoted to wing commander and commanding officer of 463 Squadron RAAF.

'Berlin was a priority target and the fifteen attacks of the Battle of Berlin in the winter of 1943/1944 were a nightmare for the crews. The strengthened defences beginning with radar-guided heavy gun batteries along the coastline followed by constant attacks from the radar-controlled enemy fighter force meant a long gruelling battle before the Lancasters flew into the defence inferno surrounding and over the target. Hitler promised his people that Berlin would never be attacked and he did his best. Over the city the massive anti-aircraft gun barrage, flares, fighters, searchlights, exploding Lancasters and bomb bursts on the ground made an experience the crews did not wish to repeat. But they did, time and time again. Then there were the long return flights. The flak and fighters which would have landed, refuelled and rearmed, would be waiting. Back over England the tired pilots and navigators had to find their airfield in a winter that was one of the worst on record. Low cloud or fog at times closed Waddington and the returning Lancasters would be diverted to a distant airfield where they would arrive, desperately short of fuel.'

At Witchford, Aubrey Howell and his crew on Lancaster 'Y-Yorker' on 115 Squadron had now flown twenty-nine operations and anxiously awaited the last one to finish their tour:

'We had been trying to think of a suitable crew emblem to decorate our 'Y-Yorker' and to give us some identification as a crew. The basic idea of using my surname, 'Howell' along with the aircraft letter 'Y' eventually led us to 'The Ys 'Owells', the original sketch being done by my father. Then an artist friend was pressed into service and he eventually came up with a magnificent canvas three feet square depicting baby owls as the crew members 'operating' from the back of the father owl flying across a huge yellow moon.

'I collected it during my leave early in September 1943, but on return to the squadron I was shattered to hear from Squadron Leader Jim Starkie my flight commander that 'Y-Yorker' had pranged and was a write-off. He had taken it on a trip while we were on leave and was badly shot up by fighters. The aircraft was diving out of control when he gave the order to bail out and only after some of his crew had actually jumped did he managed to regain control at a very low level and fly the badly damaged aircraft back to crash-land it at Ford in Sussex. He managed to salvage Joe's St. Christopher medallion which we had pinned above the doorway and as he handed it back to me with a rather guilty look on his face, he said, 'Sorry

Pilot Officer Eugene Francis Frank McEgan RAAF and crew who were lost on Berlin on 22/23 November 1943.

Major Eckart-Wilhelm 'Hugo' von Bonin.

Marie 'Missie' Vassiltchikov.

'Hajo' Herrmann.

The 33-year-old Pilot Officer Ralph Henderson DFM on 83 Squadron PFF who was KIA on 22/23 November 1943.

Hitler's architect and Reich Minister for Armaments, Albert Speer, with his children in his BMW Kübelwagen in the Obersalzberg in 1943.

Elephant at the Bahn Zoo killed by the bombs in the raid on 22/23 November 1943.

Gunners on the roof of the massive Bahn Zoo flak tower. To the right is the 'L' (*Leitturm* or 'leadership') or 'Lower' tower, which housed the radar equipment.

Gerda Kernchen.

Australian Squadron Leader William Alexander Forbes who flew Walter King of the *Sydney Morning Herald* on the Berlin operation on 2/3 December 1943.

The Bessent twins – 'Bill' and Henry – who served on 405 'Vancouver' Squadron RCAF at Gransden Lodge.

Sergeant Dick Stuart who was KIA on Wednesday 29/Thursday, 30 December 1943.

The 20-year-old Pilot Officer Richard Anthony Bayldon and crew on 9 Squadron at Bardney. All seven crew were killed on the night of 16/17 December 1943.

The 27-year-old Major Prinz Heinrich Alexander Ludwig Peter zu Sayn-Wittgenstein.

'Pip' Beck.

Ted Cachart, aged 17, on completion of the Air Gunnery course in spring 1943.

Flight Lieutenant Aubrey Howell, a pilot on 115 Squadron at Witchford near Ely.

Pilot Officer S.R. McDonald of Sydney, NSW and crew on 460 RAAF Squadron before boarding their Halifax for the raid on Berlin on 20/21 January 1944.

The remains of a Lancaster crew shot down over the Reich.

On 28/29 January 1944 'U-Uncle' piloted by Squadron Leader J. Eric Hockey of Kentville, Nova Scotia was abandoned following a night-fighter attack over the target area. All eight crew members including Flying Officer Jack Ferguson of Regina, Saskatchewan the navigator bailed out and were taken into captivity. Hockey had been best man at Ferguson's wedding.

No. 77 Squadron before the raid on Berlin on 30 January 1944.

The 28-year-old New Zealand Warrant Officer John Edward Rule of Auckland City who was KIA on 30/31 January 1944.

Flight Sergeant Geoffrey Charles Chapman-Smith RAAF on 156 Squadron outside Buckingham Palace with friends and relatives after receiving the Conspicuous Gallantry Medal for his actions on 15/16 February 1944 when his right ankle was hit by a cannon shell and his leg had to be amputated

Pilot Officer Joseph Alphonse Leon Louis Renaud (left) and crew on 425 'Alouette' Squadron RCAF who were KIA on 24/25 March 1944.

Berlin burns after a raid by Mosquitoes on one of seven nights in June 1944.

The 24-year-old Flight Lieutenant Donald Frank Constable RAAF who was KIA on 24 March 1944 flying Halifax LV903 which was shot down and crashed near Eisenach.

The 28-year-old Pilot Officer Leonard Myles McCann of Ottawa, Ontario on 115 Squadron who was KIA on 24/25 March 1944.

The 28-year-old Canadian Pilot Officer Norval Hodges Jones. He and his Halifax crew were killed on their fourth operation on 24/25 March 1944.

Wing Commander Joe Northrop.

A 4,000lb 'cookie' bomb with 'Happy Xmas Adolf' chalked on the casing is manoeuvred into position at Wyton prior to a night bombing operation by Mosquito XVI MM199 on 128 Squadron. On 4/5 February 1945 this aircraft was shot down by flak on an operation to Hanover. Flight Lieutenant James Knox Wood RAAF and his navigator Flying Officer Raymond Poole were killed.

An RAF airman of Bomber Command killed on a bombing raid on the Reich.

Coffins being filled after an air-raid.

A scene of destruction on the Köthener Straße which borders the Potsdamer Platz in the Kreuzberg district of Berlin.

German 'rubble women'.

Victims of an air-raid.

An aerial photograph of Berlin on 26 February 1945.

Hungry Berliners, 1945.

The Bahn Zoo flak tower is demolished by British explosives on 28 February 1948.

that's all that is left of your aircraft.' Fortunately, a brand-new Lancaster had just been delivered, so we christened another 'Y-Yorker', the ground crew doped the new emblem onto the fuselage just below my window on the port side and we were back in business again.

'Several trips were laid on and then cancelled due to bad weather and we were all on edge at this time. Then we were briefed again for a trip to Berlin, but before we went out to the aircraft I was sent for by Wing Commander 'Bobby' Annan to be told that a signal from Bomber Command had temporarily reduced the number of operations for a heavy bomber crew from thirty to twenty-five ops due to the very heavy losses in recent months. We were immediately stood down from duty, but could not leave the base for security reasons as we knew the target. So we relaxed with a few beers while the rest of the squadron took off, but I think each of us wished we had been able to do the last one to finish off our tour of ops. Perhaps it would have been one too many. Flight Lieutenant Roy Barnes DFC and his crew had also completed twenty-nine ops at the same time, but opted to go straight on to 7 Squadron PFF at Waterbeach for another tour. They failed to return from their first trip, on 15 February.'

Aubrey Howell's crew had, on another occasion, taken Squadron Leader Baigent as 'second dickey' just prior to him taking over as 'B' Flight Commander. He paid them the compliment of falling asleep during the return journey, but was rudely awakened when both the starboard engines cut out. Before dozing off Baigent had omitted to change the petrol cocks over to the other tanks.

New Zealand Squadron Leader Cyril Henry Baigent, usually known as 'Mac' or 'Baige', was born at Ashburton on 16 January 1923. Now on his second tour, he had flown thirty-two operations on 15 Squadron and would fly thirty-three operations on 115 Squadron. Of his seventh trip to Berlin since the opening of the battle, he wrote:

'Our Lancaster, 'N-Nuts' was approaching Berlin at about 20,000 feet. There was thick cloud away below, the base lit up by many searchlights giving the effect of an illuminated white sheet on the floor of a dark room. Across this white sheet black insects – aircraft in our bomber stream – were progressing steadily. They stood out clearly and it was a simple matter for the Hun night-fighter to stay above and pounce down every so often to pick off a trundling bomber. One of them made a pass at us but my gunners did not see him until the last moment when they yelled a warning and I began weaving smartly. My enthusiasm for weaving was encouraged by a shower of tracer and exploding cannon shells all around. The Lancaster was hit in several places and the port outer engine set on fire. We got it feathered and luckily the fire went out. We made our bombing run.

'Then just as the bomb-aimer called 'Bombs away', a fighter gave us another sharp shower of cannon shells. The controls went 'haywire' but we managed to level up at about 3,000 feet and headed for home. Both the engineer and rear gunner were wounded. Very slowly, it seemed and very lonely we made our gradual way back, seeing the odd fighter looking for us, but always managing to find a convenient bit of cloud. The elevators had been hit, necessitating a big push forward on the stick for the rest of the flight. We managed to wedge something large between the stick and the seat to stop us from stalling all the time and in this fashion we eventually reached our base near Ely. On landing we found one tyre completely missing which helped to make the landing an interesting one.'

'Mac' took over as commanding officer of 75 (NZ) Squadron on 6 January 1945 while ten days short of his 22nd birthday; the youngest squadron commander in RAF Bomber Command. Despite the baby face and clear complexion, he was tall and physically quite strong. He was also very popular and acknowledged for looking after new crews, often taking them on their first ops. Tragically Cyril Baigent passed away aged just 33 on 10 November 1953 in Nelson, New Zealand.

For the raid on Berlin on 20/21 January 467 Squadron RAAF had named sixteen crews, but one Lancaster broke down before take-off so fifteen got away in the end. The usual crowd of WAAFs and ground crews watched the take-off. The first aircraft, 'H-Harry' with Flying Officer Henry Stuart Lindsay Crouch of Pymble, Sydney at the controls got away at 1616, with each successive Lancaster following an average of about ninety seconds thereafter. Apart from one early return when Flying Officer Jack Colpus in 'N-Nuts' 'boomeranged' with an unserviceable rear turret and icing inside the fuselage, all aircraft from Waddington got away safely.

At her home, an anxious Mary Crouch, who worked in a factory making springs while her husband was at war, always feared the sight of messengers who handed out telegrams with tragic news. After her brother-in-law was killed in New Guinea she hated the sight of the telegram boy. 'When you saw him on his bike, you just got that sinking feeling,' she said. There were times when she nearly lost her husband, like on the evening of 20 December 1943 when first one engine on his Lancaster failed and he lost a second on the way home from Frankfurt, but calm airmanship by the crew enabled them to reach Waddington safely. On 30 June 1944 he was awarded the DFC. After the war he resumed the law training he had begun before joining up and practised as a solicitor until his death at age 69.

It was a fine day and the bombers took off in late afternoon but the night was filthy. The 'Lion' Squadron – 427 RCAF at Leeming – originally mustered sixteen Halifax Vs for the raid but two aircraft returned early, one due to the failure of the starboard inner engine and the other when 'Gee' went u/s. The dozen remaining aircraft continued to the target. The diversions by twelve Mosquitoes on Düsseldorf, four to Kiel and three to Hanover were not large enough to fool the German defences. The bomber stream was detected at 1709 hours when it was still 160 kilometres out over the North Sea over Terschelling by the MS *Togo*, a Würzburg-Reise ('Giant Würzburg') gun-laying radar-equipped vessel equipped with direct-link communication equipment to German night-fighters.

Over Germany the bombers ran into the cloud of a cold front and cloud tops over Berlin varied from 10,000 to 15,000 feet. Horizontal visibility was good, especially in the earlier stages, until columns of smoke began rising up and up to 18,000 feet. The timing of the blind markers was reported to be 'excellent'. They scattered their markers slightly at first, but soon settled down and achieved an extremely accurate and concentrated pattern of 'sky-markers' for the main waves that were detailed to bomb during the twenty minutes between 1933 and 1954 hours. The crews on H2S aircraft thought that the attack fell on the eastern districts of the city, but the consensus of opinion was that the German capital had suffered a major disaster.

This fact was borne out by the series of explosions, some very large, that occurred and one reflection was visible for 75 to 100 miles on the homeward journey.

On 428 'Ghost' Squadron, the crew on 'P-Peter' piloted by Flight Sergeant Frederick F.E. Reaine were flying their first operation and twenty minutes from the target when they were hit by flak which punctured at least one of the petrol tanks. Reaine then ordered the bomb load to be released as they were losing height and were down to 12,500 feet. After releasing the bombs they managed to reach 19,000 feet and turned on a course for home. Petrol was pouring from No. 3 petrol tank and the engineer, Flight Sergeant William E. Fell, estimated they had enough fuel for another ten minutes' flying. Reaine had little choice but to give the order to bail out.

North-east of Châlons-sur-Marne the Canadian navigator, Flying Officer Alvin R. Fisher, Fell and mid-upper gunner Sergeant Leo Fryer, together with the Canadian rear gunner Sergeant William Wynveen, all jumped from the front escape hatch. Fell's straps hit him in the face, cutting him about the jaw and mouth when his parachute opened, but he made a safe landing. The Canadian bomb-aimer, Flying Officer Yves Lavoie, had been sick and when he jumped his feet were facing aft, so that his parachute pack got caught on the edge of the hatch. He put his elbows out and was unable to jump free. The wireless-operator, Sergeant Thomas W. Banner, tried at first to pull him back in but was unable to do so; eventually Lavoie got himself free. As the pilot left the aircraft, the port outer engine cut. Reaine opened his parachute but only one strap was attached and the other had pulled open, so he landed heavily, hurting his spine. Fryer landed in a pine tree. After climbing down he spent the rest of the night under cover. In the morning he took down his 'chute and started to walk in a southerly direction. He eventually arrived in Switzerland on 3 February and finally set foot in England on 11 September. Banner also fell into a tree and when he released his parachute, fell 15 to 20 feet and was knocked out. He later crossed the Pyrenees with the Bourgogne escape line at the beginning of March. All the crew, apart from Wynveen who was taken prisoner, evaded capture and, helped by the Bourgogne escape line, eventually returned to England.

Conditions were particularly favourable to night-fighters since a layer of cloud at 12,000 feet illuminated from below by searchlights provided a background against which aircraft could be silhouetted. About 100 twin-engined fighters were sighted in the Berlin area and they shot down all 35 bombers (22 Halifaxes and 13 Lancasters) that failed to return. Three of the missing Halifaxes came from 76 Squadron at Holme-on-Spalding-Moor.

'Q-Queenie' skippered by 24-year-old Pilot Officer George Corbett Ive from South Perth was attacked by an enemy fighter at 18,000 feet in the target area which set the starboard inner engine, the overload petrol tank and the bomb bay on fire. Ive ordered the crew to bail out. The escape hatch was opened by Sergeant Kenneth Frank Hutson the navigator and Flight Sergeant M.F. Curry the wireless-operator was the first to leave at about 16,000 feet as the aircraft went into a spin. Sergeant K.C. Buchan, the air bomber, managed to put on his 'chute but could do nothing owing to the centrifugal force. After the aircraft dropped thousands of feet it exploded and Buchan was blown out before the Lancaster crashed in open countryside. He and Curry were taken prisoner, but Hutson and the others died in the aircraft.

'R-Robert' flown by 26-year-old Canadian Pilot Officer Victor 'Red' Parrott of Redlake, Ontario was lost with all seven crew. The third loss on the squadron was 'X-X-ray' skippered by Pilot Officer G.G.A. Whitehead, who recalled:

'As the bombs left the bomb bay of our Halifax there was an almighty crack as we were hit in the nose by flak at 20,000 feet. The 25-year-old bomb-aimer, Flying Officer Harold 'Don' Morris, was killed instantly and the wireless-operator, Sergeant L. Stokes, was badly wounded. There was a large hole in the port side of the nose, involving the navigator's compartment and all his instruments, charts etc., were sucked out of it. There was some damage in my department, the worst of which was to both compasses, which were completely inoperable. One engine failed and the aircraft was difficult to control but we turned westwards and I told the navigator that I would keep Polaris in the starboard cockpit window and although that would involve flying over more enemy territory than was healthy, provided our luck held we might make the shorter sea crossing to the UK. There was 10/10ths cloud below and Polaris was our only navigational aid.

'We held on like this for ages, gradually losing height. Fuel was a problem. Although we had plenty on board, the flight engineer reported that he was unable to use the starboard tanks because of damage to the fuel-cock mechanism. Both port engines began to overheat. I saw the clouds ahead were breaking and I told the crew that if there was land below they should be prepared to 'get out and walk'. I instructed them to prepare Stokes for a static-line parachute exit if I deemed it necessary to give the order. We were at 3,000 feet when we reached the break in the cloud but it was not possible to identify anything on the ground. I adopted the 'I am lost' procedure by calling 'Hallo Darkie' on the radio several times but got no reply. We were down to the last half-pint of our useable fuel so I gave the order to bail out [over Liévin in the Pas-de-Calais]. All the survivors got out and landed safely. The aircraft had a mind of its own and wanted to do aerobatics as soon as I let go of the controls, but I made it and it passed me on the way down! We had hoped that the land might have been Suffolk or Essex but on the way down I realized there were no coal mines in these counties. I landed in the back garden of a miner's cottage in Lens, in north-eastern France!'

Stokes crawled to a farm and was given first-aid before being taken into custody with two others on the crew. The navigator, mid-upper gunner and rear gunner were given shelter by a farmer in the Pas-de-Calais and were liberated by the Canadian Second Army in June 1944. Pilot Officer Whitehead began walking and while crossing a plain he looked up and saw the large Canadian memorial on Vimy Ridge. He walked through Arras, right past the German HQ near the station. Then he walked further south down the road to Bapaume, round Péronne and on to Ham where he was helped by the Resistance. He travelled along the escape line and arrived in Gibraltar on 2 May 1944. He was in the UK two days later. He found out that their forecast wind was from 270° but during the evening it had unexpectedly veered round to due north, thus forcing them south of their intended track.

Three of the missing Lancasters were on 83 Squadron at Wyton. At Bourn there was no word from 'K-King' on 97 Squadron, which was flown by 27-year-old

Pilot Officer Cyril Arthur Wakley of Streatham Hill, London who was killed along with three of his crew. The 28-year-old rear gunner, Technical Sergeant Benjamin Howell Stedman USAAF of Woodstock, McHenry County, Illinois whose remains could not be found had completed ten operations. Sergeant Rendle George William Climo, the 29-year-old WOp/AG had worked for the Post Office in London prior to enlisting. Sergeant Jack Tye, the 32-year-old mid-upper gunner, left a widow, Winifred of Horbury, Yorkshire. The three other crew members were taken prisoner, the navigator of whom, 25-year-old Sergeant Edward Lowe, on 9 September 1945 married Wakley's widow Winifred Grace and they moved to Nova Scotia, Canada with her two children.

Canadian Flight Lieutenant George E. Coldray piloting 'S-for-Sugar' on 405 'Vancouver' Squadron RCAF was attacked by a Ju 88 and a Focke-Wulf 190. After seeing tracer over the port wing, Coldray put the Lancaster into a diving turn to port. The Ju 88 made an attack from dead astern and broke off above the bomber to the left. The mid-upper gunner, Flight Sergeant Joseph Gerard Renaud, fired about fifty rounds at the Junkers as it did so. The Focke-Wulf made its attack from dead astern and at the same level. 'Sugar's rear gunner, Flight Sergeant Roger Henry Jules Daoust, fired a short burst but in the exchange the Lancaster received extensive damage. The Ju 88 was claimed as probably damaged. Daoust was killed in action on 6 January on Stettin. Squadron Leader Couldray and crew were shot down by a German night-fighter on 2/3 June 1944 on the raid on Trappes and he and Renaud and two other crew members were killed.

'C-Charlie' piloted by Canadian Flight Lieutenant J.M.J. Bourke on 514 Squadron was attacked near Berlin at 0313 hours. His rear gunner, fellow Canadian Sergeant Albert Williston reported a twin-engined aircraft which turned out to be a Bf 110 to starboard at 800 feet. Williston ordered a 'corkscrew' to starboard at the same time as he opened fire as the 110 closed in. He suffered stoppages in two guns, but despite this his tracer appeared to hit the fighter, which broke off into the darkness. A second attack came at 0340 on the homeward journey, 25 miles east of Leipzig. Williston was again alert, spotting a twin-engined aircraft, which he later identified as a Ju 88, on the port quarter. He again gave the order to 'corkscrew' and fired a four-second burst, but again suffered stoppages. The 88 made one firing pass and was lost in the night.

On the night of 21/22 January 'C-Charlie' and Bourke's crew were lost on Magdeburg, believed shot down by Heinrich Prinz zu Sayn-Wittgenstein who claimed five bombers before being shot down, most likely in a final exchange of fire with Albert Williston and Sergeant Les Brewer, the mid-upper gunner. Wittgenstein was killed, as were Williston and the flight engineer. Bourke and four of his crew survived and were taken prisoner.

No. 6 Group lost a Lancaster on 426 'Thunderbird' Squadron and ten Halifaxes. At Croft 434 'Bluenose' Squadron RCAF lost four Halifaxes. Just as 'C-Charlie' piloted by Canadian Flight Sergeant F.W. Johnson was releasing its load of incendiaries at 19,000 feet the aircraft was hit twice by flak. The first flak strike was towards the rear of the bomb bay and the second hit the fuselage near the wing root. The resulting damage was severe: the rudder control was sheared off, there was no oxygen supply or electrics from the rest position backwards, all the aircraft's aerials were missing and some of the electronics were destroyed. 'C-Charlie' remained airborne and the remainder of the bomb load was jettisoned, although a number of remaining incendiaries caught fire in the bomb bay and filled the cockpit with smoke. This fire was later put out and Johnson made for home using only aileron controls to steer the aircraft. The engines had not been damaged and there was no problem with the speed or height being lost. As the aircraft reached the British coastline the intercom between the pilot and Sergeant A. Hession the wireless-operator failed and soon after crossing the coast with Johnson beginning to lose control and out of fuel they abandoned the aircraft somewhere in the Driffield area. Some of the crew suffered heavy landings; Johnson sustained head injuries and Canadian Sergeants Jim Campbell the bomb-aimer and Donald M. Tofflemire the rear gunner both sustained head and leg injuries.

On 427 'Lion' Squadron RCAF at Leeming 'S-Sugar', better known as 'Sierra Sue' and flown by Canadian Pilot Officer Norman Earl Cook was shot down at 2005 hours, possibly by Hauptmann Leopold Fellerer for his twenty-third victory. All the crew were killed. Anxious listeners waited in vain for word of his return but nothing was heard after the ETA passed. There was no further word also from 'N-Nuts' piloted by 20-year-old Flying Officer William Arthur Cozens, a bridegroom of a month having married Dorothy, his fiancée from Wimbledon, but possibly he was low on fuel and it was hoped that he had put down at another aerodrome as soon as he had cleared the Norfolk coast. At Westwick close to the fighter airfield at RAF Coltishall near Norwich, farmer Joe Mutimer and his wife Noele were preparing for bed in their home at Orchard House. Almost overhead Cozens was trying desperately to get 'N-Nuts' down safely on the single runway. Twice he was forced to abort. He went around again for a third attempt, but he was too low and the starboard wing of 'N-Nuts' hit high-tension wires and smashed through some tall trees in a nearby wood, shearing off the wing and its two engines. The remainder of the Halifax carried on through the trees, finally coming to rest in a ball of fire within yards of Orchard House. The navigator, Flying Officer Laurence George Biddiscombe, was killed instantly.

Startled, Joe and Noele Mutimer immediately got out of bed and almost immediately realized that an aircraft had come close to destroying their home. Because the crash had cut all the power and telephone lines to the house, Joe asked his wife to cycle up the road to alert Mr Eldred the local ARP man and notify him of the crashed aircraft. While his wife was struggling on her bicycle in the wind and rain, Joe bravely went to rescue the surviving crew members trapped in the burning bomber. Constable Emmerson from North Walsham, who just happened to be passing the scene at the time, also helped in the frantic rescue of the crew. Thanks to their bravery, air gunners Flight Sergeants C.L. Bernier and Ross Bell Nairn RCAF were pulled out alive from the burning Halifax and taken to Orchard House where Dr Morgan from North Walsham looked after them until the crash crews from RAF Coltishall arrived at the scene to take over.

Flight Sergeant H.P. Whittaker, the mid-upper gunner, also survived. Unfortunately Bill Cozens died of his injuries later that night and flight engineer Sergeant John McGowan and Sergeant William Stockford the bomb-aimer died in hospital two days later. In due course, Joe Mutimer travelled to Buckingham Palace to receive the BEM from HM King George VI. Pilot Officer Ross Nairn was posted to 405 Squadron on 11 May. On the night of 25/26 August he was flying on ops to Russelsheim when his Lancaster was attacked and damaged by night-fighters. The rear gunner was injured in the attack and control was briefly lost. Nairn and two others took it upon themselves to abandon the Lancaster over Germany before the pilot had given the order, but their skipper regained control and flew the Lancaster safely back to England. Nairn may have landed in the Homburg area, possibly safely, but was then captured, murdered and his body hidden in a wood.

Three Lancasters on 83 Squadron failed to return to Wyton. 'L-London' piloted by Australian Flight Lieutenant Roland King DFC on 83 Squadron had taken off at 1611 hours on this, his eleventh operation. He arrived over the target without incident, but after bombing his control stick suddenly went dead in his hand and the rudders failed. He found too that he had lost his helmet and intercommunication gear and that the aircraft was full of smoke. During the next few seconds King tried to check on his crew's condition, but he could see only two of them. Flight Sergeant Ken Farmelo the engineer seemed to be curled up on the inside of the roof, apparently held there by the forces acting on the falling bomber. King released his harness and immediately he too was shot upwards. He hit the roof, and then fell back into his seat again. Seizing the stick once more he tried to pull the bomber out, but it was useless. King believes he lost consciousness; the next thing he remembered was falling through the air, his parachute unopened. He pulled the ripcord and it spread out above him. He was descending immediately above the target and the attack was at the height of its fury. Bombs were raining down all around him and the sky was alight with massed searchlights and bursting flak. The noise then was terrific. He pulled the shroud of his parachute in an attempt to drift outside the city and believes that he did actually drift some little way to the south-west of Berlin, for he came down in a ploughed field. Soon after he landed he heard the Berlin 'all-clear'. He freed himself of his parachute and then, by the light of incendiary bombs burning in a hole nearby, searched for his cigarette case, but could not get at the lighter. His right arm seemed fixed across his body and quite useless. His left hand was smashed and he was wounded in the head. There were no other survivors on the crew.

Eventually, King was picked up by the Germans and taken to the Hermann Goering Luftwaffe hospital. He remembered sitting on the bed while the Germans cut off his clothes, then no more. He woke up on the operating table. His elbow had been severely injured and he had five operations on it and two blood transfusions. He spent two and a half months in the hospital and had a 'ringside view' for ten weeks of the terrifying attacks on Berlin. RAF air attacks occurred almost every night. The patients were hurried down to the air-raid shelters in the cellars and there they would listen to the ten- or fifteen-minute broadcasts of the approach of the bombers. Every time there was an attack the hospital windows were blown out. When the heavies were not over the capital the Mosquitoes 'stoked the fires' in the capital. After ten weeks King was taken to Stalag Luft III. A year later he went to Lamsdorf by hospital train to be exchanged with a German prisoner. When eventually he arrived back in England he was reunited with his wife and saw his baby son for the first time.

Seven Halifaxes were lost or missing on 102 Squadron which had dispatched sixteen aircraft from Pocklington. One of these was 'X-X-ray' piloted by Warrant Officer R.G. Wilding, which was shot down on the outward leg by Hauptmann Ludwig 'Luk' Meister and abandoned in the vicinity of Neuruppin. All the crew were taken into captivity.

'H-Harry' captained by Pilot Officer A.W. Dean was hit by flak at 19,500 feet over the target and after 'Bombs away' and then finished off by a night-fighter. 'Harry' was abandoned and crashed at Ahrensfelde 13 kilometres from the centre of Berlin. Dean and four of the eight-man crew survived and were taken prisoner. Sergeant Arthur Landen, the 36-year-old flight engineer, Flying Officer James Nelson, the 28-year-old bomb-aimer, and Sergeant Alan Watson, the rear gunner were killed. Only Flight Sergeant E. Render, piloting 'N-Nuts' survived when the aircraft was shot down and he was taken into captivity. Sergeant Fred Moss the bomb-aimer and Sergeant Earl Smith the Canadian air gunner were killed.

'Y-Yorker' piloted by Sergeant R. Compston was abandoned by five of the crew before it crashed at Neu-Zittau, 27 kilometres south-west from the centre of Berlin.

After the briefing at Pocklington, Flying Officer Laurie Underwood, the bomb-aimer on 'F for Freddie', better known as '*Old Flo*', had sat down in his Nissen hut and written a letter to Beryl, his fiancée in Middlesbrough. He told her that he had a premonition that they would not be coming back, but he told that he would be coming back eventually and would she wait for him? For the first time in his life he clipped on his parachute before take-off without telling the rest of the crew. '*Old Flo*'s skipper was Pilot Officer George A. Griffiths DFM aka 'Gag' who had completed a first tour in the Middle East. Sergeant Kenneth Frederick Stanbridge, a 22-year-old pilot from Salisbury, South Australia was flying as 'second dickey' for experience.

Flight Sergeant Charles Gordon Dupueis, the 20-year-old Canadian mid-upper gunner from Regina, Saskatchewan was, like Underwood, superstitious and always carried a rabbit's foot as a good-luck charm. He had not let on to the rest of the crew that he had flown a relatively easy leaflet-dropping flight with another crew to get his thirteenth trip in. Flight Sergeant Eric Arthur Church, the 24-year-old wireless-operator, came from Tottenham, North London. He had married his fiancée Gladys on 24 January 1943. Offered a commission, he had at first refused as he did not wish to be separated from his wife, but when she discovered that she was pregnant he had accepted the promotion. Pilot Officer Reg Wilson, the 20-year-old navigator, was from Goodmayes, Essex; Sergeant John Bremner, the 21-year-old flight engineer, was from Fenham, Newcastle upon Tyne. Sergeant John H.L. Bushell, the 20-year-old rear gunner, was from Bedford where he worked in the small family newspaper shop with his mother and two aunts.

After releasing its bombs from 18,000 feet and as the bomb doors started to close, '*Old Flo*' was hit by flak over the target, which set the starboard wing and the bomb bay on fire. Their attacker was Hauptmann Leopold 'Poldi' Fellerer in a Bf 110G-4 who claimed the Halifax for the first of his five victories this night. Flying underneath '*Old Flo*', out of sight and with upward-firing cannon, he fired into the starboard wing fuel tanks. (Fellerer had scored forty-one victories by the end of the war and was awarded the Knight's Cross). Reg Wilson recalled:

'*Old Flo*' caught fire from wing to wing, with over 1,000 gallons of fuel still in her tanks. At 17,000 feet she went into a spiral dive over Oberspree. Then there was an explosion of fuel. Of our crew of eight, four survived, all of us having had remarkable escapes, sustaining just a few cuts and sprains.

'Seconds before the spiral dive, Laurie Underwood and I, having kicked out the jammed escape hatch, bailed out at 17-18,000 feet into the upcoming flak and tracer of Berlin.'

A minute or so later 'Gag' Griffiths and Johnny Bushell were blown out with the explosion of fuel. Both were unconscious and in free fall, but they regained consciousness enough to be able to open their parachutes fully only a few hundred feet before they hit the ground. Laurie Underwood and Bushell were caught by the military. Griffiths and Reg Wilson were apprehended by the civil police and they too were taken into captivity. Stanbridge, Eric Church and John Bremner had no time to bail out before '*Old Flo*' crashed into woodland at Hirschgarten Friedrichshagen on the outskirts of Berlin. Flight Sergeant Dupueis, who was ten days short of turning 21, has no known grave.

'U-Uncle' skippered by Flying Officer Dennis H. Phillips DFC had its starboard engine set on fire by a night-fighter but made it home. 'O for Orange' flown by Flight Sergeant Richard Proctor crashed between Intwood Hall and the Norwich to Wymondham LNER railway line at Cringleford on the outskirts of Norwich. Proctor was injured; Flying Officer James Alexander W. 'Jock' Turnbull, the 20-year-old bomb-aimer from Ashkirk, Selkirkshire was more seriously injured and he was pronounced dead at the Norfolk & Norwich Hospital. 'P-Peter' skippered by 27-year-old Flying Officer Alexander Henry Hall was hit by flak at 18,000 feet and the No. 3 petrol tank was punctured. On the return the undercarriage could not be lowered and on regaining the Yorkshire coast Hall ordered the crew to bail out, after which he crash-landed at Clitheroe Farm, 5 miles north of Driffield airfield. There were no injuries but the aircraft was wrecked. The crew would lose their lives on the night of 23/24 April on a 'Gardening' sortie in the Baltic when they were shot down by Leutnant Walter Brieglieb.

At Waddington 'The consensus,' wrote Flying Officer Alan McDonald, 'was that it was an easy night's work.' Sadly, tragedy struck the 463 Squadron Lancaster piloted by Pilot Officer 'Freddy' Merrill. The crew encountered trouble with their oxygen system and all were in some way or other affected by it. Sergeant 'Bertie' Turner, the mid-upper gunner, was affected worst of all and was unconscious by the time the crew left the target area. All efforts were made to disentangle him from his turret and every effort was made to revive him for fully two hours, but this was of no avail and Turner was dead on arrival at Waddington.

While the Air Ministry in London announced simply that there had been another heavy and concentrated attack on Berlin, the Toronto *Globe and Mail* reported that

'Berlin has been blasted again. Nine RCAF squadrons helped carry the 2,300 tons which smashed the German capital Thursday night. So, Berlin will be destroyed, beaten into the dust, a thing despised. The thrill, the sheer delight, which news of the Canadians contributes to these raids sends through the nation each time it is repeated comes not from the satisfaction of destroying. It resides in the pride which all the people have in the courage and stern idealism of the young men of the RCAF.'

Since photographic flights over Berlin at this time were not possible because of cloud cover, the extent of damage caused to Berlin and other German cities was often gleaned from newspaper reports in neutral countries and in particular the Swedish press, which were picked up and quoted at length by *The Times*:

'There is no longer any block or buildings in Berlin that had escaped damage,' wrote the Berlin correspondent of the Dagens Nyhter. 'Fires so large and numerous that it takes several days to put them out and many persons are buried in cellars; but life still goes on, although in a very primitive form.' Describing his walk home [the Berlin correspondent of Allehanda] says he 'spent a full hour wandering past blocks where the fires were still burning and through streets where the pavements were encumbered with mountains of furniture and household goods.... Even for those who lived through the catastrophic Berlin days around November 23rd, the impressions of the bomb-storm then pale before what we have experienced in these days.'

On the night of Tuesday 21/Wednesday, 22 January 102 Squadron lost a further 4 Halifaxes when 648 aircraft were dispatched in four waves to Magdeburg, 60 miles west of Berlin. Winds en route to Magdeburg were stronger than forecast and the outward route was not dissimilar to that of the night before.

'There was some groaning when we were told at briefing we were to fly over Holland and Germany heading straight for Berlin and then fool the Germans by turning about 80 miles short of the "Big City" to bomb Magdeburg,' recalled 'Bertie' Lewis, the American wireless-operator on Ron Champion's crew on 102 Squadron. 'Butch' had been turned down for air crew in the RCAF because he had not completed high school (which in the USA meant being in school until 18 years of age):

'Hearing that most people in Britain quit school at 14 (like me), I went to the main Canadian seaport of Halifax and got a job as a trimmer on a small Norwegian ship carrying timber to England. The job required shovelling coal to the stokers below. As it was amidships and below the waterline I could see why the job was open. These small ships, it seemed, were more expendable and were placed alongside of the slow-moving convoys.

'Putting in on the Isle of Lewis in the Hebrides we took on a couple of anti-aircraft gunners as we were going down the North Sea, open to roving enemy planes. But none showed and it was interesting to see at times, pairs of British fighter aircraft hovering over us. On a bright summer's day we could see many masts of sunken ships sticking out of the waters of the Thames estuary. We docked at Surrey Docks in east London and noted how the area was flattened – by bombing no doubt.

'After passing the air crew selection board in London I was on my way towards my purpose; striking a blow against a vicious enemy. If I had known that it would be two years before I saw any action when I went to the air crew selection board in London, I would have about-faced and re-joined the merchant ship on which I had crossed the Atlantic. Being a target wasn't to my liking, however, unlike the Air Force where we could also strike a blow at the enemy.'

A feint by twenty-two Lancasters and a dozen Mosquitoes of 5 and 8 Groups that bombed Berlin was largely ignored. Just one Lancaster, piloted by 20-year-old

Flight Sergeant John Walter Homewood on 630 Squadron at East Kirkby, was shot down with no survivors, possibly by Feldwebel Andreas Hartl on the approach to the 'Big City'.

'Unexpectedly, when we got over Magdeburg there was little enemy night-fighter activity,' continues 'Butch' Lewis. 'We could hardly believe our good luck; the trick worked! But shortly afterwards on our way back there were exploding planes all over the sky and it was fighting all the way back to the coast. It seemed the enemy, knowing we would not really aim for Berlin, ordered their fighters to the likely target of Leipzig. That guess meant the enemy night-fighters crossed the bomber stream's route home. We lost fifty-seven aircraft – phew!'

This was Bomber Command's heaviest loss of the war so far.

Major Sayn-Wittgenstein, bordfunker 'Fritz' Ostheimer and bordmechaniker Unteroffizier Kurt Matzuleit were airborne again in their Ju 88C-6, taking off from Stendhal shortly before 2100 hours on a 'Tame Boar' sortie secking to add to the three Halifaxes the Prinz had claimed on Berlin the night before when he had almost collided with the third burning Lancaster, which went into a dive and came very close to his own aircraft. Wittgenstein regained control of his just-flyable aircraft, Ostheimer established contact with the airfield at Erfurt and Wittgenstein belly-landed the aircraft safely. On inspection they discovered that about 2 metres (6 feet 6 inches) of the wing had been cut off by the Lancaster's propeller.

Now, Major Sayn-Wittgenstein claimed three Lancasters and two Halifaxes in the Magdeburg area, but he was again in trouble. While getting into position for a new attack he was ready to shoot when their Ju 88C erupted in 'terrible explosions and sparks'. It immediately caught fire in the left wing and began to go down. The canopy above Ostheimer's head flew away and he heard on the intercom a shout of 'Raus!' ('Get out!'). He tore off his oxygen mask and helmet and was then thrown out of the aircraft. After a short time he opened his parachute and landed east of the Hohengoehrener Dam near Schönhausen. He and Kurt Matzuleit survived, but early next morning the body of Prinz Wittgenstein was discovered close to the crash site at Lübars. On bailing out, his head had probably struck the tailplane, rendering him unconscious and unable to pull the ripcord.

'Missie' Vassiltchikov dined with Count Friedrich-Werner Graf von der Schulenburg, a German diplomat. Born on 20 November 1875 at Kemberg in the old German Empire, he had served as the last German ambassador to the Soviet Union before Operation 'Barbarossa'. Midway through dinner Schulenburg said that Major Heinrich zu Sayn-Wittgenstein had been killed. The announcement had been made in the Wehrmachtbericht, an information bulletin issued by the headquarters of the Wehrmacht. 'Missie' froze. Schulenburg looked at her in surprise, as he was not aware that she and the Prinz were such close friends. The last time 'Missie' had seen Wittgenstein was in Potsdam when he had 'dropped in for supper' looking 'pale and tired'. She had urged him to take some leave but he only wanted to do so at the end of the month. Now the papers were full of his exploits. Only a few days earlier Wittgenstein had telephoned 'Missie' telling her 'I have been to see our darling!'

He had just been to Hitler's HQ [to receive the Swords to his Knight's Cross] and was surprised that his handgun had not been removed before he entered, so that it might have been possible to 'bump him off' right then and there. In her memoirs, Tatiana von Metternich reported that Wittgenstein planned to kill Hitler after the ceremony at which he received his Knight's Cross of the Iron Cross in 1943. He said: 'I am not married, I have no children – I am expendable. He will receive me personally. Who else among us can ever get as near to him?' 'Missie' warned that it might be better to continue the conversation elsewhere and when they did, he speculated about the possibility of blowing himself up with Hitler when they next shook hands!

His mother, Princess Walburga, commented that: '... he was boundlessly disillusioned and boundlessly disappointed. It was only out of sense of honour and duty that Heinrich went on fighting, carried along by the ambition to overtake Major Lent in his score of enemy aircraft shot down.'

There were three nights of rest for the Main Force following the Magdeburg debacle and a Bomber Command raid planned for the weekend of 25/26 January was 'scrubbed'. Berliners and the crews of Bomber Command did what they could to enjoy the brief respite, but life in the German capital and on the home front, morale was severely tested.

'The Battle of Berlin did cause morale to sag,' recalled Pilot Officer Joe Sherriff, a Canadian wireless-operator on 57 Squadron at East Kirkby. 'Crews were weary and angry, strained and more fearful of their next trip than usual, cursing "Butch" Harris for his unrelenting demands and his apparently uncaring attitude towards his own men. The results didn't appear to come anywhere near justifying the losses and the hardship. I knew three crews during the Battle of Berlin who obviously were in bad shape because of fatigue and should have been rested. Two didn't survive. One of the crews had several close calls and the pilot was a nervous wreck. On one trip they were hit by flak and the navigator and wireless-operator were injured. On another trip they were sprayed by shells from a night-fighter. One shell came through the windshield right in front of the pilot – the shoulder of his jacket was sliced through. He was not injured, but his journey home was a nightmare because of the blast of air through the hole in the windscreen and manhandling a Lancaster which had some of its controls damaged. It was obvious that this crew had had its nine lives and was so shattered by fatigue and tension that there was little chance of them surviving if they continued to operate. They were not rested and they perished.

'In attacking Berlin, we paid dearly for a morsel.'

Chapter Twelve

'Chop City'

'God, the losses over Berlin! The "Big City" is now referred to as "Chop City" by some. Seem to remember that over four raids at the beginning of 1944, 158 kites bought it. A slugging match with masses of night-fighters all along the route with even more over Berlin itself; and the heaviest concentration of flak in all Germany.'

Pilot Officer Campbell Muirhead,
a Lancaster bomb-aimer on 12 Squadron.[1]

The main Battle of Berlin had begun on the night of 18/19 November 1943. RAF Bomber Command had attacked the German capital in some strength on ten nights up to and including 20/21 January 1944. The main offensive of the war against the 'Big City', as it was known to RAF bomber crews, would continue to the end of that month and it would see a grand total of 14 large raids and 7,403 sorties on the German capital at a cost of 384 aircraft. The German night-fighter defences would prove that Bomber Command could not maintain a strategic offensive on deep penetrations of Germany. The Luftwaffe had, by January 1944, fitted the FuG 220 Lichtenstein SN-2 radar to most of the 'Tame Boars' employing freelance or Pursuit Night-Fighting tactics to augment the Lichtenstein sets. Now the fighters had such a marked superiority over the bombers that bomber crews were instructed not to use H2S, or to use it only for short periods when vitally required for navigation or for blind marking on long-range targets. There was no other technique available.[2] However, the accuracy achieved against the Ruhr and against Hamburg could not be achieved on long-range targets such as Berlin and the attrition from fighters became too great to sustain.

The night of 27/28 January 1944 would be the second of the four raids on Berlin which prompted the scornful sobriquet 'Chop City'. It came after six nights' respite during which the only raid on the German capital had been on 21/22 January when twenty-two Lancasters and a dozen Mosquitoes had carried out a diversionary raid on the 'Big City'. Only one of the Lancasters was lost but fifty-seven aircraft had been lost on the Magdeburg raid.

Wing Commander Reggie 'Sunshine' Lane DSO DFC had taken command of 405 'Vancouver' Squadron at Gransden Lodge on 22 January when long-serving Johnny Fauquier had been posted to a desk job at 6 Group. Lane's squadron detailed fourteen Lancasters for the Berlin raid on 27 January. He wrote:

'Every time the crews came into the ops room the route would be up on the map and they'd look at the map and they'd say, 'God! Berlin again!' The old usual chit-chat that would go on had died; it was just not there. It was like walking into the jaws of death another night, because the losses on the Berlin raids were very heavy.

'During that difficult time when every night it was Berlin, Berlin, Berlin and the morale was down, I can remember one occasion when Mac and Bennett – both were Squadron Leaders – came into the Ops Room and you could hear a pin drop. They took one look at the map. Old Benny put on his glasses and picked up one of the coffee mugs and grabbed a handful of pencils and put them in it. Mac got into the act and he grabbed a ruler and used it as a cane and put on dark glasses and they both came down the aisle like blind men and said, 'Can anyone tell us where we are going tonight and how we are going to find it?' Well of course, it just broke the tension immediately and everyone roared with laughter and that was it; it was just great.'[3]

All fourteen of Lane's Lancasters would return. On 27 January 13 Lancasters on 405 'Vancouver' Squadron RCAF were on the battle order, which totalled 515 Lancasters and 15 Mosquitoes. Six Wellingtons and seventy-four Stirlings were detailed to lay mines off the Dutch coast and twenty-one Halifaxes would do the same near Heligoland; both with the intention of drawing German fighters up early. No. 100 Group were putting up nine aircraft on RCM sorties and a dozen Mosquitoes on 'Serrate' interception patrols. A further eighteen Mosquitoes were to drop imitation 'fighter flares' away from the main bomber routes to and from the target.

At Bardney at 10.00 am that day, 19-year-old Flight Lieutenant Stanley James and his Lancaster crew on 9 Squadron expected to fly their twenty-third operation. James, who was from Harrow, had joined the RAFVR at 16 and was known as 'Jimmy' after the famous comedian. Pilot Officer George Robert Tomlinson, his 21-year-old flight engineer, was a Lancastrian from Clitheroe. Flight Sergeant Austin William Archer was the navigator and Flight Sergeant A. Howie the bomb-aimer. The wireless-operator was 22-year-old Sergeant Ronald Ernest Burke from Andover. Sergeant Mike Chivers was the mid-upper gunner. Flight Sergeant 'Hal' Croxson the rear gunner had started as a trainee pilot in America, but he was sick for some while and could not catch up on the course, so he re-mustered as an air gunner. To Croxson life on the squadron seemed 'a little like flying and boozing – one night on ops, one night drinking, but of course the nights in the pubs were more enjoyable.' After lunch came briefing and preparation for the operation. The weather forecast supplied to the Air Staff at 1600 hours indicated that the weather should be 10/10ths cloud with tops at 8,000 to 10,000 feet but 90 mph winds were expected at 20,000 feet increasing to 95 mph at times. At 1630 hours 9 Squadron assembled at their Lancasters, went through final checks and at 1715 hours 'Jimmy' James took 'M-Mother' off. They were in the second wave of the five attacking waves. This was the crew's seventh consecutive visit to Berlin. After this trip they were on a posting to 617 Squadron.

The German running commentary control was heard plotting the build-up of the bomber stream over the Norwich area as early as 1736 hours and from 1806 hours night-fighters were being sent to intercept the bombers over the North Sea. The diversion by the Halifaxes fooled the JLO into sending about half his night-fighters north, but half the German night-fighter force was duped into flying north by a diversionary force of Halifaxes laying mines near Heligoland. The remainder was sent up earlier than normal, flying out 75 miles over the North Sea from the Dutch coast to meet the oncoming bomber stream before Berlin was reached and about six Gruppen were pitched into battle with the Main Force.

One of the first claims was heard at 1945 hours near Alkmaar and four more occurred between Minden and Magdeburg, seven over Berlin and two more by single-engined fighters near Frankfurt.[4] The bombers' route was partially obscured by clouds which increased in intensity, so that the target, except for one or two breaks, was soon completely covered. However, route-marking was exceptionally good. Hindered only by intense flak in the Rhineland and occasional more or less ineffective searchlights, the bombers ploughed on to their destination. Half the German night-fighter force was duped into flying north by a diversionary force of Halifaxes laying mines near Heligoland and only a few enemy fighters attacked the bombers before Berlin was reached.

On 408 'Goose' Squadron Lancaster 'S-Sugar' piloted by Warrant Officer2 John Douglas Harvey who was born in Swansea, Ontario on 7 August 1942 encountered a Bf 110, which was first sighted below and slightly to port, range 600 yards, commencing an attack. The rear gunner, Flight Sergeant Stanley Enos Campbell of Drumheller, Alberta instructed Harvey to turn port towards the dark side of the sky. The fighter appeared to be trying to position himself to fire rockets. The rear gunner opened fire at 300 yards with long bursts of approximately 300 rounds. He observed his tracer entering the 110's starboard wing, hitting the engine and knocking off one of the rockets. The fighter broke off down to port and Campbell instructed Harvey to climb starboard, do a banking search and then resume course. Campbell again sighted the 110 right below at a range of 300 yards and opened fire with another long burst of 300 rounds, his tracer entering the rear of the fighter's cockpit. A large blue flash appeared in the cockpit and every light came on. The 110 started to weave, going over to port quarter down and back again underneath the bomber and commencing an attack with all his lights still on. Campbell again opened fire with another long burst of 300 rounds, his tracer entering the fighter's cockpit. The 110 caught fire, rolled over and went down out of control, disappearing beneath the clouds with flames completely enveloping the fuselage. This was seen by the gunners and the wireless-operator. Then a glow appeared beneath the cloud, which was assumed to be the fighter hitting the ground.

Over the target the Pathfinders again excelled themselves and dropped an excellent pattern of sky-markers but the strong winds blew them rapidly along the line of the bombers' route and bombing was 'spread well up and down wind'. Widespread fires were observed through fleeting cloud-breaks and several explosions were noticed, while the glow was visible for 150 miles after leaving the target. Anti-aircraft fire was moderate with the light flak seeming to concentrate on the sky-markers. Considerable night-fighter activity was reported both over the target and on the way home, but searchlights in and around Berlin were unable to pierce the clouds. All in all this was an excellent effort as testified to by Mosquitoes who were over Berlin an hour after the departure of the heavies.

Of course the same conditions were experienced by the German night-fighter crews, as Oberleutnant Wilhelm Johnen, a Bf 110 night-fighter pilot at Insterburg in East Prussia, recalled:

'The Met reported a cloud ceiling of 150 feet with solid cloud up to 13,000. From 3,000 feet there was danger of icing. 'You're not thinking of taking off in this are you Herr Leutnant? Even the Chief's left his bicycle at home and has come on foot.'

We had to laugh as we climbed into the cockpit. I switched on all my instruments and gave them a thorough check-up. Facius fiddled with his apparatus and tuned in to the notorious Soldatensender Calais station, a British black propaganda broadcaster operated by the Political Warfare Executive. It pretended to be a station of the German military broadcasting network. The sugary-sweet music was suddenly interrupted by the well-known 'V for Victory' and we heard the announcer say: 'Berlin, you were once the most beautiful city in the world. Berlin, look out for eleven o'clock tonight!'

'We were dumbfounded.'[5]

The target was cloud-covered and 'sky-marking' had to be used. This appeared to be accurate, but the strong winds blew them rapidly along the line of the bombers' route and bombing was 'spread well up and down wind'.

All told, the 27/28 January raid proved a costly night for the RAAF and RCAF squadrons, with fourteen of the thirty-three Lancasters lost. The Canadian 6 Group, which contributed forty-eight aircraft, of which two returned early, cost eight Lancasters or 16.6 per cent of its aircraft. Seven of these were from Linton-on-Ouse, home to 426 'Thunderbird' Squadron RCAF and 408 'Goose' Squadron RCAF.

The 'Thunderbird' Squadron lost four Lancasters. 'W-William' was piloted by 29-year-old Flight Lieutenant Arthur Tempest Martens, born on 27 December 1914 in Toronto, the son of Arthur Herman and Camilla Martens of Bishopgate, London. Martens took the Lancaster off at 1803 hours. What happened after that is unknown. He may have been shot down by a night-fighter or hit by flak. What is known is that Martens and four of his crew were killed and the navigator and air bomber were taken prisoner.[6]

'D-Donald' piloted by 27-year-old Canadian Flight Lieutenant Thomas Robert Shaw had had a narrow escape on the raid on Brunswick on the night of 14/15 January when they were attacked by unidentified single and twin-engined aircraft and an Fw 190, which was claimed shot down after being hit repeatedly before catching fire and crashing to the ground. 'Tom' Shaw was born at Kapuskasing in Ontario and left for Toronto in 1939 to study aeronautical engineering, later gaining employment at Victory Aircraft in Malton when he enlisted in January 1941. On the Berlin trip the crew of five Canadians and two RAF crew members were shot down with just one survivor. 'Tom' Shaw has no known grave and is remembered on the Runnymede Memorial. He left a widow, Mary Fleming Shaw of Etobicoke, Ontario whom he had married in June 1942 before going overseas.

'U-Uncle' captained by Flight Lieutenant M. Wilson was intercepted by a night-fighter over the target area and attacked three times. It was abandoned, on fire and out of control, crashing at Rausslitz, 6 kilometres north-north-east of Nossen. Wilson and two of his crew survived to be taken into captivity. The four others were killed on the aircraft. There were no survivors of the eight-man crew of 'R-Robert' skippered by 25-year-old Canadian Pilot Officer Ray Edgerton Countess, which carried a second pilot, Warrant Officer Leo Harkness Patterson. 'Robert' was lost without trace. Flying

Officer Kjarten Ari Solmundsson, the 22-year-old navigator, was of Icelandic origin. During his service he spent fifteen months on loan from the RCAF to 330 Norwegian Squadron RAF and flew Northrop N-3PB float planes assigned to patrol the North Atlantic convoy routes from bases in Iceland. Prior to enlisting, Kjarten had worked for Winnipeg City Hydro. He left a widow, Margaret, and a son.

On the 'Goose' Squadron, which put up eight-man Lancaster crews, 'P-Peter' was captained by 24-year-old Canadian Flight Lieutenant Eldon Eastman Kearl DFC. Eldon had attended a military summer camp in 1940, but news of the Battle of Britain inspired him to join the Air Force. It was 1941, he was 21 and like many young men at the time he was excited about becoming a pilot. He earned his wings in Fort Macleod and returned home to visit his family before shipping out to Europe. He and his younger brother Harold – three years apart, who followed in his older brother's footsteps – grew up in southern Alberta and when they were not doing chores on the family farm they hiked, fished and camped between Chief Mountain in Montana and their home town of Cardston.

Harold remembered his brother as a calm and thoughtful fellow, a good dancer popular with girls. During high school, Eldon worked part-time as an assistant to the town tailor. On his final day in Cardston, Eldon stopped in to say goodbye to him. 'Bill,' he said, shaking the man's hand, 'I probably won't see you again.' Promoted to flight lieutenant, Eldon especially welcomed the responsibility and challenge of flying over Berlin in his Lancaster, heavily laden with bombs and incendiaries. 'If I have to go missing,' he often told a friend, 'I hope it's over Berlin.'

The date of 27 January marked his eighteenth operation. It was also Eldon's 24th birthday. 'P-Peter' was shot down by a German fighter with only the navigator surviving to be taken prisoner and the bomber plummeted into the Reichswald Forest on the approaches to the Rhine, south-east of Berlin. A kind German farmer named Karl König, who had seen Eldon's plane crash in a ball of flames, buried the crew and planted flowers on the grave sites. Among those killed was the 22-year-old 'second dickey', Pilot Officer Elmer Reginald Proud of Eden Grove, Ontario.

'A-Apple' skippered by 26-year-old Canadian Squadron Leader Charles Woodward Smith DFC and 'X-X-ray' flown by 23-year-old Flight Lieutenant Sven Roy Walfrid Laine DFC of Port Arthur, Ontario were lost with all sixteen crew killed. 'A-Apple' collided with the Bf 110G-4 piloted by 26-year-old Oberleutnant Werner Baake south-west of Aachen at around 2250 hours. Baake's Messerschmitt was hit by return fire, but he managed to bail out of his doomed fighter. His bordfunker, Feldwebel Heinz Waldbauer, was killed in the collision. Baake survived the war with a total of forty-one victories and became a flight captain with Lufthansa. He was killed in a car accident at Heilbronn on 15 July 1964.

This raid was the first time that the Flare Force marked with 'Supporters' from non-Pathfinder squadrons; until now, the 'Supporters' had all been from 8 Group. Supporting the Flare Force meant arriving at the target at the same time but flying at 2,000 feet below them to attract the flak and enable the PFF to carry out a straight and level run. After drawing the flak the 'Supporters' would then re-cross the target to drop their bombs. Twenty-eight of the most experienced crews in 1 Group acted as 'Supporters', two of which were shot down, though one was lost far from the target.

Eleven of the losses came from 1 Group. On 460 Squadron RAAF at Binbrook the aircraft piloted by 23-year-old Australian Flight Sergeant William Robertson McLachlan crashed well to the east of Berlin with the loss of all seven crew members. McLachlan, who had been born in Paisley, Scotland on 19 November 1920, was laid to rest in Poznan Old Garrison Cemetery.

'K-King' had been taken off from Binbrook at 1740 hours by Squadron Leader Lorraine Joseph Simpson DFC. 'Laurie', as he was known, was born on 22 August 1918 in Deniliquin, New South Wales and he enlisted in Melbourne. 'K-King' radioed that the crew had serious fuel problems and efforts to establish their position failed. The aircraft was abandoned when it finally ran out of fuel in the Saint-Malo area on the return flight. Six crew were taken prisoner immediately. Simpson was captured on 2 February and taken to Rennes civil prison and then to a prison in Paris. After interrogation at Dulag Luft in Frankfurt-on-Main he was incarcerated at Stalag Luft III.

'B-Baker' was flown by 20-year-old Australian Warrant Officer Richard John Power. Born on 6 February 1941 in the township of Echuca on the Murray River, Richard Power had grown up on the family's Barfold Estate in central Victoria. One of five children, he was the only son. Named after his father, he was known as 'Jack' to his family. His mother died when he was 9 and his sisters were placed in an orphanage while Richard was sent to Xavier College. A keen sportsman, he was a member of the school's First Eight and First Eighteen Australian Rules team. At just 17 years of age, he was invited to train with the Richmond Football Club in Victoria. In September 1941 Power enlisted in the RAAF and soon commenced training as a pilot. During his time training at the No. 4 Service Flying Training School at Geraldton in Western Australia, Power and Leading Aircraftman Paul Edward Willoughby of Adelaide were flying an Avro Anson aircraft when the engine failed at 600 feet. Both men survived a forced landing.

'B-Baker' was shot down and crashed into a field near the town of Stücken, 25 miles south-west of Berlin. None of the seven crew members – five Australians and two Britons – survived. In Murwillumbah, New South Wales, Joan Kelly waited for news of her 21-year-old fiancé Flight Sergeant John Francis Worley, the mid-upper gunner on the crew. He had trained in Kingaroy, Queensland and Evans Head, NSW before being posted overseas. After the loss of 'B-Baker', the commanding officer of 460 Squadron wrote to Richard's father that his son 'was a very popular member of the squadron and had carried out his duties in an extremely conscientious manner'.

At Kelstern at about 0117 hours a last message was received from 'W-William' on 625 Squadron whilst homebound after supporting the PFF. This Lancaster bore a cartoon portrait of 'Billy Brown' the 'Tutor of Travel' made famous in England by David Langdon and fifteen bombing mission symbols. Pilot Officer Roy James Cook DFM, the 23-year-old pilot, a Canadian from Vancouver, British Columbia was on his fourth Berlin trip. In June 1941 Roy had left Victoria, British Columbia with four other young Canadians, all intent on joining the RAF in England. They had their passages booked across Canada to Halifax, as well as steamer accommodation allotted them on a ship sailing for England from the Nova Scotia port, when they were notified that their space had been requisitioned for urgent military reasons.

Furthermore, it could not be determined definitely when they would be able to be accommodated for the Atlantic crossing. In stepped the redoubtable Captain Henry Seymour-Biggs. Born in Bombay, India, Harry Biggs had run away to sea and saw action in the Boer War and the First World War, retiring from the Royal Navy to Canada in 1923 to a house and garden on Vancouver Island. He offered to purchase accommodation for the would-be recruits on a Pan American Airways clipper from La Guardia, New York to London via Bermuda and Lisbon. Four of them duly travelled to England via Canadian Pacific train to Montreal and then took a 'Lady' ship of the Canadian National Steamships from Montreal to Bermuda, Pan-American clipper from Bermuda to Lisbon and a British airliner to England, while a fifth flew to Montreal, made the steamer trip to Hamilton, Bermuda and there boarded an aircraft flying directly to the 'Old Country'.

After bombing Berlin from 22,000 feet Cook's navigator, Flight Sergeant V.H.N. Thompson had a problem with his plotting before reaching the Rhine, where a route-marker was expected north of Koblenz and course was well south of track. The Lancaster was then badly hit by anti-aircraft fire over Leipzig, which stopped both starboard engines and set fire to the fuel tank in that wing. Suddenly there was a great sheet of flame from an explosion in No. 2 tank and Cook put the aircraft into a dive hoping to extinguish the flames. The Lancaster plummeted down at a rate of about 1,000 feet per minute and it was at 13,000 feet before the fires were extinguished. The starboard inner was restarted using petrol from No.1 tank. Eventually, with only twenty minutes of petrol remaining, Sergeant R. Henderson the wireless-operator asked for and got a fix for Southampton. At this time their estimated position was north-west of Paris so a second fix was requested which placed them north of Guernsey. Roy Cook managed to keep 'W for William' airborne for more than an hour before his petrol ran out and managed to get as a far as the Gournay area of France. After all engines cut Cook gave the order to bail out. The brave pilot died on the aircraft when the bomber plunged to the ground at Bézancourt.

Flight Sergeant J. Berger the bomb-aimer got the front hatch up and jumped out first, followed by the navigator and Flight Sergeant D. Brown the flight engineer and then the pilot. Sergeant Jack Ringwood DFM, the 37-year-old rear gunner, in jettisoning all the surplus weight in the aircraft had accidentally thrown out his 'chute and he and Sergeant R. Weller the mid-upper gunner appear to have gone out by the rear door and on one parachute. Ringwood was killed but Weller survived. Ringwood left a widow, Muriel Mary Ringwood of Shepperton-on-Thames.[7] Flight Sergeant D. Brown evaded capture and with the help of the 'Shelburn' escape and evasion line finally made it home from the Brittany coast on 16/17 March 1944 in a Royal Navy motor gunboat attached to Operation 'Bonaparte III'.

Two Lancasters on 61 Squadron failed to return to Skellingthorpe. One was 'Y-Yorker' and Bob West's crew who, after their debut operation on Berlin on 16/17 December, had flown three more ops to the 'Big City' in January. The trip on the 27th of the month would have been their fifth overall. All seven crew are buried in Hanover. When he got home from school Audrey Clark and her son David's extended family were all sitting around the table and David was told that his father was 'missing'. About eighteen months elapsed before 'Bunny's family knew that he was dead. David Clark never really came to terms with his death. He was always expecting him to walk in at his home.[8]

'Q-Queenie' captained by Pilot Officer Eric Albert Williams was the other Lancaster on 61 Squadron that was lost. On the outward journey his port engine was hit by flak over Hanover. Eventually, when north of Guernsey, Williams gave the order to take up ditching positions. The 21-year-old flight engineer Sergeant William Beach, who was washed into Portinfer Bay, was buried on 9 February in Fort George Military Cemetery at St. Peter Port. The two gunners, Sergeant Cyril Arthur Acombe-Hill and 19-year-old Sergeant Terence Bowden, failed to reach the dinghy and have no known grave. Williams, his air bomber, the wireless-operator and the navigator, who suffered a back injury, were rescued at 1800 hours on the 28th. Williams was subsequently awarded the DFC on 2 June 1944 for his actions on the night.

At RAF Wickenby 11 miles to the south-west of a blacked-out Lincoln, where the spires of the cathedral, though no longer illuminated like gold filigree, was still a familiar landmark for crews on 12 and 626 Squadrons returning from their nightly operations, the White Hart pub 2 miles down the road had been adopted by the air crews, and the publican always knew, before the crews did, what targets were scheduled for the next day. (His uncanny forecasting ability was later traced to his listening to 'Lord Haw-Haw' broadcasting in English from Germany.) Further to the north lay Market Rasen with its Friday night town hall dances providing a goodly selection of 'popsies' for companionship on the nights when no operations were scheduled.

Four Lancaster crews would never again see Lincoln or Wickenby; their 'brief sweet life was over'. They had 'got the chop', their nightly ops were done and there would be no more evenings with 'pretty popsies' for dances in Market Rasen.[9]

Three of the missing Lancasters were on 12 Squadron with six men killed, fourteen taken prisoner and four evading capture. Australian Flight Sergeant E.A. Webb and his crew were taken into captivity after they ran out of fuel on the way home and had to abandon their Lancaster north-east of Frankfurt. Sergeant W.R.W. Moller DFM, a Queenslander, was the only survivor on the Lancaster piloted by 26-year-old Squadron Leader Hayden William Goule DFC, which exploded after a German night-fighter attacked and blew the aircraft to pieces near Ehren before any order to bail out could be given. Goule was on his second tour after having flown forty-eight operations. He left a widow, Alma Joyce Goule of Newbury, Berkshire.

'E-Edward' skippered by 25-year-old Flight Lieutenant Colin Patrick Haworth Grannum was hit by flak three times on the bomb run. Grannum was born Colin Eisner in Kingston, Jamaica on 18 September 1918 but had been adopted by his aunt and uncle. The port inner engine was knocked out, the roof of the cockpit blown off and extensive damage caused to the entire port wing, which eventually put the port outer engine out of action. All the petrol tanks had been holed and when down to 20 gallons, Grannum gave the bail-out order before 'Edward' crashed 13 kilometres south-west of Verviers in Belgium. Grannum bailed out at 9,000 feet and was told later that when he left the aircraft it rolled over onto its back. He landed on the side of a hill and in so doing hurt his knee.

Grannum and Flight Sergeant John Quinn the navigator were helped by the 'Dragon' and 'Comete' escape lines and on 9 May they reached Switzerland. Pilot

Officer Roland George Hoare the wireless-operator landed successfully at Bannoux near Sprimont, Liège province. Fifteen kilometres from Liège, Hoare met up with Pilot Officer David Raymond Murphy, the bomb-aimer from Northern Ireland. They split up to make their way separately, but on 12 May Murphy was captured by a German patrol in Tarbes, Hautes-Pyrenees and sent to Stalag Luft I. Pilot Officer Robert Henry Taylor, the flight engineer from Nottingham and a former actor, was hidden until he was liberated by American troops on 10 September. The war over, he was killed on a Wellington on 81 OTU on 18 May 1945. John Quinn and Roland Hoare were evacuated by the 'François' Group and reached the Pyrenees and Gibraltar where they were flown back to England on 24 June. The two air gunners, Ken Singleton and H. Owen, were captured.

Flight Lieutenant Bill Belford's crew on 626 Squadron, having abandoned 'Tommy 2' over the North Sea returning from Stettin on 7 January, had been given 'Sugar 2'. When the operation planned for the night of 25/26 January was cancelled they had left their parachutes in this aircraft and went off to see *Yankee Doodle Dandy* at the local cinema. The parachutes could wait until another night. A 'stand-down' then lasted for three nights and it was not until 27/28 January at around dusk that Bill Belford and his crew finally boarded 'Sugar 2' at their dispersal. It was Belford's eighth attack on the 'Big City'. Once in the aircraft navigator Arthur Lee thought his parachute felt damp and, with a strong instinct of self-preservation, decided to exchange it but the rest of Belford's crew decided this was an unnecessary chore involving a long ride around the perimeter track to the parachute store. Damp or not, they would take the parachutes that were already on board. It was a decision they would come to regret.

Helped by a strong tail-wind, 'Sugar 2' arrived over Berlin two and a half hours after leaving the airfield. Following a 'Wanganui' attack, Belford had swung south for the Czechoslovakian border before turning west into the headwind to crawl snail-like across the map of Europe towards the Rhine, the Channel and England. Just before eleven o'clock when 'Sugar 2' was 20 miles short of the Rhine and 10 miles south of track, it was brought down by the 'Schräge Musik' cannon of a stalking Bf 110:

'There was no warning of the attack,' wrote Arthur Lee. 'Cannon shells struck the starboard wing with what felt like three blows from a giant hammer. The shock and noise of the impact was transmitted through the main spar to the interior of the fuselage. I emerged from behind my curtain with the aircraft in a steep dive and the starboard wing in flames. I made ready to abandon the aircraft by removing my helmet with intercom and oxygen connections and attached my parachute. I must have "blacked out" at this point for I remember no more until becoming conscious of lying face-down on the floor of the aircraft at the top of the steps leading to the bomb-aimer's compartment. The cabin was well alight and appeared to be empty. I saw that the forward escape hatch was open and assumed that I had been left for dead. I struggled to drag myself down the steps to the hatch but could not move. I felt that my harness was entangled but it was more likely that centrifugal force from the spinning aircraft was pinning me to the floor. I could smell my hair burning and the heat was intense. There was a moment of terror at the thought of being burnt to death but as I seemed to be hanging head-downwards into the bomb-aimer's compartment it came as a relief to realise that I would soon hit the ground head-first! The certainty of death had a strange effect. I felt no fear, only an intense moment of sadness. I remember the thought, "I shall not be going home on leave any more."

'I resisted the temptation to pull the ripcord of my parachute "just to see if it would have worked" and relaxed into a period of calmness in which time seemed to be passing in "slow motion". At this point, I was ejected violently from the aircraft – observers from the ground later reported a mid-air explosion – and I found myself apparently on my back grasping one of the carrying handles of my parachute. There was no sensation of falling. I frantically pulled the carrying handles, thinking "the bloody thing won't open" before sanity returned, enabling me to transfer my grasp to the metal handle of the ripcord. The parachute billowed above me and the flaming wreckage of 'my' aircraft hurtled past me into the clouds. I quickly followed and within moments was on the ground, my fall broken by trees at the edge of a wood on a hillside. The aircraft had crashed into the wood where I could see it burning and hear the ammunition exploding. Large chunks of the aircraft were burning within 20 feet of where I had landed so I assume that I had left the aircraft at a low altitude.'

The Lancaster had been attacked by Oberleutnant Albert Walter who claimed the aircraft as his eighth victory. Walter went on to claim ten Nachtschüsse before he was killed on 24/25 February 1944, almost certainly by return fire from Halifax LW427 on 429 'Snowy Owl' Squadron, which was also his last kill. 'Sugar 2' fell from 23,000 feet in a blazing spiral dive towards Katzenelnbogen, a village in the beautiful wooded hill country known as the Taunus, 20 miles south-east of Koblenz. The village has a history going back many hundreds of years and boasts an ancient castle. Rudi Balzer, a 22-year-old soldier in the Wehrmacht, was on home leave which was interrupted at 2300 hours by the noise of an aircraft and the alarm was raised. He recalled: 'The population ran into the bunkers or basements. I was standing on the street with open eyes and ears searching the sky. Shortly thereafter I saw tracer bullets and heard the sound of aircraft guns. Within seconds there was an explosion combined with a large darting flame. One wing had come down near a house; the engine came down with a large noise a few kilometres further afield. The aircraft fuselage came down like thunder in the forest near a thick beech tree known as a local landmark. There it exploded once again. In the glare of the fire I could see a parachute coming down.'

Balzer set off for the crash site on his father's motorcycle: 'Crawling on my belly I attempted to reach the place of impact but because of the great heat and exploding ammunition, I could not. While the airman was on my mind, numerous people's voices could be heard. There was a standing order that all surviving air crew members had to be shot on sight. Arriving on the edge of the forest, I could see the airman tied to a tree (he had been put there by a search party which had found him earlier). With a torch I cast some light on his body and noticed that he had injuries from cuts and burns. I freed his hands and took him to my own doctor, who provided medical care. We had no more than ten minutes with the doctor, when two Hitler Youth brought the message that the airman was to be taken to the mayor's office. At the same time a policeman appeared in the corridor and wanted to lynch the English airman. I said that the Englishman was a PoW and was under my protection. When the policeman attempted to draw his pistol, I drew quicker. Unmistakably I made it clear that I would shoot instantly in the event that he should draw his pistol. He (the policeman) threatened me with a court martial. Here was a person, the Englishman, who needed help, a human being and not an enemy any more. After the doctor had finished his treatment, I took the airman to the mayor's office. A few other men were already present but none could speak English, therefore the director of the district (police) court was sent for.

'After personal particulars had been established, everybody was dismissed. The airman was given something to eat by the family of the mayor. I was alone with the mayor in the office and witnessed a telephone conversation where the mayor called the Nazi Group leader and said: 'Well, Wilhelm, now you have your Englishman and you can shoot him.' From that moment I knew that I could not let the Englishman out of my sight. I explained to the mayor that he was a PoW and was under my protection and should anyone dare, I would immediately make usc of my firearm. Hitler Youth brought the airman's parachute and boots. Using the parachute, I made a bed for the needy man and covered him with a heavy military coat. He immediately fell asleep. On the next day I brought the flier Arthur Lee to my old school, gave him something to eat and drink; in the afternoon he was picked up by a Luftwaffe officer.'

Arthur Lee was convinced that he was the last of the crew to bail out of the aircraft before it crashed. It was only when they failed to show up that Lee wondered if the damp parachutes had figured in his friends' deaths. On the afternoon of 28 January, a Luftwaffe truck arrived and took Arthur to a guardroom cell at an airfield near Wiesbaden; the first stage of his journey to the PoW camp where he was to spend the rest of the war. All the other members on Belford's crew were laid to rest in Rheinberg War Cemetery.

In 5 Group four Australian crews were lost at Waddington. On 467 Squadron RAAF, 22-year-old Pilot Officer Stephen Charles Grugeon of Manly, Sydney and crew were killed on 'G-George' which crashed east-north-east of Kassel. The skipper left a widow, Merle Phyllis Grugeon of Woolooware in southern Sydney. There were no survivors of 27-year-old Australian Pilot Officer Cecil O'Brien's crew on 'P-Peter' which crashed in the Berlin suburb of Kopenwick, 8 kilometres south-east of the city.

On 463 Squadron RAAF, 26-year-old Australian Flying Officer Alan James Durham Leslie and crew were killed on 'L-London', which crashed near Teltow, 16 kilometres south-west of the centre of Berlin. 'R-Robert' flown by 27-year-old Squadron Leader William Lloyd Brill DFC of Grong Grong, New South Wales had been struck by incendiaries falling from high-flying aircraft over the target which started fires in the fuselage and a wing, impairing rudder controls and rendering the compass unserviceable. Bill Brill had begun his second operational tour on 1 January. He and his crew were close to bailing out until Brill regained control and got the Lancaster home safely. For his leadership, skill and gallantry, he was awarded the DSO in May and he took command of 467 Squadron. In July, while bombing supply depots for V-weapons near Saint-Leu-d'Esserent his successful efforts in evading three German night-fighters earned him a Bar to his DFC. Having completed fifty-eight sorties, he returned to Australia in January 1945.

Having completed the bomb run, 'M-Mother' on 9 Squadron piloted by Flight Lieutenant 'Jimmy' James suffered a 'Schräge Musik' attack about fifteen minutes after the target. 'Hal' Croxson said that there was a 'thump' and that 'the entire aircraft shuddered and then carried on.' Flight Sergeant Howie bellowed into the intercom: 'We've got fire in the bomb bay!' Some bombs had not been released because the bomb release gear would often freeze solid and there would be odd hang-ups. Austin Archer had been hit in the leg by a piece of flak and George Tomlinson said one engine had gone down. After the initial shock of the attack and the panic that ensued, Howie dealt with the fire through the inspection door and at the same time he released some of the hang-ups. Ronald Burke treated the navigator's wound. James reckoned that even with three engines they would fly home, but about twenty minutes later another engine packed up. 'Jimmy' James told Croxson to jettison anything he could. He got the flare 'chute away and the Elsan out. He thought, 'I wonder whose head this will land on!' He also got the arrest bed out and 12,000 rounds of ammunition, which would feed the rear turret but left several hundred rounds in case he should need them.

By now the Lancaster had fallen to just 4,000 feet and soon they would be flying over the high ground of Bavaria. Croxson took the parachute from its little rack outside the turret with elastic ropes over it, clipped it onto his harness and got back into his turret. James called out: 'I've got to go. Good luck, chaps and everybody out.' Only three men made it. Howie got out through the front and Sergeant Chilvers the mid-upper gunner came down from his turret and got out of the side door. Croxson brought his rear turret round to full port, opened the slide doors at the back, took care to get hold of his oxygen feed, his electric suit and his intercom cord and get it all out of the way. Then he got his feet on the gun butts and kicked himself out into space. Suddenly he was hanging in the air in total silence with the breeze swishing through the cords of the parachute, an enormous black cloud above him. Descending into what he thought was a thick black cloud he hit the ground hard. It was not a cloud, but one side of a valley. Away in the distance he saw the sky light up as 'M-Mother' crashed, close to Trimburg Castle. He pulled on the shroud lines of his parachute which stopped him being pulled along the ground. Croxson had lost a boot in the jump and felt as though the whole of Germany was looking for him.

Taking out his .38 revolver Croxson cocked it and put it ready by his side. He thought that it would be ready to use or to hand over! To calm his nerves he lit a cigarette without thinking that the light might be seen. He did not finish it because he laid back and fell asleep for about a quarter of an hour or so. When he awoke he discovered that his fingers were cut and bound them with strips of parachute silk, keeping them bent to stop the bleeding. Shortly afterwards he set off into some woods where he buried everything he did not need, including his flying helmet. On the front was written 'Horizontal', a nickname from the crew, because in his spare time he would lie down horizontally and either stink or sleep! Despite having only one boot, Croxson evaded capture for three days, dodging German patrols, but he was picked up by a hunting party with dogs and shotguns.[10] Howie and Chivers were also rounded up and taken into captivity. The bodies of the others were removed from the Lancaster and initially buried at Sulzthal.

The 22-year-old Leonard 'Dusty' Miller was piloting a Lancaster on XV Squadron at Mildenhall on the raid. Born and bred in East Ham in London's East End, he began his working life as an engineer apprentice in the London docks where 'they were bombed to pieces' but he was always untouched and, not unreasonably, he considered himself a 'born survivor'. On the bomb run a shell came through into the cockpit of Miller's Lancaster and hit his flight engineer, Sergeant 'Alf' Pybus, in the head. The crew did not know if Pybus was mortally wounded or just badly wounded and could only wrap him in Irvin jackets and blankets, the only warm clothing that they had, roll him up and put the portable oxygen cylinder on him to help him breathe. Miller reasoned that the best thing was to get back home with him as quickly as possible. 'He died beside me on the floor,' says Miller. 'He had been a very close friend and we had plans to do things together after the war.'

Immediately after this raid, nights on 'stand down' now becoming rare, a maximum effort by 677 bombers – 432 Lancasters, 241 Halifaxes and 4 Mosquitoes – was ordered for the night of Friday 28/Saturday, 29 January. It was the thirteenth time in the series of Berlin raids which had begun the previous November. A full range of diversionary operations was put into operation. Eighteen 'Oboe' Mosquitoes raided four of the most significant Nachtjagd airfields in Holland and sixty-three Stirlings and four Pathfinder Halifaxes dropped mines in Kiel Bay five hours before the Main Force raid on the 'Big City'. Six more Mosquitoes bombed Berlin four hours before the main attack went in, and another four of them made a diversionary raid on Hanover.

'Nuisance' raiding by the RAF had begun in April 1943. Mosquitoes went in up to an hour before the main attack, descended slowly and released their 'spoof' cargoes of two 500lb bombs, two target indicators (TIs) or 'sky-markers' (parachute flares to mark a spot in the sky if it was cloudy) and bundles of 'Window'. German fighter controllers immediately sent up their night-fighters, so that when the 'heavies' did arrive, the Nachtjagdgeschwaders were back on the ground having to refuel. No. 139 Squadron first tried 'spoof' raiding on the night of 18 November 1943 when flares and bombs were dropped on Frankfurt. Various plain colours with starbursts of the same or a different colour prevented the enemy from copying them. On 26 November three Mosquitoes on 139 Squadron, flying ahead of the Main Force, scattered 'Window' on the approaches to Berlin and returned to drop bombs.

'Working with the heavies was the most interesting,' wrote 21-year-old Pilot Officer Jim Marshallsay DFC, a Mosquito pilot on 627 Squadron at Oakington. 'We made "spoof" raids, laid dummy fighter flare lanes and TIs with the idea of drawing off the night-fighter force from the heavies.' By 24 November 1943 he and his navigator Flight Sergeant 'Nick' Ranshaw had completed fourteen LNSF trips on 139 Squadron, beginning with the big Hamburg raid of July 1943.

'At Oakington we continued with this work, sometimes just a handful of Mossies would set out for the big German cities, usually in the 'moon period' when it was much too bright for the 'heavies'. If, on these trips the weather was cloudy, it was possible to take off, climb into cloud, travel to Germany, bomb the target on ETA and return to base, having seen nothing but the runway lights at Oakington on take-off and landing. If, however, the night was clear, moonlight and stars, then you could get a hot reception from predicted flak and from the massive searchlight cones, especially at 'Whitebait', the code-name for Berlin. If you saw one of the attacking Mossies coned over the target, you took your chance, slipped in, bombed and slipped out again while the poor unfortunate in the cone was dazzled and blasted. When you got back for interrogation, if you had been the one in the cone, you got no sympathy from the other crews, just a lot of banter like 'Brave lads, taking the flak from us.'

On 28 January Marshallsay and Ranshaw in their faithful 'A-Apple' were one of three Mosquito crews that made very early evening take-offs and they flew to Berlin by direct route:

'Our early attack was intended to make the enemy think that the LNSF had hit the 'Big City' and then the Main Force would go elsewhere. As forty-nine heavies were shot down, I don't think it worked.

'We did a fast return trip to Berlin in three hours fifty-five minutes. After we had landed we met the 7 Squadron crews in the Mess doorway, just heading out to their Lancs for take-off. They asked 'Are you going tonight Jim?'

'I cannot repeat their language when I replied, 'No, I've just been.'[11]

At Wickenby Pilot Officer Jack Currie on 'A' Flight on 626 Squadron was nearing the end of his tour of thirty ops with one op left to do. Currie's second-to-last trip had been to Berlin the night before and he was expecting to finish with a relatively 'easy' target but to his chagrin his crew again appeared on the battle order for what would be their ninth Berlin raid. When Currie made his feelings known, his flight commander Squadron Leader Bill Spiller had suggested that it would be better to 'get it over with' rather than 'hanging around waiting for their last "op" getting more and more jittery'. As Berlin was to be an early (1900 hours) take-off, Spiller told him, 'You'll be home by three and you're finished before you've had a chance to worry about it.' Take-off time, however, was postponed twice before finally being fixed for midnight. To pass the time the crew went to the camp cinema to watch *Casablanca*. It was just after midnight when they taxied from their dispersal and shortly after got the green light to take off.

At Lissett 6 miles south of Bridlington near the Yorkshire coast, Flight Sergeant D.A. 'Robbie' Robinson's Halifax crew on 158 PFF Squadron were due home leave and they went in to get their leave passes, only to be told that two crews had not returned. 'If they get back in time to get bombed up you can go,' they were told, 'but if they don't…' Sergeant Les Cardall, the flight engineer who had volunteered for the RAF on his 19th birthday on 11 November 1939, recalled:

'There were two crews standing by; mine and another. One crew got back! We tossed up and lost so we had to take the place of the crew that didn't get back. We went to briefing and found it was Berlin – oh Christ, no! Not again! We'd been there twice before. It was a bad place. The defence was very hot, very strong, apart from the fact that you had a long journey over enemy-occupied territory. You'd got fighters coming at you all the time and all the way back.'

Cardall had already sent a telegram home to say 'expect me at 3 o'clock in the morning' and hadn't had time to cancel it. Once operations were 'on' no one was allowed to make a telephone call.

Robinson's crew would be flying 'J-Jane'. Air crews tended to be superstitious and many disliked flying bombers lettered 'M-Mike' as it is the thirteenth letter of the alphabet.

'"J" was our own Halifax,' recalled Cardall. 'It had a big portrait of "Jane" out of the *Daily Mirror* on the nose. We always called it "J-Jane". "Q-Queenie" seemed to be a jinx aircraft because every "Queenie" was shot down. They tried to do away with "Q". Crews would carry mascots and wouldn't fly without them. On every raid Stan Chapman the bomb-aimer would take his personal mascot "Percy the Penguin" with him. Like many others a mascot answered some unexplained need and he believed "Percy" brought the crew good luck. "Robbie" Robinson would never enter the aircraft until he had first tapped on the door. I had a very favourite tune at the time which was *Begin the Beguine*. Whenever I heard it we always had a rough time on operations. It got so bad that in the end everyone used to rush to the wireless to turn it off.'

Reluctantly Cardall got ready for his fifty-ninth operation.

The routes to the target went north over northern Denmark on both the outward and return flights in an effort to dissipate the night-fighter force. 'Instead of flying over 800 miles of heavily-defended territory (over Holland and north Germany) it was less dangerous to fly over the lightly-defended Denmark, through the Kattegat, over the Baltic Sea and cross the enemy coast east of Rostock before a 150-mile dash for the target,' wrote Bertie 'Butch' Lewis, the American wireless-operator on Ron Champion's Halifax crew on 102 Squadron at Pocklington.

At Holme-on-Spalding-Moor Warrant Officer William Barlow Ward on 76 Squadron took Halifax 'G-George' off on his sixteenth operational sortie. Shortly after he clipped a tree and crashed. Ward was born on 29 September 1914 in Manchester and was educated at Manchester Grammar School for Boys via a scholarship. He joined the RAF as an aircraft hand sometime in 1933 but sometime later re-mustered as an air gunner and served in the Middle East from 28 January 1936 to 22 December 1938. He was serving with 604 Squadron at Middle Wallop by 23 September 1940 as an aircraftsman. Sometime after he was selected for pilot training and by early 1944 he was serving on 76 Squadron. Ward was seriously injured in the crash of the Halifax in which Sergeant Gordon Channon, the 19-year-old navigator of Feniton, Devon and Sergeant Donald William Munson, the 21-year-old mid-upper gunner from Ipswich were killed. After initial treatment at the base sick quarters, air gunner Sergeant Leslie Wilkins and the bomb-aimer Flight Sergeant James Dawber Ashton were later treated at Rauceby Hospital, but because of the burns they received they were then transferred to East Grinstead Hospital in March 1944 and became two of the famous 'Guinea Pig' patients. William Ward was taken to RAF Northallerton Hospital. The injuries he sustained in this accident prevented him flying operationally again and once sufficiently recovered he saw out the war serving as a flying instructor.[12]

The bomber crews found broken clouds over the North Sea and severe icing conditions up to 20,000 feet in the Denmark area. One in ten bombers turned back over the North Sea. Flight Sergeant Randolph Rhodes, mid-upper gunner on a 35 Squadron Halifax captained by Squadron Leader Keith Cresswell who was on his fourth trip, recalled:

'Icing began shortly after we crossed the enemy coast and due to the rapid build-up the Skipper decided to lose height in an attempt to reach the warmer air below. From the mid-upper turret I could see the heavy ice layers and realized this might well be my third and last operational flight. Such was the weight of the ice we carried that our journey downwards was no longer a matter of choice and we jettisoned the bomb load and returned to base.'

As the bombers proceeded the weather improved until in the target area there was from 8 to 10/10ths thin-layer cloud through which ground markers and the effects of bombing could be easily discerned. Little opposition was offered on the outward trip, but the Jägerleitoffiziers in their 'Battle Opera Houses' to orchestrate Nachtjäger movements and pinpoint individual target aircraft still managed to concentrate large numbers of fighters over the target.

Despite continued efforts of the ground defences to shoot down the sky-markers, the Pathfinders maintained a continuous pattern for the various waves of bombers. Just east of the target area several crews noted many searchlights, but owing to the clouds these were largely ineffective. So centralized was the attack that huge fires broke out, interspersed with particularly violent explosions, one of which was very prolonged. Many lesser blasts kept up an almost continuous glare in the eyes of the jubilant crews as far as the Baltic coast. Flak was somewhat heavier than on the previous night and consisted of moderate to intense heavy, accurately predicted at first, which later gave way to a barrage of heavy and light flak. In the target area and on the homeward journey as far as the Danish coast fighter flares were much in evidence and encounters were fairly frequent.

The early Pathfinders identified twenty single and twin-engined aircraft, of which the majority attempted an engagement and were evaded while two were claimed as destroyed. Conditions had improved over the target with areas of broken cloud permitting some ground-marking, a rare luxury on Berlin ops.[13]

One of the Rhodesians who took part in the raid was Flying Officer Terence Hugh Flynn of Gatooma. It was his eleventh operational flight and his seventh to Berlin:

'I thought it was a very good attack. When we arrived, many fires were burning. The whole attack seemed well concentrated. I saw two explosions, the second when we were about to come away from the city. In each case, the cloud was lit up for miles around. The ground defences fell off as the attack developed and at one stage they seemed to be overwhelmed.'[14]

Pilot Officer Mike Beetham's crew on 50 Squadron at Skellingthorpe had not got to bed until 0430 hours the previous day and had been up by 0900 to pick up a 463 Squadron Lancaster from Waddington as a replacement for their aircraft which was u/s. Take-off had been scheduled for fifteen minutes to midnight. Beetham's bomb-aimer Flight Sergeant Les Bartlett had intended to get about three hours' sleep before the off, but instead started a card game which did not finish until around 0930. Bartlett recalled:

'The first opposition we met was crossing the enemy coast not far from Flensburg where two bombers were seen to go down. Searchlights were more active than usual, showing us through a few very large breaks in the clouds, but the Pathfinders were on top form and put down our route-markers very accurately, which enabled us to keep out of the most hazardous areas. We were in the fifth wave and as we approached Berlin I could see that the attack was in full swing. With the target in my sight I could see numerous large fires and one particularly vivid explosion, which seemed to light up the whole of Berlin with a vivid orange flash for about ten seconds. At the critical moment I called for bomb doors open and then released our bombs bang on target. Just as I was taking my usual checks to ensure that no bombs had hung up, Beetham yelled: 'There's a bloody fighter dead ahead attacking a Lancaster.' It was a Ju 88. I jumped straight into the front turret and started blazing away. It did a slow turn to port and then spiralled down to earth. From then on we saw absolutely nothing but occasional short bursts of flak, but no searchlights and no fighters at all.'[15]

About 30 miles from the target on the homeward route, Bartlett at last had time to check the bomb bay only to discover a bomb had failed to release. At the same time, through a break in the cloud he saw the lighting system of a German airfield, so he threw the jettison bars across and out went the bomb and much to his delight the lights went out also. On their return they found the cloud base down to 800 feet, so Beetham had to exercise great care when breaking cloud. He did this and to his great surprise they were right over the English coast at Skegness. They landed at Skellingthorpe at 0840 feeling tired and hungry. In the recommendation for Les Bartlett's DFM, this trip was mentioned with the shooting-down of the Ju 88.[16]

The 1 Group Summary for 28/29 January said: 'Berlin was again the target for 125 aircraft of this Group, which took off to find 10/10ths cloud in the target area with tops up to 10,000 feet. The cloud layer was thin enough for a fair proportion of the crews to see the ground markers. The PFF opened the attack punctually and a very good concentration both of Release Point flares and Ground Markers was achieved. Those crews carrying navigational aids found that the area marked agreed with their own indication of the central city area. Very large fires were soon started and soon became very exceptionally well concentrated and even those crews bombing later in the attack reported that there was very little scatter. Several experienced crews report that in their opinion this was the most effective and concentrated attack that they had yet seen on Berlin. Slightly more opposition was encountered from ground defences than in the previous night's attack. Heavy opposition was encountered from the night-fighter defences in the target area where all but two of the ten reported combats occurred. The only other areas where enemy fighters were seen was off the Danish coast and in the Rostock area. Seven aircraft were abortive, all due to technical reasons and four aircraft are missing, nothing having been heard from them after take-off. Crews generally believed this to have been a raid of exceptional concentration.'

The 6 Group report talked of 'huge fires' and 'particularly violent explosions'. The 'jubilant crews' could see the results of their work all the way to the Baltic coast and talked to the Intelligence officers about 'the best yet', 'the best of eight', 'really wizard', 'a first-class do'.[17] Although the raid did some significant damage in Berlin (among the buildings hit were the new Chancellery around the corner on Vossstrasse off Wilhelmstrasse and completed in early 1939; four theatres; the Französischer Dom (French Cathedral) on Gendarmenmarkt; six hospitals; five embassies and the Reichspatentamt or State Patent Office in Gitschinerstrasse); and seventy-seven other places outside the capital were also hit. It was estimated that 188,000 people were Ausgebombt ['bombed out'].

The Jägerleitoffiziers were able to concentrate fighters over the target area where most of the twenty-six Halifaxes and eighteen Lancasters that failed to return were shot down. Over Denmark Lancaster 'S-Sugar' better known as '*The Saint*', flown by 32-year-old Flight Lieutenant Horace Robert Hyde of 83 Squadron at Wyton and 'S for Sugar', a Lancaster on 463 Squadron RAAF piloted by Australian Flight Lieutenant Norman Percival Cooper were involved in a fatal collision while the latter was attempting to turn for home after major problems. Both Lancasters crashed on the small island of Als, killing all fourteen crew members, who were buried in Aabenraa Cemetery on 2 February.

'B-Baker' on 83 Squadron flown by Pilot Officer William Simpson was attacked by a Ju 88C crewed by Hauptmann Gerhard Raht, his funker Feldwebel Anton Heinemann and bordmechaniker Unteroffizier Werner Hesse and controlled by the radar station 'Star' at Lütjenhorn in northern Germany. At 0237 the Lancaster exploded in the air and the wreckage was spread over a radius of 2.5 kilometres just north of the village of Varnæs. Sergeant Thomas Kinnoch McCash, the 21-year-old flight engineer, and Flight Sergeant John James Martin, navigator lay dead in fields near Bovrup. One crew member was not wearing a parachute. Australian air gunner Flight Sergeant John Robert Tree had landed in the sea off Ålesund and drowned. Simpson, Pilot Officer Ronald Pilgrim the air bomber, wireless-operator Sergeant W. Livesey and Flight Sergeant J.A. Fell, air gunner, were taken into captivity. Two Lancasters were lost with their crews in a mid-air collision over Alsace.

At Waddington Australian Flight Lieutenant Ivan G. 'Joe' Durston DFC, a pilot on 467 Squadron RAAF who had completed his tour, decided that he would fly one more op so that the four Australians on the crew of 'L-London' could finish together. The crew was delayed in taking off for two hours until 1249 hours because of a fault on the rear gun turret. Durston's brave gesture was in vain. The Lancaster still had its bomb load including a 'cookie' and more than 900 4lb incendiary bombs on board when the bomber was shot down by a Focke-Wulf 190 on the approach to Berlin. The explosion when the bomber was hit sent it plunging to earth where it left a 12 foot crater and the remains of six of the crewmen. The skipper, his navigator, 21-year-old Flight Lieutenant Fry from Ilford, Sergeant Francis Aver, the 23-year-old engineer from Goole, East Yorkshire and Pilot Officer Sidney Griffiths, the 22-year-old bomb-aimer from Cardiff and Durston's fellow Australian crew members, wireless-operator Pilot Officer Robert Ludlow and gunners Flight Sergeants Phillip Gill and Jack Sutherland all died. Griffiths was discovered dead in woods soon after the Lancaster went down. The other airmen lay undetected in a German field for almost sixty years until part of a parachute attached to human remains was unearthed by air enthusiasts 3 miles away from the woods in 1999 and identified over the following two years.

At Witchford two Lancasters on 115 Squadron were missing. 'G-George' was skippered by 27-year-old Scottish Pilot Officer Farquhar Gray George Tinn of Kirkhill Castle at Colmonell in Ayrshire. Pre-war he had been an actor and had married the Russian ballerina Nina Tarakanova. Tinn and five of his crew were killed. They were buried at the Berlin War Cemetery. 'S for Sugar' piloted by 20-year-old Flight Lieutenant Keith Harris, a quiet, thoughtful, sandy-haired West Country lad from Knowle Park, Bristol went down with no survivors. Three men on the crew, who had twenty sorties to their credit, were Canadian. Pilot Officer Joe Horsley's crew on 166 Squadron at Kirmington also was lost with no survivors.

While altering course north-east of Berlin on the way home, 'W-William' piloted by Australian Flying Officer Colin Gregory Phelps who was on his twenty-fifth operation (his eighth trip to the 'Big City'), collided with another aircraft at 18,000 feet. Moments later a violent explosion blew the nose off the aircraft, throwing the laconic South Australian and Canadian Pilot Officer Earl D. Nesbitt clear into the air. They survived and were taken into captivity. The dead included the navigator, Master Sergeant W.W. Mitchell from Michigan.

Writing to his parents much later, Phelps said: 'I would not have been quite so disappointed if I had been shot down by the Germans but I came down in a collision with another machine. I know it is not the first time I have run into something but my conscience is quite clear this time, no-one kept a better lookout for other aircraft than I did but it is almost impossible to see other machines in the great blackness. I did see the other machine before we collided but I could not do much, it was only 100 to 200 yards away when I first saw it and we were both travelling at over 200 mph.'

In just eight days in January 1944, he and his air crew went on four bombing raids, three of them to Berlin. On 7 February Phelps' family received the telegram advising that he was missing. More than two months later, on 28 April, his relieved parents were notified that he was a prisoner of war in Stalag Luft III. On discharge in October 1945 Colin visited all the relatives of his six dead crew, including those in the US, and then he returned to the tranquillity of the family market garden and vineyard, later grew almonds in Willunga and channelled some natural-born need for speed into a career as a champion motorcycle rider.

Of nineteen Lancasters on 97 Squadron that took off for Berlin, one had returned early and Flight Lieutenant Charles Thomas Wilson DFC and crew and Flying Officer Frank Allison's crew were missing. Allison had flown forty-eight sorties and had been awarded the DFM in 1942 when he was flying Wellingtons in the Middle East. Having failed to find the 'Big City', 31-year-old Flight Lieutenant Henry Stewart van Raalte, piloting 'O-Orange' on his fifth operation, bombed Kiel instead and returned on three engines. Flight Sergeant Lionel George Laurie, Van Raalte's 23-year-old rear gunner was decapitated by flak in his turret.

On 23 June 1944 Van Raalte's crew was involved in a collision with another Lancaster during a formation flying practice. 'Geoff' King, who after his first tour on 57 Squadron at East Kirkby had been posted to 97 PFF Squadron at Coningsby, recalled:

'The first of our daylight formation-flying exercises was quite successful, although the Lancaster was not the best aircraft for close formation work. On our second exercise though, a horrific accident occurred. We were about an hour into our manoeuvres, flying in our formation of three, with Van Raalte in the outer port position. Another skipper [24-year-old Flight Lieutenant Edward Leslie John Perkins] was in the centre and we at the outer starboard. Our flight leaders were in three other aircraft, above and just ahead of us.

'We had just completed a small manoeuvre to port when Van Raalte's aircraft was caught in the slipstream of one of the leading aircraft above. He suddenly swept across above us, missing our aircraft by a few feet, then plunged over us again and straight into the side of Ted Perkins' aircraft. Both immediately started to disintegrate and dived into the fields north of Sleaford. The squadron was immediately ordered back to base and this was the end of our formation-flying exercises. We were all badly shaken up at seeing so many of our friends killed in this manner.'

Only Sergeant Cowan, the wireless-operator on Perkins' aircraft, bailed out and miraculously survived. Perkins' two wild Canadian gunners who had been sent to the Aircrew Refresher Centre at Sheffield in punishment for smashing up the sergeants' mess one night thus missed the crash that killed their pilot. Earlier that morning Perkins' tiny Fiat car had been hauled onto the top of a large air-raid shelter at Coningsby by fifty pairs of arms and left there. Crews were still laughing when they took off. The little Fiat was quietly removed from the top of the air-raid shelter by the chastened young crews. Six weeks after the collision another crew took Cowan on another training flight. He landed shaking, was later diagnosed as a tuberculosis case and never flew again. Van Raalte left a widow, Mary Ellen in Albany, Western Australia.

The Halifaxes, although they constituted just 35 per cent of the force, represented 56 per cent of the losses on 28/29 January. Four Halifax IIs on 77 Squadron at Elvington were never heard of again. Of twenty-three 'Hallies' on 10 Squadron that took off from Melbourne, seven turned back for a variety of reasons, while four were shot down, leaving the remaining twelve to press on with the raid. No. 6 Group's casualties amounted to nine Halifaxes, 7.2 per cent of its force. On 429 'Bison' Squadron at Leeming, Halifax V 'K-King' captained by Warrant Officer J.L. Wilkinson was attacked by two fighters en route to the target. Wilkinson managed to evade and continued his trip. Then a third fighter pounced. The attack killed Sergeant Harry Charles Clay, the 21-year old American rear gunner, and wrecked the controls. Unable to handle the aircraft any longer, Wilkinson ordered the crew to bail out. He had to use the call light because the intercom was working only spasmodically. However, at that precise moment, a violent explosion hurled the bomber on to its back. The overload fuel tank in the bomb bay – a much-loathed necessity on long trips – had blown up. 'I was thrown out of my seat and the helmet was torn off my head,' Wilkinson later reported. He remembered 'going around and around' inside the aircraft. Then he passed out, to wake up in the air. He barely had time to pull the ripcord of his parachute and landed with a badly sprained back.[18]

Three Halifax IIIs on 433 'Porcupine' Squadron – motto *Qui s'y frotte s'y pique*, meaning 'Who opposes gets hurt' – failed to return to Skipton-on-Swale. One of these was 'H-Harry' flown by 22-year-old Flight Sergeant Jack Eldin Mitchell of Saskatoon, Saskatchewan, one of five Canadians on the crew. Flying Officer John Kenneth Jack Shedden, the 22-year-old navigator came from Calgary, Alberta. Flying Officer Henry Cox, the 26-year-old rear gunner who was born in Lancer, Saskatchewan was from Comox, British Columbia. Flying Officer 'Rod' D. Wilson the bomb-aimer hailed from Vancouver. Warrant Officer2 Stewart McDougall and Sergeant J.F. McDonough the mid-upper gunner made up the rest of the Canadian contingent. Sergeant George Lumsden the RAF flight engineer was from the Newcastle area. The crew had not been on the squadron long. On arrival at

Skipton they had turned up late and after some searching had found an unoccupied and freezing cold Quonset hut with no fuel for the stove, so the ever-resourceful colonials tore up the linoleum floor and used that to get a fire going![19]

'H-Harry' was approaching Berlin at about 22,000 feet when without any warning tracers went by Mitchell's port window and there was vibration on his left rudder. He immediately took evasive action, diving to port and returning to level:

'It was not a good idea to do too much manoeuvring around with 999 other aircraft in the vicinity,' he said later. 'Luckily we threw him off without sustaining any more damage; apparently it was a Junkers 88 who came up from below us and our gunners never saw him until he fired a burst. The gunners were not injured during the attack. As a matter of fact I had reamed them out after we headed for home because they had not spotted him or fired a shot. We continued on through the target and dropped our bombs and then made a gradual 180-degree turn and headed north towards Denmark. We got reports from the crew to see if we could determine how badly we were damaged; some of the wing tanks had been holed on the port side and the left rudder was just about destroyed, then it was finally decided that we could possibly make the coast of Britain with the fuel we had left; the alternative was a PoW camp in Germany or ditch in the North Sea. After flying over Denmark we headed straight west for Britain. We gradually lost altitude as the engines failed one after the other. We eventually reached the coast with one engine still supplying enough power to keep almost level when I gave the order to abandon the aircraft. Stewart McDougall handed me my 'chute and then he and George Lumsden and Jack Shedden and "Rod" Wilson went out the front hatch.'

They had bailed out 8 miles north-east of Thirsk. Jack Shedden landed in a ploughed field about 100 yards from a farmhouse. Disentangling himself from his harness, he trudged along the muddy furrows and knocked on the door. A middle-aged man answered. Shedden enquired whether he could use the telephone. The man responded by slamming the door in the Canadian's face! Shedden knocked again. This time a girl answered. Shedden repeated his request and was admitted. Apologizing, the girl explained that her father had taken Shedden for a German, 'because of his funny accent'.

Jack Mitchell was still in his seat when the aircraft dived straight for the ground: 'It must have been when the tail gunner's 'chute hit the right rudder. Henry Cox opened his parachute too early and became caught up on the aircraft and died when it crashed near Cowesby Hall. I dived from the pilot's seat directly through the front hatch without touching a thing, then pulled my ripcord. I could hear the plane spiralling down and then crashing and then I hit the ground. It was just getting daylight when I first looked around to find I was in the front yard of a big manor house. The owner, I assumed, came out and I told him what had happened so he phoned Skipton and told them where we were. It was only about an hour before someone arrived to take me to base.'[20]

Flying Officer John M. Gray's new Halifax III 'D-Dog' with his own crew on their first operational sortie was hit by heavy flak just as it crossed the enemy coastline. Fuel poured out of No. 3 tank and it quickly became apparent that if he went all the way to Berlin, the crew would not have enough fuel to make it back to Skipton-on-Swale. Nevertheless, Gray decided to continue and deliver his bombs.

During the return flight the wireless apparatus and some navigational equipment became unserviceable. The enemy coast was crossed, but some time later the engines cut over the North Sea 15 miles off Hartlepool. Gray did an excellent job of ditching the Halifax in the rough sea. Not one of his crew was hurt and they all got safely aboard the dinghy and were picked up by Air-Sea Rescue. Gray was awarded an immediate DFC.

Low on fuel and in bad weather on the return, Flight Sergeant William Alfred Stiles of Innisfail, Alberta, the 26-year-old pilot of HX285 was instructed to divert and make a landing nearer the coast at Catfoss airfield. As a young man he worked at a number of jobs in Innisfail, latterly at a creamery. He joined the Canadian army in October 1940, serving with the Calgary Highlanders briefly before transferring to the 15th Alberta Light Horse Regiment. He enlisted for RCAF service on 29 July 1941 at Calgary. Because of poor visibility Stiles overshot the first attempt at landing and flew a circuit of the airfield to make a second attempt, but while making a turn to make a final approach to land, the fuel ran out and the engines failed. At 0800 hours the aircraft lost height and flew into trees in the grounds of Brandesburton Hall about 5 miles west of Hornsea. Stiles was killed and Sergeant Henry Glen Boissevain the Canadian bomb-aimer and Sergeant R.L.B. Ludlow the rear gunner suffered injuries but were not seriously hurt.[21]

Five Halifax Vs on 434 'Bluenose' Squadron RCAF never returned to Croft. While over the target area 'S-Sugar' skippered by Pilot Officer Murray Franklin Flewelling of Calgary, Alberta was attacked by a fighter which knocked out the port outer engine and holed at least one fuel tank. The crew bombed the target and made for home, but as they neared and then crossed the Yorkshire coast the fuel supply was nearly exhausted and the starboard inner engine cut out. Flewelling ordered his crew to bail out and he was last to leave the aircraft which crashed at Flixton, 5 miles west-south-west of Filey in Yorkshire at around 0800 hours. Sergeant Joseph William Raul Demeres, the 21-year-old rear gunner of Quebec City, is thought to have released his parachute too soon or it had fouled the aircraft as he left it. The parachute caught on the tail of the aircraft and he only became free when the 'chute tore but this did not break his fall and he was killed on impact with the ground. The remaining crew landed safely, although Sergeant Dobney sustained minor injuries.

There were no survivors on 'X-X-ray' piloted by 21-year-old Canadian Flight Lieutenant Russell Henry Alvin Stanley. None survived on 'V-Victor' piloted by 26-year-old Canadian Squadron Leader Lloyd Martin Linnell. His grave bears the inscription 'He dropped everything to serve his country'. He left a widow, Marianne Elizabeth Linnell of Vancouver, British Columbia. 'D-Dog' flown by 23-year-old Canadian Pilot Officer Edward Philip Devaney was lost with all seven crew. 'U-Uncle' piloted by Squadron Leader J. Eric Hockey of Kentville, Nova Scotia was abandoned following a night-fighter attack at 21,000 feet over the target area. All eight crew members, including the navigator Flying Officer Jack Ferguson of Regina, Saskatchewan, bailed out and were taken into captivity. Hockey had been best man at Ferguson's wedding when he married the former Rita Cuffe of New Barnet, Hampshire whom he had met while attending the marriage of his skipper to her sister.

No. 431 'Iroquois' Squadron, which shared Croft with the 'Bluenoses', lost four Halifaxes. 'H-Harry' piloted by Flight Sergeant Jack Maher from Chatsworth, Ontario was hit by flak at 20,000 feet while homebound and eventually crashed at Webelsfelde. Three crew members were killed; Maher and three others were taken prisoner. 'Q-Queenie' flown by 22-year-old Pilot Officer William Russell Hewetson of Saskatoon, Saskatchewan was lost with no survivors.

Returning to Croft, 'F-Freddie' flown by Australian Pilot Officer J.C. King ran low on fuel and diverted to Dishforth where it swung out of control and the undercarriage gave way but no-one was injured. 'N-Nuts' skippered by 23-year-old Warrant Officer2 Joseph Thomas Raymond Corriveau of Rivière du Loup, Province of Quebec was hit by flak. After reaching the coast of Lincolnshire the crew was ordered to bail out. All landed in the sea from where four of them were rescued by the combined efforts of three naval MS trawlers, *Property*, *Prospect* and *Varanga*, which reached the scene about half an hour after the Halifax ditched but by then Corriveau and two of his crew had died.

At Leconfield, 466 Squadron RAAF had dispatched fourteen aircraft, but four Halifax IIIs failed to return. After bombing, 'A-Apple' piloted by Squadron Leader Allan Owen McCormack of Melbourne, Victoria was attacked by a night-fighter, which holed the petrol tanks and the Halifax came down in the Baltic. McCormack ordered the crew out before he took to his 'chute at 3,000 feet. Everyone except the 23-year-old Australian navigator, Pilot Officer Jack Wilfred Tylor of Katanning, Western Australia, whose body was washed up at Fåborg on the coast of Denmark were rescued and taken into captivity.

'C-Charlie' flown by 32-year-old Australian Flight Lieutenant Frank Wharton Mack was shot down at 19,000 feet by a night-fighter shortly after bombing. Only two men on the eight-man crew got out alive and they were taken into captivity. Mack left a widow, Hilda. 'Y-Yorker' flown by Pilot Officer G.B. Coombes was shot down from 20,000 feet by a night-fighter, crashing at Biesdorf, 10 kilometres from the centre of Berlin. Three of the crew were killed. Coombes and the three other members of his crew were taken into captivity. Out of fuel on the return, Canadian Pilot Officer D.D. Graham tried to land 'G-George' at Matlaske, a fighter strip in Norfolk, but he ground-looped to avoid hitting a group of workmen and then collided with a partially-constructed hangar, seriously injuring two of his crew.

There were no losses on the two Wickenby squadrons. Jack Currie's trip was quite uneventful and after dropping their bombs they were winging their way home. Welshman Sergeant George Protheroe, the mid-upper gunner, summed up the thoughts of everyone on the crew when he began singing on intercom, 'So Long Chop Land and if I never see you again it will be too soon'. When they landed in the early hours of the morning a crate of beer was waiting for them, courtesy of Squadron Leader Bill Spiller. (Spiller's crew would be on the battle order for the next operation to Berlin on 30 January.) Currie was told that the CO was in the dining room and was invited to join them. Then it was off on two weeks' leave to London.

Ron Champion's crew on 102 Squadron got iced up on entering the Baltic area and dropped from over 20,000 feet to below 5,000 feet:

'Luckily, now below the icy cloud, the ice dropped off our wings and we were on our way,' recalled 'Butch' Lewis. 'Now we realised that after losing so much height and a slow climb back to our operating height, we were far behind the end of the stream. It would be almost impossible to reach Berlin, as alone we would stand out as an easy target for any roving night-fighter. Even if we were fortunate enough to reach the "Big City" the fires would make it like daylight and the fighters would be queuing up for such an easy target. "Press on regardless" does not win wars so we dropped our bombs on the first likely target on the coast and returned home safely.'

Two Halifax IIs on 102 Squadron were lost. One was 'S-Sugar' flown by Flight Sergeant Dai M.E. Pugh on only the crew's second operation, which was hit by flak as they came off the target. The rudder controls and Nos 5 and 6 starboard wing tanks were damaged. The flak had actually severed the block tube control at the rear of the aircraft. Sergeant Alexander Addison Burgess, the rear gunner, received a nasty head wound when a flak shell burst near to his turret. The explosion threw him against the side of the turret, knocking him out and causing him light concussion. When he came round he swapped places with Sergeant C. Williams, the mid-upper gunner. Sergeant Royston Frederick Purkiss, the 19-year-old flight engineer, managed to repair the rudder controls when they reached the Danish coast, but they were losing fuel fast and finally, with the aircraft down to 2,000 feet, Pugh gave the order to prepare to ditch. It was 0845 hours and they were about 60 to 90 miles east of Dundee.

Sergeant A. Cohen the wireless-operator had put the IFF to distress at 15,000 feet after leaving Denmark and at 2025 he had sent out an SOS. Purkiss had just announced that they were down to 150 gallons of fuel while the crew took their ditching positions. The bomb-aimer Sergeant Everard Campbell was lying on the starboard rest position with his feet braced on the front spar. Flight Sergeant James Craig Graham, the 27-year-old Canadian navigator, was on the opposite rest position, his intercom plugged in to listen to the pilot. Burgess was placed with his back to the main spar. Then Williams collected the axe and No.7 pack with attached paddles and dinghy cover and sat on the port side with his back to the spar, having collected the dinghy radio and handed it and the kite container to Everard Campbell. Purkiss stood at his position until the last possible moment so he did not have time to reach his ditching position. He placed himself against the wireless-operator and braced his feet against the centre rest strut of the front spar. He had already grabbed the Very pistol and cartridges. All the hatches were open, the pilot's jettisoned for him and each member of the crew had collected rations and torches.

The sea was rough with waves up to 20 feet high, but it was daylight and the weather was good. Pugh ditched successfully and the crew scrambled into their dinghy, but later the next day a heavy wave capsized their craft and all the crew were flung into the sea. Pugh, Cohen, Williams and Graham managed to clamber back into the dinghy but Burgess, Campbell and Purkiss remained in the sea, clinging to ropes. The men in the dinghy tried vainly to get them into the craft but they were too exhausted and one by one the three men in the water drifted off silently and alone and they were never seen again. Two days later the dinghy was spotted by a Warwick, which dropped two Lindholme dinghies in the rough sea to no avail and next day when another Warwick dropped another dinghy the four men were too exhausted to reach it. Finally, after three days adrift in the open sea Pugh, Cohen, Williams and Graham, all suffering from hypothermia, were picked up by a high-speed launch (HSL) from Montrose in Angus. Graham died before the HSL reached Scotland.

When 'Robbie' Robinson's crew on 'J-Jane' reached their target it was well alight:

'We had a Master Bomber and our call-sign was "Ravens",' recalled Les Cardall. 'We must have been absolutely spot on time because they called up and said, "Hello Ravens! Hello Ravens! Ignore reds, ignore reds; bomb greens, bomb greens!" We were making our bombing run on the reds and we changed course and we'd no sooner changed than WHOOMPH! Anti-aircraft shells!'

It was at around 0320 hours; about the time Cardall had telegrammed home to tell them that was when his parents should expect him. It was only later that he discovered that his mother had woken her husband that very moment and said, 'Les is downstairs; go and let him in!' Les would throw a stone up at the window and his father said, 'No, I can't hear anything!' When his father did not get up she got up, went to the window and saw her son standing at the gate but when she went down to let him in, he wasn't there! She went back upstairs and told her husband and he just said 'Go back to sleep!' Next morning she received the telegram to say that her son was missing.

All Cardall remembered was a brilliant white flash and then a terrific explosion: 'I looked and the target was up above, so I knew we were upside-down! I looked out through the astrodome and one wing was on fire, so we immediately pressed the fire extinguishers – and it went out. There was a terrific wind; everything was blowing about all over the place. Bloody great accumulators were floating past. But finally it got straight and we tried to get everything heavy into the nose. To hold the nose down everybody had to move forward to try and keep the weight there because we were continually going up. That's how we came back, right the way across Germany till we got to Texel. It was becoming daylight then and they really pumped everything at us. You could see it going in through the floor and out through the top. It looked as if they came up ever so slow until they got to you. My parachute was useless, all shot to pieces, in little bits. My pilot said 'take mine' but by that time we were only at about 250 feet – no chance.'

The aircraft sustained such damage that Robinson was barely able to steer the Halifax. Stan Chapman recalled:

'The following hours were spent flying over a blacked-out countryside on our own and every so often the aircraft was permitted to 'take up' its climbing and turning attitude under partial pilot control. The reason being our second pilot [Sergeant D.A. Wilkinson] had to sit alongside the Skipper and hold the control column forward by sheer brute leg power, keeping this position until cramp overtook when he had to remove his leg, replacing it with the other one.'

'J-Jane' was scheduled to arrive back at Lissett at approximately 0737 hours but at around 0600 it was still somewhere over the northern Netherlands. Les Cardall drew attention to their petrol situation which was causing him some concern. The Halifax was down around 13,000 feet when an unhealthy burst of flak brightened the clouds around with dabs of orange. Robinson put the nose down, at the same time turning back towards the Dutch coast. He asked Chapman to keep a lookout for the coast and to bail out when certain they were over land. Eventually, the crew could see the dark outline of a coast a few miles ahead. Their height was now between 4,000 to 5,000 feet and it was getting lighter outside. Chapman reported this to his skipper, who replied 'Out you go first Stan; best of luck.'

Chapman stuffed 'Percy the Penguin' inside his flying jacket, put on his parachute, opened the escape hatch, sat for a few seconds with his feet dangling in the slipstream, looked up to where he could see 'Wilky' Wilkinson's flying boots and gave Dave the navigator's face the usual thumbs-up sign. Then he lowered himself until the slipstream took over and whisked him smartly away. As his 'chute opened it felt as though his neck had broken. Looking down Chapman could make out some farm buildings and an orchard, plus an uninviting barbed-wire fence almost beneath him. He cleared the fence and finished up with his silk covering a small fruit tree and hanging with his feet about 2 feet from the ground. Two cyclists in uniform with rifles slung across their backs came along the road in his direction. Their arrival was meticulously timed, dropping their cycles against the hedge as Chapman 'dropped in'! They asked two questions: 'Are you RAF?' and 'Are you armed?' Chapman was then marched in front of his captors towards the village with a rifle pointing at his back. It was the start of his journey to Stalag Luft III at Sagan in Silesia.

Though he had been shot down, Chapman was philosophical about his capture: 'Our losses were forty-four aircraft that night; the vast majority of these crews did not witness the dull dismal dawn of the 29th, which looked pretty good to me.' Perhaps 'Percy the Penguin' had proved lucky after all.[22]

The rest of the crew also escaped unhurt. Sergeant C.N. Durdin, the Canadian mid-upper gunner, was the only crew member to initially avoid captivity but later, near Arnhem, he was arrested. As 'Robbie' and Les Cardall were getting ready to abandon the aircraft, they discovered that Cardall's parachute had been damaged by the anti-aircraft fire so they executed a perfect crash-landing just outside the village of Zandeweer in northern Groningen. When the aircraft had come to a standstill, the two men exited the aircraft and started inspecting the considerable damage to the tail. Eventually the two crewmen were arrested by a Dutch police officer and later captured by German soldiers.

At the Frankfurt interrogation centre Les Cardall saw none of his friends for a fortnight:

'After two days of that a German officer came in. He spoke perfect English and wanted me to sign the form for the Red Cross – well, we were warned about that – it had details you were not supposed to answer so I refused. They took me into a massive room with a German officer sitting at a desk and he spoke very good English too. He asked for my name, rank and number and I told him. He opened a book and for two or three minutes turned the pages over. 'Oh yes,' he said, 'we've been expecting you for a long while!' And he told me more about myself than I knew!

'Oh yes,' he said, 'you come from Moray Road, Finsbury Park?'

'I said, 'Yes, that's right.'

'You went to Montem Street School?'
'That's right.'
'You became a wall and floor-tiler?'
'That's right!'
'Well,' he said, 'I lived in Blackstock Road for years!'

Chapter Thirteen

Wild Colonial Boys

'They were a queer conglomeration, these men – some educated and sensitive, some rough-haired and burly and drawn from all parts of the Empire, Great Britain, Canada, New Zealand and Australia.... Some, of them were humming, some were singing, some were laughing and others were standing serious and thoughtful. It looked like the dressing-room where the jockeys sit waiting before a great steeplechase.... [At take-off] the control officer flashed a green ray for a split second, which was the signal that this plane was designated for take-off. Its roaring grew louder and louder as it dragged its heavy tail towards the starting-point like a slow, nearly helpless monster. About twenty yards away we could just discern a vast dinosaurish shape; after a moment, as if stopping to make up its mind ... it lumbered forward, raising its tail just as it passed us and turning from something very heavy and clumsy into a lightly-poised shape, rushing through the night like a pterodactyl. At this instant, a white light was flashed upon it and a Canadian boy from Vancouver who was standing beside me put down its number and the moment of departure. It vanished from sight at once and we stood, staring down the field, where in a few seconds a flashing green light announced that it had left the ground.... A great calm settled over the place as the last droning motors faded out in the distance and we all drove back to the control room where staff hang onto the instruments on a long night vigil.... I went to sleep thinking of the youngsters I had seen, all now 150 miles away; straining their eyes through a blackness relieved only by the star-spangled vault above them.'

General Raymond Lee, the US Military Attaché in London, who early in the war observed RAF bomber crews at a station 'somewhere in England'.[1]

'Pip' Beck, the WAAF radio telephone-operator in Flying Control at Dunholme Lodge, had soon come to like the easy, pleasant manner and lack of formality of the Rhodesians on 44 Squadron at Dunholme. 'They were so unmistakably not English. Their appearance was often highly individual during working time at least, with sheepskin jerkins worn over tunics and roll-neck pullovers; cap-comforters in place of forage caps and battered flying boots or rolled-down Wellington boots with thick white socks inside. Of course, our own ground-crew resorted to similar clothing out on the flights, but the Rhodesians managed to make it look far more outlandish, with their air of tough independence, skins bronzed by warmer sun than ours and eyes used to wider distances. Their independence and disregard for the finer points of discipline was a by-word on the camp. Their accent was clipped and unfamiliar and their speech sprinkled with words or phrases in Afrikaans.'[2]

No. 44 Squadron had been renamed the 'Rhodesia' Squadron in 1941 in honour of that colony's contribution to Britain's war effort and also to recognize that up to 25 per cent of the ground and air crew were from Southern Rhodesia. The squadron had moved to Dunholme Lodge airfield while Waddington's grass runways were tarmacked but never returned to Waddington and during the next sixteen-month period of operating from Dunholme, the squadron lost 461 air crew on operations.

'As CO, I am told what the target is to be and the strength of the raid,' wrote Wing Commander Robert Lawrence Bowes DFC*, officer commanding 44 ('Rhodesia') Squadron. Born in April 1908, he held a private pilot's licence prior to being commissioned on the Reserve of Air Force Officers in early 1933. Advancing to flying officer in September of the following year, he transferred to the Royal Air Force Volunteer Reserve in January 1938 and was advanced to flight lieutenant on the outbreak of hostilities. He then served as a flying instructor in England and Southern Rhodesia until 1942. During an attack on Peenemünde on the night of 17/18 August 1943, his Lancaster was hit by an accurate burst of light flak during the run-up to the target. The bomb-aimer was seriously wounded and the bomb-sight completely smashed, but in spite of these difficulties a most determined and accurate attack was carried out. Awarded an immediate DFC, three of Bowes' crew were duly gazetted for DFMs in the New Year. Again, in the Berlin attack on 18/19 November, his aircraft was hit by flak shortly before bombing and one engine put completely out of action. A second and successful run-up was, however, made, after which he flew his damaged aircraft back, eventually landing it without further damage in adverse weather conditions at an aerodrome on the south coast of England.

'I inform my Group of the number of aircraft that I can supply for the operation; fix details of aircraft to be used and quantities of petrol to be carried, which may be as much as 2,000 gallons or more, to each aircraft, according to the route they will take. Aircrews are selected for the night's work. The armoury Staff is preparing the bombs and ammunition to be loaded up later. The ground staff are re-examining and testing the planes that are going to be used. The aircrews take the aircraft up for a final flying test. In the mess kitchen, sandwiches are cut and coffee made. Emergency dinghies are checked and the hundred and one other pieces of equipment packed carefully into their special stowage places aboard the aircraft. By midday or soon after, if all goes smoothly, everything will be practically finished and ready for the night's operation. The ground crews are as keen as the aircrews that nothing should prevent an aircraft taking off at the appointed time. I have been discussing the routes to the target and the general plan of attack with the station commander and the Met officer, who tells us all that can be predicted about the weather. We may start with as many as three alternative routes, the final route to be selected nearer the time of take-off. The longer the route to be followed, the more petrol will be needed and the smaller the bomb-load can be carried.'

'Every aircraft's part in the attack, exact time of take-off and required arrival over the target. Finally, at what is known as the Flight Planning Conference, details of the group plan of attack are settled by telephone among all the squadrons taking part. By lunchtime, all that remains to be done is the briefing of the aircrews. This is a very intricate affair particularly for the navigators, who are responsible for bringing the aircraft to a point perhaps six hundred miles over Germany within one and a half minutes either way of a given time. Any straggler may find himself in Queer Street, as he will at once be made the individual target for the defence organization, so accurate navigation is all-important. The bomb-aimer gets a ground plan of the target and information regarding Pathfinder technique for the attack. Then, the main briefing, which follows, makes the opportunity for all crews to get together and pool their individual information. Every man knows exactly what he has to do and when he has to do it. As dusk falls, the whole sky seems to vibrate with the roar of the bomber force as it climbs to gain altitude before setting out. The ground crews will be waiting again to take over in the icy winter night when our planes return in eight hours' time.'[3]

In the early hours of Saturday morning, 29 January 1944 accredited photographers visited Dunholme Lodge to record Flight Lieutenant A. Moore and the crew of 'C-Charlie' on 44 ('Rhodesia') Squadron on their return from their ninth trip to Berlin which would complete their tour of operations. The photograph appeared on the front page of the London *Sunday Graphic* newspaper the following morning. Also appearing in that issue was a photograph of two young men standing beside the Lancaster in which they had thankfully returned from the trip to the German capital on the morning of the 29th, having landed at 0826 hours. Australian Pilot Officer Norman Joseph Lyford, his bomb-aimer Flight Sergeant G. Owen of Bury, Lancashire and their crew-mates were fortunate to have survived a very near miss from a flak shell which caused significant damage to 'F for Freddie'. Squadron records noted: 'Damage to aircraft caused by heavy flak. Port wingtip shot off. Port fin damaged. Holes in starboard mainplane, port mainplane, port inner engine cowling and starboard elevator trimming tab.'

In the photo Norman Lyford looks as though he preferred to be anywhere other than in the limelight. Lyford was born on 4 December 1921 to George and Lillian Lyford of Pymble, Sydney. He went to North Sydney High School and went on to become an insurance clerk. He applied to enlist in the Royal Australian Air Force shortly after turning 18 but had to wait ten months to be accepted, during which time he served in Australia with the 30th Battalion of the militia. He was accepted by the RAAF in November 1942 and underwent six months' training in Australia before transferring to Canada for further training under the Empire Air Training Scheme which trained pilots and air crew from Commonwealth countries for service in the Royal Air Force.

Having arrived back at Dunholme Lodge around breakfast-time, crews were thankful for a stand-down that (Saturday) evening. Norman Lyford recalled: 'We were rather badly shot up by flak over the target, but this did not affect the mission.' The crew was given 'C-Charlie', which was no longer required by Flight Lieutenant Bert Wright and crew.

Crews had just the one night's rest before the bombing of Berlin resumed on the night of 30/31 January for the third raid in four nights on the 'Big City' when 534 aircraft – 440 of them Lancasters – were on the battle order. The crews were understandably unhappy about it, with Flight Sergeant James Brown, a Lancaster mid-upper gunner on 50 Squadron, summing up the thoughts of many when he said, 'If that isn't flying the arse off people I don't know what is.'

It was also the start of a new moon period and a quarter- to half-moon was expected during the outward flight. Also, the only diversionary raids were by twenty-two Mosquitoes on Elberfeld and five more on Brunswick. Not surprisingly, some crew members were fatalistic. The omens were so bad that 23-year-old Sergeant Stanley Kenneth 'Chalky' Chalkin, the flight engineer on 'M-Mother' on 207 Squadron at Spilsby, thought that there could be only one outcome for the crew skippered by Pilot Officer Harold Douglas Broad. After his first trip Chalkin was now convinced that he would not return from this next one. Following the Berlin briefing he approached fellow flight engineer Sergeant Stan Carter with a large cardboard carton addressed to his mother in Tonbridge, Kent. He asked Carter if he would please post the carton when Carter returned. Carter told Chalkin to post it himself when *he* returned. Chalkin replied, 'I wish I could believe I will be coming back.'

While the outward route for the Main Force was again a northerly one it was not as far north as the previous raid on Berlin. Throughout most of the route and over the target the customary complete cloud cover was found, but the way was well-marked and horizontal visibility was good. The path chosen was free of trouble so that little difficulty was experienced. The attack was extremely concentrated and during the eighteen minutes the Main Force was over the target area a continuous stream of well-placed markers was maintained. Assessment of results was more difficult than usual due to the density of the cloud formations, the blinding brilliance of the moonlight and the illumination provided by countless flares. However, later waves returned to base with stories of a monster explosion and a most reassuring glow visible for 150 miles. The target area was ringed with fires and there was every indication of a successful attack.

The night-fighters were unable to intercept the Main Force over the sea and the bomber stream was well on the way to the target before they met with any opposition. About 50 miles from and fifteen minutes short of the 'Big City' 'C-Charlie' on 44 ('Rhodesia') Squadron was attacked by a night-fighter, which caused so much damage that Norman Lyford ordered his crew to bail out. The Australian skipper held the Lancaster under control long enough for all six of them to safely exit the aircraft to become prisoners of war before the wreckage of 'C-Charlie' came down at Geisenhorst, a tiny rural hamlet 44 miles from Berlin. Norman Lyford's remains were recovered and buried in the parish cemetery at Dreetz on 4 February.

The bombing took place in complete cloud cover and was scattered once more. At the head of the bomber stream was Pilot Officer Cecil Hopton who had arrived on 156 Squadron from 12 Squadron at Wickenby on 7 November. The 25-year-old pilot, who was from Montreal, was a multi-talented sportsman, the son of a British émigré to Canada. Before enlisting in the RCAF at Niagara Falls, Ontario in August 1940 he had worked for the Imperial Bank as a clerk. Three weeks before embarking for Britain he had married his fiancée Dorothy Symes.

He wrote: 'Target was attacked at 2013.12 hours from 20,000 feet. We were first to bomb. TIs fell into cloud before cascading but as we left the target there was a good concentration of sky-markers. Through a small gap TI [Target Indicator] Red was seen burning on the ground and TI Green seen through the cloud cascading. Sky-markers continued to be well concentrated with two stragglers to the west, possibly dummies. One photo attempted.'

Squadron Leader Hopton DFC's luck ran out on his twenty-eighth sortie on the night of 7/8 June on the raid on the Versailles railway marshalling yard when flying as the deputy master bomber, he was shot down by night-fighters after leaving the target. All seven crew were killed.[4]

Warrant Officer Stanley William George Neighbour, a 22-year-old North Londoner who skippered 'L-London' on 156 Squadron, wrote:

'Target was bombed from 18,500 feet at 2016.55 hours. At 2013.7 hours the first R/P [Release Point] flares were seen and at time of bombing about five release point flares had dropped forming a close circle estimated at not more than a few hundred yards in diameter. Immediately after bombing two more R/P flares fell singly slightly south-west of main concentration. Towards the end of the attack release point flares formed a line east-west. Only one TI was seen – a Red at 2016 hours. Thick cloud prevented further observations and searchlights were ineffective. Slight heavy flak and moderate light flak. One photo attempted. Bomb load was 1 x 4 flares red/green stars, two x TI green L/B, 2 x TI green, 1 x 4,000 Heavy Capacity, 4 x 1,000 Medium Capacity and 1 x flare red steady.'[5]

Flying Officer William Scott Breckenridge piloted a 626 Squadron Lancaster whose crew comprised three Scotsmen, three Canadians and an English mid-upper gunner, Pilot Officer William B. Baker, a keen amateur boxer and a talented illustrator and cartoonist signing his work 'Biff'. On the approach to the bomb run the aircraft was attacked by a night-fighter. Its initial burst of fire killed Sergeant 'Jimmy' Hall, the wireless-operator, and 'Biff' Baker was wounded in the right side of his face by cannon shell fragments as it burst inside his turret, tearing away his oxygen mask and the right-hand earpiece of his flying helmet. Sergeant Joe Schwartz, the Canadian rear gunner, was wounded in the foot. Both men fell unconscious. Canadian bomb-aimer Sergeant 'Val' Poushinsky dropped the bombs, but a minute later the night-fighter came in again firing a long burst. Breckenridge took violent evasive action, but the aircraft was once again hit and this time the navigator was seriously wounded. After a further two minutes the night-fighter attacked a third time, closing in from the starboard quarter at 400 yards and let forth yet another devastating barrage. This time the skipper was hit, a passing bullet grazing his legs. By the time the fighter was shaken off, their height was down to 15,000 feet. Luckily, no further attacks came their way.

Just after leaving the target Baker regained consciousness. He discovered he had no intercom, no oxygen and his turret was put out of action; he climbed out of the turret and found James Hall dead and the rear gunner slumped forward on the rest-bed. Baker clambered into the still-serviceable rear turret, even though he was injured and without oxygen, and remained in the turret throughout the homeward flight, except for a short time when he and Alex Stephenson, the engineer, went aft to extinguish an electrical system fire. Joe Schwartz also revived, extricated himself from his turret, crawled up the fuselage to the rest-bed, but again collapsed. 'Val' Poushinsky rendered first-aid to both Schwartz and Warrant Officer Richard Jack Meek, the 36-year-old navigator from Vancouver, before taking up a position in the astrodome.

Meek, who was on his sixth op, had received a bullet through his left shoulder blade and a piece of shrapnel had gone clean through his middle, entering at the right side of his back and emerging at the left front, just below his chest, missing his heart by inches. However, despite loss of blood and great pain he remained at his post throughout the entire journey. His navigational gear was wrecked, but the accurate data on the winds on the route in now came in useful. All he could do was dead reckon on these, but in reverse. He could not hold up the sextant for his left arm kept dropping down, finally becoming completely useless. Luckily, his figures were good for they took them right back on track. He also took observation of landmarks he knew. When he saw searchlights or flak over German territory he would say to the skipper, 'That's Hanover. Go so many minutes in such a direction then bear so much west.' Two hours after leaving Berlin he was able to get a 'Gee' fix, despite feeling lightheaded from loss of blood and lack of oxygen. They were now over the Zuider Zee and only 3 miles off track. The open bomb doors caused severe drag and Breckenridge could not make much speed, though he did manage to hold altitude. All were chilled through due to the many gaping holes, while the lack of oxygen was taking its toll.

Thirty miles from the English coast the 'Gee' packed up. A distress signal was sent out and in less than a minute the searchlights were homing them in to Docking, on the Norfolk coast. A crash-landing was inevitable but the hydraulic system had been shot away, the bomb doors would not close nor, as they found later, would the wheels lower. One petrol tank was holed, three rev counters and three boost gauges useless, as were the direction-finder and gyro-compass. The elevators and rudders were also badly damaged. With the crew at crash positions, the skipper brought the battered Lancaster in, but it was difficult to control and he had to overshoot. On the second attempt he brought her in like a baby, ran forward on the tail-wheel, nose well up and then slowed. The open bomb doors hit the ground, snapped shut and suddenly all was quiet. They were down. There was no fire.

Bill Breckenridge and 'Biff' Baker each received the DFC. Jack Meek was awarded the Conspicuous Gallantry Medal. He recovered from his wounds and returned to finish his operational tour on 626 Squadron, later receiving a commission. In August 1944 he was awarded the DFC, having completed twenty-eight operations over enemy territory.

'X-X-ray' on 50 Squadron captained by Pilot Officer Edward Weatherstone was attacked by a Ju 88 on the homeward journey at 22,000 feet. Flight Sergeant Collingwood, the rear gunner, again saved the crew's bacon. He saw the fighter dead astern down at 400 yards closing rapidly. The Ju 88 opened fire immediately and Collingwood ordered 'corkscrew starboard' to get into the attacker's blind side and opened fire with a short burst point-blank. Hits were seen on the fin and rudder. The Ju 88 broke away at 250 yards port quarter upon climbing perpendicularly and Collingwood opened fire again with a short burst. The Ju 88 then turned over and made a diving attack on port quarter and the rear gunner opened fire with another short burst. The Ju 88 burst into flames with the underside of the fuselage burning and continued to dive completely enveloped in flames. It was later claimed as definitely destroyed.

Heavy damage was caused to the 'Big City' but seventy-nine towns and villages outside the capital reported falling bombs, most of these exploding in open countryside. The German night-fighters were able to follow the bomber stream until well into the return flight. At the target the bombing was made through complete cloud cover. Twin-engined 'Tame Boars' wreaked havoc, continuing their attacks until well into the return flight and they accounted for all twenty-eight Lancasters and four Halifaxes that were shot down. Lancaster 'U-Uncle' on 101 Squadron at Ludford Magna skippered by 23-year-old Flight Sergeant Douglas William Froggatt is thought to have been shot down by Oberleutnant Josef Kraft with the aircraft crashing at around 2000 hours in the Alexanderhof area of Berlin. Froggatt and four of the crew, including Flying Officer Moie Marder, the special operator born in Regina, were laid to rest at the Berlin War Cemetery. The three others were taken into captivity.

At Waterbeach two Lancasters on 514 Squadron were missing. The crew on 'G-George' skippered by 25-year-old Flight Lieutenant George Boyd DFC, probably one of three Lancasters shot down over the North Sea, were lost without trace. 'A-Apple' captained by 22-year-old Canadian Flight Lieutenant George Joseph Chequer was shot down by a night-fighter equipped with 'Schräge Musik' at approximately 2030 hours approaching Berlin. Flight Sergeant R.L. Gulliford, the 'second dickey', heard a shout from the rear gunner to 'corkscrew' and stated that the aircraft was then hit by upwardly-fired cannon shells which immediately ignited the petrol tank.

Their attacker was probably Oberstleutnant Günther Radusch who destroyed three Lancasters in the area between 2024 and 2030 hours. Chequer and Sergeant John O'Brien, the 23-year-old Australian mid-upper gunner, bailed out too low for their parachutes to deploy, while Sergeant Robert Montgomery the WOP/AG apparently drowned after landing in a lake. Flight Sergeant Alex Robertson the Australian rear gunner walked south-west for five nights before being captured near Magdeburg. The flight engineer Sergeant J. Carey and the navigator Flight Sergeant Ken Mortimer were captured and taken into captivity. Mortimer was subsequently killed on 19 April 1945 when Typhoons shot up a PoW column near Boizenburg.[6]

In 100 Group Mosquitoes flew seven 'Serrate' patrols from Norfolk airfields and two crews returned with claims for a victory apiece. Although the 30/31 January operation could be considered successful – it was a well-concentrated attack and major fires broke out in the centre and south-western sectors – it did not achieve the degree of concentration necessary for the systematic destruction of a city the size of Berlin. In the course of fourteen raids, 24,000 tons of bombs had fallen on Berlin, yet Harris had still not succeeded in doing what he set out to do.

'Markers well concentrated,' claimed the 6 Group reports. 'Four large explosions – glow of fires on cloud.' In total, 6 Group contributed forty-seven of the aircraft on the operation. Two returned early and one was lost. All told thirty-two Lancasters and one Halifax – 6.3 per cent of the force – were shot down. The Canadians, whose Halifax losses had been grievous of late, were more fortunate than the RAF on this sortie for the simple reason that Harris did not include the obsolescent Mark IIs and Vs on the battle order. One Halifax III, 'L-London' on 433 Squadron at Skipton-on-Swale piloted by 20-year-old Flight Sergeant Gerald Ernest Hagerman of Saint John, New Brunswick was lost. Only the mid-upper gunner, fellow Canadian Sergeant M.D. Park-Taylor survived and he was taken prisoner.

Three crews on 405 'Vancouver' Squadron RCAF at Gransden Lodge failed to return. Outbound, 'S-Sugar' captained by Canadian Flight Sergeant A. Bonikowsky was hit by flak and set on fire. The Lancaster crashed at Teschendorf, south-west of the Dretzee. Bonikowsky, his flight engineer Sergeant F.S. Cole, Canadians Flying Officer J.A.R. Laberge DFC and Warrant Officer2 G.R. Buchanan parachuted to safety and were taken prisoner. The bomb-aimer, mid-upper gunner and rear gunner were killed. One of the supporters, 'J-Jig' skippered by 23-year-old Flight Lieutenant Warren Ainsley Roberts of Birtle, Manitoba, crashed at Loburg with the loss of all the crew. Roberts was on his ninth operation.

Shortly after 'bombs away' at 20,000 feet 'R-Robert' flown by Flight Lieutenant Henry L. Shackleton who had flown four PFF trips to Berlin without mishap was attacked repeatedly by two night-fighters which set the port wing on fire and the Lancaster spiralled out of control. Shackleton shouted 'Abandon aircraft'. His wireless-operator 'Red' Williams put on his navigator-type chest parachute and then decided to get a bar of chocolate from his desk. Taking off his parachute he put it in his tunic and then he put his 'chute back on again. A violent explosion occurred, catapulting Shackleton into the air. Williams jumped out of the hole in the cockpit and landed in a Berlin street and was immediately taken prisoner. After being blown out of the cockpit Henry pulled on what he thought was his parachute release, but it was the release of his seat harness! When it fell away he searched again and to his relief the parachute opened before he fell onto a bush in a Berlin park. Henry hid by day and walked by night, but on the third night, just after people had come out of their shelter during another bombing raid, some children surrounded him and he was taken to the Burgermeister's house where kind ladies bathed his face and gave him food. However, a pompous and drunken Wehrmacht officer took Henry to a Berlin police cell (which was warm!). A few days later he met 'Red' Williams at the Frankfurt Interrogation Centre, who told him he had been taken to a crashed Lancaster and understood their five crew members had lost their lives.

The rate of losses led to a hardening in attitude on the part of the 405 Squadron Commander, Wing Commander 'Sunshine' Lane:

'Our losses got to the point where when a crew came down from 6 Group I didn't even bother with their last names. I just tried to catch their first names, that was all, because there was no point in trying to remember the last names because they probably wouldn't be there two or three days hence. It was a habit I got into that I never did really shake ... it was just not worth the effort. If they stayed around then I got to know their last names, if they lasted. But it was a question of 'Welcome to the Squadron' and probably two nights later I was writing a letter to his mother.'[7]

The loss of 33-year-old Flight Lieutenant Albert Henry John Sambridge and five of his crew on 'C-Charlie' on 83 Squadron was the thirteenth Lancaster and crew the PFF squadron lost in January, eleven of them on Berlin. 'Charlie', which was one of the first three Lancasters fitted with H2S in November 1943, was attacked from astern by a night-fighter. Pilot Officer Harry Owen Scatchard the flight engineer managed to open the forward escape hatch and bail out. He was captured later.[8]

At Waddington it was 463 Squadron's worst night with four Lancasters out of fourteen attacking Berlin shot down and twenty-eight crewmen killed. 'J-Jig' which included five Aussies (an all-Australian crew – even on an Australian squadron – was a rarity) was believed crashed at Lützkendorf 5 miles north-west of Pölitz. Flight Sergeant Lindsay Samuel Fairclough of Midlands, Western Australia and five of his crew were killed. Australian Flight Sergeant P.K. Giles was taken prisoner. 'G-George' skippered by Australian Pilot Officer George Laurie Messenger was shot down from 21,000 feet by a night-fighter, crashing at Jabel 3 kilometres west-north-west of Wittstock. Messenger and four crew members died; the two survivors were taken prisoner. 'A-Apple' captained by 22-year-old Australian Pilot Officer Douglas Chapman Dunn of Evendale, Adelaide was first off at two minutes past the midnight hour. Flight Sergeant Edward Fitzgibbon Gloster, the 20-year-old Scottish rear gunner of Morayshire, almost immediately reported that his turret was out of action, but Dunn decided to continue on the operation. 'Apple' was attacked near Neuruppin by a night-fighter and only Harry Deakin the mid-upper gunner was able to return fire. Fire broke out in the bomb bay and as the Lancaster went into a shallow dive, Dunn gave the order to abandon the aircraft. Marshall Smith the air bomber was the only survivor and he was taken prisoner. He believed that 'Apple' must have entered into a spin or blew up in the air.

'O-Oboe' captained by Australian Pilot Officer Peter Edward Hanson is believed to have crashed at Repente, a small village north-east of the Grosser Zechlinersee. The pilot and five of his crew were killed; only the flight engineer Sergeant E.A. Hughes survived to be taken prisoner. Hughes was subsequently repatriated in February 1945.

Ten Lancasters on 467 Squadron RAAF had taken off from Waddington with a bomb load of 1 x 4,000lb, 64 x 30lb and 1,200 x 4lb incendiaries. Nothing had been heard from 'C-Charlie' after taking off at 1712 hours. 'Charlie' was skippered by 28-year-old Flying Officer Alexander Douglas Riley, who was described as 'a pukka RAAF member having been employed as clerk of stores at Richmond, NSW before the war'. Born on 27 January 1916 at Granville, Parramatta, New South Wales, he had enlisted on 3 October 1938 at Richmond. Post-war it was established that the aircraft exploded in the target area following a direct hit from flak, killing Riley and five members of his crew.[9]

In a later statement the Canadian air bomber Warrant Officer2 Jan R. Valastin said:

'I was beside Flying Officer Riley in part of the aircraft which received direct fire from the enemy. I was hit but have no definite knowledge as to whether he was hit. A few seconds later the aircraft went into a spin. He was still in his position when I was preparing to bail out and when the aircraft exploded. I was informed two weeks later by an unknown German officer at Dulag Luft that Riley had been killed.'

Valastin returned to the United Kingdom on 20 April 1945 and then returned to Canada. Riley left a widow, Maxine.

Scottish Flight Lieutenant Thomas Henry Blackham, a Lancaster pilot on 50 Squadron who was born and raised in Dunoon, had been to Berlin on the previous two nights and would make five trips to the 'Big City' during his tour. Now, on the night of 30/31 January, he was flying 'S-Sugar'. On the outward flight the aircraft was hit by anti-aircraft fire and the elevators were damaged. Soon afterwards he was attacked by a fighter whose approach had not been seen or detected. The hydraulics and oxygen supply were damaged by shell splinters. Flight Sergeant J. Shuttleworth, the Australian rear gunner from Brisbane, was wounded and slumped unconscious in his turret. The port fin and rudder and the tailplane were shot up in the attack; the hole later found was large enough for a man to crawl through. The mid-upper turret had also been hit and the gunner wounded in the head. They were later to discover the left tyre had burst and a cannon shell had gone through the port tailplane. It also holed the outer petrol tank, but the self-sealing there had held. There were cannon shell holes all along the fuselage, but despite this carnage, Blackham carried on and bombed the target, an act for which he was awarded the Distinguished Flying Cross.

Sergeant Charles Richard Ernest Walton, the 28-year-old flight engineer from Birmingham, went back with an oxygen bottle for the rear gunner who was trapped in his turret. He feebly waved to him, his face covered in blood. He tried to work the dead man's handle to release him but because of the lack of oxygen, Walton kept passing out. The Scottish bomb-aimer, Sergeant Stewart James Godfrey from Paisley, went back to find out what was happening. When he too failed to come back, the WOp, Sergeant Sidney Charles Wilkins went aft, and he too passed out. It was left to the 24-year-old Welsh navigator, Pilot Officer David Gwynfor Jones, to help. He found Godfrey, brought him round and then went back to sort out the engineer, but then Jones too passed out. The WOp, who then came too, gave a running commentary to Blackham: 'The navigator is down; no it's the flight engineer, the navigator is up, no he's down, the engineer is kicking him, yes the 'nav's on his feet….'

Walton came round and Jones got back to his seat. They were now about thirty minutes from the French coast and nearly out of oxygen, so Blackham got the aircraft down to 4,000 feet to cross the coast. They flew over the North Sea with their wheels down; it took the engineer twenty minutes to pump them down by hand. The rear gunner remained trapped until the aircraft was about to land when Sergeant Herbert George Ridd, the 29-year-old mid-upper gunner, also from Wales, hacked the doors free with an axe and pulled him out. Despite a burst tyre they landed safely, although petrol spilled out of ruptured fuel tanks. Shuttleworth had an operation on his damaged eye, as well as on a fractured forearm.

A few nights later 'Tom' Blackham again displayed praiseworthy skill and resolution in a successful attack on Augsburg. Blackham was on his twenty-sixth operation on the night of 3/4 May 1944 when he and his crew were shot down on Mailly-le-Camp soon after clearing the target area. With the aircraft on fire, Blackham fought to keep it flying until all his crew had bailed out safely, after which a sudden explosion knocked him senseless, hurling him through a glass panel. He recovered consciousness to find himself surrounded by flames and jumped clear moments before the aircraft blew up. Six of the crew including David Jones, who was flying as the second pilot, Charles Walton and Herbert Ridd died on the aircraft. Stewart Godfrey bailed out safely and evaded capture. He was assisted by Madame Deguilley of Romilly-sur-Seine before being passed to a Resistance group, but was killed by the Germans on 24 June while in the company of the French Resistance when the Wehrmacht attacked their camp. He has no known grave. For months

Blackham lived and fought with the Maquis until he was sent to Paris for return to England along the 'Comet' line.

In Paris on 27 July he was betrayed by Jacques Desoubrie, the illegitimate son of a Belgian doctor who worked for the Gestapo.[10] After interrogation Blackham was imprisoned in Fresnes prison where he was beaten, stripped of clothing and put under cold showers, surviving on weak sauerkraut soup and sleeping on filthy lice-infested straw. At one point during his two-week incarceration at Fresnes, Blackham was among a group of inmates who faced a firing squad manning machine guns, but for some reason the order to fire was never given. He was sent to the Buchenwald concentration camp where the airmen were fully shaved, starved, denied shoes and for three weeks forced to sleep outside without shelter.[11]

Meanwhile, on their seventh trip to Berlin, there was a remarkable escape for several of the crew on 'O-Oboe' on 550 Squadron at North Killingholme flown by 22-year-old Flying Officer Godfrey Arnold Morrison of Scarborough. About 22 miles north-west of the 'Big City' at 2006 hours, the 25-year-old rear gunner Sergeant John McKenzie reported confidently a Lancaster behind. About a minute later 'Oboe' was attacked by a night-fighter. Morrison immediately took a deep diving turn to port then climbed to port and managed to shake off their attacker. The bombs were then jettisoned on the aiming-point, only to be attacked by a second fighter. 'Oboe' was hit repeatedly by cannon fire and both rear and mid-upper turrets were put out of action and 23-year-old Sergeant Jack Marshall Cantor and McKenzie were killed. The navigator Flying Officer Fred Bennett and flight engineer Sergeant Percy William Wise were on their knees, which was fortunate for them as they saw a stream of tracer passing above their heads along the fuselage, with Wise suffering a slight glancing wound on his shoulder. 'Oboe' became more or less out of control and dived 5,000 feet. Morrison managed to resume control at 14,000 feet.

During the first evasive action Morrison had instructed parachutes to be donned. The front escape hatch was blown off and with it went Bennett's navigation charts. To make matters worse, the controls were damaged and Morrison needed the help of the bomb-aimer, Flying Officer R. Warren, in holding the rudder. Warren momentarily let go of the rudder bar to adjust his mask. The intercom had been put out of action in the attack and Morrison signed with his fingers for Warren to continue to assist. Presumably mistaking the gesture as an order to bail out, the bomb-aimer promptly jettisoned the escape hatch beneath his feet and exited the aircraft. He was subsequently taken prisoner.

'O-Oboe's port outer engine had been stopped and the rear and centre fuselage heavily damaged. Course was set to clear Hanover by about 20 miles, which was difficult as both the DR and P.4 compass were out of action. With the wireless-operator Sergeant Gilbert and the flight engineer giving assistance despite the latter lapsing into unconsciousness for several short periods, Morrison got 'Oboe' to the Eindhoven area at 11,000 feet on three engines where they were subjected to some intense and accurate bursts of heavy flak which inflicted some additional damage. Four bundles of 'Window' were hurriedly dropped, which caused the flak to drop behind and cease. Under the impression that they were over Kent (due to a wrong 'Gee' pulse indication), Morrison circled an airfield with its perimeter and flare lights on for approximately fifteen minutes but they were in the funnels when he realized that they were on the wrong side of the North Sea. It was Overflakkee in Holland!

Assisted by star observations, Sergeant Gilbert organized the working of signals from the dinghy wireless set, but found that the transmitter was only partially serviceable so endeavoured to send SOS messages. Morrison managed to nurse the ailing bomber back to East Anglia and landfall was made at 2,000 feet about 10 miles north of Orfordness. A 'Darkie' call was made and searchlights homed the Lancaster to the emergency airfield at Woodbridge where he needed most of the 1,500 feet runway to bring 'O-Oboe' to a halt. The squadron records later spoke of Morrison's 'exceptionally' good landing in view of the fragile condition of the aircraft, which had to be scrapped. On 9 February 1944 Morrison received an immediate DSO. Posted to 103 Squadron at Elsham Wolds on 24 April 1944, Flight Lieutenant Morrison was lost on the night of 22/23 May on Dortmund when he and his new crew, including American flight engineer Sergeant Hugh Kerr Grant, who was from Philadelphia, were killed. Godfrey Morrison left a widow, E.P. Morrison of Pickering, Yorkshire.

All the crew on the 640 Squadron Lancaster piloted by 22-year-old Pilot Officer Douglas Affleck that crashed near Catfoss Manor were killed. A Halifax crashed at Coltishall with its wheels retracted, the undercarriage being inoperable after combat with a fighter.

Throughout November and December 1943 Pilot Officer Edgar Thompson Jones on 103 Squadron at Elsham Wolds, born in Moose Jaw in 1920, flew eight operations, six of which were to Berlin. On 30/31 January he skippered one of 103 Squadron's Lancasters on the crew's fourth journey to the 'Big City' and was hit on its way to the target by a hail of bullets which suddenly erupted through the floor of the fuselage close behind the rear turret. Flying Officer J.R. Bob Boyes, an American who had enlisted in the RCAF and had become one of hundreds of 'Yanks in Canadian clothing', saw the dark shape of an Fw 190 streak away upwards as it passed by. There had been no warning of an approaching night-fighter, nor had they been caught by searchlights. The damage suffered was extensive. The starboard tail fin and tailplane were riddled with holes and effectively useless. The rear turret was jammed solid and one of the bomb bay doors had been shot away. As Boyes watched, the German fighter turned gracefully and came diving down to attack again. Jones threw the heavy bomber into a turning dive, but the German managed to hit the starboard wing and put one engine out of action. A third attack took place a few minutes later, but this time the German missed the bomber and dived away to be seen no more. Realizing that the bomber would be unable to reach Berlin and return, Jones coolly flew his aircraft towards the known location of some heavy flak batteries and bombed them instead. He then turned for home, nursing the aircraft through the skies across the North Sea to return to base.

At Warboys sixteen Lancasters on 156 PFF Squadron took off for Berlin. Some were loaded with five 2,000lb Heavy Capacity bombs for their role as 'supporters'; others with 1 x 4 red/green flares; 2 x TIs, green L/B; 2 x TIs, green; 1 x flare steady and a 4,000lb Heavy Capacity 'cookie' and four 1,000lb Medium Capacity bombs similar to 405 'Vancouver' Squadron's blind marker illuminators. Three hours later two of the Lancasters returned with mechanical problems. The others were over the target at around 2020 hours. 'Z-Zebra', captained by 28-year-old New Zealand Warrant Officer John Edward Rule of Auckland City, was shot down and crashed in the Noordoostpolder, just north of where the village of Marknesse now stands. Rule, navigator Flight Sergeant Kenneth Richard Ball, flight engineer Sergeant Edward Arthur Shorter and the two air gunners, Sergeants John Johnstone Sloan and George Albert Race, were killed. Sergeants Walter W. Cottam and P. Coyne, who was blown out of the aircraft, were captured in Antwerp on 7 August and taken into captivity.

'W-William' piloted by Warrant Officer P. Batman was shot down by a night-fighter operating over the target area. Four of the crew were killed. Batman and two of his crew survived and were taken prisoner. Nothing was heard from 'Q-Queenie' on 106 Squadron after take-off from Metheringham at 1719 hours and it was believed that the Lancaster crashed into the North Sea. The body of the pilot, 26-year-old Pilot Officer Kenneth Herbert William Kirkland of Bellingen, New South Wales was washed ashore five weeks later on 5 March on Nordstrand on Vlieland in the Dutch Frisian Island chain. The other six crew members have no known grave and their names are commemorated on the Memorial to the Missing at Runnymede.

At Spilsby 207 Squadron lost three Lancasters too. There were no survivors on 'V-Victor' flown by Pilot Officer Arthur Moore. 'K-King' piloted by Pilot Officer Richardson Dick Burnet was clearing the target area at 19,500 feet after 'bombs away' when a night-fighter raked the Lancaster with cannon fire. The port wing caught alight and the order to abandon was given. Sergeant Arthur Pulman the rear gunner was killed. Burnet and the rest of the crew parachuted to safety and were taken into captivity. No word had been heard from 'M-Mother' since taking off from Spilsby at 1715 hours. The only information came later when notification was received that Flight Sergeant Eric William Devere Downey, the wireless-operator, was a PoW. The remains of the rest of the crew had been found, but these were not sufficiently individually identifiable to go in separate named graves, so they were buried together in a collective grave in the Berlin War Cemetery.

Stan Carter dutifully posted the cardboard carton containing Stan Chalkin's effects to his mother, Mrs Kate Elizabeth Chalkin in Tonbridge.

During January 1944 Bomber Command as a whole had lost more than 300 four-engined bombers and more than 2,000 air crew plus another 40 or more aircraft to crashes in England. No. 6 Group alone had lost forty-eight aircraft and crews, the equivalent of two entire squadrons. The Group had become active a few minutes after midnight on 1 January 1943 when airmen of eight RCAF bomber squadrons in England had wished each other a 'Happy New Year'. Some of the Canadians on RAF squadrons transferred to the Canadian squadrons; others, like Canadian navigator Pilot Officer (later Flight Lieutenant) J. Ralph Wood DFC from New Brunswick who had flown a trip to Berlin on a Whitley on 7 September 1941, preferred to stay with the RAF. 'We got along fine with the Limeys and besides, we thought that where we were "on loan", we might get away with a little more murder and less discipline.'

The vast majority of Canadians objected to being referred to as 'colonials'. Canada was not a colony but a Dominion, they said. Canadians behaved well;

Canadians were gentlemen; Canadians were not crude. As Ralph Wood was once heard to remark: 'I thought about that goddam 'Butcher' Harris, the deserved nickname of the RAF chief of Bomber Command. He didn't give a damn how many men he lost as long as he was pounding the shit out of the Germans. He was willing to sacrifice Englishmen as well as Canadians. It all depended on the individual.'[12]

Fellow Canadian Pilot Officer Jack Bonet, an air bomber on 35 Squadron, had a different view: 'Bomber Command was a marvellous experience. The spirit, everything; it was all these.' Bonet had been shot down on Leipzig on 3/4 December 1943 and taken prisoner. 'On the way to Leipzig on a train we followed the Ruhr partway there. You know, we didn't see a single house left standing for a hundred miles. Everything was flattened! We clobbered the Germans! We really did.'

By the end of the war no fewer than 814 aircraft and 4,272 air crew members (or almost 75 per cent) in 6 Group were lost.[13] Many men of Bomber Command did complete their tour, but of the 10,000 Australians who enlisted for service in RAF Bomber Command, 3,486 were killed in action and 546 died in training accidents.

Bad weather held up flying for two weeks after the raid on Berlin on 30/31 January. During the month the Nachtjagd had scored an all-time monthly record of 308 Bomber Command aircraft shot down but the Reich defences were in need of an overhaul. Though I Jagdkorps claimed at least 223 victories (including 114 during the three Berlin raids on 29 January-1 February), it had lost 55 aircraft and crews, which reduced its front-line strength to 179 operational aircraft and crews by 31 January. It was clear too that new British tactics and new countermeasures would be necessary before a resumption of raids deep into Germany.

Replacement crews and aircraft were on their way and existing crews were told that they would not be required for operations for nearly two weeks. The moon period gave a respite for the weary crews; a time to complete all the maintenance on the aircraft; a time to go on leave and forget about the 'Big City' for a while. A time to take stock, to count the losses and lick the wounds before the nightmare began again. In the meantime, the bomber crews let their hair down at every opportunity. On nights of stand-down it meant another party:

'During the periods of stand-down,' wrote 'Jonah' Jones, one of the Intelligence officers at Kirmington, 'there were frequently ENSA shows on the Station, some of which were of excellent quality, some not so good and usually with completely or relatively unknown artists. However, the audience could always be relied upon to make up for what was lacking in the shows and to liven up the proceedings. I remember one really classic example of crude but absolutely shattering humour. A sketch was being performed and one of the actors came onto the stage to discover the 'body' of a somewhat scantily-clad female on the floor, supposedly murdered. He wrung his hands and said, 'Oh, dear, what shall I do?' and a voice from the back of the darkened hall shouted: 'Stuff her while she's still warm.' The whole place just erupted in an uproar of laughter. How those poor artists were able to carry on afterwards I shall never know. I was still laughing when the artists were entertained in the Mess afterwards. Mess parties were also held on occasions and, although I was a non-drinker, I always went along to the impromptu parties (I always tried to dodge the official ones).

'Usually the parties started off quite mildly with such antics as the 'Muffin Man' walking on the ceiling and some 'debagging', but when the sounds of *Goodnight, Ladies* began to issue forth, this was the signal for any WAAF (or other service females) to remain at their own risk. It was at this stage that the really bawdy songs started to come out. The songs progressed from *I touched her on the knee* to *The Ball of Kirriemuir, The Big Wheel, I stuck my finger in a woodpecker's hole*, etc. and the *Zoological Song*. In this song, which was usually rendered by one particular officer, various animals of the zoo were defined in rather bawdy terms. For example, one of the more innocuous ones was the *Laughing Hyena*: 'Ladies and Gentlemen, this is the laughing hyena. He only copulates once a year, so what the hell has he to laugh about?' Disgusting, are you saying? It might have been at some other time and under different circumstances, but remember that these young men just in their twenties (and some even younger) were always living under the threat of a violent death, severe mutilation or a PoW cage. I have conducted briefings on many occasions for 200 or more aircrew members, knowing that if things went badly that night, a percentage of them would be missing from the Mess the next morning, not necessarily all dead but certainly some of them would be. They were afraid – and so was I when I went with them on operational flights – but letting their hair down was their way of hiding their fear and making sure that nobody noticed their fear. Aircrew were not judged by their bawdy songs and party frivolity – they were judged by their results and their actions in the face of the dangers which faced them in the darkened skies over enemy territory. They were a great crowd and I was proud to serve among them and to fly with them.'[14]

At Kirmington crews were also actively encouraged to visit the library; the Intelligence Library: 'Some of the Security and Safety posters displayed in the Intelligence Library were not only very ingenious but were also very amusing and designed to catch the eye,' wrote 'Jonah' Jones. 'My favourite example was that of a navigation poster which portrayed a tiny blushing navigator being led by the hand by a near-naked, well-endowed, gorgeous blonde, with the caption "A Heavenly Body will always get you home", a plug to encourage navigators to keep up their astronavigation. Another poster, one of the famous "Prudence" series, showed a gorgeous blonde in a scanty evening gown with an air crew member wearing an incorrectly secured parachute harness. The caption read: "Prudence relies on her straps to save her modesty; why not secure yours correctly to save your life?" These posters were very popular and extremely useful, but only if they were changed periodically. We always encouraged crews to try their hand at slogans which could be displayed in the Intelligence Library. Some of them could not as the WAAF Officer and the WAAF clerks frequently tidied up and assisted with the display material and they were considered not quite broadminded enough for some of the slogans.'

As far as 460 Squadron RAAF was concerned, parties were normally in the back room at the 'Marquis of Granby' in Binbrook village where Rene Trevor sang for the boys and played the piano. The tradition was that each man who completed their tour was held aloft while he wrote his name on the ceiling of the back room. Rene had been left to run the 'Granby' with the help of a staff of seven ever since her husband had been called up for the RAF and sent to the Middle East in 1940. She sewed on buttons and decorations, mended jackets and cooked meals for the young men. Sausage, two eggs and toast cost 1s and 6d [8 pence], or at the weekends, a full Sunday roast could be had for 2s 3d [11 pence].

Anne, the landlady's young daughter, proved to be very popular with the Aussies and they would often ask her to sing to them. When she was 3 she had run through from the bar screaming 'Mummy, mummy, the Germans have arrived!' The little girl had never heard an Australian accent before. Her pet donkey was tethered at the back of the pub and one night some of the boys got a bit tight and they took the donkey back with them to the sergeants' mess and painted the animal Air Force blue. They brought it back next day. Quite apologetic they were too! On another occasion the sergeants' mess was turned into an impromptu polo arena. Cycles were horses, brushes mallets and a teacup was used as a ball. The following day there was not a surviving cup in the mess. The piano needed replacing at least once a fortnight because of the amount of beer poured into it.

When Liberty buses were arranged to Cambridge (where the 'Yanks' wanted to know the best place to pick up girls and were told the 'Green Man', 'The Bull' and The English Speaking Union, but the consensus was that for real sure-fire 'nookie', the Sunday afternoon tea dance at the Regent couldn't be beaten), or Peterborough, the 'Golden Lion' at St. Ives or the 'Pike and Eel' at Holywell, which did their usual roaring trade as Warboys air crew met friends and rivals from Wyton.[15] 'The Saracen's Head' at Lincoln, the 'George Hotel' at Grantham, the 'White Hart' at Newark and 'Betty's Bar' in York were popular with RAF airmen. 'Eddy' Collyer, a RAF flight engineer on 425 'Alouette' Squadron RCAF recalled: 'In York we often met old pals from other squadrons who had aged physically in a matter of weeks. I think we were all aware that none of us might complete a tour.'[16] On average crews had a one in three chance of completing a tour of operations of thirty sorties. Many didn't. Girls were often seen waiting outside the white-tiled entrance to the Savoy Picture House on a corner in Victoria Street, Grimsby waiting for Binbrook air crew that had gone missing the night before.

Chapter Fourteen

A 'Yank' in Bomber Command

'Listen, you guys. This is a milk-run and we'll have some fun. What we do, we make the bomb run and then we go down real low and shoot the shit outa the sons of bitches.'

First Lieutenant Lail K. Dawley USAAF.

First Lieutenant Lail K. Dawley, a married man from Detroit, Michigan on attachment to the Royal Air Force silently appeared out of a thick pea-soup fog that blanketed South Yorkshire. It was December 1943 and the WAAF driver sent to meet him was huddled in the cold of the open jeep. She heard the sounds of revelry as the pubs closed and knew it was after ten o'clock. Due to the fog the train bringing the American officer north to 1656 Conversion Unit at Lindholme near Doncaster was hours late. Dawley had been born on 18 April 1918 in Manhattan, Kansas. The USAAC, in which he had enlisted in 1940, had regarded him as too old for fighters and too short-limbed for bombers and he had become a temporary Canadian to find a way into the war. Having obtained his wings, Lail Dawley had been accepted back into what by then had become the USAAF, which promptly loaned him to the RAF; he now received as much pay as any four of his British colleagues put together and was not subject to the King's Regulations and Air Council Instructions by which their lives were circumscribed.

As Dawley's jeep eased slowly through the fog, it was hailed by six revellers on foot facing a 6-mile hike back to Lindholme. Over protestations of the driver, they clambered aboard and urged the WAAF to 'press on'. Bomb-aimer Mike Allen, a 20-year-old Yorkshireman, perched himself on the bonnet and gave directions to the driver, 'LEFT, LEFT' … STEADY…R-I-G-H-T', standard bomb-aimer jargon for guiding a pilot to a target. 'BACK A BIT!' shouted 'Jock' Stephens, the mid-upper gunner. The others laughed as though the joke were an original. The 23-year-old 'Red' Redshaw was the navigator; Joe Pickering, aged 18, was the flight engineer. Joe Williams, 20, was the wireless-operator and Edward Arthur Percival was the rear gunner. A little older than the others, Ted was married to Maud Lillian Percival of Barking in Essex. Michael Victor Allen had met a 'Georgia Peach' while under training in the Southern States, attempting – and, like many others, failing – to become a pilot. Dawley, unused to English humour, took comfort from the .45 automatic cradled in its shoulder holster under his coat. Pilot and crew were informally introduced for the first time. The Fates chuckled at their deviousness. Mike, Allen and 'Jock' were scheduled for court-martial hearings the next morning and had been confined to quarters, but they had crawled under the fence and hitched a ride to town where they had been given a send-off party by the other members of their crew.

Mike and 'Jock's court-martial hearings were the result of an earlier confrontation when they had left a sergeants' dance at midnight. Scheduled to leave for a squadron the following day, the crew had discovered that their pilot had chickened out at the last moment. Overnight he had decided that he could not be a party to bombing 'defenceless women and children'. He had been relieved of duty. This was the second time the crew had been on the verge of getting into action. Their first skipper had a nervous breakdown and froze at the controls on their final checkout flight. It took the combined efforts of the crew to bring the bomber down to a safe but somewhat unorthodox landing.

After leaving the dance the commanding officer's Hillman Minx staff car stood invitingly in Mike and 'Jock's path. The CO and his adjutant were inside paying their respects to the latest graduating class. 'Jock' noted that the CO's dress cap with 'scrambled egg' insignia lay on the seat. The keys were in the ignition. Between the sergeants' mess and the WAAF quarters was a footpath bordered by a white picket fence. While 'Jock' donned the CO's coat and cap, Mike aimed the Minx down the narrow path. The oversize hat hung over 'Jock's ears. The coat dragged on the ground. Sweat rolled down his swarthy face in rivulets. 'Stand by your beds for inspection!' roared Mike, flipping on the lights. Awakened from deep sleep, the WAAFs automatically obeyed, seeing only the insignia of authority. As 'Jock' weaved down the line of beds, murmurs of disbelief became screams of hysteria. The two were bodily ejected.

Undaunted and thirsty from their efforts, they next headed for the officers' mess. It was a repeat performance with instant recognition. After allowing them to quench their thirst, they were sent on their way with admonishments to return the car and trappings to the spot where they had found them. The car, as yet unmissed, was returned. Mike and 'Jock' set off again, on foot this time.

The parade ground was immaculate. With a fresh coat of tarmac, it had just that afternoon received its final embellishment: white lines to identify various assembly-points and gamin areas. The striper, still primed, stood invitingly in their path. A giant egg-faced Kilroy in the centre seemed appropriate to the occasion. The white line then veered off diagonally in the direction of the officers' billets.

Their late pilot, now confined to his quarters in disgrace, was not alone. Mike and 'Jock' pounded on his door. Faces appeared at other doors to see what the ruckus was about. Unable to quiet them, the pilot, now in tears and stark naked, ran down the hall and out into the night. 'Jock' entered the room to find a damsel truly in distress and shivering under the bed. He promptly passed out on the floor. Mike, doubled over from uncontrolled laughter, leaned too far over the stair rail and fell to the floor below.

The culprits were not hard to trace. Charges were filed from all directions and the two confined to quarters pending formal hearings.

Next morning as he read the personnel files of the crew members assigned to him, Dawley recalled snatches of conversation from the previous night. It soon became apparent that what he had inherited was what he feared the most. This was the crew that Lieutenant Dawley had to face. His pep-talk brought murmurs of scorn and 'now we get a bloody "Yank".'[1] However, the American differed from previous captains of the jinx crew in that, when flying, he insisted upon carrying a loaded .45 revolver in a shoulder holster and in that, far from suffering a breakdown or feeling qualms about his conscience, he had attempted – unsuccessfully – to loop the loop in the Lancaster on their final training flight. In the days that followed, Dawley gained grudging recognition from his newfound crew. In record time he checked out on the Lancaster and proved to be an able pilot despite his size. Shortly they were assigned their own plane, 'V-Victor', which they would fly to their future squadron. On the final checkout flight, Dawley took the plane to 20,000 feet. Putting the nose down in a power dive, he pulled the stick back into his stomach in an attempt to loop the heavy plane. The Lancaster stood vertically on its tail, shuddered and fell forward. That night, for the first time, he was invited to join the rest of the crew to celebrate their posting to 12 Squadron at Wickenby in 1 Group RAF Bomber Command. Departure was delayed while 'V-Victor' underwent replacement of wing rivets that had popped from the strain of a manoeuvre for which it had not been designed.

Upon landing at the base, Dawley was told that a 'maximum effort' was scheduled for that night. He was instructed to have his crew report for briefing at 1100 hours in case they should be needed to fill vacant slots on other crews. As the curtains were pulled back there was a groan, 'Berlin again'. All but Mike Allen were assigned to other crews.[2]

'Losses in the Battle of Berlin had been averaging about 6 per cent of late,' wrote Clayton Moore, 'and this figure was disturbingly high for anyone hoping to complete a tour. There was no question of the Germans not having adapted to the effect that 'Window' had given earlier. For one thing, they had changed the wavelength of their radar systems, so that we were now obliged to drop strips measuring almost twice the size of the originals. Although the chop rate was steadily mounting, so too was the degree of success we were having in hitting the enemy where it hurt. The techniques being developed by the innovative Pathfinder Force were beginning to show promise and a lot of crews were showing an interest in joining AVM Bennett's "Blue-eyed Boys".'

'Bill Siddle had called a crew meeting to propose that they might also make the move to the Pathfinders. 'The vote,' wrote Clayton Moore, 'went in favour of the proposal and the application was lodged the next day. Little time was wasted in processing it and acceptance was confirmed almost immediately. PFF would be an entirely new ball game. Emphasis would centre on a crew's ability to navigate within precise limits, with timing to within a tolerance of plus or minus ten seconds at the target being the maximum error allowed. We also learned that each member of the crew would receive an automatic bump up in rank on completion of the training.'

The Berlin offensive was supposed to have recommenced on Sunday, 13 February when 'Bomber' Harris decided to mount a maximum effort on the 'Big City', but the operation was cancelled because of bad weather. The operation was laid on for the next day, but heavy snowfalls caused the operation to be cancelled again.

It was not until Tuesday the 15th that the Battle of Berlin could re-start. This time the German capital was the target for 891 aircraft, 561 of which were Lancasters, the first time that more than 500 Lancasters had been dispatched thus far in the war. The rest of the battle order consisted of 314 Halifaxes and 16 Mosquitoes, the increased number of Halifaxes being due to the return of 420 'Snowy Owl'

Squadron and 424 'Tiger' Squadron from the Middle East. (Another Canadian squadron – 425 'Alouette' RCAF – would be ready with its Lancasters for the next raid.) When diversion and support operations are taken into account, the total effort for the night totalled 1,070 aircraft. Altogether, this was the fifteenth time in the series of attacks on Berlin during which more than 8,300 aircraft were dispatched.

After leaving Bardney for 83 Squadron PFF Bill Siddle's crew had found RAF Station Wyton to be a large peacetime airfield with excellent runways and accommodation and Clayton Moore at once became aware of the multi-national element within the air crews that made up 83 Squadron:

'As a result of this, there was ever present a businesslike atmosphere, yet I found conditions around the flights and in the Mess to be relaxed and unassuming. Everybody just got on with the job and there was ever-present an air of friendliness between the ranks that was not to be found on most other squadrons and stations that I had served on.

'We were issued with badges to signify our membership of the PFF force. This took the form of the brass albatross worn as a cap badge by commissioned officers, but was to be worn by us on the left breast pocket flap of the Number One Blues uniform. Prior to receipt of the badge, we were required to sign a declaration stating that we would not permit ourselves to be photographed while wearing it and that it would not be carried or worn during operational flying.'[3]

Bill Siddle's crew were down to fly their first PFF op that night, in 'N-Nan': 'The flight was to be the first of six trips as "Supporters", wrote Clayton Moore, 'and it was with some trepidation we learned at the briefing that our target was again to be the "Big City". Because we were to go in with the leaders of the pack, our take-off was set for the early time of 2130 hours and our load would be made up entirely of high-explosive and incendiary bombs. All things considered, there was no denying the fact that we were being thrown in at the deep end for this one.'

The operation would be Flight Sergeant Kenneth Patrick ('Pat') Doyle's crew's eighth visit to the 'Big City'. They had led a nomadic existence since coming together at 1667 HCU Faldingworth in 1943. The crew completed just eight ops on 625 Squadron at Kelstern before getting the chance of transferring to 7 PFF Squadron at Oakington on 1 January, but they had hardly settled in when they were posted to at Warboys near Chatteris in Huntingdonshire to help make good recent losses on 156 PFF Squadron.

'Pat' Doyle was a Londoner. He and five of his crew were all RAF. Flight Sergeant Douglas Keller Green, the 32-year-old wireless-operator, was from Golders Green in Middlesex. Flight Sergeant Syd Richardson the flight engineer had been brought up between Hayfield and New Mills in Derbyshire. He recalled that over Berlin early in their tour 'Pat' Doyle called navigator Dave Winlow forward to have a look at the target. Winlow came up, took in the bomb-bursts and flames, the cascading markers, the flak, the tracers looping upwards, the fingering searchlights, the shapes of other Lancasters, some so close…. 'Jesus Christ!' he muttered and went back to his cubby-hole, after which he kept his curtain closed and that was the way it was staying. From what Richardson heard, 'he was not the only "nav" to do his tour-and-a-half like that.'

Fred Astle, the 29-year-old bomb-aimer whose wife Dulcie lived in Swindon in Wiltshire, had no such concerns about leaving his position in the aircraft and would come forward when he needed to arm the bombs or man the front turret. Sergeant Eric Fletcher was the crew's original mid-upper gunner.[4] Flight Sergeant Geoffrey Charles Chapman-Smith the rear-gunner had been born at Marrickville, Sydney on 3 February 1919 and was fondly referred to as a 'colonial' and a 'rear-end-Charlie' by the crew. Sometimes they were known in RAF parlance as 'rear gunners' but never 'tail gunners' which was the American term.[5] On 2 December 'Smithy' had shot down a Ju 88 on his first operation on Berlin.

At Breighton on 15 February one of the Halifax crews on the 78 Squadron battle order was skippered by Sergeant Jack Boswell, his fourth operation of the war. Born on 27 July 1923 in Dargaville, known as the kumara (sweet potato) capital of New Zealand on the North Island, his parents were English ex-pats, Florence and Frank Boswell from Norfolk. Frank had become a dairy farmer in New Zealand and survived the bloody 1915 ANZAC campaign in Gallipoli. The growing depression during the 1920s hit the family dairy farm hard and they came back to England when Jack was aged 2. He went to Norwich Grammar School and the Technical College there before enrolling at the University of London, only to see his studies interrupted, like so many, by the outbreak of war.

He and his crew had arrived at Wressle railway station in Yorkshire on 30 November. Although training continued, while on the squadron there was very little of the 'bull' encountered at some of their training stations. On one occasion when the crew walked along the perimeter track they were passed by a very senior visiting officer in his be-flagged car. Receiving no salute, the officer ordered his driver to drive around again and stop by the airmen. On opening the door to berate them for their lack of discipline, he was met by 'Thank you very much for the lift, sir' and the airmen sat down beside him! Distances between the hangars, aircraft dispersal bays and flight HQ buildings were far-flung and without a cycle it was a long walk around the perimeter track.

On the Berlin operation on 29 December 1943 Jack Boswell's crew had bombed the target from a height of 19,000 feet on four green flares. One night the other crew in his Nissen hut was reported missing and the SPs [Service Police] had the unpleasant task of collecting all their belongings and forwarding them to the next of kin. With a half-empty hut Boswell's crew was moved to other accommodation on the site. Whenever there was a stand-down, some of the crew would head for Selby (a town that had thirty-six pubs), York or Leeds or to one of the local pubs in the Breighton area. A few enjoyed a pint in the mess, played snooker, darts or 'Shove Ha'penny' and at weekends a dance may have been held in one of the messes.

Take-off was timed for 1723 hours. This would be the largest force sent to Berlin to date and the largest non-1,000 bomber force dispatched to any target. The previous record was 826 aircraft, which included Stirlings and Wellingtons sent to Dortmund on the night of 23/24 May 1943. A series of diversion and support operations was mounted. Chief among these, 23 'Oboe' Mosquitoes were to attack 5 night-fighter airfields in Holland, 43 Stirlings and 4 Pathfinder Halifaxes would lay mines in Kiel Bay and 24 Lancasters of 8 Group would attack Frankfurt-on-Oder.

On 625 Squadron at Kelstern, Sergeant Bill Ashurst's eleventh Lancaster operation began badly when, due to a mechanical fault, 'Y-Yorker' took off twenty-five minutes later than the other aircraft at 1725 hours. At Leconfield Ken Handley, a British flight engineer on 466 Squadron RAAF, prepared for his first Halifax operation. He would find the trip less frightening than he expected. There were no searchlights owing to 10/10ths cloud base, 2,000 feet tops and 6,000 feet over the target and only light flak below them. They bombed at 22,300 feet and came off the target at 24,000 feet. There were numerous fighter flares around the target and on the return trip and evasive action was taken, but their luck held and they had no combats with fighters. Handley, however, endured a tense last half-hour on the seven-hour, thirty-minute flight when No. 4 tank iced up and they had 'no joy' with it for ten minutes.

Flight Lieutenant Kenneth H. Berry DFM on 103 Squadron at Elsham Wolds was on the battle order to fly his seventh operation on his second tour in 'A-Apple'. The 20-year-old pilot from Walthamstow, Essex had completed twenty-nine ops on his first tour from September 1942 to the end of January 1943. In all that time he had not visited Berlin once, but tonight he would be making his third trip to the 'Big City', having flown two ops to Berlin in January. His crew was very experienced and included 22-year-old Flying Officer K. Wilcock of Stretford, Leicestershire who had been his flight engineer on his first crew. Squadron Leader Harold Lester Lindo DFC acted as bomb-aimer. Born in Kingston, Jamaica on 6 July 1917 he had enlisted in the RCAF in June 1940 and had later made his home in Northwood, Middlesex. Lindo first joined 103 Squadron in the summer of 1941 and he had survived a ditching in a Wellington. Spending a second spell on the squadron in 1942 as bombing leader, he was now on his third stint on the squadron.

A Halifax crew of flight sergeants on 51 Squadron at Snaith skippered by 20-year-old 'Johnny' Hollander, a diminutive Cockney pilot known to his friends as 'Dutch', were flying their first operation with a new navigator. The crew had only completed two operations and had been badly mauled on both occasions. On the first trip their Halifax had been severely damaged by flak and 'Dutch' did well to make an emergency landing on a wire-mesh runway at Gatwick. On their second trip they were attacked by night-fighters and were fortunate to struggle back to base. They had been briefed for their third raid and were actually standing on the concrete dispersal ready to climb into the Halifax when the navigator broke down. He refused to fly on the grounds that 'this is going to be the trip when we all get "the chop". No way will we be coming back from this one.' 'Dutch' and the others argued and pleaded with him, but nothing would persuade him to enter the aircraft. In the end, reluctantly, they had to call up control and explain the situation.

As the other Halifaxes had taken off for Germany, the crew had stood disconsolately in the darkness below the aircraft and the CO arrived. Their comrade was put under arrest and taken away. He later faced a court martial, was stripped of his rank and disappeared from their lives. Hollander's crew were returned to the Heavy Conversion Unit to await the arrival of a new navigator who went by the name of 'Ben' Bennett, who had been recalled from leave to join them. They were given three or four cross-countries at the conversion unit before rejoining the squadron. Even then, it was over a month before they were considered ready for operations.

For the first time Clayton Moore was seated inside the modified and greatly-improved FN 120 tail-gun turret. Although the space available to him was still somewhat limited, the layout of the Perspex canopy was much improved, thus making possible a less restricted view of the sky around and this had been further enhanced by the removal of most of the Perspex from the front of the turret. He had been issued with the standard pilot's seat pack parachute, so the small seat cushion (normally a feature of the FN 20) had been removed, together with the minute piece of armour plate intended as a means of affording some degree of protection to the 'family jewels'. Because there were within the air gunners' fraternity some who complained that the plate was not in any case of sufficient dimension to give complete protection, its removal was not entirely regretted:

'The outward flight proved no more traumatic than any of the previous Berlin raids in which I had been involved. Again, weather conditions were a problem, mainly because of the cold and we were forced to come down below our designated operational height when condensation trails were seen to be forming behind us. These were a dead giveaway to any fighter that happened upon them and both Gerry and I had strict orders to report these to the skipper whenever they appeared, whereupon Bill would bring us down a hundred feet or so. I was also having problems with my microphone due to the condensation of my breath. This quickly turned to ice, thereby making conversation with the rest of the crew almost impossible. Because of the importance of me being able to give clear orders during a possible attack, I had to dislodge the ice at frequent intervals during the flight by giving my oxygen mask a sharp rap with my gloved hand. At a later date, the vexing problem was to be overcome by the extension of the heated clothing to include a small heater within the mask itself, an improvement which was to earn the gratitude of many.'[6]

'Dutch' Hollander's crew crossed the North Sea at only 1,500 feet, climbing to 18,000 after passing over Denmark. It was while crossing the Baltic that things went wrong. 'Dutch' came on the intercom:

'What's the fuel situation, Douggie?'

'Time to change tanks, Skip,' replied the flight engineer.

'OK. Go ahead.'

Douglas Parkinson made his way amidships, intending to switch over the fuel cocks located under the rest-bed. He re-plugged his oxygen tube into the nearest point. Within moments of his departure all four engines started to cough and splutter and then suddenly cut dead and the Halifax started to drop like a stone.

'What the hell shall we do?' someone yelled.

'We can always glide!' suggested 'Ben' fatuously.

'Get back and see what's happening, Tommy, quick as you bloody can!' ordered 'Dutch', wrestling with the controls.

Tommy MacCarthy, a Geordie from Wallsend, scrambled up the steeply-diving Halifax until he reached Douggie who was lying unconscious on the floor. Although Tommy was the bomb-aimer he knew exactly what to do. Thrusting his hands under the rest-bed he adjusted the fuel controls. The response was immediate as fuel flooded back into the starved engines. The Halifax came out of its plunge and resumed level flight.

They had lost thousands of feet in a matter of seconds. 'Ben' was busy with his calculations:

'Not a chance of getting back to 18,000 feet by the time we reach Berlin, Skipper, not with this bomb load.'

'What do you suggest, 'Ben'?'

'Only one thing to do. Sticking to our 180 mph indicated airspeed and pressing on at our present height of 10,000 feet, we'll reach the target on time.'

'And have the whole of Main Force dropping their bombs on us from a great height. Sounds healthy!'

'No bloody option, I'm afraid.'

They bombed on time with thousands of incendiaries and hundreds of 4,000lb high-explosive bombs hurtling past them from above and then came all the way back at 10,000 feet.

'We were routed via a point east of Denmark and then direct to Berlin,' remembered 'Tom' Forster on Brian Lydon's crew on Lancaster 'L-for-London' on 103 Squadron who were flying their fourteenth op from Elsham Wolds. All went well until they ran into fighter and ack-ack activity close to the island of Bornholm on the southerly flight to Berlin. There was a tremendous explosion and the gunners reported an attack by an Fw 190. Paul Collings the mid-upper gunner and Alfred John 'Jackie' Bristow, the Cockney rear gunner who was from Bethnal Green in the East End of London, must have wondered if they would make it back and sink their customary pint in the 'Oswald' in Scunthorpe!

'During violent evasion action,' remembered Forster, 'Brian Lydon reported he had been hit as splinters cut the side of his face and his right arm. The flight engineer then reported that No.1 petrol tank on the starboard side had been hit and the petrol gauge recorded N/W, so we had lost a huge quantity of petrol. It was decided that we could not reach the target and the bombs were dropped over the Bornholm defences and Brian asked for a course to bring us back to base. I had not until then switched on the H2S as Brian believed, correctly, the H2S enabled the enemy to home on to the Lancaster. I immediately switched on the H2S and could clearly see the outline of the islands and coast beneath us and gave Brian a rough westerly course to fly, but I could not just identify any feature on the map. Then I realised that in the evasive action the DR compass had been "toppled" and the H2S picture was upside down. I corrected this by re-orientating my compass repeater to point north at the top. I was then able to map-read my way home, avoiding known areas of peak activity, Heligoland etc.

'Before we made the decision to return to base we discussed, over the intercom, the question of whether we had enough fuel to cross the North Sea and whether or not Brian was fit to fly the plane. I suggested we might make for neutral Sweden and become interned, but Paul Collings and "Jackie" Bristow were dead against this as it would mean goodbye to their pint in the "Oswald"! "Ben" Benroy the engineer felt we had sufficient reserve of petrol to make it back to England.'

There was some bad flak and a small amount of icing but to most of the bombers it was merely a quiet flip over complete cloud cover. The cloak of cloud lying over the land continued all the way to the target where the tips rose to between 15,000 and 17,000 feet. Nine Lancasters and six Halifaxes were acting as primary 'blind markers', dropping their flares two minutes before the arrival of eleven special Lancasters equipped with H2S acting as backers-up. They dropped their markers at the rate of one every two minutes and were followed by three Lancasters and eleven Halifaxes flying in pairs. After these came come the visual 'backers-up'; 20 Lancasters dropping flares at double that rate and their 'supporters', 58 Lancasters and the Halifaxes and finally, the Main Force, divided into 5 waves of an average number of 140 aircraft. 'Window' was dropped throughout the attack until supplies were exhausted. The aiming point was marked by red and green stars and the 'blind backers-up' were ordered to keep it marked throughout the raid with green TIs.

One of the 'supporters' was the Lancaster on 83 Squadron flown by Bill Siddle: 'This was the first time we had gone in with the primary marker aircraft,' wrote Clayton Moore. 'And we found the German capital unusually quiet as we began our run-up. As on previous occasions, there was almost total cloud cover in the area, but this time there was nothing to indicate that the city had a defence to offer. Darkness reigned, there being no searchlight beams to be seen anywhere in the area and this, together with the marked absence of a flak barrage, led one to believe that we were nowhere near our intended objective. I was later to learn that the Jerries often "played possum" in this way, hoping that the Pathfinder crews would go on to drop their marker flares over one of the many decoy targets that had been laboriously and skilfully constructed in the vicinity of the more important German cities. Berlin was not without one of these and there was no doubt that more than a few crews had in the past been fooled into dropping their markers on these "cardboard" cities. But our marker crews were not to be duped this time. The H2S set was behaving well and Dick Lodge the navigator was confident that we were on track and on time. We already had the bomb doors open when we saw the first target indicators go down just ahead of us. That was the signal for all hell to break loose around us.

'Suddenly the city beneath took on the visual impact that we had all come to expect of it. On came the scores of searchlights as if by the throwing of a single switch and I again sensed the feeling of naked exposure as the sky around and beneath us became flooded with the all-revealing illumination that I hated so intensely. In almost the same instant, the flak barrage opened up with deadly accuracy and I again heard the familiar "whump" of the shells bursting near us and the metallic rattle of the shrapnel against the aircraft as we flew steadily onwards on the bombing run. This was the part of a raid that we all feared the most. There was nothing we could do except sit it out and hope to God that our luck stayed with us. Dead astern, somebody's luck let them down and their aircraft suddenly exploded in a ball of white heat and coloured marker flares, indicating that it had been a Pathfinder. Off to starboard, two others were going down, one in flames, the other with no sign of fire but apparently out of control as it spiralled down in the direction of the opaque cloud tops. In all probability the controls had been damaged, or maybe the pilot had been killed or injured. Whatever the cause, I was too busy to reflect on it. I had seen a twin-engined fighter silhouetted against the clouds as it passed from port of starboard a couple of hundred feet beneath us, so the situation required that I exercise the utmost vigilance, otherwise we too might join our unfortunate friends in their death dive.

'At last the bombs were released and the snapshot had been taken for posterity, thus freeing us for evasive action as we winged over to head for the comforting darkness beyond the city. There now lay ahead of us the 300-mile flight over enemy territory that would take us out across Holland to the comparative safety of the North Sea. Indications were that it wasn't going to be an easy trip. Even though we were in the forefront of the attacking force, the German fighters were already in the bomber stream, as was evinced by the number of aircraft we could see going down on either side of us and astern.'

The attack, which lasted for thirty-nine minutes, was remarkable for its precision, though no glimpse of the city was seen. Aided by the expert target-marking, the raid developed rapidly, successive waves pressing home a most concentrated attack which resulted in a record 2,643 tons of bombs being dropped by 806 aircraft that cut a swathe from the working-class districts of Wedding and Pankow in the north to leafy Zehlendorf in the south-west,[7] though many parts of the surrounding countryside again reported bombs falling. Damage was extensive with almost 600 large fires and 572 'medium' fires and the last arrivals were able to report the glow of large fires and a column of smoke rising 30,000 feet into the murky air. Over 140 war industries, the most important being the Siemens and Halske works which manufactured electrical apparatus, were hit. Several of its many buildings were gutted including the switch-gear and dynamo workshops. Also hit were a power station, two gasworks, Dr Goebbels' broadcasting station and five tramway depots. Almost 1,500 houses and temporary wooden barracks were destroyed.

The Jägerleitoffiziers had plotted the bomber stream soon after it left the English coast but the swing over Denmark for the approach flight proved too far distant for many of the German fighters. Flak in a wide barrage form was tremendous around the aiming-point, but the effectiveness of the searchlights was minimized by the heavy clouds. The diversion to Frankfurt-on-Oder failed to draw any night-fighters away from the Berlin area but the JLO ordered his fighter pilots not to fly over the capital, leaving the target area free for the flak. So although fourteen combats took place above the 'Big City', the night-fighters sought for the most part to intercept the bombers on their way in and out and left the defence of the target area itself to the guns.

After leaving Denmark there were twenty-two attacks by German night-fighters and upwards of fifty sightings. Clayton Moore was reporting such sightings every few minutes:

'It was clear that the Jerries were having a right old turkey-shoot. Bill had issued an order for all non-essential crew members to assist in scanning the sky around us for signs of a possible attack and both Gerry Parker's mid-upper turret and mine were constantly on the move. Our vigilance paid off and we spotted two fighters during the return flight. Gerry let go a burst at the second one (an Me 109), but we managed to lose him in the darkness before he could launch an attack on us. I was later to have a word with Gerry on the matter of his having opened fire first. This was a policy favoured by a lot of gunners, but it was one with which I disagreed strongly, not only because the sight of his tracer bullets had served to betray our position to the enemy.'[8]

A 77 Squadron Halifax, a 419 Squadron Halifax and a 619 Squadron Lancaster went down in the waters of the Baltic. There were no survivors on any of the aircraft. Halifax 'O-Orange' on 158 Squadron flown by Flight Sergeant William C.M. Hogg ran into flak over Denmark. Flight Sergeant Robert McDonald recalled:

'Our port inner engine burst into flames and the aircraft went into a vertical dive. Our Skipper regained control after 10,000 feet, but our port outer was now on fire. He extinguished the fires, feathered the props and jettisoned the load, but could not maintain height. Not sure whether we were over sea or land, we decided to stay with the aircraft. The starboard inner was now faltering as we skimmed a house and crash-landed in a snow-covered field. The nose burst open on impact, as did the overloaded fuel tanks and one engine tore loose. But miraculously there was no fire and all seven of us stepped out of the wreckage.'

They had come down near Grasten in Denmark. All the crew were taken into captivity.

'Y-Yorker' on 625 Squadron was attacked by a night-fighter and the Lancaster was set on fire. Bill Ashurst instructed Flying Officer Harry Proskurniak, the Canadian bomb-aimer, to 'get rid of the bomb load' which included a 'cookie'. The aircraft was out of control and losing height and Harry frantically tried to open the forward escape hatch. He says:

'I must have lapsed into unconsciousness when trying to open it. When I came to it must have been the abrupt jerk of my parachute opening which really woke me up. The parachute really saved my life but I'll never know how I opened it! For me it was a miracle! I still keep asking myself the question, 'Why was my life spared and not that of any of my comrades?'

In the village of Fjelstrup the occupying Germans left the scattered bodies of Bill Ashurst and five crew members for several days before collecting them for a military funeral. Harry Proskurniak was eventually taken prisoner.

Four Lancaster IIIs on 7 (PFF) Squadron were missing in action. 'L-London' piloted by Flight Lieutenant Peter K.B. Williams DFC was hit by Hauptmann Erhard Peters and exploded over the Baltic, throwing Williams and the only other survivor, Flight Sergeant George S. Staniforth, the air bomber, clear. Williams landed in the sea off the island of Skarø. He managed to get up in his dinghy and shouted for help. He was heard by Åge and Hans Strange Rasmussen who set out in a small boat and brought him ashore. Staniforth landed in a field on the island of Skarø and broke a leg. He did not manage to release the parachute and was pulled across the frozen field, hitting his head on rocks. The dead bodies of the rest of the crew were brought ashore and laid to rest on Danish soil. There were no survivors on 'W-William' piloted by Flight Lieutenant Roy Laurence Barnes DFC. On 'Y-Yorker' flown by 40-year-old New Zealand Squadron Leader John Alfred Hegman DSO DFC only Flight Sergeant F.L. Cook the rear gunner survived to be taken into captivity. There were no survivors on 'D-Dog' captained by Squadron Leader Richard David Campling DSO DFC.

Thirty miles from the 'Big City' the trouble began for 'Pat' Doyle's crew on 156 Squadron. Chapman-Smith was searching the port beam when, from the corner of his eye, he saw three white lights. He swung his guns, saw a green light and realized that it was an enemy fighter with its identification lamps on. They had been singled out for a joint attack by a Focke-Wulf 190 and a twin-engined fighter. 'Smithy' gave the warning and 'Pat' Doyle dived the Lancaster to port as four lines of tracer streamed from the wings of the twin-engined fighter, now close enough to identify as a Messerschmitt Bf 110. The two attackers liaised very cleverly, the 110 waggling its wings and flashing its navigation lights but initially remaining just outside the effective range of the bomber's guns, the Focke-Wulf closing surreptitiously and letting the bomber 'have it'. Smith poured 150 rounds into the 110; there was a mighty flash and it blew up. Four more lines of tracer appeared; an Fw 190 was coming in from behind. The Lancaster dived and lost the enemy, but a cannon shell had hit Smith's right ankle and exploded. He was in great pain, his turret was unserviceable and his parachute bag was on fire.

Other shells had plastered the Lancaster from its tail along its fuselage up to the mid-upper turret. The tail wheel had been shot off, while the hydraulics were so badly damaged that the bomb doors would not open and the flaps were left dangling. They were only 15 miles from the target, their bombs were trapped on board and they reluctantly decided to turn back. Crossing a flak belt, the Lancaster was hit again. A lump of shrapnel hit the throttle box by Doyle's feet and severed the controls to the port engines. Of immediate concern was the propeller on the port outer which was setting up such a severe vibration that 'Pat' Doyle had great difficulty in maintaining control. At a nod from Doyle, Syd Richardson stopped the damaged engine and feathered the prop. Two engines had stopped when at last Doyle got clear of the defences and crossed the coast out to sea. Then, seeing that his pilot had regained at least some measure of control, Syd Richardson made his way to the rear.

Doyle called his crew to check for casualties. There was no answer from Sergeant A.C. Clark, the mid-upper turret gunner, and the pilot sent 'Doug' Green back to see what had happened. Clark was on the floor without his oxygen mask, almost unconscious. His turret had been hit. Though wounded by a cannon shell and his left leg fractured when he fell out of the turret, he had tried to beat out the flames of burning oil from a burst pipe, using his helmet before lack of oxygen had overcome him. 'Doug' Green busied himself getting the mid-upper gunner forward over the spars to the rest position where he could be given a shot of morphine and jammed an oxygen tube in Clark's mouth just in time to save him. Then he climbed into the mid-upper turret to watch for fighters. Dave Winlow dealt with the burning parachute.

Doyle called Smith on the intercom and told him he was sending help, but the Australian refused to be moved and he continued to work the guns by hand. Fred Astle and Syd Richardson went aft to free Smith. Arriving at the rear turret and peering through the clouds of smoke billowing from what turned out to be 'Smithy's burning parachute, Syd Richardson found 'an awful mess'. 'Smithy's right leg was shattered and twisted around the ammunition belt and controls. The turret was drenched in blood.'

Having beaten out the flames with his gloves Richardson turned to the turret, to find that its doors had been so seriously damaged they could only just be opened. Fred Astle had to chop it away with an axe. Smith's oxygen mask had frozen and he had taken it off and was breathing the dangerous rarefied air. When

Richardson tried to extricate 'Smithy' he would have none of it. 'Just leave me alone,' he insisted. 'As the mid-upper gunner's out of action I'm needed here.' He was adamant and so Richardson had to leave him there. Indeed the Focke-Wulf did make another attack, but meeting determined resistance, fired low, passed beneath the Lancaster and disappeared for good. Making his way forward again Richardson discovered that the gale whistling through the holes in the aircraft had made a shambles of the navigator's station. Dave Winlow's charts and logs had gone 'heaven only knows where'. Not surprisingly, having to work under these conditions upset his calculations so that some while later they strayed over Texel in the Frisian Islands and came under heavy fire, one shell hitting the throttle box and causing the starboard inner to run so wild that 'Pat' Doyle had to start in all over again to maintain control.

Finally, the moment they reached the Channel, Syd Richardson managed to reach the forward hydraulic jacks on the bomb doors via the bomb-bay inspection hatch. He dismantled the connections on the hydraulic system in order to release the pressure to allow the doors to open when they jettisoned the bombs on top of them. All except one of the 500-pounders fell through the open doors and they were forced to carry it back with them. It was the second time they had been forced to let their load go over the sea.

Only now, when they were well clear of the enemy coast, did 'Smithy' allow them to set about releasing him from the turret:

'It took some doing,' wrote Syd Richardson. 'Indeed, by the time Fred Astle, Doug Green and I, with the fire axe, had broken down the doors, then got him forwards, Dave had already brought us to a landfall that enabled "Pat" to set up for an approach at the same long, wide, emergency-landing airfield we had used before, at Woodbridge.

'It was clear that the landing would be fraught but there was no question of bailing out with two seriously wounded men on board, more especially as the fire had reduced Smithy's parachute to a smouldering mess. So, a crash-landing it had to be. The rest of the crew put their backs to the main spar, Fred and Doug supporting "Smithy" and Eric. For my part I took station beside "Pat", ready to assist him in any way I could.

'He made one approach but wasn't satisfied and so went around again to get a better line-up. With no wheels he was forced to touch down on the bomb-bay doors, which he duly did, if with something of a bump. Pat had a full Sutton harness restraining him, but as for me, having no chance to move aft as the theoretical drill called for, I had to brace my boots against the instrument panel. Even so, I was propelled forwards and got a bang on the head which knocked the senses out of me.

'The saving grace was that there was no fire. Just the same, the aircraft was in such a state that the rescue crew decided that the best way to remove our casualties was to chop through the fuselage.'[9]

Chapman-Smith's leg was amputated above the knee next morning at the RAF Hospital, Ely. The surgeon told the crew that had they moved him from the freezing-cold turret into the relative warmth of the fuselage any earlier he would certainly have bled to death. A Conspicuous Gallantry Medal, one of the last made to an Australian for an attack on Berlin, was awarded to Flight Sergeant Geoffrey

Smith. The Aussie's only comment, however, was 'If it hadn't been for the Skipper we'd none of us have got back.' Geoffrey Chapman-Smith was discharged from the service in November 1944.[10]

'Q-Queenie' on 460 Squadron RAAF also put up a strenuous fight for survival after being attacked by a Ju 88 and an Me 210. Pilot Officer Robert William Burke DFC, who was from New South Wales, had just celebrated his 22nd birthday and he and his crew were on their ninth op. In the action the Ju 88 was shot down and the Me 210 damaged, but 'Queenie' had been damaged in the starboard wing and rudder and the starboard inner engine was holed by cannon fire. The starboard outer engine was also holed and there was a jagged hole in the fuselage. Burke got 'Queenie' back to Binbrook, but he would not live to see his 23rd birthday. He and five of his crew were killed on the night of 9/10 April 1944 when their Lancaster crashed in Denmark on a 'Gardening' trip.

Ken Berry's crew on 103 Squadron had made it to Berlin and out again after dropping their bombs, but near Texel off the coast of Holland at 2250 hours they were attacked by Leutnant Kurt Matzak and the Lancaster was lost with all seven crew. Brian Lydon's crew made it home safely to Elsham Wolds just as 'Ben' Benbow, his engineer said they would. Lydon was taken to hospital by ambulance and operated on by the squadron MO, Flying Officer Henderson, who removed bits of metal and shrapnel from his head, face and right arm. 'Doc' Henderson had quite unofficially done over sixteen raids to various targets and Padre Ratledge had also done his share of unofficial trips. While he was in hospital Lydon's crew were stood down. A new crew needed a replacement gunner on 19/20 February for the raid on Leipzig and 'Jackie' Bristow and Paul Collins decided by the toss of a coin who would fly with Warrant Officer Frank Law. Bristow lost and he went on the trip. Law's Lancaster was one of three Elsham Lancasters lost on Leipzig that night. Bristow and Law and three others were killed. It was another sad night in the 'Oswald' in 'Scunny' that night.

A press correspondent who spent the night at one bomber station described how 'punctually at midnight, the air became full of the sound of the returning aircraft. Lights on the ground made the night like day as the bombers, their navigation lights winking, circled round the airfield. Anxieties were soon relieved. Thirty-five aircraft from that station took part in the operation and thirty-five came back. None showed even a scratch.'

However, forty-three bombers – twenty-six of them Lancasters and seventeen Halifaxes – were shot down on the Berlin raid. Nachtjagd, which deployed 143 crews, claimed 39 victories, mainly over the Reich capital, for the loss of 11 night-fighters. In the target area thirty fighters were seen and fifteen fighters were encountered on the return. Three kilometres south-east of Ribuitz Oberleutnant Paul Zorner shot down the Lancaster on 166 Squadron piloted by 30-year-old Warrant Officer George Arthur Woodcock-Stevens for his twenty-sixth victory. The 'Lanki' crashed near Jabel with the loss of all seven crew.

Halifax 'A-Apple' on 76 Squadron at Holme-on-Spalding-Moor was intercepted by Hauptmann Leopold Fellerer, whose fire set light to the port inner before it went down for his twenty-eighth victory. All seven on Flight Sergeant D.A. Eaton's crew bailed out but Sergeant Eric Basil Upton, the 19-year-old mid-upper gunner who was standing in for the regular gunner on the crew, plunged into the ice-covered Schweriner See and drowned. At Elvington three Halifaxes on 77 Squadron were lost with no one surviving on any aircraft. Four Halifaxes failed to return to Leconfield.

As they crossed the coast of England Ken Handley on 466 Squadron RAAF looked at his fuel gauges, which showed that their Halifax had no fuel remaining for the return to Leconfield. His pilot asked permission to land immediately without any 'stacking'. This they did, Handley expecting the engines to cut at any moment. 'What a relief to be taxiing along the runway and perimeter track,' Handley wrote later. It was not until the following morning that the ground crew said that they could not get any fuel into the bomb-bay tank: it was still full. Handley had forgotten to pump the 230 gallons into tanks 1 and 3 after leaving the target area!

The Canadian 6 Group had lost three Halifax aircraft and a Lancaster shot down. On 424 'Tiger' Squadron everyone on the Halifax crew skippered by Canadian Squadron Leader Aloysius Valentine Reilander was killed. On 434 'Bluenose' Squadron everyone on 'Y-Yorker' piloted by 24-year-old Canadian Squadron Leader Frank Ernest Carter was lost without trace after the Halifax reached the rendezvous-point over the North Sea. Carter left a widow, Catherine Ellen of Williamsburg, Ontario. The Lancaster that was lost was piloted by Canadian Flight Sergeant Basil William Pattle on 426 'Thunderbird' Squadron at Linton-on-Ouse, which crashed in the Ijsselmeer with no survivors.

The crew on Halifax 'T-Tommy' on 420 'Snowy Owl' Squadron RCAF piloted by Canadian Flying Officer Harold Edward Damgaard were on their first op. They experienced altimeter trouble, the wireless equipment also failed and then the No. 3 engine began overheating. The Halifax continued to the target and descended from 22,000 feet to the bombing height of 19,000 feet. Sergeant Stanley Fletcher, the RAF flight engineer, wrote: 'The ground below seemed to be one sheet of flame ... parts of it white, almost incandescent....' There was little flak and no sign of enemy fighters. However, shortly after leaving the target area they were attacked by a Ju 88 and the gunners returned fire and claimed it as a 'probable'. Due to the radio fault the crew were not aware of an order to divert to another base because of the poor weather and Damgaard kept on course for Tholthorpe. On reaching the airfield he made three attempts to land in swirling fog. All three resulted in overshoots. On the fourth attempt on going around again Damgaard mistook a railway fog light for a Drem and landed on the York to Liverpool railway line. The impact tore the undercarriage off and the remains of the Halifax finished up in a grove of trees. Warrant Officer1 Lloyd Leslie Whale of Toronto, Ontario, the 25-year-old WOp/AG and the 23-year-old rear gunner Sergeant Bernard Downey of Doyles, Great Codroy, Newfoundland were killed. Whale's tour was to have ended in April when he was to return home and marry in August that same year. Three of Damgaard's crew were injured while two escaped injury. Fletcher returned to the squadron after many months but he never flew on operations again.

Damgaard later stated that the altimeter had stuck at 300 feet during one of the overshoots and had read around 700 feet when the crash occurred. Born in Kamloops, British Columbia in 1914 and a bus driver prior to enlisting, Damgaard had been injured in a crash on his first sortie when he flew as second pilot on a 'nickel trip' on 1664 HCU. His next trip had not been until 27 January when he had flown as second pilot on the raid on Berlin. In September 1944 he was later awarded the DFC.[11]

Leaving the target the undercarriage on Halifax III 'A-Apple' on 78 Squadron pilot by 23-year-old Flight Lieutenant Robert Nathan Shard DFC DFM fell down and locked. Bob Shard had been brought up at Knutsford and had been employed by a firm of Altrincham printers. He volunteered for the RAF in the summer of 1940 and had married Vera Joyce Bowler in December 1941. He was a 'second tourist' who had completed fifty ops including several of the 1,000 bomber raids over Germany.

As the crew of 'A-Apple' neared the English coast out of fuel and thinking they were over land, Shard ordered his crew to bail out but they were still 17 miles north-north-east of Flamborough Head and they all landed in the sea. Only Flying Officer William Uyen, the 23-year-old bomb-aimer from Hamilton, Ontario made it ashore but the others drowned. Only a month later Uyen was killed during the disastrous 31 March raid on Nuremberg.

Sergeant Jack Boswell and crew on 'L-London' returned early owing to compass trouble and were fifteen minutes late on reaching the enemy coast. The furthest point reached was Sylt where the bombs were jettisoned 'safe'. The mystery of the 'inexplicable' compass failure was solved when the ground crew realized that 'Jack's service pistol in his bomber jacket had deflected the compass. He had not long before the flight swapped a camera of his with another airman's gun. However, he strongly believed this probably saved their lives. If they had gone on they might not have survived. Boswell and his crew would attempt to bomb Berlin again on 23 March, but on that occasion 'N-Nan' suffered an electrical failure and once again the bombs were dropped on the alternative target of Sylt. This time the bombs were dropped 'live' but no results were observed. The crew always tried to make it back to Breighton, but on one return and running short of fuel they landed at another 'drome by mistake. One or two others did the same. At the next briefing the CO requested that they take particular care and hoped that everyone would land back at Breighton on return. Everyone did except for the CO![12]

'J-Jig', a 630 Squadron Lancaster which was being flown by a 619 Squadron loan crew, overshot East Kirkby on return due to another aircraft being slow to clear. The skipper, Pilot Officer Kimberley 'Kim' Roberts, a pipe-smoking Australian from Perth, made another circuit at 700 feet. When coming into the funnel it hit the ground near Old Bolingbroke and was wrecked. The rear turret was torn off and was caught in the branches of a tree. Sergeant Lionel Virgo, the Australian rear gunner from Adelaide, a keen poker-player who went by the nickname of 'Lucky', suffered a broken jaw, two broken arms, a leg and seven ribs. The rest of the crew suffered minor injuries. Roberts received the DFC and was promoted to flight lieutenant. Perhaps Virgo was lucky after all because on 7 June 1944 'Kim' Roberts and three of the crew including the replacement rear gunner were killed on the operation on Caen when they were shot down by a Ju 88. Sergeant Jack Forrest the flight engineer and Flight Sergeant Reg De Viell, the 29-year-old bomb-aimer from Kingsbury, Middlesex bailed out and were taken prisoner.[13]

Two Halifaxes on 640 Squadron crashed in Yorkshire. 'V-Victor' piloted by Flight Sergeant Edgar Thomas Bridson Vicary born on 3 May 1915 in

Rockhampton, Queensland was hit by flak at 22,000 feet during the bomb run on the target. A navigation aid failed and the bomber crashed at Coxwold low on fuel. Two of the crew were injured in the crash. 'H-Harry' captained by 22-year-old Flying Officer Hugh Alastair Yuille Barkley of Weybridge, Surrey crashed onto a 300 feet hillside at Cloughton, 4 miles north-north-west of Scarborough. There were no survivors. The two other Leconfield losses were on 466 Squadron RAAF. No word was received from 'F-for Freddie' piloted by 21-year-old Australian Flight Sergeant Jack Dudley Wormald which was shot down over Holland with the loss of all the crew, all but one of them Australian. 'M-Mother' flown by Australian Flight Lieutenant J.D. Cairns was abandoned near Papenburg due to engine failure caused by a malfunctioning overflow pump. Cairns, the four other Aussies on the crew and two Englishmen were all taken prisoner.

Altogether, six aircraft returning from Berlin crashed in England. While avoiding another Lancaster, 'K-King' on 106 Squadron at Metheringham skippered by Flying Officer Reginald William Dickerson went down at Timberland Fen, killing its pilot and four of the crew. A fifth crew member, Sergeant Walter Charles Hills, died of his injuries later that day.

For 'N-Nan's crew on 83 Squadron, the seven-hour, forty-minute flight ended with touch-down just after 5.00 am on the 16th. On arrival at dispersal they inspected the aircraft and were not surprised to find that 'Nan' had picked up a couple of flak holes, 'but,' wrote Clayton Moore, 'nothing serious had resulted.'

This raid was the last trip for Pilot Officer Michael Clifford Foster, a Halifax pilot on 51 Squadron who had Squadron Leader Kentish as second pilot. Foster was glad to report that it was a very quiet and peaceful operation, quite different to one he had flown on 5/6 September 1943 when, during a sortie against Mannheim, his aircraft was severely damaged in an encounter with a fighter. One engine was put out of action, the starboard mainplane and the ailerons were damaged. A fire broke out in the starboard wing and burned for more than an hour. The aircraft became very difficult to control, but Foster flew it safely back.

Foster's letter home contained a prediction: 'On the whole I shall say Berlin had rather a rough night with the heaviest attack ever. We were almost first in before they got organised. Everything indicated that Berlin is finished and I think we will probably be in at the death. That will be a fitting finish, just as Hamburg was a fitting start.'[14]

In London the Thursday edition of *The Times* announced that: 'The largest force of RAF bombers which has so far attacked Berlin bombed the city on Tuesday night at the rate of over eighty tons a minute, dropping 2,500 tons between 9.15 pm and just after 9.45 pm. Of the force of more than 1,000 aircraft dispatched by Bomber Command the greater number were Halifaxes and Lancasters and all of these went to Berlin except the Lancasters which made a feint attack on Frankfurt-on-Oder. Originally it was reported that 45 of our aircraft were missing, but later the number was reduced by two. More than an hour after the main attack Mosquitoes were still making the work of Berlin's fire brigade difficult and dangerous and their crews reported an enormous pall of dense black smoke over the city, rising to a height of 20,000 feet. Under the cloud which covered the city in a thick layer up to nearly 10,000 feet, a great pear-shaped glow of fires stretched across the target. Flak was so violent when the first sky-marker bombs were dropped that it was evident that the main night fighter force was late. Scattered fighter flares later began to appear in the sky, but even in the last stages of the attack many of our crews bombed without opposition from fighters.

'A station commander, describing the tremendous work involved in putting up Tuesday night's great force, said, 'it took roughly 4,000 men to get the bombs into the 1,000 aircraft and the work took over five hours. Seven thousand flying personnel were briefed. There was something like 50 men working on the ground for each bomber that got into the air. We used well over 1,000,000 gallons of petrol.'

After the raid Flight Sergeant Dennis Cooper, a Lancaster wireless-operator on 630 Squadron at East Kirkby, had broken out in boils under the crotch and on the buttocks. 'Lack of Moral Fibre' was a label which frightened everyone because, if you stopped flying, you were stripped of rank and posted out as an AC2 to some other station. There was a case of a gunner who twice damaged his turret so that the aircraft had to turn back; no aircraft could continue unless fully serviceable. Station Medical Officers had instructions to keep aircrew off the sick list and the SMO still passed me fit for flying. As a result, on my next op, I sat on the metal of my parachute harness and crushed the boils. With the pain and the cold, I was very uncomfortable until landing. After debriefing, I went to Sick Quarters where a very hard medical officer told me to drop my trousers and using a scalpel, cut them. In spite of the fact that I fainted, I was on ops the next night. Bomber Command was terrified of too many people going sick and reducing the available force and that other crews might catch the 'don't want to fly' bug. Crews were beginning to look untidy in dress and manner and even the ground sergeants, who had previously thought nothing of us because we got our stripes too quickly, began to have pity on us as they could see what we were going through. Many of us could see no hope of completing a tour the way losses were showing. We drank and smoked too much when we were not flying and things were generally depressed.

On 19 February Flying Officer Keith Ross Holland RAAF, a Mosquito pilot on 540 PRU Squadron at RAF Benson, Oxfordshire, made four runs over Berlin to take the first reconnaissance photos of the destruction caused by the bombing. On the last run the former surveyor and civil engineer, who had enlisted in Melbourne on 5 December 1941, came under intense ground fire but returned safely. Next day Flight Lieutenant Lionel Hamilton Scargill of 541 PRU found the city clear of cloud and he covered the whole area of Berlin. For this work Keith Holland was awarded the DFC. On 27 October 1944 he and his navigator, Pilot Officer Geoffrey John Bloomfield were killed when their Mosquito PR.XVI crashed at Steinfeld near Rostock while heading for the Stettin-Berlin area to carry out further photographic reconnaissance. Scargill failed to return while flying a Spitfire XIX on a Damage Assessment sortie to the Bielefeld viaduct on 4 March 1945 but eventually made his way back to Britain.

The raid on 15/16 February marked the close of the true Battle of Berlin which was supposed to produce 'a state of devastation in which surrender is inevitable.'

Since the end of November 1943 Harris had dispatched thirty-four major assaults on Germany, sixteen of them against the 'Big City', yet still no German surrender was in sight. Berlin must have seemed a 'busted flush'.

The next big raid by Bomber Command was on the night of 19/20 February when the target was Leipzig and its aircraft assembly factories, as part of a true round-the-clock offensive in concert with the American Air Forces. The Main Force lost seventy-eight bombers, Bomber Command's worst casualties so far. At one American base the door was flung back and a group of fly-boys lurched in, singing with drink-sodden voices: 'Coming in on a wing and a prayer.'

'They made up in volume what they lacked in harmony. Someone turned up the radio to drown them into a giggling silence. Over the radio a woman's voice was telling the recipe for the morrow, which was Woolton Pie. It sounded revolting to an American palate. The BBC news came on. We mostly didn't listen, because its content was really designed for the British ear. But towards the end we crewmen caught a flash that made our ears prick up: 'Royal Air Force bombers last night raided Leipzig. Large sections of the city were left in flames with considerable damage to the railway yards…' Then in the crisp British accent: 'Seventy-nine of our aircraft are missing…'

'Jesus H. Christ!' said somebody. 'I didn't know they had that many.'

Generalfeldmarschall Milch, speaking on 23 February 1944 at a conference held in Berlin, said, 'the English have worked out exactly how many attacks they need to make on Berlin – probably twenty-five. Now they have done fifteen that leaves ten. Furthermore, we know that when Berlin has been dealt with they will go on to the central German industrial region: Halle, Leipzig, Dessau and so on. These are all involved in the production of armaments and equipment. There is only one way to overcome this threat and that is with fighters.'

Sir Charles Portal had agreed that RAF Bomber Command would participate in a devastating and concentrated Allied offensive against the German aircraft industry, but at the Air Ministry the air staff had become 'distressed and angered' with Harris's fixation on Berlin with the resumption of attacks. It was not until the end of February 1944 that 'Bomber' Harris finally sent his bombers on five raids on elements of the German aircraft industry, which had to be completed by 1 March in order to free the USAAF and RAF heavy bombers for other operations in support of Operation 'Overlord'.

By and large, Harris continued to use most of his heavies on German cities, starting with Cologne on 20 April. Meanwhile, the Americans persisted with precision bombing of targets – aviation or otherwise – in the Reich and on 13 April overall command of the Combined Bomber Offensive and the US Eighth Air Force would officially pass to General Dwight D. Eisenhower, the newly-appointed Supreme Allied Commander.

During stand-downs when poor weather conditions brought the air war to a halt, morale ebbed. At Wickenby Mike Allen and 'Jock' Stephens on Lail Dawley's crew set rabbit snares in the woods behind their Nissen hut and skinned and cooked their catches over an open fire. The crew that had become a disciplined unit in the air fought and bickered among themselves on the ground. Only occasionally could Dawley get them all together for a few beers. Once a month, they would fly south to an American base to collect Dawley's ration of candy and 'Lucky Strike' cigarettes. A cross-country training flight took them over Yorkshire and close to the town of

Halifax nestled in the Pennine hills. It was an afternoon that residents of suburban Illingworth would remember for many years after.

'Hey, I can almost see my home,' said Mike over the intercom. 'Let's go see,' drawled Dawley, pulling the plane around in a wide circle. With Mike giving directions, Dawley brought the Lancaster down to ground level across the golf course at Ogden. Those on the eighteenth fairway scattered like scared rabbits as the plane thundered by up the narrow valley. Mike's home lay just below the church and Dawley brought 'V-Victor' round and down and straight on target. Mike's mother, caught in the bathtub, was clearly seen bare-breasted, waving her towel from an upstairs window. They flew so low that Mike looked up at the church tower clock and saw the time frozen at ten to four.

The incident was never formally reported. The air reporter, on duty at the time, was a friend of the Allen family and guessed who the culprits were. There were, however, casualties of sorts. A window-cleaner fell off his ladder and sprained an ankle. Major Youngman, commander of the Home Guard unit, in freshly pressed uniform, was reading his evening *Courier* before a cosy fire when 'V-Victor's slipstream swept his chimney clean and in the process doused the major in soot from head to toe. The local vicar, entertaining ladies over tea, shook his fists skyward and was heard to loose some un-godlike epithets. The crew, high spirits restored, returned to base.[15]

Each time Lail Dawley and the crew of 'V-Victor' returned from ops unscathed, the 'hard luck' crew became, by default, the senior squadron crew on returning from their thirteenth mission. It was on 3 May 1944 that 'V-Victor's luck nearly ran out. The target, a Tiger tank factory at Mailly-le-Camp, was thought to be a 'milk-run'. After the briefing Dawley confided his own tactical plan: 'Listen, you guys. This is a milk-run and we'll have some fun. What we do, we make the bomb run at 4,000 feet and then we go down real low and shoot the shit outa the sons of bitches.'[16]

It was a night when everything went wrong. The bombers were ordered to circle flares and await instructions from spotter planes to start their bombing runs. The flares silhouetted the planes for the German night-fighters to pick off one by one. The operating wavelength clashed with an American Forces Network station playing *Deep in the Heart of Texas*. They heard the calm voice of the spotter pilot, 'Firepump One. Am hit and going down.' The situation was chaotic. Dawley, disobeying instructions to wait, started his bomb run. Ted Percival yelled 'Fighter!' as tracers slammed into the wing 6 inches from Joe Williams, the wireless-operator. The combined fire-power of 'Jock' and Ted scored a bull's-eye on the fighter. The fighter, now flaming, flew wingtip to wingtip with 'V-Victor' as though its pilot could not decide whether or not to ram and take them both down. Time froze. The Me 109 slipped by and underneath and headed for the ground. Mike said 'dummy run' and the crew groaned.

The bombs were dropped on target and 'V-Victor' headed out into the safety of darkness homeward bound. The stench of gasoline was overpowering. Joe Williams reported that they were losing fuel through a holed tank. Dawley elected to make it back to base. In daylight a German tracer was found to have passed through a petrol tank, coming to rest in one engine. The tracer had failed to ignite. Of 362 Lancasters taking part, 42 failed to return.

Dawley's determination to make home base was not without reason. On landing, it was learned that his wife back in Detroit had delivered a baby girl. To honour the occasion, 'V-Victor' was christened *Mari-Jac* and a picture of a stork carrying a diapered bomb was painted above the sixteen mission markers on the nose.[17]

Lail Dawley's crew's final eleven operations were flown in fifteen days, culminating on 18 June 1944 with an abortive trip to Aulnoye. It was barely light when 'V-Victor', with bomb load still intact, swept low across the airfield at Wickenby. Its wingtip passed within feet of the control tower and below eye-level of the air controller on duty. Minutes later it touched down on the runway and came to rest at its dispersal point. That night, while the crew slept, Lail Dawley packed his gear and slipped quietly away.

Dawley and newly-commissioned officers 'Red' Redshaw and Mike Allen were awarded the DFC, their pilot receiving his medal in June 1945 during retreat ceremonies at Hammer Field, a Fourth Air Force Night Fighter training base near Fresno, California. The rest of the crew, except for Joe Pickering for reasons never clarified, received the DFM. On his second tour on 214 Squadron in 100 Special Duties Group Ted Percival parachuted out of his disabled Fortress III while on RCM support on the raid on Hagen on 15/16 March 1945. He was kept in Bühl prison before being transferred by foot into Luftwaffe custody on 17 March, the very day his wife Maud was expecting a baby. Upon reaching Huchenfeld he was locked into the boiler room of the Neuen Schule (New School) along with six others of his crew. A crowd of civilians demanded access to the seven men, demanding revenge, and dragged them outside. Three escaped to be recaptured. Percival and four others were taken to the cemetery and shot. Ted was 30 years old. He was posthumously awarded a Mentioned in Dispatches which was recorded in the *London Gazette* published on 4 June 1946.

'Jock' Stephens received an emergency discharge after his father and two brothers were killed when their deep-water fishing boat struck a mine. Lieutenant Dawley became an appliance salesman for a department store in Royal Oak, Michigan. The balance of the crew faded back into civilian life. Mike Allen returned to the Southern States to find his 'Georgia Peach' but when that proved abortive he made a westward diversion to the state where 'the corn is as high as an elephant's eye', something he had wanted to do ever since Lail Dawley had made him listen to the songs from *Oklahoma*. There he met and married an 'Okie' with whom he eventually set up home in Houston, Texas.

'We were lucky to be so young and indestructible,' he said many years later. 'After our last op, the ground crew told us that they never once doubted our safe return, whereas they had often had accurate forebodings about other crews. Later, I was to learn the importance of PMA – positive mental attitude – which was what Dawley instilled in us and what Churchill instilled in the British people.'

Chapter Fifteen

Once the Most Beautiful City in the World

'*We are just outside Berlin, Fräulein. There is a raid. The train must wait for the British to evacuate their bowels.... We could be waiting, could we not, on the outskirts of Hell?*'

An SS officer, a Latvian from Riga, in black with forked lightning insignia – exactly like an image illuminated in nightmare – speaking to Christabel Bielenberg.[1]

Berlin's Anhalter Bahnhof had become a symbol of disintegration; its huge domed roof, once glassed in, stood out like a skeleton greenhouse against the sky. Along the platforms the propaganda posters hung unnoticed in red and black tatters from the shrapnel-pitted walls: 'Führer we thank you'; 'To Victory with our Leader'; 'National Socialist Order or Bolshevik Chaos'. Every day the windowless trains trundled in and out in the few hours left for living between the American mass daylight raids and the sporadic British night attacks; they carried a rudderless crowd of soldiers, civilians, refugees and evacuees along diverse routes to uncertain destinations. The day that Christabel left Berlin to return to Rohrbach was no exception.

'You need a compass to get across Berlin now,' Christabel Bielenberg's friend Lexi von Alvensleben told her immensely tall companion, 'Night after night it's a hell hole.' Lexi's flat in the Budapesterstrasse had been partly converted into an office. On one of her visits when Christabel reached the Gedächtnisplatz and passed the truncated Gedächtniskirche, she had been surrounded by a frozen sea of shattered ruins. Christabel had never seen bombing like it before. In the Budapesterstrasse house after house was an empty shell; not one single building had survived. The rubble had been neatly stacked to the gaping windows of the first floors. There was a thin powdering of snow, which had only been disturbed before her by the wandering tracks of a dog. She was alone 'in a silent ghost town'. In the summer of 1943, Christabel and her husband had decided that their children should not go through another winter in Berlin.

Although she had become an ardent supporter of the black market, throughout the following year the food situation had worsened month by month. Also when the nights grew longer she knew that they could reckon once more with RAF raids. 'The damage done by these "Night Pirates" was not yet great,' she wrote. 'They usually turned up when the skies were overcast, but when they did so they had a nasty habit of keeping it up bomber by bomber, bomb by bomb, all through the night.'

Heavy Allied bombing had eventually forced Christabel and her children to leave the centre of Berlin, capital of Hitler's mighty empire, which he had boasted would last 1,000 years and finally settle in the village of Rohrbach, near Furtwangen im Schwarzwald in the Black Forest.[2]

Wing Commander E.W. 'Bill' Anderson, an experienced PFF navigator on the staff of 8 Group Pathfinder Headquarters would have sympathized with her:

'There was no glamour in this winter Battle of Berlin,' he wrote, 'and the crews got no kick out of it apart from the fact that it was the capital of the Reich that they were attacking. The trips were long, dull and dangerous. Lining the route, we would see strings of fighter flares, generally in threes and every now and then the gunners would report an aircraft falling in flames. You just sat and waited for your turn to come.'

Sergeant Frederick Charles Blackmore, a Halifax flight engineer on 578 Squadron at Burn, carried out thirty-six bombing operations, mostly as a spare engineer. Luck would play a large part in his survival before he was posted to Transport Command in late October after he had asked to be 'screened'. At the age of 4 'Fred's family moved from Heavitree near Exeter to Rectory Cottage, Gittisham to enable his father to take up the post of chauffeur/gardener to the rector. It was only during the latter years of his life that Fred came to appreciate the wonderful environment the family enjoyed during their eleven years at the Devonshire village where he attended the village school and sang in the choir until he was 11. Fred's father thought hairdressing would suit him as a job for life but after a few months of working fifty-four hours per week, Fred gave in his notice, which really upset his father (who had served and was injured during the First World War). In 1936 Fred's mother died. She never recovered from losing Fred's sister Barbara. Fred next worked for a short while for a dairyman. It was great fun learning to ride a three-wheeler bike, but at that time he hated discipline so he left for pastures new.

At about this time war broke out and in July 1942 he received his call-up. He eventually crewed up with Flight Sergeant Stan Sparks and the crew was posted to 578 Squadron being formed on the new Halifax IIIs at Snaith on 14 January 1944 and then moved to Burn, 2 miles south of Selby in North Yorkshire, on 16 February.[3]

The beginning of the spring offensive was the dominant feature of March 1944 and RAF Bomber Command operated in varying strength on every night save one. In addition there were only eight days on which some representative of the Command did not make a daylight sortie into enemy territory. Stand-downs were of short duration that month, but when 102 Squadron at Pocklington became the last in 4 Group to re-equip with the Mark III Halifax that could fly as high and fast as the Lancasters the squadron was, for a time, non-operational. The respite was brief but it could not have come at a better time for the air crews. Peter Geraghty on 102 Squadron recalled:

'On one particular day we had been briefed in the afternoon. The plan was to put as many bombs as possible, in the shortest time possible, on Berlin. This huge city seemed to represent all that was evil. I personally felt that at last I was in the action – frightened but fulfilled. Of all the targets, Berlin was the big one. The briefing finished at 1600 hours. Take-off was set for 2300 hours, seven hours of tension before we could get going. I decided to go to my Nissen hut and lie down for a while, pretending to sleep but finding my mind in turmoil of dread. I stayed there for a couple of hours and then heard a loud rattling of the latch on the door followed by my flight engineer saying, 'What are you doing in there? Ops are scrubbed.' I don't think I've heard such welcome words.'

By now 'Bomber' Harris realized that blind marking was unlikely to prove successful against German cities, principally Berlin, and so he waited patiently for clear conditions over the 'Big City'. At 'morning prayers' on Tuesday, 21 March the weather forecaster informed his chief that conditions appeared favourable and Harris ordered another maximum effort. In his message read out to crews, Harris said:

'Although successful blind bombing attacks on Berlin have destroyed large areas of it, there is still a substantial section of this vital city more or less intact. To write this off, it is of great importance that tonight's attack should be closely concentrated on the aiming-point. You must not think that the size of Berlin makes accurate bombing unimportant. There is no point in dropping bombs on the devastated areas in the west and south-west. Weather over the target should be good. Go and do the job.'

However, a later forecast revealed that cloud would probably cover the German capital and the attempt to mount the sixteenth (and final raid) on the 'Big City' was cancelled at 1800 hours. No raids on Berlin were possible on the Wednesday or the Thursday either.

The first weather reconnaissance on Friday, 24 March took off from Wyton forty minutes after midnight, following a request from the Eighth Air Force which was planning a big daylight attack in the Berlin area. It would not be the Americans' only involvement in the attack on 'Big B' this day. Major Tom Gates, a 50-year-old Texan with slow speech and an attractive way with him who commanded the newly-formed tiny Intruder Detachment at Little Snoring in the wild and lonely reaches of North Norfolk, had decided he too would participate in the day's unfolding events. Earlier in the year HQ Eighth Air Force had agreed to allow some of its escort fighters to be used to supplement the work of the intruder element of 100 Group RAF stationed throughout the county. Wing Commander Roderick Chisholm had helped establish a small unit comprising a single P-38 Lightning and a pair of P-51 Mustangs for training and trials. The detachment was now about to become operational for Gates announced that he was going off 'to see the boys' and the next thing Chisholm knew was that his name came through on the night's operations programme. Tom would be taking one of the P-51s to Berlin and back to see the city for himself.

Meanwhile, the weather reconnaissance Mosquito dispatched from Wyton had penetrated as far as Nordhausen, 80 miles south-west of Berlin to find solid strato-cumulus unbroken from the German coast onwards. Flight Lieutenant John Maurice Winnington Briggs DFC DFM, born in Burnley, Lancashire in 1920 with Pilot Officer John Custance Baker DFC as navigator returned after four hours in the air and on the basis of their report the American attack was cancelled; while the substance of this reconnaissance was available for Sir Arthur Harris's morning conference, it did not affect his decision to lay on a full-scale operation that night. It was far too early in the day and his chief met officer held out the likelihood of an improvement later.[4] Planning went ahead and another weather sortie was ordered.

At 1030 Squadron Leader J.M. Birkin DSO DFC AFC, Officer Commanding, 1409 Weather Reconnaissance Flight took off with Flight Lieutenant Cowan to cover the route across the North Sea and Lower Denmark where they found frequent gaps in both the medium and low stratus cloud; an obvious improvement over the past few hours supporting the forecast produced by the Command Met Staff. At the midday review of the weather the situation was deemed good enough for the work of aircraft preparation and crew briefing to go ahead. Nevertheless, the threat of poor conditions over the home bases persisted and the risk was, for the time being, accepted: 'Reverting to the Met forecast for the night…. Fog will develop at 0300 in Lincolnshire and East Anglia … all Groups will have at least half their bases until 0200 with visibility 1,500 yards or more.'[5]

Crews went into their briefings not entirely sure what lay in store for them. The day of 24 March was a memorable one for Pilot Officer Ron Walker's crew on 57 Squadron who were waiting to fly their first operation. They had arrived at East Kirkby from 16 OTU Upper Heyford on 17 March, having crewed up in time-honoured fashion.

Sergeant Roland Alfred 'Ginger' Hammersley, the 21-year-old, 5 feet 4.5 inch WOp/AG from King's Langley came from a family of four brothers and a sister and his home was a three-bedroom council house with a fair-sized garden in which vegetables were grown plus a few apples and soft fruit. Hammersley had met his future wife 'Nan' Webber serving with the WAAF at Barford St John. 'My luck was in,' he wrote, 'Ron Walker was physically a well-built, strong man who since leaving school had managed his father's farm in Sussex; he was a natural pilot and a quick learner. I believe that he could have flown a Lancaster blindfolded. Later in our flying career, his physical strength saved our lives, or at least saved us from having to land in enemy territory with a wounded crew member and a damaged aircraft.

'On arrival at the Flight Office we found our names on the battle order for the night's operations. The aircraft we were to fly was "T-Tommy". We set off on bicycles that had been issued to each one of us, to look the aircraft over and check the equipment. The ground crew responsible for the maintenance of "T-Tommy" were a fine bunch and gave us much information as was possible about it as we went through the checking procedure. The bomb load was one 4,000lb, 48 x 30lb and 600 x 4lb. Later we were fully briefed, both as individual crew members and then all crews together.'

While Ron Walker's crew were new to the game, Pilot Officer Tommy Farmiloe's crew on 61 Squadron at Coningsby were old hands. Howard Hatherall Farmiloe was born on 21 August 1921 in Birmingham and educated at Chipping Camden School and Birmingham University. A keen motorcyclist, he intended to join the Royal Signals but had responded to a call for volunteers to be air crew, joining the RAF in 1940 and training as a pilot in the United States. At the beginning of 1944 61 Squadron had forsaken the ramshackle base at Skellingthorpe 2 miles to the south-west of Lincoln in 5 Group, which they had shared with 50 Squadron after an acute accommodation problem arose and the 'Lincoln Imps' had forsaken 'Skelly' to move to Coningsby on the edge of the fens about 15 miles south of Lincoln on a three-month detachment. It meant sharing with 619 Squadron, though Coningsby at least offered more in the way of home comforts.

'The month of March was the height of the Bomber Command Offensive and we on 61 Squadron were being very active indeed,' wrote Farmiloe. 'Losses were mounting. If a new crew lasted three or so ops we reckoned that they had a reasonable chance of making ten and then they may possibly complete their first tour (thirty ops). The Lancasters, despite the sterling efforts of the hard-pressed ground crews, always seemed to have "faults". Much as we loved her, my aircraft, "*H-Hellzapoppin*", gave us problems. We were doing Berlin runs quite often – and on two occasions we had to feather a faulty engine, each time on the way to the target.'

On 640 Squadron at Leconfield if the raid went ahead it would be First Lieutenant Edward Dawson Kornegay and crew's sixth operation and their first on Berlin. Kornegay, commonly called 'Doss', was a Texan born on 2 December 1914 who had joined the RCAF in Canada before America entered the war. He successfully transferred to the Eighth Air Force, but effectively pleaded to remain with the RAF and his crew and they would complete fifty-six operations. His cosmopolitan crew included two Canadians, two Scotsmen, a volunteer from Brazil and a Londoner. Sergeant Kenneth Percy Bellew Grantham, the WOp/AG who was from Hastings in Sussex, wrote:

'Our Halifaxes had overload tanks on, so we guessed we were in for a long flight. The pre-raid weather report said that there was a good chance of clear skies at Berlin but added that there was a possibility of 10/10ths thick stratocumulus and so an alternative target, Brunswick, more likely to be clear of cloud, was included in the Battle Order. The final decision would be made just before take-off as to the city which would be attacked. If the choice was 'A' we would go for Brunswick; if it was 'B' then it was the big one. We hoped for the lesser evil. The aircraft had their overload tanks on, so we guessed we were in for a long night. Up on the rostrum the target map was unveiled … a thin red line commencing at Hull ran across the North Sea to Denmark, then out over the Kattegat and on to a point just south of Sweden – making a turn into the Baltic and the Island of Bornholm; from there in a straight line to Berlin. Another red line was pinned to the map which ran southwards into France.

At dusk we were dressed and ready, standing by our Halifax, laughing and joking among ourselves. The CO's little car drove fast into our dispersal bay. He said two words: 'It's B.' We climbed aboard and it didn't seem funny anymore. As we taxied into position at the end of the runway the ground staff and WAAF were lined up on either side to wave us off. It seemed a nice gesture – nice to know some wished us well. Engines run up to full revs – brakes hard on – final check and then we were rolling, leaving the runway at 1900 hours exactly and heading for the first turning-point over Hull; then out over the North Sea but keeping low to stay beneath the German radars for as long as possible. After two hours or so would come the words which put everyone on the alert: 'Enemy Coast Ahead.'[6]

The battle orders were that 811 aircraft – 577 Lancasters, 216 Halifaxes and 18 Mosquitoes – would take off for Berlin and 147 aircraft from training units were detailed to fly a diversionary 'sweep' west of Paris. Fifteen Mosquitoes were to 'spoof' raids on Duisburg, Kiel and Münster and twenty-seven more were to bomb night-fighter airfields in Belgium, Holland and France. Aircraft of 100 Group would fly four RCM sorties and ten Mosquito 'Serrate' patrols.[7]

At Kirmington Flight Lieutenant William R. Jackson's crew on 166 Squadron had by now completed seven ops and Berlin would be their eighth. Sergeant Roy V. Keen, the flight engineer, married and originally from Redhill in Surrey, recalled:

'Jackson was a Canadian who we called 'Rex'. Flight Sergeant Ken Mitchell the mid-upper gunner had done thirty-two trips. Bill Jackson, Flying Officers George Carlisle Reed, navigator and Benjamin Cynddylan Jones, air bomber, got together before we all met and then Sergeant Frank Fountaine the wireless-operator and Ken Mitchell and Sergeant 'Pete' Fenner the gunners joined them. When we had joined the squadron, we took over aircraft that were normally flown by crews who were on leave at the time but on the night of 24th March 1944 'I-Ink' was brand-new, on its first trip. Before we took off, I'll never forget Fountaine saying: 'We're going to get the chop tonight.' The skipper immediately pounced on him.'

On 158 Squadron at Lissett sixteen Halifaxes including 'C-Charlie' flown by Flight Sergeant Bruce Douglas Bancroft were on the battle order. Bancroft was born in Rochdale, New South Wales, Australia on 29 October 1916. He enlisted in the Royal Australian Air Force on 28 February 1942, gaining his 'wings' as sergeant pilot in Canada in March 1943 and he arrived in England the following month. He was eventually posted to an Operational Training Unit at Abingdon, Berkshire on Whitley aircraft where he formed his crew. Bancroft flew his first op, to Magdeburg, on 21 January as 'second dickey' on a 10 Squadron Halifax crew at Melbourne. After he and his crew joined 158 Squadron he flew another 'second dickey' trip on the attack on Stuttgart at the end of February. On Friday 24/Saturday, 25 March Bancroft's crew were detailed as one of the 'windfinder' aircraft in the bomber stream. A number of aircraft were detailed as 'windfinders' on every raid. When the navigator had calculated the actual wind speed and velocity they were transmitted back where an average wind speed was calculated from those sent back by aircraft and then relayed to the Bomber Force to use on their journey.

On 115 Squadron at Witchford Pilot Officer Frank Leatherdale, the 21-year-old navigator on the crew skippered by Pilot Officer Donald 'Mac' McKechnie, a native of Ottawa, viewed the trip philosophically:

'It might have been worrying but for the leadership shown by our Flight Commander – Squadron Leader George Mackie – who put himself on the battle order, making it his eighth trip to the 'Big City'. This was typical of the man and most reassuring to the rest of us. For this night our rear gunner was Charles E. Koss from Illinois whom we borrowed from Flight Lieutenant Halley's crew. 'Chuck' had quite a lot of operational experience, but his real claim to fame was that he was a top sergeant. He was an American who had joined the RCAF before the USA entered the war but after Pearl Harbor he transferred to the USAAF and so enjoyed a greatly increased rate of pay. However, he wanted to remain with his crew and the RAF and so here he was. He wore USAAF khaki uniform and he habitually had the peak of his 'doughboy' hat turned up, looking like a cartoon character from the Bronx.'

'There was always tension going into Berlin,' recalled Squadron Leader George Mackie.[8] 'I always tried to get in early. I tried to get in with the Pathfinders when

I could, because I fancied that I was as good as any Pathfinder. When you went in all hell let loose. They had extraordinary devices that exploded with a tremendous bang and lit up the whole sky to frighten you. The Pathfinders were remarkably good. You saw the flares and incendiaries go down. Then six hundred bombers were all around you. The risk of collision was very great. Looking down you gradually saw the city explode with bombs dropping and with incendiaries. Looking back you saw Berlin burning. This was the turning-point at which extreme caution had to be exercised. If everyone did not turn at the same time, the risk of collision was very great.

'On one particular night two Lancasters collided in front of us and one of them exploded and went straight down. The other did two upward rolls with all four engines burning and exploded right in front of us, a hundred yards away. The pilot shouted to the gunners to turn away so that their night vision would not be impaired. One gunner asked why and when he was told, his knees shook. Quite an extraordinary scene.'

'At the briefing,' wrote 'Ginger' Hammersley, 'we had been told at what time there would be signals broadcast from Bomber Command; when we would receive weather reports; where the searchlight belt and anti-aircraft guns were known to be and also the positions of known German night-fighter units and airfields en route. A weather report was given by the Station Met Officer, the indications being that the weather conditions were not too good and we would be meeting quite strong winds at 18,000-20,000 feet. We were issued with amphetamine ("Wakey-Wakey") tablets; these were taken just prior to take-off and would keep the crews wide-awake and on a "high" for the duration of the flight. If the operation was cancelled, it meant a sleepless night which, for the most of the crews, meant that a wild night of drinking would take place in both the Officers' and Sergeants' mess until the effects of the drug wore off and sleep could take over.

'It was customary for a meal to be prepared for the crews before we flew. We were then issued with a flask of tea or coffee, with chocolate, sandwiches and an apple; armed with a 0.38 revolver and parachute. Codes and Very pistol with cartridges which when fired would give the coded colours of the day. We were even given what were understood to be those in use by the German forces that day. After emptying my pockets and locking my personal items into my cage-type locker, I joined the crew in the crew bus with WAAF "Connie" Mills at the wheel. She often drove the bus that collected the crews from near the control tower. We were then taken out to "T-Tommy". We had another look around the aircraft with the ground crew and about an hour before we were due to take off we settled into our places to await the take-off order. When the first part of the take-off procedure commenced, we were lined up on the airfield perimeter with seventeen other Lancasters from the squadron. All crews would by now have taken their amphetamines and would be wide awake.'

Hammersley saw the first Lancaster given the 'green light' from the mobile watchtower:

'We watched as it slowly climbed away. The remainder all slowly moved around the perimeter track towards the runway and then it was their turn for destination Berlin! The smoke from the engines and the smell of burning high-octane fuel eddied across the airfield. Sixty tons of explosives and incendiaries were to be dropped by 57 Squadron and the sight of seventeen Lancasters, each under full throttles roaring away into the evening sky was an awesome spectacle. Sergeants Frank Beasley and Leslie Wakerell with their ground crews and a number of other well-wishers watched us away before returning to while away the long hours before our return. The smoke and smell slowly thinned and drifted away over the silent airfield and we were on our way to our first bombing operation with the squadron. We were airborne at 1845 hours. This was to be the order of things for some time to come.'

At Metheringham, Pilot Officer Dick Starkey on 106 Squadron taxied 'C-Charlie' out for take-off. On this, his twentieth operation, the crew's ninth to 'the city', they were to act as one of the 'windfinders':

'For dark take-offs at night a line of lights, like cats' eyes, had been installed across the runway 800 yards from the end to give pilots a guide to the distance remaining for take-off. These were very important because getting a Lancaster off the ground, fully loaded with bombs and petrol was a mouth-drying experience as the end of the runway rushed towards you; the last thing you would want or remember was an engine failure. The take-off after straightening the Lancaster on the runway was started by holding the aircraft tightly on the brakes and pushing all four throttles fully open. The aircraft would start moving forward and you gradually released the brakes, at the same time pushing the control column fully forward in order to get the tail up as quickly as possible and build up speed. At that point Johnnie Harris the flight engineer operated the throttles by pushing them through 'the gate' to get extra boost. This could only be maintained for two minutes before he brought them back to normal maximum revs. The two minutes would give us time to get into the air as I concentrated on lifting her off the ground.

'Meanwhile the engineer would call the speed out as it slowly built up – 90 … 100 … 110 mph, at which point I started easing it off the ground, which sometimes it was reluctant to leave and by that time we had left the 800 yards marker well behind and were thundering towards the end of the flarepath. You were then fully committed and had no chance if you had to cancel take-off, it would be the aircraft and the crew. I remember waiting to take off one night when two bright flashes lit up the sky as two Lancasters exploded at nearby airfields – no doubt crashing due to engine failure.

'At 120 mph the wheels came off the ground and as the speed built up I started a flattish climbing turn out of the Drem system with the inner wing barely 50 feet off the ground. Sometimes I left our Drem system with insufficient speed to turn and would approach another airfield's system nearby who were also dispatching aircraft, so we had to be very alert and keep clear of their aircraft. As the altitude increased very slowly I brought the aircraft round to fly over the airfield and set course given to me by Colin Roberts. We left the coast at Skegness and then Wally Paris fused the bombs and I turned off the navigation lights.'

Doug Bancroft on 158 Squadron had lifted 'C-Charlie' off from Lissett at 1859 hours:

'We were briefed to attack in wave three of the five waves of the complete force between 2236 and 2239. Zero hour on the target was timed at 2230 with each wave being allocated three minutes over the target area. The met report at briefing advised good weather conditions all of the way with little cloud and winds only light and variable. We were detailed to fly below 1,000 feet across the North Sea to keep below the enemy radar screen until Anrum Island – about 100 miles from the enemy coast – at which point we were to begin our climb to our bombing height of 20,000 feet. From previous experience we knew that 'C-Charlie' would be struggling to reach 18,500 feet but it so happened that this was the least of our worries.'

At precisely 1909 hours Pilot Officer Tommy Farmiloe revved '*Hellzapoppin*'s powerful Merlin engines at the end of Coningsby's main runway. He released the brakes and shortly afterwards took off into a dark but clear starlit sky. In the airfield circuit they could clearly see Tattershall Castle, of Norman origin but all that remained was the keep, a fine rare medieval brick tower with stone mullion windows and corbelling. The tower's red warning lights coupled with the silver ribbon of the River Witham was a useful navigation aid on night sorties and a very welcome sight to many a bomber crew. After clearing the circuit the crew settled down in their positions as the Lancaster turned north-east over the small fishing port of Boston and the 242 feet-high church 'stump' to join the bomber stream over the North Sea on the first outward leg of the route to Berlin.

This was the crew's seventh trip to the 'Big City' and the third time they had flown the favoured northerly route over Denmark. The return route, however, was potentially a dangerous one. First of all over the north German plain, south of Hanover, then squeeze between flak batteries to the north of the dreaded 'Happy Valley'. With 800 other Main Force aircraft '*Hellzapoppin*' headed north-east over the North Sea. Two hours later the Lancaster crossed the coast of Denmark just north of the island of Sylt, only a couple of miles off track, thanks mainly to the skill of the experienced second tour navigator, Pilot Officer Stan Halliwell. At the crew briefing they had been told to expect strong north-westerly winds up to 60 mph at 20,000 feet. The reality was nearer 125 mph when they made their turn south-east for Berlin, and yet Sergeant Eddie Davidson, the WOp/AG, was still getting a lower wind velocity forecast from Group: 'It was a ludicrous situation. Due to the high tail wind we were at our final turning-point over the Baltic south of Denmark early and found ourselves in the first wave of the bomber stream. Apart from that everything seemed to be going very well.'

On Halifax 'D-Dog' on 78 Squadron at Breighton it was Flight Lieutenant Eric William Everett's crew's fourth visit to the 'Big City' as the wireless-operator, Sergeant Jim E. Johnson, recalls: 'We took off along with the other aircraft from our squadron and headed for Flamborough to join up with the Main Force and set course. To me it was always an awe-inspiring sight to see so many aircraft in flight at the same time all heading for the same target.'

'Apart from flashes in the North Sea as some crews jettisoned their bombs, it was hard to believe there were 800 bombers all closely flying in a stream approximately ten miles long and five miles wide,' wrote Dick Starkey.

Doug Bancroft was on track as verified by fixes taken by his navigator, fellow Australian Flight Sergeant Alwyn Fripp, until over halfway across the North Sea where Bancroft commenced his climb to bombing altitude:

'On reaching the Danish coast Fripp advised that we had drifted over 50 miles south of our flight-plan track and that he had calculated a wind velocity of 100 mph from the north and that our ETA target would be 2252 – fifteen minutes late. The wireless-operator, Sergeant Leonard Dwan[9] was instructed to immediately advise Group Control of the wind velocity and direction and the navigator to give me a new course directly to the northern side of the target area in an endeavour to make up some of the time. We would then be able to attack the target on the planned heading. We arrived in the target area still ten minutes late and I could see that the bomber stream was very widely scattered, no doubt by reason of the fact, as was revealed later, that quite a large number of the crews were adhering to the met forecast winds. Anti-aircraft fire was very concentrated but we were able to make a good bombing run up to the target and get our load of incendiaries and high-explosives onto the target. Enemy fighter aircraft were very active in the search-light area and even in the flak area but as several searchlights converged to form a cone I pushed the control column forward and we dived through the space which they had left clear.'

Flight Lieutenant Ralph Edwards, captain of Lancaster 'S-Sugar' on 7 Squadron at Oakington, wrote: 'The weather report indicated clear skies and the old hands pursed their lips; no cloud meant searchlights; flak and fighters were lined up for a field day. And to rub it in we were told to expect much night-fighter activity.'

'At 20,000 feet the Met forecast a North-westerly wind increasing in strength as we went eastward to a speed of 45 knots,' wrote Frank Leatherdale. 'I found the wind was already stronger than forecast by the time our "Gee" was jammed by the Germans as we got about halfway across the North Sea. As we crossed the Danish coast Ken Demly, our bomb-aimer from Herne Bay down in the nose, got a pin-point which showed we were well south of track. He was positive that he definitely recognised where we were from his map. This gave me a wind from the north-west but at 65 knots. I used this for navigation. We did not see the ground again. Soon the seventy-mile long bomber stream ran into one hundred-knot winds instead of the anticipated sixty-knot tailwind. Over the Baltic the jetstream was so strong that aircraft were registering ground speeds approaching 360 mph, which scattered the aircraft and made navigation tricky. The bomber stream was spread out over fifty miles of sky and stretched back for another 150 miles. When crews made landfall on the Danish coast many navigators realised that they were much further south than they should have been.'

Pilot Officer Mike Beetham's crew on 50 Squadron had just returned to Skellingthorpe after nine days' leave to find that they were on ops this night. Beetham's crew also experienced problems as his bomb-aimer, Flight Sergeant Les Bartlett recalled:

'The winds were so variable so instead of passing the northern tip of Sylt we went bang into it and had to fly up the island's west coast and then around the top. Chaps were off course all over Flensburg. The next leg took us across Denmark and then down the Baltic coast. Many chaps then got into trouble with the defences of Kiel, Lübeck and Rostock; I saw at least four go down in a very short space of time. We had a near squeak at Rostock as the wind blew us into their defences and we were coned by about four searchlights but after a few violent manoeuvres we managed to shake them off before the flak got into range; they were very tense moments for us. With a strong wind behind us we were soon approaching Berlin.'[10]

Dick Starkey was advised by Sergeant Colin Roberts his navigator that the wind speed was approaching 100mph and should he broadcast his findings back to Bomber Command?

'I said if he was satisfied with his calculations he must transmit them to England. I ordered my navigator to work from his own calculations and ignore the wind speeds being sent back to us because they were far too low. By the time the Danish coast was crossed we were many miles south of track as a result of the high wind speed from the north. (At that time nobody had heard of the jetstream. Bomber Command met this phenomenon on this night.) The force was scattered over a very wide front as we approached Berlin well before zero hour. Some captains ordered their navigators to work to the winds broadcast from England and found them hopelessly off track. Others navigated on their own findings and were reaching points well in advance of ETA but they were not as far off as the others were. We arrived over the target early and I decided to risk going round the city on the eastern side, by which time the PFF markers would be going down, and start our bombing run.'

Flight Lieutenant Ralph Edwards on 7 Squadron wrote: 'As we flew across the North Sea the visibility was so good we could pick out the coast fifty miles off and there was plenty of evidence as to the activity of the defences. Our route took us to the German-Danish border where we turned south-east, not so far from Kiel where we saw vast skeins of searchlight beams – gigantic lattices – hundreds of them. As we got closer I observed great pyramids of light and at the apex glittered a silver fish – a Lancaster surrounded by flashes of orange and red light which winked and flashed as the shells exploded. Several aircraft were caught and as I watched, the glistening object suddenly dissolved into a brilliant red mushroom – like a child's rocket on Guy Fawkes Night and then it blossomed out and fell as red rain. We knew it was a Lancaster with seven tons of bombs, two thousand gallons of high-octane and a full crew on board – going down in fragments – a burning incandescence. As the final moments came and a 'kill' registered, the beams would extinguish; then, a moment later, quiver into brilliance again having locked on to another quarry.'

The bombers on the diversionary raid west of Paris had already turned for home and when the Main Force had crossed the German coast east of Rostock and bypassed Stettin the JLO became convinced that the target was Berlin. He concentrated forces at points in the Hamburg-Heligoland area as well as to the north-west of Berlin and fed them into the bomber stream all the way from Sylt to the target. Others were held in readiness to follow the bombers once they had left the target. Actually, fighters achieved comparatively little success, because the strong north wind that scattered the bomber stream proved unfavourable to consistent interception. The Nachtjagd made thirty-six attacks; mostly over the target but many bombers were engaged over defended areas off track, notably at Sylt, Magdeburg, Münster, Osnabrück, Kiel and Rostock; also at Leipzig, Kassel and the Ruhr. The night-fighters claimed 18 victims: 6 at Sylt, 2 at Flensburg, 2 at Rostock and Prenzlau, 4 over Berlin, 1 at Nordhausen, 1 over Osnabrück and 2 over Holland. It was reported that at Berlin the heavy guns fired a slight to moderate barrage from 17,000 to 22,000 feet with moderate to intense light flak up to 16,000 feet. Numerous searchlights illuminated the cloud base and formed cones through the gaps. No fewer than 45 aircraft were estimated to have been lost to flak: 17 on the outward route, 7 over the target and 21 on the way home. Seven were shot down over the Ruhr, six at Osnabrück, four at Flensburg and four at Magdeburg.

As a result of a strong tail wind Flight Lieutenant Lou Greenburgh DFC on 514 Squadron who had successfully ditched returning from Berlin on 29/30 December arrived well before the Pathfinders. 'C-Charlie' was coned by searchlights and then, having just released the bombs over Berlin, was attacked head-on by a night-fighter. Luckily Sergeant Les Weddle the flight engineer had spotted the dark shape below and shouted to the skipper to 'go starboard for chrissakes!' The second he did so cannon shells slammed into the two starboard engines. Having instantly swung his turret forward, Fred Carey the mid-upper gunner saw the cannon shells strike home. The Lancaster turned onto its back and went into a flat spin, plunging from over 20,000 feet to barely 8,000 feet. Greenburgh ordered the crew to bail out. The two nearest the front escape hatch, Les Weddle and Don Bament the Australian bomb-aimer, wasted no time in leaving and both parachuted to safety and into captivity. For the five remaining in the out-of-control bomber their horrible fate seemed certain, especially for the navigator 'Paddy' Butler whose parachute disappeared through the open front escape hatch along with all the tools of his trade. Suddenly a bump was felt under the Lancaster and for some inexplicable reason the aircraft's attitude changed to almost level flight. Greenburgh and Butler, believing they were the only two left aboard, got a shock when three others of the crew appeared. 'Connie' Drake had got stuck in his rear turret and Fred Carey and 'Strommy' Stromberg the wireless-operator had gallantly stayed behind to assist him.

Showing amazing courage, Greenburgh managed to get back into the cockpit. As the Lancaster continued its rapid descent, Greenburgh skilfully pulled the Lancaster out at 4,000 feet over Berlin. However, they were not yet out of danger. A fire was raging in the fuselage. 'Strommy' Stromberg fearlessly fought the flames, extinguishing them before the fire did any more damage. With tremendous effort, Greenburgh managed to restart one of his damaged engines and was able to pull the bomber up to 6,000 feet so that they could fly back to base at Waterbeach on three engines.[11]

'Some distance ahead of us,' continues Flight Lieutenant Ralph Edwards, 'the first target markers were falling to open the attack and the ground defences redoubled their efforts to knock down the Pathfinders responsible. Searchlights swept upwards and red flashes from exploding flak shells engulfed the aircraft. Untouched by these horrors we rode through it and released our bombs; then we were on the far side of the city congratulating ourselves on a merciful escape when it happened.... Suddenly, from below sprang a quivering beam of intense light which transfixed "S-Sugar"; a single master beam had picked us out and in a split second we became the centre of a web of blinding searchlights. Our turn had come – we were well and truly 'coned'! The first reaction was one of being robbed of all vision and sense of direction: the white light penetrated every chink and the Perspex astrodome became a shimmering hemisphere, intensifying the glare. The first salvoes of high-explosive arrived with a shattering roar, bracketing the Lancaster which bucked and shuddered in the shock waves.

'There was nothing to be gained by looking outside; the only course was that of lowering my seat and starting the evasive action with eyes glued to the instrument panel – ignoring the maelstrom of fury surrounding us – and hope for the best. I twisted and turned diving and climbing as salvo after salvo came up from below until there came a tremendous bang right in front of the nose and instantly all was darkness on the flight deck – as if a great canopy had been flung over the Lancaster, shutting out all light. It was bewildering and I wondered what diabolical trick had been played. The sudden exchange from dazzling light to utter darkness was frightening and the mid-upper gunner called to say his turret was blanketed with a black substance. Here was a fine situation! We were at 18,000 feet harried by flak and blind as a bat. Then the rear gunner called me to say he could see and I took directions from him to avoid the flak bursts, "Down port – hold it – sharp starboard – keep diving …" and eventually the bursting shells were left behind. All this time I was flying on instruments and wondering that the hell had happened – but as we discovered later the explanation was simple enough: the main hydraulic feed to the nose turret had been shattered by the burst under the nose and high-pressure oil had been released … covering everything.

'Fierce and bitterly cold draughts came through the jagged holes in the fuselage and a fire was burning in the lower end behind the oxygen storage and main spar. Flames were belching from the port inner engine and the exhaust stubs had been blown off – the smell of cordite was strong – but all four engines were running sweetly. Though we did not know it at the time, the fuel jettisoning pipe had been blown from its housing in the mainplane and was dangling in the slipstream with a small but steady leak from the outer tank. The oil still lay thick on the windscreen; the fire in the fuselage was out and with freezing blasts from the torn nose panels we set a course for the North Sea coast. There were hundreds of miles to go before we would reach it and fuel was draining away; the loss of the hydraulics did not worry me; with any luck the undercarriage could be blown down by air pressure from the emergency bottle, but the thought of all that water and the prospect of a ditching were uppermost in my mind. She was not handling too well but I was determined to get her back to Oakington again. My crew never seemed to doubt we could do it but it was a long flog.

'We were picked up again by searchlights but no flak arrived and I assumed they were co-operating with night-fighters so we kept the sharpest lookout every inch of the way, but I was still virtually blind up front and flying by the instrument panel. The film of oil that covered the side windows was very sticky and not likely to clear without external help so I knew the landing might be tricky, but put this problem to the back of my mind for the time being.'

Flight Lieutenant Peter Sherriff, captain of 'P-Peter' on 100 Squadron at Grimsby, was over Berlin at zero hour:

'Very little cloud or haze over target. PFF marking very unsatisfactory … bombed on mixed red and green TIs accompanied by release-point flares red with yellow stars. Five minutes later we saw still further red and green TIs. Both groups were bombed. Incendiaries were dropped all over the place. There was a little flak over target but intense searchlight activity. Extensive decoy oil sites with decoy red markers (short-burning) active to north of target. Winds 30 mph faster than forecast. Many aircraft strayed south on way arousing defences as far off track as Kiel. Over Denmark defences very hot.'

All crews reported an increase in cloud as they drew near the city. Squadron Leader Keith Cresswell piloting Lancaster 'B-Baker' on 35 Squadron was one of the twenty-five Blind Marker Illuminators opening the attack at Z-5 minutes (zero hour was 2230). The Pathfinder Marking Sequence or the 'Berlin Method' designed to cover all eventualities was necessarily complex. Seventy 'supporters', which had no marking role, were necessary to mask the Blind Marker Illuminators and were to be followed by forty-four more PFF aircraft in sequence over the city. These consisted of six Visual Markers commencing at Z-3 minutes and eighteen 'Blind Backers-Up' and twenty 'Visual Backers-Up', both commencing at Z-1 to Z+15.[12] The bombing was made on red sky-markers at 6,000 feet at a speed of 165 mph. The attack was very scattered at first and some of the TIs were seen burning about 10 miles south-west of the target. The raid developed into a 'terrific overshoot' because of the strong winds.

John Searby wrote: 'Some crews overshot Berlin altogether – blown south – but stoutly returned and tried again – though by the time they got back into position the rest of the party had beaten it for home. This was commendable – since they were virtually alone over Berlin, providing an easy target.'[13]

Keith Cresswell's mid-upper gunner, Sergeant Randolph Rhodes, who was on his fourth operation recalled:

'The pyrotechnic display was a sight never to be forgotten – the ack-ack shells exploding, the fiery red and green trails of the target indicators, bombs exploding below, bombers blazing from end to end all served to make the night skies over Berlin almost as light as day. The enemy fighters sat up high out of range of the flak where they could see bombers silhouetted against the general conflagration. I searched the sky diligently – saw the brief reflection from a propeller – and wasted not an instant… 'Fighter – Fighter – corkscrew port…' but Cresswell had already dropped the nose and wing as the enemy opened fire, making a large hole in the tailplane. The red and green tracer shells streaked past no more than a foot from my head; a fraction of a second delay on the part of the pilot and I would have caught it. Then the fighter pilot made a fatal error: instead of breaking away below where we could not possibly have hit him, he pulled up the nose exposing his underside to our combined guns at close range. I saw the puny .303s bounce off without doing any obvious damage, but this was not the case for he levelled off above us, his undercarriage dropped and he began diving down into the blazing city. If we had had .5 guns we could have ripped him apart. I confess I acted more from instinct than from certainty but upon such things rested our survival: a split second's indecision could have resulted in sudden death.'[14]

Flight Lieutenant 'Ed' Moore, navigator from Edson, Alberta on Jack Hollingsworth's crew on 426 'Thunderbird' Squadron recalled:

'When the Pathfinder flares went off behind us … we turned around and dropped our bombs on target about twenty-five minutes late. Since the planned bombing run had been from the north-west, we were bucking a strong headwind and flying against the main stream of aircraft leaving the target area. We would be bucking high winds all the way home and thus would be short of fuel. Finally we would be travelling alone and would be vulnerable to fighters. Common sense should have dictated that the bombs be jettisoned and a course set for home. Nevertheless we all agreed with the skipper. "We've come this far; we'll drop the bombs in the right place." People like myself with no H2S assistance relied on broadcast winds which were quoted at about 75 mph rather than 120 mph. That put you about 50 miles from where you thought you were at the end of each hour.'[15]

Pilot Officer Frank Leatherdale on 115 Squadron wrote: 'At the time I calculated we should be over Berlin there was no sign of enemy searchlights nor flak, nor of our Pathfinder's Target Indicator (TI) markers. Then suddenly all hell broke loose behind us as the first PFF flares started to cascade and the defences opened up. Doubtless they had been silent hoping we would fly past them to go somewhere else. The ground was hidden by a solid layer of cloud so the Pathfinders were dropping sky-markers. These were special parachute flares which burnt with a given colour, either red or green, and sometimes they emitted stars of a different colour which fell from the main flare in order to distinguish our markers from German decoy 'sky-markers' fired from their anti-aircraft guns. The PFF aimed their sky-markers using their H2S radar, but for the main force to hit the target on the ground the bombs had to be dropped on a given heading. In our case it meant we had to turn round and fly back across Berlin before we could turn again onto the correct heading for bombing. As we flew back I realised for sure that something was awfully wrong. It took us twenty very worrying minutes to fly northwards across Berlin; this meant our speed over the ground was only 55 mph. For that to be true it followed that the wind was now blowing at 120 mph or more. This was quite unbelievable; but the facts were there very plainly. No one had heard of 'jet streams' – the words simply did not exist.

'This flight back over Berlin was quite frightening as we risked colliding with friendly aircraft coming towards us in later waves and our slow ground speed must have made us a sitting duck for the flak, but our luck held and we safely got into position from which to bomb. We eventually bombed the target twenty to twenty-five minutes late. I used the new wind I had found to re-calculate our course for home.

'Soon after leaving the target our main compass failed, which meant that 'Mac' McKechnie had to steer by the P4 compass; this was difficult for him to see and was not so accurate. We got back to Witchford without further trouble, having been airborne for seven hours and twenty-five minutes. We subsequently learned that Bomber Command had lost over 100 heavy bombers that night: some had been blown off course and had straggled across the Ruhr where the defences had a field day. George Mackie had also realised there was an unprecedented wind speed and decided to come down and fly below the clouds, which he did map-reading his way along the Dutch coast. Many navigators had not been as fortunate as we had been in finding new wind velocities and had relied upon what was called the 'zephyred wind'. This was a wind which was broadcast to the main bomber force from HQ Bomber Command and which was the met men's estimate of what the wind was, based on wind velocities sent back at each degree of longitude by certain PFF aircraft. With their H2S these PFF navigators knew where they were and what the wind really was, but the met men in England did not believe them – and who could blame them when no one had experienced such strong winds before. Everyone learnt a lesson that night.'

The Pathfinder assessment was that 'the attack opened punctually at the planned zero hour by the 'Blind Marker Illuminators' and eleven of those detailed had marked the target and in the majority of cases, released 'sky-markers' over the target by Z-1. Cloud conditions prevented visual identification and as a result the attack was purely 'Parramatta' and 'Wanganui' [code-names for blind 'ground' and 'sky-marking']. Only four 'visual markers' were able to drop target indicators visually and as a result the ground-marking between zero and Z+7 was thin. At Z+7 the Blind Backers-Up came into play and from then until the end of the attack a good continuity of 'ground-marking' was attained.'

For the first time since the raid on 23/24 August 1943 a master bomber, Wing Commander Reggie 'Sunshine' Lane DSO DFC, the amiable, soft-spoken Canadian CO of 405 'Vancouver' Squadron who was on his third tour, was used. Wing Commander Lane's radio call sign was 'Redskin'. Wing Commander Bill Anderson who was lying on some cushions in the nose of a Mosquito of the Meteorological Flight was deputy master bomber. His call sign was 'Pommy'. Anderson wrote:

'Wing Commander Lane was heard in spite of jamming and although unable to give little positive direction to the crews he nevertheless gave much general encouragement in a distinctively Canadian and often excitable series of remarks such as 'Those bastards wanted a war; now show them what war is like.'

Warrant Officer J. Porter, a Halifax captain on 10 Squadron at Melbourne who heard the master bomber 'exhorting crews', wrote:

'At 2227 the glow of fires ahead indicated our approach to target. Red TI seen to cascade followed by others. Sky-markers already burning. 5/10th cloud with tops at 5,000 feet – mass of searchlights and many cones forming. Got south of track leaving Berlin – touched north of Ruhr – four bombers seen shot down between Dortmund and Duisburg. Glow of Berlin fire seen 140 miles away.'

Flight Lieutenant J.H. Stevens, a Halifax pilot on 466 Squadron RAAF, remembered that 'the master bomber was pleading with PFF crews to achieve a better concentration.' Pilot Officer Ronald C. Reinelt, captain of Halifax 'Q-Queenie' on 433 'Porcupine' Squadron RCAF at Skipton, felt that 'the Master of Ceremonies was more a morale help than tactical.'[16] The Bomber Command Intelligence narrative after the raid would agree with him. '"The Master of Ceremonies" was generally more helpful in giving encouragement than in directing the bombing,' it said. Other men remember the calm and cultivated English voice of the deputy master bomber occasionally contributing a remark.[17]

Flight Sergeant Alan Ludvig Olsson of Montreal, Quebec on 426 'Thunderbird' Squadron RCAF at Linton-on-Ouse reported:

'Marking was punctual at 2230 hours with red and green TIs … with some red and yellow flares. The concentration was fair but results difficult to assess owing to cloud. Bombed at 2233 from 22,000 feet – defences normal. Not much heavy flak and searchlights obscured by cloud five to seven-tenths cover. Good breaks occasionally permitting glimpses of buildings on fire … some overshooting, possibly due to strong winds … flak activity was considerable at all defended areas, especially south of Magdeburg.'

Olsson was second pilot on the Lancaster captained by Squadron Leader James 'Bert' Millward DFC of Sherbrooke, Quebec who had taken off at 2024 hours. The aircraft was coned in searchlights before reaching the target and fired upon by flak. Millward took evasive action and escaped the searchlights, but the aircraft had been damaged by flak which had damaged the hydraulic system. With the damage sustained the crew dropped their bombs over Bremen at 2345 hours and made for home.[18]

When Doug Bancroft's crew arrived in the target area there was about 9/10ths cloud cover. 'We were able to get glimpses of the ground area from time to time and were actually able to bomb visually on to the aiming-point. The PFF marking was very scattered and so was the bombing generally. Some markers and bombs were as much as 10 miles off-target and a number of crews bombed as much as 15 miles short of the area in their haste to set course for their home bases. I witnessed several mid-air collisions, no doubt caused by aircraft which had gone wide of or to the south of the target area turning back directly into the main stream which was entering the area from the NNE. Anti-aircraft gunfire was very concentrated (I am advised that there were some 1,500 guns protecting the city) and masses of searchlights ringed the city. In addition, groups of night-fighter aircraft began their attacks well before the target area was reached and these were also very active even amongst the flak. We were able to make a good bombing run up to the target and drop our load of incendiaries and high-explosives right in the target area from our height of 18,000 feet without being attacked by a night-fighter at that crucial stage or being hit by the mass of anti-aircraft shells exploding around us, although we were bounced about considerably by the force of these explosions.'

On 640 Squadron 'Doss' Kornegay and crew flew over Denmark just north of Esbjerg at 14,000 feet, climbing and turning slightly to avoid Copenhagen.

Ken Grantham wrote: 'There was little enemy activity at this stage – isolated flak and tracer shells climbing skywards. Time to start 'Windowing'; I tore the wrapper and pushed the lot into the 'chute which would send the strips flying into the slipstream to jam the German radar scopes. One a minute – pick up – tear – throw; a monotonous rhythm which would not end until we were clear of enemy territory. In between times I spun the dial of the radio receiver over the short-wave band searching for the voices of the German fighter controllers. When I picked one up I tuned in the microphone located in one of the engine nacelles. If it was done quickly the instructions from the German controller to his waiting fighters were blotted out by the racket from my transmitter.

'Then below us lay neutral Sweden and we saw something we had not seen for a very long time – towns and villages lit up! There was no blackout anywhere and I was fascinated to see twinkling lights. Suddenly, one of the gunners reported fighter aircraft on our beam, and he was puzzled because they made no attempt to engage us. We could see them quite plainly – ghostly white aircraft flying alongside the bomber stream. We watched them for a while as they came and went and concluded they were Swedish – making a token gesture of defending their neutrality. To the north of our track we saw streams of light flak and assumed this to be from Swedish ground batteries – not trying to hit us but performing a similar duty. The fighters accompanied us well out over the Baltic, perhaps curious to see where we were going. Then they vanished.

'It was about this time that Flying Officer G. Prosser our navigator started to have serious doubts about the wind speed and direction being put out on the Group broadcast. By their reckoning it was in the region of 80 mph but our navigator was calculating wind in excess of 100 mph. Later we discovered he was much nearer the mark. We had encountered this phenomenon now known as the 'jet stream'. This was a wind of very high velocity blowing at a particular height – something like a tide-race at sea – but at that time nothing much was known about it and the bomber stream was straying all over the sky due to the conflicting opinions. By now the enemy had guessed our destination and the fighters we had seen previously had changed to dark prowlers in the night sky. Hundreds of fighter flares were coming down to light up the bombers and assist the Messerschmitts and Focke-Wulfs to attack from the darkness whilst our own gunners were blinded by the powerful lights and we met heavy flak which increased in intensity. Almost before we realised it we were over Berlin. Now the heavy ack-ack was the menace and a veritable curtain of bursting shells faced us. Up front Flying Officer G. Williams the Canadian bomb-aimer was exclaiming over and over in a broad Canadian accent, 'Jesus Skipper – look at that flak … just look at it will ya … we'll never get through it … Jeez, just look at it.' Then the Skipper's tense voice silenced him.'

Berlin was already burning when Kornegay's crew arrived over the city. Sergeant Ken Grantham's own view of events was mercifully obscured by the bulk of the Canadian navigator, Flying Officer G. Prosser and the bomb-aimer:

'At times I preferred not to look and the glimpses I got were frightening enough. It was mayhem down below – bombs bursting – photoflashes blinking and a pall of fire-lit smoke over everything. Nothing can ever recreate that moment. The tight muscles, the dry mouth and the buffeting the aircraft received whilst the Skipper fought to keep it steady as we swam through the slip-streams of a hundred other aircraft and bounced to the ack-ack bursts. It was an unbelievable experience. Three years of training – hours of circuits and landings – nights spent on cross-country navigation exercises – all leading up to this moment – to Berlin – and we were there.

'The bomb-aimer spotted the PFF flares and adjusted his sights. There was silence in the aircraft as he went through the familiar routine. 'Steady … steady…. Left a bit…. Right…. Hold it…. Steady.' Then the moment when everyone lets out a sigh of relief: 'Bombs gone'. The aircraft leapt as the weight dropped from her belly, then the Skipper's Texan voice over the intercom: 'OK. Bomb doors closed – let's get the hell out of here.'

'Once the bombing photograph was taken,' wrote Doug Bancroft, 'it became a matter of getting out of the heavily defended area as quickly as possible and trying to avoid being caught in the beam of the searchlights, especially a blue-coloured radar-controlled master light. I put the nose of the aircraft down and increased power on the motors to gain more speed and when several lights converged to form two cones in the sky, we were able to dive through the space between the cones and then to head for our turning-point for the route back to base. Still using the wind velocity and direction as calculated by Flight Sergeant Fripp, we were able to maintain the original flight-plan tracks for the whole of the homeward flight without incident, although whilst north of Osnabrück we could see well to the south, over the Ruhr Valley area, that many aircraft had drifted down there and were caught in the heavy defences of that area and many were being shot down there.'[19]

Weaving slightly to throw off the fighters, 'Doss' Kornegay on 640 Squadron flew south, pushed along by a vicious tail-wind:

'Near Leipzig,' recalls Ken Grantham, 'we were in a belt of searchlights – great pillars of blue light weaving back and forth like flying through a vast cathedral … cones of several lights coming together to trap some poor devil while the flak batteries pumped their shells into him. We turned northwards on to track, as we thought, for a more lightly defended route out via Emden. Flying at 24,000 feet the navigator again queried the broadcast wind since we were rapidly drifting south of track. Then we were once more into heavy concentrations of flak and searchlights and realised we had drifted over the Ruhr – the most heavily defended area in Germany. Struggling to make headway at one stage our groundspeed was down to a mere 30 mph and once again the searchlights hit us – the aircraft suddenly lit up as if the sun had risen and the flak started to pound us as the Skipper put us into a steep dive; the light was left behind and we plunged earthwards in total darkness. We didn't complain.'[20]

'The attack was in full swing when we arrived,' wrote Bill Anderson, 'and through the thin wisps of low cloud we could see red and green ground-markers which the boys had dropped as well as the sky-marker flares. The defences were firing away busily, but the searchlights were not working so well together as usual. The cones were not so clear-cut and odd beams were straying about. I think the cloud was foxing them a little. And I saw something new, peculiar rows of lights that floated slowly upwards. I didn't realize what they were until I went to a cinema some weeks later and saw London's rocket defences in action.

'Everybody has watched a man painting a fence. There is always an irritating little bit that he will keep missing, so that you long to grab the brush and just give one dab to cover it. There was a patch right in the centre of Berlin where nothing had fallen. I wanted to stretch out my hand and smear some of the other lights over it. Luckily for my peace of mind, some obliging type, possibly a painter by trade himself, did the job just before the end with a nice dollop of incendiaries.

'We felt so bad about turning up late that we hung about for a while after the attack should have been over. Having exhausted all the stock of expressions including the odd quotation from Shakespeare and having decided that the bombing had now finished completely and that there was no great future in staying any longer, I produced the carefully-worded and highly indelicate "good night" to Hitler. Hardly had the last rich syllable rolled unctuously off my tongue when a voice came back out of the darkness; a rich Canadian voice, "Cut the cackle and drop us off another flare, I can't see a fucking thing." So we stayed and talked with him a little to mollify him and then pushed off home.

'On the way back we were coned by searchlights for some time. And lying in the nose of the aircraft, I had leisure to analyse my exact feelings. I was scared; there was no doubt about that. Yet I knew that this was like my lumbago, an uncomfortable sensation but somehow beside the point. What really did matter was that I had let the party down by arriving late. That it had not affected the operation was beside the point. I had broken the first rule of the Pathfinder Force that I had so often drummed into others, which is not that you must be clever, nor that you must be brave but simply that you must be reliable. On the way home I saw six aircraft shot down by night-fighters. They each started as a little flame getting gradually bigger and then suddenly falling, an explosion of light as they hit the deck and then a patch of fire burning quite steadily.'[21]

Wing Commander Lane recalled the homeward journey: 'Airplanes were all over the bloody place. I was over Berlin for about half an hour I suppose and we didn't have any trouble. Then we started to go back and by golly, as we went back I called Glen Elwood my navigator up. I said, 'You don't need to navigate, just come up here', because of course by that time most of the bomber force was ahead of me and I said, 'We can map-read our way home' and literally every defended area in Germany from Berlin west was alive. Searchlights, flak … many of the bomber crews were shot down over the Ruhr because they had drifted south in this wind and they were all flying right over the most heavily defended area of Germany. So we did; he came up and he stood up beside me and we literally map-read our way home. I just flew in between the defended areas; I knew exactly where we were the whole damn time, with people being coned and being shot down. It was a disaster.[22]

'Luckily, over the target a thin layer of stratus cloud had formed which made it difficult for the searchlights to pick us up,' wrote Mike Beetham, 'so we had little trouble during the bomb run. Shortly after, however, things started to get hot as the enemy fighters were waiting for us. Although we saw fighters we were lucky that none attacked us as we dodged the flak and kept out of the defences of Leipzig, Brunswick, Osnabrück and Hanover. Along this leg we saw several combats with kite after kite going down in flames.'

Soon after leaving Berlin, Flight Lieutenant Richard William Picton DFC, the 24-year-old skipper on Lancaster 'D-Dog' on 550 Squadron at North Killingholme, was in combat with another Fw 190.

Born at Letchworth, 'Dickie' Picton was educated at St Christopher School and joined the editorial staff of the *Hertfordshire Express* at Hitchin, later entering King's College, London, further to study journalism. While a student there he joined the RAFVR and was commissioned in June 1943. After qualifying as a pilot he was for some time an instructor in elementary flying.

Sergeant W.M. Keen, the Canadian mid-upper gunner, and Sergeant J.W. Porteous in the rear turret received serious injuries from cannon fire. The wireless-operator, Sergeant Ken Williams, went into the astrodome and warned Picton and gave him evasive instructions. With the attack apparently over, he then went back to the rear gunner whose oxygen tube had been severed, gave him his own oxygen mask and assisted him out of the turret. Williams later sent a radio message back to base, giving details of the casualties so that medical aid was waiting when the aircraft landed. 'Dickie' Picton took part in twenty-four big raids on 550 Squadron.

He and Kenneth Percy Charles Williams, who received an immediate DFM for his action on the trip to Berlin, were among those killed on 10/11 April when their Lancaster was shot down by a night-fighter on Aulnoye.

Pilot Officer (later Squadron Leader DFC) Kenyon Bowen-Bravery, the skipper on Lancaster 'J-Jig', which he rechristened '*Bad Penny II*' as bad pennies always come back, had his rear turret put out of action and bombed a flak emplacement on the west coast of Denmark. Soon afterwards the '*Bad Penny*' was attacked by a single-engined aircraft and the mid-upper gunner gave it a short burst from very short range. A short while later a burning aircraft was seen going down by three of the crew and then burning on the ground. Kenyon Bowen-Bravery was born in Cardiff on 19 December 1922 and educated at Barry County Grammar School. He joined the RAF in September 1941 and trained as a pilot at the RAF College Cranwell. On the night of 5 June he and his crew, veterans of more than twenty bombing operations, set off in the '*Bad Penny II*'. They were part of an armada of 1,012 bombers flying in support of Operation 'Overlord' and had been ordered to attack the heavy gun battery at Crisbecq on the Normandy coast. At 1134 hours they released fourteen 1,000lb bombs, the first to fall in support of the airborne and amphibious assault which was about to commence. After D-Day, Bowen-Bravery attacked other targets in France and on 23 June bombed the marshalling yards at Saintes. It was his thirtieth and final operation and he was awarded the DFC.

On 156 Squadron the bomb-aimer on Lancaster 'Z-Zebra' flown by Pilot Officer R. McLean had just got his bombs away at 2228 hours at 19,000 feet when two minutes later, flak tore away the Perspex nose and the starboard inner engine was put out of action, yet McLean pressed on without charts or navigating equipment to land back at Warboys at 0202 hours. Nothing was heard from Flight Lieutenant Ronald Richmond and crew on 'T-Tommy' after take-off, the aircraft crashing at Grosthuizen while homebound. Only the flight engineer survived to be taken into captivity.

Sergeant William Henry Burnell, mid-upper gunner on Lancaster 'C-Charlie' on 166 Squadron at Kirmington flown by 22-year-old Australian Flight Sergeant Ernest Brown, wrote:

'We reached Berlin, dropped our bombs at 25,000 feet and as we were leaving the target area, our two port engines were hit by flak and set on fire. My skipper ordered us to abandon the aircraft but at that point a German fighter, attracted by our plane on fire, came in to attack us. A shell from the fighter seared across the top of my head and knocked me out. When I came to I was in the wreckage of the bomber. It had crashed into the side of a huge pine forest. I was much bruised. The only injury I received was from the shell of the German fighter; my head was split wide open. I then gave myself up at a German railway signal crossing. Next day, I found out that all six of my crew were killed when they bailed out of the 'plane. It was said that my 'plane was seen to spiral down and hit the side of the ground.'[23]

The raid was the last of Clayton Moore's six trips to Berlin: 'Our mount for the night was 'Q-Queenie'.[24] A visit to the 'Big City' was always a daunting prospect, but this was to be the worst. Our problems began on the outward leg, when we found that the information on wind speeds supplied by the Met Office was far from accurate. Dick Lodge, our navigator, was quick to realise that something was wrong and he directed us to carry out a series of time-wasting dog-legs in order to compensate for the strong winds that were pushing us on to the target ahead of time. Despite this, we still arrived too early, only to find the raid in full progress, since most of the other crews had not questioned the error.

'It was after we had dropped our bombs and turned for home that the real trouble started. Now we were heading almost directly into a wind [later to be recognized as the jetstream] which Dick estimated to be more than 100 mph – almost twice the predicted speed. As a result, our rate of progress was almost halved and we were being blown off course by the hurricane which was attacking us from a north-westerly direction. Fortunately, the skies were reasonably clear above us and Dick was able to take a few star shots with the sextant, thus enabling him to plot our position. From this he was then able to get a fairly accurate estimate of the true wind speed. The clear skies would also have provided the defending fighters with an advantage, except for the fact that they too were faced with the same problems that we had. Not so the searchlight and flak batteries, however. For them, the conditions were ideal and the degree of co-operation between the two forces was to be admired. Because of the mix-up, many bombers were straying over heavily defended areas where they were being shot to pieces by the ground defences.

'Dick was only one of the many navigators who had calculated the correct wind speed and the information had been radioed back to Group. But, because the information was so unprecedented, each of the numerous reports was considered exorbitant, so was ignored. Winds of such speeds had never before been encountered over Western Europe. As a consequence, the entire force was strung out all over central Germany. Those crews which, like us, had elected to ignore the broadcast winds and work to their own findings had a chance. The considerable remainder were in deep trouble. Lost, well behind schedule and with fuel stocks running dangerously low, they blundered on in bunches, straight into the waiting ground defences, where they were picked off one by one. When the tally was finally arrived at, it was learned that a total of seventy-two bombers [forty-four of them Lancasters] had been lost during the action. 83 Squadron had not contributed to this number, however, and we all looked upon this as a reflection of the undoubted efficiency of the crews (the navigators in particular) rather than luck.

'The carnage we witnessed was uppermost in our minds when, two nights later, we were briefed to do a raid on Essen, right in the heart of the Valley itself.'[25]

'C-Charlie' was one of four Lancasters on 166 Squadron that were lost on the operation. On the homeward flight '*Dante's Daughter*' which had completed more than seventy sorties crashed near Kempen, killing six of the crew skippered by 21-year-old Flying Officer Thomas Leo Whigham Teasdale of Vancouver. Only fellow Canadian Flying Officer Jack Barton Auld survived to be taken prisoner. Tommy Teasdale and his twin brother Harry Leo Teasdale were born on 28 October 1922 at Drumheller, Alberta. Warrant Officer1 Harry Teasdale, who enlisted in the RCAF on 14 November 1941, was on 11 Squadron when he was killed in action on 19 February 1945 at the age of 22.

'D-Dog' flown by 27-year-old Flying Officer Jack Lawrie 'Mac' McGill of London, Ontario was also shot down on the homeward flight, crashing near

Treuenbrietzen south-west of Berlin. As the nose of the Lancaster was blown off, the 22-year-old air bomber, Flying Officer Conrad Melvin Torget RCAF of Walnut Creek, British Columbia was blown out of the aircraft. 'Con' was born in Sydney on 29 May 1921 and had emigrated with his family via Norway and England in 1925. He was unconscious but regained consciousness as he passed through the clouds and was able to open his parachute. He was the sole survivor of the crew of seven, was captured and became a PoW for fourteen months.

Sergeant Roy Keen on 'I-Ink' piloted by Canadian Flight Lieutenant Bill Jackson recalled that 100-knot winds were experienced instead of the anticipated 60-knot tailwind. 'And we could not climb above 21,000 feet. I tried all ways to get more height, but we couldn't. The bomb load was normal at about 12,000lb. The skipper tried trimming the plane, but nothing would work. It's like a car; you sometimes get one that won't do what it's supposed to. We got coned by searchlights on the way in over the coast and we had to jink about like hell to get out of it. George Reed our spot-on navigator was going barmy! Because the winds were stronger we were over the target twenty minutes early and we were too long over the target. I don't think it paid to hang about over Berlin longer than you needed to! We couldn't find anything to bomb the first time, so we went round again.'

Jackson said later: 'It was a mistake to go around again. We were shot down east of Berlin by what we believed to be a night-fighter which manoeuvred beneath us and strafed us from a top-mounted gun, along the whole length of our Lancaster. The plane caught fire and I ordered the crew to abandon the aircraft. After determining that five of the crew had been killed in the attack, my engineer and I bailed out. The plane appeared to blow up about one and a half minutes after this. Because of the high winds, we landed about 30 miles south of Berlin.'[26]

After hospitalization, Keen and his skipper were put in a cattle truck [eight horses or forty men!]; destination Stalag IIIA.

Mike Beetham's crew received a message that they must divert to Docking in Norfolk. They found it and flew into the circuit with another aircraft on 50 Squadron but as they circled, a third aircraft in the landing order crashed on the flare-path, which meant that as they were No. 6 in line, they were not able to land. They were given Coltishall as an alternative and here they landed safely. It was Beetham's twentieth trip of his tour.[27]

'At long last the Dutch coast came up,' wrote Flight Lieutenant Ralph Edwards, 'but the fuel was getting low in the tanks; we called up Woodbridge, the emergency strip and I believed we would make it, but most of all I wanted to get her home. She was our "S-Sugar" and I did not want to abandon her on a strange airfield; she had carried us safely over many miles of Occupied Europe and was the best of all Lancasters. Well, we got her to Oakington and put her down gently at 4 o'clock in the morning – bursting a tyre as we touched down, causing a swerve to port which sent us careering towards the Flying Control Tower and she came to a shuddering stop right in front. I cut the engines and silence descended. It was uncanny after the racket of the past eight and a half hours. We were home.'

After debriefing Flight Lieutenant Ralph Edwards got up and wandered into the mess ante-room in time to hear the one o'clock news next day: 'A strong force of Lancasters were out over Germany last night. Berlin was the target which was heavily attacked … causing many large fires … 72 of our aircraft are missing.'[28] 'Missing' did not include losses in men and machines caused by aircraft that crashed in England or those that returned with dead and wounded on board.

That night a relieved Sergeant Ken Grantham on 640 Squadron at Leconfield wrote: 'We left the enemy coast by Texel – well to the south of where we should have been – opened up the flasks of coffee and we ate our Mars bars. England slid beneath us near Great Yarmouth and we landed at base after seven hours in the air. We had been to the 'Big City'.

Chapter Sixteen

The Winds of Change

'...there in the cloudy night sky hung a huge colourful lantern, from the centre of which dripped vivid reds, greens, blues and yellows. Oily black smoke rose from the irregular mass. It was so close I felt I could have leaned over and touched it.'

Sergeant Russell Margerison,
a mid-upper gunner on 625 Squadron.

The night of 24/25 March 1944 has gone down in RAF folklore as 'the night of the strong winds'. At Binbrook Squadron Leader Foggo, the airfield controller who reigned as king in his control tower, waited for the bombers to return. He was ably supported in marshalling the Lancasters off and back on again after each raid by WAAF operators whose welcome voice was heard as the various aircraft checked in when approaching the 'drome on their return. They were something like mother hens gathering all their chicks home and fretting over those who did not turn up:

'The usual patter was: '"Leary" from "Oboe"!'

'"Over!"

'"Oboe" 1500!'

'"Oboe" 1500! Out!'

'Oboe' then circled the 'drome at the height given until further instructed. 'Leary' was the call-sign given to Binbrook. Depending on just how many Lancasters were stacked up at 500 feet intervals, eventually the call would come: '"Oboe" 1000.' This was acknowledged and 'Oboe' let down and joined the circuit following the Drem lights that encircled the 'drome.

When on the downwind leg 'Oboe' reported '"Oboe" downwind.' At this point the undercarriage was lowered and flaps set at 15 or 20 degrees to give the pilot greater control at lower speeds. The flaps went down to 40 degrees when turning crosswind and letting down to 600 feet and then, when the final turn was made on to the runway, 'Oboe' reported '"Oboe" funnels!' The Drem lights at this point formed a funnel leading down to the start of the runway. 'Leary' then came back with '"Oboe" pancake!' meaning land or '"Oboe" overshoot!' if there was any problem ahead, such as an obstruction on the runway. Maybe the previous bomber had burst a tyre or was slow in clearing the runway.

Once the go-ahead was given, the pilot ordered 'Full flaps! Fine pitch!' The engineer responded, slackening the throttle control screw at the same time to give the pilot easy control of the four throttles. He would then descend so as to come over the fence at about 100 feet and 110 mph and, once over, it was 'Power off!' The engineer then dragged the throttles right back and virtually hung on them to make sure they were off and the pilot then had to juggle the bomber down on to the ground.

The last message to the control tower would be '"Oboe" clear!' as the bomber turned off the runway. There would be no response from 'Leary' except that, on its last trip, 'Leary' did respond with 'Congratulations "Oboe"!'

Two Lancasters on 460 Squadron RAAF were missing. 'M-Mother' which crashed near Osterbrock with the loss of 25-year-old Australian Flight Lieutenant Allan Francis McKinnon DFC, a 'second tourist', was probably shot down by Feldwebel Rudolf Frank who claimed two Viermots which he destroyed in six minutes in the Meppen area and later a third north of Almelo in eastern Holland. Everyone on 'M-Mother', except the Australian mid-upper gunner, Pilot Officer G.D. Fitzgerald, who was taken into captivity, was killed. 'S-Sugar', the Australian squadron's other loss, flown by Pilot Officer Milford 'Mil' James Cusick of Newcastle, NSW who was on his eighth operation, crashed on a hillside near the village of Hollenstein, south-west of Hanover. Only the wireless-operator Australian Flight Sergeant Percival Allan Forrest survived to be taken prisoner.[1]

Bomber Command's losses in action on 24/25 March were 44 Lancasters and 28 Halifaxes or 9.1 per cent of the force but proportionally, 6 Group's losses – 13 Halifax IIIs (11.5 per cent) – were worse. The Canadian 6 Group had contributed 113 aircraft: 23 Lancasters on 408 and 426 Squadrons and 90 Halifaxes on the 7 other squadrons. Thirteen Canadian bombers returned early. The rest went over Berlin at between 19,000 and 24,000 feet, releasing 48,000lb of high-explosives and 409,000lb of incendiaries.

No. 1 Group was the worst hit of all the Groups with nineteen Lancasters unaccounted for. At Elsham Wolds two Lancasters on 576 Squadron flown by 21-year-old Flying Officer Peter Upton Brooke and Flight Sergeant Leslie John Collis were missing. The telegram that followed informing Brooke's father the Reverend W.E. Brooke and his wife in Bognor was a bitter blow and his death was mourned by pupils at his alma mater, the Chichester High School for Boys where he was remembered as 'another fine fellow, modest and unassuming but with a great heart and sterling qualities.' The Lancaster exploded and crashed near Köhra. Only Sergeant A.A.S. Evans the wireless-operator survived. Technical Sergeant Stanley H. Chidester USAAF, the navigator of Cayuga, New York was laid to rest at the US Military Cemetery in Luxembourg.

The Lancaster piloted by 27-year-old Leslie Collis, which was possibly hit by flak, crashed at Beeck, 5 kilometres from Duisburg on the way back from Berlin, killing the skipper and Sergeant Edward Smith his flight engineer who was also 27 years old. The others were taken into captivity. Collis, who had completed only two operations, both to Frankfurt, left a widow, Constance Mary Collis of Sidcup, Kent. Smith was the husband of Winifred May Smith of Foleshill, Warwickshire.

On 103 Squadron, which shared Elsham, 'C-Charlie' piloted by 21-year-old Squadron Leader Kenneth George Bickers DFC who was on only his third operation of his second tour on the squadron, was lost. 'Bick' was brought up in a working-class family in Southampton during the 1930s, attended Bitterne Park Boys School and joined the Royal Artillery where he was promoted to corporal, having taken control of a searchlight during the blitz. He came to the end of his first tour of operations on 29 May 1943, having successfully completed thirty sorties over enemy territory in just under three months and he was still only 20 years old. His award of the DFC was for his actions on the night of 9 April 1943. There may be no finer epitaph to Ken than that contained in 'Don' Charlwood's gripping first-hand account *No Moon Tonight*, in which the author describes coming across Ken just after his DFC exploits:

'In the morning I heard that Bickers' crew had had a shaky do the night before. The rear gunner had been killed and for 'Bick' himself there was talk of an immediate DFC. Their plane had been attacked by fighters and damaged beyond belief. In the crew room 'Bick' was being congratulated. To everyone he gave the same brief answer, 'It was a crew show. The way they stuck together got us back.'

'Looking at Bickers, I felt that in him our last seven months were typified. For a Flight Lieutenant he was more than usually young. His face was finely formed and unsmiling; his eyes direct. And in his eyes was that enigmatical ops expression I had noticed so often before. I wondered what he had been before the war. I thought of him as a bank clerk, university student, even a schoolboy, but each was poles removed from the Bickers before me.

'It was as though he had been created to wear the battered ops cap; the battle dress with its collar whistle; the white ops sweater; to be a man to whom years did not apply. But most of all, it was as though he had been created for this very hour, to stand in this drab room of many memories hearing the congratulations of his fellows.

While based near Leicester 'Bick' had met a girl called Joan who he planned to marry on 5 April 1944. 'C-Charlie' was shot down on the way home, near Luckenwalde. Only three bodies were recovered and now lie in the Berlin War Cemetery and four of the crew are commemorated on the Runnymede Memorial.

'M-Mother' which Flight Sergeant Fred Brownings had taken off from Elsham at 0930 was also missing. When over the Danish coast Sergeant Ronald Bob Thomas, the 20-year-old rear gunner, spotted a Ju 88 but Brownings managed to shake it off and went on to bomb the target successfully. As they cleared the target they saw a fighter coned by its own searchlights and with flak all around it. The fighter pilot fired off a red and white Very star flare and the searchlights ceased tracking and the flak stopped. Sometime later Thomas yelled 'Corkscrew' as an Fw 190 'Wilde Sau' started an attack.

Brownings could not shake it off and 'M-Mother' was raked with 20mm cannon fire from stem to stern, which shattered both rudders, shot away both flaps and holed the petrol tanks. The instruments were smashed and the intercom was disrupted so Brownings did not know the extent of the damage or if any of the crew had been injured. Flight Sergeant Jack Spark the bomb-aimer went aft with a clip-on oxygen bottle to find out. Sergeant Ken Smart the mid-upper gunner was safe, though his foot-rest had been shot away and the hydraulics that powered his turret had been shot out. In the tail Smart found Bob Thomas dead in his turret. He had taken a direct hit to the chest. Both turrets had been put out of action. There was a 5 feet gap in the top of the port wing, one of the tanks was open to the elements and the flaps damaged beyond repair, both rudders were shattered and most of the cockpit instruments were smashed. Brownings had to use his legs to control the column to prevent the aircraft from stalling. He told the crew to strap on their parachutes but Spark found his in shreds, having been hit by a cannon shell. They were then coned by searchlights so Spark, remembering the fighter's flare shot, fired off three reds and three white stars, the searchlights went out and the flak ceased.

With only about twenty minutes of fuel left Brownings made it to Dunsfold airfield, but all the lights were out as German intruders had been over the south of England that night. A red Very cartridge was fired at intervals and eventually the lights came on. Brownings attempted a landing but he was too high so he went round again. On his second attempt he managed to get down but then 'M-Mother' slewed off the runway and hit '*Passionate Witch*', a 452nd Bomb Group Flying Fortress that First Lieutenant Bob Cook had crash-landed at the base after bombing Frankfurt on 20 March. On the Lancaster there were no injuries to speak of and the body of the rear gunner was removed from his turret. In July four of the Lancaster crew were decorated. Fred Brownings was commissioned and together with wireless-operator Pilot Officer Norman Barker and the flight engineer Flight Sergeant Arthur Richardson received the DFC. Jack Spark got the DFM. '*Passionate Witch*' soon returned to action but on 28 March flak hit the No. 4 gas tank, the right wing broke off and the Fortress spun in and crashed near Châteaudun airfield in France. Seven of Cook's crew were killed but he and his radio-operator survived. The tail gunner, who was severely wounded, died in hospital the next day.

Six of 1 Group's missing Lancasters were at Wickenby, home to 12 and 626 Squadrons that between them dispatched thirty-one Lancasters. Four of the losses were from 12 Squadron. They included 'L-Leather' flown by Flying Officer Galtan Joseph George de Marigny, who was from the Amirante Islands, a group of coral islands and atolls that belong to the Outer Islands of the Seychelles. East of Leipzig the Lancaster was attacked by Hauptmann Paul Zorner of 8./NJG3 who had taken his Bf 110 off from St Trond and had flown eastwards to meet the returning bombers. The German ace became very hopeful when his bordshütze obtained an SN-2 contact at 6,700 metres. Two minutes later Zorner spotted his target and made his first attack with 'Schräge Musik', but the device was not properly adjusted and he saw no result. Zorner aimed again, at the left wing, firing two more bursts, but saw the rounds exploding well behind and above the bomber. Sergeant George William Henson, the 23-year-old mid-upper gunner and Sergeant Ernest Alfred Anthony the 20-year-old rear gunner did not return fire and in less time than it takes to tell, the German pilot made his next attack from the rear using his forward-firing cannons, aiming two bursts at the left wing which immediately began burning fiercely.

'L-Leather' went down steeply near Kindelbrück, Zorner noting that it crashed on a bearing of 150 degrees from light beacon 'Xanthippe'. De Marigny, his two gunners and Sergeant Stanley George Bentley, the 20-year-old wireless-operator, perished in the aircraft. The flight engineer, navigator and air bomber survived and were taken prisoner. Zorner returned to St Trond to record his triumphal thirty-ninth victory. On 25 July 1944 Zorner survived the crash of his Bf 110G-4 after an engine fire and he emerged unscathed after being shot down during combat near Cloppenburgh on 17 April. He rapidly increased his score and on 11 June shot down four '*4-mots*' in the Dreux area. He would survive the war with a score of fifty-nine abschüsse.

'K-King' on 12 Squadron piloted by Flight Sergeant C.J. Bates crashed at Kolrep in Brandenburg. Bates and Sergeant H.F. McPherson survived to be taken prisoner. 'Q-Queenie' captained by 23-year-old Flight Lieutenant John Hopkinson Bracewell DFC of Burnley, Lancashire was shot down and crashed at Harzgerode in Saxony-Anhalt. There were no survivors.

Having dropped their bombs on Berlin, 30-year-old Flying Officer Frederick Charles Hentsch and crew on 'Y-Yorker' were homeward-bound when near Duisburg the dark sky suddenly changed. Hentsch shouted over the intercom to Flying Officer Carl Rudyk, the 27-year-old navigator from Edmonton, to take a look. When he reached the cockpit he saw a massive wall of light as enemy searchlights lit up the sky around them. As the Canadian returned to his navigator's seat, Hentsch started turning the Lancaster this way and that trying in vain to get out of the beams. Then an anti-aircraft shell exploded, sending dozens of steel fragments into the aircraft. One piece tore the flesh off the calf muscle of Rudyk's right leg. The fuel tanks were also hit and petrol spread to the fuselage and instantly ignited.

Despite his injured leg, Carl Rudyk picked up his parachute, snapped it on and passed Hentsch who patted him on the shoulder. The navigator made it to the forward escape hatch which fortunately had been opened by Sergeant Albert Keveren the bomb-aimer, who had already bailed out. Rudyk's foot got caught in the hatchway as he tried to dive out of the doomed aircraft, but eventually it came loose and he made it safely to the ground.

After he was hospitalized Rudyk's thoughts wandered back to Edmonton where three days later his anxious wife Louise and their 2-and-a-half-year-old son Evan received the bad news that he was missing. On 9 May Louise received a second telegram which said that the International Red Cross had learned from German sources that her husband had been killed. On 4 June news finally arrived that Carl was a prisoner of war. Sergeant Alfred Summers, the mid-upper gunner, was also a prisoner. Later, Rudyk and other badly-wounded PoWs were repatriated home via Switzerland. Hentsch, Sergeants Robert Cringle the 20-year-old flight engineer and Eric Birch the wireless-operator and Flying Officer Denys Wimlett the rear gunner died in the aircraft, which crashed at Geldern-Veert.[2]

After he bailed out, Albert Keveren evaded capture, walking in a westerly direction until he reached Holland where he swam across the River Maas. On the other side he was contacted by a Dutch boy who took him to the local Dutch Resistance HQ where he remained for four weeks until he was moved to Belgium where he remained until the liberation.

No. 626 Squadron had dispatched sixteen Lancasters, though Pilot Officer Stewart had to abort with supercharger failure. Wing Commander Quentin Weston Aldridge Ross, the officer commanding, was due to complete the end of his tour on this his thirtieth op after deciding to take Sergeant Fred Bladon's crew and fly on the Berlin raid. Born in Buncombe, North Carolina, at age 19 Quentin Ross was a student when he arrived in England in 1929. He joined the RAF in 1932 and returned to America for a vacation in August 1933. Quentin married Diana Hope Ritchie on 11 September 1941 at Malmesbury Abbey, Wiltshire. Bladon, who was from Measham, Leicestershire had been commissioned and was stood down reluctantly from this sortie. He had captained the crew on their last five operations. Flight Sergeant Stanley William Jones, the 19-year-old Australian rear gunner, was from Toowong, Queensland. Sergeant Tommy W. Bint, who hailed from Berkshire, was the mid-upper gunner. Sergeant Hance Watt, the 20-year-old flight engineer, came from Coatbridge in Lanarkshire. Flight Sergeant Cecil 'Nat' Nathanson, the 24-year-old bomb-aimer, was from Tottenham in London. Pilot Officer John Gibson RCAF, the 30-year-old navigator, was born in Boksburg, North Transvaal, South Africa on 25 September 1913, the son of a gold-miner. The family migrated to England when John was only a few months old. In 1919 he and his mother moved to Saskatoon, Saskatchewan, receiving his education in Vancouver and becoming a postal clerk before enlisting in the RCAF in October 1941. Flight Sergeant Charles 'Chris' Christie was the wireless-operator and came from Cleadon Park, South Shields.

Quentin Ross bombed the target at 2250 hours and was on the homeward route when, not far from Berlin, the Lancaster was shot down by 22-year-old Major Heinz-Wolfgang Schnaufer for his fiftieth victory. The Lancaster crashed and burst into flames at Neuwarendorf, 4 kilometres west of Warendorf where all seven crew were laid to rest. After the war the bodies were exhumed and buried in the Reichswald Forest Cemetery. Schnaufer would finish the war as the top German night-fighting 'Experte' with 121 victories, only to die in a motoring accident in France in July 1950.

The Lancaster piloted by 21-year-old Flight Sergeant Keith Harry Margetts was also shot down by a night-fighter, again with no survivors. In a letter dated 25 March to his parents at 1 Tennyson Road, Rushden from Group Captain Phillip Haynes, station commander at Wickenby, they learned of the death of their eldest son. The final paragraph reads:

'Although Sergeant Margetts had not been with us very long, he had made many friends and was very popular on the Squadron. Personally, I had the utmost confidence in him for he had proved himself to be courageous and able. All officers and men of the Squadron join me in offering you our heartfelt sympathies in your great anxiety.'

At Kelstern one of the Lancasters on 625 Squadron returned early, leaving seventeen aircraft to head for Berlin. One of these was flown by 28-year-old First Lieutenant Eugene 'Max' Dowden, a tall, rangy, craggy-faced, pre-war bush pilot from Santa Cruz in California.

'We got through to Berlin unmolested by fighters,' wrote Sergeant Russell Margerison, the 20-year-old Lancastrian mid-upper gunner from Blackburn, 'but having had to contend with some very heavy flak in the form of box barrages. This, however, whilst being more alarming, was preferable to the deadly and very active night-fighters. It was whilst flying through a curtain of flak that Gilbert "Gib" McElroy the rear gunner and I got a good close look at a mammoth explosion on the starboard beam which blew us violently sideways, like a dried leaf on a windy day, and there in the cloudy night sky hung a huge colourful lantern, from the centre of which dripped vivid reds, greens, blues and yellows. Oily black smoke rose from the irregular mass. It was so close I felt I could have leaned over and touched it.

'"Max" steadied the Lanc and we left the spectrum dripping its colours as if being squeezed by some unseen hand. On the bombing run I rotated my turret on the beam and out of the corner of my eye saw wireless-operator Dick Reeves in the astrodome jabbing his finger upwards in an attempt to catch my attention. "Bomb doors open," said "Brick" Brickenden the bomb-aimer as a Lanc, some eighty feet up and directly above us, opened its huge belly. I stared in horror at the 4,000lb "cookie" and 500-pounders which hung, clearly visible, in its bomb bays. We waited with bated breath as the two aircraft moved in unison, as if connected, unable to do a thing at this vital stage in the operation.

'"Bombs gone," shouted "Brick".

'God knows where the other bombs fell, for I only had eyes for the big one, as I sat there dry-lipped watching that "cookie" from above slide between our wing and tail. Completely disregarding the very low temperature, sweat had formed on my brow and I watched it freeze on the back of my glove when I wiped it off, the rest of the crew being blissfully unaware of the event. Dick grimaced and disappeared from view, no doubt getting back to his "Fishpond" radar screen, used to search underneath for the fighter sneaking up from below.

'The return journey was difficult for Dave Weepers our Canadian navigator as he slogged away in an attempt to keep us on course, constant alterations of which he kept giving to "Max". We eventually found ourselves flying north of the Ruhr in a quiet sky well off course, but at least away from "Happy Valley" where many unfortunates were succumbing to a pounding from the ground.

'"Pass me the can Frank," "Max" requested over the intercom.

'"Just one minute Skip, Dave's using it," Frank Moody the flight engineer from Huddersfield, a tall, slim, sharp-featured lad of nineteen, returned.

'"Brick" chipped in. "Jeez, I'm tired of emptying your guys' piss down this chute. It's full of icicles now."

'It was at this point that my aching bladder burst and I soaked myself, enjoying every second of it. I had tried using the Elsan toilet at the back of the aircraft in the past. It entailed unplugging my intercom and electric suit, disconnecting from the oxygen, unclipping my seat and groping with my foot for the single foot-rest. Then in the fuselage, connecting to an emergency bottle of oxygen in total darkness, removing three pairs of gloves, making sure no cold metal was touched with bare fingers, for they would surely stick and tear the skin, unzipping two flying suits and unbuttoning my trousers, then searching for my "Old Man", which by this time had completely disappeared into its shell. Repeat the whole performance with freezing hands. And in view of the fact that leaving the turret on operations was an unhealthy procedure I had long since decided the effort just was not worth it. I was by no means on my own in this matter – most gunners came to the same conclusion.

'A lone pale blue searchlight suddenly encompassed us in its brilliance – one second darkness, the next blinded – and pale blue meant only one thing – radar-controlled.

'"Dive port," "Gib" shouted, but before he had got it out, "Max", foreseeing the danger, sent her screaming down in a curving dive. The searchlight followed, then stopped dead and we raced into darkness. Another Lanc up and to starboard glistened silver like a length of tinsel in a fairy light's gleam. There was a searing flash and down it spiralled – a blow-torch, no less. Just one shell had been fired and the whole episode took about twenty-five seconds.

'Relieved to be out of it all we flew across the North Sea calling up "Peak Frean", our base call sign before we hit friendly shores, for it had now developed into a race as to who would get back first and never yet had we beaten Cosgrove and his crew. The earlier the call was received, the earlier an aircraft joined the circuit. We were the third to touch down – Cosgrove the first, after having been airborne six hours and 45 minutes.

'"I'll get down before that Limey one of these nights," vowed "Max". His forecast dramatically came true a few weeks later.'[3]

On 21/22 May 1944 'Max' Dowden's crew were shot down on the raid on Duisburg. The American pilot and Frank Moody were killed. The others bailed out and were taken prisoner.

'V-Victor' on 625 Squadron piloted by Flight Lieutenant Norman Arthur Wadham 'Nobby' Clark was hit by flak and came down over the German frontier on the outward journey. The skipper, who was from London and was on his fifth operation, was taken prisoner, as were the 20-year-old Canadian air bomber Flying Officer Alex Bull and navigator Flying Officer George Brand. The flight engineer, Sergeant 'Curly' Donald Beckwith, a Yorkshireman, bailed out and landed 3 miles east of Haaksbergen. He was found by a farmer and taken in by the Underground. During August he fought with the Maquis in France and at the beginning of September he contacted the American army and was soon on his way home. The 20-year-old Australian WOp/AG, Flight Lieutenant 'Pete' Charles Tuston Armytage from Victoria, landed on the German side of the Dutch/German border and he eventually reached Holland. He was later picked up in Antwerp and sent to Stalag Luft III. The two gunners, Sergeant John Remington aged 19 from Wolverhampton and Sergeant 'Tish' Munro aged 18 from Fort William, Ontario evaded capture.

The third Lancaster lost on 625 Squadron was 'W-William', which 20-year-old Flight Sergeant Ronald David Whamond Jamieson had taken off at 1836 hours. He was shot down over Lagensalza by Oberleutnant Günther Rogge at 2330 hours for his fourth confirmed victory of the war. All seven crew were killed. Jamieson had been born in Ceylon, where his father Ronald Barrie Jamieson was a tea-planter, but he died quite young in 1928. 'Ron's mother 'Babs' then returned to Scotland and bought a board-and-room property in Kirriemuir. She sent her two boys Ronald and John to boarding school, from which they then both joined the RAF. John, known as 'Barrie', also a pilot, was killed at the age of 19 flying a Whitley on 18/19 August 1941 on 51 Squadron; all but two of the crew lost their lives.

So far in the war the crew on 'T-Tommy' skippered by 23-year-old Canadian Warrant Officer2 John David Jack Owen had completed twenty-three trips to enemy targets. Five of these had to be aborted due to equipment problems, including engine trouble, oxygen failure and rear turret malfunction. Ten trips, including this last one, were to Berlin. Warrant Officer2 Frank Berry 'Spanky' Magee, the 25-year-old bomb-aimer of Salmon Arm, British Columbia, wrote later:

'We set course from base about 2000 hours and headed for target. One of our navigational aids failed about an hour out, but we still had to carry on. The winds during the whole trip were a way different from what we had been told on leaving base. We were in the first wave and as the wind was more or less behind us we arrived and overshot the target, no markers having been dropped as yet. We had a

100 mph gale to contend with heading back towards the target. We never did reach the target as it was time for all the bombers to head home. So, we just dumped our load and headed for home. We dodged flak and searchlights … and were way off track and I think about an hour late. It was a clear night and I believe I saw the coast of Holland when the navigator [20-year-old Sergeant John Charles Anthony Lavender] called up to the engineer [21-year-old Sergeant Wilfred Bill Henry Broadmore] and asked him if we had enough fuel for an hour's flying, as it would take that long to reach England.

'The engineer said we were very low on fuel and doubted if we would make it. Just then we heard shells tearing through the kite and as they came from exactly below we presumed it was flak.[4] The plane was full of smoke and Jack opened the bomb doors to drop anything that might have stuck up and been on fire. However, everything was gone and the draught cleared away the smoke. The mid-upper gunner [22-year-old Canadian Sergeant Harry 'Al' W. Nixon] suggested that we do evasive action in case it happened again. Jack said OK. He just started to do this when we were hit. I could see tracer bullets flying past the nose so we all knew then that it was a fighter.

'The plane immediately went into an almost vertical dive and Jack shouted that he couldn't control the 'kite' and shouted for the engineer to help him. I couldn't get the escape hatch open during the dive, but … Jack and the engineer … managed to pull the plane out for a second or two. I flung open the hatch just as the intercom was cut. I could hear nothing over it. The engineer shouted my name and I saw him reaching for his 'chute, so I jumped. I went down OK and landed in a small field just inside the Dutch frontier. I received immediate assistance from the Dutch Underground and was down in Belgium when Allied troops liberated the country. Two days after I landed, the Dutch told me they had found the plane with five bodies in it. Apparently the Germans had found the sixth. Jack was a darn fine fellow and a good pilot.'

'Spanky' Magee parachuted to safety between Almelo and Hengelo near the Dutch-German border and was immediately taken in by the Dutch Resistance, spending several days on a farm where a young Dutchman named Henk van Guens worked and hid to avoid slave labour in Germany. Magee was moved to Hengelo by two members of the Dutch Resistance and sometime later was transferred, along with several other Allied airmen, to Belgium. After six months in Belgium, he was liberated when the town he was in was overrun by the Allies. On returning to England his first task was an unpleasant one. He had to tell Vera Simpkin that her RAF wireless-operator husband of three months, 22-year-old Sergeant Percival 'Casanova' H. Simpkin, had not survived the plane crash. [Sergeant William 'Hugam' Clark, the 22-year-old rear gunner, was the other member of the crew who was killed.] After the war in Europe ended Magee returned to Canada. Vera followed two years later and the couple married in 1947.[5]

In 6 Group Canadian Flight Sergeant Alan Ludvig Ollson on 426 'Thunderbird' Squadron RCAF found on his return to Linton-on-Ouse that the undercarriage would not lower normally so the crew used the emergency air bottle to lower it. They landed safely at base at 0135 hours with a claim by air gunners Pilot Officers Kenneth Albert Nordheimer of Toronto and William Mead Maxwell DFC of New

Jersey, USA for a Bf 109 destroyed. On 26/27 March Pilot Officer Ollson and his own crew were shot down by flak on Essen; the Lancaster exploded, killing all seven crew.

At Tholthorpe 425 'Alouette' Squadron RCAF lost two Halifaxes and 420 'Snowy Owl' Squadron one. On the 'Alouette' Squadron, the entire crew of Pilot Officer Joseph Alphonse Leon Louis Renaud, born on 16 June 1923 in Quebec City, was killed, probably in an attack by a 'Wilde Sau' night-fighter. The 28-year-old Canadian Pilot Officer Norval Hodges Jones and crew who were on their fourth operation were all killed on Halifax 'C-Charlie', which is believed to have crashed in the mouth of the Elbe. Norval Jones was one of three brothers from Deschênes, Quebec and had worked in the North Country at Larder Lake and Jason gold mines before enlistment. His older brother Leonard was stationed at Victoria Island in Canada. A younger brother, Leading Aircraftsman Earl H. Jones was on the ground crew that serviced Norval's aircraft. Whenever it returned to Tholthorpe, Earl had always been the first to greet Norval on landing.

Norval was listed as 'missing without trace' and his parents never gave up hope that their son was alive. A picture that later appeared in the *Ottawa Journal* brought hope with a photograph of French patriots being reviewed by an American officer. Norval's mother Elizabeth Agnes Jones was first to notice the resemblance between her son and one of the men in the picture and a moment later her husband Edgar exclaimed that he was sure his son was in the picture in the *Journal*. Sadly they were cruelly mistaken. Three crew members were buried in Germany. Four of the bodies were never found.

Three Halifaxes on 429 'Bison' RCAF failed to return to Leeming. One of them was piloted by 21-year-old Pilot Officer Stanley Arthur Wick of Conquest, Saskatchewan. On 18/19 March, on their first operation he and his crew had almost been shot down by a Halifax on the bomb run. 'The rear gunner evidently mistook us for an enemy fighter,' recalls Warrant Officer Stan Boustead, the RAF wireless-operator. 'We took two bursts but fortunately no one aboard was hit.' Now, as they were making their way home from Berlin, their luck finally ran out. At about 2245 Boustead received a wireless message from HQ giving details of wind direction and speed and he passed on the information to the navigator, Warrant Officer2 Roy Clendenning who was talking to Flying Officer John Howard Warkentin, the 21-year-old Canadian bomb-aimer, about the heading. Boustead recalled: 'We were pointing directly towards heavy flak and searchlights, obviously Magdeburg. Roy said we would track south of Magdeburg due to the heavy winds. I turned back to the wireless.'

At that instant flak smashed into the Halifax. To Bob Kift, the mid-upper gunner, it sounded as if someone was hitting the aircraft with a heavy hammer. Flames streamed back from the overload fuel tank amidships. Boustead heard the three or four thuds of direct hits plus the sound of tearing metal. He quickly switched back to intercom. The skipper seemed remarkably sanguine about the situation, asking each crew member in turn for his opinion of damage. It rapidly became apparent that the situation was hopeless. Wick ordered the crew to bail out. Kift pulled off his helmet and felt the flames singeing his hair. When Boustead drew back the curtain of his compartment he saw flames 'licking down the inside of the fuselage like the inside of an oil-fired burner'. The reek of fuel filled the trembling fuselage. Clipping his parachute to his harness, Boustead saw Roy Clendenning exit through the escape hatch in the floor. Boustead followed, but got stuck in the narrow aperture. He remembers how the bomb-aimer '... helped me out with his foot and I expected him to follow me but he never made it.'

Moments later the Halifax blew up. Stan Wick, Sergeant H. Hull the flight engineer, Sergeant Louis John Keeley the 22-year-old rear gunner from Windsor, Ontario and Flying Officer Warkentin died instantly. It was while he was stationed at Leeming that Keeley had met Kathleen Stevens of Northallerton. They were married in October 1943 and had a daughter Margaret Rose. Boustead, Bob Kift and Roy Clendenning survived to be taken into captivity.[6]

The 25-year-old Pilot Officer E.A. Giles RAAF and crew were shot down at Kiel. Only the rear gunner Flight Lieutenant A.W. Larochelle survived and he was taken prisoner.

Canadian Flying Officer Robert Fitzgerald Conroy, known as 'Gerald', who was at the controls of 'V-Victor', had only recently returned to operational flying following a successful evasion in the wake of the Düsseldorf raid on 11/12 June 1943 when he went down in Holland flying a Wellington. By a quirk of fate, on that occasion he had been the sole survivor and over a period of three months, the Underground spirited him to Spain and he reached Gibraltar where he made his way back to England. This time Conroy remained at the controls of 'V-Victor' long enough for Squadron Leader Jerrold Walton Bell DFC, the 'B' Flight Commander who was flying as navigator, and the five other crew members to bail out safely after he told them, 'Get out. Get out now.' They were the last words spoken.

Conroy was the second youngest in a family of thirteen and one of four brothers to serve in the war and was just about to turn 24. Born in a small rural Nova Scotia community, he had developed an affinity for the country way of life at an early age. He began his adult years working for a forestry company and then enlisted in the Canadian Forestry Corps.

His devotion to duty cost him his life. Next morning when the people of the village near the field where the Halifax crashed reached the aircraft they found Conroy, wearing his RCAF uniform and a white sweater, dead in his seat with his head leaning forward as if asleep. He would be remembered as 'Hollywood handsome' with a beautiful tenor singing voice.

On the 'Lion' Squadron the Halifaxes flown by Warrant Officer1 W.F. Magdalinski, Warrant Officer2 Adolf Edward Yaworski and 21-year-old Flight Sergeant Stanley Geddes Dowdell of Toronto, Ontario all failed to return. On 'V-Vic' Magdalinski and two of his crew survived to be taken prisoner. On 'J-Jig' Yaworski and four of his crew were killed. The 20-year-old Canadian pilot was engaged to be married to Audrey Thomason of South Garforth, Newcastle upon Tyne. 'K- Kitty' flown by Stan Dowdell was on its home run when it was probably shot down by flak, crashing in the vicinity of Ahlen. Only the flight engineer Sergeant J. Nescom and the Canadian rear gunner Sergeant Leonard Joseph Lozo survived.[7]

At Skipton-on-Swale two Halifax crews on 433 'Porcupine' Squadron RCAF were missing. Flight Sergeant William Francis Russell, the Canadian pilot on 'B-Baker', and two of his crew were killed. The four other crew members were taken into captivity. The 24-year-old Flight Sergeant Howard Walter Lossing of Norwich, Ontario and crew on 'H-Harry' are thought to have been shot down by 24-year-old 'ace' Oberleutnant Heinz Rökker at 1841 hours for his nineteenth victory. They were all killed. The third Halifax lost from Skipton was 'R-Robert' on 424 'Tiger' Squadron RCAF flown by 20-year-old Flying Officer William Ernest Krampe of Quebec City, which was shot down on the way home. Krampe and his 25-year-old bomb-aimer, fellow Canadian Flight Sergeant William Gerard Tillmann, were killed; the others were taken into captivity.

At East Moor Pilot Officer Jim McIntosh DFC on 432 'Leaside' Squadron RCAF who had brought his ailing Halifax back from Berlin on 2/3 January to crash-land at Woodbridge, was shot down flying Halifax 'O-Orange'. McIntosh, Pilot Officer Bob Elvin, bomb-aimer, Flying Officer Alex Small and Pilot Officer Clyde Schell the wireless-operator survived and were taken into captivity. Sergeant Leo Bandle and Sergeant Andrew de Dauw and Sergeant Walter ('Wally') Charles William King, the flight engineer who was from Norwich and the only Englishman on the otherwise all-Canadian crew, were killed. Bandle, Elvin and Schell all came from Toronto. After the war Jim McIntosh married his fiancée Gerry and worked on logging camps on Vancouver Island and near Prince George before going to work in Rocky Mountain House, Alberta.[8]

In 4 Group fifteen Halifaxes were missing and two more crashed on the return. Operating from Snaith, 51 Squadron had now flown the most Berlin raids and most sorties to the capital than any other squadron in 4 Group.[9] Thus far the squadron had lost seven aircraft bombing the 'Big City'. Some on the squadron, like bomb-aimer Flight Sergeant Tony Partridge, had led a charmed life. When his crew arrived at Snaith and had an interview with the CO he had told them, 'Don't worry, we'll start you off on something easy.' Two nights later they were on Berlin and they went there five times in the next two weeks![10] LW539 piloted by Flying Officer G. McPherson and MZ507 flown by Flight Lieutenant Roy Curtis took the squadron's final Berlin losses to nine with thirty-three men killed and thirty taken prisoner. McPherson's bomb-aimer, Sergeant Dennis Frederick Bowthorpe, was the only man lost. Curtis was rammed by a Bf 110, the bomber crashing near the town of Kreien at 2210. The skipper and four of his crew were lost without trace. The bomb-aimer Sergeant A. Sidebothom was taken prisoner. Rear gunner Sergeant Alfred Leonard Taylor survived the crash, but was severely injured. He had sustained broken ribs and legs when he bailed out. He died exactly one year later on 25 March 1945 from peritonitis.

At Burn, where fifteen Halifaxes on 578 Squadron were away by 1908 hours for a target time of 2230 hours, three of the bombers made early returns and three were shot down. On 'H-Harry' skippered by 21-year-old Pilot Officer James Malcolm Row, only air gunner Flight Sergeant W.R. Crick and wireless-operator Flying Officer Reginald James Hayhurst DFC survived on the crew, which included an eighth member, Pilot Officer George Alfred Pope, the 27-year-old second pilot who left a widow, Winifred May Pope. On 'C-Charlie' flown by 22-year-old Sergeant Robert Geoffrey Arthur only the navigator and one air gunner survived. There were no survivors on 'Y-Yorker' which was captained by 28-year-old Pilot Officer Duncan Albert Long DFM.

Fifteen Halifaxes on 158 Squadron had taken off from Lissett, but two failed to return to the base. 'S-Sugar' captained by Canadian Warrant Officer2 Allan Ross Van Slyke was low on fuel and he ordered the crew to bail out. Five did so, but Sergeant Robert Whitelaw the flight engineer refused, deciding to help his pilot to make a wheels-up landing but the aircraft crashed at Pausin and Van Slyke and Whitelaw were killed. Whitelaw has no known grave and is commemorated on the Runnymede Memorial. Pilot Officer J. McGillivray, the Canadian navigator from Central Blue, Saskatchewan, Flight Sergeant John Norman Albert McDonagh the bomb-aimer from Hamilton, Ontario, Sergeant Harry Ball, wireless-operator, and Sergeant William Alexander Grant were taken prisoner. Sergeant Kenneth David Mardon-Mowbray, air gunner, was killed.

At 2240 hours while over the Dutch coast 25-year-old Pilot Officer Keith Shambler Simpson from Mackay, Queensland flying Halifax 'T-Tommy' called his base at Lissett saying that his port and starboard outer engines were damaged and that the sortie was being abandoned. Nothing more was heard until he was reported having crashed onto the sand dunes just above Winterton-on-Sea at Horsey Gap on the Norfolk coast at 2311 hours. The aircraft exploded as it hit a mine, killing all seven crew. Sergeant 'Tom' Barnett, the 39-year-old flight engineer, left a widow, Nellie May. Maisie Patricia Hindley, the wife of Flying Officer Norman Hindley DFC the 27-year-old navigator, also waited in vain for good news. Civil defence workers were quickly on the scene and after removing the bodies from the shattered remains of the fuselage they dealt with an unexploded bomb found lying nearby. Having nursed his crippled bomber back across the North Sea and succeeding in making a crash-landing on the beach, this was a tragic end for a gallant crew.

At Breighton 78 Squadron suffered the greatest number of losses on the raid (six). 'H-Harry' was flown by 24-year-old Australian Flight Lieutenant Donald 'Mac-Con' Constable DFC from Victoria, who was on his twenty-first operation. With him went 22-year-old Flight Sergeant George Thomas Alfred Lovell on his 'second dickey' trip. Flying Officer Harold Arthur Mace the wireless-operator wrote later:

'We had bombed Berlin and were on the way home when a German night-fighter, unobserved by our gunners, opened an attack from behind. With his first long burst of gunfire, he shot us completely out of control and set our petrol tanks on fire. We had no chance to do anything. 'Don' realized the situation was quite hopeless and immediately ordered us to abandon the aircraft.'[11]

Harry Mace and the navigator Sergeant Calum Murdo 'Mac' McLeod bailed out safely before the aircraft crashed near Eisenach. McLeod was rendered unconscious when his parachute opened. Being the first to leave the stricken aircraft he did not learn the fate of the rest of the crew until Mace told him that he had seen the bodies of the others beside the aircraft and that he was the only other survivor. Sergeant Ted Byford, the mid-upper gunner, was only 19 years of age and Canadian rear gunner Flight Sergeant Thomas Lorne 'Schy' or 'Bugwood' Schioler was 20, as was the air bomber Flight Sergeant Terry Ratcliffe. The flight engineer Sergeant Des Cash was 21.

'G-George' flown by Flight Sergeant Henry Jackson was shot down by a night-fighter on the return journey after being blown off course and crashed at Les

Hautes-Rivières in France with the loss of all seven crew. Jackson left a widow, Annie Jackson of Warrington, Lancashire.

'A-Apple' captained by 21-year-old Flight Sergeant Henry Keith Barden from St Anne's-on-the-Sea in Lancashire was shot down with no survivors. 'K-King' flown by 21-year-old Sergeant Basil Thomas Smith crashed in the target area. He and air gunner Sergeant Leslie Daniels were killed, the five others being taken prisoner. The 21-year-old Flying Officer Michael Arabin Wimberley's crew had taken off from Breighton at 0659 hours and a fix on the Halifax was made at 1045. Later a message was received 'Aircraft returning to base – one engine u/s,' followed by another fix at 1055 when the Halifax was given permission to land at Cranfield. It crash-landed about a mile short of the runway and all seven crew were killed. Michael Wimberley's brother Peter Arabin Wimberley, a pilot on 37 Squadron, was already languishing in a prison camp in Germany after his Wellington was shot down on 18 December 1939.

Berlin was 'unlucky thirteenth' for Flight Lieutenant Eric W. Everett's Halifax crew on 'D-Dog'. Wireless-operator Sergeant Jim Johnson recalled:

'After crossing the enemy coast there was the usual flak bursting all around and tracers streaking upwards and we, like every other crew in that mighty air armada, each had our individual duties to carry out. Soon it was the last leg in to the target and bomb-aimer Flying Officer Joe Green had just released the bombs when we were hit by a burst from a fighter, which set our rest position on fire. What happened after that has never been quite clear, but I know some of us grabbed fire extinguishers and went back and with the help of the Skipper's diving and weaving, the fire was put out. The flight engineer, Sergeant 'Taff' Jones then checked the damage and from that moment on we all knew we would never make it back home. We had been very badly damaged – fuel cocks shattered, bomb doors still open, port wheel down and the flaps half down. However, the Skipper battled with the controls and we limped on. Soon the port engine started cutting and finally stopped. By this time we were over Holland, but were losing height and we limped on until finally the Skipper gave the order to abandon aircraft. Including Sergeant 'Jock' Stewart, navigator, Sergeant Ralph Graham, mid-upper gunner and Pilot Officer Alan Sinden, rear gunner, we all got out safely. The last thing I saw while floating down to earth was our aircraft bursting into flames as it hit the deck.'[12]

'D-Dog' had come down near Rockanje, south of The Hague. Sinden was helped by Dutch farmers who tried to return him to England, but this was not possible and he was moved from house to house until December when he was captured and sent to Stalag Luft I at Barth, where he was reunited with the other members of the crew.

In 3 Group 115 Squadron at Witchford had also lost four Lancasters. 'G-George' was set on fire by a night-fighter during the outward flight and was steered by Flight Sergeant Ieuan Glyndwyr Williams towards Sweden, but the Lancaster ran out of height and only Sergeant E. Meikle the bomb-aimer succeeded in abandoning it seconds before it crashed at Kropelin near Mecklenburg in northern Germany. Nothing further had been heard from 'J-Jig' flown by 28-year-old Pilot Officer Leonard Myles McCann of Ottawa, Ontario since taking off at 1849 hours. It was skirting Leipzig on the way home when the Lancaster was shot down by a night-fighter flown by Oberleutnant Dietrich Schmidt. The skipper and four others on his crew including Sergeant 'Johnnie' Watson, the 19-year-old rear gunner from Dagenham, Essex were killed. The two crew members who survived were taken into captivity. 'N-Nan' flown by 23-year-old Pilot Officer Thomas Elliott Vipond had reached Holland before it was pounced upon at 0020 hours by 26-year-old Hauptmann Martin Drewes, who sent it crashing to earth at Epse, 4 kilometres south-east of Deventer, for his seventeenth victory. There were no survivors.

'K-King', known to 21-year-old Flight Sergeant James Arthur Newman and his all-sergeant crew as '*Werewolf*', had been hit by flak over Frankfurt before they reached Berlin. Shortly after dropping the bomb load they were finished off by Oberleutnant Heinz Rökker, Staffelkapitän, 1./NJG2 flying a Ju 88R-2. South-west of Bernberg Rökker, who had earlier claimed a Lancaster in the Berlin-Leipzig area for his eighteenth abschuss, now took his score to nineteen when his cannon and heavy machine guns set the starboard wing and fuselage on fire. Sergeant (later Warrant Officer) Nicholas S. Alkemade's rear gun turret received a direct hit from a cannon shell, blowing out all the Perspex and setting part of the hydraulic gear system on fire. Alkemade was the son of a Dutch father and English mother who was born in North Walsham, Norfolk. He had joined the RAF in 1940 at age 18 and served in Air-Sea Rescue launches until, 'wanting more excitement', he transferred to Bomber Command as a rear gunner, joining the crew on 'K-King'.

By mid-March the 21-year-old rear gunner had flown a dozen ops. His thirteenth arrived on the night of Friday, 24 March. 'K-King' was set on fire and was losing height rapidly and Newman gave the order for the crew to bail out. Alkemade, however, was not wearing his parachute. It was still stashed away in the fuselage, apparently ready for an emergency. Alkemade went to fetch it, but the wall of flame between the turret and the rest of the aircraft made it impossible. By now as the smoke filled the gun turret and the flames reached his rubber gas mask clamped tight over his mouth and nose began to melt, his clothes were already alight and he had first-, second- and third-degree burns on his face and hands and burns on his legs. He decided that the prospect of dying by fire was simply too horrible:

'I had the choice of staying with the aircraft or jumping out. If I stayed I would be burned to death – my clothes were already well alight and my face and hands burnt, though at the time I scarcely noticed the pain owing to my high state of excitement.... I decided to jump and end it all as quick and clean as I could. I rotated the turret to starboard and not even bothering to take off my helmet and intercom, did a back flip out into the night. It was very quiet, the only sound being the drumming of aircraft engines in the distance and no sensation of falling at all. I felt suspended in space. Regrets at not getting home were my chief thoughts and I did think once that it didn't seem very strange to be going to die in a few seconds – none of the parade of my past or anything else like that.'

He had thrown himself out into the night sky, 18,000 feet above the ground.

Blissfully, he passed out and then he came to three hours later on the ground. His fall had been broken by pine trees in the Arnsberger Wald near Schmallenberg and deep snow cover and his 120 mph terminal velocity had been safely cushioned by foliage and branches. He had a twisted right knee, a deep splinter wound in his thigh, a strained back and slight concussion but he was still alive! Unable to move, Alkemade blew his whistle to get attention. He was found by local members of the Volkssturm (national militia). No-one believed his story that he was an airman who had landed without a parachute and Alkemade was placed in solitary confinement on suspicion of being a spy. Eventually the harness of his parachute was examined. Rivets which held his harness snap hooks flat to his chest and would break once the ripcord was pulled were still intact and the Germans realized that his story must be true. Sergeant Geoffrey R. Burwell the wireless-operator and Sergeant John P. Cleary the navigator were the only other members of the seven-man crew to survive. Burwell was blown out of the aircraft and fell unconscious for 20,000 feet and came to, parachute trailing unopened. He pulled the ripcord, the 'chute opened and about five seconds later he hit a tall tree. His only injury was a cut lip which he got as he jumped to the ground. Cleary hit a pine tree and quickly lost consciousness, hanging in his harness from the tree. Villagers found him in the morning suffering from severe frostbite and having suffered a collapsed lung. He was taken to the small hospital at Meschede where nuns managed to save his leg. After six months in hospital he was repatriated in February 1945.[13]

At Mildenhall there were three early returns and two Lancasters were missing. 'L-London' piloted by 21-year-old Flight Sergeant Leslie William Charles Wheeler was homebound when it was shot down, probably by a Ju 88C flown by Oberleutnant Friedrich Tober and it exploded over Teltow south-west of Berlin, killing all the crew. 'T-Tommy', flown by Flight Lieutenant William George Grove, crashed near Bonn with no survivors.

At Waterbeach 514 Squadron had dispatched nineteen Lancasters, one returning early. 'C-Charlie' piloted by Flying Officer John Rollo Laing whose crew were on their fifteenth operation, was attacked by a night-fighter probably flown by Hauptmann Heinz-Horst Hissbach 20 to 50 kilometres west of Berlin; his second claim of the night. The Lancaster crashed near Wörlitz, with Flight Sergeant Ron McAllister, the Canadian mid-upper gunner, the only man to survive.

On Flight Lieutenant 'Lou' Greenburgh's crew, despite having lost their flight charts, 'Paddy' Butler the navigator navigated the bomber safely back to Waterbeach. On return Butler and Drake were given a rest; the latter going home to Australia and Butler to an Air Ministry establishment to be trained as a meteorologist. Flight Lieutenant Louis Greenburgh returned to operations with a new crew and was shot down again on 7/8 June on the raid on Massy-Palaiseau in France. All of the crew bailed out just before 'C-Charlie' exploded in the air. 'Lou' and four of his crew evaded but Fred Carey was later captured. 'Strommy' Stromberg, who got caught up in telegraph wires and was badly injured before he was captured, died later in hospital in Amiens. Both gunners and the flight engineer were taken prisoner. The intrepid Greenburgh evaded capture for several weeks before returning to England and receiving a Bar to the DFC from King George VI in a ceremony at Buckingham Palace on 11 December 1945.[14]

The Canadian squadrons in 6 Group had lost a total of eleven Halifaxes and two Lancasters. In 8 Group PFF, 7 Squadron at Oakington lost two Lancasters, 35 Squadron at Graveley one and 97 Squadron at Bourn two. When homeward-bound, 'A-Apple' on 35 Squadron flown by 22-year-old Squadron Leader Richard Thomas Fitzgerald DFC of Namban, Western Australia was attacked by a night-fighter and exploded in the air, crashing near Welsleben. Fitzgerald and four of his crew died instantly. The bomb-aimer Flight Lieutenant W.S. Muego and air gunner Flight Sergeant S.H. Boulton were catapulted out of the aircraft by the explosion and were taken prisoner. On 97 Squadron 'H-Harry' skippered by Flying Officer P.H. Todd was damaged by flak over the Ruhr and came down in the sea. Six of the crew were picked up by the Germans but the flight engineer Sergeant Sidney Robson had drowned. 'A-Apple' flown by Pilot Officer William Darby Coates DFM whose award was for his action on the raid on Berlin on 'Black Thursday' the previous December was shot down on the homeward journey from Berlin at about half-past twelve near Luyksgestel, 12 miles from Eindhoven. The crash was so violent that it was impossible to identify individual remains and all seven crew were buried together in a common grave at Woensel General Cemetery.

In 5 Group two crews on 44 'Rhodesia' Squadron failed to return to Dunholme Lodge. 'C-Charlie' skippered by 22-year-old Pilot Officer Albert Evans which was shot down at Angermund by flak on the return journey at 0001 hours was lost with no survivors. Evans had been a cub reporter on a local newspaper in Wednesbury, Staffs before joining the RAF in May 1941.[15] Six crew on 'A-Apple' including the 26-year-old skipper, Pilot Officer Bernard Michael Hayes and his 19-year-old Canadian air gunner, Sergeant Kenneth Lloyd Radcliffe of Rivers, Manitoba were killed when they were shot down by a night-fighter probably flown by Oberleutnant Josef Nabrich. The Lancaster crashed at Lage Mierde in North Brabant at 0030 hours. The only survivor was Sergeant M. Fedoruk, the 23-year-old Canadian bomb-aimer who evaded. Hayes left a widow, Ena Beatrice Hayes of Putney in London. Five months earlier on 19/20 October 1943, the Radcliffe family had lost their other son, 21-year-old Albert, a leading aircraftman, during a transportation flight in a Liberator which ploughed into Montagne Noire (Black Mountain) near St-Donat, Quebec in bad weather, killing all six crew and the eighteen passengers.[16]

Six crews failed to return to East Kirkby. On 630 Squadron Warrant Officer James White DFM captaining 'I-Ink' was killed and his crew taken into captivity. 'W-William' skippered by 22-year-old Pilot Officer Clifford Leslie Eldridge Allen was one of three victories claimed this night by Feldwebel Rudolf Frank. The navigator was the only survivor.

Flight Sergeant 'Geoff' Hather the navigator on 'U-Uncle', a brand-new aircraft with just twelve hours, (being flown by Flight Sergeant A. John Perry) was, in Hather's opinion, the cause of the downfall on their last op. 'There's a lot to do to get an aircraft operational. One of the items is the flight test. Because we were due at the briefing mid-afternoon, we had no time to do this. In fact the first time we flew the thing is when we went to Berlin that evening. I must say we were all keyed up for the 'Big City'. It was awe-inspiring.

'When we were halfway across the North Sea and an engine started to play up we were nonplussed to say the least. After a few minutes, John and 'Jock' (flight engineer, Sergeant Jim Morrison) decided to feather the engine. The Lancaster would fly on three engines with no problems, but as we were only a short way on the trip, they were worried about the remaining three overheating, so this meant that the airspeed was dropped and in consequence it looked as though we would be late at the target. I did a quick calculation and gave John a new course to fly which meant we would be there on time, which we did. But with our lower speed we were going to be back late as the course was straight home. We couldn't take any shortcuts. I don't really know what happened next [they were probably hit by flak]. I pulled out my intercom plug so I didn't hear the instruction to bail out. The first I knew something was amiss was when I saw Ted (Sergeant Naisbit) putting on his parachute. I plugged in and got an earful from John, who told me we were on fire and to get out. I went down to the bed where I had left my parachute and saw Ted pushing Frank (Sergeant Giblin) out, followed by 'Monty' (rear gunner, Sergeant Todd), then he jumped. John, Jim and 'Jock' must have gone through the front exit. What happened then I don't know. I felt myself falling through the air, then hitting some trees rather hard, then landing very heavily on the ground and although I knew I had stopped falling, I still had the feeling that I was. It was terribly cold; in fact there was deep snow on the ground. It could have been this which stopped me from losing my leg, which was a bit of a mess. So ended our sixth and last op.'[17]

On 57 Squadron, which shared East Kirkby with 630 Squadron, Pilot Officer Eric Percy Cliburn and the crew on 'S for Sugar' and Australian Pilot Officer George Alfred Hampton and four crew on 'I-Ink' were killed; two were taken into captivity. Pilot Officer Ron Walker's crew on 'T-Tommy' also failed to make it home to East Kirkby, but they were safe and sound as 'Ginger' Hammersley recalled:

'As the weather reports had come in and I decoded them it became apparent from [Flying Officer Bertram 'Mack' MacKinnon's] findings that they were not as he expected them. We were faced with greater wind speeds than those indicated in the signals being sent out to us from Command, so we used our own. We were late arriving over the target and we could see there were great fires as the run-in towards the target commenced. Having bombed successfully we headed back towards home, only to be told that we would have to land at the fighter airfield at RAF Coltishall in Norfolk. The time we had spent flying was seven hours, thirty minutes. We were debriefed and fed and then shown to our sleeping quarters. We made the thirty-five minutes flight back to East Kirkby the following afternoon, leaving at 1500 hours by which time the fog that had prevented our landing the previous night had cleared. Of the seventeen Lancasters from the squadron that flew this operation, one made an early return and two others failed to return. We made our reports at the squadron office before heading for our huts to await the evening meal.'

Four Lancasters failed to make it home to their base at Coningsby. On 619 Squadron, which shared the station with 61 Squadron, there was no word from 'L-London' flown by New Zealand Pilot Officer Paul Thompson. They had crashed at Tetlow and everyone was killed. 'W-William' captained by Pilot Officer Denis Carbutt had crashed near Gehrden. There was only one survivor and he was taken into captivity. On 61 Squadron 'G-George' skippered by 22-year-old Flying Officer John Grant Cox, a New Zealander, crashed at Rimbeck with the loss of all seven crew. This just left Tommy Farmiloe's crew on '*Hellzapoppin*' unaccounted for. The WOp/AG Sergeant Eddie Davidson recalls the events that had unfolded after nearing the target:

'As we approached the German coast between Lübeck and Rostock, bomb-aimer Ken Vowe reported heavy flak and searchlights ahead. Shortly afterwards the gunners reported a burst of air-to-air tracer very close on the port side and shortly afterwards saw an aircraft explode and fall away in a number of burning fireballs. It was always a sickening sight to see one of our own aircraft go down. Soon afterwards the visual 'Monica' equipment pinpointed an enemy night-fighter only 500 feet away at 2 o'clock. Both gunners shouted almost together over the intercom, 'I can see the bastard' followed by Ray Noble the rear gunner shouting over the intercom, 'Dive to port skipper.' All six Brownings of the rear and mid-upper turrets started firing as the skipper dived at the start of the corkscrew manoeuvre, which was so sharp and steep that after hitting my head on the roof, I ended up on the floor with all my signals books scattered around me. My stomach was in my mouth as the corkscrew seemed to go on forever, then the skipper pulled sharply out of the dive and flew straight and level while Ray Noble and Wally Patchett, the mid-upper gunner, scanned the sky. It had worked; the enemy fighter had lost us.

'After getting a new course from the navigator Stan Halliwell the skipper started to climb, hoping to get back to 20,000 feet. After picking up and sorting out my papers I realised it was time to listen out for the half-hourly Met Report from Group, which again gave no indication of the true wind velocity. About half an hour later I saw another blip on the 'Monica' screen indicating an aircraft about 600 yards away at 11 o'clock and as I opened my mouth to yell a warning, Ray Noble shouted, 'Corkscrew starboard go.' This time I stayed in my seat having fastened my belt and heard the gunners opening up, but I could still see the blip on the 'Monica' screen following us down on the port side and I instructed the skipper 'Corkscrew port.' We could feel the kite shudder as the skipper tried to level out and George Jerry, the flight engineer screamed, 'For Christ sake Tommy, take it easy or you will tear the bloody wings off.'

'The violent corkscrew manoeuvre worked for we lost the fighter and as we tried to gain height Ken the bomb-aimer said, 'I can see a glow right in front of us; it must be Berlin.' Sure enough, as we climbed we could see the glow spreading and there was a sigh of relief when the skipper said, 'We're early but I'm going in.' The high winds had scattered the Main Force and some aircraft bombed Berlin half an hour before the Pathfinders marked the target area. It was time to listen out again for the half-hourly reports from Group. With all the excitement I had missed the last two reports, so as usual I disconnected myself from the intercom and listened out on the W/T for the wind speed broadcast. Reading the message I could see they still were not reporting the actual wind speeds! Switching the set off, I suddenly became aware of a high-pitched whine coming from one of the engines. In a panic, I switched back into the intercom system and heard the flight engineer saying the revs on the port outer had increased to 3,800 rpm and the skipper telling him to shut down the engine and feather the prop.

'The runaway prop,' says Farmiloe, 'created a fearsome noise and sent ice splinters against the fuselage. I tried to feather it but without success and it was not long before there were indications of fire. I tried diving, etc., but nothing, including the fire extinguisher, solved the problem and the fire continued on and off all the way. Worse, the port inner also gave problems and had to be feathered, this time fortunately successfully. Flying just above stalling speed and rapidly losing height, I managed to keep the plane under control and continue towards Berlin.'

'Eddie' Davidson was standing in the astrodome on fighter watch when he saw flames pouring out of the faulty engine and thick smoke trailing back over the wing and tail. 'We were ordered to prepare to abandon aircraft. With both port engines dead we were in a desperate situation. The port outer was still burning with its unfeathered prop windmilling, thereby making the aircraft very difficult to control even with full rudder trim and full opposite rudder. By now we were approaching the illuminated target area and still on course for the aiming point. Shouting over the whine from the port inner the skipper ordered 'Stand by, let's go in and drop the load and get out of the target area as quickly as possible, then we will bail out.' Without a word Ken Vowe got back into his position in the nose of the aircraft. Ahead, red and green target indicators could be seen going down punctually at 2230 hours and in the glow of the following bomb flashes on the ground and enemy searchlights I could see hundreds of black flak clouds exploding against the illuminated background. This indicated only too clearly the fierce flak barrage put up by the defenders against our attacking aircraft. With all these distractions going on around him I could hardly believe I was hearing Ken's seemingly unconcerned, quiet but distinctive Yorkshire accent begin his patter to the skipper 'Left, left, no right, left again, steady!'

'In the meantime molten metal and flames still poured out of the port outer and incredibly, the enemy's searchlights, fighters and flak batteries ignored us. Still losing height we continued our bombing run and at 2235 hours, with a green target indicator in the bombsight, Ken dropped our bomb load on the burning city below. Not waiting for a target point photograph to be taken, the skipper quickly closed the bomb-bay doors and turned away onto a westerly course of 208 degrees, which led to position 'E' on the return route. Then started the debate over the intercom, should we bail out so close to the target area or try to get as far away as possible. Of course we really had no choice. If Tommy ordered us to 'Bail out' we would have to go. I for one did not fancy bailing out and was delighted when he decided to keep going as far as possible. We were now down to 13,000 feet. By keeping the air speed at 140 mph, just above stalling speed, the skipper found the fire and whine of the port outer was at a minimum but the physical effort of controlling the aircraft was taking its toll on him. At this point Ken came out of the bomb-aimer's position and wrapped his arms round the rudder bars and braced himself, thus taking some of the strain off the skipper's legs. In the meantime the flight engineer tried to trim the aircraft by draining petrol from the port tanks into the two starboard wing tanks.

'Despite everyone's efforts we continued losing height and at 9,000 feet we decided to jettison as much equipment as possible. Opening the starboard rear door I started by chucking out the flame floats, rest-bed and even the Elsan toilet. As I passed the D.C. power accumulator I glanced at the dial and saw it was indicating zero. Not believing it, I tested my radio receiver. It was almost dead and even the interference mush was faint. I called the skipper to tell him the bad news that our electrical power was almost gone and I couldn't use the wireless transmitter. Only the generator on the starboard inner engine was working; the port outer, because of the fire, was dead. We decided to switch off everything electrical apart from essential equipment so that with luck we might build up enough power in the accumulator to send out a SOS. The two gunners were ordered to leave their turrets. If they tried to rotate them the accumulators would be completely drained. After much argument they agreed to dismantle their guns and with my help the six Brownings were thrown out along with all the ammunition. This left us feeling naked and defenceless. Unbelievably we had not been attacked by night-fighters or been caught by flak and searchlights. We had the feeling that 'somebody was looking after us'.

'The navigation 'Gee' box, identification friend or foe set (IFF), oxygen bottles and anything else I could lay my hands on was thrown out. The mid-upper and rear gunner, with nothing else to do, sat near me with their backs against the main spar and learned the secret of the wireless-operator's crew position in Lancaster aircraft. Being near the main hot-air duct it was the warmest place on board. With the 'Gee' box gone and the radio direction finding (RDF) compass unserviceable the bomb-aimer obtained a visual fix of a river east of the Zuider Zee and a course alteration was made. In order to confirm this position the skipper asked me if I could try to get a radio fix. Switching on, I tuned to the emergency frequency and sent out an SOS. At 0120 hours I logged a third-class fix and a request for details, in code, of our situation. Nine minutes later I was given a first-class fix and a further request by Group Air Traffic Control for information. Halfway through my reply the power went, but this fix showed that we were heading south, down the Belgian coast. We were now down to 4,000 feet and still losing height so the skipper decided to set a westerly course for the Norfolk coast and he ordered the crew to prepare for ditching. Donning our life jackets, we prayed we would not have to ditch in the cold North Sea.

'We were struggling to hold 4,000 feet,' recalls Tommy Farmiloe, 'and we were slowly losing height. Once over the coast the order to "prepare to jump" was changed to "prepare to ditch". We got shot at by coastal flak ships [actually a British convoy proceeding up the North Sea] but managed to survive. Then my wireless-operator got a home bearing in response to his Mayday call. As we neared the East Coast (lucky it was not the South Coast, as we would not have got over the cliffs!), a single searchlight came on and pointed us in the direction of Little Snoring, a long runway emergency aerodrome.'

'After what seemed like an eternity,' says Eddie Davidson, 'we crossed the coast near Cromer at about 500 feet. The skipper then used his VHF R/T set to send out a Mayday call and received the reply, "Give details." In the circumstances, "Tommy"s reply was quite polite. "Just look up and you will see the problem for yourself. We are on fire." There was a pause and then a voice said, "Follow the searchlights." Immediately on our port side a searchlight came on making an "O" on the clouds and then it came down to lay a beam along the ground. As we reached the end of its light, another searchlight came on and pointed us forward. This happened three times until the runway lights of an airfield came on and we were told, "Circle at four hundred feet." The skipper replied, "For God's sake I am at 150 feet now. I'm coming straight in." In preparation for a possible crash-landing the navigator joined the two gunners and me as we sat facing the rear with our backs against the main spar. Ken, the bomb-aimer, refused to leave his position holding the rudder bars and the flight engineer also refused to move. They both very bravely stayed to help the skipper land the aircraft. The undercarriage was then lowered [using the emergency air bottle] but nobody knew if it was locked and would stay down or if the brakes would work. With tremendous effort the skipper got us down in one piece in spite of the runway lights being switched off halfway down the landing run.'

'With the port outer still burning and no "services",' continues Tommy Farmiloe, 'we were unable to signal our approach but struggled in with no flaps at 140 mph. We reached the centre of the runway but to my horror, instead of slowing down, we went faster and faster, eventually going off the end of the runway into complete darkness. We shut off everything that could be shut off and rolled through hedges and across several fields until we hit wet ground. The plane stopped and tipped up on its nose with the tail straight up in the air. We got out FAST, ran away and sat in a group laughing ourselves silly! My crew said that it was the only good landing I ever made, but I like to think that there was at least one other! Then we set off to follow the wheel tracks back to the Little Snoring field and control tower. It was still pitch dark. The control staff was amazed, as we had not been noticed! All I cared about was getting all my crew home safely and that we did!'

'Eddie Davidson says: 'The engine fire at last went out and it was only when we climbed out on to the fuselage we saw the nose of the aircraft was embedded in a water-filled ditch. "Just my luck," said Tommy, "to fall off here and drown in some rotten ditch." Someone quickly answered "Not you skipper, you could walk on water tonight." As we waited by the side of the aircraft we were puzzled why no fire engine or any other emergency vehicle had followed us to investigate our predicament. So I climbed back into the aircraft through the cockpit escape hatch to get the Very pistol and cartridges. After climbing out again I stood on the wing and started firing off some red distress flares. It was the first time I had ever had the opportunity to use the Very pistol and I enjoyed it. About half an hour later a wagon drove up and we were taken to flying control where we found out we had landed at RAF Little Snoring, a Mosquito base near Fakenham in Norfolk. Later the skipper and navigator were driven away to the officers' mess while the rest of us were taken to a very cold and empty dormitory hut for what was left of the night. In the morning after inspecting the damage to "*Hellzapoppin*" we waited for our squadron to send an aircraft over to collect us. Shortly after lunch "O-Orange" arrived and we returned to Coningsby. Later we learned that the exceptionally strong winds experienced during the operation had scattered the Main Force and many aircraft flew south of the intended return route over the strongly-defended Ruhr area with disastrous results.'

At Metheringham there was no sign of Pilot Officer Dick Starkey and his crew on 106 Squadron. This being their twentieth trip, many must have thought that the crew's luck had finally run out and that they had 'bought it'.

'The activity in the sky over the city was awesome and frightening, as were all raids on Berlin. The sky was full of sparkling flashes as anti-aircraft shells from 1,200 guns, the equivalent of an ammunition dump, burst in a box barrage every two minutes. I estimated that anyone getting through that would be very lucky indeed, especially as the aircraft had to be flown straight and level with bomb doors open during the bombing run and take photographs after dropping the bombs. There were also hundreds of searchlights, making two cones over the city, which the bombers had to try and evade. The fighters no longer waited outside the perimeter of the target where they were in little danger from their own flak because we were now severely damaging their cities. They flew amongst us in this area of death ignoring their own safety, meeting the anti-aircraft fire in order to get amongst us and many a bomber was shot down when most vulnerable with bomb doors open. When we were on our bombing run with two other Lancasters whose bomb-aimers had chosen the same markers as my bomb-aimer Sergeant Wally Paris, a twin-engined fighter flew past our nose with cannon and machine guns firing at one of the Lancasters. There were tracers flying all over the sky as my gunners, Sergeants 'Jock' Jameson, mid-upper gunner and Sergeant Joe Ellick, rear gunner and the others in the third aircraft joined the targeted Lancaster to return the fire. However, the stricken Lancaster turned over on its back and went down in flames. We did not see anyone escape because we were concentrating on the bombing run.

'The Luftwaffe were now using single-engined fighters in the battle, generally over the target and as I took a quick glance down at the fires I saw twelve of them circling up line astern towards the bombers whose bellies were red from the reflection of the flames below. The searchlight cones held two bombers like moths round a candle; the pilots were tossing their aircraft all over the sky but they were held like stage artists in a spotlight. The next move was from the fighters who came in and inflicted the coup de grâce, the bombers plunging down in flames before exploding and cascading in balls of fire to splash among the inferno below. A pilot had to take whatever action he could to get across the target area. One practice was to fly near a coned aircraft and hope the action against it would help him get across. This wasn't always possible because although the brightness was less intense they could be seen. When a raid was at its peak with 800 aircraft bombing in a twenty-minute period, the illuminations had to be seen to be believed. The target indicators – red and green chandeliers, 200 feet in length – cascaded down with a shimmering brightness, flak was bursting; filling every part of the sky with twinkling bursts and as you flew towards them there was no escape. You thought you would never get through it.

'After bombing the target I gained height to 25,000 feet and with relief at surviving the anti-aircraft, searchlights and night-fighter defences but we had another fight on our hands before we reached England. The strong headwinds and night-fighters had not finished with us. It soon became apparent that our ground speed was very slow and we did not appear to be making much progress. As we crawled our way west to the next change of course, which was to take us north-west between Hanover and Osnabrück, the navigator was continuously amending his air plot to try and keep us on course but we were being blown south of our intended track. It soon became apparent that the conditions were getting worse and because of the effect of the wind on navigation found ourselves further west than the point where we should have turned north-west to fly between Hanover and Osnabrück. Instead we amended our course to fly between Osnabrück and the Ruhr, making sure we kept well clear of the latter area.

'We had seen many aircraft shot down since we left Berlin, proof that the force was well scattered and aircraft were being picked off. As we looked towards the Ruhr we saw many more that had wandered over that area shot down, so they had flown into the two heaviest-defended areas in Germany – Berlin and Ruhr

– in one night. I was concentrating our efforts to get to the coast without further trouble when a radar-controlled searchlight was suddenly switched on just below the aircraft. (These searchlights had a blue-white beam and more often than not hit the aircraft at the first attempt.) The searchlights knew they were near us because the beam started creeping up in front of the aircraft. I put more power on and raised the nose to maintain our position above the beam but it still continued creeping towards us. I was just on the point of putting the nose down and diving through it when it was switched off. Talk about a dry mouth. If the searchlight had found us it would have been joined by others and as was the customary practice a night-fighter in the vicinity would have attacked us as we were caught in the beam.

'Our last turning-point was near the Dutch border. Although our ground speed was very slow, the intensity of the defences had slackened off and for the first time in the raid, fighter activity had ceased. Maybe they had landed to refuel because we were approaching their airfields in Holland. We did not have any further trouble and eventually reached the North Sea coast. I pushed down the nose of the aircraft and did a very fast descent to 2,000 feet to the relief of the crew who were thankful to have the raid almost behind them. The wireless-operator Sergeant George Walker received a signal ordering us to divert to Wing, an OTU near Luton. It was a dark night and normally as you approached the coast you saw the odd searchlight. But we did not see one light. I was surprised when the navigator told me that according to his calculations we had already crossed the coast and gave me a course to Wing. We were by then well inland with navigation lights on flying at 2,000 feet but could not see a thing. Suddenly a searchlight switched on to us followed by two more. They could not have been practising because they could see the lights of our aircraft. I cursed as they held us, thinking back to the hundreds we had evaded over Germany only to be caught in the beams of a searchlight battery in England. I was told afterwards that a crew of ATS girls operated the lights.

'We eventually landed at Wing after a flight of seven and a half hours on the last big raid to Berlin. It made me feel quite like a veteran with twenty operations completed.'

Of the nine operations the crew had now flown to Berlin, three were on four nights at the end of January when they were in the air for twenty-four hours out of ninety-six.

'The Battle of Berlin was a period of changing situations,' Starkey wrote later. 'You could be watching *Alexander's Ragtime Band* featuring Tyrone Power, Don Ameche and Alice Fay in a cinema in Lincoln at 8 o'clock one night and the next night at 8 o'clock, be over Berlin. On one of our Berlin operations our 4,000lb "cookie" exploded near the Reichstag; this was confirmed by the photo of the burst which must have damaged the building.'

Bombs were not the only thing the crew dropped on operations. When he had gone home on operational leave Starkey had often visited his local where some of the customers asked him to take small items to drop on the 'Big City': 'One of these was an ancient pair of pantaloons belonging to Polly Kirk, an octogenarian who wrote a less than complimentary message on them for Adolf Hitler. They landed on Berlin, so for an old lady the operation was successful!'[18]

The bomber losses on 24/25 March were a high price to pay for the delivery of 2,493 tons of bombs on Berlin's vital war factories. Bombing generally was very scattered with more than 100 towns and villages around Berlin being hit and very little commercial damage done in Berlin itself. No major industrial targets were hit, although some damage was done to five military establishments including the Waffen SS depot in Lichterfelde. Civilians were hardest-hit again with 20,000 made homeless and 150 people on the ground killed. A further thirty people were killed in other areas bombed by the scattered force. Berlin reported that fourteen aircraft were shot down by night-fighters over the target area alone and it was believed that about fifty aircraft were brought down by flak. The 516 empty beds on the bomber stations included those of 133 men taken prisoner; four would evade capture and return to England.

In north Norfolk in the early hours of Saturday morning a lone Mustang touched down at Little Snoring. Major Tom Gates had got to Berlin safely but on his return he had strayed over the Ruhr and he, probably the only Allied airman over the Ruhr that night, got everything they had. 'After that,' wrote Wing Commander Roderick Chisholm, 'we just saw him at the planning conferences and then he would be off "to see the boys".' He and they did several more trips but they saw no opponents and this plucky experiment was abandoned.[19]

The 24/25 March raid on Berlin was the last major RAF raid on the city by RAF Bomber Command and it was followed by another morale-shattering blow a week later when just over 100 crews were lost in a disastrous raid on Nuremberg on the night of the 30th/31st of the month. 'The enemy defences,' recalled 'Butch' Lewis on 102 Squadron, 'had reached the height of success. It seemed impossible to carry on with night-bombing of Germany.'

Nuremberg brought, for a brief period, the virtual cessation of heavy attacks because without 'radical and remedial action', the prospect of sustained and massive long-range operations deep into Germany was impossible. Nuremberg was – as Winston Churchill recorded in his history of the war – 'proof of the power which the enemy's night-fighter force, strengthened by the best crews from other vital fronts, had developed under our relentless offensive.'

Yet the previous December, when Harris wrote to the Air Ministry saying he expected in the next three months to have forty Lancaster squadrons that would be able to drop 13,850 tons of bombs a month, sufficient to destroy between 40 and 50 per cent of the principal German towns, he had concluded that 'from this it appears that the Lancaster force alone should be sufficient but only just sufficient to produce in Germany by 1st April 1944 a state of devastation in which surrender is inevitable.'

Chapter Seventeen

Berlin or Bust

'The RAF went to Berlin so often that they even had their own song: "And so it's Berlin or Bust; Oh, we didn't want to do it, but we must, boys; Berlin or Bust; Someone started kicking up a fuss, boys; Tell them the truth we loudly roar; So it's Berlin or Bust; Oh, we didn't want to do it but we must."'

Originally formed from 3 Group, using volunteer crews, Light Night Striking Force had started as a specialist Pathfinder Force (PFF) on 15 August 1942 under the direction of Group Captain D.C.T. 'Don' Bennett and was headquartered at Wyton. On 13 January 1943 the PFF became 8 (PFF) Group and 'Don' Bennett was promoted Air Commodore (later Air Vice Marshal) to command it. The tough-talking Australian ex-imperial Airways and Atlantic Ferry pilot wanted Mosquitoes for PFF and target-marking duties. Bennett's Mosquitoes were to prove so successful that he carried out an expansion of his Mosquito force. Ultimately, eleven Mosquito-equipped squadrons operated in 8 (PFF) Group.

Attacks on the 'Big City' now became the almost nightly preserve of the 'Wooden Wonders' in the 'Light Night Striking Force', with as many as seventy Mosquitoes unloading their 'cookies' in all kinds of soupy weather when the Halifaxes and Lancasters were grounded. Churchill had decided that as a propaganda ploy, Germany should be bombed for 100 nights in a row and Berlin became the 'favourite' destination for the Mosquito squadrons, better known as the 'Light Night Striking Force'. 'A' and 'B' Flights at 8 (PFF) Group stations were routed to the 'Big City' over towns and cities whose air-raid sirens would announce their arrival overhead, although they were not the targets for the Mosquitoes' bombs. Depriving the Germans of much-needed sleep and comfort was a very effective 'nuisance' weapon, while a 4,000-pounder nestling in the bomb-bay was a more tangible calling-card. The 'night postmen' had two rounds: after take-off from Wyton, crews immediately climbed to height, departed Cromer and flew the dog-leg route Heligoland-Bremen-Hamburg; the second route saw departure over Woodbridge and went to the Ruhr-Hanover-Munich.

The German people were not the only ones losing sleep in this war: 'We usually slept until the last minute on nights when operations were "on",' wrote Ralph Wood, now a Mosquito navigator on 692 Squadron at Graveley, which the squadron shared with 35 Pathfinder Squadron, flying Lancasters. Ralph was a 'second tourist', having flown on Whitley and Halifax bombers on his first tour. Andy Lockhart, his Canadian pilot, an old school chum from Moncton, was on his first tour. Their first Mosquito op was on 6 July, when the target was Gelsenkirchen. It was Ralph's twenty-eighth op of the war and his pilot's first over enemy territory:

'On 7th July we went right to the 'Snake's home' (Berlin). We were quite keyed up, too, but were not letting on to each other. A typical trip to Berlin would be a feint attack on a couple of cities on the way to our target and throwing out 'Window' to foul up the radar. Once over Berlin we were usually caught in a huge cone of searchlights, so blinding Andy that he couldn't read the instruments. 'Are we upside-down or not?' he'd ask. I'd look down at the bombs exploding below and assure him that we were right side up. As the anti-aircraft crap seemed to surround us, Andy would throw our '*Moncton Express*' around the skies, trying desperately to get out of the searchlights. On three occasions we lost an engine about now and had to limp home, as one set of searchlights passed us on to another set and so on, until they ran out of lights. When over the target, we'd bomb and get out as fast as we could. This was when I'd sit in my seat, the blood draining out of my face and my stomach in tight knots. Jesus, this could be it, I thought. And after tight moments like this I'd say, 'Andy, pass the beads.'

'The trip was successful, but packed with excitement. As we did our bombing run into the centre of Berlin, our starboard engine seemed to catch fire. Andy feathered it immediately in case of the fire spreading. We finished our run, dropped our 'cookie' and were immediately coned by a great number of searchlights. After five minutes we got out without damage. On the return journey we were coned and shot at again in the Hamburg district. Finally we reached the English coast and landed at the nearest airdrome with about twenty gallons of petrol left. We returned to base the following day after our engine was repaired. We have now been over the hottest target in Germany and feel quite good about it. One of our crews failed to return.[1]

'Our billets were huge tin Nissen huts, situated some distance from the mess, which we tried to keep heated with toy stoves and a niggardly ration of coal. We would make a mad dash for the mess before the doors closed. Most of us had this timed pretty well; so well that me and Andy decided to upset the pattern by piling as many bicycles as possible on top of the latrine building. Of course, a great many missed their breakfast that morning, including the CO, Wing Commander Joe Northrop DFC AFC whose bicycle was also included.'[2]

Having just finished on heavies, Wing Commander Northrop had assumed command of 692 in July after Wing Commander Stephen Delancy Watts DFC, a New Zealander from Morrinsville, had been killed on 10 July. Joe had been 'on cloud nine' when Don Bennett had offered him the job, with the proviso that he would be limited to two or three operations a month. Joe was now a master bomber, having been the controller of a force of 242 Lancasters and 12 Mosquitoes attacking the railway yards at Revigny and Villeneuve on the night of 14/15 July. His navigator, Flight Lieutenant A.R. 'Sandy' Galbraith DFC born in Auckland, New Zealand on 20 April 1918, who had been a clerk before joining the RNZAF in 1940, was particularly cut up at the news that Joe was leaving for pastures new, but before Northrop left Wyton he promised he would send for him as his navigator on Mosquitoes. After an early breakfast at Wyton, saying 'cheerio' to his friends on 83 Squadron and obtaining clearance from the few sections on the station, Joe packed up the last of his kit into his little 1926 Baby Austin Seven he'd acquired for £20 and set off towards the Boston Road for Graveley.

On arrival, he was ushered in to see the station commander, Group Captain Menaul DFC AFC. Joe had known 'Paddy' Menaul earlier in the war at Wyton where he had been a flight commander on 15 Squadron flying first on Blenheims and later on Wellingtons. Like Joe, he had begun his RAF career as an aircraft apprentice at Halton. He whisked Joe off in his service car for a quick tour of the main sections on the station. At the end of the tour he drew up at a motley collection of Nissen hits of various sizes housing the offices and crew rooms of 692 Squadron. He introduced his new arrival to Flight Lieutenant Northover, the bespectacled adjutant with the air of a bank manager (which is in fact what he was in civvy life). That night Joe sat in on the briefing for the raid on Bremen.

Joe was already a great admirer of the Mosquito and he soon decided he wanted to fly more than the two or three operations a month to which he had been restricted:

'It was the cat's whiskers. We would have been well away at the beginning of the war with a few Mosquito squadrons. We could have hit Berlin for a dozen in the first few weeks – you could afford to fly one of those things in daylight. In winter we could take off at about four o'clock in the afternoon, in the dusk. By the time we got over the Dutch coast heading towards the target, which was invariably Berlin, you were up at about thirty thousand, pretty safe, away from everything. You could steam into Berlin, in the knowledge on many occasions that you had fog on the Continent. The Mossie made such a superb night-bomber operating at heights and speeds far in excess of the Lancasters and Halifaxes that flying times to all major targets in the Third Reich were literally halved.

'During the short summer nights when the heavies had to confine their attacks to short-range targets to keep within the hours of darkness and acceptable loss rates, Mosquitoes of the eight squadrons of the Light Night Striking Force hit Berlin and all major German cities at will, keeping the air-raid sirens wailing night after night throughout Germany. Only the very worst of bad weather grounded them and the high intensity of operating, together with an extremely low loss rate, became so routine that the normal tour of operations was set at fifty as against thirty on the 'heavy' squadrons. Even so, there was a big turnover of tour-expired crews and the Mosquito Operational Conversion Unit was hard put to churn out sufficient crews to meet the needs of the squadrons. In the winter months it was often possible to fit in a sortie between afternoon tea and late dinner in the mess and have a drink afterwards before the bar closed. It was quite common for crews to complete their full operational tours within three months of first joining a squadron.

'We'd send about 100 aircraft, converge on Berlin, having done a bit of dog-legging around the place to alert the fighters and make them try to get up and fox them a bit. We'd collect over the target, drop a load of 4,000lb 'cookies', the air-raid sirens would be cracking and so on, down they'd go fairly accurately, and back everybody would steam. Used to take about three and three-quarter hours, roughly, and you'd be back in the mess by half-past eight, having a normal dinner. You'd have tea before you went, dinner when you got back. What a way to fight a war!'[3]

The operational use of the Mosquito bomber had forced the Nachtjagd to reconsider the 'Wilde Sau' method to hunt the high-performance aircraft at high altitude with Focke-Wulf 190A-5s and A-6s and Bf 109Gs with 'Neptun' AI radar and a long-range fuel tank. Oberleutnant Fritz Krause, a Staffelkapitän in the experimental I./NJGr10 at Berlin-Werneuchen commanded by Hauptmann Friedrich Karl Müller whose main task this was, took off at 0040 hours on 8 July in 'Weisse Elf' ('White 11'), a FuG 217J2 ('Neptun')-equipped Focke-Wulf 190A-5 and destroyed a Mosquito near Brandenburg, his only abschuss in this unit. Krause describes his victory:

'I was flying over Berlin at a height of 8,500 metres when I saw a twin-engined plane flying west caught in the searchlights. I closed in until I was 700 metres above, gave full throttle and dived. I went in too low and opened fire from approximately 200 metres from below and behind and kept firing as I closed. My first shots hit the right motor and an explosion followed. There was a burst of sparks and then a thick white trail of vapour.

'As I had overshot I had to stop the attack momentarily and found myself on the right, alongside the enemy aircraft, whose cockade and external fuel tanks I saw clearly and so was ablc to identify it without a doubt as a Mosquito. I fired ESN to draw the attention of the flak and the searchlight to my presence. The enemy 'corkscrewed' in an attempt to evade. Because of the thick 'white flag' of vapour I was able to follow him, although he had already left the searchlight zone in a north-westerly direction. Following the trail, I managed to attack twice more. At the third attack I noticed a further explosion on the right wing and an even stronger rain of sparks. At 2,000 metres he disappeared, turning at a flat gliding angle under me. I did not see the impact on the ground as this was hidden from my angle of view.

'On my return flight, passing Lake Koppeln I could estimate the crash-point as 60 to 70 kilometres north-west of Berlin. When I returned to base a report had already reached them about the crash of a burning enemy aircraft west of Kyritz. My own plane was covered in oil from the damaged Mosquito.'[4]

On 10 July Andy Lockhart and Ralph Wood were on the 'Milk Run' again or 'Berlin or Bust' as the latter put it. 'Of course, we had to get coned and shot at again over the target. As if that wasn't enough, the boys of Heligoland had a crack at us too, but the trip was exciting and a good one. Andy and I saw a lot of action in that direction as we passed it. Andy liked the choice of names I used for the 'Hun' when he let us have a barrage of flak. We were still keen and a bit more Berlin-minded. We were coned for nine minutes there this time. On return we just made the English coast and landed with 5 gallons of petrol left. We were getting along fine together and our teamwork was improving.

'One unusual return from enemy territory and most satisfying included a dive, beginning at the French coast from 32,000 feet to 10,000 feet, to Southwold on the English coast. This 88-mile journey was completed in eleven minutes, which was fast, even for a Mosquito. With our 'cookie' gone, our two 50-gallon drop tanks discarded and our fuel load pretty well depleted, it wasn't too hard to accomplish this feat. Andy and I were at 25,000 feet completing our air test in preparation for the night's operation when I happened to look up from my lap table. There was Andy, out cold and slumped over the controls. We were dropping like a lead weight – straight for the ground. My blood drained into my shoes as I managed to place my oxygen mask over his face in time for him to revive and pull the plane out of the dive.

'After a trip to Hanover on 14 July it was Berlin on 15 July, on the 'Milk Run' again; my favourite dislike. On the way there, via the Ruhr, we managed to anger the bastards and they threw up everything they had at us. After what seemed ages, we shook them off and proceeded to the target, where we were fortunate in steering clear of trouble. Coming home, we had a few more taking pot-shots at us, but returned to base okay. The fog at base caused us to land at our training station a few miles from base. Looking at our kite the next day we saw several flak holes: one below in front of us; one below and behind us on the bomb-bay doors; and one entered the engine covering underneath. 'A miss is a good as a mile', so here's the next trip.

'On 17 July it was Berlin again – making four out of six trips to the 'Big City'. This was more than I expected. It was a satisfaction to know that they respected our raids. That might be due to the fact that we carried a 'cookie' with us. If it didn't give them a headache, it would at least keep them awake! One lad on the way in was coned in about 100 searchlights and was getting enough shrapnel in his direction to sink the *Queen Mary*. The poor guy stooged over Hamburg by mistake. (I'd have to watch that; it might have been us!) At the target the boys were coned here and there but no flak was shot up the beams, which indicated that enemy fighters were present. At interrogation next morning we learned that a few of the boys were chased persistently by those fighters. Joe's halo (that's mine) must have been working overtime! It was a good trip for us, though.

'We were on again the next night too and we hoped it would be a short trip this time. No luck. It was Berlin again. The trip proved quite nerve-racking, as we were both on edge all the time due to not being able to get enough sleep and working rather hard lately. We were first over the target and got coned as we waited for the markers to fall. As we let our 'cookie' drop, the markers dropped beside our bomb burst. Andy threw the kite around in every direction to get out of the searchlights. At one time he nearly stalled her and thought we were upside-down. I told him I could still see the searchlights by looking down, so we must be right side up. On the way out we were nearly coned again over Magdeburg. Andy was a little too quick for them this time and we returned home without further trouble, definitely all in and slightly fed up. Our leave on the 21st would certainly be welcome. So far we had been to Berlin five times out of seven trips.'

George Cash, another Mosquito navigator, had been on ops for nearly a year. Tuesday, 18 July began like any other day, but little did he know what lay in store! George was the elder of two sons born to George and Lylie Cash who lived in a cramped Victorian back-to-back terraced house in West Ham in London's poverty-ridden East End before the war. They realized that education would be their sons' salvation and they scrimped and saved to give their two boys the opportunities they never had. George matriculated in July 1938 and was working as a junior in a chartered accountant's office, studying for exams, when some of his former schoolmates returned from Dunkirk. The evacuation brought a new sense of urgency and Cash decided to abandon his ambitions in the world of accountancy. When the blitz destroyed the family home and they fled to Dagenham, Essex, he decided that he would become a fighter pilot. He enrolled in the RAF in July 1941 at Oxford with the intention of becoming a pilot, for which he had already grown a bristling moustache to go with his pilot's wings. His outstanding ability at mathematics, however, made him realize that he would be of more use to the war effort as a navigator. In May 1943 he was posted to 1655 Mosquito Conversion Unit at Finmere and he went on to become equally adept as an advanced navigator, a wireless-operator, bomb-aimer and gunner:

'On the evening of 18 July, when we went into briefing, I had no undue feelings of trepidation – certainly not like the 'butterflies' that I had when I first flew on ops. During training and flying time, I had formed quite firm friendships with various fellows. Friends had gone on different postings from mine and we'd parted. Crews on ops had gone missing or had been killed. One was saddened for a short time but life went on and they went out of mind; that was the way of things. Like many others, I suppose, I thought that nothing would ever happen to me and that I would just go on until the end of the war, or until such time that I felt like packing up. Experience and the knowledge of what to expect helped to allay one's fears although, however much experience a man had, I don't think that any airman could truthfully say that he did not feel some apprehension before setting off on an operation.

'This time, I saw that 'A' Flight – ours – was to go to Cologne and 'B' Flight to Berlin. Accordingly, I began to get out maps and charts of the Ruhr in readiness when I noticed that our names were not on the 'A' Flight list. I pointed this out to my pilot, who was always known as 'Doddy'.

Squadron Leader Terence Edgar Dodwell DFC* RAFVR, 29 years old, whose wife, Olive, lived in Thorpe Bay, Essex, had completed part of a Mosquito tour with 1409 Met Flight before joining 571 Squadron. Before this he had completed a tour with Squadron Leader Peter Ashley on 110 'Hyderabad' Squadron, flying Mk IV Blenheims.

'Doddy' nodded and remarked that we were going to Berlin instead. 'There's a "sprog" crew in "B" Flight,' he said, 'so I offered to take their place – they can go on a short trip sometime to break them in gently.' In the Services, one was always told never to volunteer for anything. A dangerous job in the line of duty was one thing, but you did not stick your neck out needlessly and go looking for trouble! Somehow, deep inside me, I had an uncomfortable feeling that this was 'It'.

'We had the usual briefing: target, routes into and away from the 'Big City', deployment of defences along these routes, met report and so on. During the briefing, the Intelligence officer warned us of the Germans using experimental jet-propelled night-fighters over Berlin. I didn't pay much heed to this for I had heard it all before (big head!). After preparing my flight plan and marking my maps and charts with information that I would need, I packed my things and 'Doddy' and I walked across to the crew room to get our Mae Wests, 'chutes and dinghies. We were unusually silent and I wondered if he sensed what I was thinking.

'It was time to go. The crew bus arrived, we clambered on and soon we were dropped off at our dispersal. We climbed into the aircraft, stowed our gear and while I fixed my charts and flight plan, 'Doddy' carried out his pre-flight check.

'When he came to run up the engines he found that the port engine had a mag drop and consequently was u/s. We collected our things, climbed out of the aircraft and sent one of the ground crew to get a van to take us over to the reserve aircraft ['V for Victor' MM136]. By now, the rest of the squadron had taken off and were on their way. We raced round the 'drome to the reserve aircraft, climbed aboard and after hurried checks all round, took off well behind the rest. All this rush and frenzy had been most unsettling – it was a very bad start. We were more than fifteen minutes behind and could never make up that time which meant that we would be 'tail-end Charlies' out behind the mainstream. This would make us very vulnerable – an easy target for flak or fighters as we knew from experience – and yet, strangely, I remember that I wasn't particularly perturbed by the prospect.

'As we climbed to our operational height – 28,000 feet – we began to settle down and by the time we levelled out, we were quite calm and I was too busy with my navigation to worry about anything else. We were approaching the enemy coast and, as normal, we began to siphon fuel from our overload tanks to the outer tanks in the wings to replace fuel that we had used.

'We had just crossed the Dutch coast when near Arnhem a stream of tracers from below indicated that enemy fighters were on to us. 'Doddy' immediately took vigorous evasive action – always difficult with a 'cookie' on board. For a few hectic minutes that seemed like an age, we ran the gauntlet of what we thought were a couple of Ju 88s. We felt a few thuds in the fuselage but there did not appear to be any serious damage. We shook them off eventually and resumed our course, each of us in our own way breathing a sigh of relief. I suddenly realised that, in the heat of the moment, we had forgotten to turn off the petrol siphons. The outer tanks had filled and we had been discharging precious fuel into the slipstream. We must have lost a considerable amount and it crossed my mind that we might not have enough to get us home. This must have occurred to 'Doddy' too, as he gave vent to a few choice phrases but, once again, I wasn't particularly bothered. It seems, in retrospect, that I was subconsciously preparing for the worst – that we wouldn't be coming back anyway. This had put us further behind and, although the next part of the route was a dog-leg round a heavily-defended area near Wittingen, we decided to take a chance and fly straight across. I worked out the new course and just as we were thinking that we had got away with it, all hell broke loose. Shells burst round us too close for comfort. 'Doddy' put up the nose, opened the throttles and climbed as fast as we could go. It seemed ages before we got away but not before a huge lump of shrapnel had smashed through the back window into the 'Gee' box by my side – another few inches and I wouldn't be telling this tale!

'At the turning-point in our route which was to take us on a dog-leg to Stendal – our last turning-point – in the distance I saw that the target indicators had already gone down over the railway marshalling yards north-west of Berlin – the target. Ahead of us were searchlights and bursting flak. The raid had begun. We decided to fly straight there to make up for all the lost time. I worked out a course to steer and then began to 'Window' 'like mad'. Unfortunately the route took us over the flak at Wittingen, which immediately opened up on us. Suddenly we found ourselves in a box of heavy predicted flak with shells bursting all around. Shrapnel rattled down on to the cockpit of the aircraft and we could smell the cordite. 'Doddy' put the aircraft into a steep dive; a chunk of flak smashed through the fuselage and hit the 'Gee' set, putting it out of action. The evasive action finally took us clear of the flak and on an ETA for Stendal we climbed back to 32,000 feet. 'Doddy' decided to skirt round the defences and come in from another direction but, just then, we were coned. We were blinded by the glare. 'Doddy' once more threw the kite around, diving and banking, turning and climbing in an effort to get away but to no avail. Then, suddenly the searchlights dipped – we had shaken them off – but we ought to have known better!

'We were now in sight of the target indicators and I noted in my log: 0200 hours. Target sighted, preparing to bomb. I stowed my equipment and knelt down ready to crawl into the nose to the bombsight. I had hardly moved when we felt a quick succession of thumps as cannon shells smashed into the fuselage. A tremendous 'whoof' and the port petrol tanks exploded. The port engine burst into blames. I realised, all too late, why the searchlights had left us. A night-fighter had homed on to us and had flown up beneath us to deliver the coup de grâce – we had been a sitting duck. With the cockpit now well ablaze, 'Doddy' said, 'Come on, we've got to get out of here!' I pulled up the cover of the escape hatch and threw it into the nose. When I got up, I found that I was on my own. 'Doddy' had exited smartly through the top hatch. I couldn't blame him – his seat was on fire! (In dry runs on the ground, we had practised getting out in a hurry through the conventional exit below the navigator's position. We had to aim at getting out in ten seconds. With all our cumbersome gear, Mae Wests, parachutes and harness and dinghy, we couldn't get out in ten minutes!)

'It was dangerous going out of the top (to be done only if the aircraft ditched or crash-landed) since, in flight, there was the great risk of striking the tail fin and rudder or the tailplane. But, there I was, in a blazing aircraft, spiralling out of control with a 4,000lb bomb still on board. The 'G' pressure was like a heavy weight, pressing me down on to my seat. I did what any man in my position would do: I breathed a quick prayer, 'God, help me.'

'Suddenly, despite the heat in the cockpit and my perilous position, a calmness came over me and my mind was clear. A fierce draught fanned the flames so that the whole cockpit was ablaze and full of smoke. There was nothing for it – I had to go: out of the top hatch. I struggled round on my seat to reach behind me to get my parachute from its stowage. As I turned back, my elbow caught the ruined 'Gee' box by my side, knocking my 'chute from my hand. It fell down the escape hatch but fortunately it stuck halfway down where I could reach it and clip it onto my harness. In those few seconds, I suddenly remembered reading an account in *Tee Emm* magazine about how a Mosquito navigator had bailed out by climbing out of the top hatch and rolling on to the starboard wing before letting go. I took three deep breaths of oxygen, took off my mask and helmet, threw them down and proceeded to do likewise. I was carried away by the slipstream, clear of the aircraft and, after counting the requisite 'One, two three' I reached up to my parachute pack, which was now above my head and pulled the release handle. Nothing happened! I reached up with both hands and pulled open the flaps of the pack.

'There was a plop as the canopy sprang out and filled with air. There I was floating through the quiet, peaceful sky. Then I looked down and, immediately below me, or so it seemed, there was our Mosquito in a field, blazing away with the 'cookie' still on board. If it had gone up then, I would have gone up with it. I continued drifting a little way away then, suddenly, innumerable fingers were scrabbling at me – I had the fleeting thought of falling into the hands of a lynch mob. But they were twigs

– I had come down in a tree! I was dangling there, my night vision completely gone and I couldn't see or feel the ground. I needed to get away as fast as I could. I pressed the release button and I fell 10 feet into a bush below the tree. Except for a few scratches, I was unharmed. I was on terra firma, albeit enemy terra firma, but I was down and that was how I qualified for the Caterpillar Club. For my claim to fame – if it can be called such – I am one of a very few men who bailed out from the top hatch of a Mosquito and lived to tell the tale. Also, I am one, probably of many, who climbed down from a tree which he had not climbed up!

'I set off walking in a westerly direction, putting as much distance as I possibly could between myself and the blazing 'Mossie'. The 'cookie' did go up after about ten minutes, with a great crump and a terrific orange glow – I felt the blast even at that distance. I was now on my own; my last link with home had gone. I kept going for nearly two days but, on the way through a small village just outside Magdeburg, very late at night, I had the misfortune to walk into a Volkssturm patrol out looking for the crew of a Flying Fortress that had been shot down earlier in the day. I spent the next three days in the civvie jail in Magdeburg before I was transported to the Interrogation Centre at Oberursel, just outside Frankfurt-am-Main. A few days later, I was entrained with about 200 others – 180 Americans and 20 British – to Barth in Pomerania on the Baltic coast. I marched into Stalag Luft I with this contingent on Tuesday, 1 August 1944 – my 23rd birthday – just two weeks after I had taken off from Oakington for the last time. I was to spend nearly ten months in Germany before returning home at the end of the war.

'Apparently, we had been tracked and shot down by a German night-fighter ace: Oberleutnant Heinz Strüning of 3./NJG flying a Heinkel 219A-5 'Owl' which was armed with 'Schräge Musik' (the code word for upward-firing guns fitted to the aircraft). To enable them to keep up with faster aircraft, as we were, their engines were fitted with nitrous-oxide boosters which could be used for about ten minutes or so to enhance their speed. Heinz Strüning was awarded the Oak Leaves to his Knight's Cross with Swords and Diamonds on 20 July 1944 for shooting us down! From an account in the German archives, the body of Squadron Leader T.E. Dodwell had been discovered, with his parachute unopened, in a clump of trees near Laudin, 35 miles west of Berlin, close to the site where the aircraft had crashed. From the appearance of the body, it had been deduced that he was dead before reaching the ground having been fatally injured by striking part of the aircraft (the tail?) on bailing out; hence the unopened parachute.

'Strüning had been promoted to Hauptmann a few weeks after our incident and posted to 9./NJG as a Flight Commander. He enjoyed considerable acclaim as a night-fighter ace with a squadron of Me 110s flying from Holland. On Christmas Eve 1944 a force of our heavies was out and Strüning's squadron took off to try to infiltrate them. Unknown to him the heavies were accompanied by a couple of squadrons of Mosquito night-fighters. Strüning's aircraft was shot down by a Mosquito night-fighter and crashed near Bergisch-Gladbach-Rheinland. The radar-operator and air gunner bailed out safely, but Strüning hit the tail of the Me 110 when he bailed out and was killed. His body was found two months later and interred.'

Ralph Wood and Andy Lockhart on 692 Squadron flew their thirteenth trip on 13 August to Berlin, 'their lucky city'.

'We paid it a short visit with our usual calling-cards of 4,000lb bombs,' wrote Ralph. 'It was a good trip, but we had a bit too much excitement attached to it. In short, our luck wasn't of the high standard it had been since our leave. We were coned for a hell of a long time between Hamburg and Lübeck. No flak came up, so I strained my eyes looking for the inevitable fighters while Andy concentrated on getting us out of a cone of from fifty to a hundred searchlights. As the night was black, the lights had a fine time with us. It sure made you feel naked! We were next coned over Berlin and again when we were nearing the enemy coast on the way home. I saw a fighter, but he evidently didn't see us. When we landed at base all our petrol gauges registered zero. And so ended another trip to the "Big City".

'On 16th August it was Berlin again. It was a good trip in spite of a lot of things going wrong. One of our compasses went unserviceable before we were airborne; then, over the North Sea wc lost a carburretor stud on the port engine. Over Berlin we dropped our wing tanks along with the "cookie", as the ground crew had it wired up wrong. We were coned over the "Big City" but got out of it in four minutes with only one hunk of flak in our wing. We had an uneventful trip home and were quite tired. A feed – our rum ration – and bed, all looked pretty good to us.

'Ops on 17th August, to Mannheim, and 23rd August, to Cologne and then on the 26th it was back to Berlin again. It turned out to be rather pleasant in spite of our being coned over the target. We were hit by flak and we lost an engine before reaching home. Andy made another single-engine landing.'

On 26 August as conditions were again favourable, Joe Northrop lost no time in placing the newly-arrived Sandy Galbraith and himself on the battle order once more. They had finally become operational on the 13th with a first trip in a Mosquito, which Joe found 'an exceedingly tight fit in the cockpit after all the room in the Lancaster "office"' and on the following two nights he had briefed his crews for operations on Berlin, followed by a 'shortie' on Mannheim and then another Berlin trip. He was keen to get on the battle order again after what he considered was a decent interval, but at this stage the weather had turned really bad and for the next three days no operations had taken place.

'As our force of fifty-three Mosquitoes bombed Berlin, to the north and east the heavies were attacking Kiel and Königsberg at extreme range and suffering quite heavy losses.[5] My flying time for the Berlin raid amounted to four hours and twenty-five minutes, the easiest and fastest operation I ever made against the capital city. The last trip of the month was against Frankfurt with no losses whatsoever for the squadron during the whole of August.'

Joe was not quite correct, however, for 28-year-old Squadron Leader Walter Douglas Wilberforce Bird and 21-year-old Flight Sergeant Francis William Hudson were killed when they returned short of petrol and crashed into a house at Park Farm, Old Warden near Bedford. It was believed that Hudson had misread his altimeter.

On 8/9 September Ralph Wood flew his fiftieth op of the war when he and Andy Lockhart were among the forty-five Mosquitoes that went to Nuremberg. On the night following, it was Brunswick, which was visited by thirty-nine Mosquitoes.

'We were nearly half-finished now,' he wrote. 'The Hun was now sending more fighters up after us as we were proving to be more than just nuisance raiders.

According to a press report, the Luftwaffe now rated Mosquitoes on night attacks so high that when and if a Jerry shot down a Mosquito he was allowed to count it as two [*sic*].[6] Sometimes I wished we had some guns, too.

'On 10th/11th September it was the old "Milk Run" again – Berlin [which was visited by forty-seven Mosquitoes]. We had to land away from base, as an earwig plugged the starboard jettison tank. We had more trouble at the place we landed and didn't get home until 1800 hours the next day. At 1830 hours we were having our flying supper for another trip to the "Big City". We were coned near Hamburg on the way in and again over the target. Another one of our crews failed to return.'

Terry Goodwin DFC DFM, a 692 Squadron pilot at Graveley flew this operation, his last on the Mosquito. He had a rather anxious time, as he recounts:

'After Hugh Hay had finished his tour I had several good navigators with nothing to worry about. However, when my last trip was coming up there was a new navigator posted in. He was a Warrant Officer with no trips in at all. I just could not figure that out when all crews at that time had a tour under their belts and knew what the score was. I took him for a cross-country, which was not satisfactory as he had trouble with the 'Gee'. I did not know whether it was a 'short' or a 'long' trip: either the Ruhr or Berlin. It turned out to be the 'Big City'.

'The night was clear. The take-off with the 4,000lb 'cookie' was good. The aircraft was singing right along with all gauges OK. The track was out over the North Sea towards Denmark, then a sharp turn right south-east to a point just west of Berlin, then straight east for the bombing run. When we were approaching this turning-point it was clear with no moon. I could see the coast outline right from Denmark south. The tram trolleys of Hamburg were still making their blue sparks and then shut down fully. Then the 'sprog' navigator said to me, 'I don't know where we are!' I told him to get the course from the turning-point and I would tell him when to start all over again. He did and got us just west of Berlin on time, or at least I thought we were on time. I told him to log the time, then go and dump the 'Window' down the chute. There was no action outside as we ran up looking for the 'TIs'.

'Jerry was playing it very careful, giving nothing away. Where was that PFF type? The TIs should be going down! Then all hell broke loose. Every searchlight in the city came on right on us and the flak was too damn close. I turned sharp right and dived 2,000 feet, straightened out back on course, held it, turned left and climbed and got more flak but further away. And this kept on and on. Finally the lights were bending east so I thought we should be through the city. I turned back west and still no PFF. I told the navigator to drop the 'cookie' (I don't think we got a proper picture) because the flak was hard at us again. Then the TIs went down right ahead of us so we were pretty close. But the flak kept on and I twisted and dived and climbed and kept that up.

'I knew we were down to about 17,000 feet when I suddenly saw the light flak opening up. You knew it was pretty if it was not so damn serious. I turned and climbed out on the west side of Berlin. I told the navigator to log the time. We had been in it for eleven minutes with the Jerries' undivided attention. Were there any fighters? Not that I saw; maybe I was just too busy. It would not have been a safe place for them with all that flak around. We did get home and logged four hours and thirty minutes.

'The next morning the Flight Sergeant found me and then showed me the aircraft. It was full of flak; the main spar of the tailplane was getting an 18 inch splice. He dug a piece of flak out for me. One piece had just nicked the intercooler rad; then the fairing for the main rad, but not the tubes. It was spent as it bounced around the engine.'

Ralph Wood's trip to Berlin on the 11th/12th when forty-seven Mosquitoes went to Berlin was, in his words, 'quite respectable and we got back to base without any trouble. We were coned over the 'Big City', but managed to get out of it with a little effort. We were now over the hump and on our downward journey, with twenty-four ops left to do.'

This raid on Berlin did not go well for Flight Lieutenant Norman Griffiths and Flying Officer Bill Ball on 571 Squadron in B.XVI MM127 'K-King'. Bill Ball wrote:

'There were wavering clusters of them all around the city, in the city and on the approaches to the city. A complete forest of blazing lights. Some were almost stationary, holding one or more of the early arrivals. Others were waving about like tall trees in a high wind, seeking the Squadron's Mosquitoes. Bombs were going down all the time as we approached. Great flashes and fires on the ground showed where the blockbusters were bursting. Flares and target indicators added to the illuminations. The whole sky on the bombing run and over the target was filled with vivid, vicious flashes and ugly grey and white puffs of smoke. The flak was crabbing nearer, bursting all around; a deadly barrage just above the cockpit, outside the port window and all along the starboard fuselage … it was so near I could feel 'K for King' shuddering with the impact. So close I could see every detail of the cotton-wool puffs slowly unfolding! ('K-King' limped back towards the Norfolk coast on a rapidly depleting fuel supply and was abandoned over the sea. The aircraft came down in a beet field near the village of Bacton, having missed houses in the village by a fair margin.)'

Warrant Officer 'Tommy' Tomlinson and Flying Officer Dick Richards in B.XVI PF394 were also given 'the full treatment', as Richards recalls:

'We dropped, but while still held in the glare the guns stopped. Twice fighters attacked us and the second attack smashed all our hydraulic systems. Eventually we got away and 'Tommy' (I was lucky enough to do most of my trips with the tearaway Warrant Officer 'Tommy' Tomlinson) remembering Magdeburg wanted to do another low-level night cross-country across Germany. (On 25 August to Berlin we had an engine shot out near Magdeburg. We returned the compliment with our 4,000lb 'cookie' and turned for home. The aircraft would not hold height and we were contemplating jumping but with the throttle through the gate we staggered home at lowering altitude with 'Tommy' loving every minute of it.) I persuaded him that, with two engines operational, it was silly to lose the advantage of height. He reluctantly agreed and eventually he made his usual immaculate landing at Woodbridge, but this time with no undercarriage or flaps and at a speed close to 200 mph.'

Two Mosquito bombers that failed to return from the attack on Berlin on 13/14 September were claimed shot down south-east of the capital by Oberfeldwebel Egbert Jaacks of I./NJG10 and at Brunswick by Leutnant Karl Mitterdorfer of

10./JG300. Squadron Leader Charles René Barrett DFC, a 31-year-old Londoner, and Flying Officer Edward Sydney Fogden on 608 Squadron were killed and Pilot Officer Gwilym Rhys Thomas and 30-year-old Flying Officer John Herbert Rosbottom on 692 Squadron also died. Both aircraft crashed near Nauen.

Berlin was all too familiar to Flight Lieutenant 'Chas' Lockyer DFC who had flown a tour on Hampdens on 106 Squadron at Coningsby in 1941 before beginning his second tour of operations as pilot of a Mosquito B.XX on 608 Squadron at Downham Market. His navigator, Flying Officer Bart 'Jock' Sherry DFC*, another second tour man, was a big, cheerful Glaswegian with a laugh that could stop a bus at twenty paces. He had completed a tour on Lancasters in 1943.

Lockyer recalls: 'Naturally enough, with 635 Lancaster Squadron and 608 Mosquito Squadron sharing the same airfield at Downham Market there was a lot of good-humoured rivalry and banter between the respective air crews. Our cause wasn't helped by some idiot naming the Mosquito squadrons of 8 Group 'The Light Night-Striking Force', which left us wide open to sarcastic suggestions that the qualification for service on a Mosquito squadron was presumably an inability to see in the dark! It was later changed to 'The Fast Night-Striking Force'; equally clumsy but less ambiguous.

'We were fortunate at Downham in having a FIDO installation: the fog dispersal system consisting of a double line of burners running parallel to either side of the runway, which burned large quantities of petrol on the Primus stove principle. The intense heat so generated burned off the fog and thereby enabled the airfield to remain operational when the rest of the area was blanketed in fog. Coming in to land when FIDO was operating was rather like descending into the jaws of hell and proved a very useful incentive to keeping straight after touch-down!

'The Mossies were given a wide variety of tasks including such niceties as dropping route-markers and target-indicators over a false target while the Main Force pressed on elsewhere. With the introduction of the 'pregnant' Mosquito version adapted to carry a 'cookie', we became a reasonably lethal bombing force in our own right, particularly as we could operate in weather conditions that grounded the heavies. The inhabitants of Berlin would be the first to acknowledge that 100 Mosquitoes each carrying a 'cookie' weren't the most welcome visitors night after night. When bad weather grounded the Main Force, small groups of Mosquitoes could be sent to a wide variety of targets in the Reich. Their objective was to get a large part of Germany out of bed and into the shelter so there were very few nights when the sirens were silent.'

'Chas' Lockyer's and 'Jock' Sherry's first operational trip in a Mosquito was to Berlin on 15/16 September, when twenty-seven Mosquitoes went to the 'Big City'. It was Andy Lockhart's and Ralph Wood's third time running, which Wood considered was 'too much'. 'Our journey there and back was fine and we missed all the hot spots. The target proved quite hot and we were coned for a while. It was a horrible naked feeling, especially as there was no flak in the cone which got us. Hence, a damn good set-up for a cat's-eye fighter. It was okay, though and we hoped for a smaller target the next time.'

'Chas' Lockyer and 'Jock' Sherry had just released the bombs and had completed the requisite straight and level run for the benefit of the camera when a master searchlight switched straight on them and they were immediately coned as its satellites 'joined in the fun':

'At the same moment,' continues Lockyer, 'Jock', who had scrambled back from the bomb-aiming position in the nose, spotted a Focke-Wulf 190 closing in on us but slightly high. The pilot obviously hadn't seen us yet or his cannon shells would have blown us out of the sky by now and we were apparently in the blind spot created by the 190's large radial engine. This situation posed a bit of a problem as any sort of diving turn on our part would undoubtedly bring us into his line of vision and a highly probable early end of our tour. The only alternative seemed to be to try to stay in his blind spot. I throttled back slightly until he was immediately above us. For about the next ten minutes we performed a graceful pas de deux over the city, watching him like a hawk and responding as soon as we saw his wing dip as he searched left and right for his prey. Finally and to our profound relief he gave up and turned steeply to starboard while we turned equally steeply to port and high-tailed it for home. We had a few chuckles on the way back trying to guess the gist of the conversation which must have gone on between the 190 pilot and his ground controller. The latter probably asked what sort of short-sighted dummkopfs the Luftwaffe were recruiting these days, the pilot responding by asking the controller kindly to clean his screen as he didn't want to spend the rest of the night being vectored on to fly dirt.'

The one Mosquito that failed to return from this raid, 'G-George' on 608 Squadron, crashed into the railway station at Rangsdorf at 0230 hours. Flight Lieutenant 'Bert' Howard Smith RCAF and Sergeant Leonard Frederick Pegg both perished. They were buried in a joint grave at the Berlin 1939–1945 War Cemetery.

Three Mosquitoes and a Stirling of 199 Squadron in 100 Group were lost on Bomber Support. Leutnant Kurt Welter claimed two of the Mosquitoes, one south of Berlin and the other north of Aachmer, and Feldwebel Fritz Reichenbach of 10./JG300 one other north-west of Wittenberg. One of Welter's victims was a 515 Squadron FB.VI in 100 Group flown by Squadron Leader Charles Brian Best DFC and Flight Sergeant Harry Dickinson, both of whom were killed. Squadron Leader John Harry MacKellar Chisholm and Flight Lieutenant Eric Lawless Wilde on 157 Squadron disappeared without trace. Reichenbach's victim was an FB.VI on 239 Squadron flown by Flying Officer Edward Walter Osborne and Pilot Officer George Victor Acheson, who were both killed.

On 16/17 September Andy Lockhart and Ralph Wood returned to Brunswick: 'It wasn't a very spectacular raid because of cloud. However, it was one trip nearer 'Home Sweet Home'. This trip was a piece of cake and we had very little trouble. Berlin again on 18/19 September (when thirty-three Mosquitoes were detailed to bomb Berlin) was anything but a nice trip. It was our thirteenth trip to the 'Big City'. We had the 'twitch' while waiting for take-off. Over Berlin we were coned and got caught in a huge barrage of flak. It was very unpleasant and ineffective. (Twenty-nine Mosquitoes visited Berlin and all returned safely.) The following afternoon we were due to start a nine-day leave and we could certainly do it justice. Though we decided we might wait and go Wednesday morning as we would like to have got thirty trips in before our leave, we went.'

When they returned from leave Andy Lockhart and Ralph Wood visited a succession of targets starting with Karlsruhe on 29/30 September, and then as they started their 'last lap', Ralph's seventieth op on Monday, 23 October was to 'Berlin or bust'. 'We had a very pleasant trip there and back, watching others get into trouble instead of ourselves. The target itself, however, proved very, very warm. It was such that we were really shaken for a few minutes. Personally, I was just waiting for a hit in a vital spot, which I expected at any moment – then to see if I could bail out. In short, the gunners below were in top form. We were over the 'Big City' at 1930 hours. Andy and I now had seven more to do and then it would all be over.'

It looked like they were going to finish the hard way. On 30 October it was Berlin again and Ralph's heart was really in his mouth as they lost their starboard engine and came home nearly all the way on one engine. He had visions of finishing his tour in Stalag Luft III, but Andy Lockhart did a good job as usual and they made a one-engine landing at base.

It was Berlin again on 3/4 November when fifty-five Mosquitoes were dispatched to the 'Big City'. After a couple of operations like their first two in September, Chas Lockyer and 'Jock' Sherry were thoughtful about their chances of doing another fifty-three trips to complete their tour. Lockyer noted that 'the 'good old Law of Averages' prevailed and the next half-dozen trips were comparatively 'uneventful'. But whilst taking off the Mosquito swung to the left due to the port engine suddenly losing power. I closed the throttles but I was unable to prevent the aircraft from crashing into the radar hut at the other side of the perimeter track.'

Both men's front teeth were knocked out, but they were fit enough to fly again three weeks later. As their tour drew towards its end, they completed it in style with nine of their last eleven trips to Berlin and they finally finished about three weeks before the German surrender.

The 3/4 November trip was Geoff Wood and his pilot's seventeenth operation together and the Canadian navigator hoped was the last; the one that he had wanted to write about for quite a while. 'We took off at midnight. I'd never felt so keenly about a trip in all my life. I certainly lived every moment of it. There were numerous fighter flares and fighter contrails all the way there and back. We saw one jet fighter. The moon was rather bright, too. The raid was wizard, though. Andy and I exchanged congratulations and shook hands on it before we got out of the kite. Gosh, we were a couple of happy kids. '*Moncton Express III*' came through with flying colours. I could have written pages about our feelings, our 'twitch' and our relief when we got back again, but so ended my second and last tour.

'Suddenly it broke through my slightly spinning head that I had now completed seventy-seven ops and for me my war was finally over. It looked like I'd made it after all, though why, I couldn't understand. All I knew for certain was that I was very glad to be alive. I'd come very close several times to discovering all about death. Perhaps in the years ahead I might be lucky enough to find out something about life.'

Chapter Eighteen
A Night on the Spree

'*Berlin tonight – again. A night on the Spree, and it will create chaos. The city is jam-packed with refugees fleeing from the Russians on the Eastern Front.*'

Squadron Leader (later Air Marshal)
Sir Ivor Broom KSB CBE DSO DFC**

Michael Henry Astolf Topham Bayon was born the son of a doctor on 30 April 1922 at Shenley, Hertfordshire but grew up in rural Cambridgeshire. Educated at Marlborough, where he excelled at classics and sport, his studies at Peterhouse College, Cambridge were interrupted by the war. A gifted rugby and hockey player, he just missed a Blue; he also qualified for Junior Wimbledon. He had been a frustrated fighter pilot since he was a boy when he watched Spitfires flying from Duxford a few miles from his home. 'Of course, I would be a fighter pilot. Nothing else occurred to me as even a possibility,' he wrote. 'And so I went to school, and took longer than the average to fly solo and on my first solo landing bounced so high that my instructor suggested that I should have switched on my oxygen again. At the end of the course I failed ignominiously. I was summoned to the selection committee; "you will be a navigator" said the voice of authority. So, more tests. I couldn't really see the letters with one eye; luckily they tested my good eye first and I memorised the letters.

'We stayed in huge blocks of flats in Saint John's Wood and heard the lions roaring at night in the Zoo. We went first to the Grand Hotel and then to the Hotel Metropole at Brighton. There a Messerschmitt came in low from the sea, machine guns blazing. We all dived for the floor. There was one casualty – a bloke was scalded as the tea urn was riddled with bullets.

'We were sent up to Manchester. I was put to swilling out the cookhouse with John Sidgwick, a slightly effete musical scholar from King's College, Cambridge. From there we went to Canada and I began to learn to navigate. If your pilot asked where you were, you put your thumb firmly down on the map, covering perhaps 100 square miles and said confidently 'just there'. Then he felt secure and you could sweat it out in peace. I flew across Montreal and was told to photograph a bridge over the St. Lawrence but I pressed the wrong tit and dropped a bomb on it instead. I must have missed as I heard no more of it. I went to bombing school in Ontario and discovered that I was rather good at it. Quite a surprise. The rest of the course was sent to heavy bombers, to Coastal Command, to photo-reconnaissance. I alone was sent to Mosquitoes, Pathfinders – the elite of Bomber Command. We were to be a brand-new squadron [128], three British, one Canuck, the rest Aussies. For some reason, I was the only member of flying crew on the whole unit who was not an officer.

'The first evening, over drinks in the Mess, all the blokes teamed up. Next day we turned up for briefing. I was the only one without a pilot. I looked at the various pilots and I thought, "There's the one I'd like as my pilot." A tall, raw-boned blond Aussie called Doug Swain. We all went along to the decompression chamber to test our ability to withstand low pressure. One navigator dipped out – Doug Swain's. He got agonising bends, so did I – but I decided not to say so.

'So Doug and I were now a partnership. Doug said, "Right, now – my ambition is quite simple. I want us to be the best bloody aircrew in the RAF and that means in the world. As for you, you can make any bloody mistake you like ('that's good of him,' I thought contentedly) – 'ONCE'," he added menacingly. We went up for our first flight together and Doug decided to feather one engine. What he did not know was that you could not restart an engine in mid-air, so our first ever landing together was a single-engine landing.

'I decided that if radar was the key to success, I would master it; we used to have two nights of operations and then one night off. On my nights off, I would go along to the radar unit, where a thin, dark radar aircraftsman and his plump jolly girlfriend would teach me all they knew. I became an expert, accurate at finding my position anywhere on the airfield to within six feet, sight unseen. This was to save our lives, later on.

'If you were flying that night, in the morning you would contact your ground crew and when they gave the OK it was ready for a test flight. We had a magnificent ground crew, they really were our friends, and they would work any hours to get things right for us. We'd fly for perhaps half an hour, testing, testing. Or perhaps we'd fly for almost two hours, including a trip to the practice bombing range on The Wash.'

On the night of 10/11 October 1944 Doug Swain and Mike Bayon began their tour. 'On one flight, as they left the target, Bayon's nose started to bleed. 'Nothing I could do with my oxygen mask on, so it contentedly bled on till I'd lost between half a pint and a pint of blood; and then it stopped of its own accord. When I got out of the plane, the front of my uniform was sodden and red with blood. 'Mike's wounded – get the blood wagon,' said one of the ground crew. I took off my oxygen mask to say that it was only a nosebleed. The blood had clotted and congealed. 'Christ, they've shot his face off,' said the young fitter and he fainted. Not a nice cushiony sort of stage faint, with the legs buckling. No, he fell straight back like a board and I heard the crack of his skull on the concrete. The blood wagon tore up; he was put on a stretcher and away he went. This was the sort of thing that tended to upset Rose.

'One night of appalling weather only two Mosquitoes from another squadron and Doug and I from Wyton took off. The idea was for us to do a 'Cook's tour' – come very close to Hamburg, then veer off; the same for Bremen, Kiel, Hanover, Essen etc., so as to alert the air-raid wardens, fire-fighters, flak crews, searchlights, night-fighters – the lot; and rob them of their sleep.'

When they had twenty-one ops under their belts Bayon thought he was near halfway on his second tour. 'But it was announced that to complete a tour on Mosquitoes the number had been increased to fifty-five. This meant that if I was to successfully complete the tour I would have done well over eighty bombing operations. You'd think that bombing Germany was challenge enough and at first it was but then, we wanted to swagger a bit, to take an early bath, to field close to the bat. We knew that if we switched on our radios (which should only be used as you bailed out to let the rest of the squadron know you were alive or unwounded as you left the plane), the Germans could home in on us. Yet our squadron had a tuneless little ditty and as we swung away after the photographic run one harsh 'Aussie' voice would come over the air and then another and another and another would join in the refrain. And we'd be laughing with the sheer risk of it.'

Bayon tried not to think of cities and people and treasured possessions and pets and children. 'London had been in the grip of the blitz. If you went up you would sleep in the Tube shelters, all along the platforms. Not a restful night – babies might cry and trains started at 4.30 am. But there was a great feeling of camaraderie – no theft, no mugging. From Cambridge nightly we saw the glow in the sky, 50 miles away. I tried to concentrate on the essential. If Germany won, the whole world would be enslaved. Then one night Ivor Broom the CO said, 'Berlin tonight – again. A night on the Spree (Berlin is on the River Spree), and it will create chaos. The city is jam-packed with refugees fleeing from the Russians on the Eastern Front.'

'That night I had a nightmare. I dreamt that I saw, in the cold light of dawn, a great heap of bricks and rubble. Drifts of thin smoke wafted around. A woman, swathed in black, was clawing desperately at the rubble. I could see that her breath was rasping in her chest but everything was completely silent. I could see her nails tearing, her hands bleeding and the desperation in her. Suddenly she saw a child's thin bony hand poking out of the rubble. She called out and clawed and scrabbled even more desperately, and as she cleared almost to the elbow the hand just went limp and I woke, sweating. I did not sleep for the rest of that cold, frosty night. I just walked round the deserted airfield with Sheba, my muzzled spaniel. There was a full moon, the stars were very vivid and it was very cold. I found a £5 note, sodden, in a ditch. From then on, almost every night and long after the war was over, I had that same dream. Yet I was happy. I was doing something important, something which had to be done, and I was doing it well. We were strongly individualistic. Unthinking obedience was anathema to us, yet we were disciplined, deeply disciplined. We had very little time for indiscipline.

'I remember flying over Alconbury, an American base. If the 'Yanks' got back to base damaged, or with wounded aboard, they'd contact control and take their place in the circuit in order of priority. The Yanks were back from a daylight raid. The airwaves were throbbing with their cries of 'May Day'. Then they abandoned control altogether and came in huggermugger – downwind, crosswind, any old how. No less than five collided about at the junction of the runways and a great pall of smoke rose. It made me very angry.

'In spite of our casual dress, behaviour, cars and moustaches, we were surprisingly caring of our 'best blue', or new forage caps, or gloves; like the Guards Officers at Waterloo, oddly dandified.

'The Mosquito boys had another chore, which we did not much enjoy. We would set off, on the same route and almost at the same height as the Lancasters and Halifaxes – the heavy boys; then they would swing off one way and we would swing off on our own route. BUT – we had to drop thousands and thousands of strips of tinfoil ['Window'] to simulate a heavy stream of aircraft to the German radar. It was fiddly work splitting the packages and pushing them down the chute, cold too; and the slight pressurization we had in the plane would dissipate. But worst of all, to entice the enemy fighters away from the soft target of the heavies, we had to fire off vivid flares and Very lights every few hundred yards. It's not very nice to be told that you don't count and that you're expendable!

'But now we had done twenty or thirty trips; we were good and we knew we were good. By hours and hours of work in the radar shed I had become an expert on radar. And I, who can't even mend a fuse and who usually puts in the petrol and leaves my companion to see if we need any oil!

'Donald Bennett had me to dinner a couple of times with his wife Elsa ('Ly'), to see if I could explain exactly how I knew which were our radar signals on the screen and which were the German ones. I couldn't. I just knew. I would sometimes be getting accurate radar fixes 50 miles further east than anyone else on the raid. It gave us a great edge and Doug was pleased. If we were dropping a 4,000lb bomb – which we often were; its terminal velocity in falling was something like 460 feet per second. In other words, if we had gone into a dive we could easily have passed it.

'It was a great big clumsy thing, like a cylindrical hot water tank. So, you would release it and all of us had enough pride of performance to do a very steady run-up to the bombing; however, the flak might rattle and the plane would give a great surge as the bomb left it. An anti-aircraft shell bursting nearby could feel much like this, actually. Then you had nearly a minute before the bomb burst. Obviously, standard practice was to take evasive action directly the bomb left, with the navigator timing it to photograph the bomb burst. Once, 'Mick' Solomon took off with a 4,000lb bomb aboard. One engine cut out at 10,000 feet so he jettisoned his bomb, safe – not fused. The bomb did not care; it went off anyway and almost blew him out of the sky. That's at a range of 2 miles. Next day was very hot. Mick was wearing an overcoat, gloves and a scarf and he was still cold. Shock, of course; but we thought it hilarious. He had to go, of course. They should have known earlier when he refused to join 571 Squadron – because it added up to thirteen.

'By now we had worked out a way of always being first back. Sure, we did come back in a straight line but so did lots of others. Our secret was to climb to 32,000 or higher for the return journey, when bombs or petrol didn't weigh us down. On the indicator, the reading was very low for our airspeed, owing to the thinness of the air; and the climb did take time. But at that height we went like a bullet. In fact, every time I suffered from bends; but it seemed ungenerous to mention it. Doug would stay at height till the last possible moment and then scream down to take first place in the circuit. Obviously, our ears could not cope with this change of pressure. Later, when I shared a room with Doug, whoever woke first would hold his nose and blow and the high-pitched squeal as the pressure equalised would wake the other.

'If the forecast was appalling four-engine bombers with their crews of eight men were not to be involved. Icing at height would distort the wing shape so that you just fell from the sky. Heavy fog on return, or towering cumulus clouds containing

100 mph up and down draughts within a few feet of each other were strong enough to toss a Lancaster around like a leaf. Send in the Mosquito boys. A plywood body and a crew of only two were expendable. We had no defences, except our speed and manoeuvrability with which to elude an enemy fighter. It did make one feel somewhat wimpish! A tour of operations was thirty for the heavies who bombed at 15,000-18,000 feet; fifty for Mosquitoes, who bombed at 25,000 feet, so we were much less vulnerable. One night of appalling weather only two Mosquitoes from another squadron and Doug and I from Wyton took off.'

On 23 October the weather was fine and the forecast for later in the night, when thirty-eight Mosquitoes were detailed to bomb Berlin and other cities, would change very little. 'A' and 'B' Flights on 128 Squadron at Wyton were assigned different cities: ten Mosquitoes on 'A' Flight commanded by Squadron Leader Ivor Broom DFC* was given a 'spoof' raid on Wiesbaden; 'B' Flight was allotted Berlin. Another two Mosquitoes went to Aschaffenburg. Like all German cities these targets were heavily defended by anti-aircraft guns and searchlights, but no aircraft were lost on these three operations. The following night the largest Mosquito raid was on Hanover which was visited by fifty-seven of them. Again no aircraft were lost. It was the same story on the night of 27/28 October when sixty Mosquitoes attacked Berlin and twenty-one others visited six other targets and the next night also, when thirty Mosquitoes went to Cologne. During October just nine Mosquitoes of the LNSF were lost on operations.

At Wyton during the early morning of 23/24 October 1944 Flying Officer 'Bertie' Boulter, a pilot on 128 Squadron, was on the 'A' Flight battle order for that night's 'spoof' operation to Wiesbaden. (Ivor Broom and his navigator Tommy Broom – no relation, who was ten years older than Boulter – thought that as the new pilot looked so very young he should be called 'Bertie the Boy' and 'Bertie' he became.) His parents had emigrated to Canada and he had grown up in Saskatchewan, but in 1938 he returned to England and in 1941 he enlisted in the RAF and qualified as a pilot, taking up his flying duties on 128 Squadron in October 1944.

Boulter and Sergeant Jim Churcher his navigator had mixed emotions about the coming operation before they went out to B.XXV 'D-Dog'. They were overjoyed to be part of a team at last and they were excited and apprehensive in equal measure. They knew that the Mosquito was almost too fast to catch and they had the cover of night and the plane had a track record of minimum casualties. Like almost every other young crew, they had that wonderful 'It won't happen to me' mentality. 'But above all else,' recalls Boulter, 'there was the determination not to let your chums down. That covered your crew, your ground crew, your flight, the squadron and above all else the other air crews you flew with.'

'B' Flight, meanwhile, had been allotted Berlin. One of the crews comprised Flight Lieutenant Patrick James Duncan AFC and his navigator, Sergeant Charles Parker, who was from London. He had experienced the blitz as a 17-year-old and was determined that 'these people had to pay for this' and so had joined the RAF. He crewed-up with Duncan, with whom he had flown on navigational training flights in Oxfords. 'Dunc' simply said, 'Are you willing to risk your life with me, sergeant?' Parker took one look at his AFC ribbon and said, 'Yes!'

Charles Parker was apprehensive: 'The 'Mossie' was considered a 'lady' and as such needed careful handling. Normally, a pilot would do a 'second dickey' flight, but you couldn't do this in a 'Mossie' so Berlin was our first op together. We took off at 1714 hours. It was dark until we reached the searchlight batteries. [Altogether, they would fly twenty trips to the 'Big City' and all would follow roughly the same pattern.] Berlin had radar searchlights. We'd be stooging along when the icy-blue searchlight in the distance would suddenly swing over to us and immediately all the others latched on until we were coned by white light. It was like daylight in the cockpit. Two minutes caught in the beams seemed like two days. I'd duck down. Pat would lose 10,000 feet in diving. Then the flak would get closer. If you couldn't hear it, then it wasn't intended for us – it had someone else's name on it. If you could smell it, well … it was bloody close.

'At ETA I said: 'We should be there by now Pat.' He banked and looked down. We were at 25,000 feet and there, only 15 miles in the distance, was the start of the raid, so I was quite pleased we were that close. We didn't have a Master Bomber that night. Another PFF's TIs went down, bursting at different heights. (We seldom got an overshoot on the TIs; normally they slipped back: human nature.) We'd been told to drop our four 500lb MCs [Medium Capacity bombs] on the green markers. I flicked the bomb selection switch and immediately got down into the glass nose. It was difficult. You could quite easily get snagged on the oxygen knob and the 'Window' chute sticking up on the door underneath my feet. 'Window' came in a brown wrapper with a loop around it. The idea was to hold the loop while shoving 'Window' out. Usually, there were upwards of fifty bundles piled up in the nose and all had to be thrown out in two minutes before using the bomb-sight.

'Half-crouching, I'd throw out the 'Window' and then switch on the Mk XIV automatic bomb-sight. On my knees now, I peered into the illuminated cross, shaped like a sword, the point to the front. The bomb-release cable in my right hand was like a bell-push. I gripped it and directed Pat on the intercom: 'Right, right, left, steady, steady…. Bombs gone!' With four bombs you didn't have the gigantic leap you had with a 'Blockbuster'. You didn't wheel away. We still had to fly straight and level for the camera in the rear to take its two photos. Activated by the bomb release it took the first frame and with the shutter open a time switch shot the second half a minute later as the bombs exploded. The flight lasted four hours, twenty minutes. When we got back to Wyton we landed and sat in the cockpit a moment, shook hands and said something like, 'Well, that's the first of many – we hope!'

'On a later op, when we were 'Windowing' for the 'heavies', seven minutes were allowed because we carried 250 bundles. I felt OK but I heard Pat ask: 'You all right Charles? Your oxygen's off!' I'd knocked the knob to 'Off' with the edge of my 'Mae West' as I clambered into the nose. He turned it back on and I came up gulping for air. OK again, I started back down to the nose.'

'Pat said, 'You going back down there?'

'What do you think we're here for?' I said.

Like all German cities, Wiesbaden was heavily defended by anti-aircraft guns and searchlights and 'Bertie' Boulter and Jim Churcher returned to Wyton having been shot at by an 88mm radar-controlled gun, but although the shell bursts were very close they had come through unscathed.

During October eleven Mosquitoes of the LNSF were lost on operations. New squadrons joined the force, with 142 Squadron re-forming at Gransden Lodge on 25 October and flying its first operation when its only two Mosquito B.XXVs were dispatched to Cologne. Berlin was attacked on the night of 30 October and the LNSF returned to Cologne again the following night.

At the beginning of November Sergeant Johnnie Clark, a Scottish navigator, flew his first ops on 571 Squadron at Oakington. He and his pilot, a New Zealander from Auckland by the name of Bill Henley, had crewed-up at 1655 OTU Warboys. Henley had been instructing for the past eighteen months and like Johnnie Clark, had yet to fly his first operation. Henley's brother had been killed in the fighting in Crete in the Middle East campaign. 'Good God,' thought Johnnie Clark, 'is no family going to be untouched by this war?'

Their first op – to Gelsenkirchen on the night of 5/6 November – and the next three were routine but their fifth trip on the 24th/25th came as something of a shock. Johnnie Clark had just finished lunch when Bill Henley came over to him. 'We are on the Battle Order for tonight Johnnie,' he said. 'Briefing is at three o'clock.'

'At the appointed hour Bill and I presented ourselves for briefing.

'Ye Gods,' muttered Bill, 'do you see where we are due to go tonight? Berlin.' The route tapes were pinned to the map.

'So, it's the "Big City" tonight,' drawled the Canadian at my elbow. 'Is this your first to the "Big City"?'

'I nodded. It was funny how everyone took the same place at briefing. Still, it was more comfortable that way.

'The Intelligence officer soon filled us in on where the 'heavies' were bombing that night. We were going to bomb the centre of Berlin, with a view to drawing off some of the flak and searchlights from the main forces. The Germans may have had a 'busted flush', to use the Canadians' poker language, but they were still a force to be reckoned with; a fact of which the paratroopers' disastrous landing at Arnhem was but one example. Their fighters, flak and searchlights were others. That we were winning no one doubted, but it was going to take a big heave yet. The Germans were fighting for their lives with their own lives.

'We were given our time on the target, which would be marked by the H2S Mosquitoes of 139 Squadron. H2S was airborne radar. 'Oboe' aircraft couldn't mark as far as Berlin. Their activities were confined to the Ruhr and its environs, although their range was extending as the armies on the ground advanced. The 'Oboe' marker was very accurate and very 'hush-hush'.

'You'll find the flak and searchlights really concentrated around the "Big City",' remarked the Intelligence officer. Cold comfort for us, I thought, as the briefing progressed. When it ended I turned to the Canadian: 'You been there before?'

'He nodded. 'Two or three times and as yet not a scratch to show on us.' He pointed to his pilot. 'We're hoping our luck lasts.'

'We got airborne just after five o'clock, thanks to the short days at the end of November. Running up to Hanover, the 'Gee' blips grew fainter and eventually guttered out like two spent candles. After collecting our share of flak over that city we pointed our nose towards Magdeburg. We turned towards the north-east and headed for the 'Big City'. The TIs went down on time and then the searchlights came into play. First the bluish ones, operating singly and radar-controlled, wandered haphazardly, or so it seemed. As we were running up to the target a bunch of searchlights caught us. I was completely blinded by the light and couldn't see the TIs, far less bomb on them. 'I've overshot the TIs – we'll have to go round again,' I said into my mike, adding automatically, 'Bomb doors closed.'

'Oh, bloody hell,' replied the somewhat strained voice of Bill. 'Which way do you want me to turn the damned thing?' It was the first and only time I had ever heard him swear. After a moment's thought I replied, 'Make it a wide right turn. All the others will be making a left turn after dropping their loads. We don't want to run into any of them.' Bumping into another aircraft's slipstream was no fun, either, as I had found out over Hanover when night-fighters had attacked us. Our right turn seemed to fox the searchlights. Presumably, they had anticipated we would be making a left turn, heading for home. Anyway, we lost them and were shrouded in darkness again.

'I resolved to concentrate on the markers and ignore what was going on around me. This I found rather hard to do; it was difficult to tell which were bombs bursting and which were aircraft either on fire or blowing up. It seemed to me that Dante had underestimated his description of Hell. I went through the patter on our second run-in, dropped the TIs, waited for the photographs and then headed for the Cromer beacon and home. 'Sorry about the run-in to the target. I couldn't see a thing; the searchlight blinded me,' I said rather lamely.

'Not to worry, Johnnie, we're still in one piece. It was a good idea of yours to make a right turn – it caught the Jerries on the wrong foot.'

'I didn't explain to him that I had been thinking more of the aircraft following us than of the German defences.

'We landed safely. Bill, following the laid-down instructions, opened the bomb doors at dispersal before cutting the engines. I was doing my usual – having a pee and spitting out the wad of chewing gum which had kept my mouth moist during the trip – when an armourer of the ground staff approached me. 'I say, sergeant, come and see this. It looks a bit queer to me.'

'Nothing wrong, I hope?' We ducked into the empty bomb bay together.

'Do you know where you collected that?' He pointed to the whole side of a flak shell embedded in one of the main spars.

'Over the "Big City" I suppose,' I answered. Bill had joined us and was looking curiously at the splinter. 'I never felt a thing hit us during the whole trip. It must have gone through the bomb doors or the fuselage. Isn't there a hole somewhere?'

'That's what's making me wonder. There's not a mark on the outer skin of the aircraft at all,' replied the armourer.

'I looked at Bill and found him gazing at me. 'Are you thinking what I'm thinking?'

'I shrugged. 'I don't know, but I reckon we could only have collected it after I'd dropped the bomb and before you'd closed the bomb doors – a matter of seconds.'

'That's what I thought,' said Bill. 'Thank God the bomb had gone.' We turned to the armourer, who was looking as if he had seen a couple of ghosts. 'Yes, a matter of seconds – the difference between the quick and the dead.'

'At the debriefing my Canadian oppo' said 'I hear you went round the target twice tonight?'

'That's right. I liked the look of the place,' I answered dryly.

On the night of 27/28 November when sixty-seven Mosquitoes were dispatched to Berlin Pat Duncan and Charles Parker went out to their Mosquito for their thirteenth operation. They watched their ground crew winch a 4,000lb 'cookie' into the bomb bay. It was almost in position when, crash! The back half fell down. Parker did the 100 yard sprint. 'Pat was more philosophical and stayed put. I stopped. I felt a bit stupid! The Squadron Leader 'B' Flight arrived. He told us to take the spare aircraft into the hangar, but we said it hadn't been bombed up. (A 4,000-pounder had to be dropped on the night. We were not allowed to land with one because it would strain the fuselage.) The Squadron Leader ordered it bombed up and told me to go to the briefing room and work out a direct course to Berlin. I drew up a new course, Cromer direct to Berlin, calculating an extra five knots' airspeed on top of our average cruising speed. Even if we left in the next ten minutes we would arrive twenty minutes after everyone else had left! Pat was halfway up the ladder when I got back to the reserve aircraft. I said, 'Pat, hold it. This is just madness.' In his perfect King's English he said, 'Come on Charles – we're going.'

'I am no hero. Flying alone over Berlin was not my idea of fun. Perhaps the thirteenth was at the back of my mind. I argued. We didn't go that night.'

Returning from Berlin on 6 December Pat Duncan and Charles Parker encountered severe problems with wind changes and gusty conditions. Low on fuel, they sent out a May Day call, adding cryptically: 'Gravy is low! Gravy is low!' Parker studied his maps and made his calculations, but the wind played havoc with their Mosquito. He could have sworn it was Grimsby when he saw fishwives on the quay below as they passed over the coast, but it was actually a French port! They finally put down at Friston on the south coast with less than 20 gallons of fuel remaining in the twelve tanks.

On the night of 9/10 December, a sixty-strong attacking Mosquito force was detailed to attack Berlin. One of five Mosquito XX Pathfinders on 139 Squadron was crewed by Flight Lieutenant Mark Wallis and Flight Lieutenant Fred Crawley DFC.

Crawley recalled: 'The programme detailing the names of crews to fly that night on operations usually appeared on the mess notice-board around mid-day. No matter how many operations one had under your belt, even the most experienced felt that tightening in the stomach that presaged night operations. The night-flying test in the afternoon, with its well-tried procedures and familiarity, coupled with the affection that exists between a particular crew and a particular aeroplane, restored the confidence. Later, at the crew briefing, when the target and route details were disclosed nerves were well under control. The route was to be: Upwood to the coast. Then north-eastwards across the North Sea to the red rock island of Heligoland (there was a fighter airstrip on the nearby sand island of Dune). Then landfall north of the wide Elbe estuary, the Great Lakes NW of Berlin – Berlin return on a straight line to the Zuider Zee and home to base. The bomb load was to be: Target Indicator (green and yellow) bursting at 9,800 feet; Target Indicator (green with red drip) bursting at 8,000 feet; photo-flash 'Red' and one 500lb HE bomb.

Weather conditions were described as good for take-off and return at Upwood with considerable cloud formations over most of Germany.'

'Upwood at 2045 hours was a busy airfield, with the Lancasters of 156 Squadron and the Mosquitoes of 139 vying with one another on the perimeter track, anxious to get airborne. Rolling now, with a touch of rudder to correct swing, we got off at 2046 hours and with wheels and flaps up, turned straight away on to the first course of 067, climbing at 160 knots to the English coast at Cromer. The twenty minutes' climb to 17,000 feet at the coast found the navigator busy using 'Gee' fixes to keep the aircraft on the planned track to the coast. (The calculation of wind speed and direction was not of much use because of the continual increase in height, but the noting of drift often gave indication of what to expect.) The coastline showed clearly on H2S and Cromer passed underneath at 2109 when navigation lights and IFF were switched off. The two-stage booster was now put into the engines and the next twenty-four minutes had the aircraft climbing to the operational height of 25,000 feet. During this time the navigator fixed the aircraft's position every three minutes by 'Gee' and calculated the wind velocity throughout the height bands. Accurate navigation throughout this stage was vital to the success of the operation when the aircraft could be flown with no interference from enemy action. On this operation, the calculated winds proved to be considerably stronger than forecast and about 10-15° to the southward of forecast. Navigation proceeded steadily until about 5° east, when enemy jamming of 'Gee' rendered the equipment ineffective.

'On DR navigation, we turned almost due east running towards Heligoland, a good H2S target and very useful, where the next turning-point, about 8 miles north of the island, would require a route-marker to be fired off for the Main Force. Although I had never seen an aircraft shot down over the island, their anti-aircraft guns could make it pretty uncomfortable if you strayed too near. The island of Heligoland appeared on the H2S screen and from the present track it was clear we were running too close to the island on the starboard side. An 'S' turn to port put this right and at 2202 hours the route-marker for the Main Force was fired to indicate the turning-point north of Heligoland. It was bitterly cold, with the outside temperature gauge indicating -50° and the heating system could not prevent thick ice forming on the inside of the side-blisters.

'Approaching the enemy coast, the coastline showed clearly on H2S and once again we had drifted 2 to 3 miles south of track of the flight plan. Another route-marker was fired crossing the enemy coast with the Main Force being informed on VHF that the marker was 3 miles south of track. Shortly afterwards two more flares went down on the port side. At 2217 radar bearings on Hamburg and Harburg confirmed that the aircraft was still 4 miles south of track plan and at 2225 hours an alteration to port was made to reach the Great Lakes at 2237 hours. At the Great Lakes the reception committee awaited. The lakes showed up so well on radar (despite German attempts to cover them to spoil radar definition) that most operations were routed to the lakes, leaving only a ten-minute run-in to Berlin. The Germans knew this and therefore used the lakes area as a marshalling point for fighters. Usually with a height advantage and with all the Mosquitoes streaming contrails, the night-fighters had a chance to intercept on the run-in to Berlin, when the Pathfinder aircraft had to fly straight and level. Heads down and sweat it out was the order of the day.

'On this occasion no night-fighters were seen but heavy ack-ack was predicted as always with remarkable accuracy and the ride was uncomfortable. The TIs were dropped at 2245 hours, Main Force being advised as the drop took place; straight and level for the photograph and then a hard turn to starboard nose down to reduce height to 22,000 feet and the hard slog home against the wind. The home trek against a 65-knot headwind meant almost a full hour's flying to reach the enemy coast. 'Gee' was ineffective and pulses would only start to appear through the jamming when approaching the Zuider Zee; the route chosen was well clear of all large towns and H2S gave little or no hope for bearings. The moon was now well up and the cloud layer well below at around 12-15,000 feet. Visibility was good and it was a question of DR navigation and wait for 'Gee' and H2S to come back on line nearing the coast. It was remarkable how lonely it was at 22,000 feet late at night with only the presence of your partner and the occasional brief comment between you to break the loneliness. The aircraft was going well and thoughts of bacon and eggs started to intrude and yet…'

Twelve Mosquitoes on 142 Squadron had their take-off scheduled for 1942 hours. The weather at Gransden Lodge started off hazy and fine but as the day progressed, conditions got worse with wintry showers sweeping in over the airfield during the evening. It was to be a rather disastrous night as far as operations were concerned, with numerous mishaps occurring. At dispersal 'A-Apple' could not take off, as the electrical system was found to have failed. Then 'U-Uncle' was found to have low brake pressure, so only ten aircraft proceeded to taxi out for take-off. Flight Sergeant D.S. Courage in 'D-Dog' did not have a good take-off and the aircraft ploughed through the top of the trees at the end of the runway, smashing the aircraft's Perspex nose cone. Courage continued to climb to 10,000 feet and then flew away from base until all the other aircraft had taken off. At 2017 the crew landed back at Gransden complete with the bomb load.

'J-Johnny' flown by Flying Officer John Whitworth and Flying Officer William A. 'Bill' Tulloch got away on time, climbed to operational height and crossed the Channel but then the constant speed unit on one of the engines packed up and the engine had to be shut down. Whitworth aborted the sortie and headed back to the bomb jettison area before making a single-engine landing at Gransden at 2107. He recalled: 'I have only a foggy memory of KB408 with which we came in to a fast landing "on one" and went through the end of the runway. It was the only kite I ever even scratched in 450 operational hours of flying.' The Mosquito ran through a hedge on its belly and was badly damaged, never to fly again.

The 22-year-old Flying Officer Kenneth Pudsey and 25-year-old Flying Officer John Reginald Dalton Morgan in 'K-King' got only a little way further than KB408. The 'Gee' set packed up on the way out and shortly afterwards a supercharger failed to engage properly. The aircraft could not maintain operational height and so Pudsey had no option but to turn back for home. He landed at base with a full bomb load at 2130.[1] At this point the squadron was down almost to half-strength, with just seven out of the twelve aircraft still en route for Berlin.

'S-Sugar' crewed by Flying Officer J.M. Ellison and Flying Officer H.J. Farquhar were the first crew to arrive over the 'Big City', which had only 3/10ths cloud cover and a ground haze. They saw the first green TIs go down at 2152 and at regular intervals following this, yellow TIs. The crew bombed a group of these from 23,000 feet.

On 'N-Nan' Flying Officer W.E. Martin and Sergeant F.L. Lilley missed the first three yellow TIs which cascaded on the north bank of the river. They went into an orbit over the city to await developments. Moments later they saw some yellow TIs going down and so they began a bombing run on these. A number of red TIs were burning on the ground two-thirds of a mile to the south-east of the yellow TIs. Many searchlights lit up the sky but none operated in cones. The flak opened up briefly, bursting between 24,000 and 25,000 feet among the attacking Mosquitoes. On 'E-Edward' Sergeant W.K. Brown observed 'bags of searchlights. No flak or fighters.'

'N-Nan' was the last squadron aircraft to bomb the target, at 2211. Martin's navigator, Sergeant Lilley, could see bombs bursting near to the red TIs, with the main effort concentrated on the yellow TIs: 'cookie' blasts which appeared near to the aiming-point started several small fires. The return trip home was without incident and everyone was back on the ground by 0029.[2]

'About 10° east and north of Hanover began the feeling of unease,' wrote Fred Crawley on 139 Squadron. 'Nothing appeared to be wrong but the feeling persisted and indeed was getting stronger. A check of fuel, engine gauges, etc., showed nothing out of the ordinary and in desperation I told my pilot I was going to have a look backwards through the astrodome (the only way you could see aft in a Mosquito). Unlike daytime when you cannot see easily into sun, at night you cannot see easily down-moon as this is the dark side of the sky. Also at night you usually do not see objects you look at directly, so the trick is to keep your head moving and hope to see from the periphery of your eyes! After a good look around and seeing nothing except our own contrails, I was about to sit down when suddenly my eye picked up something on the dark side to starboard. Once having seen something, just like radar, you can "wash" it with your eyes and you can see it. And there it was; a single-engined aircraft, slightly down and off to the starboard side, converging slowly. As the distance between us decreased and with us aware, as the fighter turned towards us we made a steep diving turn to starboard, putting us now in the dark side of the sky. Tracer went over the top of the aircraft but no hits. The westerly course was resumed shortly afterwards and when the feeling of unease returned I needed no telling our friend was back, probably having carried out the same manoeuvre as us. This time, without waiting for a sighting, a second hard turn to starboard was made, flying on a reciprocal course back into Germany for two minutes before resuming our course homewards. No more unease and I was convinced he had given up.

'I have often wondered about this episode. When I do, I always remember how deeply superstitious most aircrew were, always wearing the same things and dressing in the same order and so on, before an operation; perhaps senses were more finely attuned during those difficult times. There were no more problems coming home. The Zuider Zee came up. "Gee" came back on stream and the gradual let-down over the North Sea to land at base at 0115 hours. We were welcomed by the WAAF officer in the debriefing room with hot tea laced with real Jamaica rum and bacon and egg in the mess. It was nice to be back.'

Feldwebel Fritz Reichenbach of 4./NJG 11 claimed a Mosquito near Berlin, but the Mosquitoes that attacked the 'Big City' returned without loss.

On 18 December the LNSF, or Fast Night Striking Force (FNSF) as it had become known at Bennett's insistence, was increased when 162 Squadron re-formed at Bourn with Mosquito B.25s. Soon it was accompanying 139 Squadron on target-marking duties. Charles Parker recalls: 'Bennett thought we should be called the Fast Night Strike Force because we carried a 4,000lb bomb load to the target – fast, unlike the American B-17s and B-24s. I don't think Bennett had a very high opinion of the Americans. On at least one occasion he ordered Mosquitoes to take off and form up over Cambridge at 500 feet to show the good folk of that city that there were RAF squadrons in the area besides Americans! If he ever heard squadrons using the American phonetic alphabet (which ultimately replaced the RAF alphabet), a wigging would go to the squadron CO.'

On the night of 31 December seventy-seven Mosquitoes were dispatched to Berlin and twelve to Ludwigshafen. One of the Mosquitoes headed for Berlin was 'Z-Zebra' on 128 Squadron, which was flown by Flight Lieutenant Leicester G. Smith RNZAF, who with his navigator Warrant Officer Bill Lane completed fifty-two operations on the Mosquito B.XVI from October 1944 to April 1945. Twenty of these were to Berlin. Smith was to recall: 'The big 'cookie-carrier' B.XVI was a wonderful aircraft to fly and although it had a pressurised cabin it was not used on operations in case of internal damage from flak. Take-off time was 1615 hours. The flight plan kept our aircraft to 10,000 feet to 6° East and an indicated airspeed of 215 knots at that height. It was a glorious evening for flying, as so many evenings were and mainly over 7/10ths cloud. The reason given was to miss the cumulonimbus cloud tops. We climbed to operational height and levelled out at 26,000 feet. Flak was heavy between Lübeck and Hamburg (commonly called the 'Gap'). Shrapnel was whistling around everywhere but our sympathy went out to one Mosquito crew who was coned by at least twenty searchlights. Flak was bursting all around them, at least 2,000 feet above and below. I was about 2 miles north of this aircraft and he flew straight through it all. It was an unforgettable sight. Otherwise we had a comfortable run to the 'Big City'. Over Berlin all was quiet as the target indicators, reds and green, went down. A warning was issued that fighters were in the area but none were seen. Bill reported contrails 2-3,000 feet above. We put our 'cookie' down on schedule, took the photo and had a relatively quiet flight back to England. We were coned by many searchlights over the Woodbridge area (must have been an army exercise), landing at Wyton from an operation of five hours airborne.'

One of the 692 Squadron crews who were laid on, unexpectedly, for the operation to the 'Big City' was Pilot Officer R.H.M. 'Percy' Vere and his navigator, Flight Lieutenant (later Squadron Leader) John F.P. Archbold, who remembered that 'the crew conference was at midday and navigation briefing at 1315 so there was just time for a meal before getting ready. Our aircraft was 'K-King' (MM224), Burbidge and Ramage's kite. Rumour had it that everyone who flew 'K-King' except those two had something happen to them. We hoped that we were the exception! After the meal I went down to the billet to put on my old blue sweater, check scarf and flying boots and then biked to the crew room for briefing. 'Phil' Eamshaw was doing the nav briefing and a hell of a route it was too! Tonight's op was a maximum effort with twelve kites on the Battle Order. There was something else in the air too. Wadsworth, Burbidge, Crow, Nairn and two others hung about as if waiting for a briefing after we came out. Ron had been out to the kite to ground-run it and put in the kit. I didn't have the time.

'The route out was via Cromer, over the North Sea, with a turn towards Heligoland, then north of Lübeck before turning SE to Berlin. The return route was south of Magdeburg, through the gap between Osnabrück and Münster before turning west for the English coast. This was a route I did not like. We were going in north of Hamburg and the gunners there were pretty hot. They got bags of practice anyway so I hoped it was 10/10ths there. We plotted tracks, working out courses and times and recording them in the log, sorting out maps and charts. Then, after about three-quarters of an hour we checked our work against the Master Log for any errors (on either side) and then sat back and waited for the main briefing to begin.

'In came the Met man. He started drawing in his cloudscapes on his briefing board. It didn't look too good to me: 8/10ths stratocumulus over the sea, clearing over the Third Reich. It looked as if we could be shot at! The 'drivers, airframe' [pilots] drifted in and sat down with their navs and the CO, Wing Commander Joe Northrop followed them. We got on with the main briefing. It was 1415. First, Flying Control and Squadron Leader 'Pop' Hemming, a pioneer in photographic reconnaissance in 1940 with Sidney Cotton. He was known as 'Popeye' because he sported RFC wings and First World War medals. He wore a black eye patch permanently over one eye and with his now white hair it gave him a distinctly raffish air. He told us the runway would be the long one; no obstructions.

'There were no other comments. Then Met gave his story. 'Target will be clear with no cloud from the time you cross the coast in till you come out again. Base would be clear for the return. Forecast winds are up in the seventies and eighties.' My guess was that they may well be a little stronger than he told us. Now Intelligence: 'Usual place chaps; you've all been there before, so I can't tell you anything you don't already know. Target height, 17,000 feet.' The CO, in his slow methodical way, told us the tactics and the type of the TIs to be dropped. We were to bomb the highest concentration of red TIs, or failing that, the highest concentration of greens, or on good DR. Finally the CO detailed take-off times for each aircraft. Ours was 1608 and the full number of aircraft would set course at 1617.

'Well, it all seemed pretty straightforward so far. I caught Percy's eye and grinned. He was a bit cheesed off because his wife had come down for the New Year's Eve party and we were only put on this trip at the last minute. I could see us belting back tonight! Well, that was the end of the briefing. It was now about 1445 and we all trooped out to the crew room where old 'Chiefy' Tite had organised tea and sandwiches for us. Having munched these we went to the locker room and collected Mae Wests and navigation bag, signed for the escape kit pack and straggled out to the crew buses waiting to take us out to our aircraft. Our dispersals were at the east end of the airfield, south of the main runway. The bus duly deposited us at 'K-King'. First thing to do was to stow the 'Window' bundles in the nose while the skipper went to sign the Form 700; then cram the nav bag in on top. After this I had to check that the DR compass master unit was serviceable, that the oxygen cocks were turned on and the camera magazine was fitted; all this is in the rear hatch. Next I had to see that the navigation lights were working and that the safety pins had been taken out of the 'cookie'; an awkward job. You had to use a torch and peer through a small circular hole at the lug. All done; time for a last smoke.

'Percy was round the back having his operational pee, which he never missed. The usual curious hush had settled on the aerodrome just before the kites started up. There just wasn't a sound. A train whistled in the distance and then the silence descended again. I looked at my watch: twenty minutes to take-off. Time to get in. I took a last drag at my cigarette. Ron was getting himself strapped in. It took him some time to do this. And I put on my parachute harness after slipping a piece of gum into my mouth and got in myself. 'Have a good trip, Sir,' said the rigger, as he stowed the ladder and shut the door. Good lads, our ground crews.

'Bill Brodie the duty CO came round to each kite in turn to see if everything was OK. We gave him a thumbs-up and he went to the next kite. We were eighth off, so it was about time we started up. The first kite had already started up so Ron ran up the engines and I checked the 'Gee' and Loran to see if they were working. All were OK and I switched them off until we were airborne. The first kite taxied out in the dusk of this December afternoon. After a while we waddled forward, checked the brakes and moved slowly out on to the perimeter track and on in the queue to the take-off point. A last check: petrol on outers, pitot head heater on, nav lights and oxygen on, radiator shutters open. We got a flashing green Aldis from the ACP's caravan and taxied on to the runway. We could see the tail light of the kite in front climbing away. Ron taxied forward a little to straighten the tail wheel and then said 'OK, boy, here we go.' And we were off.

'The next few moments were pretty tense. We had the maximum load of fuel and bomb aboard. You hoped she wouldn't swing or burst a tyre because you had a rather unpleasant companion about 6 inches underneath where we were sitting. Then the tail came up and we watched the airspeed creep up to 120 knots; full boost and 3,000 revs. The red light at the end of the runway came rushing up and the kite heaved herself off the deck. (You could almost hear her grunt.) Then the skipper gave the word to raise the undercarriage. We listened anxiously to the engines. A misfire now would be decidedly unpleasant, but they didn't miss (we had a damn good ground crew) and we climbed away to the delay pattern. We passed over Little Staughton, 10 miles from base at 1,500 feet before turning back towards base, still climbing, to set course with the others.

'We crossed the coast at Cromer and headed for Heligoland. At 1712 we began climbing to 20,000 feet. We were gaining a lot of time. The kite wouldn't go less than 190 knots at 10,000 feet. That was 15 knots too fast and we now had nine minutes in hand and had to lose some time. We decided to orbit to lose four minutes. We got back on course and ten minutes later started to climb again to 27,000 feet. During this time we transferred fuel from 100-gallon drop tanks to the outer tanks. This was done automatically and a red light came on when the drop tanks were empty and you switched off the transfer switch. Slap bang over Heligoland six rocket shells rose up on the starboard beam about 2 miles away and we altered course slightly to the north and pressed on. At 1805 the yellow route-marker went down dead ahead and fairly close. Good, that meant that we were pretty well leading the stream behind the markers. 'Gee' was no longer available now and I worked feverishly to average a wind velocity to apply to courses ahead. We crossed the German coast 25 miles NW of Brunsbüttel. All cockpit lights were out now; both of us keeping our eyes skinned for flak and searchlights. It was very dark now and the low cloud had completely dispersed. The kite was going like a bomb. Wizard! Aha, there were the first searchlights, ahead and to starboard and there was flak too, 88mm stuff and rockets. You could see the rockets coming up as little red points of light moving very slowly at first. Then they suddenly sped up to your level and burst with an angry red flame. Not near us though. The searchlights were coning over to starboard. They were too far off to see if they'd got someone but it looked like it.

'At 1814 we crossed the Kiel Canal and we were right in the searchlight belt. A master searchlight picked us up and three or four others swung over on to us immediately. The bright red lamp of the 'Boozer' came on, indicating that we were being tracked by radar-controlled flak. Ron stuck his head well down in the cockpit and did a corkscrew while I kept watch aft. Wow! Just as well we did; a burst of rockets came up just where we were a few seconds before. No sign of any fighters, touch wood. Hello, someone else was coned to starboard. It looked like a Mossie too. I'll bet they were twitching like we were a moment ago. We've lost the searchlights now, or they lost us. We seemed to be getting past the worst of it and the time was 1820. Ahead and a little to port went the green route-markers. We seemed to have lost a bit of ground doing avoiding action. We still had to get past Lübeck. At 1825 the marker leader broadcast a 'Zephyr' message: 'Wind 345°/90 knots.'

'Lübeck was comparatively quiet, thank the Lord. Just past there, on course, someone yelled, 'Snappers' (enemy fighters spotted). Another colossal corkscrew and bags of rubbernecking, but we saw nothing. We resumed course and tried to get some Loran to check position but there were no signals visible, only grass. We expected the red route-marker any minute now. When it came I'd switch on the bombsight which must be done at least fifteen minutes from the target so that it could warm up. The reds went. It was 1840 and we'd just crossed over 10/10ths cloud below, which looked like going all the way to the 'Big Town'. So much for the Met briefing but a bit of luck for us. I switched on the bombsight and got the 'Window' ready to push out through the wooden 'Window' chute down through the small hatch in the floor.

'Our ground speed on this leg was about 338 knots (about 390 mph). We began 'Windowing' with eight minutes to go. The chute was on the floor between your feet and you had to bend almost double to drop the bundles. You could hear a crackle on the R7T as they opened up in the slipstream. Back-breaking job, this, and it made you sweat like blazes. Just five minutes to go. We should see the first TI in a minute. Out went the last 'Window' bundle. I stretched up and had a look out. We were still over 10/10ths cloud. Good. The first TI was slightly over to port. I dived into the bombing position. 'Dive' is a misnomer. With all the kit I had on it was more like a wrestling match! I switched on the sighting head and put the final wind velocity on the computer box and waited for the TIs to come into view. The entire nose except for the optically flat, heated bombing window was frosted up so I couldn't see very far ahead. A couple of minutes to go now.

'More red and green TIs going down,' said Ron. 'Bomb doors open.'

'Bomb doors open,' I repeated and I heard the rumbling roar as they opened and the wind whistled in the bomb bay.

'I'm running up on a bunch of three,' said Ron. 'Can you see them yet?'

'I craned my neck close to the window and looked ahead sideways. 'Yep, I can just see them.' I said, 'OK now, left-left, left-left, steady. We're running up nicely. Keep weaving a bit, we've a minute or so to go yet.' I got the TIs up on the centre line of the graticule and thumbed the release switch. I would press this when the markers reached the cross line. A couple of big white flashes under the cloud up ahead showed that the first two 'cookies' had gone down. I noticed them almost subconsciously.

'A little bit of flak to starboard,' said Ron.

'OK, keep going,' I said. 'Right, right, a little steady now, steady… BOMB GONE!' and I pressed the tit. There was a thud underneath as the lug sprang back and released the bomb. The camera whirred and the red light on the selector box came on. We had to keep straight and level for forty-five seconds to get a photo of our bomb burst in relation to the TIs so as to be able to plot the accuracy later. I scrambled back into my seat and looked down the 'Window' chute. The wait seemed endless.

'Bomb doors closed,' said Ron.

'The camera green light came on. 'Hold it,' I said. There was a great flash under the cloud. 'There she goes; OK, let's get the hell out of here' and we turned south-west to get out of the target area. I turned off the bombsight and bomb selector switches and looked aft. Some flak was coming up now and some searchlights were on under the cloud. It must have been pretty thin, but they were quite ineffective. More bomb flashes appeared as the TIs drifted slowly down into the cloud tops. It looked like quite a concentrated effort. Just after turning we saw a kite (possibly a cats-eye fighter, a 190 or a 109) shoot over us in the opposite direction leaving a contrail. He didn't appear to have seen us but we kept a sharp lookout just in case there were any more. Things being quieter now, I entered the time, height and heading of when we bombed.

'Ron said, 'Check the petrol, will you?'

'I did so and found that we had about 330 gallons left; a little less than we expected but OK. At 1919 I tried to get some Loran but the signals were very weak and I discarded them. I would try again later. Just then the expected green route-markers appeared ahead so we were OK and pretty well on track. At 1924 we altered course and we crossed the Dutch coast at 2022, altering course slightly to the north for Woodbridge and still keeping our height above 23,000 feet. We switched on the IFF and 'identify' on Channel D, making a VHF broadcast: '"Lounger K-King" identifying, out.' (This was for the Fighter Command plot so that we are not mistaken for an enemy aircraft.) I got a string of fixes across the

North Sea. The crossing always seemed to me to be one of the longest parts of the trip. The 'Scu' cloud that had reappeared over Holland near the coast was about 4-5/10ths but it dispersed completely before we got to Woodbridge, leaving a clear night. I worked out the ETA coast as 2049 and Ron increased speed a little. At 2038 he said he could see lights ahead and when I looked out for a minute or two later I could see the semi-circle of sodium lights which marked the Woodbridge circuit dead ahead. We coasted in at 2046 and began to lose height slowly, switching on the navigation lights as we did so. We were really moving now, with a ground speed of 260 knots. ETA base was 2100. I began to relax a little.

'Ron changed frequency from Channel D to Channel A (base frequency) to listen out for other aircraft. All the way in from the coast was airfield after airfield, each with its Drem system of lights illuminated and one or two searchlights (called Sandra lights) over the top, forming a sort of canopy. Someone once said that airfields in East Anglia were as thick as fleas on a dog's back. He was right. We began to look for the base lights and I set up homing co-ordinates on the 'Gee'. At 2056 we sighted two Sandra lights in an inverted 'V' with a flashing white light in between them (this was the Station identification letters 'GR' in front of Flying Control; all Station idents were lit but ours was the only one in this area to have them flashing). As soon as we saw this, Ron prepared to call up Flying Control and I started packing up my kit. As we did this, two other kites called up almost simultaneously; Chandler and 'Ginger' Wood in 'J-Johnny' and another kite. We came tearing up behind them. As we arrived over the airfield, Chandler called, '"J-Johnny", funnels' and landed. The other kite called 'downwind'. We now called up: 'Control from "Lounger K-King", over.'

'Control replied, '"Lounger K-King", prepare to land, runway 270, QFE 1029, over.'

'We replied, '"K-King" preparing to land, out,' which meant that we acknowledged permission to land and were listening out. Someone else called up just behind us.

'I switched on the downward identification light and opened the radiator shutters. We reduced height to 1,500 feet and turned downwind. Ron lowered the undercart, put down some flap and called, '"K-King" downwind, out.' This was not acknowledged by Control. Instead they called the next aircraft and told it to prepare to land. Now we were turning across wind and one-quarter flap was lowered. Two green lights showed that the undercart was down. The circuit lights were visible over the port wingtip and the funnel lead-in lights appeared with the Station ident letters 'GR' illuminated on the outer circle at their head. We turned into the funnels at 900 feet and called '"K- King", funnels, over.'

'Control replied '"K-King", land, out.' Had the runway not been clear we would have been told to overshoot and come in again. The runway lights appeared now, narrowing into the distance. Two flashing lights either side of the threshold were the glide path indicators, or GPIs, which showed the correct glide path. Now Ron hunched himself over the stick, put down full flap and concentrated on his landing. We went sliding in at 125 knots. The runway lights came up quickly at the end. We gave the usual heave as Ron checked her and closed the throttles, touching down on the main wheels at about 95 knots and trundling down the runway to the accompaniment of the usual crackles and pops from the exhausts of those wonderful Merlins. We turned left at the end of the runway, pulled up the flaps and called, '"King" clear' and then taxied back to dispersal with the engines purring away as if they'd only just started up. At dispersal we were waved in by the ground crew and we stopped and opened the bomb doors. (You got reproachful looks from the ground crew if you forgot this, for they then had to pump them down by hand; a tedious exercise.) Ron pulled the cut-outs and the engines rumbled to a stop. We switched everything off and climbed out stiffly with a mutual grin of congratulation at completing another trip safely. This was our 27th.

'We collected our kit and stalked over to the waiting crew bus laden with parachutes and harness, nav bag, camera magazine and the rest and were driven back to the crew room for interrogation.

'Back at the crew room we dumped our kit and went in to be interrogated. First, the CO had a word about the trip in general, then Intelligence. They wanted to know in detail about the bombing: how concentrated was it? Was there much opposition? What were the relative positions of the TIs you bombed? Draw a sketch of them as you saw them please and a host of other details. While this was going on coffee and rum was brought in and the second cigarette lit. Boy, did the first one taste good! Following this the navigators had to hand in their maps, charts and logs and pass on details of radar coverage, 'Gee' jamming, hand over signals flimsies and camera magazine, while the pilots signed the Form 700 and told the engineers about any snags. At last all was done and it was away to the Mess for bacon and eggs and the New Year's Eve party.'

Chapter Nineteen

The 'Milk Run'

'For some time now Berlin had been attacked on a nightly basis by the Light Night Striking Force – so regularly in fact that some air crews called it the "Milk Run".'[1]

Flying Officer Herbert 'Bertie' Boulter.

By 5 January 1945 Flying Officer Philip Back and his 23-year-old navigator Flying Officer Derek 'Tom' Newell Smith DFC on 692 Squadron at Graveley had flown more than thirty ops together. Derek Smith was a 'second tourist' having finished a tour as a sergeant navigator on Lancasters on 61 Squadron. He did not learn until much, much later that 'Phil' had only thirty hours' night-flying experience, but he never had the slightest cause to doubt his ability. 'He was a natural who handled the 'Mossie' with a skill well beyond his experience and always did the right thing in our more 'hairy' moments. There was something special about the bomber Mosquito pilot/observer relationship. On my Lancaster tour I flew in a very close-knit crew which was all-sergeant until near the end, but I never formed any lasting relationship as close as I was to have with 'Phil'. In the bomber 'Mossie' we sat side-by-side, almost shoulder-to-shoulder, sometimes for five or more hours, with a lot of decidedly unfriendly citizens down below for most of the time. They were no more friendly to the 'heavies' and although we relied as much on each other, we had so much more space and a little bit of the aircraft which was ours. In the 'Mossie', every move which was made was seen by the other, so maybe it served to weld us closer together as a unit.'

The start of January was hectic for them. Derek Smith wrote to his sister: 'We've done three trips in the last three nights to Berlin, Hanover and Nürnburg. It's a nice way of spending New Year's Eve, going to Berlin. Still, there was a party in the Mess when we got back so we had a slap-up meal and a good time.'

On 5 January Philip Back and Derek Smith set off yet again for Berlin in 'T-Tommy'. At Wyton 'Bertie' Boulter's Mosquito was delayed on take-off by engine problems and ground crews worked on it by torchlight. Just as Boulter reached flying speed the troublesome Merlin misfired and lost power. With a 4,000lb bomb on board and a faulty engine the Mosquito would flop over on its back and plough in, so the bomb was jettisoned and the operation aborted.

Meanwhile, Philip Back and Derek Smith were experiencing problems returning from Berlin. Back had feathered one engine over Holland: 'We had feathered one engine over Holland due to lack of power and lost some height. At about 27,000 feet the other engine stopped. We discussed bailing out but it looked such a bloody long way down and we were over the sea, we decided to try and get down. We could see the lights of Woodbridge. We crossed the coast at about 18,000 feet and requested permission to land. 'What is your trouble "T-Tommy"?'

'We have lost both engines' – long pause – 'Land, "T-Tommy".'

'We got into the circuit about 12,000 feet on the upwind cross-leg – lost all the rest of our height to cross the boundary high and very fast, wheels down and a bit of flap. God knows what our speed was. I know it was over the limits for the aircraft. The next morning I got a bollocking from the engineering officer, for they had found nothing wrong. We were collected on 6th January in the Oxford and the next day I flew back to Woodbridge and flew 'T-Tommy' home to Graveley. A day or two later I got another bollocking from Wing Commander Joe Northrop. I was expecting a Green endorsement in my log book and was somewhat miffed at completing a dead-stick landing, in a 'Mossie', at night, losing about 15,000 feet in one enormous circuit and getting the wheels down – and getting my balls chewed up for doing so!'

Derek Smith adds: 'It was a remarkable bit of flying and really deserved a medal. I can only think our otherwise amiable "Wingco" guessed we had been a little too high!'

On 14/15 January eight crews on 128 Squadron were detailed for a raid on Berlin in dangerous conditions but rather than break the sequence of continuous nightly raids on that city, the raid went ahead. One of the pilots was 'Tom' Empson. He had completed initial pilot training in New Zealand in 1941 followed by Canada and then two years as an instructor on twins before his much-desired posting to 128 Squadron with his navigator 'Bert' Dwerryhouse. Empson recalls:

'Calculated risks in time of war were considered acceptable. Sometimes they were taken for unwarranted reasons. The forecast was for pending snow storms with zero visibility. As it was not due for a few hours the planners decided a small force of [83] Mosquitoes had time to visit Berlin and return before it clamped. So the eight were selected from 128 Squadron and 'Bert' Dwerryhouse and I were one of the 'privileged' crews.'

Among the other crews at Wyton who were 'privileged' to fly this operation were Doug Swain and Mike Bayon but they had a noisy argument in the mess and it was deemed wise to assign them to other crews for the raid on Berlin. Swain swiftly forgot the quarrel. He was having none of it: 'You're the best navigator in the world and I don't trust anyone else,' he whispered to Bayon. 'Will you fly with me tonight?' Bayon agreed and hopped surreptitiously off the bus at their normal dispersal point for 'G for George'. They would fly nine operations in November of which three were to Berlin.

'Bertie' Boulter was also on the battle order. A few days earlier on 7 January he had acquired a new navigator, 'Chris' Hart, who was from Derby and they had crewed PF403, Mk XXV Mosquito as part of a 100-plus raid on Nuremberg. 'It all went rather well,' wrote Boulter, 'and uneventfully. I then had a week's leave and met up with Chris again on the 14th for an NFT in an old favourite of mine, MM204 for a raid on Berlin. This trip was not as smooth as some and would be the end of the line for MM204. For some time now Berlin had been attacked on a nightly basis by the Light Night Striking Force – so regularly in fact that some air crews called it the "Milk Run".

'It was all part of the whirlwind that Bomber Harris had promised the Germans that they would reap. A break in this retribution was considered highly undesirable.

The weather forecast during the day was not good and very high westerly winds were forecast for the evening at our operating height. It was also forecast that the weather over England at low level would deteriorate markedly later in the night and as a result, the heavy bombers would not operate at all as the trip would have simply taken them too long. However, the BBC still needed to be able to announce to the British public the next morning, "Last night our aircraft again bombed Berlin."

'The met men considered that there was a reasonable chance that the Mosquitoes of the LNSF would be fast enough to get back before the predicted front bearing rain, mist and murk arrived. Six planes each from six squadrons were subsequently detailed for Berlin. One crashed on take-off and so thirty-five Mosquitoes set off to demoralize further the citizens of the Fatherland.'

'When we left,' recalled 'Tom' Empson, 'we entered a very thick cloud at about 500 feet and we didn't break it until we were at over 23,000 feet where it was a beautiful moonlit night. The only uncomfortable factor was that we were leaving clearly defined condensation trails behind us. We consoled ourselves with the thought that the stormy conditions were forecast for all of Europe and the Luftwaffe would have more concern for their crews than those of the "mad dogs of Englishmen" and the one from New Zealand. We completed our op to the best of our ability, but we still had to get down. We started our let-down over the enemy coast as per usual, entering and breaking cloud again at the same height as on the journey out. Navigation lights on, we were just able to see a faint glow on each wingtip, although it would be almost invisible to the seven other planes heading for the same area as we were. We continued regardless with "Bert" glued to his green screen. We were down to 500 feet again, still in cloud, when "Bert" said we were overhead. About then another aircraft called for permission to land saying that visibility was very bad with the cloud base at 220 feet and it was snowing. I recognised the call sign as that of our Flight Commander Ivor Broom. This was very disturbing and I told "Bert" to lower the undercarriage and 20° of flap just to be ready for an emergency landing.

'I called up control to say we were orbiting overhead at 164 feet and needed urgent clearance and confirmation that they had sighted us. Confirmation came just as "Bert" indicated the blurred lights below. Fortunately, we were in a position from which we could do a steep turn and without power, with full flap and make a good approach. We got off the runway as soon as we could because another aircraft said it had a visual and was coming in. It was too high but the pilot wisely decided to put down rather than risk losing the 'drome in another attempt. He couldn't pull up in time and ran off the end of the runway and through the hedge beyond. We then heard control calling "Sparhawk" aircraft ordering them to climb to a safe height and bail out. They were getting near the end of their endurance and needed fuel to climb to at least 5,900 feet. The outcome of this disastrous sortie was that one crew spotted runway lights through a small gap and managed to get down just before their motors stopped. Of the others, one couldn't reach height and the crew perished. Two others did escape successfully, leaving one unaccounted for. It was not until next morning that a report came in that the eighth plane had been found a distance from the end of the take-off runway. It had crashed and miraculously not exploded or caught fire. All in all the cost of that bit of propaganda was two crews lost, with one aircraft badly damaged and four written off. Hardly worth it, they had to admit, and all because the Met had miscalculated the arrival time of the weather front.'

When Doug Swain and Mike Bayon got back to base their fuel tanks registered empty. 'Moreover,' says Bayon, 'a great blanket of warm air had slid over the cold air, trapping fog, which was forming on a nucleus of the ashes of burning London. Doug contacted base. "Why aren't the runway lights on?"

'"They are."

'"But we're right over base at only 10,000 feet."

'"There's a bit of fog down here."

'This was my chance to test the theory of blind landing I had worked out,' Bayon later recalled.

'Run down one radar line till you hit a cross-line, do a steady 30° turn port and you'd be lined up with the centre of the runway. Accurate to six feet. We tried it at 300 feet. No joy. We simply could not see the massive sodium lights. We went round again. 200 feet. Not a sausage.' "We'll just have to go lower," I said.

'"Well I'll go in at 30 feet," said Doug. "But you'd better be bloody accurate. The hangars are higher than that."

'"Oh that's OK," I replied. "It will work." We came in at 30 feet. "Crossing perimeter," I said. Then, "Start of runway." Then, "You'd better be quick – we're halfway down the runway." Doug gritted his teeth. "I hope you know what you're doing," he said. "I'll chuck her down."

'We hit the runway and seconds later we were off the runway and on the grass verge. Then we tore through the concertina wire and barbed-wire entanglements and perimeter fence as though they were cobwebs. We were still travelling at over 100 mph. Then we hit the hedge and the ditch and the main road from Cambridge to Huntingdon and still Doug was fighting to keep her straight. We hit the hedge and the ditch the other side of the road and now we were in a field of sugar beet, sodden soil. Suddenly the undercart collapsed and we skidded along on the belly of the plane. Then we were still and after all of the intense drama of the last half-minute it was amazingly silent – so silent that you felt you could have gathered great handfuls of it. I've never known a feeling like it.

'I broke the silence. "Thank you, Doug," I said. "That was good."

'Still we sat; we knew we ought to get out in case the plane caught fire, but we felt curiously drained, as though we were waiting for all our innards to catch up with us again.

'Again, I was the one to break the silence. I said, "I've got some chocolate in my navigation bag. Would you like some?" It was another of our perks, like oranges, that the aircrew got extra rations of, coarse rather bitter heavy chocolate. "Christ, yes," said Doug and suddenly we both realized that we were ravenously hungry. I broke the huge slab equally in two and both of us just stuffed the whole lot into our mouths barbarously. At that moment, the CO climbed onto the wing of the plane and battered on the Perspex of the cockpit. "Is anyone alive?" he shouted. He had come by van as far as the perimeter fence and then run through the gap left in the defences by our plane.

'Our mouths were stuffed with half-chewed chocolate. We were incapable of coherent speech. I tried to say "Don't worry, we're OK," but it was unintelligible. "Bring the stretchers – they're alive. I can hear them groaning," shouted the CO. Doug and I collapsed. We were laughing till the tears came and choking and doing the nose trick. It was all very silly really. But of course, next day when it came round to seeing what had happened to the squadron that night, things were different.

'The rest of that night is easily told. Half a dozen Mosquitoes gained height and crews bailed out, leaving crewless planes to crash. One plane aborted and came back early with radar trouble – once when we had radar trouble we just carried on. They were pretty "wet", we thought. The planes limped in, exhausted, frustrated, short of fuel and no airfield visible. One diverted to Bassingbourn and landed safely.

'"Taxi in to the perimeter," radioed control. He couldn't – he had no fuel.

'One crew who tried to land was not quite accurate enough and they landed on a petrol bowser. Even this great sheet of flame was not visible through the clinging fog. Next day the Medical Officer went to search for their bodies. All he found was one thumb and he callously trod it into the ground with his heel. John Smith, a good bloke and a bloody fine fly half at rugby, found base but could not land. "Gain height and bail out," ordered control. He tried and ran out of fuel. His navigator bailed out safely. Parachutes were designed to open within 400-600 feet. John got out at 180 feet and his parachute was still only half-open when he hit the ground. He must have hit at well over 80 mph, but he was fit and relaxed. He rolled with the fall and wasn't even bruised. When he got back he said, "I'm going to look there tomorrow. Just before I jumped I chucked out my forage cap – it was brand new." The plane hit the ground less than 200 yards from where his cap was found.'

Five Mosquitoes from the Berlin raid crashed in England and three crashed in Belgium. The 28-year-old Australian Flying Officer Treless James Stewart Adam of Watsonia, Victoria and 33-year-old Flight Sergeant Allan James Casey RAAF on 128 Squadron died when they crashed at Woodhurst, 5 miles north-east of Huntingdon trying to force-land at Wyton. The only clue to the cause of this accident was the condition of the starboard propeller, the blades of which were bent backwards, while those of the port propeller were bent forward. It is considered that loss of power in the starboard engine immediately after take-off was the cause of this accident. Both airmen are buried at Cambridge City Cemetery. The Squadron CO, Wing Commander Richard James Burrough in a letter of 15 January 1945 to Pilot Officer Adam's father in Australia stated: 'Both had been with the Squadron for eight weeks and during that time had completed nineteen operations together. They were a very sound crew and could be relied on to do their work in a most efficient manner.'

The crew of 23-year-old Flying Officer Alan Walter Heitman from Tasmania and his fellow Australian navigator Pilot Officer 'Nat' Gold got back over base, saw no runway, were told to gain height and bail out.

As Mike Bayon recalled: 'Nat opened the escape hatch and froze with fear. A red-haired WAAF was talking the planes in. In fact, she was engaged to Alan and they were due to marry on their next leave. She could hear him telling Nat to jump and then his urgency as he said, 'The engine's overheating. Christ – it's on fire. Jump! Jump!' Still Nat clung to the plane. Now Alan was losing control of the plane and the flames were beginning to lick at the cockpit. He even struggled with Nat and still he clung neurotically to the plane. Suddenly he jumped and landed safely. But by now it was too late for Alan. The plane was in a spin, burning fiercely. The red-haired WAAF could hear Alan screaming all the way down and she even heard the plane hit the ground, though by now she was on hands and knees under the desk, trying to blot out the sounds. She was sent on a week's immediate compassionate leave.

'The met men had forecast a 120-knot tail wind at 25,000 feet which we soon found out was grossly understating it,' wrote Bertie Boulter. 'We overshot Berlin, easily beating the marker aircraft to the target area. Before we had started even to realize our situation we saw two searchlights switch on with their beams vertical. Then slowly they descended and their beams converged, pointing in the reciprocal direction to our track and were then extinguished. This was repeated a second time. Now we knew for sure they were pointing to Berlin. The only troops in that area likely to do that were Russian. They must have identified us by the engine noise of our Merlin engines and worked out that we had overshot. We had hardly completed half of our 180-degree turn to sort ourselves out when we saw the PFF markers in the distance. It seemed to take a long time to return and to reposition ourselves to make a successful bombing run, but eventually we did and then turned again for home, still battling the fierce upper winds that had fooled us in the first place.

'Eventually, well over three hours' flying time later we identified Woodbridge beneath us, with the glow from the lights of their massive runway showing through a layer of cloud. We were given the cloud base of 1,100 feet and Chris estimated Wyton in twelve minutes. What a surprise it was to us when we descended in to Wyton that the weather had closed in dramatically. We could see nothing as we drew close, flying the standard beam approach for a straight-in landing. At circuit height we could still not see the lights. On final, dead on the beam, we could still see absolutely nothing. Final approach – nothing; passing the outer marker at 600 feet – still nothing; 150 feet and down to zero at the set QFE (Atmospheric Pressure at Aerodrome Elevation) on the altimeter and still not a glimmer. We instigated overshoot procedures and went round again.

'Our second and third attempts to land were equally unsuccessful. I told Chris we would not be making another approach, we had run our main tanks virtually dry until the engines spluttered and now the inners must have been almost empty. No sooner had I finished saying that and before Chris could answer, than the voice of Ivor Broom came through loud and clear on the R/T.

'"Bertie; this is Ivor Broom. This is not a request, this is an order. Climb immediately to a safe height and bail out.... Acknowledge."

'I acknowledged. At 5,000 feet I levelled out and Chris and I abandoned MM204 to her fate.

'Once again a muddy field awaited me after my second try at parachuting. It was getting to be a bad habit. [He and his previous navigator, Jim Churcher, had had to bail out near Dunkirk returning from a raid on Nuremberg.] With the wet fog clinging like a scotch mist, I wandered along the hedgerow until I found an opening onto a narrow road and turned left to see where it got me. The time would have been about 0230. Shortly after this I came to a farmhouse by the side of the road. I recall it was on my left. I walked up to the door and knocked hard. After a while the first-floor window above me opened and a voice from above my head asked what I wanted. I explained that I was an RAF pilot and had bailed out of my Mosquito returning from a raid on Berlin and asked if I could please use their telephone. The voice hardened and advised me there was a public phone box 200 yards down the road on the right-hand side. The window then slammed shut.

'Somewhat stunned at this sort of response I continued my wandering down the lane, thinking mainly how I was going to get through to Wyton. I had no money on me due to my usual pre-operation procedures and added to that was the fact that I hadn't really got a clue who to call anyway. Even when I had decided on that, would the operator put me through to an operational RAF station at that time of the morning? As these things buzzed through my mind, I became aware of the sound of engines, the rumble of vehicle tyres and a dull glow of some masked headlights coming up behind me. I looked round. Amazingly it was an American staff car, followed by a large truck with some mini-searchlights on it, scouring the hedges on the side of the lane. Bringing up the rear was an ambulance, into which I was quickly bundled.

'It appeared that a rather alert sentry at the nearby USAAF airfield of Thurleigh had heard the crash of MM204 and had alerted the chaps who now had me in their charge. As all this was at a very unsociable time of the day, I was mightily impressed. The first port of call at Thurleigh was the sick quarters where I was thoroughly checked out and had some attention to the front of my shins. Once again on bailing out, I had managed to skin them. I mentally made a note to avoid exiting any further Mossies in flight, or at least to devise for myself a less painful method of getting through that hatch. Naturally I was somewhat vociferous about my reception by the local farmer and my native Canadian accent became more pronounced the more excited I got, even after several years in the RAF, with the last one as an officer!

'The American MO tried valiantly to make me feel better by telling me that the farmer must have mistaken me for a drunken USAAF airman – it really didn't have the effect that he had hoped. Meanwhile the rescue crew had set off again in the unfavourable conditions to see if they could locate Chris. They came back an hour or so later without finding him. The next morning we found out why. Chris had worked out that being found was quite a long shot in the middle of the night. Normally he slept at night; therefore he would go to sleep now. He had vast quantities of protective parachute material to wrap around himself, which he proceeded to do, then promptly fell asleep until it became daylight. He was still asleep when a passing farm hand found him on his way to work. I really had to think more about this bailing out business. Both my trusty colleagues had got it far better sorted than I had. Jim met up with some decent coves and got well drunk and Chris realized that he might as well get some sleep, whilst both times I spent several hours each night wandering around, lost in the mist and rain with very sore shins. Someone was doing it right and it wasn't me. Later that morning the C of E padre from Wyton drove over to Thurleigh aerodrome to collect me. We picked Chris up on the way back to the airfield.

'Ivor and Tommy Broom had been on the same raid and had managed to find Berlin first time. Because of this they were back at Wyton about twenty minutes ahead of the returning squadron. The weather had already deteriorated to a near impossible situation when the "Flying Brooms" arrived back. They had visibility problems on approach too, but just as Ivor initiated the overshoot, Tommy caught a fleeting glimpse of the runway lights. He was then able to instruct Ivor on the heading and timed him round the circuit for a procedural approach. They landed successfully and were in fact the last plane to land at Wyton that night. By now, as they taxied in, Ivor was fuming. He taxied directly to the control tower, shut down, leaped out of the aircraft and bounded up the stairs. There he ordered the lights to be changed to runway 26, the longest on the airfield and the one served with the standard beam approach. He then verbally ejected the "regular" squadron CO from the tower and called all 128 Squadron aircraft still airborne to bail out.

'Of the thirty-six planes sent on that operation twelve were lost, all of them over East Anglia when they were almost home. Shortly after this the CO was posted. Wing Commander Ernest Rodley took over in his place. He was a real "flying" CO and knew how to run an operational squadron.'[2]

Next day when it came round to seeing what had happened to the squadron that night Doug said to Mike Bayon pretty solemnly:

'Look Mike, if you'd flown with Alan Heitman last night, he'd be alive now and I'd be dead.' (Alas, 'G for George' had suffered severe damage and they were subsequently given 'H for Harry'. 'The second marriage isn't quite the same,' Bayon said, wistfully.)

'If a friend was killed we were actively encouraged to get very drunk that night. Next day the day before felt quite distant. On mess nights at the end of the evening we would sing a song from *The Dawn Patrol*, a film of the Great War starring Errol Flynn and David Niven:

'So stand by your glasses, steady
Each man who takes off and flies.
So here's to the dead already;
Three cheers for the next man who dies.'

'And then we drained glasses. Unfeeling? Disrespectful? Insensitive? I don't know. Perhaps it was a kind of denial or defiance.

When Doug Swain and Mike Bayon had made forty-eight trips they transferred to another squadron 'hoping to do ninety-eight raids on the trot':

'In fact,' recalls Bayon, 'when we had done fifty-two raids the war in Europe ended. We volunteered for Japan as a crew and while we were on embarkation leave, the atom bombs were dropped. Doug went back to Melbourne. Six months later he was killed in a civil flying accident.'

On the afternoon of 14 September 1954 Captain Doug Swain, his co-pilot and a passenger aboard a Lockheed Hudson owned by the *Sydney Morning Herald* went missing, ironically while delivering newspapers on the regular 'milk run' from Mascot to Taree, Kempsey, Armidale, Glenn Innes, Inverell and Bingarra. Seven months later his son was born and his widow remarried. After the war Mike Bayon became a classics master at St Faith's, Cambridge and then Colet Court, the preparatory school for St Paul's, London. He never married, but had a string of girlfriends.

'I'd always longed to bail out,' said Bayon. 'But why did we risk death to save our planes? Why did we join the most perilous and casualty-ridden branch of the Forces? Why did we refuse to turn back when instruments failed? Were we just conditioned lemmings? I don't think so. Some of it was competitiveness, a bit was bravado; but most of all, it genuinely was pride of performance; the Olympic ideal, pursuit of excellence. I can't believe that was bad. Personally, I am happy to have been part of it.'[3]

On the night of 29/30 January Philip Back and Derek Smith on 692 Squadron flew their fortieth op, with their second mission to Berlin in forty-eight hours. Smith wrote:

'We returned to be greeted by the news that FIDO at Graveley was u/s and we were diverted to Bradwell Bay. Bradwell closed in and Coltishall advised that we should 'Get down where you can', which we did at Hethel, a USAF base [home to the 389th Bomb Group and B-24 Liberators] near Norwich. We were treated with the usual American '10/10ths' hospitality (a jeep wherever we wanted to go, pineapple, ice cream, whisky, cigs and tobacco and they would not let us pay a cent) but memory of the operational meal remains in both our minds: it was roast pork with gooseberry jam! Next morning our 'T-Tommy' came up with a very bad mag drop so we were taken the 12 miles by jeep to Philip's home at Brundall for lunch and the weather closed in so we stayed the night. Next morning Philip's father took us by car to Norwich where we were picked up by American transport for a run-up of the now serviceable 'T-Tommy' but we were at Hethel for another night due to continuing bad weather and it was 'flicks' in the evening and drinks in the club. We showed some of the boys over the 'Mossie' at midnight.

'On 1 February we woke to a sunny morning and after a good breakfast at Hethel, we were back at Graveley by 0940 to find ourselves on the battle order for Berlin that night. Because of the problems at Hethel, 'T-Tommy' had to be checked so we were in 'K-King', Burbidge and Ramage's aircraft, which had an indifferent reputation put about by them, I suspect, to keep it out of other hands!

'The trip was fairly routine until we lost an engine near Hanover and again the weather was u/s with low cloud and snowstorms over East Anglia and the 8 Group area so once more it was a matter of getting down where we could. The Mossie flew very well on one engine but it could be tricky to land especially at night and in the poor weather conditions, so we proceeded with care losing height gradually knowing we were over East Anglia. Eventually we saw a rocket come up through the low cloud and, losing more height, spotted a runway [Rougham near Bury St Edmunds and home to the 94th Bomb Group] very well illuminated by wartime standards. 'Phil' was quickly into the approach only to find a Fortress being landed; hence all the illumination. However, short of fuel, on one engine and in a snowstorm it was no place for the faint-hearted. So 'Phil' went in over the Fortress with rather too much height and speed so that we hit the runway past halfway but with hardly a bump. We shot off the end over a wide grassed area and ditch, to be brought to a halt at the perimeter by a row of tree stumps, one of which impacted with the starboard wing and slewed us around by 90°. Apart from two small cuts on my forehead, neither of us was hurt. So we were very smartly out and taking off at speed in case of fire, only to be halted by the sound of voices behind us.

'We returned to find the aircraft was across a road with an Armstrong Siddeley car between the port engine and drop tank. We found four very lucky occupants, badly shocked but not too badly hurt, although one did need hospital treatment for a head wound requiring forty stitches. Then, almost immediately, we found ourselves surrounded by GIs brandishing rifles as they thought us to be a Messerschmitt 410 intruder. On this occasion we did not receive the usual American hospitality probably due to our unannounced arrival and were left to make our own way back to Cambridge by train to await being picked up by car. Of course we were lugging our flying gear and received some odd glances from other passengers. However, we made our way to the University Air Squadron and were lavished with their hospitality. Of course, we were not very popular with Burbidge and Ramage but everyone was pleased to see us in one piece, especially the Wingco who put us in the battle order for the next two nights! However, they were Wiesbaden and Dortmund, rather easier than the six to Berlin up to that ending up at Rougham. This latter Philip described as being due to the bad judgement of a single engine approach. Many Mossie air crews did not survive to tell the tale of single-engine landings. So in my view, as the only witness, to land from a steep approach at night in a snowstorm and to be able to walk away was a small miracle aided by airmanship of the highest order.'[4]

Late that January Ivor Broom was called to see Air Vice Marshal Don Bennett at his headquarters at Castle Hill House, RAF Huntingdon. The conversation was typically short and sweet: 'Ivor, you are promoted to acting wing commander.... We are having a new squadron at Wyton.... You are in charge.... You start forming it tomorrow morning and will be operational by tomorrow evening.... It will be 163 Squadron.... Any questions? No ... thought not. Well done, off you go. Good luck.'

Ivor and Tommy Broom, his faithful navigator, became 163 Squadron's first crew and 'Bertie' Boulter and Chris Hart followed a week later as crew ten or eleven. On the night of 1 March they flew what was 'Bertie's thirteenth visit to Berlin, although he thought it better not to mention it:

'We were the last of the ten planes to take off that night and lifted off Wyton's runway at exactly 1830 hours. We logged five hours for the trip. One or two of the crews took twenty minutes longer for the same journey and all got to the target area within a minute or so of each other.'

In February the LNSF flew 1,662 sorties, the 1/2 February raid being the largest Mosquito bombing attack on the Reich capital since the formation of the LNSF thus far. In total, 122 aircraft were dispatched in two waves to bomb Berlin. No aircraft were lost. On 5/6 February sixty-three Mosquitoes attacked Berlin. In March the LNSF raided Berlin on no fewer than 27 nights, flying 1,222 sorties and losing 7 Mosquitoes on operations.

Jim Foley, a navigator on 608 Squadron at Downham Market, had flown a first tour on Lancasters. At the beginning, in the summer of 1944, when he had crewed-up with Flight Lieutenant 'Hank' Henderson, a Canadian pilot, 'the number of operations to complete a tour on Mosquitoes was fifty – it seemed a lot at that time.

'A navigator in a Mosquito was a more interesting function than in a heavy bomber. He sat by the side of the pilot, his chart on his knee, 'Gee' box to the left and the nose of the aircraft directly ahead in which was the bomb sight. Instead of being enclosed, as in the Lancaster, the navigator saw everything that was happening, but was not quite so comfortable. A consolation was that the flying time to a like target was very much shorter. For instance, my Berlin trip in a Lancaster took seven hours plus, whereas the average Mosquito op on the same city was about four and a quarter hours.'

Foley recalled: 'From February on to the end of my tour, Berlin, weather permitting, was going to be the target. The war had progressed with the Allied armies pressing towards the Rhine and the Russians advancing rapidly through Poland towards Germany. It obviously became Bomber Command policy that the Light Night Striking Force should keep the German capital awake as often as possible. These were more than pinpricks, as on each raid up to 100 tons of bombs were dropped. While it was still a long way to fly to Berlin, we were never sure of the reception we would get, as more often than not they put up a heavy anti-aircraft barrage. On one occasion no defence at all was evident – as though they were saying 'we can't do anything about these buggers, we'll just have to take it.' In February I did six trips, five to the 'Big City', one of which I flew with Squadron Leader Lawrence McArdle as 'Hank' was not able to fly on this particular trip. When we reached the target area we were completely in cloud and could not see anything. The bombs were dropped blindly on target ETA (dead-reckoning time over target). I had a week's leave in this month and spent it with Peg and visited brother Syd in Staffs. I think on this leave I mentioned to 'Pop' Sheffield about marriage and he nicely told me that he didn't think it a good idea to get married until I had finished flying operationally for obvious reasons.'

On the night of 14/15 February when forty-six Mosquitoes went to Berlin many in Bomber Command must have thought that they too would be heading for the 'Big City' once again, particularly as Operation 'Thunderclap' had begun the night before with a heavy raid on Dresden. Berlin must follow, must it not? Along with Leipzig and Chemnitz, all lay just behind the Eastern Front and were vital centres of communications and supply centres, and all of them were teeming with thousands of German refugees fleeing the Soviet advance. 'Thunderclap' had been planned for several months for just such an opportunity and that time was now. Rumours on the bomber bases were rife. On 218 Lancaster Squadron at Chedburgh, the easy money was on Berlin being the target. Australian Flight Sergeant 'Dig' Klenner's crew, Harry McCalla, their West Indian rear gunner from Jamaica, was known for his 'hunches', as Miles ('Mike') Tripp the bomb-aimer recalled in his book *The Eighth Passenger*:

'Within the hut there was a scene of unfamiliar orderliness. The crew was resplendent in best blue and brass buttons shone with intentions for a bright night out in town. Only Harry, sitting on his bed, was wearing battle-dress. Had he guessed that there was no purpose in getting dressed for town?

'Harry had a brown skin, high cheekbones and an arrogant bearing; it was not difficult to imagine that the Scottish seafarers and African women among his ancestors were proud clansmen and the daughters of tribal chiefs. Harry was 24 and the old man of the crew. Our pilot was a tall, lean Australian with blue eyes and a thin pale face. We called him 'Dig'. Late in the nineteenth century, Dig's grandparents had emigrated from Germany and settled in Australia and although he made a joke about bombing the land of his forefathers, he spoke very little about his background.

'Tripp had then found out that they 'were on'. He told them it was another minimum bomb load and that they were down to fly in 'A-Able'. While he was speaking Les Walker the navigator caught his eye and tipped his head slightly in Harry's direction.

'Harry,' I said, 'the boys don't understand your hunches. You get the gen from inside your head, nowhere else, don't you?'

'You know I do,' he said. He looked at the others. 'Everything must be explained, eh? I'd be angry if I wasn't amused.' He laughed to show amusement, but we all looked uncomfortable…. There was some general talk about the complexity of the human brain and how little anyone understood of its processes, then Paul asked, 'Where do you reckon we're going tonight, Harry?'

'Berlin, I hope.' (For some extraordinary reason, Harry had always wanted to pay one visit to Berlin.) Take-off was scheduled for 2000 hours and I went to the briefing room as soon as it was open. On the wall the red ribbon led to a town about 40 miles to the west of Dresden. I had never heard of the place as a target and I doubted whether Harry had either…. I had mixed feelings; I wanted him to prove that he did possess some sort of precognitive power because this would show that any leakage of target information was not being fed through him. On the other hand, I felt that by becoming involved in the plot I was betraying our friendship.

'The crew looked at me. I decided I couldn't pose the fateful question and simply said, 'Not much sleep for us tonight.'

'It was 'Dig' who turned to Harry and said, 'Have a shot at guessing the target, mate.'

'At this point I think Harry realized it was more than a plot; it was a trial. He moved across to where a map of Europe was pinned to the wall. It was a smaller edition of the briefing-room map and was unmarked by any ribbon.

'He put out his hand and let it stray across the map until his forefinger reached Leipzig; then he moved it across the province of Brandenburg. He paused and his finger began to move towards Chemnitz where it stopped. Had he been giving a stage performance it could not have been more theatrically effective.

'It might be Leipzig, or perhaps Brandenburg, or even Chemnitz … I think it'll be Chemnitz,' he said.

'The crew looked at me. I alone knew what the target was. 'He's right,' I said.'

As part of the diversionary operation, forty-six Mosquitoes visited Berlin and another eighty-seven flew Mosquito patrols. Post-raid reconnaissance revealed that many parts of the city were hit but that most of the bombing was in open country. Mosquitoes resumed their nightly attacks on Berlin on the night of 20/21 February when, including diversionary and minor operations aircraft, 1,283 sorties were flown. Included in this grand total were sixty-six Mosquitoes of 8 Group that went to Berlin. One of these was B.XVI MM202 'V-Victor', which was flown by Flight Lieutenant Leicester G. Smith RNZAF and his RAF navigator Warrant Officer Bill Lane who were flying their thirty-first operation on 128 Squadron. Smith recalls:

'Our flight time was four hours fifteen minutes. Many and varied are the experiences Bill and I shared over enemy territory, but that evening we certainly had our fair share.

'We were over the 'Big City' at 2010 hours. We had quite a fire raging in the cockpit prior to the release of our 'cookie' and on our bombing run. I didn't realise its importance as, at the time, my attention was on the controls, but seeing the flames a foot in length urgent action was required. At the time we were at 27,000 feet, ahead of schedule by three minutes, so climbed the aircraft for the bombing run. Within a few seconds the cockpit was filled with black smoke following from the flames, which Bill thought at first was from the outside. My first action was to dive the aircraft, thinking incendiary bullets from an enemy fighter had hit us. The flames were out before Bill could use the fire extinguisher and with target indicators ahead, we dropped the 'cookie'. The resulting dive found the aircraft at 22,000 feet, so I turned onto 296° and on the way out an enemy fighter jumped us, as indicated by the white flashing 'Boozer' light in the cockpit. I took evasive action but as nothing happened I climbed back to operational height. All told a very busy five minutes.

'However, I am a little ahead with my story. It had been a wonderful night flying the German skies with, at times, cirrus cloud for protection, but on the whole quite clear. Flying in near Hanover the plotting became serious, as the contrails were plainly visible to the enemy. At 2000 hours I switched over to the main fuel tanks, with 'V-Victor' cruising at a steady 180 knots, while Bill computed his final course to Berlin. In the distance and at operational height, we could plainly see the lights of the advancing Russian army approximately 50 miles away and east from Berlin. To the north the Germans had lit their dummy city, so that before our ETA it was quite a pretty sight. However, with our own red and yellow target indicators clearly visible, on these we bombed Berlin.

'It was during our bombing run that the fire started and so did the problems. In fact, who would feel secure at the thought of bailing out over the 'Big City' with all the 'cookies' bursting. But my chief concern was getting 'V-Victor' back to good flying condition. We had lost 5,000 feet in the dive. At a steady 200 knots and back at 26,000 feet we turned onto a course of 285°. Near Hanover the guns were opening up on the incoming wave of Mosquitoes, one of which nearly hit us. Seeing the black outline rushing towards our aircraft at an incredible speed, I just had time to ease the control column back and fly over the top of the other aircraft. Left to ourselves, the enemy plotting ceased and then was able to enjoy the glory of the German skies. With no navigational equipment serviceable, Bill pinpointed himself over the Dutch coast; the water shone in brilliance, giving perfect relief to the coastline. Over the North Sea we received a Vector from 'Largetype' [a code-word for the controller] to steer 305°, only 20° difference from Bill's original course. We returned to clear sky over England and landed at Wyton at 2153 hours, after circling base for fifteen minutes. Because Gee and Loran navigational aids went unserviceable at the same instant, we assumed the fire was the cause. On return the aircraft was checked and no sign found of a fire from the motors. We were both very relieved and again our faithful friend, 'V-Victor', brought us safely home.'

On 7 March eighty Mosquitoes visited Berlin, ten went to Frankfurt, nine to Münster and five to Hanover. One Mosquito was lost on the Berlin operation.

On 8/9 March, thirty-nine Mosquitoes were dispatched to the 'Big City', thirty-three to Hanover, seven to Hagen and five each to Bremen and Osnabrück. The night following no fewer than ninety-two Mosquitoes went to Berlin and sixteen more went on 'siren tours' of Bremen, Hanover, Osnabrück and Wilhelmshaven. On 10/11 March when no heavies were operating, sixty Mosquitoes were detailed to bomb Berlin, with four each going to Gotha, Jena and Weimar. Nine aircraft including two H2S-equipped Marker aircraft were dispatched by 162 Squadron.

Flying Officer Burgess and Flight Lieutenant Wallis suffered engine problems over the North Sea. The port engine began to give trouble and Burgess decided to shut it down. However, before he could complete the task the starboard engine suddenly began to fail. The crew decided to abort the sortie to Berlin and drop the bomb load on Hamburg. An alteration in course was made and at 2105 the bomb load was released from 24,000 feet over the city. Once clear of Hamburg, a direct course was set for base and on nearing the English Channel was notified of the problem. The aircraft was diverted to Carnaby and the crew made a landing there at 2204.

Flight Lieutenant Abraham and Flight Lieutenant Don Gannon in one of the Marker Mosquitoes on 139 Squadron arrived over Berlin to find the target covered with a layer of alto-stratus topping out at around 20,000 feet. They approached the glow of two sets of TIs which were visible on the cloud and then they made their bombing run from 27,000 feet, releasing three TIs and a 500lb MC bomb on an H2S aiming-point over the cloud. The son of a stockbroker, Donald Herbert Gannon was born on 5 August 1923 at Walthamstow and educated at Enfield County School. He joined the RAF in 1943 and trained as a navigator in Canada. Over a three-month period, he attacked Berlin no fewer than twenty-nine times. He carried out fifty-six bombing operations over Germany and at the end of his tour he was awarded the DFC. (Don would write his name into the record books in 1953 as a member of the two-man crew of the record-breaking Canberra jet bomber that won the London-New Zealand air race that year.)[5]

Flying Officer Rhys and Flying Officer Kennelly saw the first red and yellow floaters go down as they approached at 26,000 feet. TIs were seen going down at one-minute intervals until the defences were active and some flak was put up against the attacking Mosquitoes.

Flying Officer 'Ben' Knights and Flight Sergeant 'Robbie' Robjohns bombed and were hit by a flak burst about thirty seconds later as they completed their camera run. A fragment of flak partly severed a fuel pipe from one of the main inner tanks to the fuel distribution box, causing a fuel leak on the return trip. Knights recalled:

'It was a straightforward trip to the 'Big City' except that we caught a packet in the target area. As was my wont I checked the petrol gauges when I had cleared a difficult passage through heavy flak. Berlin had special flak towers equipped with 120mm AA guns, far out-gunning any other German defences. I never knew at this time but was frequently surprised by the number of small holes picked up on the Berlin raids. On this occasion my caution proved worthwhile as it soon became clear that we were losing fuel quite rapidly. We identified the holed tank and switched over to it to make use of the remainder. It then became a question of whether we could venture across the North Sea. If not, was a friendly aerodrome within reach or would we have to bail out in a suitable area? 'Robbie' had to do the calculations on the elementary computer supplied by the engine-maker and I had to set the engines to the most economical running. We used our VHF to request permission to land at Woodbridge but we were diverted to Coltishall. As it turned out, the main Drem lighting system at Coltishall was out of order and we had to land on the bumpy grass aerodrome by old-fashioned glim lamps.[6] It transpired that Coltishall was used by gun-firing Mosquitoes to intercept low-flying V-1s.'

The second Marker crew of Wing Commander John Derek Bolton and Squadron Leader Peter Henry Waterkeyn suffered a series of major equipment failures as they flew over the English coast. Both the 'Gee' and H2S sets failed. However, the crew decided to press on, Waterkeyn navigating using the compass and DR fixes assisted by the route-markers to reach the target area. They dropped a single 500lb bomb on a cluster of TIs visible beneath the cloud. Leaving the target area, what appeared to be 'dummy' TIs were seen beneath the cloud 10 miles north of the target. As a consequence of the H2S failure the TIs were not released; they were brought home. Flight Lieutenant Haden and Flight Sergeant Nichols, who bombed from 25,000 feet at the same time, saw bomb bursts around one set of TIs. Among them were one or two scattered 'cookie' blasts. Thirty seconds later Flight Lieutenant Goodman and Flying Officer Jarrett dropped their bomb load onto TIs from 26,000 feet. Because of the cloud cover it was impossible to assess the effectiveness or accuracy of the bombing.

March 21st was an almost perfect spring day and that evening some crews flew two sorties when no fewer than 142 Mosquitoes were detailed for two attacks on Berlin. The first wave of 106 Mosquitoes headed off at about 1900 hours and the second wave of a further 36 Mosquitoes following just before 0200 hours. All told, 118 crews got their bomb loads away on the 'Big City'. Seven Mosquitoes of 5 Group dropped mines in Jade Bay and the River Weser and three Mosquitoes visited Bremen. One Mosquito failed to return from the raid on Berlin and another returned early with engine trouble and crash-landed at Upwood. Both crew members survived the crash, but the navigator died of his injuries later in Ely Hospital.

The largest operation ever on Berlin occurred on the night of 21/22 March when 138 Mosquitoes attacked in two waves. It was the thirtieth successive raid on the 'Big City' and PFF HQ had invited the media to visit Wyton: 'All the newspapers and the BBC were there covering the preparations during the day, briefing, take-off and return,' recalls 'Tom' Empson DFC, pilot of 'A-Apple' on 128 Squadron.

'Bert Dwerryhouse and I were on our fourteenth trip to the "Big City". Not much significance in that except that over Berlin we caught a piece of flak in the port motor radiator. We weren't aware of this until it was noticed that the temperature was climbing rapidly. So we had to shut the motor down and feather. Again no big deal except that the motor drove all the nav radar.

'Then it was back home on one motor and Bert's dead reckoning. Down at about 17,000 feet and 150 knots and all lonesome, we attracted more than the usual attention. This we particularly noticed when we wandered over defended towns; we copped the lot. "Boozer" was working overtime, bless it, especially when a fighter beamed on to us. We all but toppled our gyros shaking him off. Called for a QDM when we reckoned we were in range. In spite of Bert's good navigational ability we were surprised to get one from Manston so far south of track so decided not to be heroic and go in there. Next day "Archie" Robinson came down in an Oxford and took us back to Wyton. Reported to the "Wingco" and he said, "Good show, but it would have been much better if you had come home and given the media a bit of drama"! We were not heroic and had forgotten all about the media anyway. We were to do another ten trips to Berlin before the Russian army took over. Towards the end we wore Union Jacks over our Mae Wests and were drilled to shout "Ya Anglicanen" if we bailed out in their vicinity.'

On 27/28 March three Mosquitoes of the Light Night Striking Force were missing from a raid on Berlin. One Mosquito on 692 Squadron was lost without trace and the other two were involved in a collision. Flight Lieutenant Leicester G. Smith RNZAF and his RAF navigator Warrant Officer Bill Lane on 128 Squadron in Mosquito B.XVI MM202 'V-Victor' who were on their forty-fourth op were on the outward leg to Berlin over Holland at 25,200 feet under a full moon when at about 2000 hours they were involved in a collision with Mosquito RV326 of 571 Squadron.

Smith recalls: 'We were waiting for the arrival of the yellow route-markers, which was but a couple of minutes away when the collision occurred. There was a sudden jolt, the sensation of which was like being bounced off a trampoline. The aircraft started to go into a spin to the right with the nose well down and for a time out of control. RV326 spun in, crashing in a cornfield near the village of Zevenhuizen, or Seven Houses, near Groningen.'

The 27-year-old Flying Officer Gordon David 'Huddy' Hudson AFC RNZAF and his 21-year-old Canadian navigator Flying Officer Maurice George Gant, who were on their eleventh consecutive sortie to Berlin, were killed. They were later buried in a single coffin at the local cemetery of Leek. Smith's starboard propeller had been torn away before it could be feathered and it cut a huge hole in the fuselage near the nose and splintered the cockpit windscreen. A small explosion followed and a fire broke out but Smith quickly extinguished it with the graviner and after falling to 16,000 feet Smith was able to jettison his 'cookie' and regain control. He nursed 'V-Victor' back across the North Sea and put down safely at Woodbridge.

Throughout the attack on Berlin the searchlights were active across the city and a jet fighter was spotted in the area on the 128 Squadron bombing run. Flight Lieutenant Jim Dearlove and Sergeant Norman Jackson's Mosquito was coned on the bomb run and it was attacked by an Me 262 of 10./NJG11 just after they had dropped their 'cookie'. He fired two short bursts of cannon fire which missed the Mosquito and Dearlove was able to take evasive action and escape.

Two other Mosquitoes that failed to return were claimed shot down by Me 262 jet fighters. Oberfeldwebel Karl-Heinz Becker flew one of 10./NJG11's three Me 262A-las this night and claimed his sixth victory. At 2138 hours and flying at 27,600 feet Becker clearly saw the RAF aircraft and opened fire at 150 metres while pulling up the nose of his aircraft. He hit the Mosquito squarely. Pulling away to the left, Becker observed large burning parts of the Mosquito falling and scattering the ground near Nauen.

Becker's victim was FB.VI MM131 XD-J on 139 Squadron, which had taken off from Upwood at 1912 hours for Berlin. Squadron Leader Harry A. Forbes DFC RCAF, the navigator/bomb-aimer escaped and was taken prisoner, but no trace has ever been found of his 28-year-old pilot, Flight Lieutenant André Jan Van Amsterdam, a Dutch escapee decorated with the DFC and the Dutch AFC. Harry Forbes recalled:

'Our Mosquito was hit without warning and went into an uncontrollable spiralling descent. André, as captain, gave the signal to bail out. The lower hatch, the normal emergency escape, was jammed and I motioned him to go out the upper hatch above his head. He did; I never saw him again. I followed, hesitating momentarily on the edge before sliding backwards off the wing. Much sooner than I expected I was on the ground, unhurt, in an open field.

'In the darkness, I removed my harness, gathered it up with my parachute and stashed it under nearby bushes and began to move away from the vicinity. André had lived in Germany and knew the language well. My presence could be a liability to him. Finding each other in the dark would be a matter of luck. Feeling very much alone, I started off across some fields and came to a road that I followed. At some point I stopped to remove the badges and insignia from the jacket of my battledress and put them in my pocket. After a time I came to a long straggling village that seemed asleep, except for what appeared to be a small army post. Through an open door I could see some uniformed soldiers. My passing did not arouse attention.

'At the first sign of approaching daylight, I began to look for somewhere to hide. I needed time to rest and to think. I found a haystack that could be reached without going close to houses and hid myself there. A dog barking furiously nearby wakened me. Very quickly a farmer appeared who made unmistakable signs that I should get up and go with him. There seemed no practical alternative, so I walked with him past his house and onto a street through a small village. He attempted to speak to me, but I had no knowledge of German, though one sentence was easily understood and remains with me: Es ist kalt. He took me to what appeared to be a police station, where I was made to wait for some time until a staff car and driver arrived with three Luftwaffe officers and picked me up. Before long the car turned into a lane through open fields to the top of a rise, from which we could see far over the low country around. Alarmed at first, I soon realised they had driven out here to watch what they told me was an attack by the USAAF on Spandau, just west of Berlin and about 30 miles from us.'[7]

'The weather in March 1945 had been much improved,' recalled Jim Foley, 'and I did eleven sorties of which eight were to Berlin. At one period I did three ops in four nights. The second, the CO, Wing Commander Alabaster, asked me to navigate him to Berlin and back; quite an honour and an indication I took of my standing as a navigator. We successfully completed the operation, but on return were unable to land at Downham Market and were diverted to Little Staughton 20 miles away, returning the next day. Towards the end of March our aircraft were modified to carry a 4,000lb bomb, twice the bomb load we had previously carried. In order to carry this 'cookie' it was not possible to close the bomb doors. This meant that once we were airborne it was inadvisable to land still carrying it and orders were to jettison at sea. The take-off technique had to be amended, needing a lot more runway to get off the ground. Excitement at carrying this huge bomb was mixed with slight apprehension, especially when we did it for the first time. Just think, this wooden two-engined aircraft with a crew of two was carrying the same bomb load as a Flying Fortress, which had a large crew and half the load carried by a Lancaster with a crew of seven. What an aircraft. Pound for pound, as they say in the fight game, we were the greatest! Inevitably the target was Berlin for our first 4,000-pounder and I must admit that I was very relieved when we got off the ground safely, as it seemed an eternity reaching take-off speed. When I released the bomb over the target the aircraft gave a noticeable lurch upwards.

'The end of my second tour was in sight and at the end of March I had one op left to do. An historic day for me, 3 April [when ninety-five Mosquitoes went to Berlin, eight to Plauen and five to Magdeburg]. Target: Berlin again and if I successfully completed this one I could look forward to three weeks' leave, getting married and the end of the war in sight. I tried to be blasé but such a lot seemed at stake; recently we had lost a couple of crews including my flight commander. We took off at 2255 carrying the, by now, usual 'cookie'. Everything went well and we returned safely at 3.00am. I had completed eighty-two operations.'

By spring 1945 Thomas Roy Asquith Dow was a squadron leader DFC with more than sixty ops to his name. Virginia 'Peggy' Scott had met her Canadian husband on Saturday, 2 September 1939 at the Maison de Danse in Yarn Lane, Stockton-on-Tees when Roy, from Fort William, Ontario, was on a navigation course nearby. In the heady war-charged atmosphere of the time, Roy and 'Peggy' Scott enjoyed a whirlwind courtship and despite little money (Roy was paid just £21 a month) and with death around every corner, they got married on 9 November. Roy whisked 'Peggy' off in his nimble Morgan Four-Four, painted British Racing Green, for a lightning fifty-six-hour honeymoon in her home town of Newcastle before rejoining his squadron at Thorney Island, Hampshire. He would fly forty-nine ops on Beauforts of Coastal Command and turn down a group captain post in Canada before finally being granted his greatest wish: he wanted to fly the Mosquito. On 23 October 1944 the 139 ('Jamaica') Squadron pilot received the coveted gilt Pathfinder eagle.

'Peggy' waved her husband off from their house close to RAF Upwood on a sunny morning, 3 April. The popular Canadian's red hair was groomed neatly under his RAF cap and his PFF badge shone proudly beneath his RAF wings on his best blue uniform. The one with the faded wings, which he wore on ops, hung, unwanted, in his wardrobe because he was not scheduled to fly that night. Before mounting his bicycle for the short ride to the base, he said, 'I'll be in for dinner, Peggy. Be a good girl!'

Later that day, 'Peggy' heard four Mosquitoes take off and thunder over the house on their nightly operation. 'Peggy' had heard the sound of the Merlins hundreds of times before. On eighty-nine occasions, Roy had come back safely and anyway, hadn't he said he wasn't on ops that night? She only began to worry much later. Lying in bed, she heard three Mosquitoes return. One was missing. She had a premonition that something was wrong. A key turned in the front door and she heard footsteps on the stairs. The bedroom door handle turned. She called out, 'Roy!' He didn't come in. She knew then that her Canadian pilot was dead.

Her husband's Mosquito, one of the Mosquitoes that went to Magdeburg, was navigated by 28-year-old Flight Lieutenant Jack Stuart Endersby. They were shot down and killed by an Me 262 of 10./NJG11. Theirs was the only loss of the night. It was Roy Dow's ninetieth op.

'Peggy' was distraught. Next morning she ran outside into the back garden, a 4lb hammer and a chisel in her hand and destroyed the Anderson shelter Roy and her father had built while on leave. Roy Dow and his navigator were laid to rest in the Olympische Strasse British Cemetery in the Russian Zone in Berlin, after the Russians had given permission for their bodies to be interred there. Endersby left a young pregnant widow, Margaret.

Having only lost one day's flying to weather conditions in March, it came as quite a surprise to 163 Squadron to lose four of the first eight days of the following month to the traditional English weather and to have pretty windy conditions for most of the rest of the time. It was, however, able to mount raids up to 5 April and to start again on the 9th. On that day the Mosquitoes were made ready for a 2200 hours take-off. They were to join a larger group, making a total of fifty-four aircraft. One from another squadron went missing, but the remaining fifty-three got through and hit their primary target.

'It was Berlin again,' wrote 'Bertie' Boulter. 'I counted in my log-book that it would be my sixteenth bombing operation on the German capital. Somehow I began to get the feeling that it would soon be the last. Rumours, whether based on fact or fiction, were flying about the camp and of course fuelled by the newspapers, all claiming victory was in sight. The opposition was becoming less and less and more often than not I was telling the Intelligence officer in the debriefing room that I had seen neither fighters nor flak. I know the other chaps were all saying much the same. This last trip to Berlin followed that pattern. Only Flight Lieutenant Hawley and Flying Officer Richardson saw anything for the whole journey and that was a single burst of tracers that went over their wings. I was teamed up with Flying Officer Howell again for this one and it would be the second of three operations we would fly together. We were last away with a take-off time for KB403 at 2217 hours. One or two crews encountered a few searchlights on the way but we didn't. We all seemed to think we had bombed pretty accurately that night and were rather pleased with ourselves. Two huge explosions in the target area were noted at 0018 hours and 0022 hours; certainly they both appeared to be much bigger than a single or even a multiple bomb burst. We must have hit something pretty effectively.

'Flight Lieutenant Jinks and Flight Lieutenant Ross managed to bring KB518 back with some tail damage, but they had no idea how it happened. Like most of the crews, they heard and saw no opposition the whole way there and back; a most odd situation therefore to come back damaged. It was, however, fully repaired and back on line within forty-eight hours, so it could not have been that serious; though as I mentioned earlier, we had a super ground crew who were not known for letting anything get the better of them.

'Chris was back with me on the 12th when 163 Squadron went back to Berlin again. The weather was fine and getting warmer, though there were a few thunder showers forming in the afternoon, but they came too little by take-off time, which was just before 2200 hours. We had a straightforward run there and back and encountered very little German activity, except for a large scattering of searchlights close to Berlin. They didn't cone us and, chatting to the other pilots after we landed, Bill Jinks was the only one who got coned and then for only two or three minutes before he shook them off. We were back on the conventional four 500-pounders for this one and they would remain our designated ordnance for the remainder of the war – which only had three more weeks to run, though no-one knew that at the time.'

Flight Lieutenant Mike Young and his navigator-observer Flying Officer Ted Jenner flew their first op on 142 Squadron on 11/12 April when 107 Mosquitoes attacked Berlin in three waves. According to Jenner the crew's arrival at Gransden Lodge on 6 April had been a chastening experience. 'On arrival Mike and I were directed to a Nissen hut to dump our kit before seeing Wing Commander Bernard G.D. 'Baz' Nathan. We were greeted by: 'Oh you'll be the replacements. Have these two beds; the bods who had them got the chop last night!' Life, all of a sudden, seemed to become very precious! Watching the take-off with the 'Wingco' later that evening, Lancasters of 405 RCAF at 1930, Mosquitoes at 2030, we were startled by a very large explosion nearby. A 'Mossie' on 692 Squadron had felt obliged to jettison their 'cookie' in the circuit! An evening or two later the crater was observed on a liberty run into Cambridge; impressive tribute to the power of the 4,000-pounder.

'On our first operation the navs were issued with topographical maps of Northern Europe with over-printed 'Gee' lattices. Somehow, we got to the target on time, dropped our 500lb bombs and turned for home. As a 'sprog' flying officer I was fairly alarmed to find 'Gee' so erratic, giving me impossible wind-speeds and ground speeds of over 600 mph. I knew that the 'Mossie' was fast but thought, 'this can't be right!' We got back somehow on time but mentioned the hairy trip at debriefing. It turned out that the problem had arisen due to the Allies' fast advance into Germany, with consequent movement of the mobile 'Gee' transmitters. We had been issued with obsolete maps relating to previous positions. Thereafter, the WAAFs double-checked the maps before issue and we had no further trouble. At breakfast the following morning one of the crews mentioned 'port engine running a bit rough on way home'. It transpired on a visit to dispersal later that an unexploded 20mm cannon shell was buried deep into their port engine boss, much to their surprise! At this time of the war, few of us ever saw an enemy aircraft, but some of them evidently saw us!

'On 19 April we took off for Berlin once more, returning to base after forty-five minutes due to a faulty fuel pump and consequent non-functioning port engine. We knew the Mosquito could fly on one engine but the 'Gee' had also gone u/s and it seemed pointless to press on to the enemy coast. Our debriefing was unpleasant: we had put up a real 'black', so we were told it was no eggs-and-bacon breakfast.'

On 13/14 April meanwhile, twenty-nine Mosquitoes were dispatched to bomb Berlin. One of the 608 Squadron Mosquito XVIs at Downham Market that took part was piloted by Flight Lieutenant George Albert Nunn, who had flown a first tour on Wellingtons, his first being the 1,000-bomber raid on Cologne in May 1942. His navigator, Pilot Officer S.T. 'Harry' Harris DFC, had flown a tour on Lancasters:

'Take-off was at 2309 hours. It was a warm spring night and the aircraft was reluctant to leave the ground as, apart from a full load of fuel, it carried a 'cookie'. A minute later the aircraft staggered into the air and started the long, slow climb to 27,000 feet. As the roof of the crew compartment was Perspex the view from both seats was very good. In addition there was a Perspex blister on the side of the canopy next to the navigator. By putting his head in the blister he could see to the rear of the aircraft. The ability to see behind us was to play a vital part in just over two hours' time. The route was via Clacton, which was reached at 2334 hours. Our height was then 17,000 feet. From there we crossed the sea to reach the enemy coast at Westkapelle at 2354 hours.

'At 2359 hours the heading was changed to fly directly to Berlin. At 0007 cruising level at 27,000 feet was reached and we settled down to another hour's run to the target. It was black all around, although the stars shone brightly above. 'Gee' was working well and fixes were obtained until 0057. The route had taken us north of the Ruhr and then between Hanover and Magdeburg, avoiding the heavily-defended areas of Germany. As we cruised at 310 mph we had no fear of enemy fighters as only jets could get at us and we thought they were few and far between. And they would not bother us when the heavy four-engined bombers were attacking other targets that night, including Magdeburg. We passed 10 miles north of it at 1300 hours. Although we knew there were Mosquitoes all around us heading for Berlin, we saw none. On a previous trip one had crossed only about 30 feet above us, the flames from his exhausts terrifyingly close.

'George and I were no strangers to flak or fighters but there was always some apprehension as the target was approached. Mine came mainly from the thought that I might have made an error in navigation and that at the appointed time there would be no sign of the TIs by the Pathfinder Force going down on the target. Tonight they would illuminate at 0111, 0112, 0113 and 0114 hours. Green coloured markers at 5,000 feet, red at 7,000 feet and yellow at 10,000 feet. The lower the markers the more accurate they ought to be. In the event the first TIs did not show until 0116. At that time I was down in the nose ready to bomb.

'As we spotted the TIs a blue beam flashed across the sky and stayed on our aircraft. This was a master searchlight, controlled by radar and deadly accurate in picking out its victim. Within seconds ten or twelve white searchlight beams lit up our aircraft. For us this was not unusual. Nearly every time we went to Berlin we got coned. The good thing about it was that when I was down in the bombing position I didn't have to fumble around with a torch to set up the bombing instruments. With searchlights it was clearer than day. But that night they came too late to help me, as the bombing run had started. As the searchlights were positioned on the outer areas of Berlin they in no way affected the bombing run. At 0118 I pressed the bomb release and the 'cookie' slipped gently off the bomb rack and sped on its destructive way. The aircraft had to be flown straight and level for the next forty-two seconds. This was the time for the 'cookie' to reach the ground and explode, the aerial camera mounted in the aircraft hopefully photographing the point of impact. At 0119 another group of TIs burst over the target, but by that time the 'cookie' had exploded.'

George Nunn continues: 'The heavies were doing their stuff on Potsdam just outside Berlin. It was fairly spectacular; they seemed to have set fire to everything around. We were caught in the searchlights, having bombed on the markers and turned for home. The area illuminated by searchlights was too big to get out of. It was just a big pool of light made by perhaps fifteen searchlights, with you in the middle. No violent weaving, because that just kept you longer in the cone. Best to get out of the area as fast as you can. The nav was watching behind us and I heard him call, 'Fighter!'

'Harry' Harris continues: 'We made a turn to the left, climbing steadily, until we were heading westwards for home. We did not even try to get out of the searchlight cone, as it would be quite impossible. The flak was below us and then it stopped. As we settled on course for home at 0125 the searchlights suddenly went out. I looked through the blister to the rear of the aircraft and saw we were making extremely thick condensation trails. These are commonly seen today in the wake of high-flying jets and are caused by the heat from the engines condensing the water or ice crystals in the air into clouds, very white clouds, streaming out behind the aircraft.

'As I looked behind I saw a red and a green light just above our contrail. I said to George: 'Some idiot is flying with his navigation lights on and is following behind us.' As I said this I realised the lights were gaining on us very fast. I then knew it was not one of ours but the dreaded German jet. At that moment a white light appeared between the red and green lights from the nose of the aircraft. As it did I shouted 'Dive to starboard. Go!'

'Simultaneously three things happened. The searchlights from the ground came on, bathing our aircraft in dazzling light. Secondly, George flung the Mosquito over to the right, pushing its nose hard down. And thirdly, a hail of coloured lights came across the top of the canopy. The fighter was firing and had just missed the cockpit, the cannon shells and tracer bullets missing us by inches. George said a rude word and pulled the aircraft over to the left. The change of attitude must have been sufficient for the light cone to flood the cockpit.'

George Nunn recalls: 'I got slightly blinded. The next thing I knew we were upside-down. The nav was not strapped in because he had been down in the nose, bombing. So, at that moment, he was up against the roof, all the gyros had toppled and so the instruments went berserk.'

Harris adds: 'As the aircraft was pushed around by George, I lost all sense of direction or attitude. I was forcibly shot out of my seat and crashed into the top of the Perspex canopy. Then I was floating in the cockpit. Also floating was my parachute, which I grabbed and clipped onto my parachute harness. This harness was worn before entering the aircraft and the parachute itself was stowed in a special container in the bomb-aimer's position. The violent movements of the aircraft had dislodged it. It has two 'D' rings, which clip onto two hooks on the harness and the parachute was then in place on the chest, ready to jump. As I clipped on the parachute George said very quietly: 'I can't see. I've been blinded by the searchlights. Bail out, quickly.' Having assured me that he would follow me out, I scrambled down to the nose, where the escape hatch was situated. It consisted of a square hole in the floor, with a door on the inside floor and another on the other side. This was the normal method of entry and exit. I found the handle, but I could not budge the door. Suddenly it was pitch black. The searchlight had gone out.

'I cursed then, as I could not see and I could not open the escape hatch, possibly due to the twisting action of the aircraft or due to pressurisation. I gave it up and went back to George. He was still in his seat. As the aircraft turned over slowly, I saw fire through the top of the cockpit. I was looking down at the ground and the fires were the result of the heavy bomber attack on Potsdam. I asked George if he could see. He had closed his eyes to try to get his vision back. As several minutes had passed since he was blinded, I asked him if he would open his eyes and look for the fires. Fortune was with us as he saw the red light of the fires, now on his left side. Using the fires as reference, he slowly and carefully brought the aircraft on to a level keel. The instruments on the flight panel were useless. All the gyro-operated ones were spinning furiously, including the artificial horizon and compass. A careful reading of the altimeter, still moving erratically, showed the height as 20,000 feet. Then, checking even more carefully, we found it to be 2,000 feet; only 1,600 feet above the ground. A check on my watch showed it was fifteen minutes since evasive action had started. The Mosquito had descended at about 2,000 feet per minute, so luckily for us it must have stayed level or even gained height at times.

'Using burning Potsdam as a datum, I was able to give George a direction to go for England and then we climbed hurriedly away, shaken but undismayed. As the gyros settled we were able to resume normal flight and 110 minutes later were over base. An inspection of the aircraft on the ground showed a hole through the rudder and through the tail fin from a cannon shell. Following this line of sight, it missed the cockpit by an estimated 3 inches. There was no trace of any other hits. While on the staff of the RAF Flying College in 1955 I read a report by a German pilot of an Me 262. On 15 April 1945 he shot down a Mosquito just north of Berlin at 0130 hours. Apparently he couldn't follow us down!'

George Nunn commented: 'I flew back on the Turn and Bank Indicator until the instruments recovered. We were minus half the tail, but this didn't affect the flying qualities of the aircraft.'

The Boulter/Hart crew did an NFT on KB395 on the 15th and again on the 16th prior to yet another run to Berlin in their favourite plane, KB403. One plane was seen going down in flames near the Dutch coast, but all 163's aircraft made it home. The raid was deemed a success as most crews witnessed good bombing concentrations and a lot of smoke and fires in the target area. They also noticed that the Russians were being a real nuisance to the defending Germans and many fires were burning fiercely along their wide advancing front. 'Bertie' and Chris encountered the odd burst of flak here and there, but were complimentary on debrief about the accuracy of the TIs that night.

On the night of the 19th/20th seventy-nine Mosquitoes went to Berlin again and thirty-five more visited Wittstock airfield while eight went to Schleswig airfield. Another forty Mosquitoes flew patrol sorties and thirty-four RCM heavies also put in an appearance. All 196 aircraft returned safely.

The Boulter/Hart crew was on the battle order for the operation to Berlin on the night of the 20th/21st when seventy-six Mosquitoes carried out six separate attacks on the 'Big City' (and a force of thirty-six Mosquitoes attacked the airfield at Oberschleissheim just a few miles north of Munich).

'Little did we know,' wrote 'Bertie' Boulter, 'that it would be the last raid on that battered city and our last in dear old KB403. We did the NFT that afternoon in some decent weather, but with the real threat of thunderstorms approaching according to the met men. We took off just before 2200 hours and got back a little after 0200 hours. There was a bit more flak about in the target area this time, mainly as we turned after the bomb run and headed for home. It seemed to explode either behind us or way above us and fortunately for us none was anything like close. We thought maybe it was one of the sites we heard that had been manned by schoolchildren and they were less accurate than the experienced adult crews. I guess we'll never know. We did see some explosions on the ground near the target though, so I suspect we were successful again. It was on this trip that Chris and I did actually get to see our first Me 262 jet fighter at long last. Everyone else on the squadron seemed to have seen at least one or more, long before we did. Chris and I were getting to feel that even the ground crew back at Wyton would get to see them before we did.'[8]

Flying Officers A.C. Austin and P. Moorhead flying Mosquito XVI ML929 claimed the last bombs dropped on the 'Big City' when they released four 500-pounders at 0214 hours GMT. All told, 114 Mosquitoes were abroad this night, with 36 of the 'Wooden Wonders' attacking Schleissheim airfield and two on patrol duty. All the Mosquitoes and three heavies on RCM duty returned safely.

In the period January to May 1945 LNSF Mosquitoes flew almost 4,000 sorties over the dwindling Reich for the loss of fifty-seven Mosquitoes shot down or written off. No opportunity, it seemed, was missed to wake up the harassed inhabitants of Berlin and the LNSF bombed the 'Big City' on sixty-one nights running (the last on 20/21 April 1945), but the main purpose was for the BBC to be able to announce to the world that 'aircraft of the RAF have bombed Berlin for another consecutive night.'

Altogether, 8 Group's squadrons flew 28,215 sorties, yet they had the lowest losses in Bomber Command – just 108 (about one per 2,800 sorties) – while 88 more were written off on their return because of battle damage. This is an incredible achievement; even more remarkable when one considers that well over two-thirds of operations were flown on nights when the heavies were not operating. The greater proportion of Bomber Command airmen who failed to return – 38,462 – were RAF. Next highest loss was the Royal Canadian Air Force with 9,919 personnel. On every night of every operation, wives and girlfriends, friends and family prayed that it was not their loved one that had 'bought it' or 'gone for a Burton' or 'got the chop', as death was termed in the idiom of the day.

On the night of 2/3 May, 'Bertie' Boulter (who had flown nineteen operations to Berlin), James Duncan and Charles Parker all flew their fiftieth operations when they took part in an attack by 116 Mosquitoes from 8 squadrons in 8 (PFF) Group on Kiel. Appropriately, they had the honour of flying on this, the last Bomber Command raid of the war.

Chapter Twenty

The Cost of Victory

'If we are victorious in one more battle with the Romans, we shall be utterly ruined.'
Plutarch.

In England on the early morning of 14 April 1945, rear gunner Flight Sergeant Lawrence 'Nick' Nicholson was sitting around the 35 PFF Squadron mess at RAF Graveley waiting for his discharge to come through. When war broke out in 1939 'Nick' was 14 years old and living in Hull. He had left school the previous year, when his father died aged just 38, to become the family breadwinner, taking a job working as a delivery boy for the local chemist. As it turned out, he was a German sympathizer who took great delight in telling everyone that the Germans would 'be here any day now and that it was simply pointless to fight or resist'. One morning 'Nick' was told to clean off a large swastika someone had painted on his shop window the previous night and he had decided, there and then, that the chemist could stick his job! The next week 'Nick' started a new job at the Blackburn Aircraft factory in Brough, deciding that, as soon as he possibly could, he would join the RAF. At age 16 he and his two best pals decided they would all join up; that way they could choose which service they entered rather than await the 'call-up' and be put wherever the Ministry of Defence decided.

One of the boys was accepted into the army and the other became a naval Commando. 'Nick', on the other hand, was rejected on the grounds of being unfit. He had contracted TB in his early teens, which had left him rather weak and short of breath and he failed one of the tests which involved blowing into a tube and holding his breath and a column of mercury at a certain level for sixty seconds. He had returned home feeling totally devastated, but that evening he noticed an advert in the local paper which read: 'Charles Atlas, holder of the title "The World's Most Perfectly Developed Man" – founder of the fastest health, strength and physique-building system known.'

The next day 'Nick' wrote off to Mr Atlas explaining his predicament and to his surprise he enrolled him in his twelve-week correspondence course, which obviously worked because exactly three months later 'Nick' was passed 'A1+' and accepted for RAF air crew. 'Nick' crewed-up in October 1943 but by March 1944 during local night flights, bombing practice and cross-country firing exercises his pilot was exhibiting a curious habit of urinating all over the wireless-operator who was positioned below him in the Halifax and so the crew refused to fly with him.

It was a stroke of good fortune when they were allocated a new pilot, a brilliant New Zealander by the name of Pilot Officer Louis Basil 'Kiwi' Lawson DFC who was born in Auckland on 13 February 1913.

'"Kiwi" was older than the rest of us, probably about thirty,' wrote 'Nick', 'and already an exceptional pilot and so, when he volunteered for the Pathfinder

Force he asked the rest of the crew if we wanted to come along with him. I hadn't even heard of the Pathfinders but it seemed like a good idea at the time and so I went along with it. The next thing I knew we were all off to 1652 Pathfinder Conversion Unit at Warboys where I was introduced to the other exceptional thing that saved my bacon throughout the war, the magnificent Lancaster bomber. And so it was that in early July of 1944 we all arrived at 35 Squadron, Pathfinder Force based at Graveley in Cambridgeshire, which was to become our home for the next eleven months.'

On 3 April 1945 'Nick' had flown his fifty-second trip, to Nordhausen, and with the war almost at an end, he and the rest of the crew began to disperse. However, eleven days later, in the mess, when the Station Gunnery Officer Squadron Leader Cedric Alexander Fraser-Petherbridge came up to him and casually said: 'We're short of a gunner, would you care to join us in the briefing room?' 'Nick' thought: 'Well, what could a 19-year-old flight sergeant possibly say to a squadron leader when asked such a direct question, other than "Yes sir"?'

At Mepal near the Ouse Washes in the heart of the Fens, just over 5 miles west of Ely, twenty-five crews on 75 Squadron RNZAF also found themselves on the battle order on 14 April. In June 1943 the New Zealand Squadron was the airfield's first operational occupants flying Stirlings initially and then Lancasters. Flying Officer Allan Ralph Baynes' Lancaster crew had only arrived at Mepal on 1 April and they might have been forgiven for hoping for an easier introduction to ops. Still, the war could not go on forever and the end must surely be nigh? Allan Melrose Sliman, the Scottish flight engineer known as Jack, was born on 27 February 1906 in Busby in Renfrewshire. Apprenticed as a carpenter, he was also a talented footballer and he turned professional. By September 1943 he either joined up or was mobilized into the RAF. He was then 36 and married. Now, finally, at age 39 he would fly his first bombing operation of the war.

At Faldingworth in 1 Group which had something of a reputation of having the worst runways in Lincolnshire, pilots saying that it was built on boggy land and it was this which caused the undulations in the main runway, 300 'Masovian' Squadron did not mind. The Poles were happy so long as they achieved their solitary aim of attacking the enemy and Berlin in particular. The capital of the Third Reich was Sergeant Henryk Drożdż's particular goal. He was the flight engineer on Lancaster 'R-Roger' captained by Flight Lieutenant Jan Kozicki. Born on 8 March 1920 on a farm in the village of Zastów near Warsaw, Henryk's first few years were spent in training for ground crew duties in various stations in England and in learning English. Yet his dearest wish was to fly and in July 1944 this wish became reality when he graduated with flight engineer's wings.

His legs had shaken on 29 November 1944 when he learned that it was to be his first sortie and his heart stopped when in the briefing room he saw on the map eight sinister letters of their destination: 'Dortmund'. Twenty-eight ops later Henryk had still not fulfilled his goal. Berlin had not been bombed since March 1944 and he was disappointed that the authorities had brought down the number of sorties from thirty-five to thirty so the chances of bombing the 'Big City' again before the war ended seemed remote. 'The strategic mission of Bomber Command was almost complete,' he wrote, but when he entered the briefing room on 14 March his hair stood on end, for the flag marking that day's target was pinned to Potsdam, a suburb in the Berlin defence zone. Henryk prayed that nothing might happen to cancel this flight such as adverse weather conditions, and if this was to be his last, then it could not have given him more satisfaction. There were no latecomers; a sort of suppressed excitement was in the air.

The old seat of Prussian power, Potsdam was a residence of the Prussian kings and the German Kaiser until 1918. Its planning embodied ideas of the Age of Enlightenment: through a careful balance of architecture and landscape Potsdam was intended as 'a picturesque, pastoral dream' which reminded its residents of their relationship with nature and reason. Potsdam had only been bombed once before, by the Eighth Air Force on 21 June 1944 when Babelsberg, once considered Europe's Hollywood, and the Teltow suburb were targeted.

'Nick' Nicholson discovered at his briefing that his pilot and master bomber was the new CO, Group Captain Hugh James Felce 'Speed' Le Good DFC AFC. His DFC had been gazetted only the day before. Born in 1912 at Wandsworth and educated at Alleyna School, Dulwich and Emmanuel School, Wandsworth, he had served in the Territorial Army before being commissioned in the RAF in August 1932. Le Good had been awarded the AFC on 11 June 1942 for services in northern Queensland, where his wife Jean was living. On the night of 13/14 February on Dresden Le Good was deputy to the master bomber, Squadron Leader Charles Peter Crauford de Wesselow DFC.

Predictions were that over Germany on 14/15 April there should be no cloud and visibility would be good. Five hundred Lancasters of Nos 1 and 3 Groups (and 12 Mosquitoes of 8 Group) were detailed to bomb Potsdam, code-named 'Crayfish', in what would be the last raid of the war by a major Bomber Command force on a German city. A few days earlier, a reconnaissance aircraft had taken aerial photographs of Potsdam and four strike points around the city centre were identified. The aiming-point was in the centre of this box. The main target was the main railway station from where many units of the Wehrmacht went to the Oder front to stop the advance of the Red Army and the intention was also to destroy the local barracks (depot of the old German Guards regiments). These, however, were of little military interest and in any event the Hauptbahnhof was on the edge of the target area.

A diversionary force of 24 Lancasters and 4 Mosquitoes were to attack Cuxhaven, a seaside town on Germany's North Sea coast and 62 Mosquitoes of the LNSF would bomb Berlin with 10 more going to Wismar. Nos 515 and 23 Squadrons would fly the first Mosquito master bomber sorties in 100 (Special Duties) Group dropping green TIs and orchestrating attacks by eighteen Mosquitoes on 141 and 169 Squadrons carrying Napalmgel bombs in the first of a series of operations code-named 'Firebash' on night-fighter airfields at Neuruppin near Potsdam and Jüterbog near Berlin. (Napalmgel is petrol thickened with a compound made from aluminium, naphthenic and palmitic acids, hence 'napalm'. White phosphorous is added for ignition.)

Another fifty-two Mosquitoes and fifty-four RCM aircraft in 100 (Special Duties) Group were detailed to fly fighter patrols and employ electronic jamming of enemy radars respectively over the diminishing Reich territory. One of these,

171 Squadron at North Creake on the North Norfolk coast, which operated Halifax bombers, was commanded by Wing Commander Michael William Renaut DFC who had just completed a spell on Halifaxes in the Middle East on 76 Squadron. Born on 29 September 1920, he joined the RAF as a bomber pilot in August 1940. He and Sergeant John William Holbrook Harwood were the first pilots to drop an 8,000lb 'Blockbuster' bomb over Germany during a raid over Essen on the night of 10/11 April 1942.[1] He was also famous for being able to write the Lord's Prayer on the back of a postage stamp!

'Our aircraft was equipped with about forty wireless transmitters for jamming purposes,' wrote Renaut,[2] 'and we formed what was known as a "Mandrel" screen across the entry to enemy territory. This screen effectively jammed all the "Hun" radio frequencies with the result that the bomber stream was able to fly through the screen and they wouldn't be plotted by the enemy until they were actually over enemy or enemy-occupied territory. Until 100 Group started operations the bomber stream was plotted over England soon after take-off and the "Hun", by radar, was able to plot the course of the bombers and guess fairly accurately which was to be the target. In those days of late 1943 and early 1944 the technique of dummy thrusts and attacking more than one target was unheard of and the "Hun" was taking a very heavy toll.

'Our Halifaxes were also modified to take "Window", which, when dropped from an aircraft, looked like a bomber stream on the enemy radar screen, and there was a chute fitted so that the operator could throw out tons of "Window" at a given signal. This chucking-out of "Window" was more difficult than it sounds: it involved the wireless operator heaving out literally a ton of paper in 28lb packets; no mean feat in the bitter cold of the fuselage and at oxygen height! We knew from our Intelligence service in Europe that these tactics were very successful and quite often the Hun mistakenly plotted two or three Halifaxes dropping "Window" as a major force approaching a target and diverted his night-fighters to the assumed route. For this reason the work was dangerous and my few aircraft often were set upon by night-fighters since they only numbered half a dozen or so.

'This job of ours was reasonably safe and I can't honestly say that I was as frightened as I had been on any of my trips on the first tour. As Squadron Commander I didn't want to pick my operations for fear that I might select the easy targets and be criticised for it, so I used to tell my Adjutant that I would fly on such a date on operations and take pot luck with the target. If it was a tough or an easy one, at least I hadn't selected it. My fears began to build up again and I had so much more to lose now with an attractive wife whom I adored and a child on the way I simply hated the thought of flying on operations over Germany but there was no one I could turn to and I had to bottle up my fears like everyone else. I wanted to discuss my feelings with someone but one was lonely and comparatively aloof as a squadron commander and the last thing was to show that one had nerves. As a squadron commander I missed the chatter and leg-pulling in the locker room before an op – I had to change in my office on the edge of the perimeter track and it was there, in complete privacy, that I was able to get into my long combs! I used to dislike being alone with my thoughts and I used to change pretty quickly (after the Lord's Prayer) and get out to join my crews.

'On 28 December I had done my first operation of my second tour and was part of a "Mandrel" Screen on the German border. During February I carried out three "Mandrel" operations and three trips to Kiel, Berlin and Potsdam in quick succession. Apart from a good deal of flak near the heavily-bombarded targets I was comparatively fear-free. However, 100 Group now had the idea that we should carry bombs as well as "Window" and this was going to make our task more hazardous. In other words the main bomber stream were to come through the screen at one point and we were to act as a diversion numbering only a dozen aircraft to some target like Stuttgart. This was bound to draw the night-fighters and I knew that my squadron losses were going to increase. To date I had only lost a handful of crews and morale on the squadron was high – replacements were arriving steadily but not at a pace, thank God, and we were a very happy and a fairly efficient unit.

'On 14 April I briefed my crews for operations on Berlin and the Main Force was to attack a target close at hand [Potsdam]. We carried bombs this time and about 2 tons of "Window" so it looked like being a warm trip. I cannot express the thoughts that went through my mind that night. This was to be our first trip with bombs and Berlin was very heavily defended, we knew.'

'After briefing and normal preparations when we were loaded like camels, we drove to the planes,' wrote Sergeant Henryk Drożdż, 'and after doing my "inspection" I boarded the plane (always the first on and last after the flight); that was my function. Take-off came at 1817 precisely. Our full capacity was 67,000lb, including a bomb load of 11,000lb.'

At 1839 hours the Lancaster with the Master Bomber, 'Speed' Le Good started up and was followed two minutes later by the deputy master bomber. At Downham Market, as 'Nick' Nicholson was about to clamber into his usual rear gunner position, he was tapped on the shoulder by Squadron Leader Fraser-Petherbridge who said, in a very friendly manner, 'That's all right, you go in the mid-upper for a change, I'll take the rear.'[3]

'There were no hitches as Pilot Officer Wadzio Kossowski charted our course,' continues Henryk Drożdż, 'climbing over Reading and then, at Beachy Head, reaching 18,000 feet. I looked down on the fading English landscape and said a silent "goodbye" – if I should not return, I left her my love and admiration.

'The blue ribbon of the English Channel now appeared before us and soon, the coastline of the Continent. We had lapsed into silence. It was our unwritten but golden rule. Each man must concentrate on the job at hand and whatever he felt privately, dedicate himself to the success of the mission and the welfare of the rest of the crew. The four Merlin engines, with their rhythmic purr, were the only sounds to dominate that strange and enclosed environment. About us and around us were more Lancasters, the light still good enough to discern their darkening silhouettes. Like a drone of deadly wasps, 426 aircraft were heading to their target. The years between have seen devastation such as we could never have dreamed, we earnestly wished we could end it all … we knew it could only come from the destruction of the enemy. My consolation lay in the fact that this hope of a speedy end to the war was shared by all of us there that night… I was not alone.

'After we reached the French coast, we changed course, heading due east for Frankfurt. So far the flight had been peaceful. We moved on, uneventfully. Then there was change – searchlights, flares and occasional artillery fire. The weather started to break – formations of tiny clouds mushroomed around us. It was fairly cloudy, which increased the risk of collision, so you had to be more watchful. Just before Frankfurt, the navigator told our skipper to alter course, so many degrees to the left and to climb a further 1,000 feet to reach 19,000 feet, which was going to be our bombing height. These manoeuvres were carried out and then we were heading for Kassel and Misburg – previous targets of ours, but not that night! These changes of course were part of our defensive tactics to throw the enemy into confusion as to our real target. At 52 degrees longitude, we were now on our last leg to the target, with Magdeburg to starboard.'

At 2201 hours the first aerial combat took place between Paderborn and Kassel and at 2213-2215 hours the diversionary attack was carried out on Cuxhaven. The leading Lancasters were already in the airspace over Hanover/Brunswick. At about 2215 the air-raid warning alarm was sounded in Potsdam as the Germans realized that the Lancasters were clearly on the way to Potsdam or Berlin. Untouched and just a few miles from Berlin, Potsdam had so far escaped major bombing and when the sirens sounded, many of its residents assumed the target to be once again Berlin and failed to take cover, even emerging from their homes to watch the bombers go over.

Between 2220 and 2233 hours, an RCM Halifax arrived over Potsdam. Wing Commander Renaut's mid-upper gunner, Sergeant Feasy wrote: 'I can remember quite well the trip on 14th April 1945, which was most exciting. The crew were Flight Sergeant 'Rusty' Willis, wireless-operator; Flight Sergeant McDonald, special wireless-operator to throw out the 'Window'; Flying Officer James, a newly-commissioned Canadian who was rear gunner; and myself, mid-upper. Shortly after take-off which was at 1835 hours, the rear gunner's intercom went u/s, after which we heard nothing from him until our return to base. We carried 5,750lb of incendiary clusters and HE, with the rest of the load made up of 'Window'.

'The trip to Berlin was uneventful – I think the engineer, Wireless Operator Gold, saw what looked like a fighter some distance off which didn't interfere. On reaching Potsdam which was about the spot where we dropped our load, we were suddenly coned by about six searchlights; several more immediately caught on until we must have had sixteen or more on us. I think we were all practically blinded but it was then that I think an Me 410 was sighted on the port beam. You were weaving violently and I remember calling to you to corkscrew. The fighter opened fire on us from quite a distance and the cannon fire passed over the top of us. I can remember calling over the intercom to you to dive first port and then up starboard, thinking that I could see the lights from a better position than you, thereby getting in a more favourable spot.

'We were coned for thirteen minutes altogether and you were weaving and diving all the time, in fact you were breathing and puffing hard from exertion. We then had another attack from the starboard side by a Ju 88 which I personally didn't see until the cannon fire went under the starboard wing. It was after this that you made a masterly move. You were at the top of a climb when you saw a fighter apparently making a head-on attack. This must have been the Fw 190. At the moment of seeing the aircraft, I remember you telling us that you kicked the rudder or did some yawing movement which made our Halifax yaw sideways at the exact moment the fighter opened fire on us. The cannon shells went under the port wing.

'This was confirmed by 'Rusty' Willis afterwards who laughingly told us that he was itching to see what was going on outside his WOp's cabin and at the moment he pulled back his little side curtain he was in time to see the cannon shells go screaming past his side window. He hurriedly pulled the curtain closed again! Miraculously we were not hit in any of these attacks.

'I always remember calling out to you, 'Up starboard, dive to port', hoping that it'd help. I often wondered afterwards why you never told me to shut up, but I felt quite exhilarated. It was all this weaving which I believe made us short of fuel. I fired my guns once during this period at a fighter which was way up above; I remember this because I could only just elevate them sufficiently to get a sight. My fire, of course, went nowhere near. After that I think we just flew out of the searchlight belt and made for home.'

Several times during that encounter Renaut felt sure that he was going to be shot down. 'I thought of my poor darling Yvonne hearing the news that we were 'missing believed killed'. My mouth went dry at the first attack and I literally felt my hair standing on end during the excitement in the target area. The strange thing was that although I was scared out of my wits, I managed to remain calm and hoped that my skill as a bomber pilot would out-manoeuvre the comparatively inexperienced night-fighter pilots on my tail.

'No one who hasn't been through this sort of night raid can possibly know what went on in one's mind – it was a mixture of jumbled thoughts, fears, apprehension and sheer terror all rolled into one. One felt so naked and exposed when coned by searchlights and it was as though one was on a stage with the arc lamps upon one. No amount of twisting and turning could rid one of the searchlights; they passed one on mile after mile and minutes seemed like years.

'I had innumerable fears as a bomber pilot but none so horrific as those of attacks by night-fighters. It was the knowledge that one was immediately at a disadvantage that frightened one. The more skilled and experienced night-fighter pilots would press home their attacks ruthlessly and in the face of strong opposition from the rear and mid-upper gun turrets and I think I was lucky throughout that my many attacks by night-fighters were not those of expert or experienced men. Maybe they were and maybe my violent evasive action was enough to send them in search of an easier victim – I shall never know. All I remember is that nothing in life has frightened me more and when one has lived through that sort of terror one could surely live through anything. The fact that it was never spoken about in the Mess was significant – men faced up to this fear and were always ready to go out and meet it. Death was just around the corner and one almost got used to it.'

At 2239 hours marking the target began on the order of 'Speed' Le Good, the master bomber. Bombs began falling on the target area a minute later and a reddish explosion with a huge pall of black smoke rising up to 4,000 feet was observed. The intersection of lakes in the vicinity was identified visually with red TIs just south of it. PFF marking was described as 'good', although some green TIs fell in the south-western lake, but were cancelled by the master bomber, whose instructions were 'good but faint at times through interference'.

Henryk Drożdż's heart was hammering at the thought of nearing the target: 'The enemy below was prepared – flak became intense and too many searchlights scoured the sky. Up went one's blood pressure. The crucial time would soon be to hand, as beneath us, we saw that all hell had been let loose. The Pathfinders had done their job well. It took place on the ground and in the air amidst hundreds of searchlights and flares and smoke. The 'markers' went down – there were masses of little red stars. Streams of fire dotted the earth below.

'Now the planes one after another arrived over the target. The passing moments seemed like hours and we were still not over the target. The speed is 170 mph and it seems to me like a snail's pace. Artillery is ever nearer, I get up from my seat and draw my parachute closer – my one hope of salvation. My legs shook, the searchlights had found us, but we ducked slightly and flew on. Not long now, artillery blasts all the time, thousands of flashes all around us and on the ground exploding 'cookies'. We were near; we could see the target – the city – quite clearly. The artillery was going mad, firing straight at us – we won't escape. A plane on the right, another on the left - Attention! Artillery from the right, another second – God – the plane was being tossed about, but we could see all the streets of the city as if it was daylight. For us, there was no longer any difference between earth and air; both were consumed with fire, light and death. Just as the flak found its target in front of us, we were caught in the relentless beam of a searchlight … it pierced the cabin and made daylight in the cockpit. We couldn't escape it; its brilliance had trapped us and we couldn't shake it away.

'We were the target now. But the voice of our skipper was calm as he ordered '3,000 revs, plus 14 boost' – maximum speed! Then Wladek Januc the bomb-aimer's voice took over, giving the pilot instructions: 'Left, left … bomb doors open … left again, now … steady … steady … steady.' Now we were over the centre of the city – 'bombs gone' at 2251 hours in good visibility. We felt the familiar jerk and a sense of relief as the 4,000lb HC and ten x 500lb MCs [Medium Capacity] were released on the centre of red TIs.

'Now, we had to make our way home.

'A strong toss of the plane and we dived down on full throttle: 19,000 feet, 18,000 feet, 17,500 feet … diving rapidly and gaining speed, 200 mph! Still artillery blasts but not so accurately. We were saved, but don't drop our guard. Januc reported that a friendly Lancaster very near passed us on our right, racing us home. The flak was still heavy, but it was getting further and further behind us. Clouds appeared and we were anxious. We entered the clouds which was dangerous but unavoidable at this height. There were still a great many aircraft in the sky, including German fighters, waiting to get us on the way back. But we emerged from the milky clouds, breathed a sigh of thanks and made haste for home. Coffee was passed round from the flask and we congratulated the skipper and each other. I worked on the petrol consumption calculations – everything was working normally.'

At 2245 hours the master bomber corrected the bombing, which had started to 'creep back' to the west. Smoke and bombing was right on the red TIs; four fires spreading later into one conflagration with much smoke. Some 'cookies' were seen to burst in the town. Four explosions, including a large orange one with black smoke, were seen at approximately 2257 hours when an ammunition train exploded in the main station. Moderate to intense heavy flak in barrage form burst below aircraft and crews reported 'numerous searchlights'. Five or six fighters were seen, but no combats. At 2300 hours the master bomber left Potsdam and the raid ended. The attack was considered 'most successful'. At 2316 hours the last late-comer left Potsdam where the fires caused by 1,780 tons of bombs could be seen for 50 miles on the return journey.

The 'Firebash' diversionary raids proved successful and from 2315 to 2321 hours the diversionary attack by sixty-two Mosquitoes on Berlin and between 2331 and 0006 hours, the diversionary attack on Wismar by ten Mosquitoes were carried out. One of the Mosquitoes was crewed by Bill Henley and Sergeant Johnnie Clark on 571 Squadron at Oakington, who recalled:

'We turned towards the north-east and headed for the 'Big City'. The TIs went down on time and I noticed another bunch on my left. Potsdam was being marked for the main force of 'heavies'. They were operating much lower than we were. Then the searchlights came into play. First the bluish ones, operating singly and radar-controlled, wandered haphazardly, or so it seemed. Suddenly, one of them darted sideways and caught a Lanc in its beam. The Lanc dived and wriggled left and right, but hadn't a hope as twenty or thirty other searchlights immediately lit the sky around it. It was caught in a wigwam of light. Then the sparks of flak began to burst around the aircraft. Some of the flak shells must have hit the starboard wing, for within a minute flames were rolling over the wing and the Lanc started to spin round and down ever so slowly, I thought. I heard myself yelling into the microphone which was clamped to my face: 'Bail out, you stupid bastards. You haven't a hope. Don't you know you're on fire?'

'As if they had heard me, the silk parachutes began to appear in the searchlight beams. I started to count them – one, two, three – then no more. Four hadn't made it. As if to underline the whole affair which was unfolding, the aircraft seemed to disintegrate as it went down. The three parachutes hung like stationary mushrooms in the cone of light. Just then there was a flash and what looked like an explosion. Two aircraft must have collided in mid-air. There would be no parachutes coming out of that, I reckoned.'

The first Lancaster Johnnie Clark saw was probably 'K-King' on 35 Squadron piloted by Flying Officer V.B. Bowen-Morris. He was unable to feather the port outer engine which caught fire in the vicinity of the target, and he ordered his crew out near the target area. The navigator Flying Officer Raymond Herbert Harvey Dyer and Flight Sergeants E.G. Silcock, air bomber, C.S. Gibbon, wireless-operator and E. Meredith DFM, air gunner, bailed out and were captured, interrogated and imprisoned. The remains of the flight engineer, Sergeant William Graham Reynolds, were never located and his name is commemorated on the Runnymede Memorial.

The other air gunner, Flight Sergeant J.W. Tovey bailed out and after two days of walking westwards on his own ran into a party of French prisoners of war. He was taken to their camp at Schiamiertz where the Germans did not notice him as there was no organization in the camp. After four days he walked out with two soldiers and continued south until they met the American First Army at Grimma not far to the north-west of Colditz five or six days later.[4] Bowen-Morris prepared to make his own escape, but the engine fire went out and he was able to regain control and he continued to fly the aircraft for two hours before the starboard inner overheated and he bailed out over Holland.[5]

The Lancaster that Clark presumed was lost as the result of a collision had probably collided with a fighter as no claims were acknowledged by the Luftwaffe high command. After the bomber was coned in the searchlights it was seen on fire by PoWs at Stalag IIIA Luckenwalde only 40 kilometres from Potsdam and 52 kilometres south of Berlin who had a grandstand view of the raid. One of the observers, Bob Hall, recounted: 'Bomber Command had a target just 15 miles from here – a huge force was in on the attack around midnight. I have never seen anything to compare with it – it was very much too close for comfort. I was scared stiff and I don't mind admitting it. It's much safer upstairs.'

Lancaster I RF143 'O-Orange' on 138 Squadron, recently transferred from Special Duties, which had taken off at 1813 hours from Tuddenham in Suffolk crashed at Drewitz, 6 kilometres south-west of Potsdam. It was flown by 23-year-old Flying Officer Granville Horsaman of Atwick, Yorkshire who was killed. The only man to survive was the air bomber, Flying Officer J.W. Neve. Horsaman left a widow, Catherine Mary Horsaman.[6]

As Flight Lieutenant Jan Kozicki's crew flew home Sergeant Henryk Drożdż noted, 'Frankfurt again and now, we retraced the course which had brought us in. At 0245 we saw the illuminated letters 'FH' on the runway beneath and we were home – this was our greeting when there was no air-raid – Faldingworth. We had been in the air for eight and a half hours and had journeyed 1,500 miles, using 1,174 gallons of petrol, of which 440 gallons were left in the tank. Our bombs had been dropped at 2250 precisely and later, our cameras were to show that they had been dropped accurately on target. 'R-Roger' our regular plane had been our friend once more – we were all endeared to it. As a flight engineer I felt our AMPG [air miles per gallon] wasn't too good – only 0875, but we were back – and alive! After landing safely we shared our experiences and emotions. It was the same after every flight and we had completed thirty of them. If the rules hadn't changed it would mean the end of our allocation, but now we still had three flights left. My dream of bombing Berlin was now past history.'

Back from Potsdam at Downham Market 'Nick' Nicholson reflected on the raid: 'It was my longest trip – eight hours fifteen minutes and as it turned out, the last raid of the war by a major Bomber Command force on a German city. For what was to be my final operation of the war on 18 April on a daylight raid to Heligoland I was reunited with my pilot on 35 Squadron [Squadron Leader] 'Kiwi' Lawson; this time as deputy master bomber where the targets were a naval base and an airfield. The bombing was accurate and the target areas were turned almost into crater-pitted moonscapes! We had become experts. At the end of it all I had flown fifty-seven trips with a total flying time of 509 hours 15 minutes and my log book was signed off by 'Wing Commander' Le Good (he had 'demoted' himself from group captain in order to fly on operational duty!). I had the very great privilege and good fortune to fly, not only with an exceptional pilot and a great 'crew' but also with a man like Le Good who was a legend in his own lifetime.'

Maurice Bishop, pilot of '*Winsome Winnie*' on 218 'Gold Coast' Squadron at Chedburgh, south-west of Bury St Edmunds in Suffolk recalls:

'This op, which took eight hours fifty-five minutes, was our most remembered. About an hour from the target my mid-upper gunner suddenly shouted, 'Down skip!' I pushed the stick forward hard and saw another Lanc sliding over the top of us on a slightly different heading, same height. My gunner saw the exhaust flame just in time as it was closing in on us. The searchlight activity over Berlin was intense and we were just sliding past one that was fixed when it suddenly locked straight on to us and I was completely blinded. I started to change height, speed and direction as taught and went into a diving corkscrew, pulling out the bottom dive quite hard and throwing the old Lanc around by feel as I was still blinded by the searchlight. Then suddenly we were clear before the night-fighters spotted us and we dropped our load on the target and came home OK.

'The next day down at dispersal the ground engineer said, 'What were you up to last night?'

'I said, 'Why?'

'He said, 'Look at this' and he took me up the steps and showed me the upper wing between the fuselage and the starboard inner. The skin had a wrinkle in it. We must have pulled out of the dive with our full bomb load on board and the old Lanc had taken it under protest.'

The returning bombers landed in England during the hours of 0200 and 0300. The diversion to Cuxhaven and the Main Force approach, across parts of Germany recently captured by Allied troops, had reduced losses to enemy action to only the one Lancaster; a loss rate of just 0.1 per cent from a total effort for the night of 716 sorties. There was another casualty, however, that no-one on the ground saw. 'T-Tommy' piloted by Flying Officer Allan Baynes was attacked by two enemy aircraft believed to be Ju 88s 20 miles south-west of Potsdam on the homeward journey. The damage to nose and cockpit suggests it suffered a blast of cannon shells, one of which tragically hit and fatally wounded Jack Sliman, who died in a Cambridgeshire hospital on 14 April, close to his squadron's base. He was buried at Chelmsford Borough Cemetery on Writtle Road on 20 April.[7]

According to the official RAF report 'a very concentrated attack developed and the target was well alight by the time the last aircraft were on their way home. Flak was slight and bursting well below stream.' Severe damage was caused in Potsdam but bombs also fell in the nearby northern and eastern districts of Berlin. Even the largest part of the southern and eastern Potsdam old town and the area north-east of the Brauhausberges were hit and suffered severe damage.

Fortunately for many inhabitants and for the treasures of Sanssouci, the summer palace of Frederick the Great, many bombs landed in the lakes surrounding Potsdam. The main target, the train station, was totally destroyed but from the Glienicke Bridge, survivors observed the burning city in its entirety. The city castle, the garrison church where, on 21 March 1933, Hitler was sworn into office and other important buildings of the city burned down. The church was not hit by the bombing, but caught fire when a neighbouring building used as an ammunitions depot blew up. Large parts of Berlin's suburbs went up in flames and parts of Babelsberg were also hit with destruction or damage of 23 per cent. The buildings in the inner part of Potsdam and the suburbs of Berlin were destroyed or damaged by up to 97 per cent. Some valuable buildings like the Einsteinturm (Einstein Tower) designed by Erich Mendelsohn survived the 'night of Potsdam', but were severely damaged. Mendelsohn was a German-Jewish architect responsible for many well-known buildings who had fled his practice in Berlin in the spring of 1933 in the wake of growing anti-Semitism and the rise of the Nazis. Ironically, in 1943 he assisted the US army and the Standard Oil Company in building a set of replicas of typical German working-class housing estates, 'German Village', which would be of key importance in acquiring the knowhow and experience necessary to carry out the fire bombings on Berlin.

The death toll for the Potsdam raid is still not known but a figure of 5,000 dead has been mentioned and in the aftermath, everyone in Potsdam was affected. In total, the town lost 24,763 inhabitants (20 per cent) due to evacuation, flight, deportation and bombing. The number of bombs, the high number of incendiaries used and the marking of the old town as a target area indicated the targeted destruction of the old town.[8] Winston Churchill wrote angrily to Secretary of State for Air Sir Archibald Sinclair: 'What is the point of going and blowing down Potsdam?' In reply, Sir Charles Portal, Chief of the Air Staff pointed out that this attack had come about following a report of the Joint Intelligence Committee, describing the evacuation of the German Air Force operational headquarters from Berlin to Potsdam. Another object of the raid, Portal explained, was to destroy 'communications leading west from Berlin through Potsdam' and 'was calculated to hasten the disintegration of enemy resistance'.

At the post-war conference in Potsdam at Cecilienhof, the home of Crown Prince Wilhelm, from 17 July to 2 August 1945 attended by the Soviet Union, the United Kingdom, the United States and Canada, the place still reeked of the dead.

With the German capital and the Third Reich in its death throes, on 26 April a small Fieseler Fi 156 Storch ('Stork'), a small German liaison aircraft flown by the test pilot Hanna Reitsch was one of the last aircraft to land on the improvised airstrip in the Tiergarten near the Brandenburg Gate. In flight, the main landing gear legs hung down, giving the aircraft the appearance of a long-legged, big-winged bird, hence its name. With its very low landing speed, the Storch often appeared to land vertically or even backwards in strong winds from directly ahead. Hanna Reitsch's passenger was Generaloberst Robert Ritter von Greim, who had been summoned from Munich by Hitler. Initially they flew from the central Luftwaffe test facility airfield, the Erprobungsstelle Rechlin, to Gatow in south-western Berlin in a Focke-Wulf 190. As the cockpit only had room for the pilot, Reitsch flew in the tail of the plane, getting into it by climbing through a small emergency opening. Having landed in Gatow, they changed planes to fly to the Chancellery; however, their Storch was hit by anti-aircraft fire over the Grunewald. Greim was incapacitated by a bullet in the right foot, but Reitsch was able to reach the throttle and joystick to land on the improvised airstrip. Once her passenger had disembarked, she took off again, leaving behind the ruins and rubble of Berlin's once-proud Nazi government diplomatic district.

The ailing Führer promoted Greim Generalfeldmarschall and appointed him commander of the Luftwaffe in place of Hermann Goering, who he had dismissed for treason. On 28 April Hitler ordered Ritter von Greim to leave Berlin and had Reitsch fly him to Plön, so that he could arrest Heinrich Himmler on the charge of treason. That night, the two left Berlin, taking off from the Tiergarten in a small Arado Ar 96 biplane. When Germany surrendered, Greim was captured by American troops in Austria. He reportedly told his captors: 'I am the head of the Luftwaffe, but I have no Luftwaffe.' He committed suicide in prison in Salzburg on 24 May.

Hans-Georg von Studnitz had penned his last diary entries: 'Sleep is out of the question. The fatherland's situation is so dire its collapse so terrible, that it is no consolation at all to know that one had foreseen it all, years ago. The more bitterly disappointed our countrymen may be, the more they will have to suffer now, I am afraid…. By tomorrow we may well be homeless again, as so often during this war. In a world in which havoc spreads far more swiftly than life can burgeon, to look more than fifteen minutes ahead is pointless.'[9]

On 6 May 1945 the BBC interrupted a *Music While You Work* programme to announce: 'The German State Radio has just announced that Hitler is dead.' The Reich capital capitulated to the Russians the following day. Not since 1806 had Berlin fallen to a foreign invader, but there was no battle then. Marshal Davout and his French army entered the city on 25 October after Napoleon at Jena had won a battle he could not lose, and at Auerstädt, Davout won a battle he could not win. Headed by their Gauleiter, the Berlin citizens came out and welcomed Davout with open arms and the local press lavished praise on the French. Now there was no such triumphal end for the Nazi Gauleiter of Berlin, Reich Minister of Propaganda Joseph Goebbels who, after Hitler shot himself in his bunker, also committed suicide.

On 8 May Britain and the rest of the free world celebrated Victory in Europe Day. When he watched the happy, dancing crowds of British people Henryk Drożdż felt a wave of sadness and pity or maybe even contempt for such short-sightedness, but then his thoughts were lost in the din and the roar of victory fanfares. 'For them the war was finished,' he wrote; 'for us calm and hope.'

RAF and American bomber crews could be forgiven for thinking they had won a pyrrhic victory; one that had taken such a heavy toll that negated any true sense of achievement, though, if nothing else, the human effort spent by Harris's 'Old Lags' and the Americans in the Eighth Air Force did pave the way for the Soviet victory in the east.

Canadian Flight Lieutenant Jack Bonet remembered 'Butcher' Harris coming to his squadron on more than one occasion and he'd give a few speeches:

'He'd tell us about the buildings and factories we were going to hit, but in actual fact we went out and bombed the shit out of the civilians. Harris discovered you could bomb the factories and they'd go underground, but if you bombed the civilians, they had no place to go. I couldn't fault Harris for what he did – he was a great leader and he had a job to do.'

At the start of the Battle of Berlin Sir Arthur Harris had predicted that the 'Big City' would 'cost between 400-500 aircraft' but that it would 'cost Germany the war'. He was proved wrong on both counts. Thirty-five major attacks were made on Berlin and other German towns between mid-1943 and 24/25 March 1944: 20,224 sorties, 9,111 of which were to Berlin. From these sorties, 1,047 aircraft failed to return and 1,682 received varying degrees of damage.

In the words of Sir Arthur Harris: 'The whole battle was fought in appalling weather and in conditions resembling those of no other campaign in the history of warfare. Scarcely a single crew caught a glimpse of the objective they were attacking and for long periods we were wholly ignorant, except for such admissions as the enemy made from time to time, of how the battle was going. Thousands upon thousands of tons of bombs were aimed at the Pathfinders' sky-markers and fell through unbroken cloud which concealed everything below except the confused glow of fires.

'Scarcely any photographs taken during the bombing showed anything except clouds, and day after day reconnaissance aircraft flew over the capital to return with no information…. Then after six attacks a reconnaissance aircraft did bring back some not very clear photographs which showed that at last we were hitting the enemy's capital hard…. Then the clouds closed in again over Berlin and the Command made eight more attacks without any means of discovering whether all or any of them had been as successful as the first six raids. It was not until March was far advanced and the nights were too short for any but Mosquito attacks that an aircraft brought back more photographs and it was possible to assess the results of the Battle of Berlin as a whole.[10]

In 1943 even Air Vice Marshal Francis Frederic Frank Inglis, ACAS (Intelligence), in the beginning the one senior staff officer to have fully supported 'Bomber' Harris's Berlin campaign, had finally been forced to admit that Bomber Command's assault on morale would produce results only through a 'slow process of attrition' and even so, would not, by itself, 'exercise a decisive influence on the outcome of the war'.

'He was a gambler doubling up on each losing throw,' said Air Vice Marshal Sidney Osborne Bufton CB DFC, the Director of Bomber Operations. 'Berlin was not "wrecked from end to end" as Harris predicted on 3 November 1943 – "if the USAAF will come in on it" – although a considerable part of it was destroyed. And the "Main Battle of Berlin" did not cost Germany the war; a grinding land campaign had yet to be fought. More than 9,000 bombing sorties were flown during the battle on round trips of about 1,200 miles to Berlin. During the same period approximately 11,000 more sorties were flown against other German cities until the services of Bomber Command were handed over to Eisenhower's command at the beginning of April 1944.'

'I often wondered, through the tears, if the sacrifice of so many young lives was worth it all,' wrote Warrant Officer Angus Robb CGM. Until he was 15, Robb, an only child, was brought up by his parents in a one-attic-room of a teeming four-storey tenement building in the Glasgow suburb of Govan. He became a telegram delivery boy for the Post Office before joining the RAF in October 1941, simply because he wanted to fly. Robb completed two tours as rear gunner on Wellingtons on 431 'Iroquois' and 432 'Leaside' Squadrons RCAF and on Lancasters on 405 'Vancouver' PFF Squadron RCAF between December 1942 and April 1945.[11]

Angus made a visit to the British and Commonwealth War Cemetery in Charlottenburg in Berlin (which was constructed between 1955 and 1957) where his best friend Warrant Officer Ronnie Hainsworth, his crew's rear gunner, is now buried, along with about 3,200 others, the majority of them air crew in their 20s. Hainsworth had been killed on 5 March 1945 during an attack on their Lancaster by three Ju 88s. Next morning Robb felt he had lost a brother:

'Nobody who hasn't been there can really appreciate the bonding between a bomber crew. I think it was closer than marriage. We were a team, depending on each other and you were saying to the others, 'Here is my life.' I wondered, again, was it worth this? [12]

'On the same trip we were taken to Dachau, the site of the infamous concentration camp which is now a memorial to the millions who died in the camps. It was in that still sorrowful place I thought to myself, if it stops anything like this ever happening again, yes, their sacrifice was worthwhile. But I would make this plea to the ones this was really written for, my grandchildren: try to ensure it never happens again. Forgive, yes, but never, ever forget.'

Sergeant Henryk Drożdż, 300 'Masovian' Squadron at Faldingworth, was demobbed in 1947; eight years after that 'naive boy' first donned his proud blue uniform. Though he was happily domiciled in England with an English wife (she and her family had lost everything in the 1940 German raid on Coventry) and three teenage children, he would always feel grateful to those compatriots of his who gave their lives while serving with him. Of his thirty sorties, seventy crew members (ten aircraft) failed to return. He never saw his parents again, but he returned to Warsaw twice in his lifetime. He found the holocaust there indescribable…. 'May we never see such a war again,' he wrote. Henryk felt completely at home in England; his wife and children loved Poland and were proud of their dual heritage. This genuine love between his families often seemed to Henryk 'to be the best thing that came out of it all.'

'Berlin was the one battle, historically, which "Bomber" Harris did not win,' wrote Wing Commander Reggie 'Sunshine' Lane DSO DFC.[13] 'As a matter of fact, he lost the Battle of Berlin badly, if you use the casualties on each of those raids as a measure of success or failure.'

The 'butcher's bill' for RAF Bomber Command in the Battle of Berlin was 4,160 aircraft. The overall casualty rate in thirty-five operations in the four months commencing 18 November 1943 and terminating with the Nuremberg raid on 30/31 March 1944 was 5.2 per cent. Some 1,047 bombers failed to return from these 35 raids, 24 of them to Berlin.

Harris's authorized biographer Dudley Saward, who had been an officer on Harris's staff, says in his book *Bomber Harris* published in 1984:

'The Official History of the bomber offensive states in emphatic terms that the Berlin campaign was a failure and that losses were at a level that made it impossible to continue the campaign. This is incorrect. The reasons for the cessation were two-fold: by the end of March [1944] the nights were becoming too short for operations against such distant targets as Berlin and secondly, the requirement for the preparation for the invasion of France…. The suggestion that the Berlin campaign was a failure is not supported by the facts. An examination of the results reveals not failure but success, but as Harris himself admits, judged by the standards of the attacks on Hamburg, the Battle of Berlin was not an overwhelming success. However, for Germany it was an unprecedented disaster.'

The Battle of Berlin was not a defeat in absolute terms, but in the operational sense it was one that Bomber Command could not win.

'Berlin won,' said Sir Ralph Cochrane, AOC 5 Group RAF Bomber Command. 'It was just too tough a nut.'

Notes

Chapter One: Berlin Season

1. *Bomber's Moon* (Victor Gollancz Ltd, 1941).
2. On the night of 18 February 1942 Kee took off to lay mines off the Frisian Islands. His Hampden was hit by flak at 8,000 feet and he ditched the aircraft off Schiermonnikoog. Two of his crew were killed. Kee and his navigator were taken prisoner.
3. *The German War: A Nation Under Arms 1939–45* by Nicholas Stargardt (Vintage, 2015).
4. *Hemingway at War* by Terry Mort (Pegasus Books , 2016).
5. *A Country Boy At War* by Geoff King, cited in *wings on the whirlwind*, compiled and edited by anne grimshaw (north-west essex & east hertfordshire branch aircrew association, 1998).
6. Ibid.
7. Pat Dwyer, a WOp/AG cited in *Flak: True Stories from the men who flew in WWII* by Michael Veitch (Pan, 2008).
8. See *The Berlin Blitz by Those Who Were There* by Martin W. Bowman (Pen & Sword, 2020).
9. *Pathfinders* by Wing Commander Bill Anderson OBE DFC AFC (Jarrolds, London, 1946)
10. Sergeant Colin Rupert King was KIA on Berlin on 2/3 January 1944. Flight Lieutenant James C. Ralph DFM RNZAF and the rest of the crew also died.
11. See also *Heroes of Bomber Command: Lincolnshire* by Rupert Matthews.
12. jcproctor.blogspot.com/2014
13. *Reap The Whirlwind: The Untold Story of 6 Group, Canada's Bomber Force of WWII* by Spencer Dunmore and William Carter Ph.D (McClelland & Stewart Inc., 1991).
14. *A Close Run Thing* by Bill Porter, cited in *Wings on the Whirlwind*, compiled and edited by Anne Grimshaw (North-West Essex & East Hertfordshire Branch Aircrew Association, 1998).
15. *The War History of Southern Rhodesia*, cited in *Pride of Eagles: A History of the Rhodesian Air Force* by Beryl Salt.
16. It took no fewer than thirty-one Spitfire and six PR Mosquito photo-reconnaissance sorties before the results of the bombing of Berlin on 18/19 November were obtained. Flights over Germany were being made more difficult by enemy action, bad weather and factors such as smoke from still burning factories and houses. BDA (Bomb Damage Assessment) became such an issue with both the RAF and USAAF bomber commands that PR aircraft were required to cover targets within hours of a raid being carried out, sometimes even before the returning bombers had landed.
17. The Germans recorded only seventy-five HE bombs falling on Berlin, of which eleven were 'duds' or delayed-action and no industrial buildings were destroyed.
18. The increasing tempo of operations in 1943 increased the incidence of LMF cases, but they still remained a very low percentage of total numbers of Bomber Command.

Throughout the war, 4,059 cases were considered: 746 officers and 3,313 NCOs. The 'charges' against most were dismissed and only 2,726 (389 officers; 2,337 NCOs) were actually classified as LMF, less than 0.4 per cent of all the air crews of Bomber Command. The NCO total was higher because there were more of them than officers.

Chapter Two: Ordeal by Fire

1. Cited in *The Berlin Raids: RAF Bomber Command Winter 1943–44* by Martin Middlebrook (Cassell & Co., 1988).
2. A number of Hochbunkers that were built were usually made of large concrete blocks and were built upward and considered to be completely bomb-proof.
3. Hamburg later got two towers and Vienna three and like the ones in Berlin none were put out of action in the war.
4. See Stephen Zaloga, *Defence of the Third Reich 1941–45*.
5. *With our Backs To Berlin* by Tony Le Tissier MBE (Sutton, 2005).
6. While the official term was Luftwaffenhelfer (HJ), the term more commonly used is 'Flakhelfer' (female: 'Flakhelferin', 'Flak-helper'). By 1945 the girls of the League of German Girls or Band of German Maidens (Bund Deutscher Mädel – BDM) were also operating flak guns.
7. Twamley was wounded in the leg during a sortie to Leipzig on 3 December and was succeeded by Wing Commander Colin Scragg MBE AFC, an American who had joined the RAF in the 1930s.
8. *Bomber Intelligence* by W.E. Jones (Midland Counties Publications, 1983).
9. *Diary of a nightmare: Berlin, 1942–1945*, by Ursula von Kardorff.
10. Mullock was destined to visit Berlin on two further occasions during the battle and eventually made five trips to the 'Big City' out of his twenty-two ops. He was recommended for the MC in August 1944. See *Bombers Over Berlin* by Alan W. Cooper (PSL, 1985 & 1989).
11. See *Bombers Over Berlin* by Alan W. Cooper.
12. 'Hajo' Herrmann, *Eagle's Wings: The autobiography of a Luftwaffe pilot*.
13. Herrmann was captured by the Soviets after the war and he was held prisoner for ten years before returning to Germany in 1955. He celebrated his 95th birthday in 2008 and continued making public appearances. He died on 5 November 2010.
14. *Inside the Third Reich* by Albert Speer (Weidenfeld and Nicolson, 1970). At the Nuremberg War Trials Berthold Konrad Hermann Speer was found guilty of war crimes and crimes against humanity. On 1 October 1946 he was sentenced to twenty years' imprisonment. He died on 1 September 1981 in London.
15. Promoted to squadron leader, Bill Stewart was KIA on 13 June 1944 on the raid on Cambrai. Ochsner and Sergeant Varley were also killed. Flying Officer W.C. Burns was taken prisoner.
16. From a story on the website of Elinor Florence.
17. Cited in *Reap The Whirlwind: The Untold Story of 6 Group, Canada's Bomber Force of WWII* by Spencer Dunmore and William Carter Ph.D (McClelland & Stewart Inc., 1991).
18. *They Led The Way: The Story of Pathfinder Squadron 156* by Michael P. Wadsworth (Highgate Publications (Beverley) Ltd, 1992).
19. www.yorkshire-aircraft.co.uk/aircraft/yorkshire/york43/nov43.html
20. Howard-Williams fought in the First World War with the East Yorkshire Regiment and from 1916 to 1918 was attached to the RFC as a Flying Officer (Observer). On

17 September 1917 it was announced that he had been awarded the Military Cross 'for conspicuous gallantry and devotion to duty in co-operating with the artillery often under extremely unfavourable weather conditions'. He joined the RAF in January 1929 and in 1930 he led a flight of Fairey IIIDs of 47 Squadron from Khartoum to West Africa and back. He rose to the rank of group captain by the start of the Second World War.

21. Pilot Officer G.K. Chapman DFM was on the crew of Flight Lieutenant A.E. Keeling DFM on 83 Squadron who were shot down on Brunswick on 12/13 August 1944 by Feldwebel Heinz Pahler of 8./NJG1. Keeling, Chapman and four other crew members were taken prisoner. One member of the crew was KIA. Keeling's award was an immediate DFM for outstanding airmanship while serving on 49 Squadron.
22. See *Bombers Over Berlin* by Alan W. Cooper.
23. *My Brother Frank* by his sister Jeanette which is featured on the RAF Pathfinders Archive.
24. In an eleven-week period from the beginning of December to mid-February 1943 no less than 9.8 per cent of Halifax sorties to Germany were shot down. The worst Halifax losses would occur in January 1944.
25. *The Bomber Command War Diaries: An Operational Reference Book 1939–1945* by Martin Middlebrook and Chris Everitt (Midland, 1985).
26. Born on 5 February 1890, Ley committed suicide while awaiting trial at Nuremberg for war crimes on 25 October 1945.
27. *The Berlin Diaries 1940–45* by Marie (Illarionovna) 'Missie' Vassiltchikov (Chatto & Windus Ltd, 1985).

Chapter Three: While Berlin Burned

1. *Berlin im Zweiten Weltkrieg* edited by Hans Dieter Schäfer.
2. Named after the brothers who emigrated from Sils in Switzerland and founded the pastry bakery Zuckerbäckerei Johann Josty & Co. in 1796. From this company emerged the Café Josty at least from 1812.
3. *While Berlin Burns: The Diary of Hans Georg von Studnitz, 1943–1945* (Frontline Books, 2011).
4. Cited in *The Berlin Raids* by Martin Middlebrook (Viking, 1998; Cassell, 2000).
5. Ibid.
6. See *Bombers Over Berlin* by Alan W. Cooper.
7. *The Berlin Diaries 1940–45* by Marie 'Missie' Vassiltchikov (Chatto & Windus Ltd, 1985).
8. See *Aircrew Remembered.*
9. See *Bombers First and Last* by Gordon Thorburn (Robson Books, 2006)/*Bombers Over Berlin* by Alan W. Cooper (PSL, 1985 & 1989).
10. Chorley.
11. *Bomber Intelligence* by W.E. Jones (Midland Counties Publications, 1983).
12. *Three Passions and a Lucky Penny* by Eric Stephenson. Reay and Mair were KIA on the operation to Berlin 23/24 November 1943. There were no survivors on Reay's crew, who were flying their first operation and their bodies were never found. Almost a year later on 4/5 November 1944 in an attack on the industrial Rhineland city of Bochum, Derek Reay's brother Flying Officer Geoffrey Reay and all the crew of his Halifax bomber died, shot down near their target. It was one of twenty-eight aircraft lost.
13. Ibid.

14. *While Berlin Burns: The Diary of Hans Georg von Studnitz, 1943–1945* (Frontline Books, 2011).
15. Julius Schaub (20 August 1898-27 December 1967), chief aide and adjutant to Hitler until the dictator's suicide on 30 April 1945.
16. *The Berlin Diaries 1940–45* by Marie 'Missie' Vassiltchikov (Chatto & Windus Ltd, 1985).
17. *Three Passions and a Lucky Penny* by Eric Stephenson.
18. Ibid.

Chapter Four: 'No Enemy Plane Will Fly Over the Reich Territory!'

1. *The Past Is Myself: An Englishwoman's Life in Berlin under the Nazis* by Christabel Bielenberg (Chatto & Windus, London, 1968).
2. Private memoir, Major Hubert Knilans, *A Yank in the RCAF* (RAF Museum, Hendon, archive B2455).
3. Scuffins wrote this after completing twenty-one and a half successful sorties, nine of which were to Berlin. He and Flying Officer Donald Leslie Davies DFC's crew were killed on 57 Squadron on 30 July 1944 when their Lancaster failed to return from a post-delivery air test and was presumed to have crashed in the Wash.
4. Cited in *Bombers Over Berlin* by Alan W. Cooper (PSL, 1985 & 1989). Group Captain Leonard Slee survived the war and retired from the RAF at his own request on 1 October 1953. He died in Hove, Sussex on 10 March 1979.
5. See *No Need To Die: American Flyers in RAF Bomber Command* by Gordon Thorburn (Haynes Publishing, 2009) and *Bombers Over Berlin* by Alan W. Cooper.
6. See *No Need To Die: American Flyers in RAF Bomber Command* by Gordon Thorburn (Haynes Publishing, 2009).
7. Thanks are due to John Proctor, author of *Does Life Hold Any More in Store?*. Sergeant Cushing was killed on the operation on Berlin on 16/17 December flying on 22-year-old Flying Officer Peter Walter Robert Pollett's crew, their Lancaster crashing at Diepholz. They had completed eight operations as a crew.
8. *Boots, Bikes & Bombers* by Eric Jones (unpublished manuscript).
9. *To Fly Lancasters* by Clive Roantree. Richardson and four of his crew were killed. Three others were injured.
10. See *To Strive and Not to Yield* by Dennis West.
11. Among the dead was the 25-year-old mid-upper gunner Sergeant Edward Francis Johnson USAAF who had been awarded the Air Medal with three Oak Leaf Clusters and the Purple Heart. He left a widow, Virginia and a daughter, Jacquelene. Strange's crew are commemorated on the wall of the Missing at the US Military Cemetery at Margraten in Holland.
12. *A Bird Over Berlin: A World War II Lancaster Pilot's Story of Survival Against the Odds* by Pilot Officer Tony Bird DFC. Bird and his crew were shot down on Brunswick on 22/23 April 1944. He and his bomb-aimer Pilot Officer F.J. Davies survived to be taken into captivity. Two of the dead were his first crew members: 'Ken' Kendrick DFM and rear gunner Harry Aspinall DFM. Davies was repatriated aboard the *Letitita*, arriving at Liverpool docks on 2 February 1945. Chorley.
13. See *Fire by Night* by Jennie Gray.
14. Pilot Officer Yell DFC was KIA on the raid on Brunswick on 14/15 January 1944. Sergeant Twitchett was KIA on the raid on Stettin on 5/6 January 1944.

15. Post-war Michael Bentine became one of the famous 'Goons' comedy team with Spike Milligan, Peter Sellers and Harry Secombe. See *The Door Marked Summer* by Michael Bentine.
16. Adapted from an article by the late Stuart Howe. 'Sugar' had to be fitted with a new wing. It went on to complete a total of 137 sorties and is now in the RAF Museum, Hendon. Flight Lieutenant 'Wally' Einarson DFC DFM was killed, aged 23, on Augsburg on 25/26 February 1944. There was only one survivor. The pilot's twin brother, Flight Sergeant Harold Bjorn Einarson had been killed off Denmark on 10 September 1942.
17. Allied bombing ruined most of the store, with one shot-down American bomber actually crashing into it in 1943. Most of the store was gutted, which caused its closure. The re-opening of the first two floors was celebrated in 1950. Full reconstruction of all seven floors was finished by 1956.
18. *The Berlin Diaries 1940–45* by Marie 'Missie' Vassiltchikov (Chatto & Windus Ltd, 1985). By 1944 1.2 million people, 790,000 of them women and children, about a quarter of Berlin's population, had been evacuated to rural areas. An effort was made to evacuate all children from Berlin, but this was resisted by parents and many evacuees soon made their way back to the city.
19. *The Bomber Command War Diaries: An Operational Reference Book 1939–1945* by Martin Middlebrook and Chris Everitt (Midland, 1985).

Chapter Five: 'An Orchestrated Hell'

1. *Lancaster Valour: The Valour and The Truth* by Clayton Moore (Compaid Graphics, 1995).
2. Ibid.
3. Adapted from *A Bedfordshire Bomb-Aimer* on the WW2 People's War website by his brother David H. Marshall. No. 44 Squadron lost two Lancasters in total.
4. Ibid.
5. Adapted from *Just Another Story*, the WW2 People's War website.
6. *No Writing Home* by Maurice Chick.
7. *Lancaster to Berlin* by Walter Thompson DFC and Bar.
8. See *No Verse Can Say* by Anne Doward (Compaid Graphics, August 1966).
9. Pilot Officer Edward James Argent RAFVR aged 20 and 23-year-old Flight Sergeant Alfred Kenneth Trevena and three other crew were killed on the operation on Brunswick on 14/15 January 1944. Two crew survived to be taken prisoner.
10. Sergeant Lawrence 'Laurie' Maurice Parker RAAF had been the ground staff sergeant in charge of 'A-Apple', Flight Lieutenant Reginald Carmichael's Lancaster. It was Carmichael, from Bourke, NSW who decided to record the crew's raids with a beer mug for every operation flown. He and his crew were killed on the Berlin raid on 3/4 September 1943.
11. *'My War': Wartime Memories of Flight Lieutenant Les Rutherford* by Les Rutherford and Marion Longbottom (Privately Published, 2014).
12. *Lancaster to Berlin* by Walter Thompson DFC and Bar.
13. Cited in *Under Cover of Darkness* by Roderick Chisholm (Chatto & Windus, London, 1953).
14. Adapted from *Just Another Story*, the WW2 People's War website.
15. Willy McLeod was KIA on 21/22 February 1945. Bill Grime was taken prisoner.
16. The night following the 2/3 December raid on Berlin, 'G-George' (JB140) lost two engines on take-off for Leipzig and the aircraft swung off the runway, collided with

JB138 on 61 Squadron and crashed into a party of ground crew watching the take-off, killing Sergeant Laurie Parker who was 25 years old, and injuring another airman. Flight Sergeant Cecil Rowland Frizzell on JB140 died of his injuries on 5 December. Wing Commander William Alexander Forbes DSO DFC RAAF, 25, was KIA on a bombing operation to Mehringen, Germany on 21/22 February 1945.

17. *Masters of the Air: America's Bomber Boys Who Fought the Air War Against Nazi Germany* by Donald L. Miller. Bennett died on 4 November 1974 at Erie, Erie County, Pennsylvania.
18. Cited in *Thanks For The Memory: Unforgettable Characters In Air Warfare 1939–45* by Laddie Lucas.
19. *Chased By The Sun: The Australians in Bomber Command in WWII* by Hank Nelson (ABC Books 2002 and Allen & Unwin 2006).
20. Ibid.
21. After completing two tours of operations, 'Punch' Thompson eventually returned to Canada with degrees from both Cambridge and Oxford. He practised law in British Columbia and also wrote books on philosophy, religion and science.
22. See *Striking Through Clouds: The War Diary of 514 Squadron RAF*.
23. Adapted from *Just Another Story*, the WW2 People's War website.
24. *Lancaster Valour: The Valour and The Truth* by the late Clayton Moore.

Chapter Six: One Night in December

1. *While Berlin Burns: The Diary of Hans Georg von Studnitz, 1943–1945* (Frontline Books, 2011).
2. *No Verse Can Say* by Anne Doward.
3. From a taped interview for the University of Victoria in 1973 cited in *Trials and Tribulation: The Story of RAF Gransden Lodge* by Chris Sullivan (Matador, 2015).
4. David Clark's BBC WW2 Peoples War website.
5. See Aircraft Accidents in Yorkshire website. If JB116 was this aircraft, it was repaired and issued to 9 Squadron where it was lost on the night of 7/8 July 1944.
6. The role of the master bomber was to ensure the 'heavies' dropped their bombs in the right place. He would be over the target area for the whole of a raid and would check on the fall of the TIs (Target Indicators). He would then tell the following bomber crews where to bomb in relation to the TIs. He would also maintain a lookout for crews who began bombing too soon. If the target needed more TIs the master bomber would call up the marker aircraft to drop fresh flares.
7. RAF Pathfinders Archive website.
8. Ibid.
9. RAF Pathfinders Archive.
10. Cited in *War In The Air* compiled by Edward Smithies (Viking, 1990).
11. Cited in *Lancaster At War 2* by Mike Garbett and Brian Goulding (Ian Allan Ltd, 1979).
12. Cited in *War In The Air* compiled by Edward Smithies (Viking, 1990).
13. See *No Moon Tonight* by Don Charlwood (Penguin, 1988). Charlwood recalled that 'Of his words I remember very little, but his dark, staring eyes I have never forgotten. I felt that they looked on the worst and, on looking beyond it, had found serenity.'
14. *He Died So Young* by J.S. 'Johnny' Johnston writing in *Thanks For The Memory: Unforgettable Characters In Air Warfare 1939–45* by Laddie Lucas (Stanley Paul & Co. Ltd, 1989).
15. *A Day I'll Never Forget* by Mrs Marie Aston.

16. *One Night In December* by Herbert C. Addy (1999).
17. Propaganda leaflets.
18. Ibid.
19. Ibid.
20. Ibid.
21. Bob Stone was killed after his parachute failed to open.
22. *Three Passions and a Lucky Penny*. The Lancaster was claimed shot down by Feldwebel Herbert Herre of 3./JG 302 flying a Bf 109G from Jüterbog-Waldlager airfield and by heavy flak. Air Vice Marshal Eric Hay Stephenson AO OBE died on 13 April 2017.

Chapter Seven: A Hymn for the Haunted

1. *One Night In December* by Herbert C. Addy (1999).
2. *Maximum Effort: The Story of the North Lincolnshire Bombers* by Patrick Otter (Archive Publications/Grimsby *Evening Telegraph* 1990).
3. Ibid.
4. *Maximum Effort: The Story of the North Lincolnshire Bombers* by Patrick Otter (Archive Publications/Grimsby *Evening Telegraph* 1990).
5. Cited in www.yorkshire-aircraft.co.uk. Flight Lieutenant John Allardyce Allen RCAF (23) and his crew were killed on the 2/3 January 1944 raid on Berlin. Sergeant Robert Anthony Hutchinson RAFVR was KIA on 14 January 1944. Flight Sergeant Alexander Morvan McGregor RCAF was KIA on 19 April 1944. Sergeant Alfred Clarence Phillips RAFVR was shot down and taken prisoner on 28 April 1944. Flying Officer George John Smith RCAF was KIA on 1 May 1944 on 405 Squadron.
6. *Black Night For Bomber Command: The Tragedy of 16 December 1943* by Richard Knott (Pen & Sword, 2007).
7. Ibid.
8. Cited in *Trials and Tribulation: The Story of RAF Gransden Lodge* by Chris Sullivan (Matador, 2015).
9. 'Charles Owen was clearly a brave and brilliant pilot, his diary littered with heroic deeds, but told in a very laconic style, typical of air crew at the time. But nowhere does he mention the horrors of the war: the funerals in Cambridge after "Black Thursday" must have been traumatic, if not as ghastly as removing the headless corpse of Flight Sergeant Laurie from the rear turret of another aircraft, as he had to do on 28th January 1944, the poor man decapitated by flak over Kiel.' See *My Father The Hero* on Oliver Owen's website and *Fire by Night: The Dramatic Story of One Pathfinder Crew and Black Thursday, 16/17 December 1943* by Jennie Gray, daughter of Joe Mack. Owen celebrated his 21st birthday on the night of 5/6 January over Stettin. He would end the war as a master bomber with a string of decorations. Charles Owen was awarded the DSO after completing his last op on 5 October 1944 which was gazetted on 15 December 1944.
10. See *War-Torn Skies: Cambridgeshire* by Julian Evan-Hart (Red Kite, 2008).
11. Ernest Clarke was awarded a Mention in Dispatches for landing the Lancaster. He and his crew were killed on 30 January 1944 when they were shot down by a night-fighter over North Holland. See RAF Pathfinders Archive.
12. Reginald Neville Stidolph was born on 3 August 1915 in Salisbury, Rhodesia. Family lore was that Reg wanted to be a pilot from the age of 10 and that he was awarded a scholarship to Cranwell to join the RAF. However, he was unable to take it up as his father opposed it and wanted him to have a 'steady job' in the Civil Service. He worked in Customs Service for a short while but hated it and went to the UK to join the RAF

anyway, commencing at the age of 20 in November 1935. He was posted to command 61 Squadron in September 1943. His DFC award was for the confirmed destruction of an enemy fighter and for returning despite extensive damage to his aircraft on the raid on Stettin on 5/6 January 1944.

13. *A WAAF In Bomber Command* by 'Pip' Beck (Goodall Publications Ltd, 1989).
14. Due to there being another bomber station in 4 Group named Pocklington, it was decided that the village of Snaith almost adjoining Pollington was to be the name of the station.

Chapter Eight: 'We won't be home for Christmas; we know that very well'

1. *Aircrew: The Story of the Men who flew the Bombers* by Bruce Lewis (Cassell & Co., first published by Leo Cooper in 1991).
2. Ibid.
3. Ibid.
4. Nomenclature used when two aircraft on the same squadron had the same individual letter.
5. Ibid.
6. See *Aircrew: The Story of the Men who flew the Bombers* by Bruce Lewis (Cassell & Co., first published by Leo Cooper in 1991) and *The Berlin Raids* by Martin Middlebrook (Viking, 1988).
7. www.576squadronraf@gmail.com
8. From research by Jason Jenkinson for *Aircrew Remembered*.
9. *Lancaster Valour: The Valour and the Truth* by Clayton Moore (Compaid Graphics, 1995).
10. See *Bombers Over Berlin* by Alan W. Cooper.
11. *A Country Boy At War* by 'Geoff' King, cited in *Wings on the Whirlwind*, compiled and edited by Anne Grimshaw (North-West Essex & East Hertfordshire Branch Aircrew Association, 1998). After his first tour 'Geoff' King went to 97 Pathfinder Squadron at Coningsby. He completed fifty operations and was awarded the DFC.
12. Cited in *Flying To Hell* by Mel Rolfe (Grub Street, 2001).
13. See the JcProctor website.

Chapter Nine: 'After Every December Comes Always a May'

1. This famous Lancaster III which undertook a record 140 operations in total from May 1943 until December 1944 had originally served on 103 Squadron, as had Morgan (576 was formed from 'C' Flight of 103 Squadron on 25 November). The Berlin op would be ED888's fifty-eighth sortie. From 10 December 1943 until 20 April 1944 Morgan's crew made nine trips to Berlin.
2. Squadron Leader George Johnstone 'Turkey' Laird DFC who was from Winnipeg and five of his crew were killed on the Nuremberg raid on the night of 30/31 March 1944 when they were in a collision with a Lancaster.
3. Cited in *Maximum Effort: The Big Bombing Raids* by Bernie Wyatt (The Boston Mills Press, 1986).
4. Frazier got his 'Jocks' muddled up. Graham was known as 'Mack'. Flying Officer John Ross 'Jock' Mearns was the flight engineer.
5. It was only after the war that it was discovered that the Germans did not use an explosive device to simulate an exploding bomber. What the men saw, in fact, was a fully-loaded bomber exploding, having either been hit by flak or night-fighter attack.

6. A 'spoof' raid was in progress.
7. At Leipzig, where the bomber stream appeared to be heading before turning north-east for Berlin.
8. 'Jock' Mearns was killed in action on 166 Squadron on the attack on the Harpenerweg benzol plant at Dortmund on 24 March 1945.
9. Neil Lambell was killed in a car accident 12 kilometres from Gulargambone on 28 November 1968. He was 46 years old.
10. Cited in *The Berlin Raids* by Martin Middlebrook.
11. On New Year's Eve Keith Parry and his crew went on seven days' leave. While they were away, on 2 January 1944, 'Zeke', flown by another crew skippered by 22-year-old Flying Officer George Arthur Tull, failed to return from the 'Big City'. The aircraft was attacked just south of Stavoren over the Ijsselmeer by a German night-fighter and crashed on fire from back to front into a hill at Bakhuizen. None of the crew survived. 'Zeke' had only sixty-four flying hours on the clock. The average life of a squadron Lancaster at this stage of the war was thirty-six flying hours.
12. Ibid.
13. *The Long Road: Trials and Tribulations of Airmen Prisoners from Stalag Luft VII (Bankau) to Berlin, June 1944-May 1945* by Oliver Clutton Brock and Raymond Crompton (Grub Street, London, 2013).
14. Ibid. Before reaching the target the Halifax, flown by Wing Commander Gerald Arthur McKenna RCAF, was damaged by flak in the fuselage which killed Cecil. The crew pressed on and bombed the target and were able to return to Tholthorpe. (*Aircraft Accidents in Yorkshire*).
15. *The Bomber Battle for Berlin* by John Searby (Guild Publishing, 1991).

Chapter Ten: Unhappy Hogmanay

1. *Diary of a Nightmare: Berlin, 1942–1945* by Ursula von Kardorff.
2. *A Lancaster Pilot's Impression on Germany* by Richard (Dick) Starkey.
3. Wing Commander Albert Robinson Dunn DFC was KIA on 22 June 1944 on 83 Squadron.
4. Adapted from *Lancaster Target* by Jack Currie, a pilot on 12 Squadron at Wickenby and *A Night To Remember* by Ronald Homes DFC AGAVA.
5. Cited in *The Berlin Raids* by Martin Middlebrook (Viking, 1998; Cassell, 2000).
6. Cited in *The Berlin Raids* by Martin Middlebrook (Viking, 1998; Cassell, 2000).
7. *The Berlin Diaries 1940–45* by Marie 'Missie' Vassiltchikov (Chatto & Windus Ltd, 1985).
8. *83 Squadron 1917–1969* published by Harper and Low and *Footsteps on the Sands of Time* by Oliver Clutton-Brock. Leutnant Wendelin Breukel was killed on 1 March 1944 when he crashed into the Harrenstedter Forest during a low-level transit flight. He had fourteen victories. On 3 January Wing Commander Donald Frederick Edgar Charles 'Dixie' Dean DFC, one of 156 Squadron's flight commanders who had captained his crew on the raid on Berlin, was posted in to take command of 83 Squadron, which lost thirteen aircraft and crews in January 1944. Indeed, the whole of the Pathfinder Force, no doubt because of the SN-2 radar sets homing on their H2S transmitters, suffered worse casualties than usual. These were such as to cause 'Pathfinder' Bennett to write later: 'This Battle (Berlin) was indeed the bitterest part of the war for me – I thought that the backbone of the Pathfinder Force was really broken.'
9. *New Zealanders with the RAF*, Vol. II.

10. Seventy-nine people were killed, including twenty-five in a panic rush at the entrance of a public air-raid shelter in the Neukölln district.
11. Known German losses are seven crew killed, four wounded and six aircraft lost: three Bf 110, two Ju 88s and a Bf 109, the latter and one Bf 110 falling to German flak.
12. Twenty-nine Lancasters crashed in Europe or were lost without traces and two more crashed on return in England. Aboard these 31 bombers, 183 crew members were killed, 33 captured and one evaded.
13. *Bombers Over Berlin* by Alan W. Cooper.
14. See *Aircrew Remembered* and *Bombers First and Last* by Gordon Thorburn.
15. See *Lancaster Down! The Extraordinary Tale of Seven Young Bomber Aircrew at War* by Steve Darlow (Grub Street, 2000).
16. See *Aircrew Remembered.*
17. Pilot Officer Frederick Horace Garnett and crew on JB642/J are believed to have been shot down outbound by Hauptmann Erhard Peters and crashed at 0200 hours at Hoya, a town straddling the Weser. All except the rear gunner were killed. There were no survivors on Pilot Officer Edwin Cecil Holbourn's crew on JB645/F.
18. Ibid.

Chapter Eleven: Berlin Back to Back

1. The origin of the name Snoring is the settlement of Snear (meaning, ironically, 'swift, bright or alert') and can be traced back to the Saxon invasions from 450AD.

Chapter Twelve: 'Chop City'

1. *Diary of a Bomb Aimer: Flying with 12 Squadron in WWII* by Campbell Muirhead (Pen & Sword, 2009).
2. About ten months were to elapse before a transmitter called 'Piperack' could be developed and deployed so as to jam the SN-2 sets and it took almost as long before a variation of 'Gee' called 'G-H' was put in service to augment H2S in target-marking.
3. Cited in *Trials and Tribulation: The Story of RAF Gransden Lodge* by Chris Sullivan (Matador, 2015).
4. *Bombers Over Berlin* by Alan W. Cooper.
5. *Duel Under The Stars* by Wilhelm Johnen. Soldatensender Calais (Soldiers' Station Calais) was broadcasting not from Calais, but from the village of Milton Bryan, Bedfordshire with a massive 500-kilowatt medium-wave transmitter on frequencies shared by Radio Deutschland.
6. See *Aircrew Remembered.*
7. See the website article by Barbara Hunter to the International Bomber Command Centre.
8. Ibid.
9. Respectfully adapted from *Requiem for an Air Gunner* by R.W. Gilbert.
10. *Bombers Over Berlin* by Alan W. Cooper.
11. Cited in *At First Sight: A Factual and Anecdotal Account of No.627 Squadron RAF*, researched and compiled by Alan B. Webb (September 1991).
12. Research courtesy of Ian Ward and *Aircraft Accidents in Yorkshire*.
13. Dunmore and Carter.
14. *Rhodesia Herald*, 1 February 1944.
15. Diary entry cited in *The Lancaster Story* by Peter Jacobs (Cassell, 2002).
16. *Bombers Over Berlin* by Alan W. Cooper.
17. Dunmore and Carter.

18. Dunmore and Carter.
19. *Reap The Whirlwind* by Spencer Dunmore and William Carter Ph.D (M&S, 1991).
20. See www.yorkshire-aircraft.co.uk/aircraft/planes/44/hx281.html Henry Cox is buried at Harrogate Stonefall Cemetery in Yorkshire.
21. www.yorkshire-aircraft.co.uk/aircraft/planes/44/hx281.html See Last Flight To Berlin by TheSYNDICATE Studios narrated by Lloyd Linnell's son Robert.
22. 'Percy the Penguin' has been part of the RAF Museum's collection since 1980.

Chapter Thirteen: Wild Colonial Boys

1. *The London Observer* by Raymond Lee (Hutchinson, 1972).
2. *A WAAF In Bomber Command* by 'Pip' Beck (Goodall Publications Ltd, 1989).
3. Cited in *The War History of Southern Rhodesia.*
4. Thanks are due to John Proctor, author of *Does Life Hold Any More in Store?*.
5. Stanley Neighbour and his crew were killed on Schweinfurt on the night of 24/25 February.
6. See *Striking Through Clouds: The War Diary of 514 Squadron RAF.*
7. Cited in *Trials and Tribulation: The Story of RAF Gransden Lodge* by Chris Sullivan (Matador, 2015).
8. See *Aircrew Remembered.*
9. The flight engineer, Sergeant Sidney Webb Tupper RAAF; navigator, 23-year-old Flight Sergeant Norman William Allen RAFVR of Hunstanton, Norfolk; WOp/AG, Pilot Officer John Nixon RAFVR; 23-year-old mid-upper gunner, Warrant Officer2, Clifford Stanley Baker RCAF of Toronto, Ontario; and 22-year-old rear gunner, Sergeant Fred Barrett RAFVR of Leeds in Yorkshire.
10. Desoubrie was responsible for the capture of many of the 168 Allied airmen. He was arrested after being denounced by his ex-mistress and executed by firing squad as a collaborationist on 20 December 1949.
11. Blackham retired from the RAF in 1977 as an air commodore with the DFC and OBE. Thanks are due to H. James Flowers and the No.50 & No.61 Squadrons Association website.
12. *My Lucky Number Was 77: WWII Memoirs of J. Ralph Wood* DFC CD (unpublished memoir).
13. *Reap the Whirlwind* by Spencer Dunmore and William Carter Ph.D.
14. *Bomber Intelligence* by W.E. Jones (Midland Counties Publications, 1983).
15. *They Led The Way: The Story of Pathfinder Squadron 156* by Michael P. Wadsworth (Highgate Publications (Beverley) Ltd, 1992).
16. Dunmore.

Chapter Fourteen: A 'Yank' in Bomber Command

1. *Hardluck Crew of V-Victor* by teeboo, WW2 People's War website.
2. Ibid.
3. Ibid.
4. Sergeant Eric Fletcher was killed on 27th April 1944.
5. 'It's a DFM for You' by Syd Richardson in *Bomb On The Red Markers* by Pat Cunningham (Countryside Books, 2010).
6. Ibid.
7. *The German War: A Nation Under Arms 1939–45* by Nicholas Stargardt (Vintage, 2015).

8. Ibid.
9. 'It's a DFM for You' by Syd Richardson in *Bomb On The Red Markers* by Pat Cunningham (Countryside Books, 2010).
10. See *Aircrew Remembered* and Una McKellar, niece of David Winlow. On 7 August, now on 156 Squadron, Winlow was one of two air crew killed at RAF Upwood when a Mosquito overshot the runway and hit the house where they were staying. Doug Green, who suffered from frostbite having lost his gloves while tending to Chapman-Smith and 'Ken' Doyle and 'Alf' Astle were killed on 24 September 1944 on their last operation, over Calais.
11. See *Reap The Whirlwind* by Spencer Dunmore and William Carter Ph.D.
12. Jack Boswell was promoted to flight sergeant by his sixth op. He was commissioned by his twelfth op and was promoted again by his twenty-fifth op to flight lieutenant. He and his crew flew thirty-seven ops in total. Boswell was gazetted with the award of a DFC on 14 November 1944.
13. See *Flying Into Hell* by Mel Rolfe (Grub Street, 2001).
14. *Bombers Over Berlin* by Alan W. Cooper.
15. Ibid.
16. See *Battle Under the Moon* by Jack Currie (Air Data Publications Ltd, 1995).
17. Ibid.

Chapter Fifteen: Once the Most Beautiful City in the World

1. *The Past Is Myself: An Englishwoman's life in Berlin under the Nazis* by Christabel Bielenberg (Chatto & Windus, London, 1968).
2. Ibid.
3. Cited in The Peoples WW2 website.
4. Briggs, who was awarded the DSO on 23 March 1945, and Baker who were reported as having been partners on 107 operational sorties were killed in the crash of Mosquito LR504 'F for Freddie' at Calgary, Alberta at 1612 hours on 10 May 1945 while engaged in flying for a Victory Loan Drive in Calgary. Briggs failed to pull up after a high-speed run over the airfield and the aircraft hit the TCA control tower, tearing off the tail and part of the port wing. Just two years earlier, Briggs had left Calgary with his newly-earned wings from #37 Service Flying Training School (SFTS).
5. See *The Bomber Battle For Berlin* by John Searby (Guild Publishing, 1991).
6. City in *The Bomber Battle For Berlin* by John Searby (Guild Publishing, 1991).
7. Flight Lieutenant Howard Kelsey DFC* and Flying Officer E.M. Smith DFC DFM in a Mosquito II on 141 Squadron who had destroyed a Ju 88 on the 23/24 December 1943 raid would destroy an Fw 190 40 miles east of Berlin.
8. Lord Mackie of Benshie CBE DSO DFC.
9. On 2/3 June 1944 on the operation on Trappes, 23-year-old Leonard Stanley Dwan was mortally wounded when Bancroft's Halifax was hit from below by a Ju 88 equipped with 'Schräge Musik'.
10. Diary entry. See *The Lancaster Story* by Peter Jacobs (Cassell, 2002).
11. See *Striking Through Clouds: The War Diary of 514 Squadron RAF*. He earned a bar to his DFC for bravery in October 1944, after having been shot down and evading capture for several weeks before returning to England. The second medal presentation by King George VI was held at Buckingham Palace on 11 December 1945. He died at his Winnipeg home on 6 July 2006. Read his remarkable story in *Skid Row to Buckingham Palace* by 'Ed' Greenburgh.

12. 'Blind' means releasing TIs and flares solely by means of H2S.
13. *The Bomber Battle for Berlin* by Air Commodore John Searby DSO DFC (Guild Publishing, 1991).
14. City in *The Bomber Battle for Berlin* by Air Commodore John Searby DSO DFC (Guild Publishing, 1991). Warrant Officer Rhodes and Flying Officer George Bradburn's crew were shot down on 11 September 1944. Only Rhodes and one other crew member survived. Rhodes by then had completed more than thirty trips of his Pathfinder tour of duty.
15. *Reap The Whirlwind* by Spencer Dunmore and William Carter Ph.D.
16. Ronald Clapham Reinelt's twin brother Sergeant Norman Clapham Reinelt RAFVR died on 10 OTU on 28 October 1942. He has no known grave and is commemorated on the Runnymede Memorial.
17. *The Berlin Raids* by Martin Middlebrook (Viking, 1998; Cassell, 2000).
18. Pilot Officer Alan Olsson was KIA on Essen on 26/27 March 1944. He is buried in Reichswald Forest War Cemetery.
19. Pilot Officer Alwyn Wesley Giles Fripp DFC RAAF, the 30-year-old navigator was KIA on 19 July 1944.
20. Kornegay successfully transferred to the American Eighth Air Force, but successfully pleaded to remain with the RAF and his crew. He and his crew completed fifty-six operations.
21. *Pathfinders* by Wing Commander Bill Anderson OBE DFC AFC (Jarrolds, London, 1946).
22. Cited in *Trials and Tribulation: The Story of RAF Gransden Lodge* by Chris Sullivan (Matador, 2015). With his promotion to group captain at the age of 24, Lane flew his sixty-fifth and last operation just prior to D-Day as master bomber on a raid to Caen.
23. Flight Sergeant Ernest Brown RAAF and Sergeant John Eric Scruton, Flight Sergeant William Mitchinson, Sergeant Russell Boyde, Sergeant Joseph Flavell and Sergeant William Charles Mason were buried in Berlin war cemetery. Sergeant Burnell was interned in Stalag Luft VI and then Stalag 357 Thorn and finally 357 Fallingbostel. Here he remained until the end of the war when in April 1945 he was injured by American attacks on the camp, causing him to lose a lung. He was flown home on 4 May 1945.
24. Now on display at the RAF Museum at Hendon.
25. Ibid.
26. Cited in *The Berlin Raids* by Martin Middlebrook.
27. *Bombers Over Berlin* by Alan W. Cooper. A high-ranking commander in the RAF from the 1960s to the 1980s, Marshal of the Royal Air Force, Sir Michael James Beetham GCB CBE DFC AFC DL died on 24 October 2015.
28. Cited in *The Bomber Battle for Berlin* by Air Commodore John Searby DSO DFC (Guild Publishing, 1991).

Chapter Sixteen: The Winds of Change

1. On the night of 26/27 April 1944 Rudolph Frank and his crew of Oberfeldwebel Schierholz and bordmechaniker Feldwebel Heinz Schneider spotted and attacked a Lancaster over the vicinity of Eindhoven. The bomber, severely hit by cannon fire, exploded and became Frank's forty-fifth and final aerial victory. Debris from the Lancaster tore off the right wing of his Bf 110 and Frank lost control of the aircraft. Schierholz and Schneider parachuted to safety but Frank failed to get out in time. He was killed when the Bf 110 crashed at Heeze a few miles south-east of Eindhoven.
2. *Amazing Airmen: Canadian Flyers in the Second World War* by Ian Darling.

3. *Boys At War* by Russell Margerison (Ross Anderson Publications, 1986).
4. They could in fact have been shells fired from a 'Schräge Musik' installation. The Lancaster was claimed by Oberleutnant Martin Drewes.
5. *Uncovering A Lost Trail* by John Albrecht; *Legion: Canada's Military History Magazine*, 1 January 2001; and *Aircrew Remembered.*
6. See *Reap The Whirlwind* by Spencer Dunmore and William Carter Ph.D.
7. From research by Michel Beckers, 427 Historical Unit for *Aircrew Remembered.*
8. He and his family moved to North Vancouver in 1956 where he worked in forest harvesting research with the Federal Government until retirement. He died on 13 September 2009.
9. *The Berlin Raids* by Martin Middlebrook.
10. Cited in *Round The Clock* by Philip Kaplan and Jack Currie (Cassell, 1993).
11. Researched by *Aircrew Remembered* researcher Roy Wilcock.
12. See *Halifax At War* by Brian J. Rapier (Ian Allen, 1987). By the end of the war 78 Squadron had flown the most sorties in 4 Group (6,337) and suffered the highest percentage losses of any Halifax squadron.
13. See *Memories of RAF Witchford* by Barry and Sue Aldridge (Milton Contact Ltd, 2013).
14. *The Long Road: Trials and Tribulations of Airmen Prisoners from Stalag Luft VII (Bankau) to Berlin, June 1944-May 1945* by Oliver Clutton Brock and Raymond Crompton (Grub Street, London, 2013).
15. *In Search of Uncle Albert* by Peter Broom.
16. See *Aircrew Remembered.*
17. 'Jock' Morrison evaded capture. The rest, including Flight Sergeant J. Duncombe, the bomb-aimer, were taken prisoner. Hather was taken to a German military hospital. He had significant internal trauma wounds and multiple fractures to his legs and spine. His life was saved by a complex operation which pinned his bones back together. He then spent three months in a flea- and lice-ridden full-body plaster cast in a PoW camp hospital, being tended by Russian PoW orderlies, subsisting on a near-starvation diet of bread and cabbage soup. He was cut out of the plaster cast on his 21st birthday, 2 June 1944, an experience he described as the best birthday present he ever had. 'I didn't see or hear about any of the others until, on a train going to Cosford in May 1945, Jim came into the compartment I was in and said "guess who is on the train?" "It's got to be 'Monty'," I said, and it was.' www.rafcommands.com.
18. Dick Starkey's crew's luck finally did run out a few nights later, on the disastrous Nuremberg raid on 30/31 March when they were shot down by a German night-fighter. Starkey and 'Wally' Paris were the only two survivors.
19. Cited in *Under Cover of Darkness* by Roderick Chisholm (Chatto & Windus, London, 1953). Nine more sorties were made before the end of the month. Working closely with 515 (SD) Squadron RAF, a further twenty-one sorties were dispatched during April, ten of which were completed. By the end of the month, it had become obvious that the American single-seat fighters were unsuitable for night intruder work and the detachment was duly disbanded. Plans for large-scale USAAF help in this direction were shelved as a result. Cited in *Confound and Destroy: 100 Group and the Bomber Support Campaign* by Martin Streetley (MacDonald and Jane's, London, 1978).

Chapter Seventeen: Berlin or Bust

1. Flying Officer F.N. Plum DFC tried to put down at Weston airfield in Somerset on the return but bounced back into the air. He opened up to go around again but the starboard

engine failed and a wing dropped. The aircraft was wrecked and Plum and his navigator were injured.

2. A complete account of Ralph's and Andy's careers are featured in *Mosquito Mayhem: de Havilland's Wood Wonder in Action in WWII* by Martin W. Bowman (Pen & Sword, 2010).
3. Cited in *War In The Air* compiled by Edward Smithies (Viking, 1990).
4. *The Mosquito Log* by Alexander McKee (Souvenir Press, 1988). Fritz Krause's victim was B.XVI MM147 on 692 Squadron, which crashed west of Granzow, 9 kilometres north-north-west of Kyritz at 0155 hours. Flight Lieutenant Philip Kenneth Burley DFC was killed and Flight Lieutenant E.V. Saunders DFC bailed out and was taken prisoner.
5. The Kiel attack cost seventeen Lancasters and Königsberg four Lancasters, and five Lancaster mine-layers were also lost.
6. In typical journalistic fashion the British press had wrongly assumed that shooting down a Mosquito warranted two victories when in fact it was worth two points towards a German pilot's Ritterkreuz.

Chapter Eighteen: A Night on the Spree

1. Flight Lieutenant Pudsey and Flying Officer Morgan were on their thirty-fourth operation to Magdeburg on 4/5 April when thirty-one Mosquitoes were dispatched and they collided with a Mosquito of 571 Squadron over the Channel. Their bodies were never recovered and they are commemorated on the Runnymede Memorial.
2. Adapted from an article by Barry Blunt in *The Mossie*.

Chapter Nineteen: The 'Milk Run'

1. *Mosquito To Berlin: Story of 'Bertie' Boulter DFC: One of Bennett's Pathfinders* by Peter Bodle FRAeS and Bertie Boulter DFC.
2. Ibid.
3. Bayon and Swain were awarded the Distinguished Flying Cross after a raid on Würzburg in which they had been the only crew to dive below cloud cover at 5,000 feet and drop their 4,000lb bomb accurately on the railway in the valley. Mike Bayon died aged 92 on 29 May 2014.
4. Cited in *The Men Who Flew the Mosquito* by Martin W. Bowman.
5. Gannon navigated the RAF Canberra piloted by Flight Lieutenant Roland 'Monty' Burton, which touched down at Christchurch forty-one minutes ahead of its closest rival – a Canberra of the Royal Australian Air Force – after twenty-three hours and fifty-one minutes in the air.
6. A type of mobile and temporary battery-operated airfield lighting used on taxiways (blue) and in parking areas (red) at night.
7. He was interrogated at Luneburg and sent into captivity at Stalag Luft III at Sagan until the war's end.
8. *Mosquito To Berlin: Story of 'Bertie' Boulter DFC: One of Bennett's Pathfinders* by Peter Bodle FRAeS and Bertie Boulter DFC.

Chapter Twenty: The Cost of Victory

1. Sergeant Harwood was first to attack, his run from 17,000 feet above the Ruhr being timed eight minutes before the midnight hour. Renaut dropped his 8,000lb bomb in the closing stages of the attack.
2. *Terror By Night: A Bomber Pilot's Story* by Michael Renaut (William Kimber, 1982).

3. Squadron Leader Cedric Alexander Fraser-Petherbridge was the squadron gunnery leader.
4. *Footprints on the Sands of Time* by Oliver Clutton Brock.
5. 35squadronresearchgroup. Bowen-Morris was operational again by 7 May 1945.
6. The others who died were the 20-year-old flight engineer Flight Sergeant Stephen Larcombe RAFVR of Chard, Somerset; the two gunners, Sergeant Thomas Anthony Cotter RAFVR and Sergeant Harold Victor Stokes RAFVR of Stafford; the 22-year-old WOp/AG, Warrant Officer Graham Morris Bagshaw RAAF of North Unley, South Australia; and the 20-year-old navigator, Flying Officer Vincent Rees Macdonald Williams RAFVR of Hirwain, Glamorgan, Wales.
7. Jack's crew did not fly again for a month. When they did, the war in Europe was over and they evacuated prisoners of war from Juvincourt, twice viewed the effects of the bombing offensive on 'Cook's Tours' and finally, on 25 June they helped test German radar equipment. For these final four operations Jack's role was taken by Flight Sergeant A. Bolton. Jack's widow, Gladys Rosina Sliman remarried in 1948 and died in Hampshire in 2004.
8. This was confirmed by documents from the RAF, which were handed over after 1990.
9. *While Berlin Burns: The Diary of Hans Georg von Studnitz, 1943–1945* (Frontline Books, 2011).
10. *Bomber Offensive* (Collins, 1947).
11. *Hell on Earth: Dramatic First-Hand Experiences of Bomber Command At War* by Mel Rolfe (Grub Street, 1999).
12. Ibid.
13. Cited in *Trials and Tribulation: The Story of RAF Gransden Lodge* by Chris Sullivan (Matador, 2015).

Index